Robin Williams

Cool Mac Apps

Second Edition

A guide to iLife '05, .Mac, and more!

John Tollett

with Robin Williams

Peachpit Press • Berkeley • California

Robin Williams Cool Mac Apps, Second Edition: A guide to iLife '05, .Mac, and more!

Cover design: John Tollett
Production: John Tollett and Robin Williams
Index: Buz Riley
Editing: Robin Williams and Nancy Davis
Prepress: David Van Ness

Peachpit Press
1249 Eighth Street
Berkeley, California 94710
800.283.9444
510.524.2178 voice
510.524.2221 fax

Find us on the World Wide Web at **www.peachpit.com**
To report errors, please send a note to errata@peachpit.com
Peachpit Press is a division of Pearson Education

ISBN 0-321-33590-2

10 9 8 7 6 5 4 3 2

Printed and bound in the United States of America

Contents

iLife

1 iPhoto

3 iMovie 133

4 iDVD

183

5 GarageBand 219

.Mac apps

6 iDisk 257

11 iSync 317

12 .Mac Bookmarks 327

Mac OS X apps

13 iCal 337

15 Mail 405

16 Address Book

17 iChat AV and Bonjour

Index

Cool apps, hot stuff

A book about cool apps is really hard to write. Not because the apps are hard to understand—they're easy to learn and fun to use. Here's the problem: These apps are such incredibly hot stuff that you can't stop playing with them. And they have the power to transform you. For example, when writing the GarageBand chapter, I realized for the first time that *I'm a brilliant musical composer*—I couldn't stop creating music. When Robin asked "How's that chapter going?" I couldn't even hear her because the headphones were blasting away, and besides, I was concentrating on which drum effect sounded best under the Southern Rock piano. Then, while writing the iMovie chapter, I discovered that *I'm a genius video editor.* I couldn't stop importing video clips and editing them, experimenting with different sound tracks and effects. It got worse as I worked on the iTunes chapter. I had an epiphany—*I'm a music connoisseur*—of all kinds of music, which just happened to be at my fingertips! The iChat chapter sent me over the edge—not just because it's fun to chat with buddies—but now I can actually have audio chats with up to ten buddies, and video chat with three or four buddies all at once! Geez! It's very hard to leave a chat with an old high school buddy in Germany just because you've got a book deadline.

Even with these obstacles, the day finally arrived when it was time to quit playing around and write this introduction. I'll make it brief, because I've got some movies that need editing and they'll be needing original sound tracks.

This book is divided into three main sections:

Section One, iLife apps covers the suite of five fabulous applications that will change your digital life. If you don't have a digital life, these apps will most likely persuade you to get one. Before iLife, we rarely used our digital camera or our video camera; we seldom bought music, and our existing music collection consisted of dust-covered, scratched CDs scattered around the house. Now we shoot photos, edit movies, create DVDs, buy songs and albums without leaving the house, and compose original music tracks for our movies and DVDs.

Section Two, .Mac apps tells all about the great software, features, and services provided with a .Mac membership (pronounced "dot Mac"). If you don't have a .Mac membership, you're missing out on some of the great fun and advantages of being a Mac user.

Section Three, Mac OS X apps explains in detail the main productivity apps that are included as part of Mac OS X—iCal, Mail, Address Book, Safari, iChat, and Bonjour.

We don't just write about these apps. We use them every day. And every night. Even when we don't have to. It's too much fun being a Mac user.

John

Section one

iLife

What is **iLife** and what does the "i" mean?

When the iMac was originally introduced, Apple explained the "i" as symbolizing both *innovation* and the computer's built-in *Internet* capabilities. That was many millions of web pages ago. Now the "i" represents the concept of a digital lifestyle and the software applications that can enhance that lifestyle. Your Mac is a *digital hub* that enables various applications and devices to work together as powerful, creative tools. At the core of the digital hub concept are five separate applications: **iMovie, iPhoto, iTunes, iDVD,** and **GarageBand.** As stand-alone applications, they're amazing—add the feature of built-in integration between them and the result is an increase in creativity and productivity that can only be described as *inspirational.* This very special collection of applications is called **iLife.**

If you have a digital still camera, digital video camera, or a CD collection gathering dust, iLife will turn them into your most important creative tools. It's unofficial, but think of the "i" as a symbol for **inspiration** in your digital lifestyle. You're certain to find yourself thinking "iLove iLife!"

iPhoto

1

iPhoto makes managing, sharing, and enhancing your digital photos both easy and fun. You can effortlessly import photos straight from most digital cameras, as well as from digital card readers, CDs, DVDs, Zip disks, or any location on your Mac's hard disk.

Organize your photos, expertly retouch blemishes, get rid of red-eye, adjust contrast and brightness, make other adjustments, then share your photos with friends, relatives, or business associates in a number of different ways.

If you have a .Mac account, use iPhoto to create web photo albums and screen saver slideshows, order custom prints online, and order large or small photo albums of your favorite digital photos.

If you don't own a digital camera or if you have quite a collection of prints, negatives, and slides from long ago that you would like to drop into iPhoto for organizing and sharing, search the web for "slide scanning" or "photo scanning" services. Avoid services that give you back images in their proprietary format, such as Kodak's PictureCD or PhotoCD—you want your images in standard .jpeg or .tiff formats. Try someplace like SlideScanning.com or DigitalMemoriesOnline.net.

Open iPhoto

Single-click the iPhoto icon in the Dock, *or* go to the Applications folder (click the Applications icon in the Sidebar of any open Finder window), then double-click the iPhoto icon. The iPhoto window (below) opens, although yours will be empty if this is the first time you're using it.

The **Library** (top item in the "Source" pane below) stores all the photos you import. You can create separate **Albums** (pages 18–19) to organize selections from the Library into easy-to-use collections.

Library: *Click here to see your entire collection of photos.*

Source pane.

Viewing area.

Recent imports.

User-created albums. Select an album to see its photos in the viewing area.

From the View menu, you can choose to show titles, keywords, or ratings beneath photos in the viewing area.

The Calendar pane.

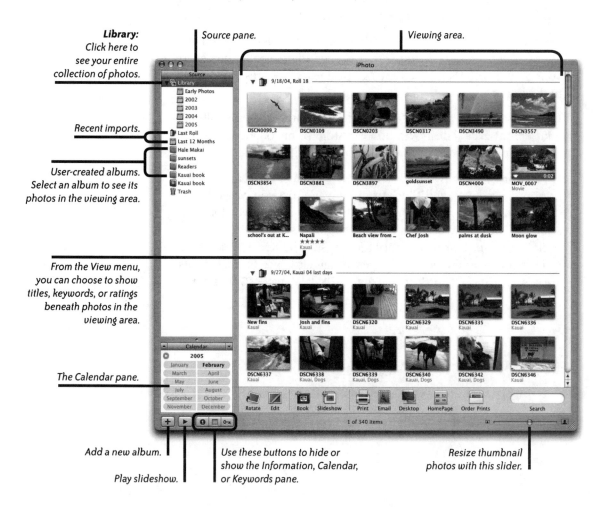

Add a new album.

Play slideshow.

Use these buttons to hide or show the Information, Calendar, or Keywords pane.

Resize thumbnail photos with this slider.

The iPhoto Main Window

Before you can use iPhoto's various features, you first have to **import** the photos into the Library, as explained on the following pages. When you import photos, iPhoto considers each import session a "Film Roll." Each time you import, the photos are grouped beneath a Film Roll icon that shows the date of the import and the import session number.

Each image is tagged with the name that your camera automatically assigned, a name like DSCN451. You can **rename** any photo, as shown below: Select a photo in the viewing area, then click the "**i**" button (shown at right) to display the Information pane in the bottom-left corner. Click the word "Title," then type in a new name for the photo. The Information pane also includes the date and time the photo was taken, the image format, the photo dimensions (in pixels), and the photo storage size. At the very bottom of the Information pane you can type comments about the photo. Comments are searchable and can help you find photos later.

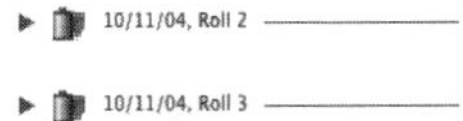

***To hide the photos** from an import session, click the disclosure triangle to the left of the Film Roll icon.*
***To show the photos,** click again on the triangle.*

Information button.

Click the disclosure triangle to reveal built-in Smart Albums that automatically organize your photos by year.

*Each import session is separated by a Film Roll icon. To select **all** the photos in a Film Roll, single-click this icon.*

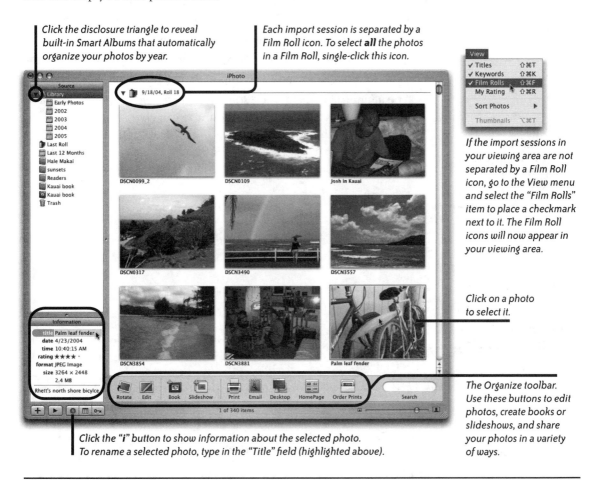

If the import sessions in your viewing area are not separated by a Film Roll icon, go to the View menu and select the "Film Rolls" item to place a checkmark next to it. The Film Roll icons will now appear in your viewing area.

Click on a photo to select it.

The Organize toolbar. Use these buttons to edit photos, create books or slideshows, and share your photos in a variety of ways.

Click the "i" button to show information about the selected photo. To rename a selected photo, type in the "Title" field (highlighted above).

Import Your Photos

When a digital camera or a memory card reader is connected to the computer with a USB cable and recognized by iPhoto, the "Import" view button is automatically selected. The next few pages explain how to import your photos directly from a camera, a memory card reader, a CD, or a location on your hard disk.

Import photos from a digital camera

When you connect a digital camera to your Mac, a disk icon appears on your Desktop named with the brand of memory card that's in the camera.

You can transfer photos directly into iPhoto if your camera has a USB port and if it is compatible with iPhoto.

1. Turn your camera off.
2. To conserve your camera's battery power, we suggest you connect the camera's AC power adapter to the camera, then plug the adapter into a power outlet.
3. Use the USB cable that came with the camera to connect the camera to your Mac's USB port. **Turn on your camera.** These things happen:
   - An icon representing the memory card in your camera (shown to the left) appears on the Desktop, indicating it has been mounted.
   - iPhoto opens to show the Import view (shown below).
4. Type a film roll name in the "Roll Name" text field, or leave it blank and let iPhoto assign a name for you. You can choose to type a description of the imported photos in the "Description" field. The description text will appear in the Information pane (bottom-left corner) when this film roll is selected in the viewing area.

*When a camera or memory card is mounted, it appears in the "Source" pane. **To unmount,** click the eject icon on the right.*

The Information pane gives information about the mounted memory card, including how many photos are on the card.

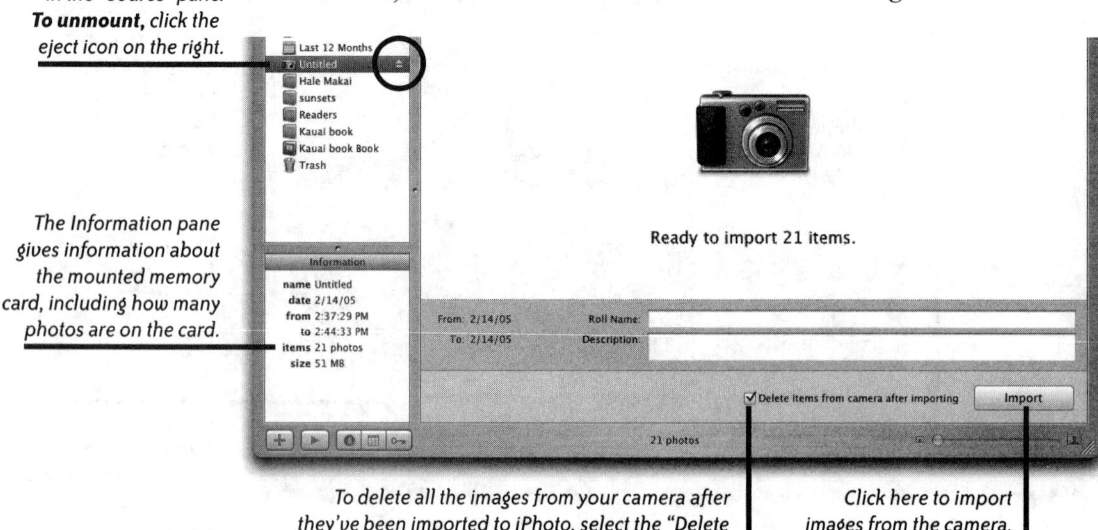

To delete all the images from your camera after they've been imported to iPhoto, select the "Delete items from camera after importing" checkbox.

Click here to import images from the camera.

5. Click the "Import" button (shown on the previous page). The "Import" button changes to a "Stop Import" button during import. **To stop an import,** click the "Stop Import" button.

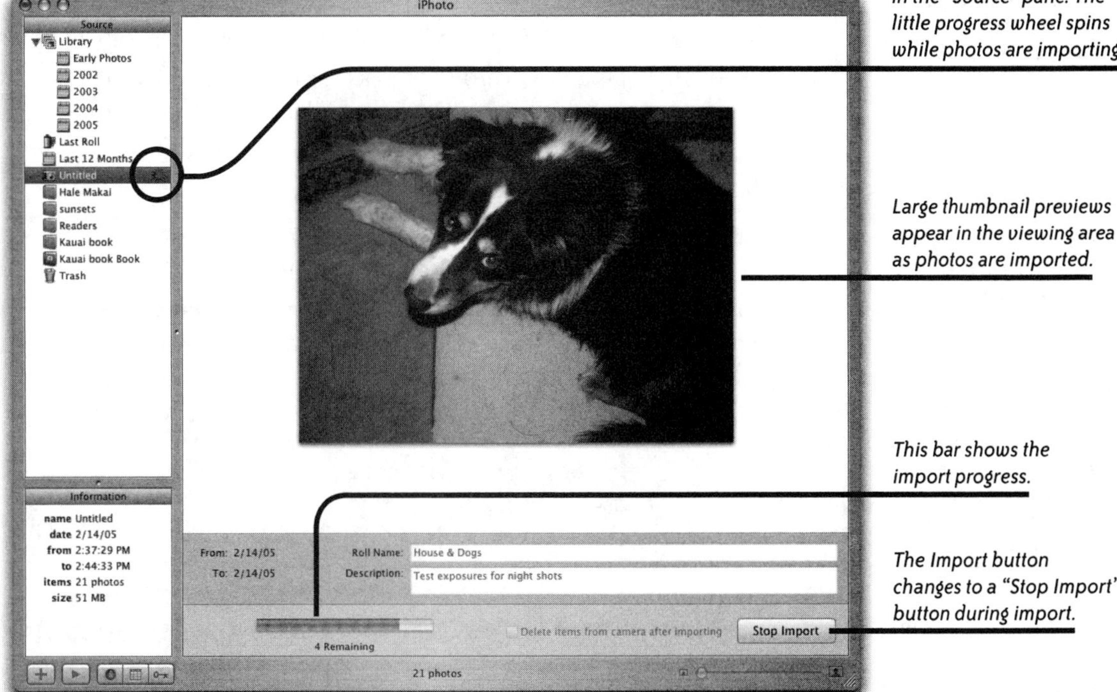

When a camera or memory card is mounted, it appears in the "Source" pane. The little progress wheel spins while photos are importing.

Large thumbnail previews appear in the viewing area as photos are imported.

This bar shows the import progress.

The Import button changes to a "Stop Import" button during import.

If there are still images left in your camera (or on the camera's memory card) from the last import, iPhoto asks if you want to import the duplicate photos.

Select "Applies to all duplicates" to apply your answer ("Import" or "Don't Import") to all duplicates on the card. Otherwise you'll have to click "Import" or "Don't Import" for every duplicate found during the import process.

6. After the photos have been imported, click the eject button next to the camera (or card) icon in the "Source" pane to unmount it.
7. Turn the camera off and disconnect it from your computer.

If you disconnect a camera or a card reader before you unmount the card, you'll get an error message warning that the device was improperly put away and you may have caused damage to the card.

All imported photos are placed in the Library.

Import photos from a digital memory card reader

The card from the camera *might be called a memory card, digital card, digital memory card, or even a memory stick! They all refer to the same item.*

You can import your photos from a **digital memory card reader,** even if your digital camera is not directly supported by iPhoto.

1. Connect an appropriate card reader to your Mac using a USB cable, one that is compatible with the type of memory card in your camera.
2. Take the digital memory card (CompactFlash, SmartMedia, SD card, Memory Stick, etc.) out of your camera and insert it in the card reader.

   The card's icon appears on your Desktop, as shown to the left, indicating it has been mounted.

This icon appears on your Desktop, named for the card that's in the reader.

3. iPhoto automatically recognizes the memory card and opens; if iPhoto is already open, it switches to the "Import" view.
4. **To automatically erase the contents of your memory card** after importing the photos, select the "Delete items from camera after importing" checkbox.

To keep your memory card empty and available for new photos, delete existing photos from the card after importing.

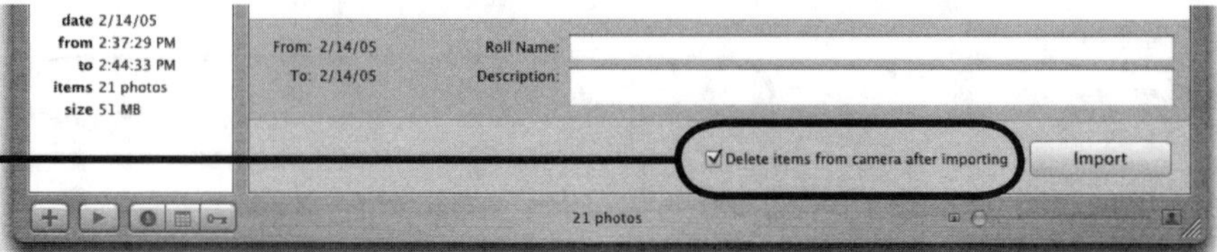

5. Click the "Import" button. After you click "Import," the button becomes a "Stop Import" button, in case you want to stop the import. Large preview thumbnails are displayed in the viewing area as photos are imported.
6. Unmount the memory card: Click the eject icon next to the mounted camera icon in the "Source" pane (shown on page 6).

   Or drag the memory card icon on the Desktop to the Trash.

   Or Control-click on the memory card icon and choose "Eject" from the contextual menu that pops up.

Imported photos are placed in the Library. They are also temporarily available through the **recent import** albums (**Last Roll** and **Last 12 Months**) that appear in the "Source" pane (shown on the left and explained on page 10).

Import photos from a location on your hard disk or from a CD

You can import any photos that you already have stored on your hard disk or that might be on a CD.

1. Insert a CD (if you have one that contains photos you want to import).
2. Open iPhoto if it is not already open.
3. From the File menu, select "Add to Library..." to open the "Import Photos" window, shown below. In the Finder window Sidebar, select the CD icon (if you inserted a CD), or choose a location somewhere on your hard disk where photos are stored that you want to import.
4. Select an entire folder of photos, an individual photo, or multiple photos, then click the "Import" button.

In the Sidebar of the "Import Photos" window, choose a volume (your hard drive, a CD, or an external hard drive), then . . .

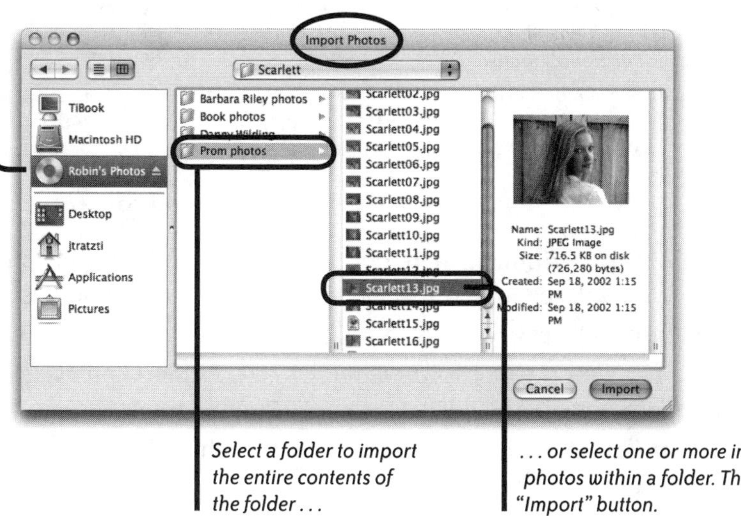

Select a folder to import the entire contents of the folder . . .

. . . or select one or more individual photos within a folder. Then click the "Import" button.

There's an even easier way to import individual photos, a folder of photos, or an entire disc of photos into iPhoto. From any location on your computer, drag your photo selection directly to the iPhoto viewing area or to the iPhoto "Source" pane. A Film Roll for the imported photos is automatically created in the viewing area (shown top-right). When you drag a photo selection to the "Source" pane, a new Album is automatically created and listed (shown bottom-right).

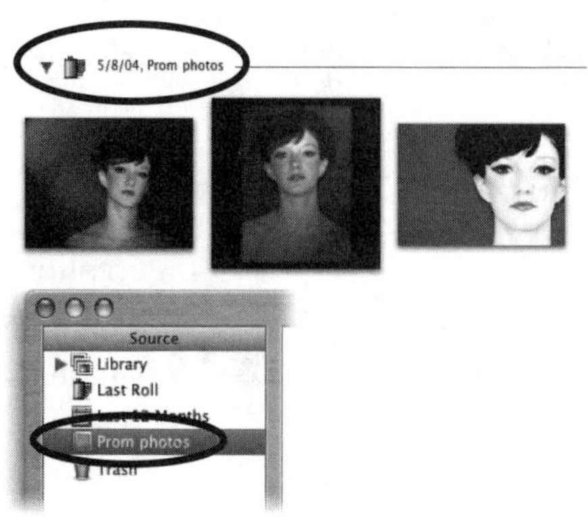

Viewing Your Photos

These are the recent import icons in the "Source" pane.

Once you've imported photos to iPhoto, there are several ways to view them within the main viewing area.

- Single-click the **Library** icon in the "Source" pane to view all photos that have been imported into iPhoto.
- Single-click one of the **recent import** albums (**Last Roll** or **Last 12 Months**) in the "Source" pane to show the most recently imported photos in the viewing area.

You can change the number of rolls or the number of months to be shown: *From the iPhoto application menu, choose "Preferences," then click the "General" icon in the Preferences toolbar.*

Enter new numbers in the "Sources" text fields, as shown to the right.

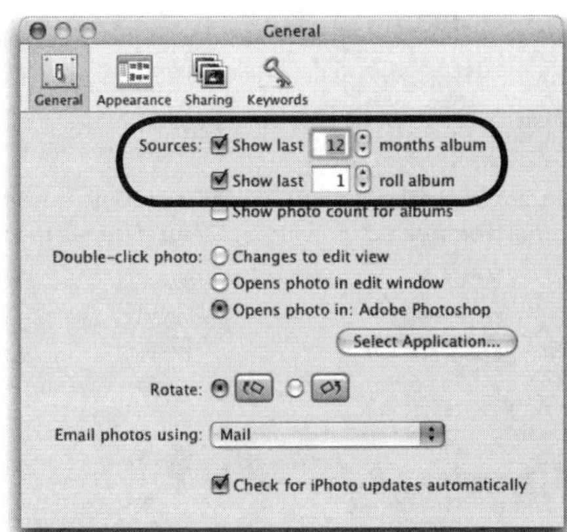

- Single-click an **album** icon in the "Source" pane to show only photos that you've placed in that specific Album (how to create and use albums is explained on pages 18–19).
- From the **View menu,** shown on the left, choose **Sort Photos,** then select one of the following views from the submenu:

  By Film Roll sorts photos into the groups in which they were originally imported.

  By Date sorts photos by the date they were taken in the camera, **if** you set the date in your camera before you took pictures.

  By Keyword sorts photos alphabetically, according to keywords you've assigned. Learn how to assign keywords on page 12.

  By Title sorts photos alphabetically by title.

  By Rating sorts photos by your "star" rating, **if** you assigned ratings to photos. Rating photos is explained on page 11.

  Manually lets you drag photos to rearrange them, but only in albums, not in the Library view or the *recent import* albums.

Checkmarks in the View menu indicate which descriptors you've selected to appear next to photos in the viewing area. Select an item to place a checkmark next to it. Select the item again to remove the checkmark.

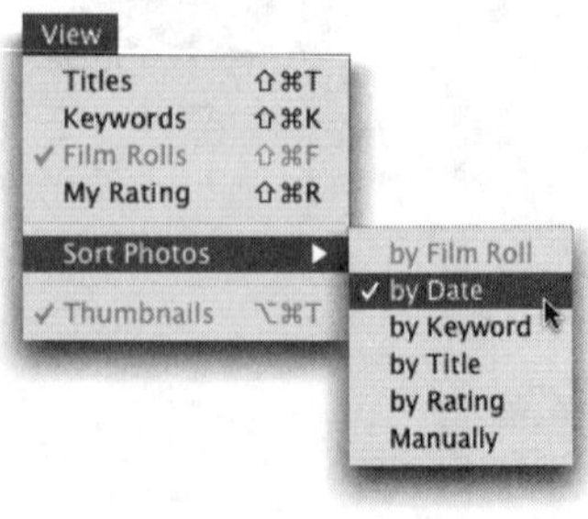

The bottom of the "Source" pane can show three different panes of information when you select one of the three buttons on the bottom-left edge of the iPhoto window (shown below).

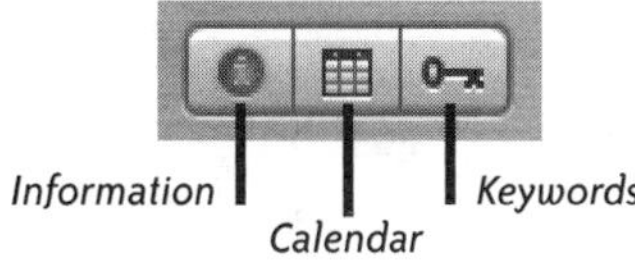

The Information Pane

Click the Information button to see information about selected photos, albums, inserted discs, or mounted volumes (such as a camera's memory card). The Information pane also lets you enter some information.

This is where you can rename photos instead of using the strange default name that may have been assigned by your digital camera (such as DSCN7021). Assigning a descriptive name can be tremendously helpful later when you search for specific photos.

Comments you add to the lower area of the Information pane can be used for books (the snazzy, printed books you can order from iPhoto—see page 37), email captions, or web pages that are automatically created by iPhoto. Comments are searchable and can be helpful when you need to find a certain photo. Learn how to search for photos on page 26.

A small dot in a bar always indicates that the bar is resizable. Press and drag this bar up or down to make the Information pane larger or smaller.

Type a photo title here.

Click on the dots to assign a rating from 1 to 5 stars.

Type any comments you want in this area.

The Information button.

To use the Information pane:

1. Single-click on a photo to select it.
2. Click the Information button to show the Information pane.
3. Click the "title" field to rename a photo. When you place your pointer over the title area, it highlights. Click once to make the title field editable.
4. Place your pointer over the "rating" field to rate a photo. When you place your pointer over the rating area, it highlights. Click on the gray dots to assign a rating from 1 to 5 stars.
5. Type any comments you want in the "comments" area.
6. Click the Information button again to hide the Information pane.

The Keywords Pane

The Keywords pane is a photo search tool. Assigning keywords to photos makes it easy to search for specific photos later. You can create as many keywords as you need. A photo can have one or more keywords assigned to it. Keywords appear in the Keywords pane (shown on the left). In iPhoto Preferences you can add, remove, or rename keywords, as explained below.

Assign checkmarks to photos that you want to single out as the best, as photos you want to edit later, or for any other purpose.

Hover your pointer over a keyword to see how many photos in the selected album contain that keyword.

Use the Keywords pane to find photos:

1. Click the Keywords button (the key icon circled, shown to the left) to show the Keywords pane. Click again to hide the Keyword pane.
2. Click a keyword in the list to show all photos that have that keyword assigned. The selected keyword is highlighted and all relevant photos are shown in the viewing area. You can choose more than one keyword at a time to search.

   Option-click on a keyword in the list **to hide** all photos that contain that keyword (the keyword button turns red). **To show** only photos that do *not* have keywords assigned, Option-click all keyword buttons.
3. Click a keyword again to remove it from the search criteria.

   You can also click "Reset" (the circle-x) to clear the search results from the viewing area and show all photos in the selected album.

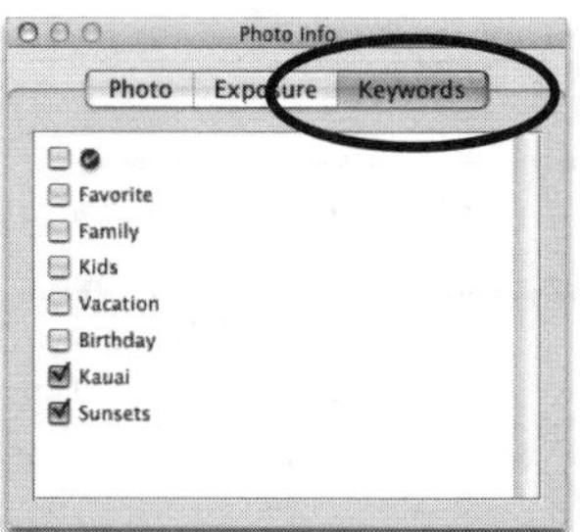

To assign keywords to photos:

1. Select a photo, or multiple photos, from the Library or from any album.
2. From the Photos menu choose "Get Info" to open the "Photo Info" window (shown on the left). **Or** press Command I.
   Or Control-click a photo, then choose "Show Info."
3. Click the checkbox of any keyword you want to assign to the selected photo (or photos).

To add, remove, or rename keywords:

1. From the iPhoto menu, choose "Preferences...," then click the "Keywords" button in the Preferences toolbar.
2. Select a keyword, then click the "Rename" button to rename it, or click the "Remove" button to remove it from the list.
3. Click the "Add" button to add a new keyword. A new keyword appears with the default name of "untitled." Type a new keyword name to replace the default name.

The Calendar Pane

The Calendar pane provides a way to search for photos by date. Choose a year, month, week, or day, and iPhoto displays all photos in the Library or a selected album that were created during that time period.

To find photos by date using the Calendar:

1. In the "Source" pane, select the Library or an album to search.
2. Click the Calendar button (circled below) to show the Calendar pane.
3. To switch between year-view and month-view, click the View arrow.

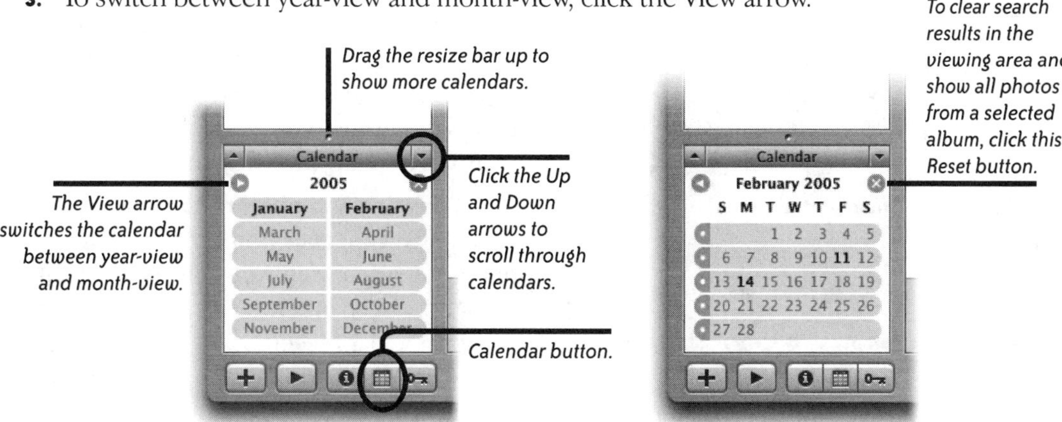

The Calendar in year-view. *The Calendar in month-view.*

Calendar dates in bold type indicate that the selected album contains photos created (or imported) on those dates and iPhoto displays those photos in the viewing area.

To show photos from specific years, months, weeks or days:

- Click on the year name ("2005" in the example above) to show photos from all months.
- To show all photos from one month, click the month.
- To show all photos from several months, click the first month, then Command-click additional months. You can also use multiple selections to show photos from multiple weeks or days.
- To show all photos from a specific day, set the calendar to month-view, then click the day.
- To show all photos from a specific week, double-click its month, then click the dot next to the week.
- To select the same month, week, or day for multiple years, press the Option key as you select.

iPhoto Preferences

To set basic characteristics that affect iPhoto's behavior and how you view your photos, go to the iPhoto application menu and choose "Preferences...."

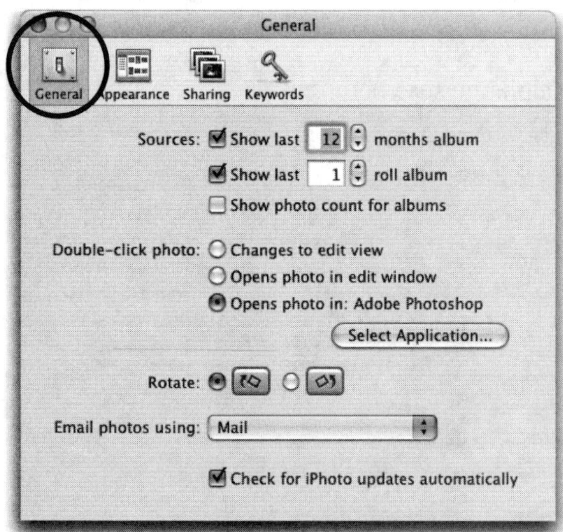

General preferences

Click the "General" button to show the General preferences pane.

Sources:

Select **Show last (number) months album** to set how many months of recent photos you'll see when you select this album in the "Source" pane. You can choose to show between 1 and 18 months of photos. To remove this album from the "Source" pane, *uncheck* the box.

Select **Show last (number) roll album** to set how many recent rolls (import sessions) of photos you'll see when you select this album in the "Source" pane. You can choose to show between 1 and 25 recent rolls. To remove this album from the "Source" pane, *uncheck* the box.

If you select **Show photo count for albums,** each album in the "Source" pane displays in parentheses how many photos it contains. This information is also available at the bottom of the iPhoto window.

Double-click photo:

Choose a preferred behavior for when you double-click an image in the viewing area.

Changes to edit view switches iPhoto to Edit view, the same as if you clicked the "Edit" view button located beneath the viewing pane.

Opens photo in edit window opens the photo in a separate edit window, complete with edit tools. Choose this option if you want to have multiple photos open at the same time, along with iPhoto's editing tools. Learn more about the edit window on page 36.

Opens photo in: If you have some other image-editing application that you prefer to edit photos in, such as Adobe Photoshop or Photoshop Elements, you can make the images in iPhoto open directly in that application. Click the **Select Application...** button; in the "Open" window that appears, select an image-editing application installed on your computer.

Rotate:

Choose a default direction for rotation when you click the Rotate button. To rotate a photo in the opposite direction, press the Option key when you click the Rotate button.

Email photos using:

From the pop-up menu, shown to the right, choose the email application you want to use when you use iPhoto's Email feature. Applications in the list that are not installed on your computer will be grayed out.

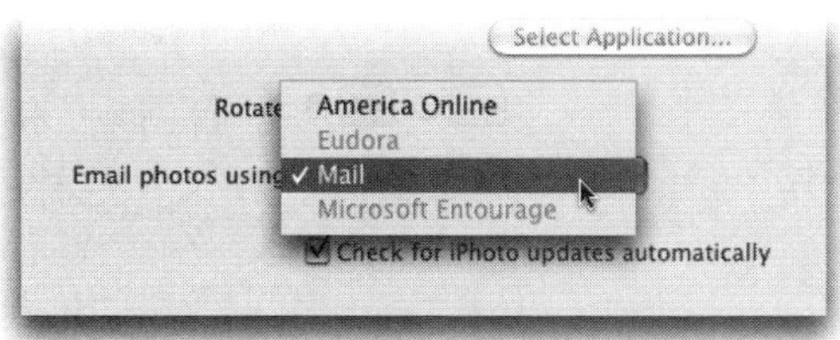

Appearance preferences

Border:

Select the **Outline** checkbox to place a small black border around thumbnail images in the viewing area.

Select the **Drop shadow** checkbox to add a drop shadow to thumbnail images.

Background:

Use the slider to change the color of the viewing area background to black, white, or any shade between.

Organize View:

Check the **Align photos to grid** checkbox to neatly organize thumbnail images in columns *and* rows.When this option is *not* selected, thumbnail images are organized in rows only, which saves a little space and may allow more photos to show at one time in the viewing area, depending on the size you show them and how many photos are present.

Check **Place most recent photos at the top** to make it easier to find your most recent photos when you have a large collection of photos in your Library.

"Source" Text:

From the pop-up menu, choose to use **Large** or **Small** text in the "Source" pane. The subtle difference in text size is shown on the right.

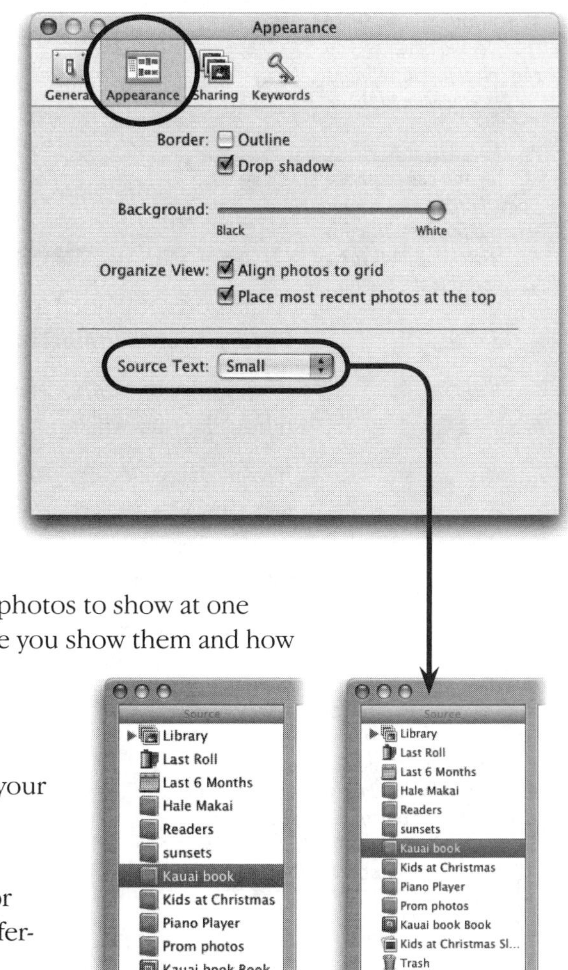

Large "Source" Text. *Small "Source" Text.*

Sharing preferences

iPhoto lets you **share your photos** with other people on your local network. When you check the **Look for shared photos** checkbox, iPhoto looks for other iPhoto users on your local network that have selected **Share my photos.**

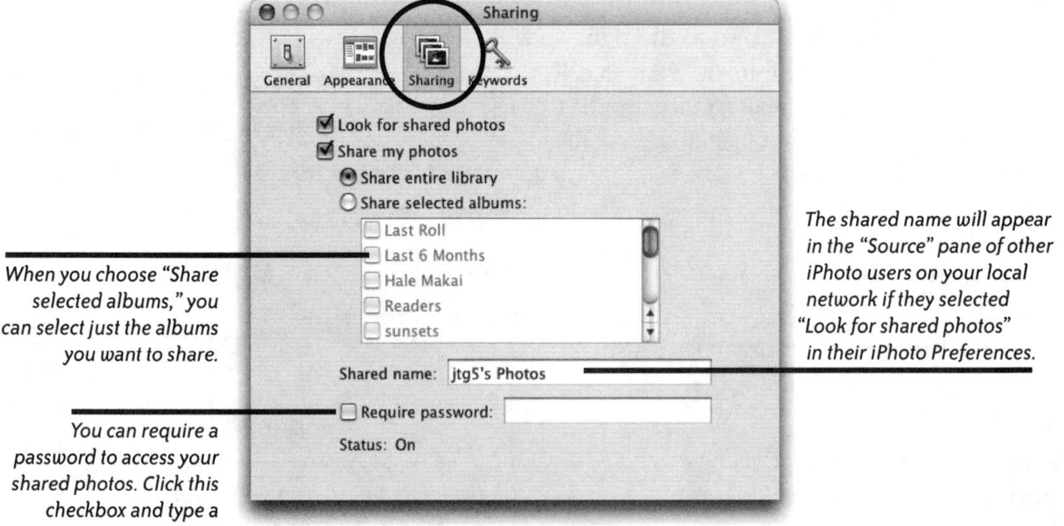

When you choose "Share selected albums," you can select just the albums you want to share.

You can require a password to access your shared photos. Click this checkbox and type a password in the text box.

The shared name will appear in the "Source" pane of other iPhoto users on your local network if they selected "Look for shared photos" in their iPhoto Preferences.

When you set iPhoto to share photos, you can then choose to **Share entire library** or **Share selected albums.**

If you choose *Share entire library,* all of the photos and albums in your iPhoto Library will be accessible to other iPhoto users on the local network.

If you choose *Share selected albums,* a list of your iPhoto albums (which were previously grayed out) becomes available for selection. Place checkmarks next to the albums you want to make accessible to others on your network, as shown above.

Assign a **Shared name:** As shown below, the assigned name you choose will appear in the "Source" pane of another user's iPhoto, **if** that user selected the "Look for shared photos" option in their own iPhoto Preferences.

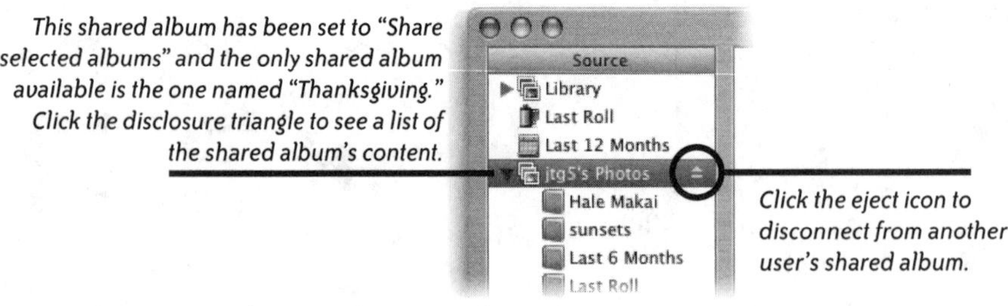

This shared album has been set to "Share selected albums" and the only shared album available is the one named "Thanksgiving." Click the disclosure triangle to see a list of the shared album's content.

Click the eject icon to disconnect from another user's shared album.

Things you can do with shared photos: You can view them, print them, attach them to email, use them to create a .Mac HomePage web site (see pages 50–51) or to create a .Mac Slides slideshow (see pages 52–53).

Things you cannot do with shared photos: You can't edit shared photos, and you can't use them to create a book (as described on pages 37–39), an iDVD project, as a Desktop picture, or burn them to a disc. Of course, you *can* do all these things if you *copy* shared photos to your own computer. **To copy shared photos,** drag one or more shared photos and drop them on the Library icon in your "Source" pane. **Or** drag shared photos into one of the album icons in your "Source" pane.

As you drag, a plus sign appears next to the pointer, a visual clue that you're about to make a copy—you are not moving the original file.

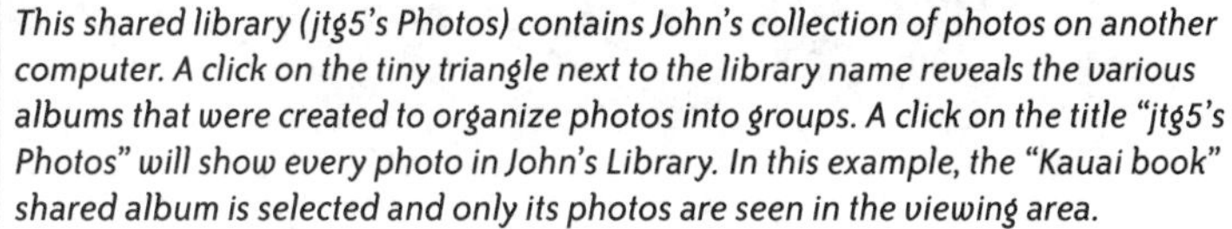

This shared library (jtg5's Photos) contains John's collection of photos on another computer. A click on the tiny triangle next to the library name reveals the various albums that were created to organize photos into groups. A click on the title "jtg5's Photos" will show every photo in John's Library. In this example, the "Kauai book" shared album is selected and only its photos are seen in the viewing area.

Keywords preferences

Click the Keywords button in the Preferences window to add new keywords to the keyword list, rename or remove existing keywords. See details at the bottom of page 12.

Create an Album and Add Photos to It

Create **albums** to organize your photos, make them easier to find, and make collections to use when you create a slideshow, HomePage, or Book.

You can put the same photo in any number of albums because iPhoto just "points" to the original photo stored in the Library (like aliases on your Desktop), which means you don't end up with multiple copies of the same photo taking up space on your hard disk.

To create a new album:

1. Click the "Add" button in the lower-left corner of the iPhoto window, shown below.
2. In the sheet that drops down, choose "Album" from the pop-up menu, type a name for the new album, then click "Create." Your new album appears in the "Source" pane.

From this pop-up menu you can also choose to create a new Smart Album, Book, or Slideshow.

Albums you create appear in this list.

Photos that you delete from the Library go to the Trash. They remain there until you empty the Trash.

To empty the Trash: *Go to the iPhoto menu and choose "Empty Trash."* ***Or*** *Control-click on the Trash icon, then choose "Empty Trash" from the pop-up menu.*

The Add button.

To add photos to an album:

Drag images from the viewing area and drop them on an album icon.

To rename an existing album:

Double-click the album name to highlight it and type a new name.

To delete photos from an album:

If you delete a photo from an *album,* it will *not* be deleted from the Library; the photo in the album "points" to the original photo in the Library. **But** if you delete a photo from the *Library,* it *will* disappear from the Library and every album that contains it.

1. Select an album from which you want to delete one or more photos.
2. Select one or more photos to delete.
3. Press the Delete key. **Or** Control-click on the photo and choose "Delete From Album" from the contextual pop-up menu.

To duplicate an album:

You may want to experiment with different arrangements of photos for a book project or a slideshow. You can duplicate an entire album. In the duplicate, you can rearrange the photos, delete some, add others, and it won't affect the original album or add to the size of your Library (because duplicate albums just *refer* to originals in the Library).

1. Single-click an album in the "Source" pane to select it, then from the Photos menu, choose "Duplicate" (or press Command D).

   Or Control-click an album, then choose "Duplicate" from the pop-up menu.
2. If you want to rename the duplicate album, double-click the new album in the "Source" pane, then type a new name.

iPhoto automatically names a duplicate album the same as the original source album, with a number added to the end of the name.

Create Smart Albums

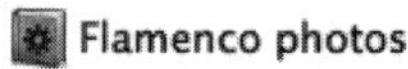

A Smart Album can be identified in the "Source" pane by the "gear" icon on it, representing automation.

Creating albums and dragging photos into them is a great way to organize your photos, but it gets a lot better than that. iPhoto lets you create Smart Albums that automatically find and organize photos that match certain conditions you've set. For instance, you can create a Smart Album that contains only photos to which you've assigned a five-star rating (see the next page). iPhoto will place all five-star photos in the Smart Album.

To create a Smart Album:

1. Click the Add button in the bottom-left corner of the iPhoto window, shown below.
2. In the sheet that drops down, choose "Smart Album," type a name for the new Smart Album, then click "Create."

The Add button.

3. A second sheet drops down that contains pop-up menus, as shown on the next page. Choose options from the pop-up menus to set the conditions that will identify photos for this Smart Album.

   To add more conditions, click the plus button on the right side of the sheet.

   To remove a condition, click its minus button.

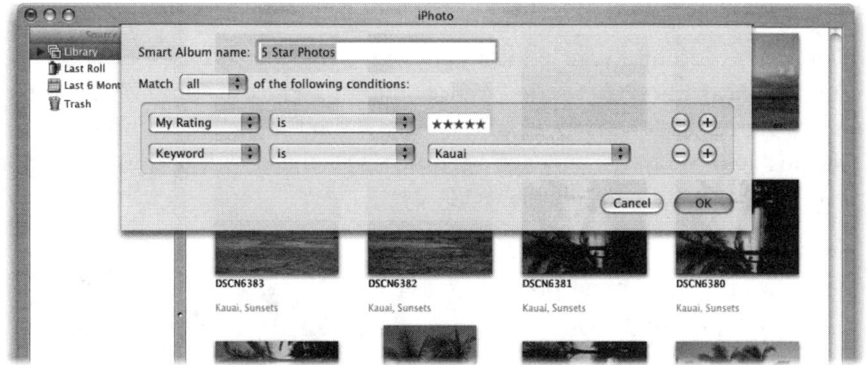

This Smart Album will automatically collect photos that have a 5-star rating and that have been assigned the keyword "Kauai."

4. If you choose more than one condition, use the top pop-up menu to choose between "Match **any** of the following conditions" or "Match **all** of the following conditions."
5. Click OK. The new Smart Album appears in the "Source" pane as shown below, automatically adding photos that meet the conditions you set.

The new Smart Album icon is selected in the "Source" pane and the viewing area shows all photos in the Library that match the Smart Album conditions.

To edit a Smart Album's settings:

1. Select a Smart Album in the "Source" pane.
2. From the File menu choose "Edit Smart Album."
3. The Smart Album sheet drops down again (as shown at the top of the page). Make any changes you want, then click OK.

Rate Your Photos

One way to organize your photos is by rating them on a scale of one to five stars. You can choose to hide or show the rating next to thumbnails in the viewing area (see the bottom of this page). You can also sort photos in the viewing area by rating (see page 10). And you can use your ratings as a condition for Smart Albums (see pages 20–21).

To rate a photo:

1. Select one or more photos in the viewing area.
2. Control-click your photo selection. From the contextual menu (on the right) choose "My Rating," then from the submenu choose a row of stars.
   Or from the Photos menu choose "My Rating," then choose a row of stars from the submenu, shown below.

Control-click one or more selected photos to show a contextual menu and assign a rating.

You can also use the Photos menu to rate selected photos.

Photo ratings are shown beneath photos in the viewing area **if** "My Rating" has been selected in the View menu. To hide ratings in the viewing area, select "My Rating" again to remove the checkmark.

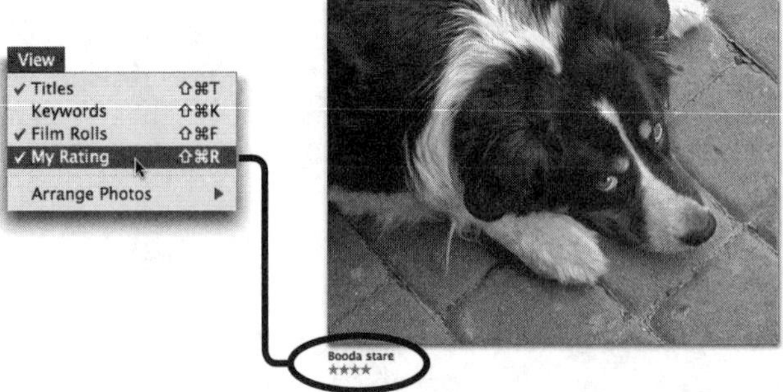

The Organize View

After you've imported all the photos from the camera to iPhoto, you can begin organizing, arranging, and sharing them. The **Organize view** lets you see and select many photos at once. The Organize pane at the bottom of the window provides all the tools you need to share your photos in many different ways.

Organize photos into albums

After you've imported photos from your camera to iPhoto, you can begin organizing, arranging, and sharing them. You can drag photos into an existing album or create a new album, as explained on the pages 18–19. If you've created Smart Albums, photos in the Library are added to the album automatically, depending on the conditions you set (see pages 20–21).

Advantages of organizing photos into albums:

- ▾ It's easy to find photos that you've collected into an album.
- ▾ Grouping photos into an album makes it easy to create a book or slideshow.
- ▾ Photos in an album can be manually sorted—dragged to a new position to change the order of appearance. Rearrange photos in an album (drag the photos) to customize their order of appearance in an iPhoto slideshow, on a HomePage, in a Slideshow, on pages of multiple prints (Order Prints), in an iDVD slideshow, or in a Book.
- ▾ When you put photos in an album, you can easily keep track of which photos you've selected for certain sharing options.

To delete unwanted photos from the Library:

Note: If you delete a photo from the Library, it *will* disappear from every album that contained it, and from iPhoto itself.

- ▾ **To delete multiple photos that are next to each other,** click on an image, then Shift-click on another image. All images between the two clicks are automatically selected. Press the Delete key to put all of the selected photos in the Trash.
- ▾ **To delete multiple photos that are NOT next to each other,** click a photo, then Command-click additional photos you want to select, then press the Delete key to put all selected photos in the Trash.

Photos deleted from the Library are moved to the Trash in the "Source" pane. They are stored there until you go to the iPhoto menu and choose "Empty Trash." **Or** until you Control-click on the Trash icon and choose "Empty Trash" from the contextual menu.

The Trash icon appears below the albums in the "Source" pane. Click the Trash icon to see its contents in the viewing area.

To retrieve a photo from the Trash, click the Trash icon to display the images that are in it, then drag the photo from the viewing area to the "Source" pane or to the Library icon in the "Source" pane. **Or** Control-click on a photo and choose "Restore to Library" from the contextual menu. **Or** select a photo and from the Photos menu choose "Restore to Library."

Sort the Order of Photos

When you create a slideshow, book, or HomePage, iPhoto builds the project with your photos in the same order as the album they're in. So you might want to rearrange the photos in an album or in the Library. There are a couple of ways to do this.

- **To sort photos in an album** (this doesn't work in the Library), drag one or more photos to the location desired. As you drag, a black, vertical bar indicates where the photos will be placed when you release the mouse button.
- **To sort photos in the Library (or in an album):** From the View menu (shown left), choose "Sort Photos," then from the submenu choose one of the options. The only option you cannot choose when sorting the actual Library is "Manually" (you can sort albums manually).

Add titles and comments

The titles and comments that you type in the Information pane are used by the Book and HomePage features to add headlines and captions. When you create a web page or a book from these photos, you'll want them to have descriptive names instead of something like "DSCN0715.JPG." Descriptive titles also make it easier to conduct a search for photos based on titles.

1. Single-click a photo to select it.
2. Click the "i" button beneath the "Source" pane.
3. Click the "title" field, then type a new name to replace any existing text in the field, such as "DSCN0715.JPG."
4. Click inside the "comments" field and type any comments you want that describe the photo, or that will make it easier to find in a search.

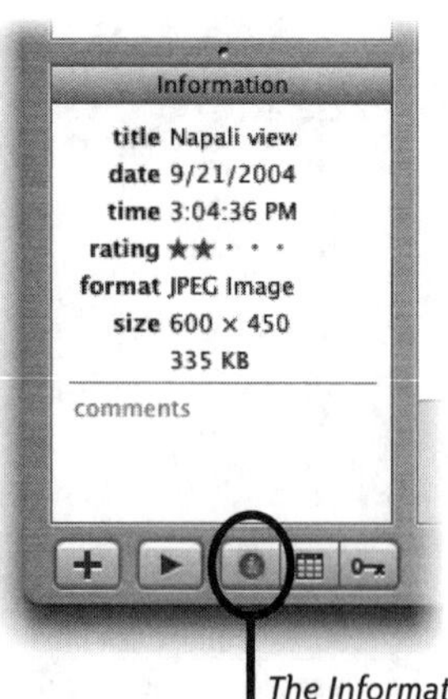

The Information button.

Keywords

Searching for photos in iPhoto is fast and easy, especially if you previously assigned keywords to photos.

To assign keywords to photos:

By assigning keywords to photos, you make it possible to search for photos based on those words. If you take the time to assign keywords, you'll save a lot of time later when you're trying to find a certain photo.

1. Select one or more photos in an album, or from the Library.
2. From the Photos menu choose "Get Info," to open the "Photo Info" window, shown on the right. You can also press Command I.
3. Click the "Keywords" button to show a list of keywords.
4. Click the checkbox next to a keyword you want to assign.

To assign multiple keywords: Select photos in the viewing area, then repeat steps 1–4 above.

To remove keywords from photos: Select photos in the viewing area, open the Keywords window (steps 2 and 3 listed above), then click a keyword checkbox to remove its checkmark.

To add, rename, or remove keywords in the keyword list: From the iPhoto menu, choose "Preferences...," then Click the "Keywords" button in the Preferences window to add new keywords to the keyword list, rename or remove existing keywords. See details at the bottom of page 12.

To display keywords next to photos in the viewing pane, go to the View menu, then choose the "Keywords" item to place a checkmark next to it in the menu. Your keywords now show underneath any photo that has a keyword assigned.

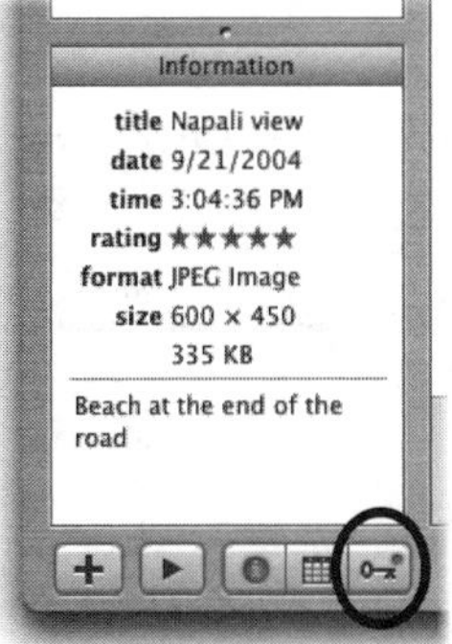

A blue dot on the Keywords button means the current selection of photos that are visible in the viewing area have been chosen by a keyword search and do not necessarily represent all photos in the selected album or Library. Click the Keyword button to see the keyword (or keywords) that is selected and being used to limit the search.

What the checkmark indicates:

The checkmark that appears in the list of keywords acts as a temporary keyword, useful for marking photos for which you haven't decided upon a keyword or category. A checkmark appears in the bottom-right corner of a photo when you select the checkmark as a keyword.

Search For Photos

When you want to search for photos, use the Search field located in the bottom-right corner of the iPhoto window.

1. Click on the album you want to search, **or** click "Library" to search your entire photo collection.
2. Type a keyword or phrase in the Search field (see the callout, below). Use a term that you remember entering in the photo title, in the comments box, or as a keyword.
3. Click the "Search" button. Photos that do not contain that word or phrase are removed from the viewing area as you type.

In the example below, iPhoto has found every photo in the Library with the word "Bermuda" attached to it, even though the search word is just partially typed in the Search field. As we type, iPhoto has narrowed the search to photos that contain the letters "Ber."

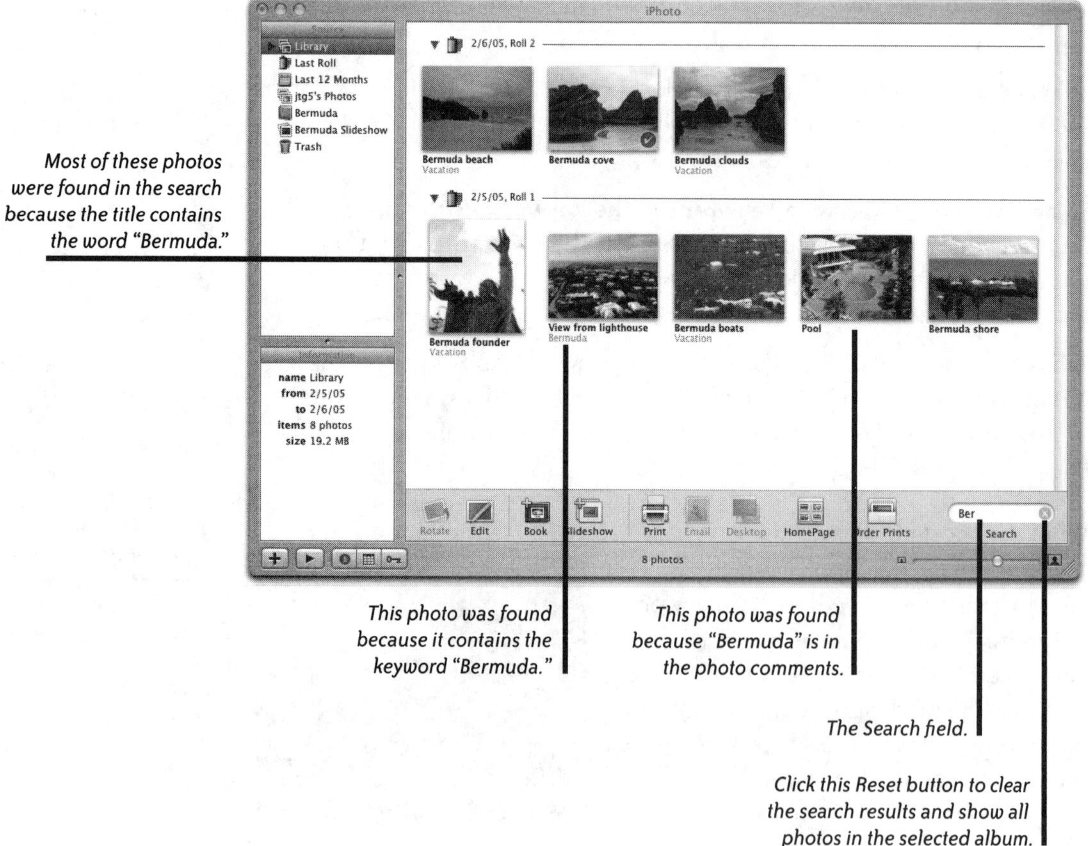

The Photo Info Window

The "Photo Info" window contains all available information about your photos, including which keywords are assigned. To open it, go to the Photos menu and choose "Get Info," or press Command I.

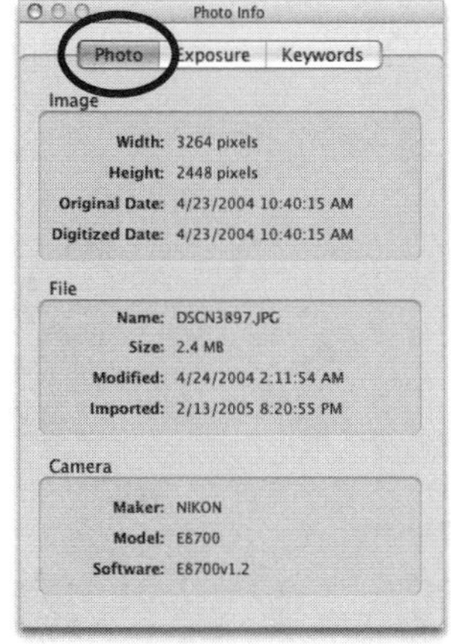

This window organizes all of the information into three categories: Photo, Exposure, and Keywords. For non-professional photograhers, some of the detailed information that iPhoto can provide is not important, but it's here if you want it.

The Photo pane

Click the "Photo" button at the top of the "Photo Info" window to see image, file, and camera information. For most of us non-professional photographers, the most useful information in this pane is the width, height, and size.

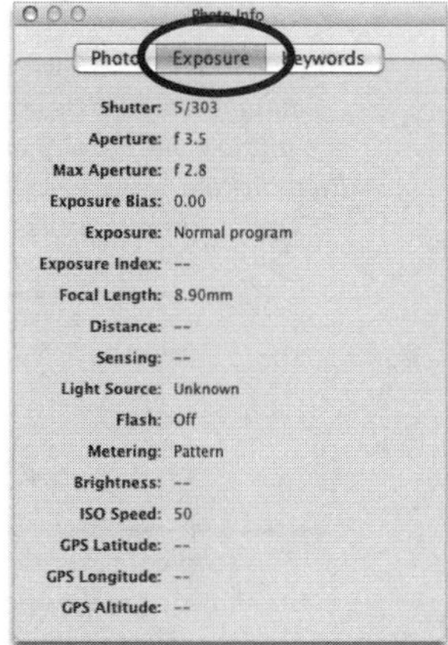

The Exposure pane

Click the "Exposure" button to see information about shutter speed, focal length, aperture settings, etc. Unless you're a professional photographer, you can probably get by without this information. For instance, most people don't care what the GPS latitude was when they snapped a photo. Don't worry if some of the categories in this pane are blank—not all cameras are designed to provide all of the information shown. The more expensive, professional camera models provide more information to iPhoto than consumer (affordable) models do.

The Keywords pane

This is the part of the Photo Info window you really care about. Click the "Keywords" button to see which keywords have been assigned to an image.

This is also where you *assign* keywords to photos. Select one or more photos (or an album), then come here and click the checkbox next to one or more keywords you want to assign to the photos.

To *remove* keywords from a photo, select the photo then come here and click a checkbox to remove the checkmark.

To add, rename, or remove any keywords, do it in the Keywords pane of iPhoto Preferences (see the bottom of page 12).

Edit Photos

Photos often need a little help to look their best. Your favorite shot may be a little too dark, too blue, or have a small blemish in the middle of the picture. Even photos that look great can sometimes be improved by cropping them to change the composition. iPhoto includes easy-to-use tools that enable the most common image editing procedures.

To view a photo for editing:

Select an album or a single photo, then click the "Edit" button beneath the viewing area. Three things happen:

- The selected photo enlarges to fill the entire viewing area.
- The toolbar displays iPhoto's editing tools beneath the photo.
- All of the photos contained in the selected album (or Library) appear in a scrollable thumbnail pane across the top of the window, where you can select other photos without leaving the Edit view.

You can rotate photos without moving to Edit view. Select a photo in the viewing area, then click the "Rotate" button. Option-click to reverse the rotation direction.

*This scrollable **thumbnail pane** shows all of the photos in the selected album or Library. Click one of the photo thumbnails to place it in the Edit viewing area.*

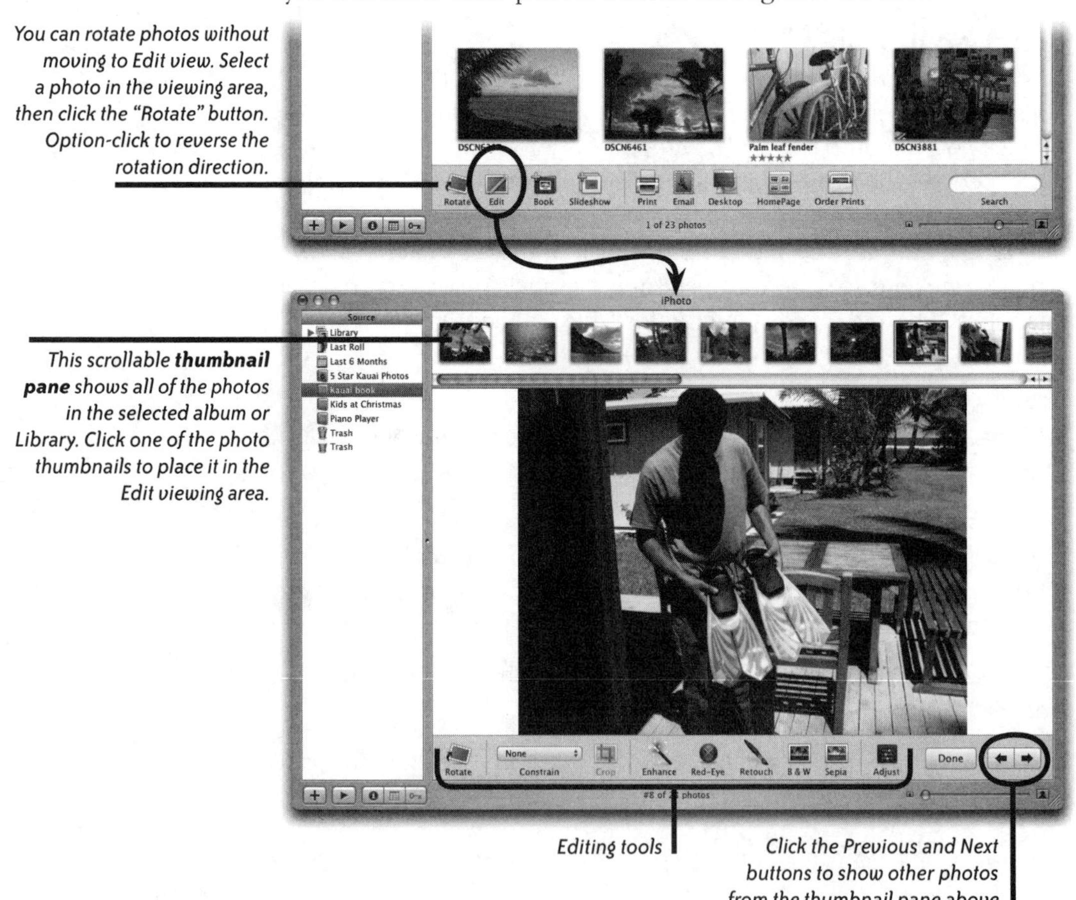

Editing tools

Click the Previous and Next buttons to show other photos from the thumbnail pane above.

Create a duplicate photo before you do anything drastic

When you drag a photo from the Library into an album, iPhoto doesn't make a separate *copy* of that photo—it creates a "link" that points from the album to the original photo in the Library. This prevents your hard disk from getting stuffed full with multiple copies of the same photo.

So when you edit a photo, you affect its appearance not only in the Library *but in all other albums in which that photo appears.* If you want to avoid changing the photo's appearance in every instance, create a *duplicate* of the photo and edit the duplicate.

1. Select a photo in the Library or in an album. When you duplicate a photo *in an album,* the duplicate appears in both the album *and* the Library; any changes you make will apply to both duplicates, since they're actually the same photo.
2. From the Photos menu, choose "Duplicate," **or** press Command D.

   Or *instead* of Steps 1 and 2, Control-click on a photo, then choose "Duplicate" from the contextual menu that pops up.
3. iPhoto automatically renames the duplicate by adding "copy" to the title, but you may want to change the name: select the duplicate, then enter a new name in the "title" field of the Information pane.
4. Select the duplicate photo, then click the "Edit" button to show the photo in Edit view and access iPhoto's editing tools.

While the duplicate is selected, type a new title.

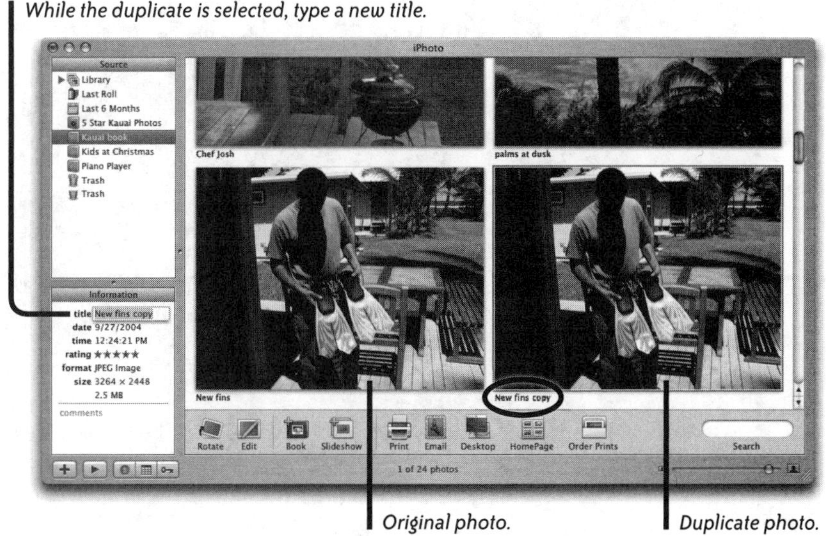

Original photo.

Duplicate photo.

Duplicate photos take up as much room on your hard disk as the original. Use duplicates sparingly to economize your computer's storage space.

As you make the editing changes described on the following pages, you can use the Undo command to undo changes, one at a time. Press Command Z, or choose "Undo" from the Edit menu.

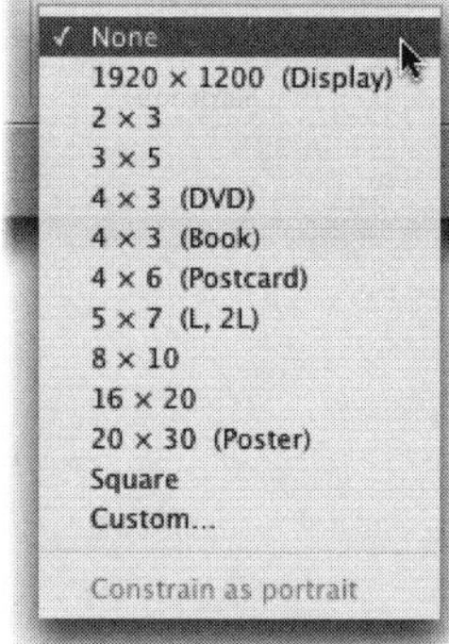

The Constrain pop-up menu contains common size and proportion options, plus a custom option for creating a photo any size.

Crop an image

The Crop tool lets you select the most important part of a picture and delete the rest of it. Thoughtful cropping makes your photos visually stronger and more interesting.

1. Select a photo.
2. Click the "Edit" button.
3. Select an option from the "Constrain" menu, shown on the left.

   Choose "None" if you don't want restraints on your cropping so you can drag-select any shape and proportion you want. Choose one of the other options to limit the cropping area to a specific ratio. For instance, if you plan to use the photo in an iPhoto Book, select the "4 x 3 (Book)" option.
4. Position the crosshair pointer at one corner of the desired cropping area, then press-and-drag diagonally to create a cropping area, as shown below. When you like the selection, let go of the mouse.

   To move the crop selection, *press* inside the cropping area and drag.

   To resize the crop selection, position the tip of the pointer on any edge of the cropping selection, then press-and-drag the edge to a new position. **Or** click outside the crop selection and start over.
5. Click the "Crop" button to apply the cropping.

Drag the crosshair pointer diagonally to draw a cropping area within the selected photo. The "faded out" area is removed when you click the "Crop" button.

Constrain the shape and proportion of the cropped area by selecting an option from the "Constrain" pop-up menu (shown above).

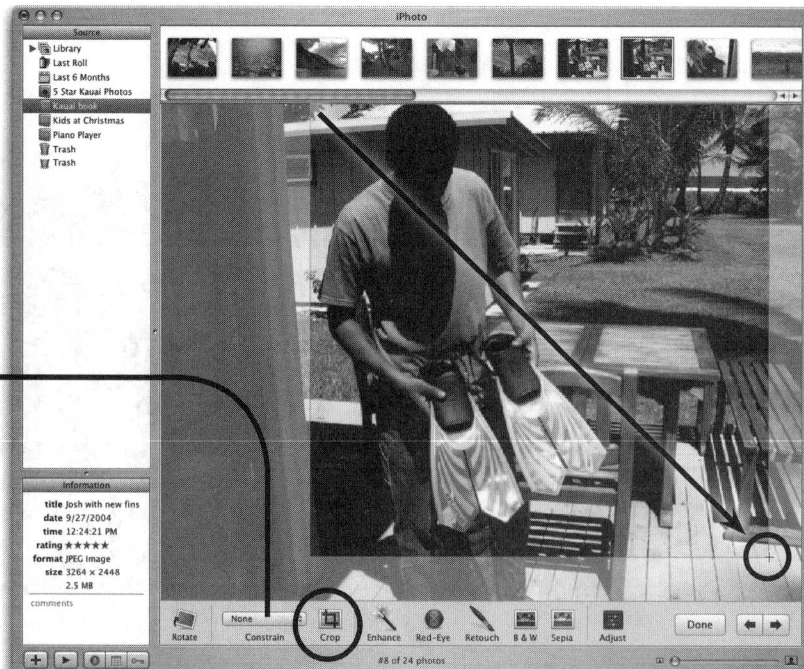

Improve photos with the Enhance tool

Sometimes you think photos look pretty good because you don't have a "corrected" version that you can compare them to. Colors may be dull and the contrast may be flat, but who notices? The "Enhance" tool analyzes an image and automatically adjusts the color and contrast. You might not always prefer the enhanced version, but it can often make dramatic improvements to photos.

To use the Enhance tool:

1. Select a photo from an album or from the Library.
2. Click the "Edit" button to fill the viewing area with the photo.
3. Click the "Enhance" button once. Check the photo in the Viewing area to see if you like the changes.

   Compare the "enhanced" photo to the original version: Press the Control key to see the original. Release the Control key to show the current effect.

   If you don't like the new version, undo the enhancement by pressing Command Z. **Or** from the Edit menu, choose "Undo Enhance Photo." **Or** from the Photos menu, choose "Revert to Original."

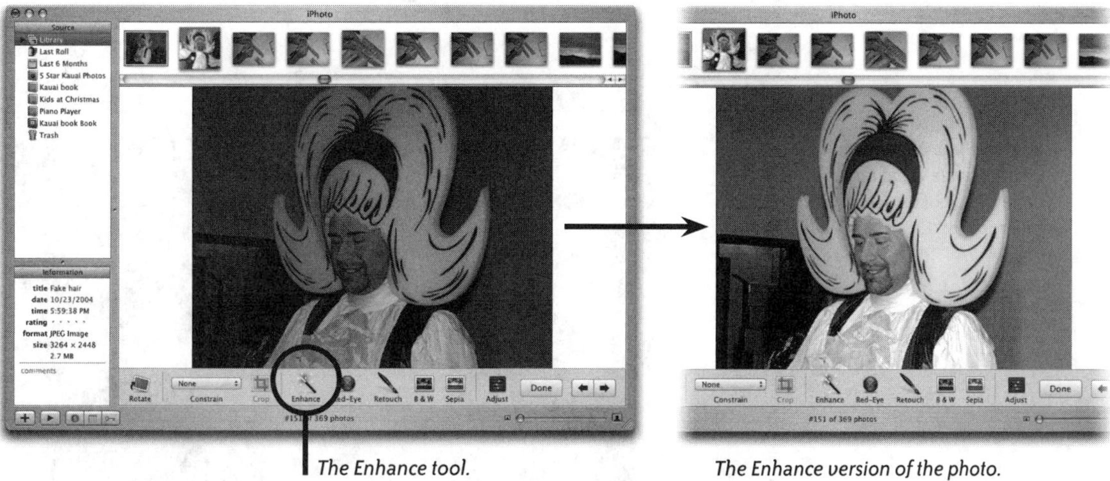

The Enhance tool.

The Enhance version of the photo.

The Enhance tool is fast and easy, but it's also a hit-or-miss solution—iPhoto does its best to analyze a photo, then applies the changes. To have more control when you enhance a photo, use the Adjust tools (see pages 34–35).

The Rotate button.

Rotate an image

You can rotate a photo from any view mode. Just select a photo and click the Rotate button (shown to the left) to rotate the image 90 degrees counterclockwise (if counterclockwise is what you chose in Preferences, pages 14–15). Additional clicks will continue to rotate the image in 90-degree increments.

Option-click the Rotate button to rotate the photo in the opposite direction indicated by the button's icon.

Reduce red-eye

Use the Red-Eye tool to remove the red glare in a subject's eyes caused by a camera's flash. The results may vary with different photos.

1. Select a photo that needs red-eye removal.
2. Click the "Edit" button (if you're not already there).
3. Click the "Red-Eye" button to select it. A green dot appears on top of the Red-Eye button to indicate the tool is active. A floating message bar appears with instructions to click the center of each eye.
4. Click the center of each eye.
5. To quit the Red-Eye tool, click the tool again in the toolbar, or click the "x" in the floating message bar.

If you're not satisfied with the results, press Command Z (Undo), or from the Photos menu, choose "Revert to Original."

You can also do this: Press-and-drag the cursor to select a rectangular area that encloses both eyes, or all the eyes of all the people in the photo. Then just click the "Red-Eye" button.

The "Red-Eye" button.

Touch up photos with the Retouch tool

Even your best photos usually have some imperfections in them. If you scanned a photo, dust or scratches on the scanner glass may be visible, and digital images straight from a camera contain artifacts or digital "noise" that appears as oddly colored pixels in the image. There's also the possibility that the model or the background could have a blemish you want to remove.

The Retouch tool does an excellent job of fixing minor problems. Acting like a combination blur and smudge brush, it blends the pixels under the crosshair into the surrounding area.

Any retouching changes you make are applied to the original photo in the Library, even if you selected the photo from an album instead of from the Library. **The retouched version will replace all occurrences of the photo in all albums in which it appears.** If you want to prevent this, make a duplicate of the photo and make changes to the duplicate.

To use the Retouch brush:

1. Select a photo to retouch.
2. Click the "Edit" button to fill the viewing area with the photo and show the editing tools. If necessary you can use the size slider (in the bottom-right corner) to enlarge the photo.
3. Click the "Retouch" button in the Edit toolbar.
4. Move the Retouch tool cursor crosshairs on top of the area you want to retouch, then click once. Click again if necessary to achieve the results you want. You can also press-and-drag the crosshairs to affect a larger area.

iPhoto's Retouch tool blurs and blends nearby pixels to acheive results.

The retouched version of this photo removed a beauty mark and shiny highlights on the nose and lips.

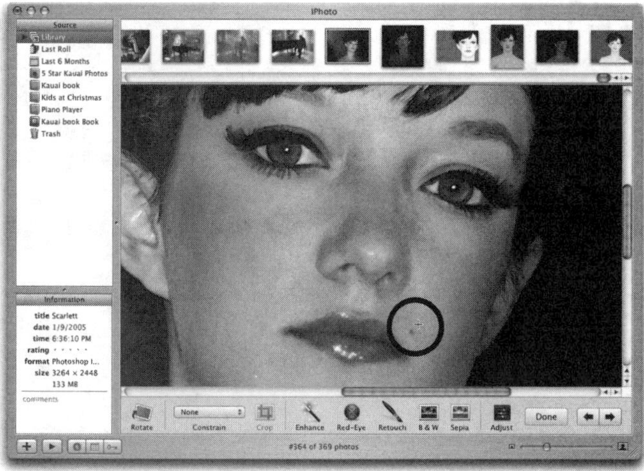

The Retouch crosshair is positioned near the area to be retouched.

Size slider.

Convert a photo to black and white or sepia

To convert a photo to black and white or sepia, select it, then click the "Edit" button. In the Edit toolbar, click the "B & W" or "Sepia" button.

Remember, this will affect how this photo looks in every album it appears in. If you don't want to affect other occurrences, first make a duplicate of the photo, rename it, and convert the *duplicate* to black and white.

Use the Adjust tools to edit images

Try this: Open the Adjust window, then use the Enhance wand to modify a photo. You'll see the Levels graph change as the photo changes appearance.

The Adjust tools let you *manually* change settings to modify the appearance of photos. This gives you much more control over the results than if you use the automatic modifications of the Enhance tool.

1. Select a photo, then click the "Edit" button in the toolbar to switch to the edit view (shown below).
2. Click the "Adjust" button to open the "Adjust" window.
3. Drag the various image modification sliders to alter the image.

   The "Levels" graph at the bottom of the "Adjust" window is called a histogram. It charts all the dark and light pixels in an image.
   To make light areas lighter, drag the right slider under the histogram to the left. To make dark areas darker, drag the left slider under the histogram to the right. You'll see the changes in the photo as you drag the sliders.
4. When you're finished with your changes, click the "Done" button to save the changes.

Tip: To change slider values in single increments, click the symbol on the left or right side of the slider.

Click here to close this window.

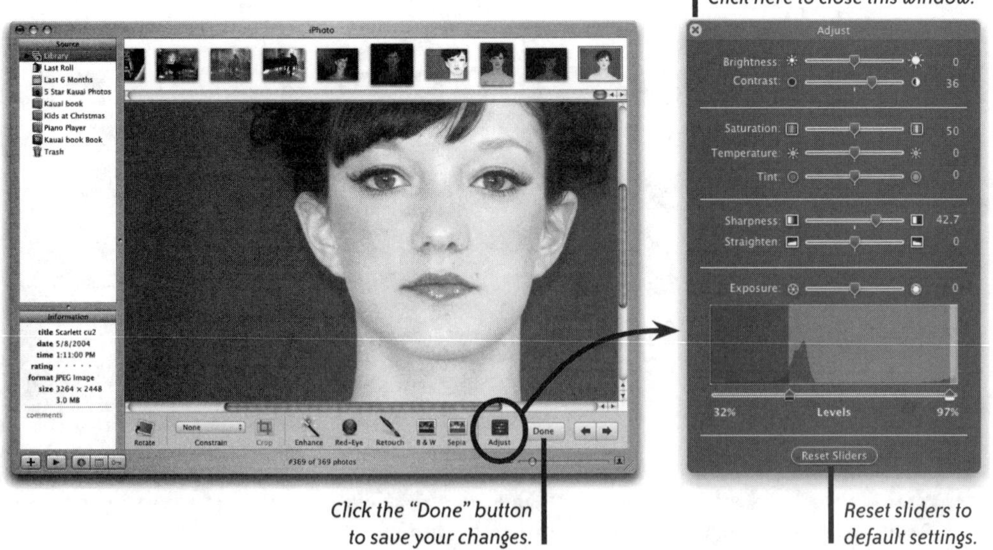

Click the "Done" button to save your changes.

Reset sliders to default settings.

When you use the Adjust sliders to modify an image, it not only gives you more control, it allows you to experiment with effects that you wouldn't ordinarily think about. Compare the two examples below to the original image on the previous page. The version on the left shows bold changes to the Levels settings. The version on the right shows even more extreme levels settings, plus a very large amount of sharpening (moving the "Sharpness" slider to the right). It's fun to experiment with the Adjust sliders.

Tip: *If you want to open photos in some other image-editing application, such as Adobe Photoshop or Adobe Photoshop Elements, set iPhoto to open another application when you double-click a photo.* *See the bottom of page 14.*

Straighten crooked photos

The "Straighten" adjustment slider lets you correct photos that need to be straightened (or tilt a photo for special effect).

1. Select a photo, then click the "Edit" button to open it in Edit view.
2. Click the Adjust button in the Edit toolbar.
3. Drag the "Straighten" slider left or right to tilt the image. A grid appears to which you can align elements in the photo.

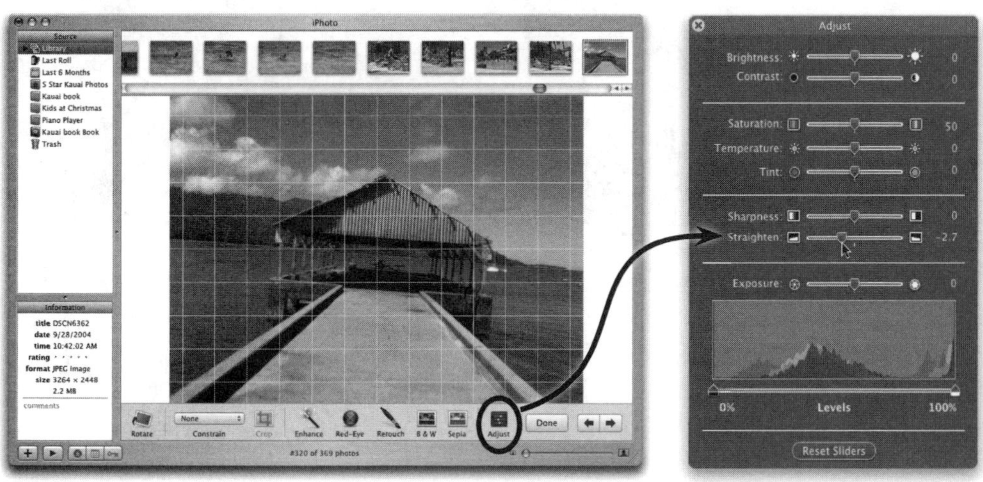

Edit a photo in a separate window

You can choose to edit a photo in its own, separate edit window rather than in the iPhoto window. This enables you keep more than one photo open and editable at one time. If you're comparing photos or editing for color harmony between photos, working with several open windows can be helpful.

To open a photo in a separate window, hold down the Option key and double-click a photo. **Or** Control-click on a photo, then choose "Edit in separate window" from the pop-up contextual menu.

After you've made image adjustments, click the red Close button to close this window and save your changes.

To revert to the original, unedited photo, Control-click on the photo and choose "Revert to Original." You can also revert to the original later from the main iPhoto window.

Tip: If you want photos to open into separate windows every time you double-click, choose "Opens photo in edit window" in iPhoto's Preferences window. See page 14.

The Close button.

Use the "Size" pop-up menu to choose what size the photo is shown in this window. When you choose "Fit to window" the photo automatically resizes when you change the size of the window.

The "Size" pop-up menu.

Use the Left and Right arrows to open other photos from the selected album in this same window.

Drag the bottom-right corner to resize the window.

iPhoto Books

iPhoto's Book feature creates a professionally printed, softbound or hardbound book you design from templates with your own photos and captions. You can use the book as a catalog, picture book, story book, portfolio, or any other sort of book you need. After you create it, you order it with the click of a button and your beautiful book will be delivered to your door.

iPhoto books are great for personal keepsakes, gifts, or used as professional presentations.

Create a book

1. First create a new album, **or** select an existing album, that contains the photos you want to use in a book. The order in which photos appear in the album is the order in which they will appear in the book that you create, so rearrange the photos before you start building your book. However, if you change your mind on the order of photos you can still make changes later. The first photo in the album is used as the cover of your book.
2. With your album selected, click the "Book" button to start the design process of building your book.

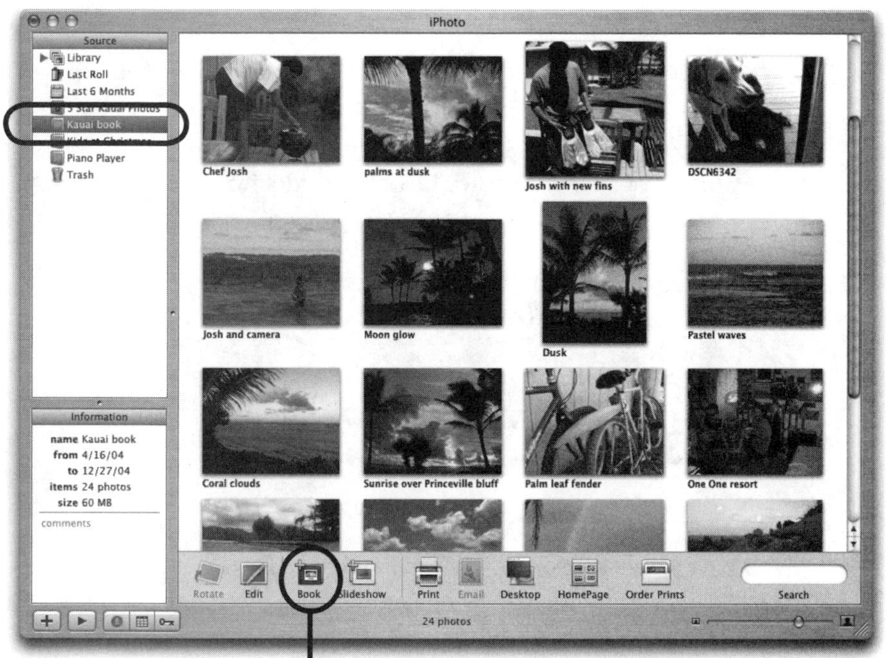

We selected the album (circled, far-left) that contains the photos we want to use in a book.

Click the "Book" button to open the selected album in Book view, shown on the next page.

—continued

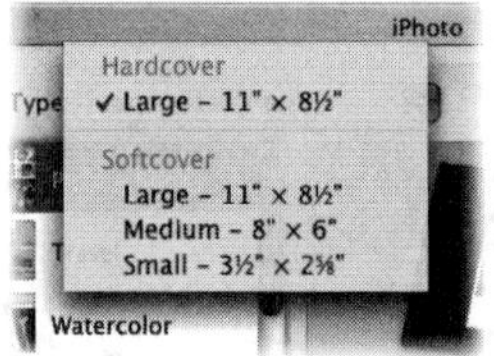

You can select from four different book styles.

3. In the Theme sheet that drops down (shown below), select a book type from the "Book Type" pop-up menu (shown left). Next, choose if you want double-sided pages (click the "Double-sided pages" checkbox), then a design theme from the scrolling pane on the left.

Choose a design theme.

Go to a web page that gives prices and more details about iPhoto Books.

4. You can add titles, comments, or captions to most photo pages, depending on the theme style or page design you choose.

   Click the "Choose Theme" button (circled above). In the message that drops down (shown below), decide if you want to place photos manually in the book, or have iPhoto automatically create a layout.

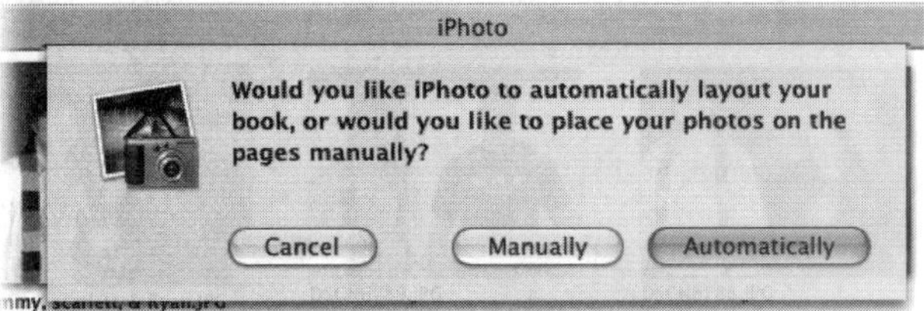

As soon as you choose "Manually" or "Automatically," the Book view opens with your layout presented in both a thumbnail version and a larger preview version (shown on the following page). iPhoto automatically creates a Book album in the "Source" pane and selects it (see the highlighted album in the "Source" pane on the following page).

- To display a book page in the Preview pane, find the page you want in the scrolling Page View Thumbnail pane, then single-click that page.
- To change the order of pages, drag pages or double-page spreads in the Page View Thumbnail pane left or right.
- You can drag a photo from the Unplaced Photos Thumbnail pane to any page in the Preview pane, even if a photo is already placed there.
- To resize the preview, drag the Size slider in the bottom-right corner.
- To delete a photo from a page, select it in either the Page View Thumbnail pane or the large Preview pane, then press Delete. Don't worry—the deleted photo is still available in the Thumbnail pane: click the Unplaced Photos button to see it and other photos that have not yet been placed.
- In the Preview pane, you can drag a photo from one side of a page spread to the other side to switch its position with the other photo.

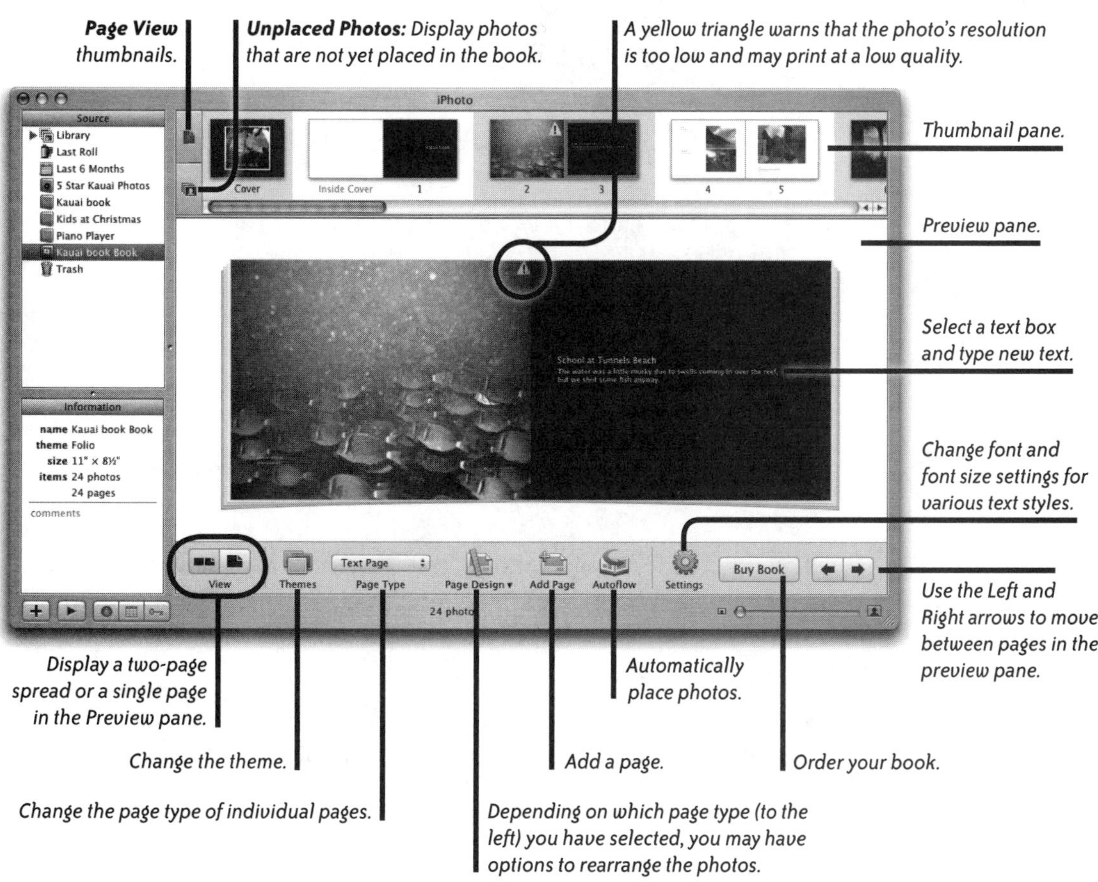
Page View thumbnails.
Unplaced Photos: Display photos that are not yet placed in the book.
A yellow triangle warns that the photo's resolution is too low and may print at a low quality.
Thumbnail pane.
Preview pane.
Select a text box and type new text.
Change font and font size settings for various text styles.
Use the Left and Right arrows to move between pages in the preview pane.
Display a two-page spread or a single page in the Preview pane.
Automatically place photos.
Change the theme.
Add a page.
Order your book.
Change the page type of individual pages.
Depending on which page type (to the left) you have selected, you may have options to rearrange the photos.
iPhoto
Source
Library
Last Roll
Last 6 Months
5 Star Kauai Photos
Kauai book
Kids at Christmas
Piano Player
Kauai book Book
Trash
Information
name Kauai book Book
theme Folio
size 11" × 8½"
items 24 photos
24 pages
comments
Cover
Inside Cover
School at Tunnels Beach
View
Themes
Text Page
Page Type
Page Design
Add Page
Autoflow
Settings
Buy Book

Order your book

After you create a book (as explained on the previous pages), you can order copies of it using your Internet connection.

1. With the book open in iPhoto, click the "Buy Book" button.
2. A sheet drops down from iPhoto's title bar (shown on the left) as the book assembly process takes place.
3. Your Mac connects to the Internet and opens the "Order Book" window, shown below. If the button in the lower-right says "Enable 1-Click Ordering," click it. You will be asked to start an Apple account and provide your name, address, and credit card information, as well as your shipping preferences. If you already have an Apple account, you will be asked to turn on "1-Click Ordering."

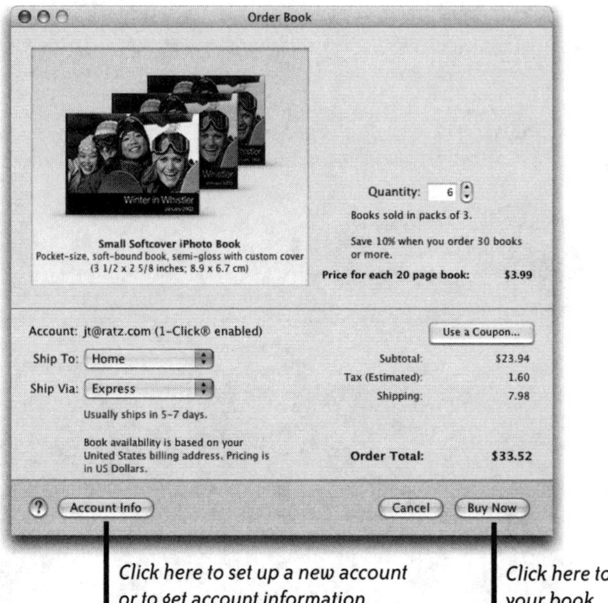

Click here to set up a new account or to get account information.

Click here to order your book.

4. In the "Order Book" window, select a color for the cover if you created a hardbound book, a quantity of books (they will all be copies of this one book), and shipping preference.
5. Click "Buy Now."
6. You'll see a "Transferring book..." progress sheet that indicates your book files are being transferred to the publisher. Your order should arrive on your doorstep in about a week.

Create a slideshow

Create a slideshow that you can play anytime you want. You can also set a slideshow to repeat and use it as a screen saver.

The quick method:

1. Select an album, the Library, or a selection of photos from either. **Or** create an album just for the slideshow and drag photos into it from the Library or from other albums.
2. Click the triangular Play button in the bottom-left corner of the iPhoto window (circled below). A "Slideshow" window opens where you choose settings for the slideshow and for the music; click the "Play" button in that window to present the slideshow.

   To skip the "Slideshow" settings window and play the slides immediately, Option-click the triangular Play button, circled below.

The "Slideshow" button as it appears in the Organize toolbar.

Slideshow

The more controlled method:

1. Follow Step 1, above. Then Click the "Slideshow" button in the **Organize toolbar** to open the Slideshow view, shown below. This view includes a scrolling Thumbnail pane that contains all of the photos in the slideshow. iPhoto automatically creates a Slideshow album, places it in the "Source" pane, and highlights it, as shown below.

iPhoto
Source
Library
Last Roll
Last 6 Months
5 Star Kauai Photos
Kauai book
Kids at Christmas
Piano Player
Kids at Christmas B...
Kauai book Slideshow
Trash
Play
Preview
Effect: None
Transition: Default (Dissolve)
Ken Burns Effect
Start
End
Adjust
Settings
Music
1 of 24 photos
Thumbnail pane.
Click any photo to show it in the Preview pane. Drag photos to change their order.
Preview pane.
Customize slideshow settings.
Choose music to play with your slideshow.
Show the previous or next photo.
Play slideshow.
Preview the selected photo and its transition.
Create pan-and-zoom effects.
Drag the Size slider to zoom in on a photo.
The Play button in Slideshow view.
Adjust the selected photo (see pages 34–35).

The Slideshow toolbar.

The Adjust window is shown below.

See the top of the next page.

See the Music sheet at the bottom of the next page.

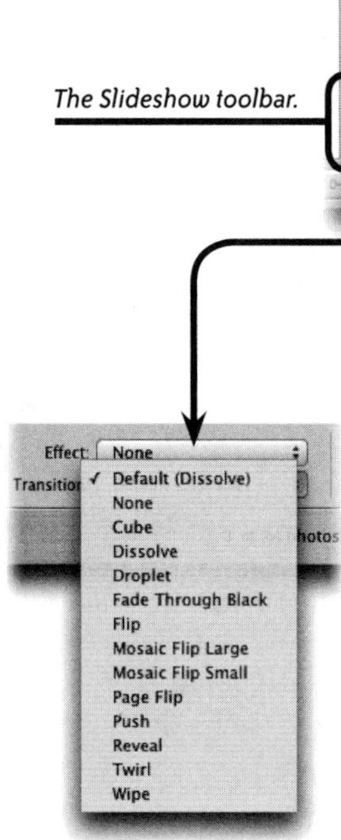

The transition you choose from this pop-up menu applies only to the selected photo.

When you create a new slideshow, all transitions are set to the default style in the Settings sheet (on the next page).

Individual transitions can be changed using the menu above or in the Adjust window (shown on the right).

2. From the "Effect" pop-up menu choose "Black and White" or "Sepia" to add that effect to the current photo.
3. From the "Transition" pop-up menu, choose a transition, or choose "None." You can set different transitions for individual photos.
4. By default, the Ken Burns Effect (a slow pan-and-zoom that adds movement to still photos) is turned on in the Settings window (shown on the following page). Click the "Settings" button to see this and other options. To apply a Ken Burns effect or to modify the existing automatic effect, check the "Ken Burns Effect" box, then:
   - Move the toggle switch to the "Start" position. Size and position the photo as you want it to appear at the beginning of the pan or zoom. Use the Size slider to zoom in close on one part of the photo, then press-and-drag the photo to another position in the Preview pane until the photo is positioned and sized as you want.
   - Then move the toggle switch to the "End" position. Size and position the photo as you want it to appear at the *end* of the pan-and-zoom effect.
   - Click the "Preview" button to test the effect.
5. To make more adjustments to individual photos, click the "Adjust" button. In the "Adjust This Slide" window you can change the duration, transition style, transition speed, or transition direction (if the selected transition is directional).

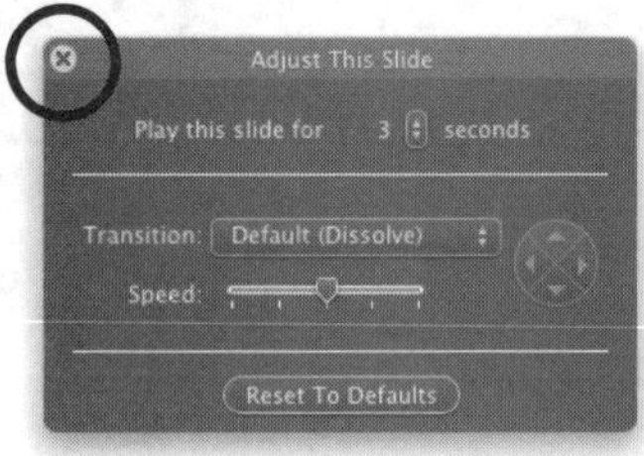

To close this window, click its Close button (circled).

6. Click the "Settings" button to change the default settings that affect the entire slideshow. A settings sheet slides down from the title bar.

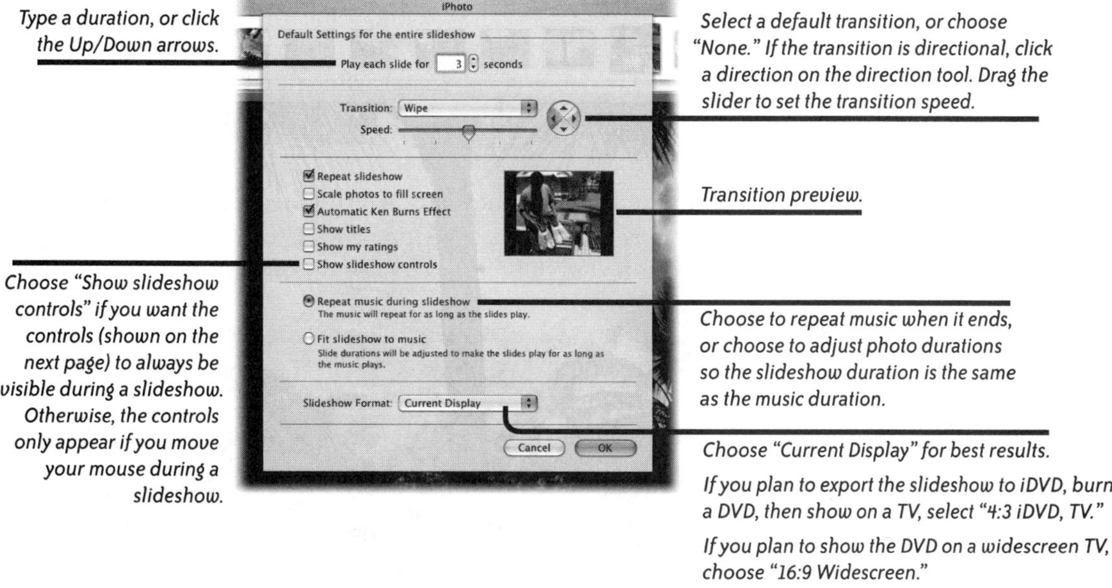
Type a duration, or click the Up/Down arrows.
iPhoto
Default Settings for the entire slideshow
Play each slide for 3 seconds
Transition: Wipe
Speed:
Repeat slideshow
Scale photos to fill screen
Automatic Ken Burns Effect
Show titles
Show my ratings
Show slideshow controls
Repeat music during slideshow
The music will repeat for as long as the slides play.
Fit slideshow to music
Slide durations will be adjusted to make the slides play for as long as the music plays.
Slideshow Format: Current Display
Cancel
OK
Select a default transition, or choose "None." If the transition is directional, click a direction on the direction tool. Drag the slider to set the transition speed.
Transition preview.
Choose "Show slideshow controls" if you want the controls (shown on the next page) to always be visible during a slideshow. Otherwise, the controls only appear if you move your mouse during a slideshow.
Choose to repeat music when it ends, or choose to adjust photo durations so the slideshow duration is the same as the music duration.
Choose "Current Display" for best results.
If you plan to export the slideshow to iDVD, burn a DVD, then show on a TV, select "4:3 iDVD, TV."
If you plan to show the DVD on a widescreen TV, choose "16:9 Widescreen."

7. Click the "Music" button to show the drop-down Music sheet. The top pane shows a folder of sample music and your entire iTunes Library, including any custom albums (collections of songs) that you created. Select the Library or an album to show its songs in the bottom pane. You can select multiple songs for long slideshows so the same song won't have to repeat over and over.

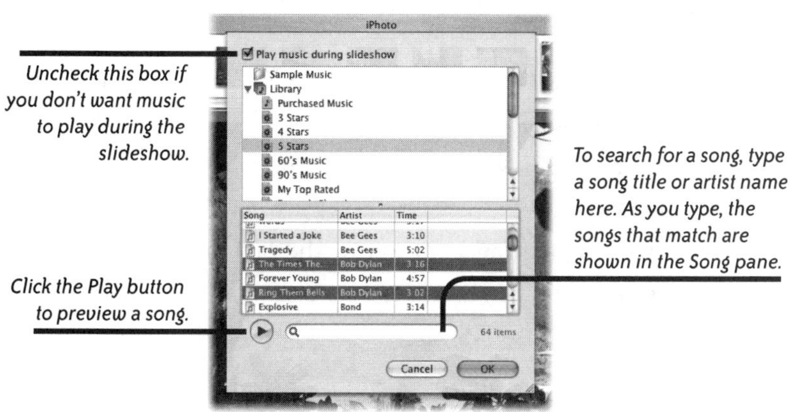
Uncheck this box if you don't want music to play during the slideshow.
iPhoto
Play music during slideshow
Sample Music
Library
Purchased Music
3 Stars
4 Stars
5 Stars
60's Music
90's Music
My Top Rated
Song
Artist
Time
I Started a Joke
Bee Gees
3:10
Tragedy
Bee Gees
5:02
The Times The...
Bob Dylan
3:16
Forever Young
Bob Dylan
4:57
Ring Them Bells
Bob Dylan
3:02
Explosive
Bond
3:14
64 items
Cancel
OK
Click the Play button to preview a song.
To search for a song, type a song title or artist name here. As you type, the songs that match are shown in the Song pane.

8. Click the "Play" button in the Slideshow toolbar to show it full-screen.

Use a Slideshow to Preview Your Albums

A slideshow is a great way to preview the photos you've just imported. As the slideshow displays the images full-screen, you can use the controls (below) to make changes such as rotate left or right, assign a rating, or delete a photo. The slideshow advances to the next photo automatically, but if you need more time to decide on a rating or to make some other decision, use the on-screen Pause control. Use the left and right arrows to go back to the previous photo or forward to the next photo.

As the slideshow plays, the controls remain hidden until you move your mouse. To make sure you always have the controls visible, check the "Show slideshow controls" box in the settings shown on the previous page.

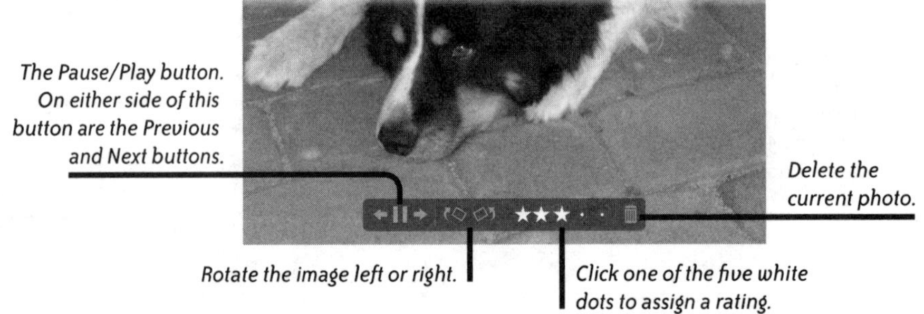

The Pause/Play button. On either side of this button are the Previous and Next buttons.
Delete the current photo.
Rotate the image left or right.
Click one of the five white dots to assign a rating.

The advantage of creating a slideshow that appears in the "Source" pane as a Slideshow album (as opposed to the instant slideshow explained on page 41) is that you can reopen the slideshow at any time to continue working on it. And it gives you access to the Slideshow toolbar which provides much more control over how the final slideshow plays.

Use these keyboard shortcuts to control the playback of your slides:

- **Up arrow:** Speeds up the slideshow.
- **Down arrow:** Slows down the slideshow.
- **Spacebar:** Toggles the slideshow between Play and Pause.
- **Left and right arrow keys:** Shows the previous slide or next slide.
- **Mouse click:** Stops the slideshow and takes you back to iPhoto.

Share Slideshows

After you've created a slideshow complete with transitions and music, you might want to share it in some way other than showing it on your computer screen. iPhoto can export a slideshow as a QuickTime movie. The QuickTime movie can be copied to a CD or, if you make the movie small enough, it can be attached to an email message. You can send a slideshow to iDVD to create a DVD that you can send to others. And if you have a .Mac account, you can publish a slideshow on the Internet that other Mac OS X (version 10.2 or later) users can see.

To learn how to publish a .Mac slideshow on the Internet, see page 52.

Export a slideshow as a QuickTime movie

1. Select a slideshow album in the "Source" pane, or choose an album.
2. From the Share menu choose "Export...."
3. In the "Save As" sheet that drops down name your movie and choose a location to save it, then click the "Export" button.

   By default iPhoto puts the exported slideshow movie in the Movies folder located in your Home folder, but you can choose any location.

If you select an album in the "Source" pane instead of a slideshow, when you choose "Export..." from the Share menu the "Export Photos" window opens, as explained on pages 60–61.

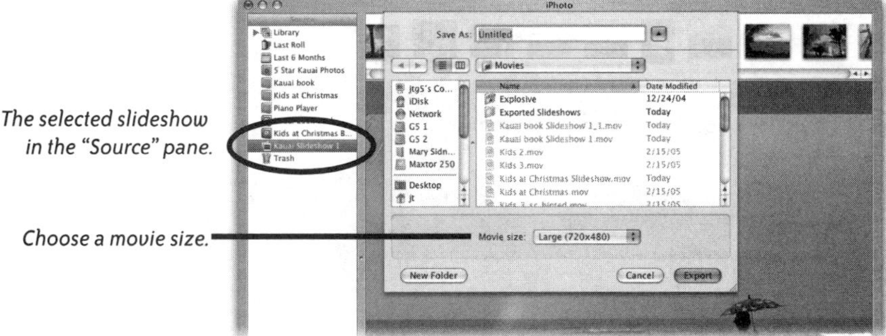

Export a slideshow to iDVD

You can send your slideshows to iDVD where it's easy to create a DVD full of slideshows. Of course, iDVD can also use movies that you create in iMovie, but for now we'll focus on slideshows.

1. Open iDVD, create a new project, then choose a design theme.
2. Select a slideshow in the source pane, or choose an album.
3. From the Share menu choose "Send to iDVD." The selected slideshow appears in the iDVD menu as a button. To add more slideshows to the iDVD project, choose another slideshow in iPhoto, then send to iDVD.

   For more details about sending photos to iDVD, see page 54.

To add your slideshow to an existing iDVD project, open that project before you do Step 3. If you don't first open the iDVD project you want to use, iDVD will automatically open its most recent project.

The Organize Toolbar

The Organize toolbar is visible when you are in the Organize view. It contains tools that let you share your photos with others in a variety of ways. You can print your photos in various formats, create a slideshow to play on your computer, export a QuickTime slideshow for others, order professional prints over the Internet, order a professionally bound hardcover book, create a web site and publish it with blinding speed, burn your photos to a CD or DVD, and more.

Print Your Photos to a Desktop Pprinter

1. Select a single photo, or choose multiple photos from an album or from the Library.
2. Click the "Print" icon in the Organize toolbar, shown above.
3. In the Print sheet that drops down, click the "Style" pop-up menu and choose one of the options. Each option will display different layouts in the Preview pane (shown below).
4. Enter the number of copies to print.
5. Put photo-quality paper in your printer and click "Print."

The "Style" pop-up menu offers these options.

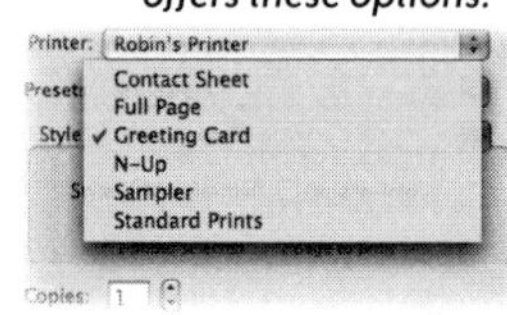

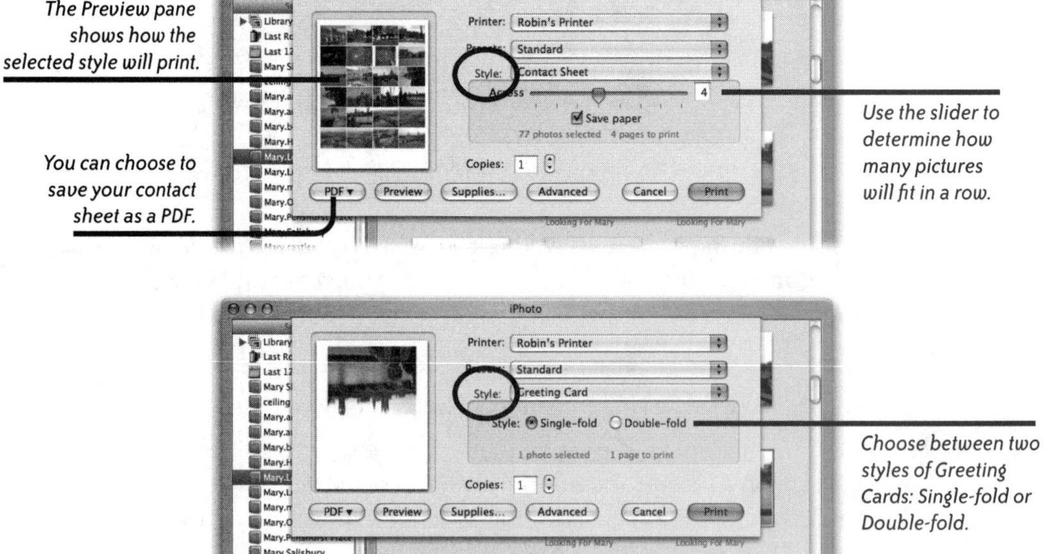

The Preview pane shows how the selected style will print.

You can choose to save your contact sheet as a PDF.

Use the slider to determine how many pictures will fit in a row.

Choose between two styles of Greeting Cards: Single-fold or Double-fold.

Share Photos through Email

One way to share your photos is to send them to someone through email. iPhoto makes it incredibly easy to do just that.

Note: **If you use AOL,** go to the Preferences and choose "America Online" as your email application. The "Email" button in the lower pane will turn into an "AOL" button and you can send photos to AOL users.

Note: **If you use any other email program,** people receiving your photos who use older versions of America Online may have trouble seeing the iPhotos you send this way.

1. Select one or more photos in the Viewing area; you can choose photos from any album or from the Library.

To select multiple photos, hold the Command key as you click on your photo selections.

Selected photos show blue borders.

2. Click the "Email" icon in the Organize toolbar to open the "Mail Photo" window (shown below-left).
3. In the "Mail Photo" window, choose a photo size from the pop-up menu, and choose whether to include titles and comments that you may have added to photos (shown on page 24). Click the "Compose" button.

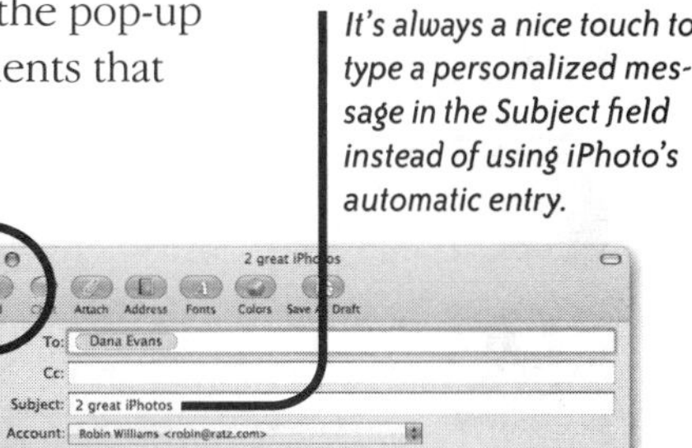

It's always a nice touch to type a personalized message in the Subject field instead of using iPhoto's automatic entry.

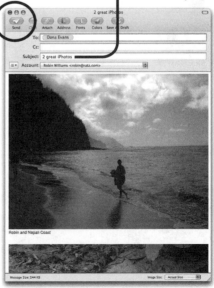

4. If you want, add a message to the email window that opens (shown to the right). Your photos are already sized and placed in the message area.
5. Enter an email address and click the "Send" button in the message toolbar. Your Mac connects to the Internet and sends the photos along with your message.

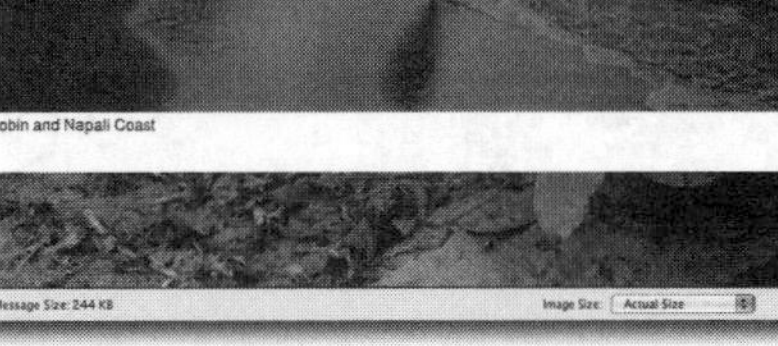

Order Traditional Prints of Your Photos

Order professional prints of any photo or collection of photos from Kodak.

1. Make sure you're connected to the Internet.
2. Select an album or a group of photos within an album or in the Library.
3. Click the "Order Prints" button (shown, left) in the Organize toolbar.

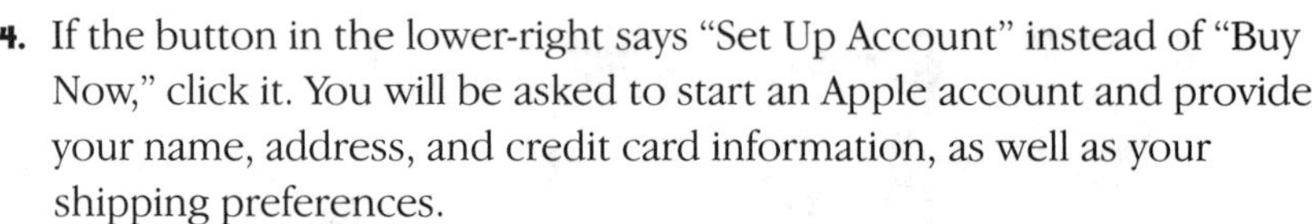

4. If the button in the lower-right says "Set Up Account" instead of "Buy Now," click it. You will be asked to start an Apple account and provide your name, address, and credit card information, as well as your shipping preferences.

   If you already have an account set up, the "Set Up Account" window that opens lets you sign in with your Apple ID and password.

5. Select the size and quantity you want of each photo in the "Order Prints" window:

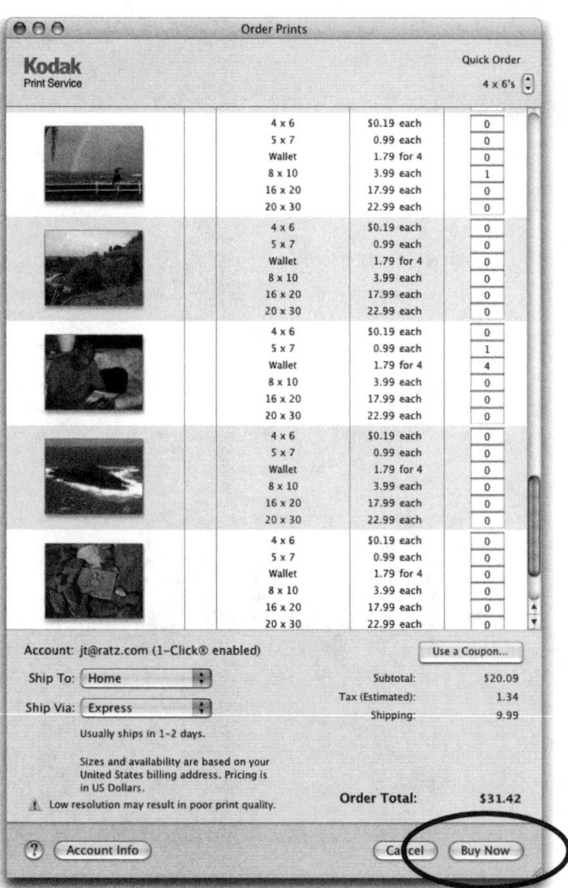

In the top-right corner you can "Quick Order" 4x6 prints. Click the top arrow button to order one 4x6 of each photo in the list.

Click again to change the order to two 4x6 prints of each photo. Every click adds to the order. To lower the quantity, click the bottom arrow button.

You can also buy individual prints of any photo you selected in iPhoto, like a 16x20 or four wallet-sized prints.

As you enter a quantity for each photo, the total cost amount is instantly calculated at the bottom of the window. To remove the order for a photo, type "0" (zero, not the letter O) in the quantity field next to it.

6. Click the "Buy Now" button. Depending on the shipping option you chose in the "Ship Via" pop-up menu, you could have your prints in just a few days. Wow.

A yellow triangle alert next to a certain print size in the "Order Prints" window indicates that photo's resolution is not suitable for a quality print *at that size.* A smaller size may be available without a warning.

A yellow triangle warns that a photo's resolution is too low for the print size listed.

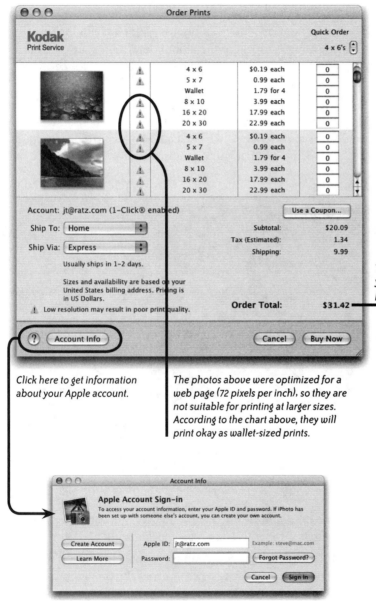

This amount changes as you add photos to or delete photos from your order.

Click here to get information about your Apple account.

The photos above were optimized for a web page (72 pixels per inch), so they are not suitable for printing at larger sizes. According to the chart above, they will print okay as wallet-sized prints.

Build a HomePage Photo Album and Publish it to the Web

If you signed up for a .Mac account (as explained in Section 2), iPhoto can automatically create and publish a web site of your selected photos and store it on Apple's Internet servers. It's really incredible.

1. Select an album or a group of photos within an album. The order in which photos appear in the album determines the order in which they appear on the web page that iPhoto creates. To rearrange photos, drag them into new positions in the album.

2. In iPhoto's Organize toolbar, click the "HomePage" button. Your Mac will connect to the Internet and open the "Publish HomePage" window, as shown below. Your selected images are displayed on a web page template that you can customize.

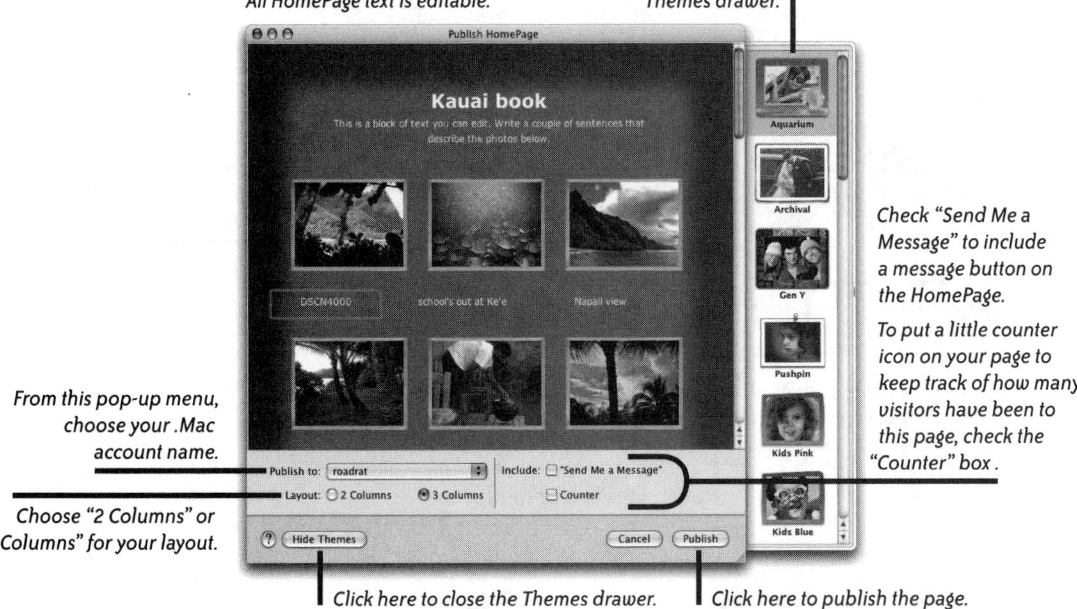

3. Click one of the thumbnail images in the Themes drawer to choose an appearance for your HomePage background and photo frames.
4. To edit the text, select the existing title and captions on the page (press-and-drag over the text) and retype. If you had previously given titles to photos in iPhoto, those titles appear as captions in your HomePage layout.
5. From the "Publish to" pop-up menu at the bottom of the window (shown above), select your .Mac account name.

6. Click the "Publish" button. After the files have been transferred to Apple's .Mac server, a notice will appear telling you the web address of your new web site; this notice has a button called "Visit Page Now." Click it to open your brand-new HomePage photo album.

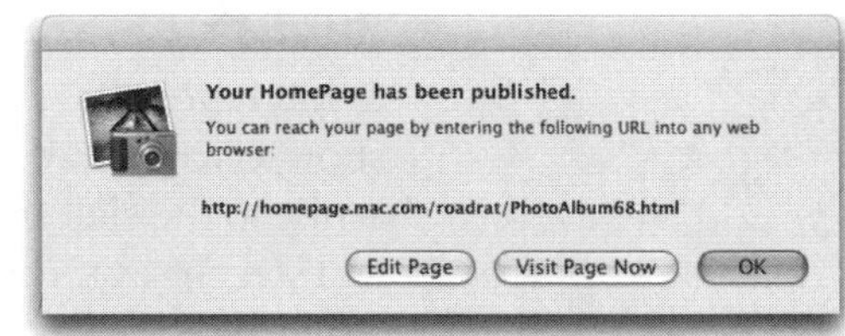

This notice gives you the web address for your HomePage photo album. Click the "Edit Page" button if you want to make changes.

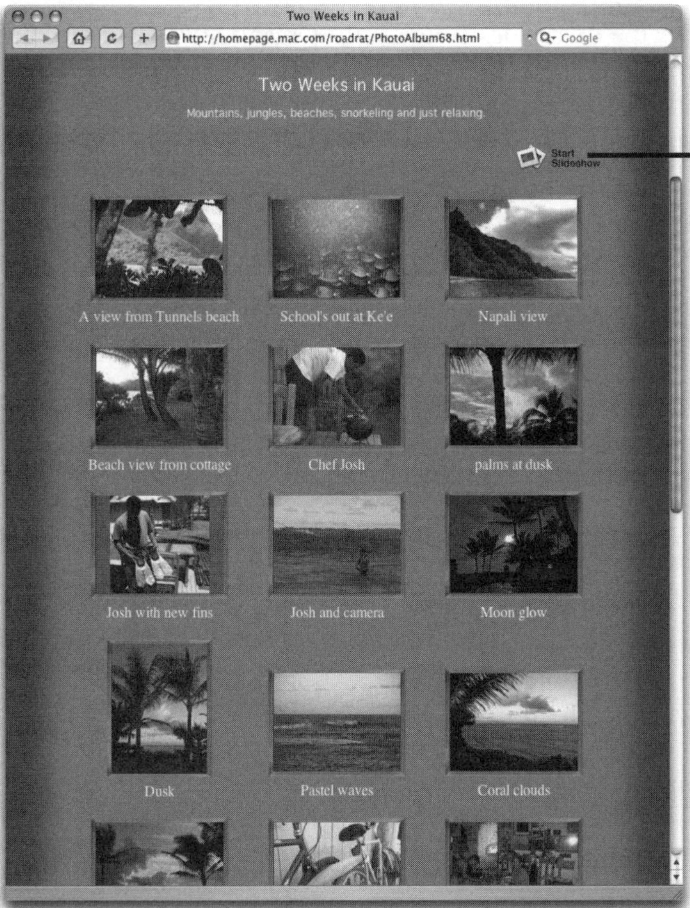

Click this icon or any photo to start a slideshow.

***Tip:* To remove a HomePage photo album,** log in to your .Mac account, then click the "HomePage" button. You'll see a list of the albums you have posted. Single-click on the name, then click the minus sign right below the list.

Send me a message

This button appears on your page if you checked the "Send me a message" checkbox in the "Publish HomePage" window shown on the opposite page.

HomePage

Send feedback

When visitors click the "Send me a message" button, a window opens from which they can send you an iCard. They can also choose an image from your photo album. When they click the arrows below the first card, they see other photos from your HomePage photo album.

Publish a Slideshow on the Internet with .Mac Slides

If you have a .Mac account, the .Mac Slides option lets you publish a slideshow to your iDisk (storage space on Apple's servers). Other people can subscribe to the slideshow, as explained on the opposite page, and it will appear as a screen saver on their own computers.

Create a .Mac slideshow

1. Click the .Mac Slides button in the Organize toolbar. If the button isn't there, go to the Share menu, choose "Show in Toolbar," then choose ".Mac Slides." The .Mac Slides button is now in the toolbar.
2. Select an album in the "Source" pane to use for the .Mac slideshow.

   Or select specific photos from the Library or from an album: Command-click on individual photos in the viewing area, or drag a selection around the photos you want to use.
3. Click the ".Mac Slides" button (left) in the Organize pane.

4. A message window opens (below). Click the "Publish" button.

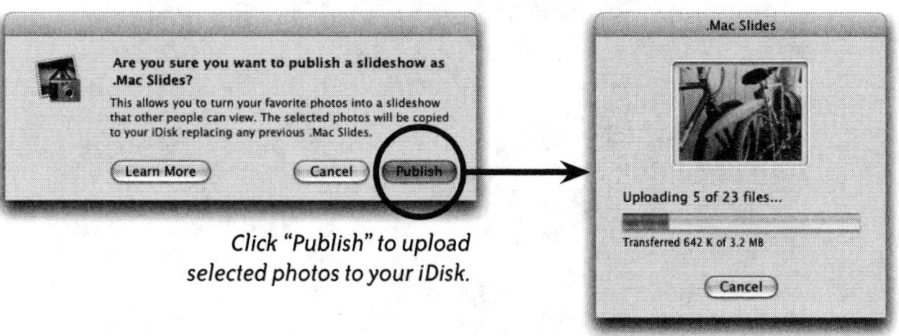

Click "Publish" to upload selected photos to your iDisk.

5. After your photos have been uploaded to your iDisk, click the "Announce Slideshow" button (shown below) to send an email announcement. An automatically generated email contains instructions for viewing your .Mac slideshow. Address the email to one or more friends, then click "Send" in the email message toolbar.

When you publish a .Mac slideshow, it replaces any other slideshow you may have previously published to that .Mac account name.

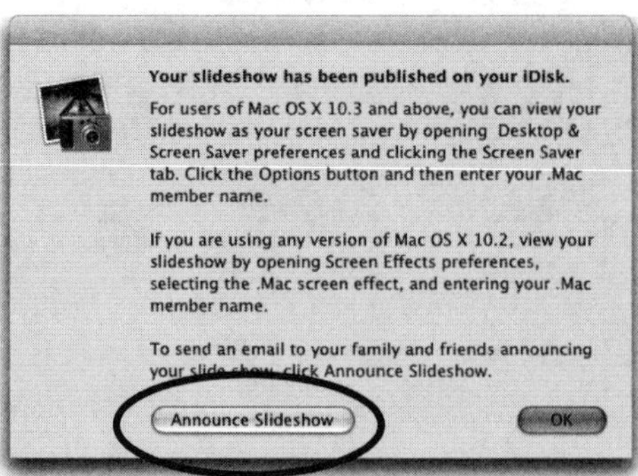

Subscribe to a .Mac slideshow

Anyone using Mac OS X version 10.2 or later with a fast Internet connection can subscribe to your published slideshow and use it as a screen saver. Here's how to subscribe to a published slideshow:

1. Open System Preferences, then open the "Desktop & Screen Saver" preferences. Click the "Screen Saver" button. (In earlier versions of OS X, open System Preferences, then click "Screen Effects.")
2. In the Screen Savers list, choose ".Mac," as shown below-left.
3. Click the "Options" button, then type the .Mac member name of the person to whose slideshow you want to subscribe.
4. Place a checkmark next to the "Display Options" you want.
5. Click OK. Now click the "Options" button again. You'll see the .Mac member name in the list of slideshows. Uncheck the box to the "Public Slide Show," then click OK.
6. Click the "Test" button. Set the duration slider and close the window.

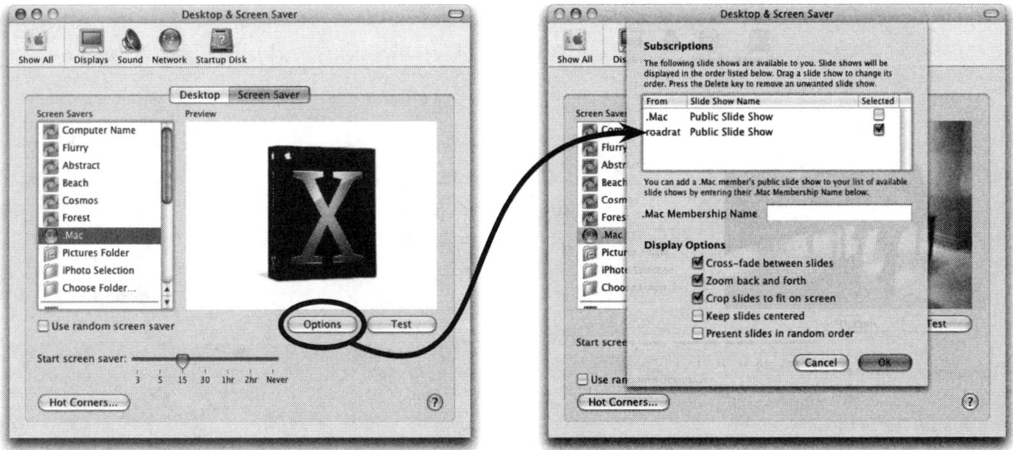

Choose a Photo as Your Desktop Background

Select one of your photos to use as a Desktop image. It's a great way to personalize the appearance of your Mac. Any photo you choose will fill the Desktop space.

1. Select **one** photo in any album or from the Library.
2. Click the "Desktop" icon in the Organize toolbar. The photo instantly appears on your Desktop.

Send Photos to iDVD

If you have a SuperDrive in your Mac (a drive that can read *and write* DVDs), you can send a selection of photos to the iDVD application to make a DVD slideshow, which you can then burn to a DVD. Because DVDs can hold so much data (4.3 gigabytes), you can put lots of slideshows in one DVD project. To learn more about iDVD, see Chapter 4.

To send photos to iDVD:

1. Open iDVD, then select a "Theme" from the iDVD Customize drawer (see Chapter 4 for detailed iDVD instructions).
2. Go back to iPhoto. From the "Source" pane, select an album, a collection of photos from an album, or a slideshow that you created.
3. From the Share menu, choose "Send to iDVD."
4. The photos are transferred to iDVD, which automatically creates a menu with a title and a menu button that links to a slideshow of your photos. If you transferred an iPhoto slideshow or an album, the iDVD slideshow button picks up the name from iPhoto. You can customize the iDVD menu in all sorts of ways, change the design theme, the font style, the music, the slide duration, and more (see Chapter 4).
5. Click the iDVD slideshow button to preview your slideshow in iDVD.
6. Click the "Burn" button in the lower-right corner of the iDVD window to burn the slideshow to a DVD. **Or** save the project so you can work on it later when you have more content to add (more slideshows from iPhoto or movies from iMovie).

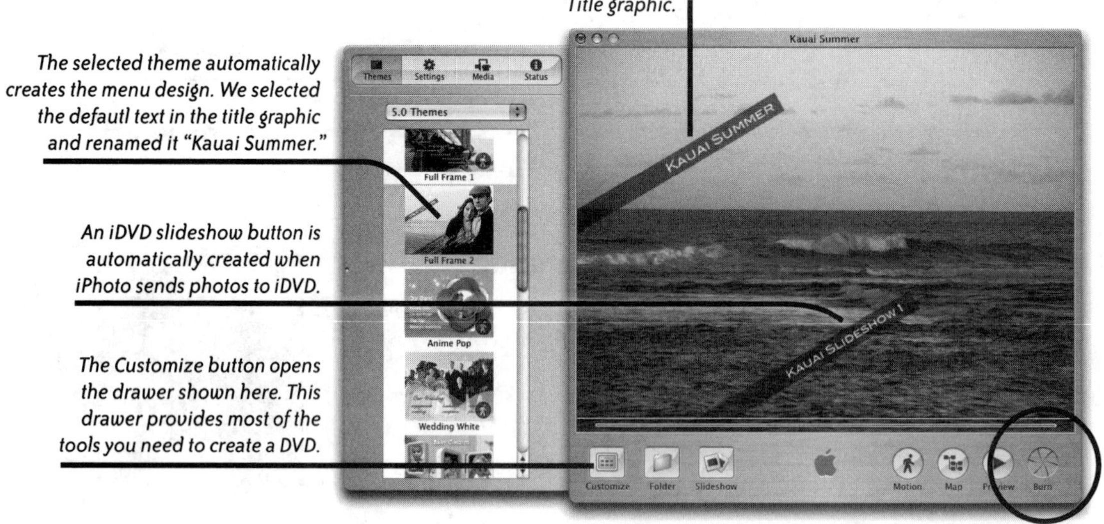

Title graphic.

The selected theme automatically creates the menu design. We selected the defautl text in the title graphic and renamed it "Kauai Summer."

An iDVD slideshow button is automatically created when iPhoto sends photos to iDVD.

The Customize button opens the drawer shown here. This drawer provides most of the tools you need to create a DVD.

Burn a CD or DVD-R of Selected Photos

To burn your photo collections onto a CD or DVD, your computer must have an Apple-supported CD or DVD drive. If your computer has a SuperDrive, it can burn CDs or DVDs. A DVD-R disc holds more than a CD—approximately 4.3 gigabytes of data, compared to less than 1 gigabyte for a CD.

Use iPhoto to burn a disc that you use as a backup or that you plan to use with iPhoto. If you want to burn a disc that you can share with others without iPhoto, don't use iPhoto—use the Finder.

First use iPhoto to export the photos to a folder, then burn the folder to a disc using the disc burning feature of Mac OS X.

Or drag a group of photos or a film roll icon from the iPhoto Preview pane to the Desktop (or anywhere on your hard disk). Then burn the album to a disc using Mac OS X's disc burning feature.

To burn photos onto a disc:

1. Select a collection of photos to burn to a disc (one or more albums, individually selected photos, or the entire Library).
2. From the Share menu choose "Burn Disc."
3. A sheet drops down (shown below) to request that you insert a blank disc. Depending on the kind of drive in your computer, the disc can be a CD-R (CD recordable), a CD-RW (CD rewritable), or a DVD-R (DVD recordable). Insert a blank disc and click OK.

4. A Burn toolbar appears above the Organize toolbar. Type a name for the disc in the "Name" field.
5. Click the "Burn" button (circled below).

The darker color on the disc shows how much disc space the selected photos take.

6. In the "Burn Disc" window that opens (shown on the right), choose an action for "After Burning," then click the "Burn" button.
7. The disc ejects when the burning is finished.

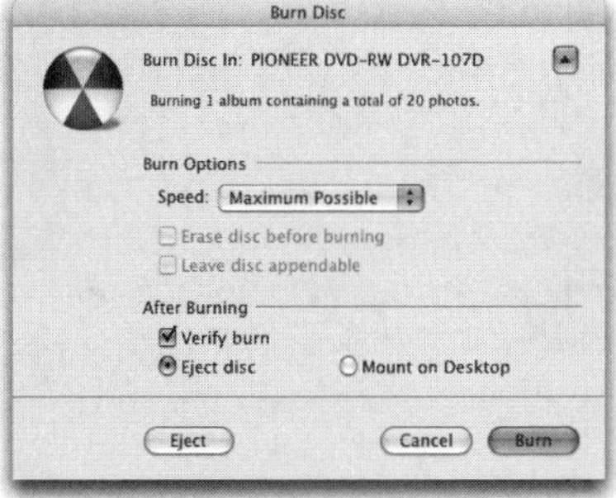

This process does not allow multiple burning sessions. After you burn a disc, the disc is "closed" and you can't burn additional data to it.

Export Photos in Various Formats

There are still more ways to share your photos with iPhoto. You can save photos into various file formats, export them as a web page, or use them to create a QuickTime slideshow.

Export copies or convert photos to other file formats

You might want to export photos to a different project folder or convert them to another file format. This does *not* remove the photos from the Library. The converted or exported photos will be *copies* of the originals; any changes you make to those copies will not affect the originals.

To export or convert photos:

1. Select a single photo, an album, or a group of photos within an album or the Library.
2. From the Share menu, choose "Export...."
3. In the "Export Photos" window click the "File Export" button.
4. From the Format pop-up menu, select a file format in which to save photos: "Original" saves photos in whatever format they currently use. The other options are "JPG," TIF," and "PNG."

   If you're not familiar with file formats, JPG is a safe choice that anyone can use. Most digital cameras create photos in this format, and it's the most common format for photos destined for web pages.

   If you plan to print the exported image, choose the TIF format.

   If you have a reason to use PNG, choose it.

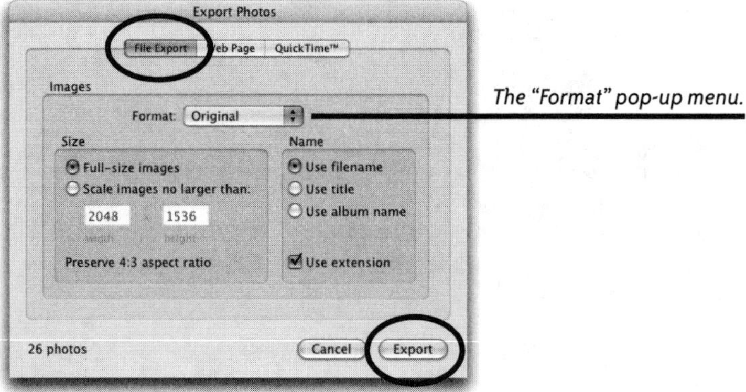

The "Format" pop-up menu.

5. **Size:** "Full-size images" exports photos the same size as the original. **Or** you can enter specific dimensions in pixels.
6. **Name:**

   Use filename: The exported photos will retain the default names your digital camera assigned (such as "DSCN0715.jpg"), unless you've renamed them.

   Use title: The photos will display the titles you gave them in iPhoto.

   Use album name: The photos will display the album name and a number for each image ("Kauai-07," for example).

   Use extension: The file format extension will appear at the end of the file name ("Kauai beach.jpg," for example).
7. Click the "Export" button. In the sheet that drops down, choose a location on your computer in which to save the exported files.

   If you want to put your exported photos into a new folder, click the "New Folder" button and name the folder.
8. Click OK to export the photos.

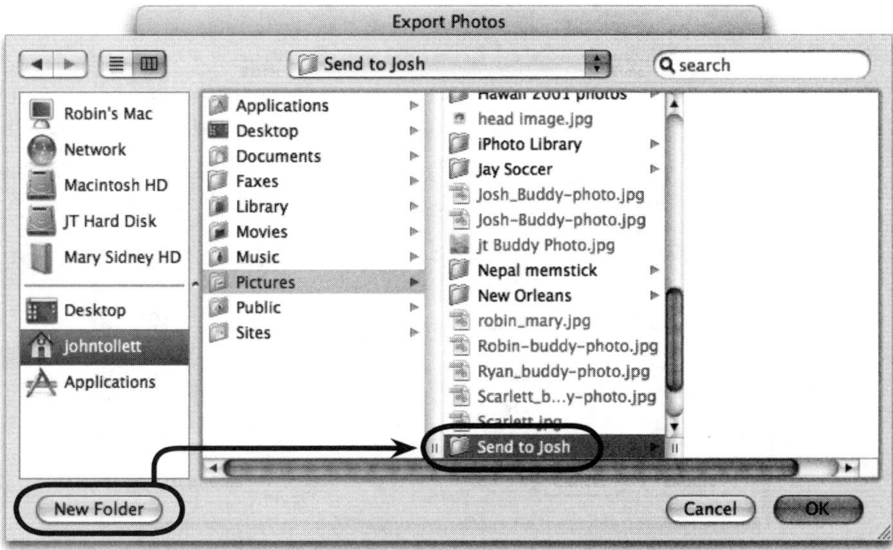

Save exported files into any folder on your computer or create a new folder in any location.

Export your photos as a web site

The "Web Page" option of the "Export Photos" window is very different from the HomePage feature as explained on pages 50–51. This web page tool creates a simpler web site and saves it on your computer—it does not post this site on Apple's server. You can upload this site yourself to a server of your choice, or you may want to burn the site to a CD to share with others.

To export your photos as a web site:

1. Select an album or a group of photos within an album. The order the photos appear in an album is the order they will appear in the web page you create.
2. From the File menu, choose "Export...."
3. In the "Export Photos" window that opens, click the "Web Page" button.
4. Make the following choices:

   Title: Enter a title for the web page.

   Columns and Rows: Choose how many columns and rows of thumbnail photographs to create on the start page (the first page of the web site).

   Background: To choose a background color, click the **Color** radio button, then click the color box for the palette. To choose a background image for the page, click the **Image** radio button, click "Set...," then from the Open dialog box, choose an image.

   Text Color: Click the box to choose a color for the text on the page.

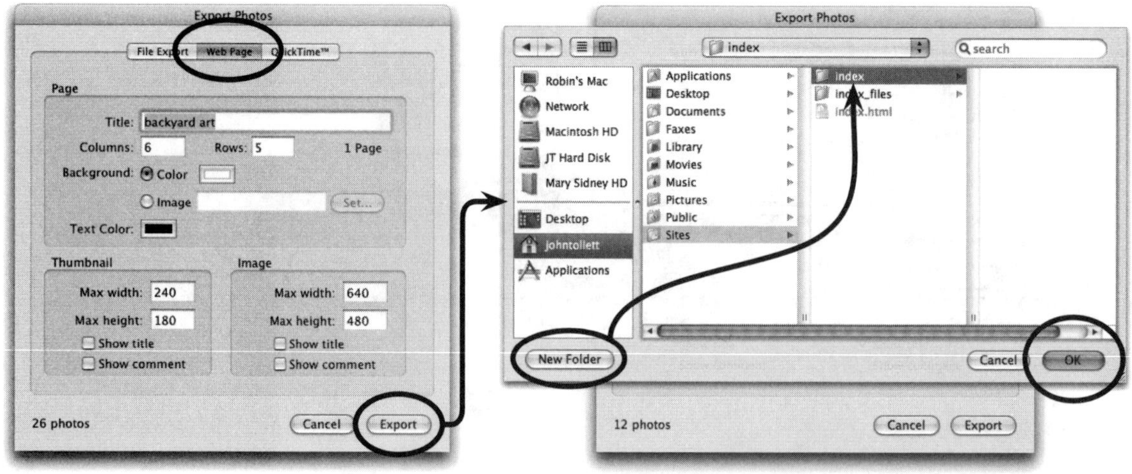

See the sidebar and Step 6 on the next page to learn why we named our new folder "index" (above).

Thumbnail: Set the maximum width and height for thumbnail images (the small photos on the "start page" or first page).

Show title: Place the title you assigned to photos under the thumbnail version on the start page.

Show comment: Show comments associated with photos.

Image: Same as "Thumbnail" settings, but this applies to the large photo pages to which the thumbnail images are linked.

5. Click "Export," shown on the previous page.
6. In the sheet that drops down, iPhoto may automatically choose the "Sites" folder in which to store your web page. You can choose any location, but you need to create a new folder *within* the selected folder to hold all the files that will be created during this export.

   So click the "New Folder" button (previous page) and name it **index**. Why? Because, unfortunately, the Web Page feature names the start page the same as the folder into which it's saved. For a web page to work correctly on the Internet, the start page needs to be named "index.html." *After* the photos are exported to the new folder, you can manually change the name of the *folder* to something unique.

   Click OK (shown on the previous page). Your new web page and all its related files will be stored in this new folder.

If the folder we export into is named "flamenco," iPhoto names the start page (the page with all the thumbnails on it) "flamenco. html." An HTML start page needs to be named "index" to work on the Internet, but if we manually change the name of the start page (after it has been created by iPhoto) to "index," the "Up" link on the secondary pages (the link that takes you back to the start page) will not work because it's programmed to link to a page named "flamenco. html." So, to make your web pages actually work on the Internet, export them to a folder named "index."

To see your new web page (which is really a web *site,* not an individual web *page*), find the new folder you just made and open it (it's in the Sites folder in your Home folder, unless you put it somewhere else).

Double-click the file named **index.html.** The site will open in your default web browser, *but it's not online!* You're actually just opening files on your own hard disk. This Web Page feature just builds the site for you—it's your responsibility to upload it to a web server if you want it online.

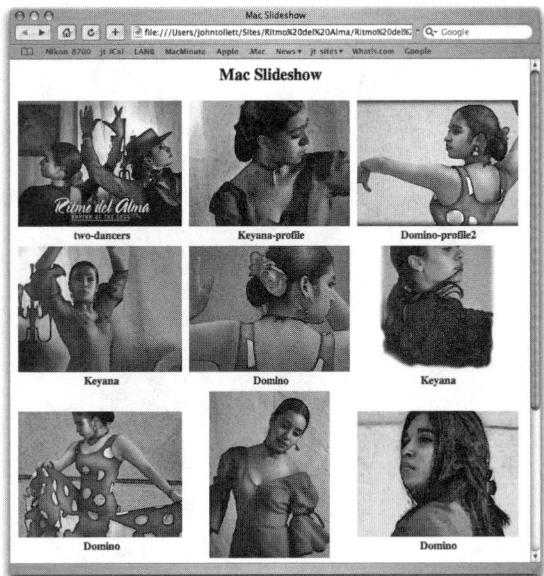

This is a finished web page shown in a browser.

Web Page creates a "start page" that contains thumbnail versions of your selected photos. Single-click any thumbnail to open a page that displays a full-sized version of that photo and navigation links for "Previous," "Up," and "Next" ("Up" means back to the start page).

Export photos as a QuickTime slideshow

You can export photos as a QuickTime slideshow that plays in the QuickTime player or in a program that supports QuickTime, such as a web browser. The QuickTime slideshow can be put on a CD and sent to friends, posted on a web page, inserted into a PDF, or placed in other software that recognizes QuickTime (such as the presentation module in AppleWorks or Pages).

To export as a QuickTime slideshow:

1. Select an album, a group of photos within an album, or photos in the Library. (The order that photos appear in an album is the order they will appear in the QuickTime movie.)
2. From the Share menu, choose "Export...."
3. In the "Export Photos" window, click the "QuickTime" button.
4. **Images:** Set the maximum width and height for the slideshow images; 640 by 480 pixels is a standard measurement that works well. In the "Display image for" box, set the amount of time that each image will stay on the screen.
5. **Background:** Choose a background color or a background image. If some of your photos have unusual dimensions, the empty background area will be filled with the color or image you choose.
6. **Music:** Click "Add currently selected music to movie." The slideshow will play the song you previously chose in the slideshow settings window, shown on page 43.
7. Click "Export."

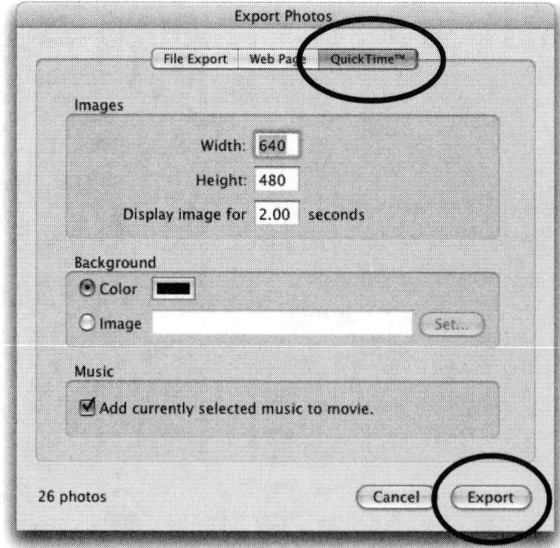

8. In the sheet that drops down, name the file and choose a location in which to save the file (shown below). iPhoto automatically selects the "Movies" folder to save the slideshow in, but you can choose any folder or disk. Click OK.

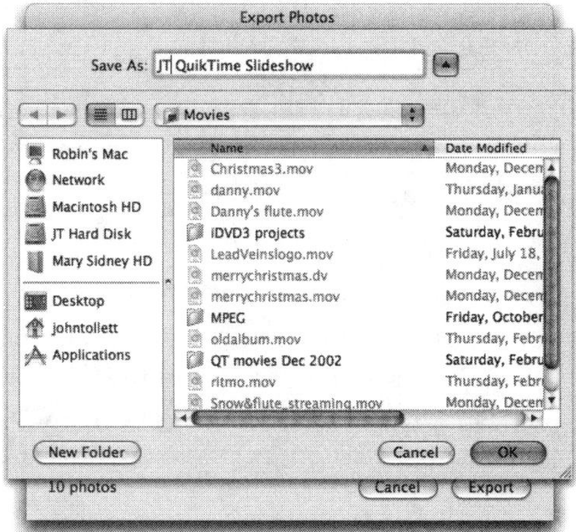

To open your QuickTime slideshow, locate the QuickTime movie file wherever you saved it on your hard disk, then double-click it to open it in the QuickTime Player.

To play your QuickTime slideshow, click the Play button on the QuickTime Player.

This is an exported slideshow, shown in the QuickTime Player.

The Play button.

Extra Tips and Information

Most digital cameras store photos in the **JPEG format,** which combines a high-quality image with effective compression to economize file size. iPhoto works best with JPEG formatted photos, although it recognizes most common formats such as TIFF, PICT, BMP, TARGA, and PNG. iPhoto also supports the RAW format used by many professional-level cameras and photographers.

iPhoto Library

iPhoto provides the viewing area in which you edit and organize your photos, but the actual photos themselves are stored in a folder on your hard disk named **iPhoto Library.** To find this folder, open your Home folder, then open the Pictures folder; the iPhoto Library is inside the Pictures folder.

The iPhoto Library folder also contains an Albums folder that contains all the **albums** you created in iPhoto. But these album folders don't *really* contain photos—they contain "references" to photos that you imported into the Library in iPhoto. This way, you can have the same photo in many different albums without overloading your computer with multiple copies.

Back up your iPhoto Library folder regularly by copying it to another disk or burning a CD or DVDs.

Search the Internet for iPhoto scripts and plugins

You'll find some very interesting freeware and shareware that makes iPhoto even better. Search Google (or any search site) for "iPhoto scripts," or go to VersionTracker.com and search for "iPhoto." A couple of useful add-ons are:

When you download and use software from freeware and shareware developers, be aware that you're doing so at your own risk and that the developers do not take any responsibility for unexpected hardware or software problems that may occur.

iPhoto Diet: When you edit images, such as cropping or making color and contrast adjustments, iPhoto keeps copies of the originals in the iPhoto Library folder so you can revert back to an original later. A convenient feature, but at the cost of using a lot of storage space. *iPhoto Diet* is an AppleScript droplet that slims down your iPhoto Library folder by moving unwanted duplicates to the Trash. Just drop your iPhoto Library folder (located in the Pictures folder, in your Home folder) on top of the iPhoto Diet droplet. Find this software at www.VersionTracker.com.

BetterHTMLExport: This iPhoto plugin creates web pages, but gives more control over the appearance of the pages than iPhoto's built-in Web Page feature. After installation, the plugin appears as an extra tab in the "Export Photos" window (from the Share menu, choose "Export…"). Visit www.DroolingCat.com to download.

iTunes

2

iTunes is an application that enables you to search for music, import it, organize it, play it, and share it with others. The mesmerizing iTunes visualizer feature creates dazzling visual-effects shows that are synchronized to your music selection. With iTunes and an Internet connection you can connect to dozens of Internet radio stations offering a wide variety of music and talk radio.

Create your own playlists that contain the songs you want, in the order you want. Then burn a CD of your favorite collections to take with you wherever you go. Create Smart Playlists that automatically organize songs into collections based on conditions that you set. If you want to play songs randomly, use iTune's "Party Shuffle" feature that shuffles songs around in a playlist, also based on conditions you set.

The online **iTunes Music Store** provides a place to search for music, preview and buy it. Thirty-second previews of more than a million songs are available, including hundreds of exclusive pre-release tracks and many rare, out-of-date albums. You can check out the top music from the Billboard 100 (going back to 1946) and the current top music charts for more than 1,000 radio stations. Watch music videos, then get the music track from the video. You can even watch the latest movie trailers at the iTunes Music Store.

iTunes is closely integrated with the other iLife applications—iPhoto, iMovie, iDVD, and GarageBand—making it easy to add music to slideshows, movies, DVDs, and to your own music arrangements.

Caution: iTunes is addictive. Just listening to the thirty-second previews on the iTunes Music Store can turn into hours of fun and relaxation.

The iTunes Interface

A quick overview of the iTunes interface is shown here and on the next page. Most of the controls you need are located directly on the iTunes interface. Almost every control is explained in detail elsewhere in this chapter.

In the example below, the **Library** is selected in the **Source pane** (the section on the left side of the window) and the Library's contents are shown in the Detail window (the large pane to the right of the Source pane). When you select an item in the Source pane, its contents show in the Detail window.

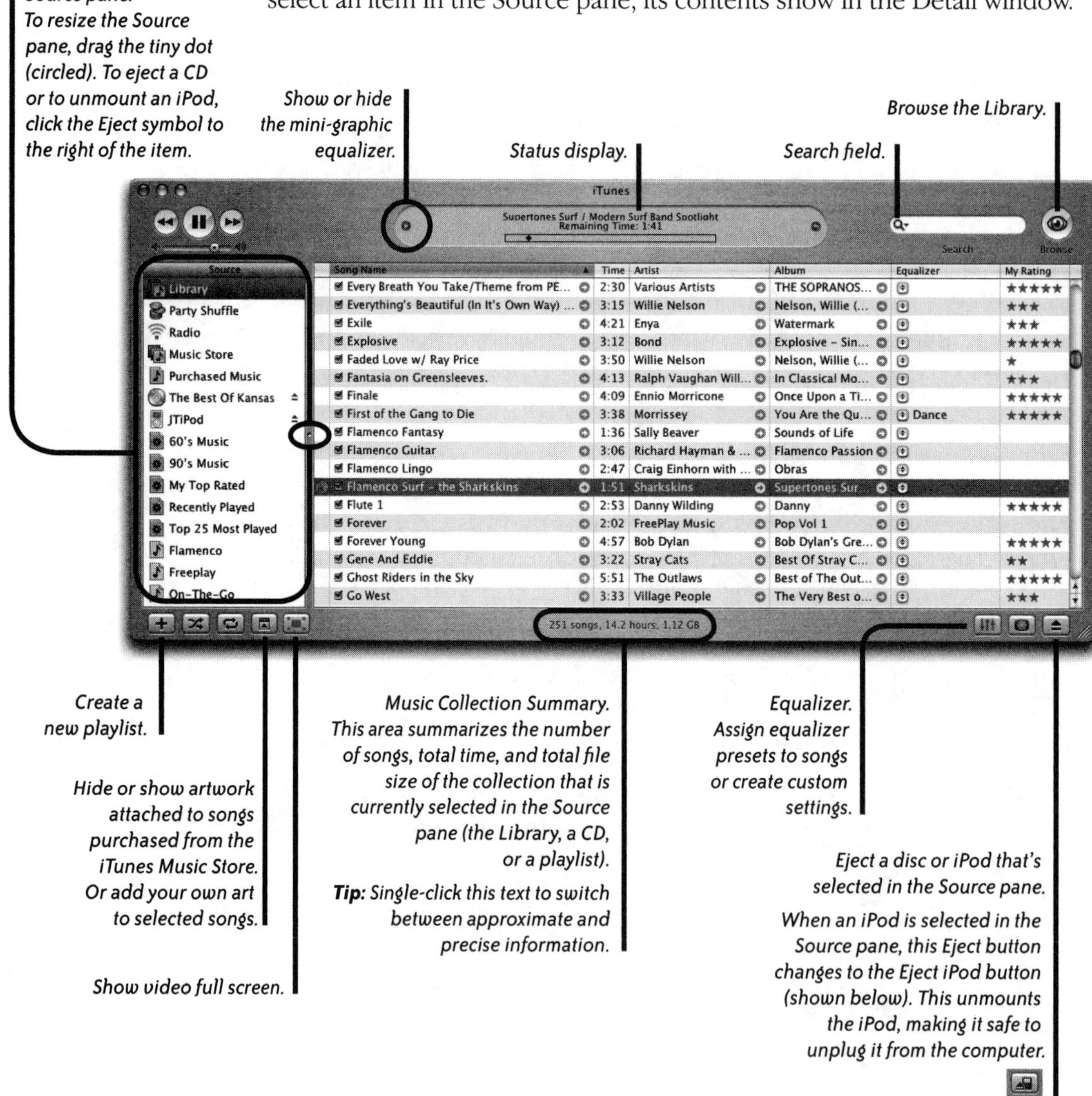

Source pane.
To resize the Source pane, drag the tiny dot (circled). To eject a CD or to unmount an iPod, click the Eject symbol to the right of the item.
Show or hide the mini-graphic equalizer.
Status display.
Search field.
Browse the Library.
Create a new playlist.
Hide or show artwork attached to songs purchased from the iTunes Music Store. Or add your own art to selected songs.
Show video full screen.
Music Collection Summary. This area summarizes the number of songs, total time, and total file size of the collection that is currently selected in the Source pane (the Library, a CD, or a playlist).
Tip: Single-click this text to switch between approximate and precise information.
Equalizer. Assign equalizer presets to songs or create custom settings.
Eject a disc or iPod that's selected in the Source pane.
When an iPod is selected in the Source pane, this Eject button changes to the Eject iPod button (shown below). This unmounts the iPod, making it safe to unplug it from the computer.

In the example below, a **playlist** is selected in the Source pane. For each item in the Source pane, you can customize the Detail window view to show the columns of information you want. See "View Options" on page 89.

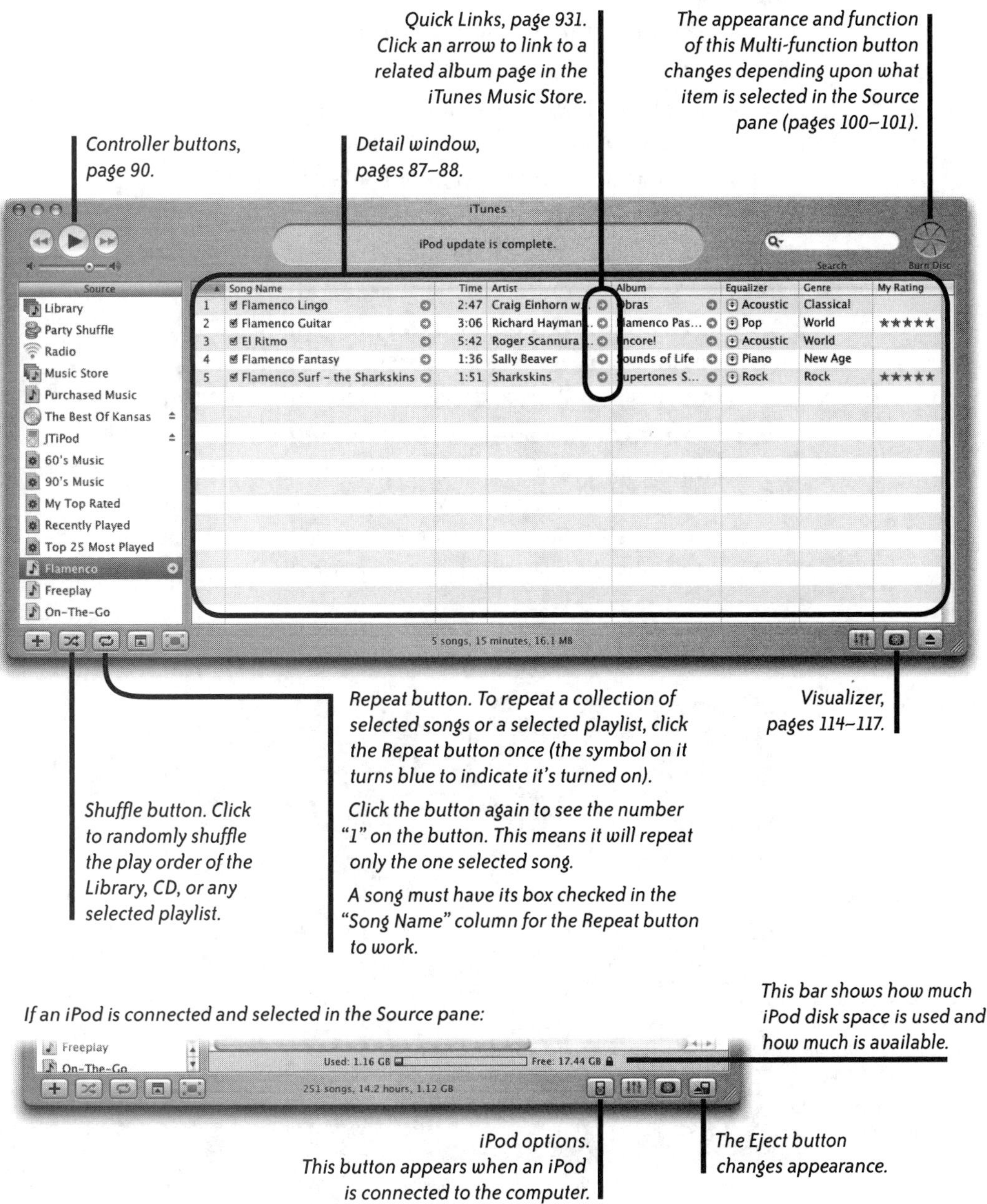

Quick Links, page 931.
Click an arrow to link to a related album page in the iTunes Music Store.
The appearance and function of this Multi-function button changes depending upon what item is selected in the Source pane (pages 100–101).
Controller buttons, page 90.
Detail window, pages 87–88.
iTunes
iPod update is complete.
Search
Burn Disc
Source
Library
Party Shuffle
Radio
Music Store
Purchased Music
The Best Of Kansas
JTiPod
60's Music
90's Music
My Top Rated
Recently Played
Top 25 Most Played
Flamenco
Freeplay
On-The-Go
Song Name
Time
Artist
Album
Equalizer
Genre
My Rating
Flamenco Lingo
Flamenco Guitar
El Ritmo
Flamenco Fantasy
Flamenco Surf - the Sharkskins
5 songs, 15 minutes, 16.1 MB
Repeat button. To repeat a collection of selected songs or a selected playlist, click the Repeat button once (the symbol on it turns blue to indicate it's turned on).
Click the button again to see the number "1" on the button. This means it will repeat only the one selected song.
A song must have its box checked in the "Song Name" column for the Repeat button to work.
Visualizer, pages 114–117.
Shuffle button. Click to randomly shuffle the play order of the Library, CD, or any selected playlist.
If an iPod is connected and selected in the Source pane:
This bar shows how much iPod disk space is used and how much is available.
Used: 1.16 GB
Free: 17.44 GB
251 songs, 14.2 hours, 1.12 GB
iPod options.
This button appears when an iPod is connected to the computer.
The Eject button changes appearance.

Play CDs

You can play any music CD in your Mac. Make sure your sound is on and turned up.

To play a music CD:

1. Insert a CD into the computer CD drive.
2. Open iTunes, if it isn't already open:

   If the iTunes icon is in your Dock, click once on it.

   If there is not an icon in the Dock, open the Applications folder, find the iTunes icon, then double-click it.
3. The CD icon appears in the Source pane, as shown below. Click the CD icon to see the song list and other information in the Detail window.

   If you're connected to the Internet, iTunes will automatically go to a CD database web site, retrieve the song titles and other data, and place the information in the appropriate columns.

   If you're NOT connected to the Internet when you insert a CD, song titles will appear as track numbers (as shown below). You can select the generic track names and type in real song names: Click once on a title in the "Song Name" column, pause, then click the title again to highlight it. Type a new name for the song.

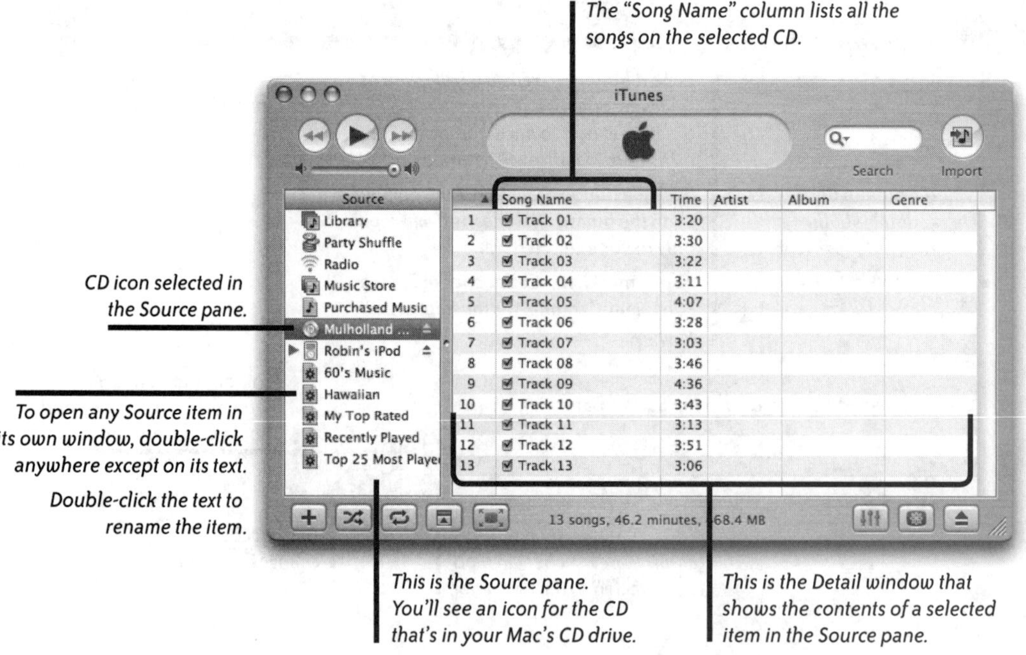

To see the actual song titles, if they have not appeared:

1. Connect to the Internet (if you're not already).
2. From the Advanced menu, choose "Get CD Track Names."

If you want iTunes to do this automatically every time you put in a CD, see the information about iTunes preferences on pages 106–107.

To choose the songs on the CD you want to play:

When you insert a CD, all of the songs have checkmarks next to them. If the box is checked, the song will play. To customize the list, check only the songs you want to hear. iTunes skips over songs that do not have a checkmark.

1. Click on the CD icon in the Source pane.
2. Click on a song in the "Song Name" column to select it.
3. Click the Play button (the middle controller button), **or** double-click a title in the "Song Name" column.

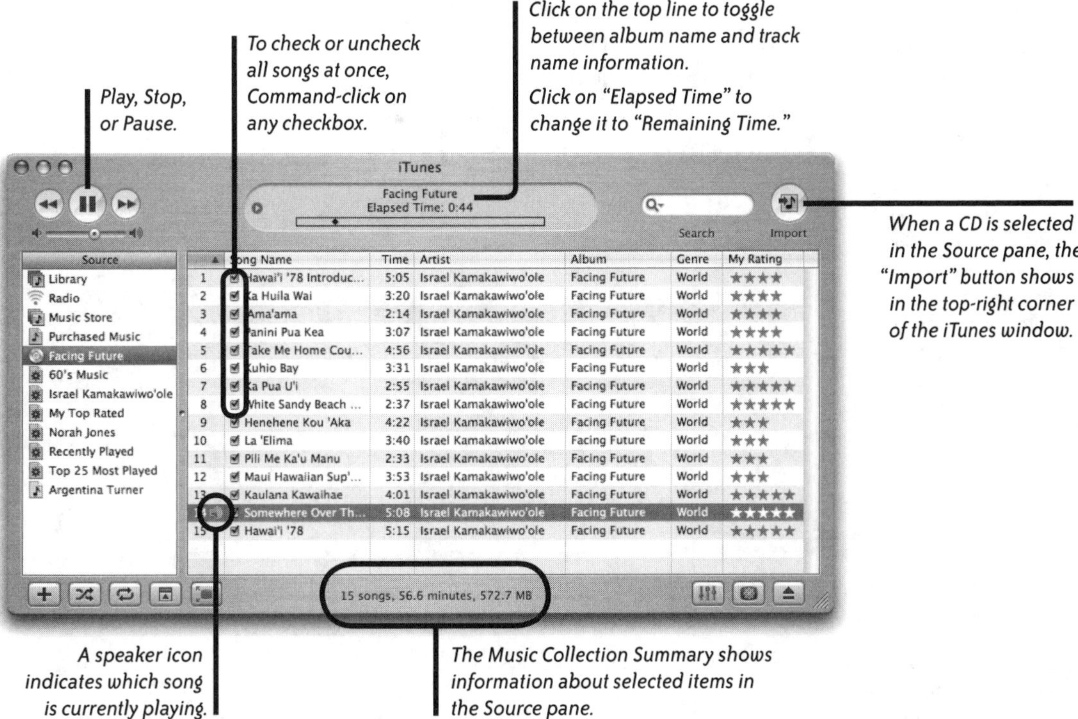

Play, Stop, or Pause.
To check or uncheck all songs at once, Command-click on any checkbox.
Click on the top line to toggle between album name and track name information.
Click on "Elapsed Time" to change it to "Remaining Time."
When a CD is selected in the Source pane, the "Import" button shows in the top-right corner of the iTunes window.
A speaker icon indicates which song is currently playing.
The Music Collection Summary shows information about selected items in the Source pane.
iTunes
Facing Future
Elapsed Time: 0:44
Search
Import
15 songs, 56.6 minutes, 572.7 MB

The iTunes Library

When you import (rip, encode) music files from a CD, iTunes encodes it as an MPEG-4 AAC file (if you have QuickTime 6.2 or later installed) and places it in the iTunes Library. If you have an earlier version of QuickTime, iTunes encodes songs as MP3, or whatever format you last chose in the Importing preferences pane (see page 109). Once a song is in the Library list, you can add it to a customized playlist, as explained on the following page. Simply playing songs from a CD does not add them to the iTunes Library.

File formats: The MPEG-4 AAC format compresses song files to a smaller size than the MP3 format without a noticeable quality difference. We encoded a 3-minute, 20-second song into both formats: the MP3 file encoded to 3.8 megabytes, the MPEG-4 file to 3.1 megabytes, a significant storage savings when you have a large library.

If you have a highly refined ear for music, set the iTunes "Importing" preferences to encode songs in "Apple Lossless" format. This format encodes CD-quality music at half the size of the original CD format.

To add songs to the Library:

1. Insert a music CD into the computer CD drive.
2. In the Detail window, click each song's checkbox that you want to add to the Library.
3. Click the "Import" button in the top-right corner of the window.

You may already have music files somewhere on your computer that you want to add to the iTunes Library. There are two ways to do this:

- **Either** go to the File menu and choose "Add to Library...," then find and select your music files.
- **Or** drag a file from any location on your hard disk to the Library icon in the iTunes Source pane, as shown below.

Tip: Each song takes up at least 3 to 5 megabytes (depending on the file format specified in iTunes Preferences) of hard disk space, so make sure you have plenty of disk space available before you go crazy importing music files!

For more about this Multi-Function button, see pages 100–101.

Drag a music file from anywhere on the computer to the "Library" icon in the Source pane. The small plus icon indicates the song will be copied to the iTunes Library.

This shows how much hard disk space is being used to store the selected music files in the Library.

Create Your Own Playlists

A **playlist** is your customized collection of audio files. You can create as many playlists as you like, and you can arrange the songs in any order you prefer by dragging selections up or down in the list. You create playlists so you can play custom collections of songs on your computer, download them to a portable MP3 player, or burn them onto CDs.

When you create a new playlist, iTunes assumes you'll want to change its name so it highlights the text for you. Just type to replace the existing text.

Create a new playlist and add songs to it

1. Type Command N, **or** click the "New Playlist" button (the **+**) in the bottom-left corner of the iTunes window. A playlist icon appears in the Source pane with the default name "untitled playlist."
2. Change the name of the new playlist to something descriptive by typing over the highlighted default name.

   You can change a playlist name at any time: Click once on the title to highlight it, click a second time to make the text editable, then type a new name in the highlighted field.

To add selections to the playlist from a CD:

1. Insert a CD whose songs you want to add to a custom playlist.
2. Click the CD icon in the Source pane to open its song list.
3. Drag desired selections from the "Song Name" column and drop them on your new playlist in the Source pane, as shown below.

Drag any song to a playlist in the Source pane.

When you drag a song directly from a CD to a playlist, the song is automatically encoded (imported) to the AAC format, or whatever format you last chose in the Importing preferences pane. The song is placed in the iTunes Library and added to the playlist.

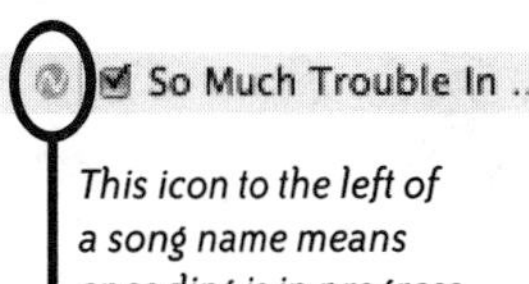

This icon to the left of a song name means encoding is in progress.

To add a song to a playlist from the Library:

1. In the Source pane, single-click the "Library" icon to display your entire Library collection in the "Song Name" column.
2. Drag a selection from the "Song Name" column to a playlist in the Source pane.

Note: When you drag a song file from the Library to a playlist collection, as explained on these pages, the song remains in the Library. *You're not actually moving the digital file*—you're creating a *directory* that tells iTunes which songs are attached to different collections. You can put the same song in as many playlist collections as you want without bloating your computer with extra copies of large music files.

There's **another method for creating a new playlist** that's even easier:

1. In the Source pane, single-click the "Library" icon to display your entire Library collection in the "Song Name" column.
2. Select all the songs you want from the "Song Name" column (see how to make *multiple selections* below).

   Note: The **checkmarks** *do not* indicate that a file is selected. The checkmarks indicate two things: songs that will *play* when you click the "Play" button, or songs on a CD that will be *imported* when you click the "Import" button.
3. From the File menu, select "New Playlist From Selection." iTunes automatically creates the playlist and adds the selected songs to it.

You can drag **multiple selections** all at once to a playlist:

- To make a *contiguous* selection of songs (songs that are next to each other in the list), Shift-click the song names. **Or** single-click on one song, then Shift-click on another song: all songs between the two clicks will be selected.
- To make a *non-contiguous* selection of songs (songs that are *not* next to each other in the list), click a song, then Command-click additional song names you want to add to the selection.

This example shows a non-contiguous selection of songs.

Smart Playlists

Smart Playlists are collections of songs that are generated automatically when imported songs meet certain conditions that you define. iTunes provides several Smart Playlists (indicated by the gear symbols) in the Source pane: '60s Music, '90s Music, Top Rated, Recently Played, and Top 25 Most Played. You can create new Smart Playlists that meet other conditions, such as your favorite Hawaiian songs, flamenco music, or certain artists.

'60s Music
My Top Rated
Recently Played
Top 25 Most Played

Smart Playlists display a gear symbol.

To create a new Smart Playlist:

1. From the File menu, choose "New Smart Playlist…." **Or** Option-click the "New Playlist" button—the "plus" symbol on the button changes to a "gear" symbol (Smart Playlist) when you press the Option key.
2. In the Smart Playlist window that appears (shown below), use the menus and text fields to set conditions for the new Smart Playlist.
3. Click OK.

Press the Option key to change the "Playlist" button to a "Smart Playlist" button.

Choose to match "any" or "all" conditions.

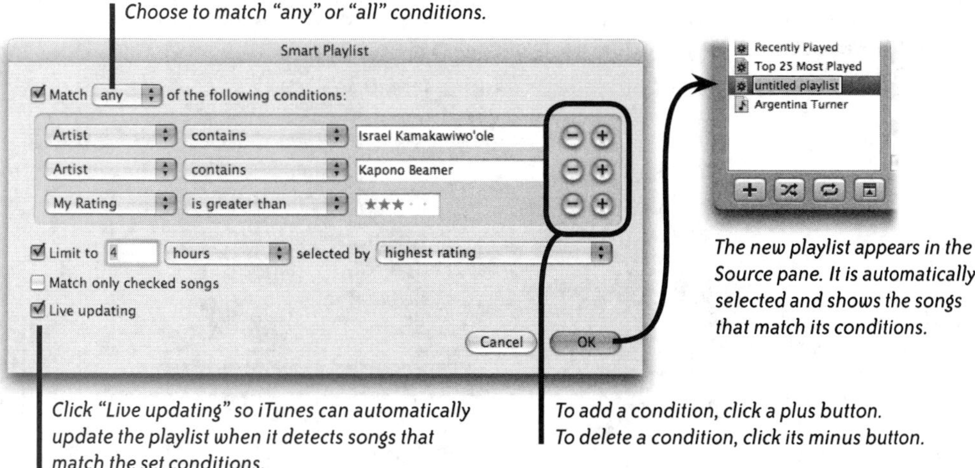

The new playlist appears in the Source pane. It is automatically selected and shows the songs that match its conditions.

Click "Live updating" so iTunes can automatically update the playlist when it detects songs that match the set conditions.

To add a condition, click a plus button. To delete a condition, click its minus button.

A new Smart Playlist appears in the Source pane (shown above-right). Any songs in your Library that meet the conditions you set are now listed in the "Song Name" column of the Detail window. Rename the playlist something descriptive.

Play the Radio

Click the "Radio" icon to open the **Radio Tuner** so you can tune into the **Internet radio stations** that are built into iTunes (or whose addresses you have entered). These stations play a wide variety of music, news, and talkshow programs (netcast in the streaming MP3 format).

To play the radio in iTunes:

1. Click the "Radio" icon in the Source pane to see the radio options in the "Stream" column (the same column that is labeled "Song Name" when the selected Source is a CD, an album, or your Library).
2. Click the disclosure triangle of a radio category to see the various choices of streaming Internet connections.
3. Double-click a stream to begin playing it. iTunes will open the designated URL (web address) and start playing the content.

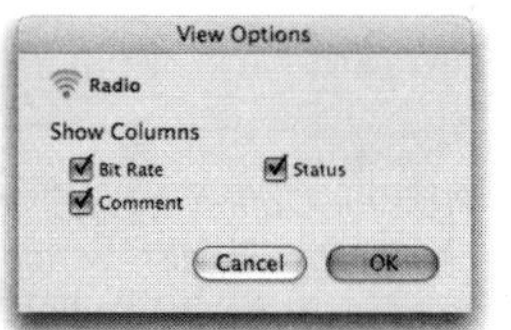

Choose which columns to display in the Radio Tuner window: From the Edit menu, choose "View Options...."

iTunes uses technology called "Instant On Streaming" that allows content to start playing immediately. It continues to download data as the file plays. If you do not have a full-time Internet connection, connect to the Internet before you double-click a radio selection.

If you lose your radio connection, click the "Refresh" button.

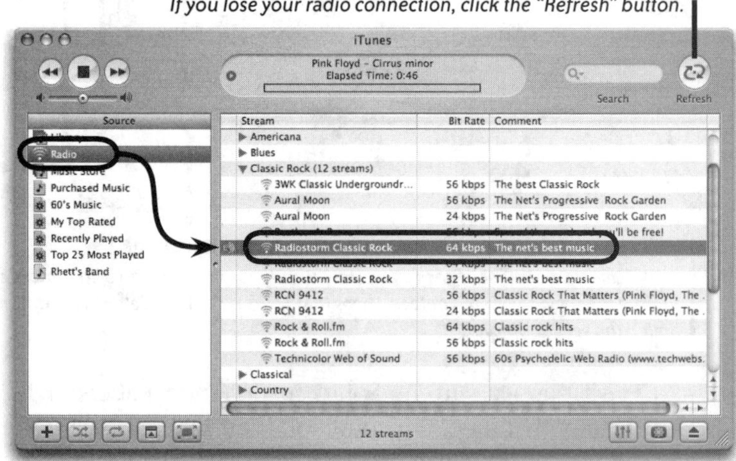

Some radio stations are available in several bit rates (kilobits per second) which affect the quality of the streams. Streams with higher bit rates sound better, but tend to break up over slow connections. If you have a dial-up Internet connection, choose streams with lower bit rates, such as 24 kbps.

To enter another radio address:

If you know the web address of a streaming MP3 radio station that's not in the iTunes Radio Tuner, you can manually enter it.

1. From the Advanced menu at the top of your screen, choose "Open Stream...."
2. In the text field of the "Open Stream" window enter the web address. The address must be a complete URL, including the stream file name.

Music File Formats

iTunes works with six **audio file formats:** MPEG-4 AAC, MP3, CD-DA, AIFF, WAV, and Apple Lossless. Using the Import feature, iTunes can encode CD-DA files from a CD to MP3, AIFF, or WAV files. It can also encode MP3, AIFF, and WAV files to CD-DA format when burning a CD. Each file format is suited for a specific purpose.

To select an encoder when importing files, see page 109.

- **CD-DA** (Compact Disc Digital Audio) is the file format used on all music CDs. When you burn a CD from a playlist, iTunes by default automatically encodes the files in the playlist as CD-DA formatted files so they'll play on CD players. In the iTunes preferences window you can set iTunes to burn files in the MP3 format, or as a data disc which will retain the original file format of song files—whatever they happen to be—but the songs may not play in a CD player.
- **MP3** (MPEG-3) is a highly efficient compression system that reduces music files up to 90 percent, but maintains a very high quality. Highly compressed, MP3s are ideal for downloading from the Internet or for storing on your computer.
- **MPEG-4 AAC** (Advanced Audio Coding) format compresses files even smaller than MP3 without a noticeable loss of quality. When iTunes imports a song from a CD to your computer, by default it encodes the CD-DA formatted song to an AAC format. MP3s and AACs are ideal for storing music on your computer, requiring 80 to 90 percent less disk space than other formats.

If you have a version of QuickTime installed that's older than version 6.2, songs are by default imported in the MP3 format instead of the AAC format.

- **Apple Lossless** encodes CD-DA files (CD music files) into a size that's half the size of the original file, without any loss of quality. This format creates files that are larger than the MP3 and AAC formats, but if you have a discriminating ear for music, the Apple Lossless format provides the best quality possible.
- **AIFF** (Audio Interchange File Format) is sometimes referred to as Apple Interchange File Format. It is a music format used by the Macintosh operating system. Web designers use snippets in the AIFF format for sound files that can play in web pages on a Macintosh computer. The file size of the Beatles song "I Want To Hold Your Hand" is 24.3 MB as an AIFF file, compared to 2.7 MB as an MP3 file.
- **WAV** (Windows waveform format) is a music file format used by the Microsoft Windows operating system. Web designers use snippets in the WAV format for sound files that can play in web pages on a Windows computer. The file size of the Beatles song "I Want To Hold Your Hand" is 24.3 MB as a WAV file, compared to 2.7 MB as an MP3 file.

The iTunes Music Store

If you have a slow Internet connection, see page 112 to learn how to improve the quality of the iTunes Music Store song previews.

The iTunes Music Store is really what makes iTunes such a cool app. More than a million music tracks are available for you to preview, purchase, and download. And the collection is growing daily. The music represents all major recording labels plus hundreds of independent labels. The iTunes Music Store also lets you preview, purchase, and download thousands of audiobooks from **Audible.com**.

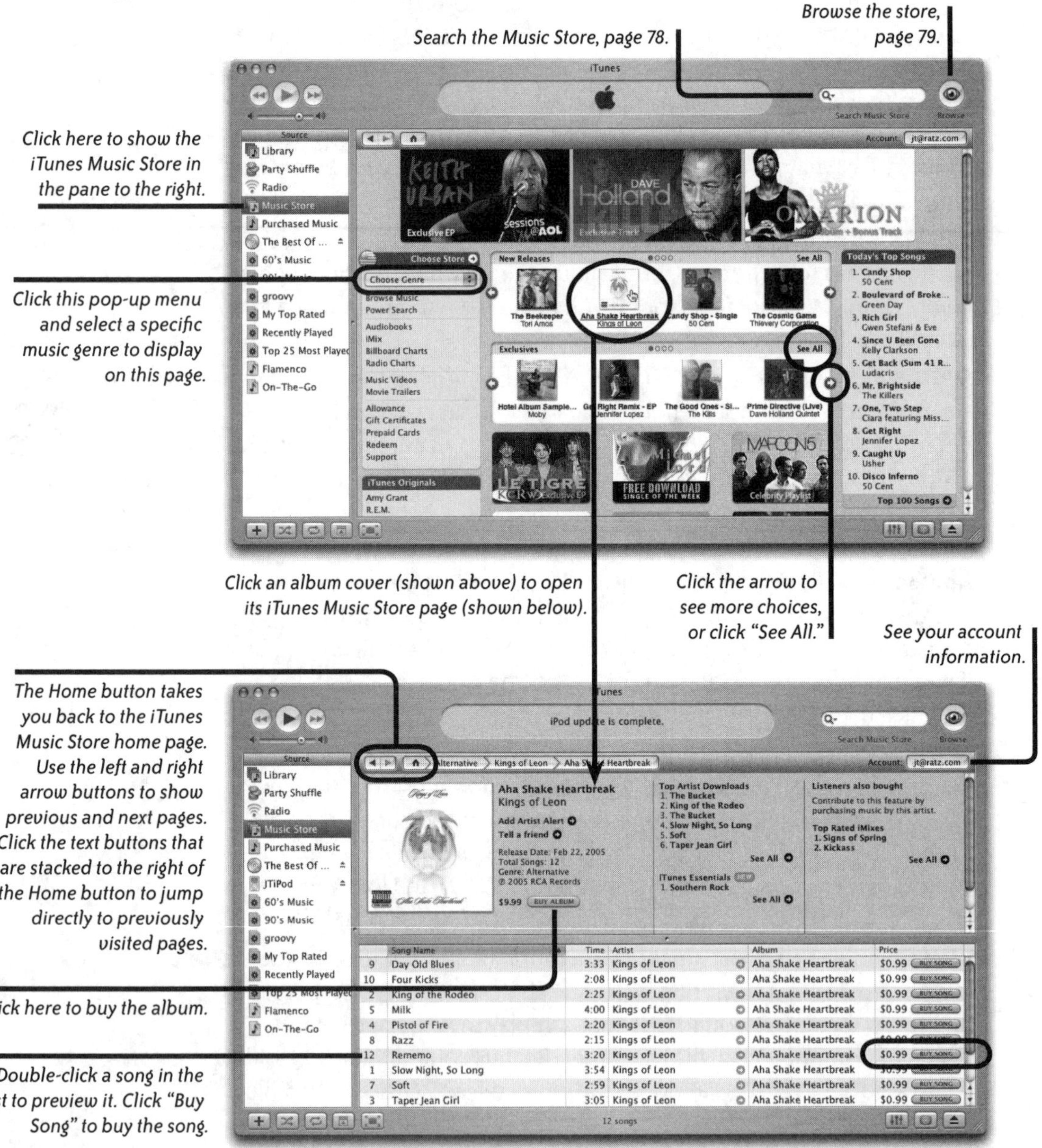

Search the Music Store, page 78.
Browse the store, page 79.
Click here to show the iTunes Music Store in the pane to the right.
Click this pop-up menu and select a specific music genre to display on this page.
Click an album cover (shown above) to open its iTunes Music Store page (shown below).
Click the arrow to see more choices, or click "See All."
See your account information.
The Home button takes you back to the iTunes Music Store home page. Use the left and right arrow buttons to show previous and next pages. Click the text buttons that are stacked to the right of the Home button to jump directly to previously visited pages.
Click here to buy the album.
Double-click a song in the list to preview it. Click "Buy Song" to buy the song.

Preview and buy songs and albums

The iTunes Music Store provides a thirty-second preview of every song and audiobook. Select an item, then double-click it to play the preview.

You can copy a song preview *link* to your computer, in case you want to preview or purchase it later—just drag the song from the iTunes Music Store to the Source pane on the left. A new playlist is automatically created, named after the song you just dragged from the iTunes Music Store. You might consider creating a special playlist just for organizing preview links in one place and naming it something like "Wish List," as we did in this example.

When you double-click a song in the Music Store, its 30-second preview shows here.

When you drag a song preview to the Source pane, the music file is not really on your computer. It's a link to the preview in the Music Store. To play it, you must be connected to the Internet.

Later, when you're ready to listen to the preview links you copied, select the playlist in the Source pane to which you dragged a song preview ("Wish List" in this example). In the Detail window you can double-click a preview to play it, **or** you can click one of the *Quick Link* buttons (circled below) to link back to the iTunes Music Store page for that particular song's page. **Or** click a "Buy Song" or "Buy Album" button to purchase and download a song or album from this window.

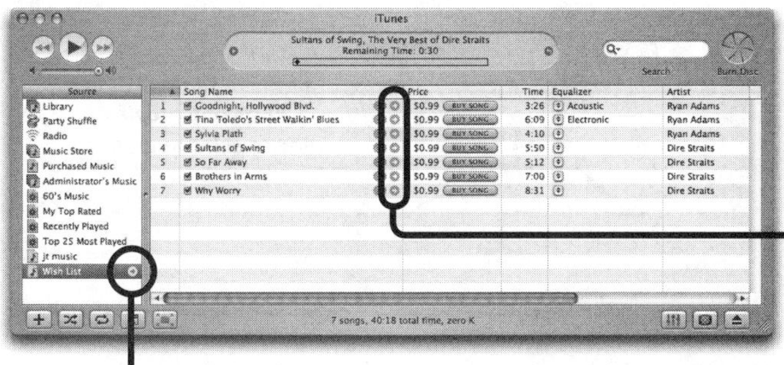

The Quick Link buttons next to the song previews take you to the iTunes Music Store page linked to that song.

The Quick Link button in the Source pane lets you create an iMix (see page 81).

Preview and buy audiobooks

The first time you try to buy music or books from the iTunes Music Store, you'll be asked to sign in to your existing Apple account or create a new account. After you finish this quick and simple procedure, you can buy songs, albums, or audiobooks with the single click of the "Buy" button.

Enter your Apple ID and password, if you have one.

Click the Help button to learn more about creating a new account.

If you have an AOL account, check the AOL button and use your AOL screen name and password instead.

If necessary, click here to create a new account.

To buy audiobooks, click the "Audiobooks" link in the Music Store window. **Or** from the "Choose Genre" pop-up menu, select "Audiobooks." When the audiobooks page opens, select a book to show the preview/purchase page for that book.

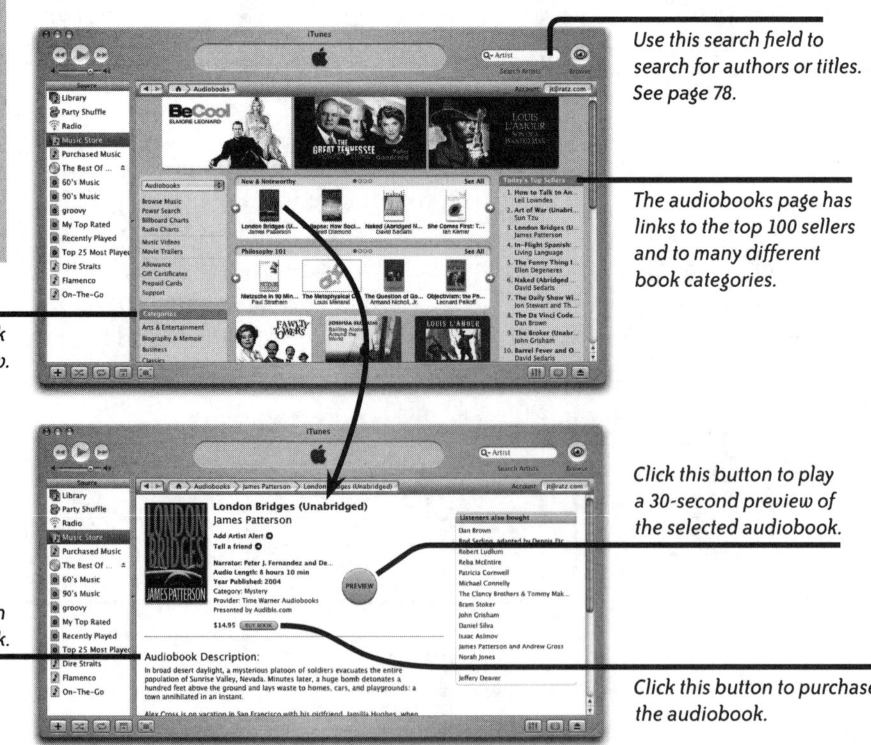

Use this search field to search for authors or titles. See page 78.

The audiobooks page has links to the top 100 sellers and to many different book categories.

Choose an audiobook category to view.

Click this button to play a 30-second preview of the selected audiobook.

Read a description of the audiobook.

Click this button to purchase the audiobook.

Copy iTunes Music Store links

Sometimes you want to tell someone about a great song or album you found. Or maybe you want to be alerted when certain artists have new music selections available on the iTunes Music Store.

If you click on a song's "Tell a friend" link (shown on the right), a message form opens (shown below) containing the associated album or book art, and a link to the song or book page in the iTunes Music Store.

To receive an email alert when more music from the selected artist is available, click "Add Artist Alert."

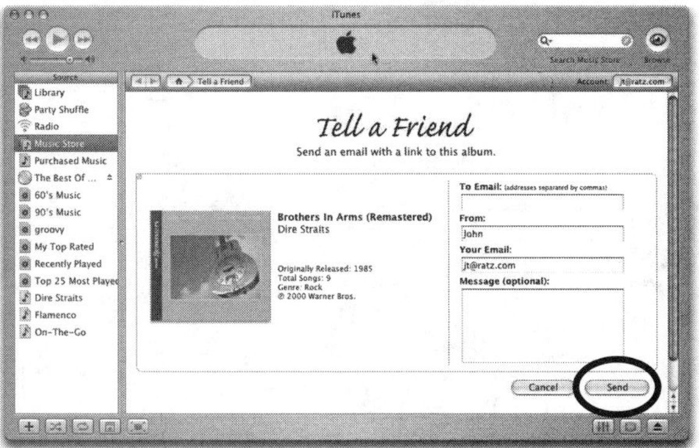

iTunes creates an email message for sharing your music discovery with a friend.

Type a friend's email address and click the "Send" button.

When you drag a link, song, or graphic from the iTunes Music Store and drop it on your Desktop or into a folder, it creates a file that links to a Music Store page. When you double-click that file, iTunes takes you to the related iTunes Music Store location. You can also drag that file into an email message and send it to a friend.

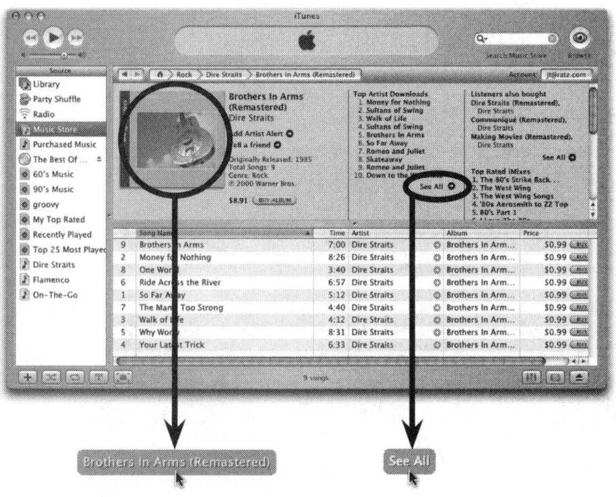

Drag almost any link, graphic, or song from an iTunes Music Store page to create a URL link.

iTunes links look like this as you drag them from the iTunes Music Store window to the Desktop.

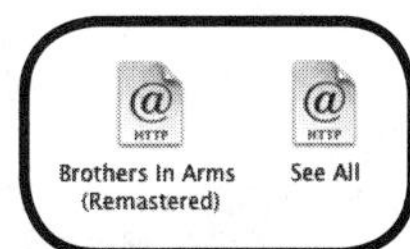

iTunes links look like this after you let go and drop them on the Desktop, into a folder, or into an email message.

Use Search, Power Search, or Browse to find specific songs

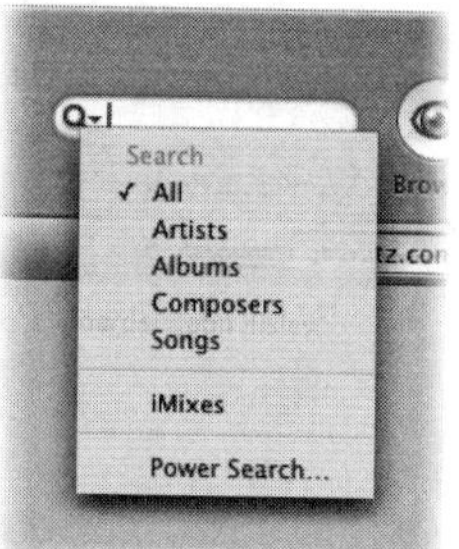

Use the Search field menu to select the music category you want to search, or to select "Power Search...."

Click on the magnifying glass in the Search field to show a pop-up menu (left) from which you choose a search category: All, Artists, Albums, Composers, Songs, iMixes, or Power Search.

After you choose a search category, the words under the Search field change to show your selection. For instance, if you choose "Songs," the Search field is labeled "Search Songs."

To **search,** type a complete or partial name in the Search field, then hit Return on the keyboard. The search results show in the bottom section of the iTunes window, as shown below.

Type an album, artist, or song name.

The top section of the search results shows albums to which the found songs belong. The bottom section shows all the found songs.

To **Power Search,** choose "Power Search..." from the Search pop-up menu. In the Power Search pane, shown below, enter as much information as possible, then click the "Search" button.

The Power Search pane.

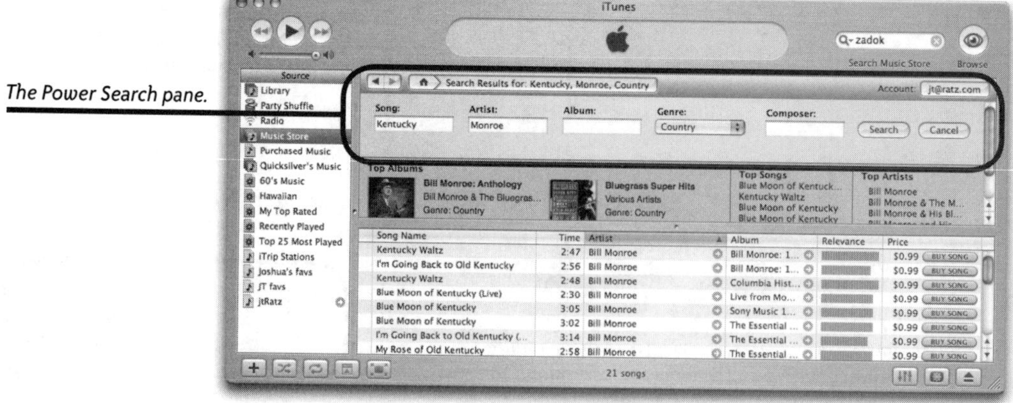

Use the **Browse** button to search for *songs* by genre, artist, and album. Click the "Browse" button to show the Browser pane, circled below. Select a genre from the "Genre" column, then choose an artist from the "Artist" column, and then choose an album from the "Album" column. After you make your selections, the matching results show in the bottom section of the window.

To leave the Browser, click the "Browse" button again. You can also click the Back button (the left-facing arrow) or the Home button.

You can also use the **Browse** button to search for audiobooks by genre, category, and author. Select "Audiobooks" in the "Genre" column. The next two columns change to the "Category" and "Author" columns. Make a selection in the "Category" column, then in the "Author" column. The results appear in the bottom section of the window.

Music charts

One way of finding great music is to select **Billboard Charts** or **Radio Charts.** Choose "Radio Charts" to access the top playlists of more than 1,000 local radio stations in major U.S. markets. Choose "Billboard Charts" to browse Billboard's top pop, R&B, and country songs, categorized by year from 1946 to the present.

The Billboard and Radio Charts can be found on the Music Store's home page or through the Browser (left).

Choose "Charts" from the Browser (left), or "Billboard Charts" from the Music Store home page (above) to browse through Billboard's top songs.

Watch music videos and movie trailers

The iTunes Music Store has evolved into an entertainment destination. Not only can you go there and listen to music previews for hours, you can watch music videos and movie trailers.

On the Music Store home page, choose "Music Videos" or "Movie Trailers" from the list of categories, shown to the left. When the movie trailer or music video page opens, single-click on the video you want to watch.

Most videos let you choose between large, medium, or small versions. *Large* is nice when you have a fast Internet connection; *medium* or *small* is much better for slower connections.

These buttons identify the page you're on.

The Movie Trailers page.

The Music Videos page.

If you have a slow dial-up modem connection (all dial-up connections are slow when you're trying to view video), the download time can be frustrating and the audio/video playback may skip or stop. You can set a couple of iTunes preferences to help improve performance of the Music Store's streaming audio and video features.

1. From the iTunes application menu, choose "Preferences…."
2. Click the "Store" button to show the Store preferences pane.
3. Select "Load complete preview before playing."

If you have a fast Internet connection and you want streaming files to start playing sooner, set the streaming buffer size to "Small." Your computer will have to pre-load less data before it starts to play a streaming file.

Also, you can increase the streaming buffer size. The buffer is the amount of streamed data that's stored in the computer's memory before the song or video starts to play.

1. Go to iTunes Preferences, then click the "Advanced" button.
2. From the "Streaming Buffer Size" pop-up menu, choose "Medium" or "Large."

Create and publish your own iMix playlist

Do you have a favorite mix of songs purchased from the iTunes Music Store that you'd like to share? If so, you can put them in a playlist and publish them as an **iMix.** iMix is an iTunes Music Store feature that publishes song mixes submitted by iTunes users. You must use music purchased from the Music Store. The published iMix plays a thirty-second preview of each song in the mix. But it's fun. And useful for sending song discoveries and recommendations to friends. Here's how to do it:

To view an iMix collection submitted by others, select "iMix" on the Music Store home page.

1. Create a playlist that contains only music purchased from the iTunes Music Store. When you select any playlist in the Source pane an iMix publish button (a white arrow in a circle) appears to the right of the playlist name (shown circled below).
2. Click the iMix button to publish the playlist as an iMix. In the message pane that opens (below), click the "Create" button.

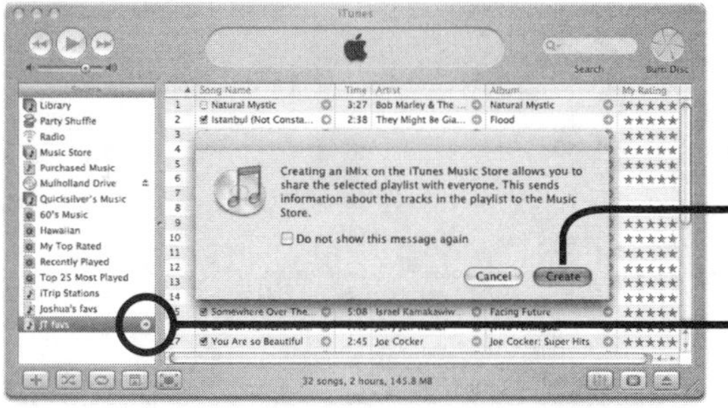

Click here to publish your iMix.

iMix publish button.

When you publish a playlist as an iMix, the iMix publish button stays visible. To modify your iMix collection at any time, click the iMix button again.

3. Sign in with your Apple ID and password, shown on the right.
4. Click the "Publish" button to sign in. On the page that opens (shown below-left), type a title and description for your song mix.
5. Click the "Publish" button.

Click "Publish" to sign in. If you don't have an account, click the "Create Account" button to set one up.

After you click "Publish," iTunes opens a page (above) in which you can "Tell a friend" or submit an iMix Rating.

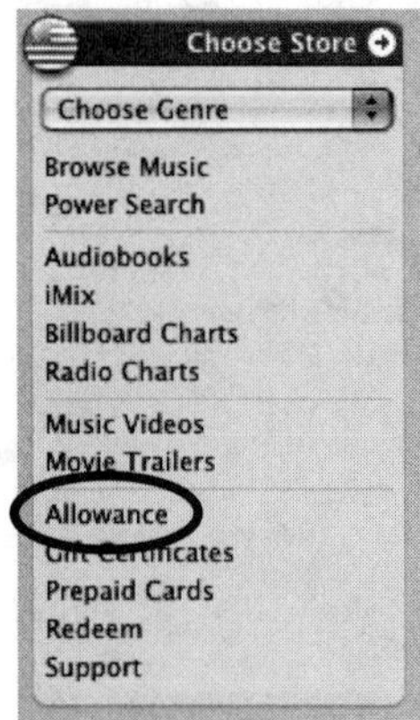

Allowance, gift certificates, prepaid cards, and shopping carts

You've seen how easy it is to click the "Buy Song" button and download music through your Apple Account. But what if you'd like to buy music for someone else and let them download it to their own computer? The iTunes Music Store provides several easy and convenient ways to do this.

Allowance: Set up an allowance when you want to let your kids buy a preset amount of music without a credit card. You can set a monthly amount between $10 and $20.

1. Click the "Allowance" link on the Music Store's home page.
2. In the set up window that opens, fill in the required information (the recipient needs an Apple Account), then click "Continue."
3. A window opens asking you to confirm your purchase. Check the information, then click the "Buy" button.

To cancel an allowance at any time, click your "Account" button in the iTunes Music Store window.

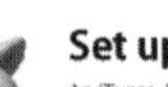

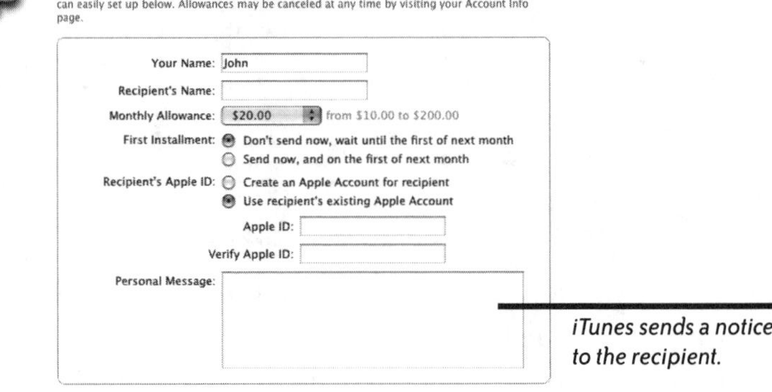

iTunes sends a notice to the recipient.

Gift certificates: Because the gift certificate can go through email, it's a great idea for last-minute gifts that otherwise don't have a chance of getting there on time.

1. Click the "Gift Certificates" link on the Music Store's home page, then choose a delivery method: "Email," "Print," or "U.S. Mail."
2. In the form that opens, fill in the required information. Use the "Amount" pop-up menu to select an amount from $10 to $200. Click "Continue."
3. Submit your Apple Account ID and password, then click "Continue." Click the "Buy" button.
4. In the "Confirm Your Purchase" window, click the "Buy" button.

Prepaid cards: Here's another solution for a gift or for someone who doesn't have a credit card—purchase prepaid cards at Target stores. To redeem an iTunes Prepaid Card, the recipient clicks on the "Prepaid Cards" link on the Music Store home page, then follows the instructions.

iTunes Prepaid Cards.

Shopping cart: Use a shopping cart if you want to store song selections and buy them later, or if you want to review the music that your children have chosen before it's purchased. To set up a Shopping Cart:

When you enable an iTunes Shopping Cart, the "Buy Song" button in the Music Store changes to "Add Song."

A new "Shopping Cart" icon appears in the Source pane, as shown below.

1. From the iTunes menu, choose "Preferences...."
2. Click the "Store" button to open the Store preferences pane.
3. Select "Buy using a Shopping Cart." Music is added to your cart when you click an "Add" button. To purchase and download a *single song* in the shopping cart, click its "Buy Song" button. To purchase and download *all songs* in the shopping cart, click "Buy Now" at the bottom of the window.

   To remove songs from the shopping cart, select "Shopping Cart" in the Source pane. Then select a song in the Shopping Cart and click the tiny Delete button that appears to the right of the "Buy Song" button.

iTunes and iTunes Music Store restrictions

Apple puts some limitations on how many computers can play the music that you purchased from the iTunes Music Store. To play purchased music, you must "authorize" your computer using your iTunes Music Store account name and password. When you try to play a purchased song on an unauthorized computer, a dialog box opens asking if you want to authorize it. You can authorize up to five computers at a time. You can use someone else's computer to buy music from the iTunes Music Store if you log in to *your* account and authorize the computer you're using, but remember to deauthorize it to prevent someone else from using your account. **To deauthorize a computer,** open iTunes, then from the Advanced menu choose "Deauthorize Computer...."

You're allowed to burn up to seven CDs of the same playlist, and you can burn unlimited CDs of single songs. You can copy your music collection to an unlimited number of iPods.

Manage and Play Videos in iTunes

Coolness, thy name is iTunes. Now you can play QuickTime videos in iTunes. They can be QuickTime videos that you made or professional videos that you've downloaded from the iTunes Music Store.

Download videos from iTunes Music Store

To open a Digital Booklet, double-click it in the Song Name column. The Booklet PDF opens in a separate preview window.

The iTunes music store includes video with some songs or albums. Some albums also may include a Digital Booklet—a PDF document that contains extra photos, music credits, and song lists. Look for a booklet icon or a video camera icon (shown below) next to song names in the Music Store. When you buy a song or album that includes either of these two extras, they're downloaded to iTunes along with the music you purchase.

Digital Booklet – Stand Up — *Digital Booklet file.*
Video – Stand Up — *Video file.*

These icons appear in your iTunes window after you've downloaded your music, as shown below. Double-click the video file to play it. The video plays in the bottom-left pane of the iTunes window (unless you set a different preference, explained on the next page). Click once on the video and it opens in a separate window, as shown at the top of the next page. Click the Full Screen button (circled below) to show the movie full screen.

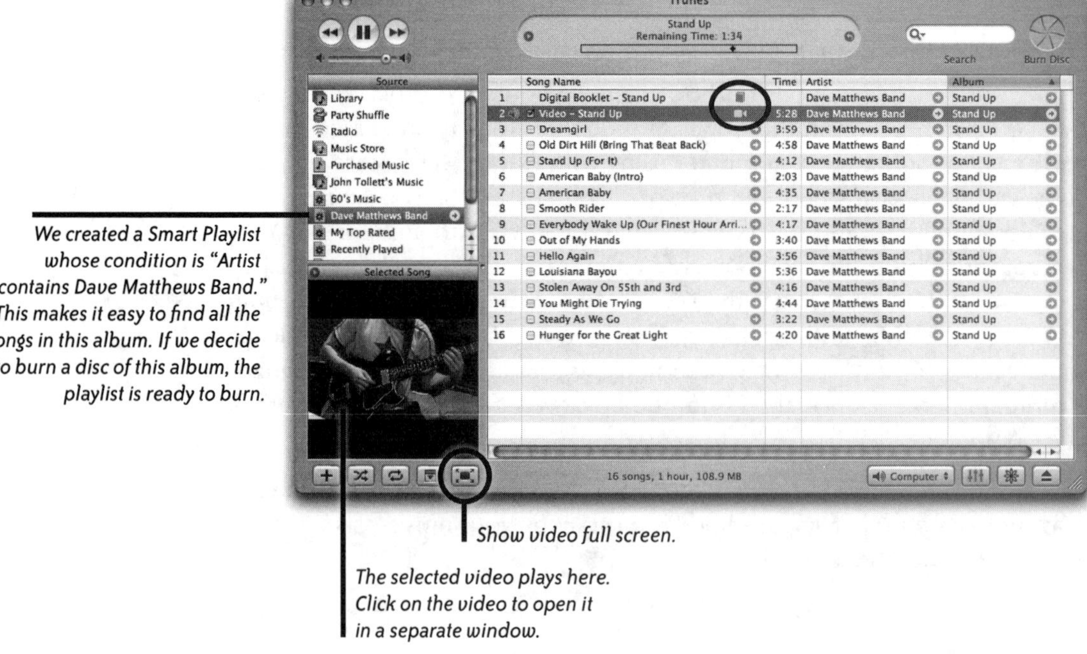

We created a Smart Playlist whose condition is "Artist contains Dave Matthews Band." This makes it easy to find all the songs in this album. If we decide to burn a disc of this album, the playlist is ready to burn.

Show video full screen.

The selected video plays here. Click on the video to open it in a separate window.

When you open a video in a separate window, you have access to the Play controls so you can place the playhead anywhere in the movie or scrub back and forth through your favorite scenes.

Control-click on the video's window to open a contextual menu from which you can change the movie size.

If you want to grab the video you downloaded from iTunes Music Store and copy it to another computer or onto a disc, you'll find it buried deep within your Home Folder's Music folder.

If you burn a disc of a playlist that contains video, the videos are burned to the disc as audio files only.

Import your own QuickTime videos

If you have a QuickTime movie that you exported from iMovie or that was imported into iPhoto from your digital camera, store them in iTunes and play them whenever you want, without having to search your hard disk for them. You can drag a QuickTime file from any location on your computer to the iTunes window to put it in the Library.

Create a video Smart Playlist

So videos will be easy to find, create a Smart Playlist whose condition says that "Kind contains QuickTime Movie" (shown to the right).

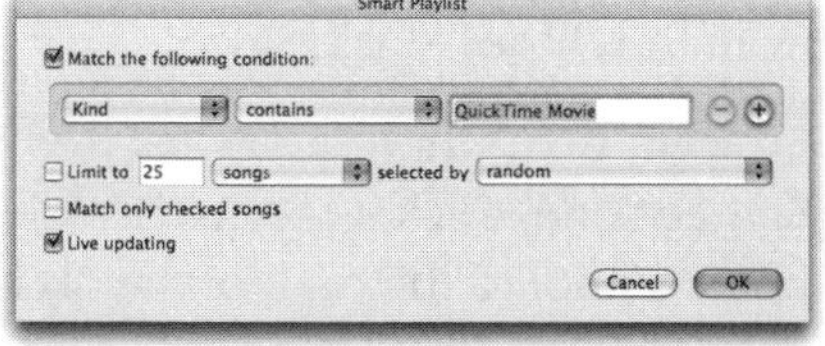

Set a default for video playback

When you select a video in the song list and click the Play button (or when you double-click a song to play it), it might play "in the main window" (the small video pane in the bottom-left corner of the window, as shown on the previous page), "in a separate window" (as shown above), or in "full screen" mode.

To set a default for how a video plays, open iTunes preferences, then click the "Advanced" button in the toolbar. Checkmark the "Play videos" option. From the pop-up menu, choose the way you want iTunes to initially show a video, then click OK.

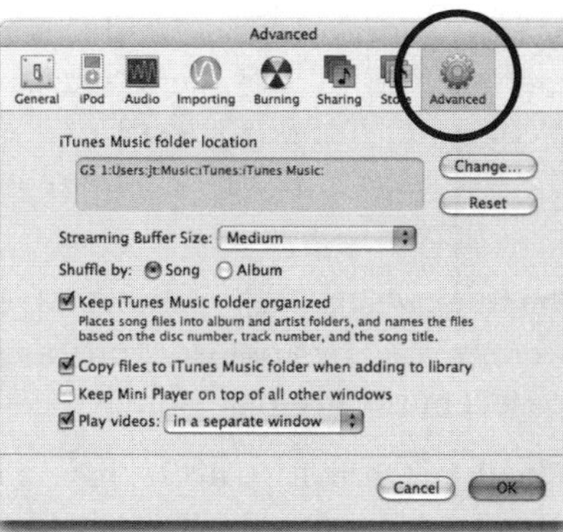

The Source Pane

If you want to delete a playlist in the Source pane, select it, then from the Edit menu choose "Clear."

***Or** Control-click on a playlist, then choose "Clear" from the menu that pops up.*

***Or** select a playlist, then press the Delete key on your keyboard.*

This is where you select the music collection that you want to display in the Detail window. Icons for the following types of sources can be found in the Source pane.

Library: This is your entire collection of iTunes music. Click the "Library" icon in the Source pane to view all the songs in iTunes. When you drag a song file from the Library to a playlist (as explained on page 69), the song remains in the Library and creates a directory that tells iTunes which songs are attached to various collections. You can put the same song in as many playlists as you want without bloating your computer with extra copies of large music files.

Party Shuffle: This is an automated playlist that selects a designated number of songs and plays them for you, constantly refreshing the playlist with selections based on your Party Shuffle settings. See page 92 for details.

Radio: Listen to streaming Internet radio stations. Learn how on page 72.

Music Store: Click this icon to connect directly to the iTunes Music Store. This is where you find, preview, purchase, and download songs or audiobooks. It's packed with powerful features. Learn more starting on page 74.

Purchased Music: This playlist keeps track of the music you've purchased from the iTunes Music Store.

CD icon: If you have a CD inserted in your CD drive, its icon shows in the Source pane. Click it to see a list of songs on the CD. To eject a CD, click the Eject symbol to the right of the CD icon.

iPod: If you connect an iPod, its icon appears in the Source pane. Select it to see the songs and playlists you've copied to it. See pages 120–127 for more iPod information.

Shared playlists: If you've set iTunes to "Look for shared music," and if it finds a Shared playlist on your local network, a new icon appears in the Source pane—a stack of documents with a music note on top. In the example shown above-left, "Quicksilver Music" is a shared music Library on a computer named Quicksilver. A click on the disclosure triangle reveals all the playlists in that Library. Learn how to share your playlists with others on your network on page 94.

Smart playlists: These automated playlists have a gear symbol on them. Some were created by Apple for you, but you can create your own to automatically collect music in a playlist that meets your preset conditions. See page 71.

Playlists: Ordinary playlists have a note symbol on them. Learn more about playlists on pages 69–71.

The Detail Window

The **Detail window** displays various columns of song information. The visible columns in the Detail window vary depending on which source you select in the Source pane and which options you choose in the View Options window (see page 89).

Press Command J to open "View Options" and choose which columns show here in the Detail window.

Select and play songs

To play any song in the "Song Name" column, double-click its title. When that selection has finished, iTunes plays the next song in the list *that has a checkmark next to it.*

When you insert a CD, by default *all* the song titles have a checkmark next to them, which means they will all play in order when you click the "Play" button. The checkmark also determines which songs will be encoded and placed in the iTunes Library when you click the "Import" button (page 102).

- **To select (check) all songs at once,** Command-click on any *empty* checkbox.
- **To deselect (uncheck) all the songs at once,** Command-click on any checkbox that has a *check* in it.
- **To select a group of contiguous songs** (songs that are adjacent to each other in the song list), click on one song, then Shift-click another song. All titles between the two clicks will be automatically added to your selection.
- **To select a group of non-contiguous songs** (songs that are not adjacent to each other in the song list), Command-click on the songs you want to select.

Resize or rearrange columns

If song titles are cut off by the narrow width of the "Song Name" column or if one of the columns is too narrow or too wide, you can **resize the column.** Place your cursor over the thin gray dividing line that separates two columns. The cursor becomes a bi-directional arrow. Press-and-drag the line to the left or right as far as necessary to resize the column to your liking.

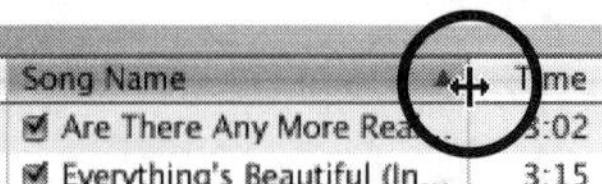

Drag the divider line left or right to resize columns.

To rearrange the columns, press on a column's title bar. When you start to drag, the arrow turns into a grabber hand as shown below. Drag the column left or right to a new position.

Above, you can see the grabber hand as it drags the "Time" column from its original position to the position between the "Artist" and the "Album" columns.

Organize the column information

The Detail window is always **organized** by the **selected** column. In the example above, the information is organized alphabetically by song name—you can see that the "Song Name" column heading is highlighted.

Click the small triangle to the right of a *selected* column name to **reverse the order** in which the information is displayed. For instance, if you select the column head "My Rating" and then click its triangle, the songs will be listed in order of how you rated them; click the triangle again to reverse the order of the ratings.

View Options

Set the Detail window to show just the information you want. Select a source in the Source pane, then from the Edit menu choose "View Options…." The top item in the "View Options" window is the name and icon of the selected source. As shown below, the options in this window change depending on the item you select in the Source pane. Check the columns you want to show in the Detail window, then click OK.

Most items in the Source pane have the same view options available as those for the Library, shown below-left. "Radio" and mounted CDs have fewer view options, as shown below. When "Music Store" is selected in the Source pane, no view options are available.

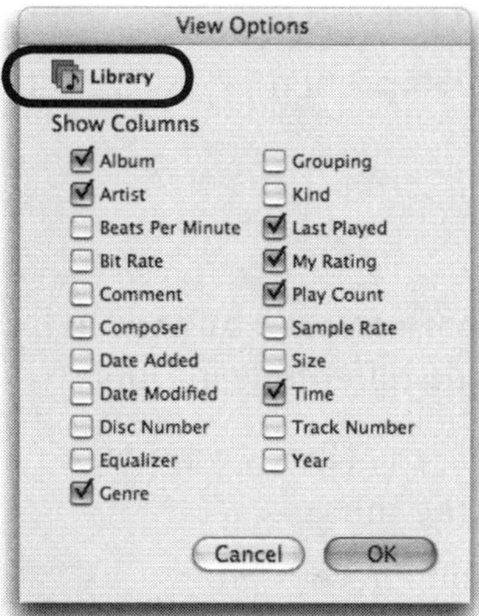

The items you choose here determine which columns are visible in the Detail window when you view the songs in the Library.

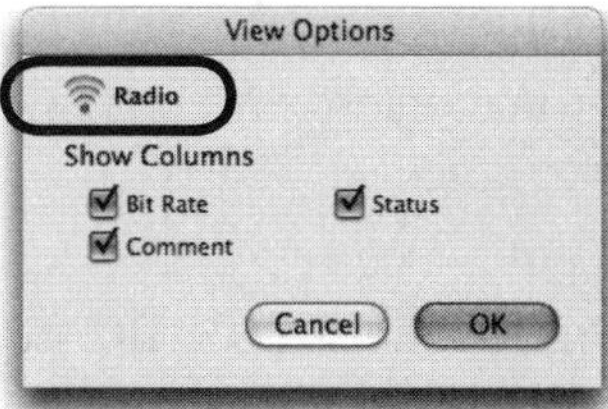

Select "Radio" in the Source pane, then choose which of these columns you want to show in the Detail window.

These are the View Options when a CD is selected in the Source pane. Select the "Disc Number" option if you want to identify multiple CDs that are part of a set.

When a CD from a set of three is mounted, its disc number shows in the Detail window as "1 of 3," "2 of 3," or "3 of 3."

When a single CD is mounted, its disc number shows in the Detail window as "1 of 1."

Controller Buttons

The **controller buttons** act just like the controls on most CD players:

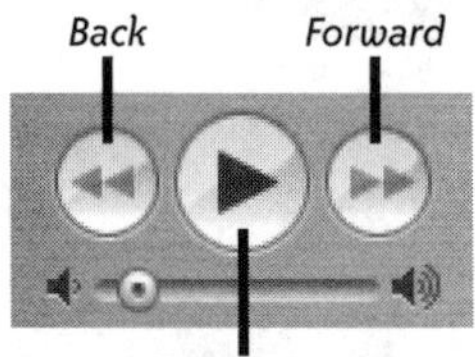

The middle button switches between Play and Pause when a song is playing.

It switches between Play and Stop when the Internet Radio is playing.

- **To select the Next song,** single-click the Forward button (double arrows pointing to the right).
- **To Fast Forward** the current selection, press-and-hold the Forward button.
- **To select the Previous song,** single-click the Back button (double arrows pointing to the left).
- **To Rapid Rewind** the current selection, press-and-hold the Back button.
- The middle button toggles between **Play** and **Pause** when a song file on your computer (or on a CD) is playing.

  The same button toggles between **Play** and **Stop** when the Radio Tuner is active.

Close, Minimize, and Zoom Buttons

As with every window in Mac OS X, you see the **three colored buttons** in the upper-left corner of the window, but they act a little differently in iTunes.

- Click the **red button** (the left button) to hide the iTunes window, even while music is playing. It won't affect the music.

  To show the player again, from the File menu choose "Show Current Song."

  Or use the keyboard shortcut Command 1 (one) to toggle between "Hide Player" and "Show Player" while iTunes is active.
- Click the center **yellow button** to minimize the player and send it to the Dock. The selected song continues to play.
  To bring the player back to the Desktop, single-click it in the Dock.

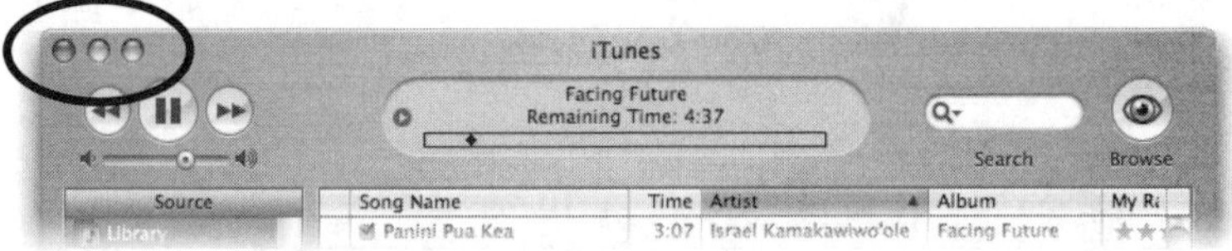

- Click the **green button** (the Zoom button, on the right) to reduce the size of the player window to its smallest possible size, as shown below. Click the green button again to return to the full window size.

The Zoom button.

This button collapses the entire iTunes window down to a compact, space-saving window.

Search the iTunes Library

The **Search** field enables you to quickly find songs from the iTunes Library, an iTunes playlist, or a mounted CD.

To focus a search, click the tiny triangle and choose a category that you want to search.

To search:

- In the Search field (circled, below), type a word or phrase that's part of the artist name, song name, or album name, or composer name.

  You don't need to hit the Return or Enter key—a list will appear instantly in the Detail window that includes only songs that contain your key words. As you type each letter, the list updates to show the matching results.

  For instance, in this example we search for a song by Bob Marley called "Crazy Baldhead." As we type the word "crazy" into the Search field, the results list instantly shows dozens of songs that have "c" in either the song title, artist name, or album name. After we type the second letter ("r") the list changes to show the only two songs that contain "cr." If we continue to type the word "crazy," the results list is reduced to only the songs that contain "crazy."

Type a search term in the Search field.

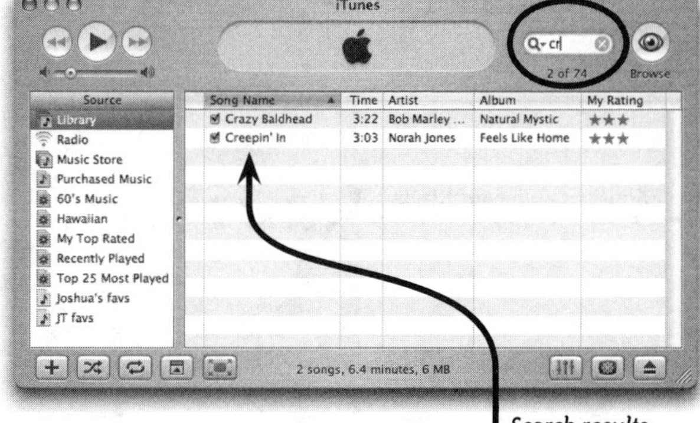

Search results.

Browse the iTunes Library

When your Library contains a large collection of songs by many different artists, you can **browse** the Library contents by genre, artist, or album.

The "Browse" button.

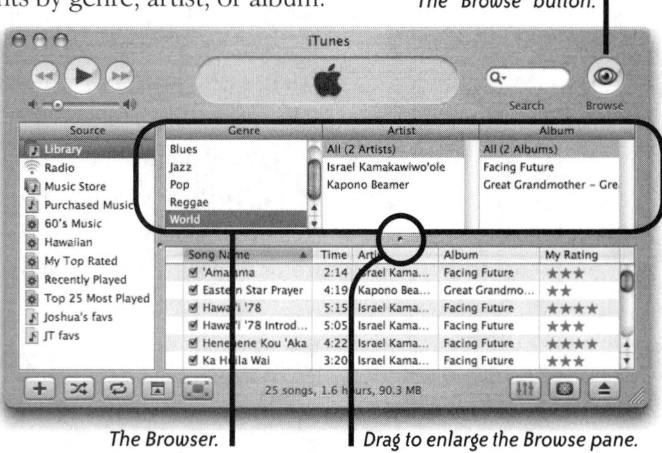

The Browser. *Drag to enlarge the Browse pane.*

1. With the Library selected in the Source pane, click the "Browse" button. **Or** from the Edit menu, choose "Show Browser." In the Browser pane that opens, select a genre, then an artist and album. The results display in the bottom pane.
2. To close the Browser pane, click the "Browse" button. **Or** from the Edit menu, choose "Hide Browser."

Party Shuffle

The Party Shuffle automatically creates a **dynamic playlist** based on your settings (shown below). It constantly updates, adding a new song whenever the current song ends. You can add songs manually, delete songs, or rearrange the order of songs at any time. Songs that you add manually stay in the list.

You can choose whether or not to show "Party Shuffle" in the Source pane: Go to iTunes Preferences, click the "General" button, then check (or uncheck) "Party Shuffle."

To create a Party Shuffle playlist:

1. Select "Party Shuffle" in the Source pane.
2. Party Shuffle instantly shows a playlist based on the option settings found at the bottom of the window, circled below.

To manually "re-shuffle" the Party Shuffle playlist, click the "Refresh" button.

Party Shuffle's automatic playlist.

Party Shuffle options.

3. Use the "Source" pop-up menu to select the Library or any playlist as a source from which Party Shuffle can choose songs. Party Shuffle will see only songs that are checked. Unchecked songs in the selected source will be ignored.
4. Click "Play higher rated songs more often" if you've *rated* your songs, as described on page 104.
5. Use the "Display" pop-up menus to set how many *recently played songs* and *upcoming songs* you want added to the list (up to 100).

Quick Links

Quick Link buttons (an arrow inside a circle) can be seen in the "Song Name" column, the "Artist" column, and the "Album" column. They are literally quick links to pages in the iTunes Music Store. Quick Links for the same song that are in different columns may go to different Music Store pages, depending on the column the Quick Link is in. If you click on a Quick Link in the "Song Name" column, iTunes will search for that particular song.

All songs and albums have a Quick Link button, but it only works if the song is actually available in the iTunes Music Store.

When you click a playlist in the Source pane, a Quick Link button appears next to it. These buttons in the Source pane are links to publish the playlist as an iMix (read about iMix on page 81). If you try to publish a playlist that contains some songs that were not purchased at the iTunes Music Store, iMix will ignore those songs and publish only the ones purchased there.

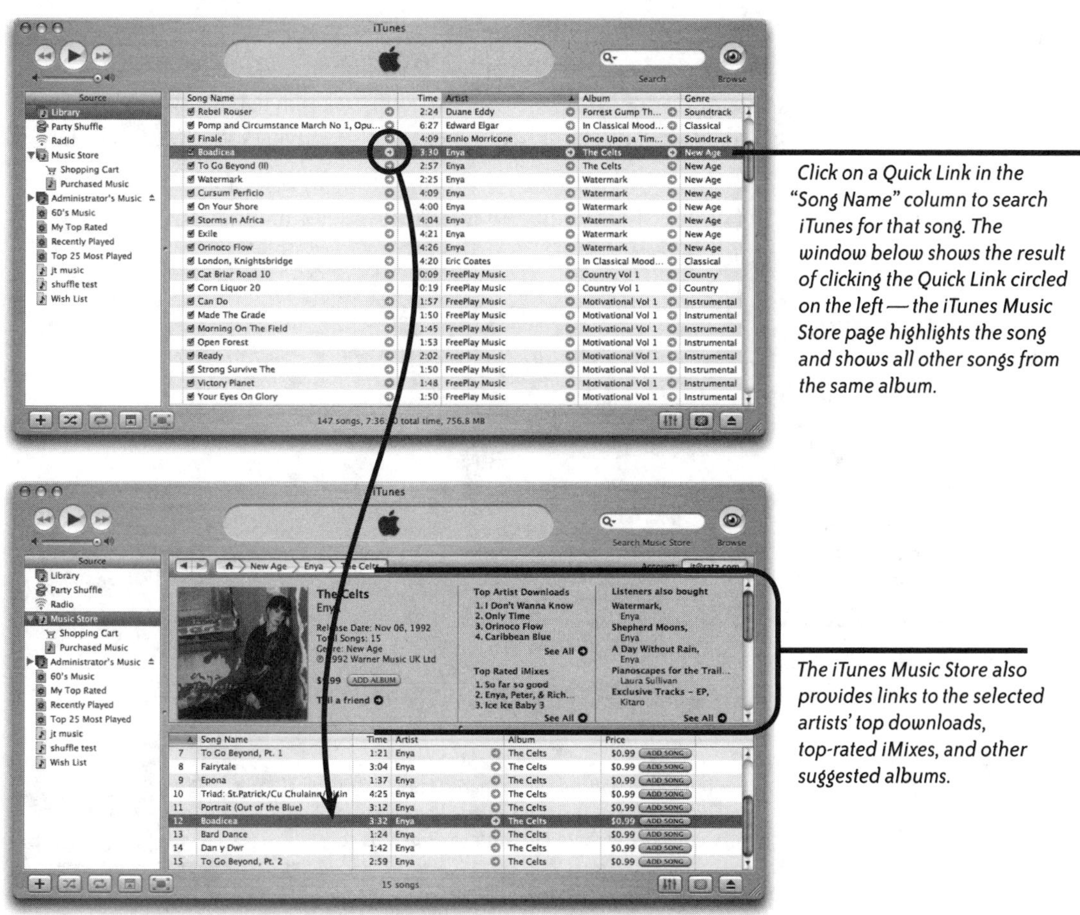

Click on a Quick Link in the "Song Name" column to search iTunes for that song. The window below shows the result of clicking the Quick Link circled on the left—the iTunes Music Store page highlights the song and shows all other songs from the same album.

The iTunes Music Store also provides links to the selected artists' top downloads, top-rated iMixes, and other suggested albums.

Share Music Over a Local Network

If you have two or more computers on a local network, users can **share their music collections** without copying any songs from one computer to another. iTunes can *stream* music files over a local area network (LAN) to a computer that has set iTunes Preferences to look for shared music. Streaming files play from one computer to another without being copied to it.

Set one (or more) of your computers to share its entire iTunes Library or selected playlists:

1. From the iTunes application menu choose "Preferences...," then click the "Sharing" button.
2. Select "Look for shared music" to make iTunes place an icon in the Source pane for any shared playlists it finds on the local network.
3. Select "Share my music" to make your iTunes music collection available on the local network to other computers that have been set to look for shared music (as in Step 2).

   If you select "Share my music," you must choose whether to "Share entire library" or "Share selected playlists." If you choose the latter, put checkmarks next to the playlists you want to share.
4. To restrict access to your music, click "Require password" and type a password in the text field.
5. Click OK.

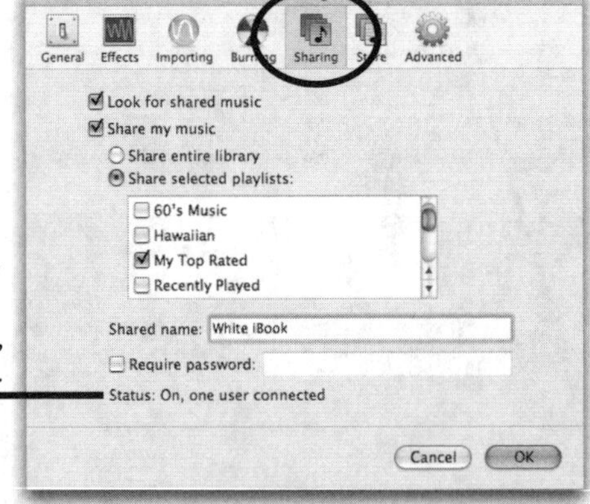

To see how many other computers are connected to your shared playlists, check this "Status" line.

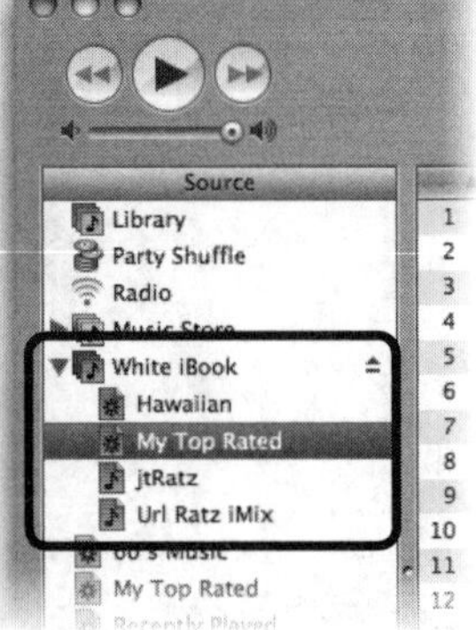

iTunes automatically finds shared music on the local network and puts it in the Source pane, as shown here. Click one of the shared playlists to display its songs, or click the shared Library icon ("White iBook" in this example) to see the contents of all the shared playlists.

Print CD Jewel Case Inserts, Song Listings, or Album Listings

Being able to burn a CD of your own customized playlists is really cool. Then you have to clumsily scrawl some kind of description on it with a felt tip pen so you'll know what's on it. Oh, wait—that was last century. Now you just select a design and let iTunes **print a beautiful CD case insert** that includes album art and a list of songs. You can also print song lists and album lists.

To print a CD jewel case insert, song listing, or album listing:

1. Select a playlist in the Source pane.
2. From the File menu, choose "Print...."
3. In the dialog box, choose one of the "Print" options: "CD jewel case insert," "Song listing," or "Album listing."
4. From the "Theme" pop-up menu, choose a layout style.
5. Click the "Print..." button to choose a printer.

The choices in the "Theme" pop-up menu change depending on the "Print" option you choose. CD jewel case themes are provided in both color and black and white.

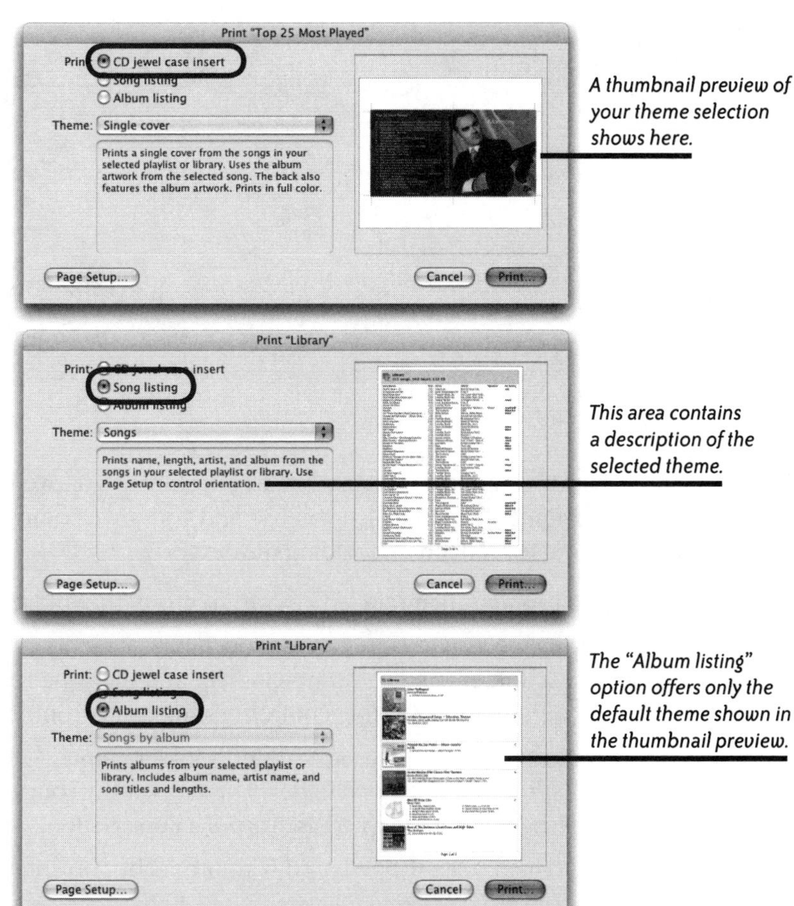

Song Information and Options

Get information about song tracks, add comments to songs, adjust the volume control, and make other adjustments in the **Song Information** window.

If you select more than one song, you'll get a different dialog box from the one shown below; see the opposite page.

To open the Song Information window:

1. Select one song track or multiple song tracks.
2. Type Command I to open the Song Information window.

If you made a single song selection, the Song Information window contains four tabs: "Summary," "Info," "Options," and "Artwork."

Summary

The **Summary** pane gives information about the *selected* song. To get information about other songs in the selected playlist without leaving this window, click the "Previous" or "Next" button (circled below-left).

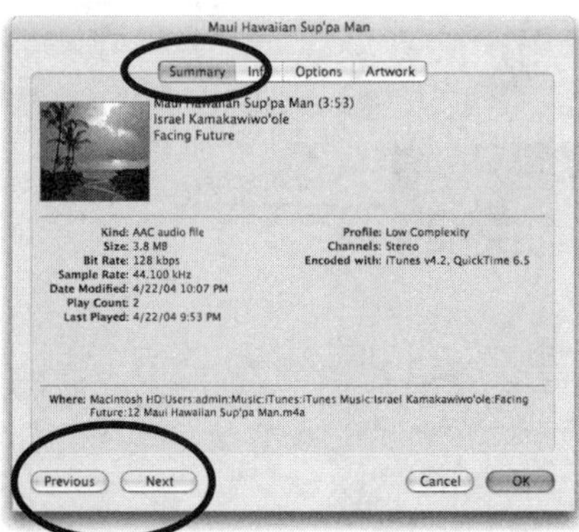

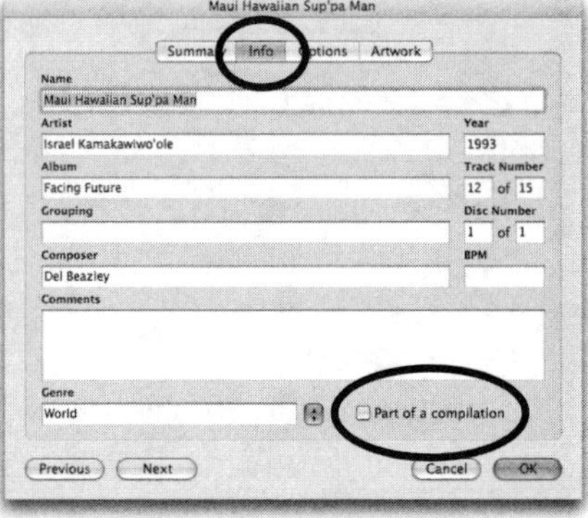

Info

The **Info** pane provides additional information, as you can see, above-right. There is also a "Comments" field in which you can add your own comments, such as "Used as theme for Amanda's wedding movie."

Mark songs or CDs as a **compilation** (circled, above) to group them together.

> When you mark a *song* as part of a compilation, a new folder is created in the iTunes Music folder named "Compilations," and the song is placed in a sub-folder named for the album the song came from.
>
> When you mark a *CD* as a compilation CD, a new folder named for the CD is placed in the Compilations folder. This causes any song you import from the CD to be marked as "Part of a compilation."

Compilations can be copied to an iPod, shared with others by copying them to another computer, or burned onto a CD.

Options

The **Options** pane allows you to set the **Volume Adjustment** for individual songs. This is cool when you're a serious rocker and cranking up the other volume controls just isn't loud enough.

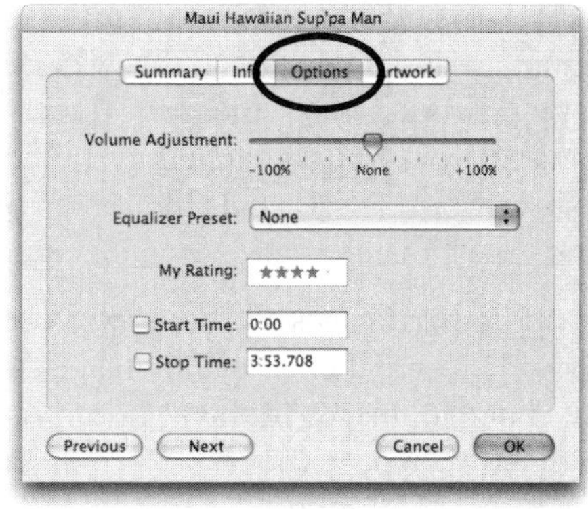

Use the **Equalizer Preset** pop-up menu to select one of the preset equalizer settings for the selected song. You can also set this in the main iTunes window if you've told "View Options" to show the Equalizer column (as explained on page 89).

Set **My Rating** for the selected song between one and five stars. This setting can also be set in the iTunes main window if you've told "View Options" to show the Rating column.

Set a **Start/Stop Time** for a song. In the event you want to **play or import just a section** of a long song, enter the "Start Time" and "Stop Time" in a minutes: seconds format (00:00). To determine which time settings you need, first play the whole song. Watch the "Status" display at the top of the iTunes window, and write down the beginning and ending "Elapsed Time" of your desired music segment. (If you don't see the elapsed time in the Status display, click whatever time display is showing until "Elapsed Time" appears.)

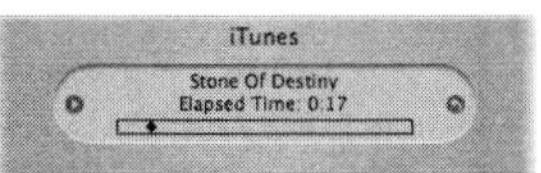

Get start and stop times from the "Status" display.

If you selected more than one song, the "Multiple Song Information" window, shown below, combines all the previous information and options into one window. The "Volume Adjustment" affects all selected tracks.

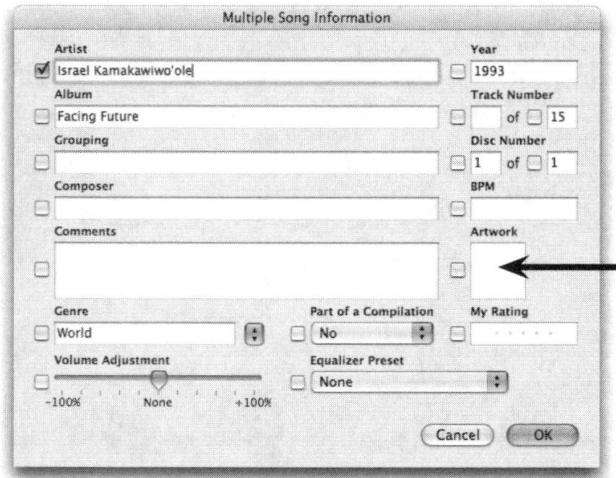

Double-click inside the "Artwork" box, then select an image that's on your computer.

The **Artwork** pane displays the album artwork associated with the selected song. Songs you buy from the iTunes Music Store automatically include the album art and it appears in this window. This album art also appears in the Song Artwork pane of the main iTunes window (bottom of page). Click the Song Artwork button, circled in the bottom example, to show or hide the song artwork. To see a full-size version of the song artwork in its own window, single-click the artwork.

You can use the album art as a screen saver. Use the Desktop & Screen Saver system preferences.

To add other images to the Artwork pane so they'll be available, click the "Add..." button, then select an image stored on your computer. When there are multiple images in this window, only the *first* image will appear in the Song Artwork pane (bottom of page). **To change the artwork,** drag the image you want to use in front of the other images in the Artwork pane, as shown below-right. Restart iTunes for your change to take effect.

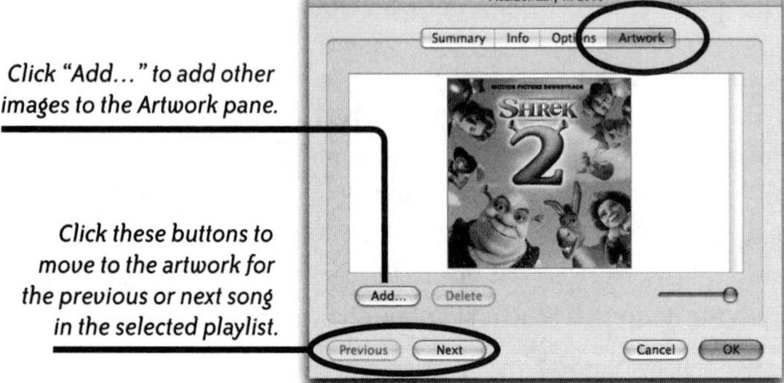

Click "Add..." to add other images to the Artwork pane.

Click these buttons to move to the artwork for the previous or next song in the selected playlist.

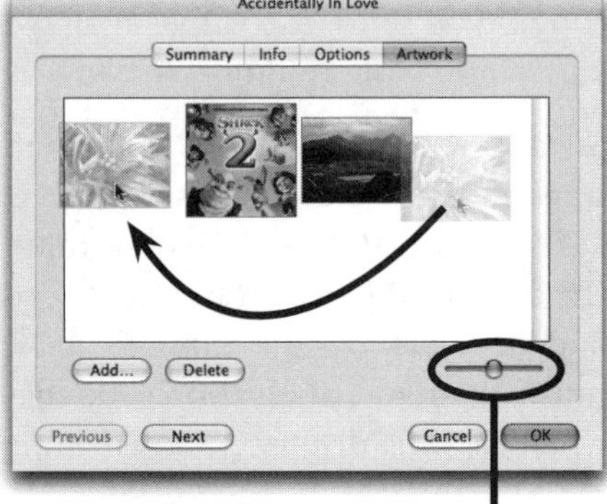

Use the slider to resize images.

Click on the song artwork to open it full-size and in its own window.

You can also Control-click the artwork, choose "Copy" from the contextual menu, then paste the image into a document such as Mail, Photoshop, TextEdit, etc.

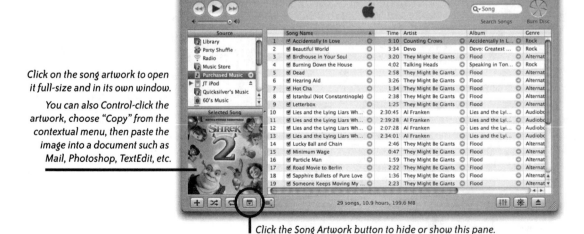

Click the Song Artwork button to hide or show this pane.

Status Display

When iTunes is playing a song selection from a CD, from the iTunes Library, or from a playlist, the **Status display** (at the top of the iTunes window) shows three lines of information: music identification, music track time, and an audio track bar.

The **music identification** (the top line) in the Status display automatically scrolls through song name, album name, and artist name. Click on the top line to manually cycle through these three bits of song information.

Status display.

The **time duration** of a song is shown in the middle line. Click on it to toggle between "Remaining Time," "Total Time," and "Elapsed Time."

The **audio track bar** on the bottom line indicates the current location of playback in relation to the entire song. **To move to any point in a song,** drag the playhead (the small black diamond) left or right. **Or** just click anywhere along the length of the audio track bar to position the playhead.

When iTunes is playing the **Radio Tuner,** the Status display is similar.

Click the top line to manually toggle between the URL (Internet address) of the radio station and its station name or call letters. The middle line shows the **Elapsed Time** of the audio stream. The bottom line is a **blank audio track** bar. You can't drag ahead or back in Radio streaming files.

No matter what you're listening to, you can turn the Status display into a **mini graphic equalizer:** Click the small triangle button on the left side of the window. This feature doesn't offer control of any kind, but it's fun. Click the button again to return to the normal display of status information.

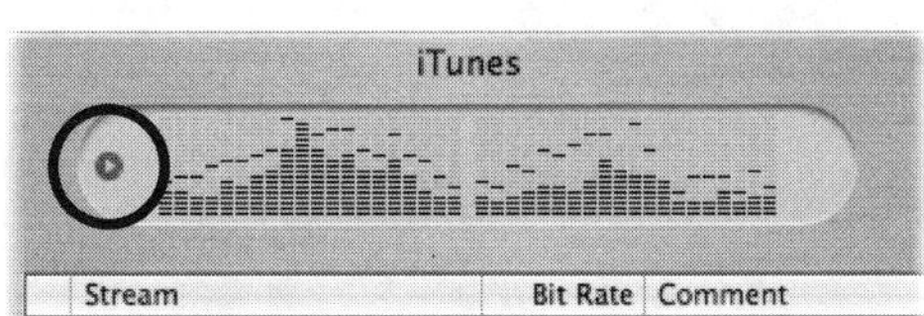

iTunes also includes a controllable equalizer; see pages 118–119.

The SnapBack button

The curved arrow on the right side of the Status display is a **SnapBack** button. The SnapBack button returns you to the song that's currently playing. For example, you play a song from a CD, then you switch to the Library, and then to the iTunes Music Store, and then to a shared playlist. You may not remember where the song that's playing is coming from, but when you click the SnapBack button, iTunes instantly shows the CD's contents and highlights the song that's playing.

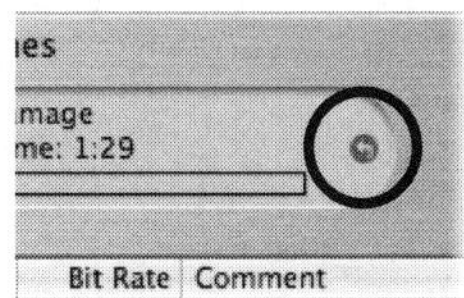

The Multi-Function Button

The button in the upper-right corner of the iTunes player changes appearance and functionality depending what is selected in the Source pane and if the iTunes visualizer is active. Since it does so many different things we call it the **Multi-Function button.** Following are its various states.

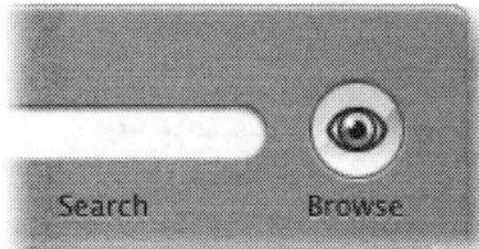

Browse: When you click on ***Library*** in the Source pane, the Multi-Function button becomes the "Browse" button. Click "Browse" and the top section of the iTunes window displays two new panes for browsing: Artist and Album. Select any item (or multiple items) in these two panes and the display below will show only songs that match the selections above. When you've located the desired song or album, you can double-click it to play immediately, or drag the selection straight from the Browse results list to a playlist in the Source pane.

To add a Genre column to the Browse area: From the iTunes menu, choose "Preferences…." In the "General" pane, check the box to "Show genre when browsing."

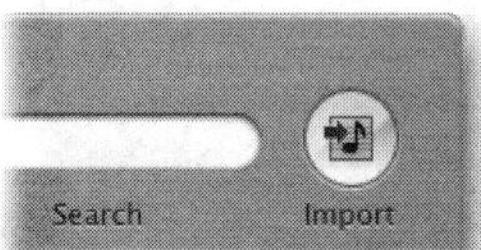

Import: When you click on a ***CD*** icon in the Source pane, the Multi-Function button becomes the "Import" button. "Import" copies selected songs into your iTunes Library. See more about importing on pages 102–103.

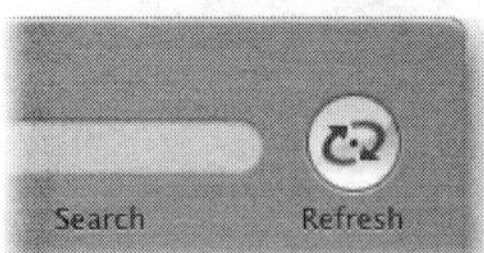

Refresh: When you click on ***Radio*** in the Source pane, the Multi-Function button becomes the "Refresh" button. Click the "Refresh" button to check the Internet for the latest radio listings available through iTunes.

You'll also see the "Refresh" button when you select the "Party Shuffle" playlist in the Source pane. Click the "Refresh" button to force iTunes to pick a new selection of upcoming songs to go in the "Party Shuffle" playlist.

Burn Disc: When you click on a ***playlist*** in the Source pane, the Multi-Function button becomes the "Burn Disc" button.

To burn a CD:

1. Select a playlist in the "Source" pane.
2. In the "Song Name" list, checkmark any songs you want recorded on the new CD. Uncheck songs you *don't* want to burn to the CD.
3. Click the "Burn Disc" button (shown top-right). The button cover opens to reveal the actual "Burn Disc" icon (shown on the right).
4. The Status window instructs you to insert a blank CD.
5. After you've inserted a disc, iTunes displays a message in the Status window instructing you to click the "Burn Disc" button again.

6. When finished, a new CD icon representing your newly created music CD appears on your Desktop.

Options: If you activate iTunes visual effects (click the Visualizer button shown below), the Multi-Function button becomes the "Options" button. Click "Options" to present the "Visualizer Options" window, shown below. You can choose to display the animation frame rate, cap the animation frame rate at 30 frames per second, always display the song information, and set a faster display or a better quality display. See pages 114–117 for details about the visual effects.

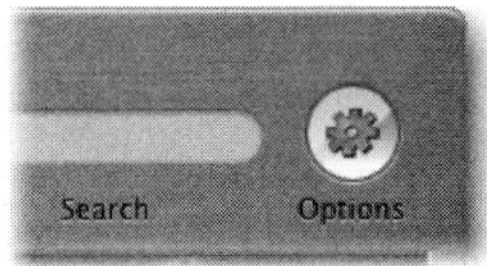

The Visualizer button.

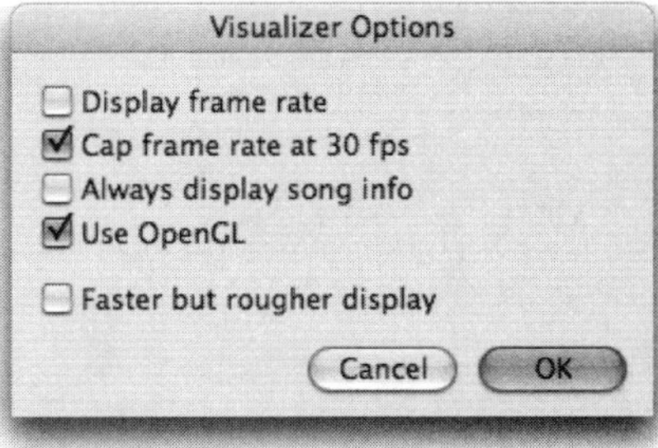

OpenGL is the industry standard for visualizing 3D shapes and textures. This option is meant to improve the performance of the visualizer, but depending on your system, it may actually degrade performance. Try it and see what happens.

Import Music from a CD

To **rip** a file is to encode it (convert it) from one format to another. To copy a CD music track **to your computer,** you'll convert it (rip it) from the CD-DA format on the CD to the AAC format, or to whatever file format you choose in the Importing preferences pane.

To rip music files:

1. Insert a music CD; the CD tracks appear in the iTunes Detail window, as shown below.

   If iTunes does not automatically go to the Internet and get the title names and other track information, go to the Advanced menu and choose "Get CD Track Names." This will open your Internet connection if you're not already online. After a few moments, the CD database will fill in the track titles, artist, album, and genre, if they're available online.

2. Select the tracks in the list you want to rip. By default all tracks in the list are checked when you first open a music CD. Uncheck any track that you don't want to save on your computer.

3. Click the "Import" button in the upper-right corner of the iTunes window. The selected (checked) tracks will be ripped (encoded) and added to the iTunes Library.

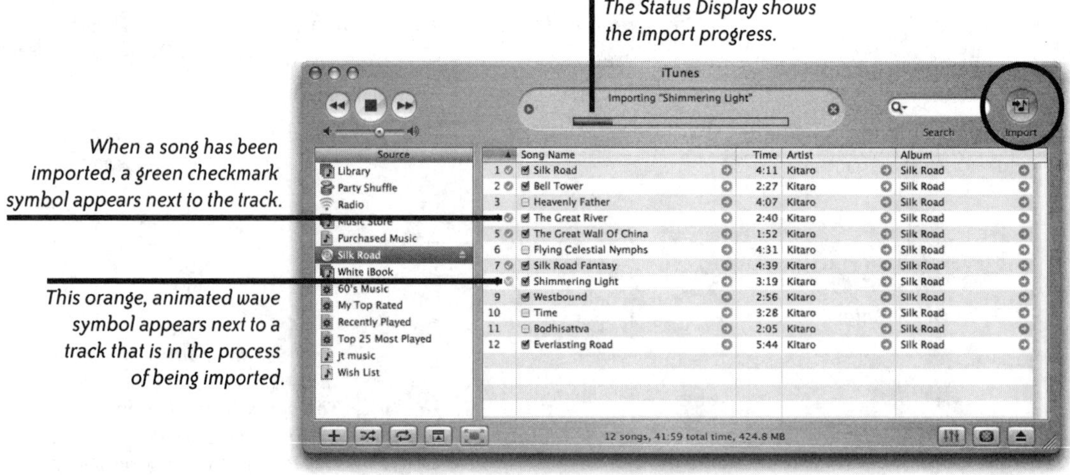

Rip multiple music files from a CD as one track

If you want to rip (import) two or more *adjacent* songs from a CD "Song Name" column so they will play as one track without a pause between the songs, use the "Join CD Tracks" command.

1. Insert a CD, then select the songs you want to join.
2. From the Advanced menu, choose "Join CD Tracks."

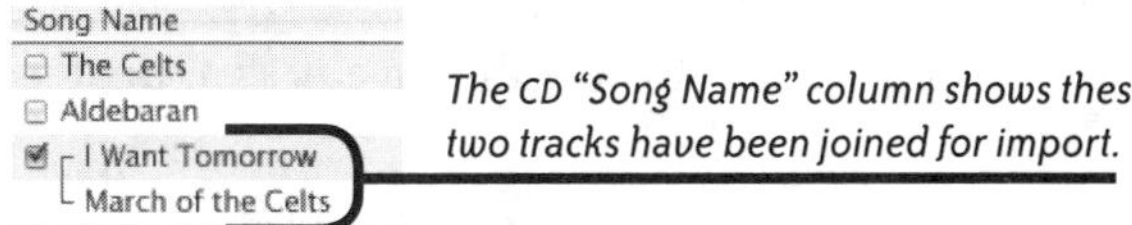

The CD "Song Name" column shows these two tracks have been joined for import.

3. Click "Import" in the top-right corner of the iTunes window.

If you have a CD with two tracks that have a cool transition between them, the transition might get lost if the songs import as two separate tracks. To keep the transition, use the "Join CD Tracks" command described here.

Rip music files to other formats

When you import music from a CD, you may want to **encode the music files to some other file format.** You can change the Importing preferences so that imported files are encoded as AAC, AIFF, Apple Lossless, MP3, or WAV formats.

1. From the iTunes menu, choose "Preferences...," then click the "Importing" button.
2. Change the "Import Using" setting to one of the supported file formats in the pop-up menu.
3. In the CD Song list, put a checkmark next to the song (or songs) you want to encode. If you plan to encode just a few songs, you can Command-click on an existing checkmark to clear *all* checkmarks, then select (checkmark) just the songs you want.
4. Click the "Import" button (shown on the previous page).

The song appears in the Library. If you already have a copy of this song in another format, you can determine which song is the newly formatted one: Control-click one of the copies and choose "Get Info," then look for the "Kind" info. **Or** set "View Options" to show the "Kind" column (page 89).

You can also **encode a copy** of a song that's already in your iTunes Library **into another file format.**

1. Set the "Importing" preference to the desired format, as explained above (AIFF, for example). Close the Preferences window.
2. Select a song (or songs) you want to encode to another format.
3. From the "Advanced" menu at the top of your screen, choose "Convert Selection to MP3." iTunes substitutes "MP3" with whatever format you chose in the Importing preferences (Step 1).

To convert songs to another format and save them in a folder of your choice, hold down the Option key as you select "Convert selection to" from the Advanced menu.

Songs you buy from the iTunes Music Store use a "Protected AAC" format that prevents them from being converted to other formats.

Rate Your Songs

You can **rate songs** on a scale of one to five **stars.** The rating can be used to sort songs, create playlists, or as a criterion in creating Smart Playlists.

1. If the "My Rating" column isn't showing in the iTunes window, Control-click on one of the column heads, then choose "My Rating" from the pop-up menu that appears. **Or** from the Edit menu, choose "View Options...," then click the "My Rating" checkbox.
2. Click on a song you want to rate. Notice that five dots appear in the "My Rating" column.
3. Click on the first dot to add a single star. Click dots further to the right to add more stars to your rating. You can also drag across the dots to add stars.

To sort the current songs by your rating, click the "My Rating" column heading. The order of songs will be rearranged with the highest-rated songs at the top of the list. **To reverse** the order of the list, click the small toggle triangle on the right side of the column heading.

You can also set a song's rating in the song information window. Select a song, then press Command I, or from the File menu choose "Get Info." Click the "Options" button, then set "My Rating" between one and five stars.

Export Playlists as Plain Text, Unicode, or XML Files

Export playlists as text files if you want to archive the song information, or if you want to import the information into another program, such as a database application.

Export as XML if you want to use the playlist in iTunes on another computer. When you import the XML file into iTunes on another computer, iTunes looks in its Library for the songs listed in the imported playlist. Songs that are not in the Library will not show up in the "Song Name" column.

Export as Unicode if you're using a double-byte alphabet such as Japanese or Chinese.

This procedure creates a file that includes information for every column in iTunes, even if some columns are not visible in your iTunes window.

1. Select a playlist. From the File menu, choose "Export Song List..." or "Export Library...."
2. In the "Save" window that opens, name the exported file. Set the "Format" pop-up menu to "Plain Text," "Unicode Text," or "XML," then choose a location in which to save it.

To create a text file (.txt) of song information that includes *only* the columns you have chosen to be visible in View Options (from the Edit menu, choose "View Options..."):

1. Select one or more songs that appear in the "Song Name" column.
2. From the Edit menu choose "Copy."
   Or Control-click on the song selection, then choose "Copy" from the pop-up contextual menu.
3. Open *another* application such as TextEdit, then from the Edit menu, choose "Paste."
   Or press Command V (for paste).

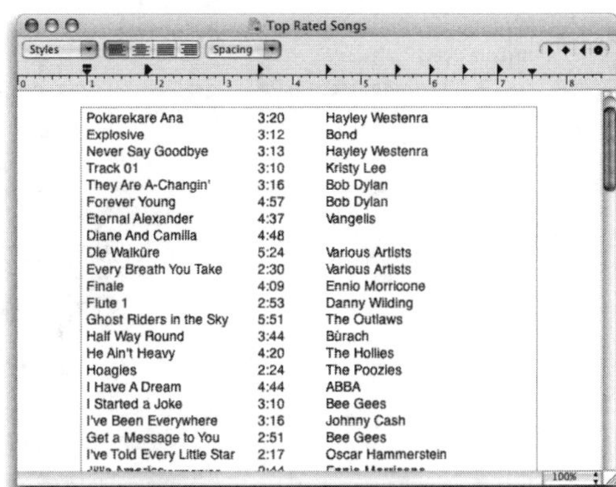

This is a TextEdit file that contains pasted song information.

iTunes Preferences

The **iTunes** preferences allow you to adjust a number of settings. From the iTunes menu, choose "Preferences…."

General preferences

Click the **General** button to see the General preferences.

- **Source Text** and **Song Text:** Choose to use "Small" or "Large" text in the Source pane and in the Detail window (the large pane of songs). The actual size difference between "Large" and "Small" is not dramatic.
- **Show Party Shuffle** or **Radio:** Select these to show them in the Source pane.
- **Show genre when browsing:** This option can be helpful when using the Browse feature (page 79) to search through a large collection of music files. It adds a "Genre" column to the "Artist" and "Album" columns that become visible when you click the "Browse" button.
- **Group compilations when browsing:** This creates an item in the "Artist" column of the Browser (see page 79) named "Compilations" (see page 94). Click on "Compilations" to see a list of albums (in the "Album" column) that contain songs marked as compilations.
- **Show links to Music Store:** This option makes the Quick Link buttons show in iTunes' Source pane and Detail window. Quick Links are shortcuts to that song's page on the iTunes Music Store site.

A compilation is a collection of songs that you choose to group together.

To make any song part of a compilation, select the song, then press Command-I to open the Song Information window. Click the "Info" button, then click "Part of a compilation."

In the Browser, the song will appear in "Compilations" under its album name.

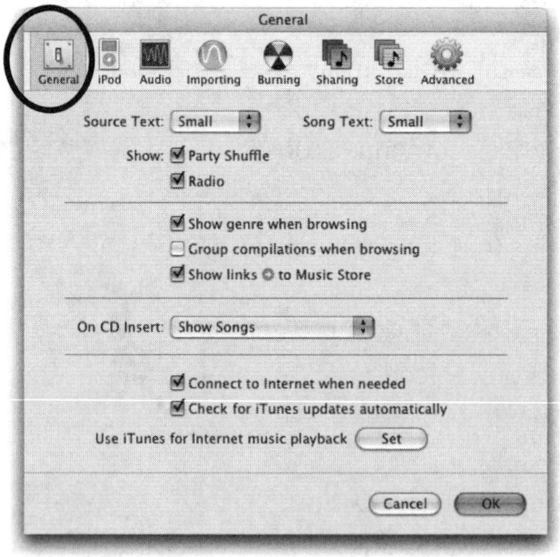

See pages 126–127 for iPod preferences.

- **On CD Insert:** This pop-up menu offers options for what happens when you insert a CD. Choose one of these options:
  - **Show Songs** displays the music titles, artist, and album information, but will not play music until you double-click a song. If you haven't retrieved the CD track names from the Internet, only the CD track numbers and times will show.
  - **Begin Playing** automatically starts playing a CD when it's inserted.
  - **Import Songs** automatically begins importing songs and placing them in iTunes' Library when a CD is inserted.
  - **Import Songs and Eject** does the same thing as above, then automatically ejects the CD when complete.
- **Connect to Internet when needed:** This option enables iTunes to connect to the Internet whenever you insert a CD so it can retrieve song titles and other information from CDDB, an Internet database of CD albums. iTunes also connects to the Internet when you select "Radio" or "Music Store" in the Source pane. And whenever you click a Quick Link button (a white arrow in a gray circle), iTunes connects to the iTunes Music Store. If you have a modem connection instead of a broadband Internet connection, you may prefer to uncheck this item to avoid having your modem dial up at unwanted times.

  If you choose to uncheck this option, you can manually retrieve CD titles whenever you like: Connect to the Internet, then from the "Advanced" menu in the menu bar, choose "Get CD Track Names."
- **Check for iTunes updates automatically:** This option checks Apple's web site for you to see if software updates are available for iTunes.
- **Use iTunes for Internet music playback:** This option sets iTunes as your default multi-media audio player when you download an audio file or click an audio file link on the web.

Audio preferences

Click the **Audio** button to change how your music plays.

- Check the **Crossfade playback** checkbox to fade music smoothly between songs without a long gap of silence. This effect is one of our favorites. The slider adjusts the amount of time it takes to fade out of one song and to fade in to the next song. Move the slider all the way to the right for the smoothest transition with the least silence between songs.
- Check the **Sound Enhancer** box to add depth and liven the quality of the music. The slider increases or decreases the effect, which is subtle but noticeable.
- Check the **Sound Check** box to make all songs play at the same volume level.

  Leave the "Sound Check" box *unchecked* if you want to vary the volume level of different songs using the volume control in the iTunes window.

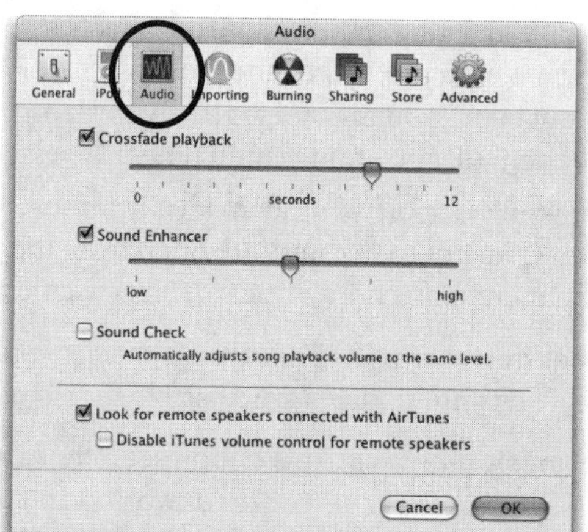

When you burn a CD, these effects do not carry over to the CD.

When an AirPort Express device is plugged into a power outlet within wireless range of your computer, iTunes detects it and adds a pop-up menu to the iTunes window from which you can select the connected remote speakers.

- Select **Look for remote speakers connected with AirTunes** if you have an AirPort Express connected to remote speakers. *AirPort Express* is a small device you plug into the wall, then connect it to powered speakers. *AirTunes* is the technology that lets iTunes stream music wirelessly to the remote speakers through the AirPort Express.
- Select **Disable iTunes volume control for remote speakers** if you want to control the volume of remote speakers from the remote speakers, instead of using the iTunes volume control on your computer. This can be very useful when the remote speakers are in a different room from your computer.

Importing preferences

Click the **Importing** button to set encoding and configuration preferences.

If you have a version of QuickTime installed that's older than version 6.2, songs are by default imported in the MP3 format instead of the AAC format.

- **Import Using** lets you choose which encoder will be used to import music files: AAC Encoder, AIFF Encoder, Apple Lossless Encoder, MP3 Encoder, or WAV Encoder (these file formats are described on page 73). The default setting of AAC is ideal for listening to and storing music on your computer because it combines maximum compression (smaller file sizes) and good sound quality.
- **Setting** is a quality setting. For most users it's best to leave "Setting" on its default settings.
- You can listen to a song as it's being ripped (encoded) by checking the **Play songs while importing** option. Encoding is very fast, usually four to ten times faster than the music plays if you have a newer system. The encoding of a song finishes well before the music has finished playing.
- Check **Create file names with track number** to force imported songs to be stored in your Music folder in the same order they appear on the CD.
- Check **Use error correction when reading Audio CDs** if you're having problems with CD audio quality. Error correction slows the importing process, but may be helpful.

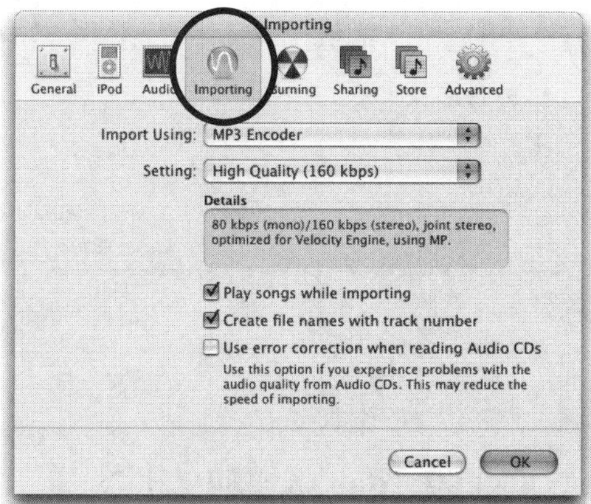

Burning preferences

Click the **Burning** button to set preferences for burning discs.

- **Preferred Speed:** Set the speed at which your CD burner will burn CDs. The default setting of "Maximum Possible" lets iTunes adjust to the speed of your hardware. If you have problems, try setting "Preferred Speed" to a low number.
- **Disc Format:** Choose a disc format for burning CDs.

  Audio CD uses the standard CD-DA format common to all commercial CD players. You can store approximately 75 minutes of music on a CD using this format.

  Gap Between Songs lets you set the amount of silence you want between songs.

  Use Sound Check creates a consistent volume for all songs.

  MP3 CD format can store over 12 hours of music, but can only be played on computers and some special consumer CD players. If you want to archive MP3 music files on CDs for backup choose "MP3 CD" for the most efficient storage solution.

  Data CD or DVD formatted discs include all files in a playlist, but may not work in many players. Use this option to make a backup of your music.

You won't see the DVD option here unless your Mac has a SuperDrive.

You can burn music CDs using either **CD-RW** discs or **CD-R** discs.

CD-RW (CD-ReWritable) discs will play in your computer, but most stereos and commercial CD players don't recognize them.

CD-R (CD-Recordable) discs can play on computers and most CD players.

Discs must be blank to record music on them. You can erase a CD-RW disc and then use it to burn a music CD. A CD-R disc cannot be erased, and it cannot be used if it already has files on it.

Sharing preferences

The **Sharing** pane is where you enable iTunes to share music with others on a local network. Instead of copying music from another computer on your network, you can have it *stream* to you (see page 94).

- **Look for shared music:** Check this box and your computer will look for other Macs on the local network that have music sharing enabled.
- **Share my music:** Select this option to make your iTunes Library or individual playlists available to others on the network. With this option selected, choose to **Share entire library** or **Share selected playlists.**

  If you choose to share *selected playlists,* put a checkmark next to one or more of your playlists that are shown in the scrolling window pane.
- **Shared name:** Type a name to identify your shared music collection when it appears in another user's iTunes Source pane.
- **Require password:** If you want to limit access to your shared music collection, select this option. Type a password in the text field, then give the password to certain people. When anyone tries to access the playlist by clicking the shared playlist icon in their Source pane (as shown on page 94), they'll be asked for the password.
- **Status:** This line of text reports how many users on the local network are connected to your shared playlist.

Store preferences

The **Store** preferences pane lets you choose how you want to shop at the iTunes Music Store, along with several other options.

- **Show iTunes Music Store:** Put a checkmark in this box to show the "Music Store" icon in the Source pane.

  If you uncheck this box, the "Music Store" icon disappears from the Source pane, and all Quick Link buttons disappear from the Source pane and the Detail window.

- **Buy and download using 1-Click:** If you have an Apple Account, when you click a song's "Buy" button in the Music Store the song is purchased and downloaded immediately. Very easy and convenient.

- **Buy using a Shopping Cart:** This selection puts a "Shopping Cart" icon in the Source pane, under the "Music Store" icon. All "Buy Now" buttons in the Music Store change to "Add" buttons. When you click a song's "Add" button, the song is added to the shopping cart until you're ready to buy. Then you can click "Buy Song" to purchase a single song in the shopping cart, or click "Buy Now" to purchase all items in the shopping cart.

  A shopping cart is useful for collecting songs you want to consider buying or for reviewing songs that your children have selected.

- **Play songs after downloading:** If you want a song to automatically play as soon as it's downloaded, click this box.

- **Load complete preview before playing:** If a slow Internet connection causes the streaming previews in the Music Store to stutter and stop, click this box to ensure a full-quality song preview. iTunes will download the complete preview stream before playing it.

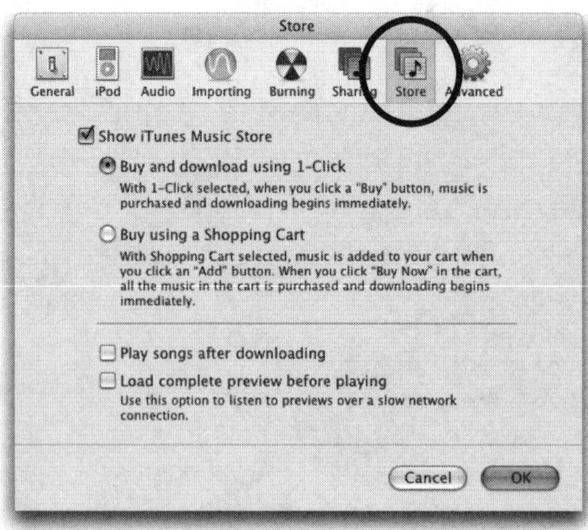

Advanced preferences

The **Advanced** button has settings to designate a location for storing your music files, as well as options for burning CDs.

- **iTunes Music folder location:** Music files created by iTunes are automatically stored on your startup hard disk. Specifically, they are stored in a folder called "iTunes Music," which is in a folder called "iTunes," which is in your "Music" folder. This folder contains all of the music files you've encoded. You can change this default location to any location you choose: Click the "Change…" button and choose another folder or hard disk.

  Every individual user account has her own "iTunes" folder inside the home "Music" folder.
- **Streaming Buffer Size:** Refers to the Radio Tuner and the Music Store preview songs. The buffer size determines how much streaming data is cached (temporarily stored) on your hard disk when you listen to an Internet radio stream or play a preview. The buffer is like padding that compensates for connection problems that would affect the quality of a direct stream. If you've determined that your connection to the Internet is low-quality, change this setting from "Medium" to "Large." A large buffer gives iTunes more downloaded streaming data to use for compensation as it deals with slow or faulty connections.
- **Shuffle by:** Shuffle the playing order of songs by *Song* or *Album*.
- **Keep iTunes Music folder organized:** This places song files into album and artist folders (in the iTunes Music folder), and names the files based on the disc number, track number, and song title.
- **Copy files to iTunes Music folder when adding to library:** Puts a *copy* of a song in the iTunes folder if you import songs from other locations on your computer. The original song remains in its original location. This is similar to the "Consolidate Library" command in the Advanced menu, which puts a copy of all songs in your Library when the original is located somewhere else on your computer.
- When you click the green Zoom button in the top-left corner of the iTunes window, the window minimizes to a small, space-saving Mini Player. Select **Keep Mini Player on top of all other windows** to always keep the Mini Player visible and on top of other windows.

iTunes Visualizer

The Visual Effects button.

The **iTunes music visualizer** is mesmerizing. Just double-click a song, click the "Visual Effects" button in the bottom-right corner of the iTunes window, and watch the show. Colors and patterns undulate and morph to the beat of the music. You can also turn visuals on by pressing Command T or by choosing "Turn Visualizer On" in the Visualizer menu.

Show Visualizer within the iTunes window in one of three **sizes:** From the Visualizer menu, choose "Small," "Medium," or "Large."

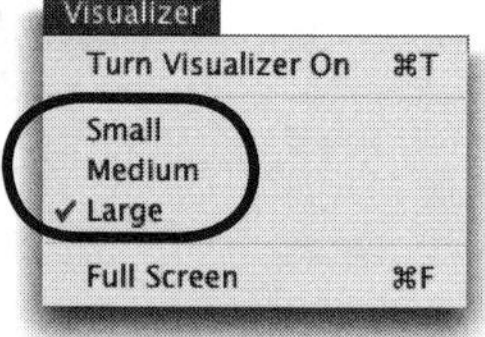

You can also show the Visualizer effects in three different sizes while in **Full Screen** mode: From the Visualizer menu, choose "Full Screen." Now your choice of "Small," "Medium," or "Large" determines how the visuals appear *while in full-screen mode.* The "Small" or "Medium" option adds black around the visual effects to fill out the extra screen space. Choose "Large" *and* "Full Screen" to fill your entire screen with beautiful visual effects.

Toggle between full-screen view and window view with the keyboard shortcut Command F. **Or** click the mouse anywhere on the screen to return to the song list without interrupting the music.

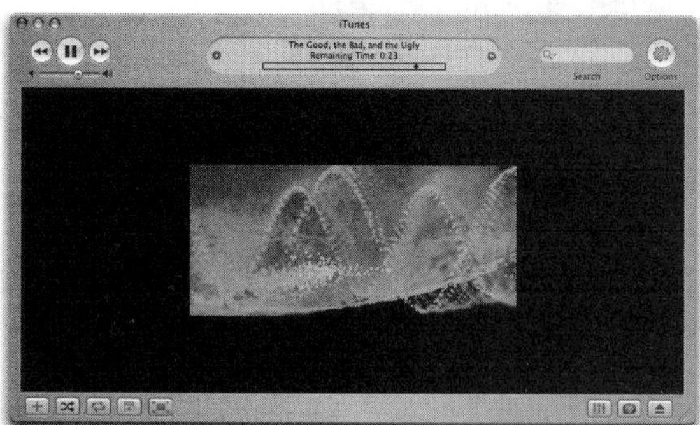

"Small" Visualizer effects as seen in window view.

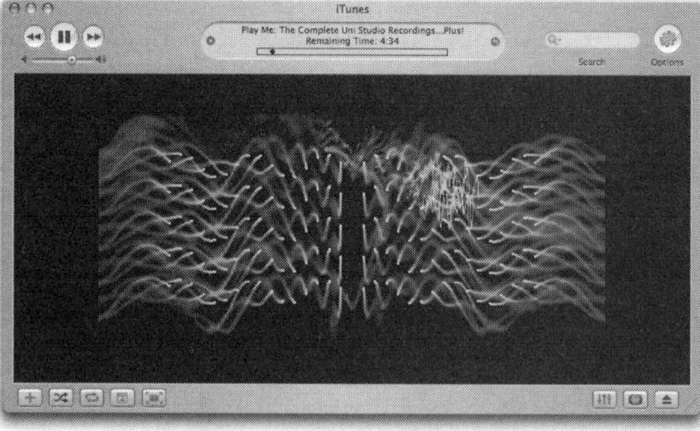

"Medium" Visualizer effects as seen in window view.

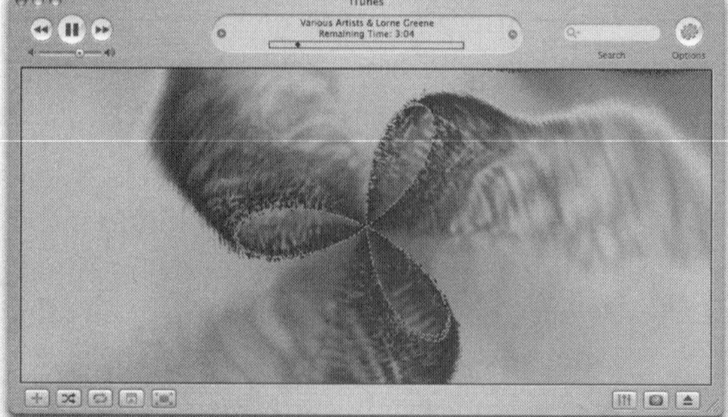

"Large" Visualizer effect as seen in window view.

Visualizer configurations

The **iTunes Visualizer** can be even more fun if you know how to control it. The Visual Effects Generator uses three different **configurations** to create visuals. You can see these listed in the top-right of the window if you press the C key while visual effects are playing (shown below). The three configurations listed change randomly and morph into one another as music plays. You can change any, or all, of these configurations while music is playing.

Press C to show the effect names in the top-right corner of the window.

The first configuration in the list affects the **foreground** of the Visualizer, the primary lines and shapes that modulate and interact with the beat of the music more obviously than the other graphics on the screen. Cycle through all the built-in effects for this configuration by alternately pressing the Q and W keys (Q for the previous selection and W for next selection).

Press Q or W to change the primary lines and shapes.

The second configuration in the list affects the **background** graphics, the shapes and patterns that stream from the primary shapes in the top configuration. Cycle through all the built-in effects for this configuration by alternately pressing the A and S keys (A for the previous selection and S for the next selection).

Press A or S to change the secondary shapes and patterns.

The third configuration in the list affects the **color scheme** applied to the visuals. Cycle through all the built-in effects for this configuration by using the Z and X keys (Z for the previous selection and X for the next selection).

Press Z or X to change the color scheme.

To manually and randomly change configurations at any time, press the R key. Press the R key in beat with the music to become the conductor of an amazing musical light show.

Press R to change everything randomly.

Click this button to set a few options. You can choose to display the animation frame rate (in the top-left corner), cap the animation frame rate at 30 frames per second (for slower systems), always display song info, and set a faster but rougher display.

***Warning:** If you have work that needs to be done, **do not** turn off all the lights, put headphones on, play great music, and click the Visualizer button. Most importantly, **do not** start pressing the R key in beat with the music. That kind of irresponsible behavior put this entire chapter in jeopardy.*

Visualizer modes

To cycle through three Visualizer modes, press the M key repeatedly:

- **To play the random visual effects** generated by iTunes, press the M key several times until "Random slideshow mode" appears in the top-left corner of the window.
- **To force iTunes to play the current configuration** until instructed otherwise, press the M key several times until "Freezing current config" appears in the top-left corner of the window.
- **To play only the configurations that have been saved as presets** under the numeric keys, as described below, press the M key repeatedly until "User config slideshow mode" appears in the top-left corner of the window.

Save a favorite configuration

When you change an individual configuration (by using the keys mentioned on the previous page), the new effect fades slowly in as the configuration description in the upper-right corner fades out. If you fall in love with an effect, you can save that particular configuration as a preset that you can activate at any time.

To save a favorite configuration as a preset:

1. Press the M key to cycle through the three different options: "Random slideshow mode," "User config slideshow mode," and "Freezing current config."
2. When you get to the "User config slideshow mode," stop pressing the M key. This mode plays configurations you have saved as presets.
3. Wait until you see a visual effect you like, or create a custom effect using the keys described on the previous page. Hold down the Shift key and tap one of the numeric keys (0 through 9) while the desired effect is playing. You can save up to ten different preset effects.

   Note: To get rid of an old preset, just save a new one over it. Use the steps above and assign the same numeric key.

   To play your preset, tap the numeric key that you assigned to your preset configuration. Try tapping different numeric preset keys to the beat of the music for fantastic visual effects.

Visualizer Help

A separate **Help** file of keyboard shortcuts is available in the Visualizer. While Visuals are turned on, press the **?** key (or the H key) to show a list of keyboard shortcuts. The "Basic Visualizer Help" list appears on the left side of the window .

Press the **?** key again (or the H key) to toggle to another list of keyboard shortcuts, "Visualizer Config Help."

iTunes Equalizer

iTunes provides an **Equalizer** that enables you to make dramatic adjustments to the sound output of your music files. Make adjustments manually or select from over twenty presets. You can even save custom settings as a preset and add it to the preset pop-up menu, as explained below.

An equalizer represents the various frequencies of the sound spectrum, or more specifically, the spectrum of human hearing. The spectrum is expressed as a measurement known as *hertz* (hz).

The iTunes Equalizer represents the frequencies of the spectrum with vertical sliders, also known as **faders.** The faders are used to increase or decrease the volume of each frequency, expressed as *decibels* (dB).

The lowest frequencies (bass): 32, 64, and 125 hz faders.

The mid-range frequencies: 250 and 500 hz faders.

The highest frequencies (treble): 1K through 16K (kilohertz) faders.

The Equalizer button.

To show the Equalizer, click the Equalizer button at the bottom-right corner of the iTunes window. Check the **On** box to activate the Equalizer.

Choose a preset from the pop-up **menu** to automatically adjust the faders.

The **Preamp** slider on the left side of the Equalizer is a secondary volume adjustment. If a music file was originally recorded too quietly or loudly, adjust the volume here. Or if you're looking for maximum room-booming sound, slide the "Preamp" knob up to the top.

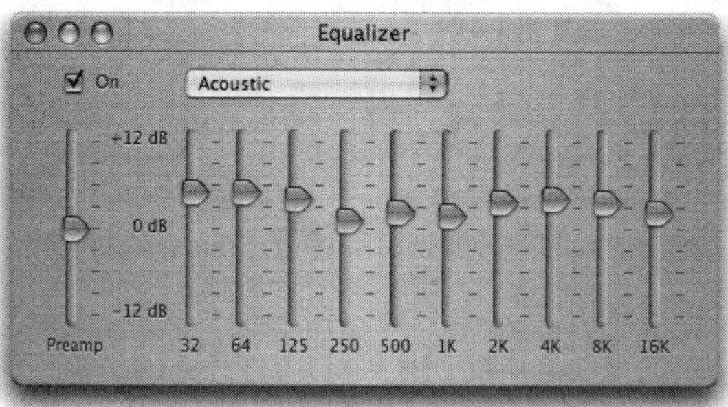

To save your custom settings as a preset:

1. Adjust the faders to your satisfaction.
2. From the pop-up menu (where it says "Acoustic" in the example above), choose "Make Preset...."
3. In the "Make Preset" dialog box, enter a name for your preset, then click OK.

   Your custom preset now appears in the pop-up menu.

If you choose, you can **rename equalizer presets** in the pop-up list, or **delete** the presets you don't use.

To edit the preset list:

1. From the pop-up menu in the Equalizer window, choose "Edit List...."
2. In the "Edit Presets" window (shown to the right), click on a preset to select it, then click the "Rename..." button or the "Delete" button.

To apply Equalizer settings to a song, use one of the following methods.

- Select a song, then click the "Equalizer" button. Select a preset from the Equalizer pop-up menu, or use the faders to create a custom setting.
- **Or** add an Equalizer column to the iTunes Detail window: From the Edit menu, choose "View Options...." Check the "Equalizer" box, then click OK. An "Equalizer" column appears in the Details window, from which you can choose a preset for each song in the list (below-right).
- **Or** Control-click on a column heading, then choose "Equalizer" from the pop-up menu that appears (shown below-left). This adds the "Equalizer" column to the window, from which you can select a preset for a song.

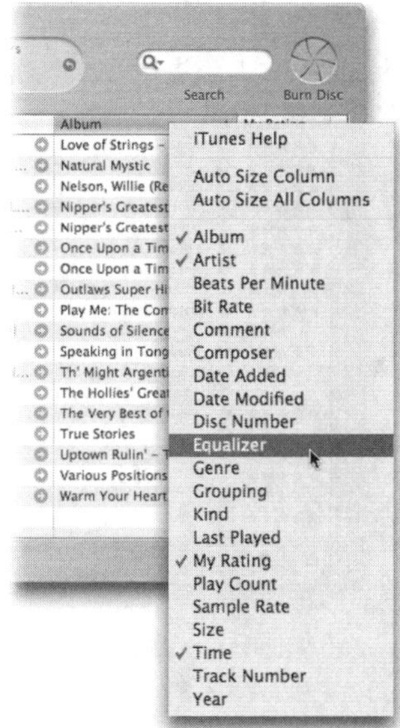

Control-click on a column heading to open a contextual menu, then select "Equalizer" to add an Equalizer column to the iTunes window.

Click a pop-up button in the "Equalizer" column to see a menu of equalizer presets.

Experiment with different sound settings by choosing various presets in the Equalizer column.

Robin's iPod

When you transfer your music collection to an iPod, a link is created between the iPod and your iTunes music library. If you connect the same iPod to someone else's computer, you'll get a message that asks if you want to delete everything on the iPod and replace it with the current music Library. Probably not.

Connect an iPod

The **iPod** is a portable digital music player designed to work with iTunes. For information about current models and prices, visit **www.apple.com/ipod/.**

In addition to storing up to 10,000 songs, the iPod can also act as a hard disk and store any computer files, including thousands of photos. With the proper accessories you can use it as a personal voice recorder. You can also import music that you create in GarageBand (Chapter 5).

iPod supports the most popular music formats: **MP3,** used by most digital music players; **AAC,** the file format used by iTunes and the iTunes Music Store; and **WAV,** a popular Windows format. iTunes encodes music to the AAC format because it creates smaller files while maintaining CD-quality audio.

Transfer songs to an iPod

1. Connect an iPod to your Mac using a FireWire or USB connection. The iPod appears in the iTunes Source pane (shown below-left).
2. Make sure the iPod is selected (click once on it). Click the "iPod Options" button to open the iPod preferences window, shown below.

If an iPod Shuffle is connected, the status bar and the iPod preferences may look slightly different from this iPod example.

When an iPod is selected in the Source pane, check its status bar to see how much iPod disk space is used or free.

*The **iPod Options** button appears when an iPod is **connected** and **selected** in the Source pane.*

3. Select how you want to update the iPod—but be careful!! Read the following to decide which results you want.

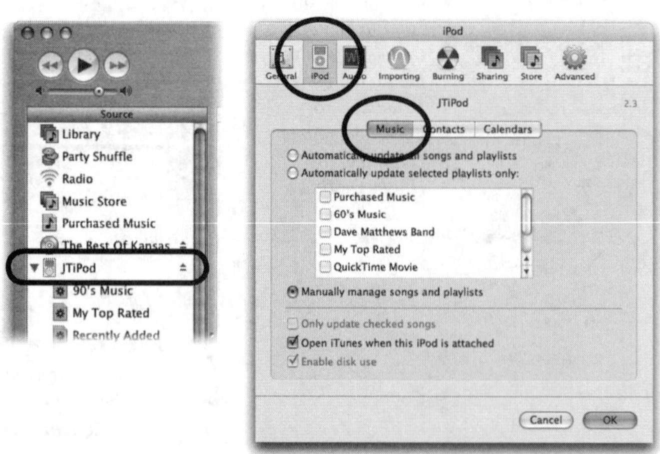

Automatically update all songs and playlists: iTunes will *automatically* load all the audiobooks and playlists that you have in iTunes. Next time you connect the iPod, iTunes will ***replace whatever is on the iPod with the current iTunes content without asking you.***

Automatically update selected playlists only: iTunes will *automatically* update only the playlists that are checked ***and all other music on your iPod will be deleted!*** (Also see Step 4 on the following page.)

Manually manage songs and playlists: You must select this option if you want to see individual iPod playlists in the Source pane, or if you want to select and play songs from the iPod through the computer. With this option selected you must *manually* drag playlists or songs to the iPod icon (or its playlists) in the Source pane. This is a good way to add music to your iPod from other authorized computers without completely replacing all music on the iPod with the current computer's iTunes collection.

Note: If you select this option to "Manually manage songs and playlists," be sure to eject the iPod before disconnecting it!

—continued

If your iPod is selected in the Source pane, you can click this button to create a new playlist directly on the iPod, then drag any songs you want into the playlist.

Anytime the iPod screen shows the warning "Do not disconnect," eject the iPod before disconnecting: Click the eject symbol next to the iPod in the Source pane.

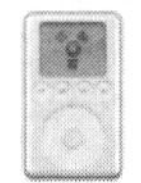

An iPod disk icon appears on the Desktop when you choose "Enable disk use."

Open iTunes when this iPod is attached: Automatically opens iTunes anytime you connect the iPod to your Mac.

Enable disk use: Use the iPod as an external hard disk; its icon will appear on the Desktop. The iPod is now a mounted volume like any other external hard disk and you must unmount it before you disconnect it or take it out of the cradle! See below for details.

Only update checked songs: This is only available if you have checked one of the automatic update options. Be careful—with this option checked, iTunes will ***instantly replace everything on your iPod*** with ***only*** the songs that are checked in iTunes!

Use the iPod as an external hard disk

Even the smallest iPod provides a huge amount of storage. In addition to music, you can use it to store or transport any kind of computer files.

1. Connect the iPod to your Mac using the provided FireWire or USB cable. If you don't see an iPod icon on the Desktop or in your Finder window Sidebar, follow Steps 2 through 4. If the iPod icon *does* appear on the Desktop, skip to Step 5.
2. Open iTunes if it's not already open.
3. Select the iPod in the Source pane, then click the "iPod Options" button (shown on page 120).
4. Click the "Music" tab in the preferences window, then select "Enable disk use." Click OK.
5. Double-click the iPod icon that's on the Desktop. A Finder window opens that shows the iPod's contents (you will not be able to see your music files, which iPod has hidden from view).
6. **To copy any files or folders to your iPod,** just drag them from your computer to the iPod window, as shown on the opposite page.

To copy files from the iPod to a computer, drag them from the iPod window to the Desktop or to any other location on the computer. You can store or transport huge folders of photos, applications, presentations, movies, or any digital files you have room for.

When the iPod is connected to your Mac and used as a hard disk, its icon appears on the Desktop. The iPod screen blinks with the message "Do not disconnect." This means you must **unmount the iPod before you disconnect** the cable or take it out of its cradle: Control-click on the iPod icon, then choose "Eject iPod" from the contextual menu, as shown to the right. **Or** click the eject symbol next to the iPod icon in the Source pane of iTunes or in any Finder window's sidebar.

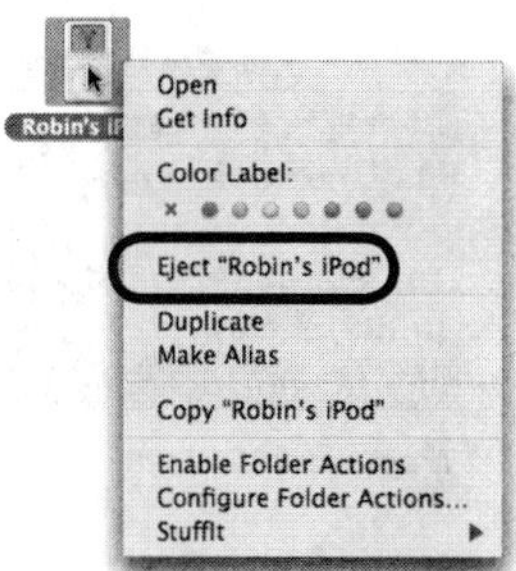

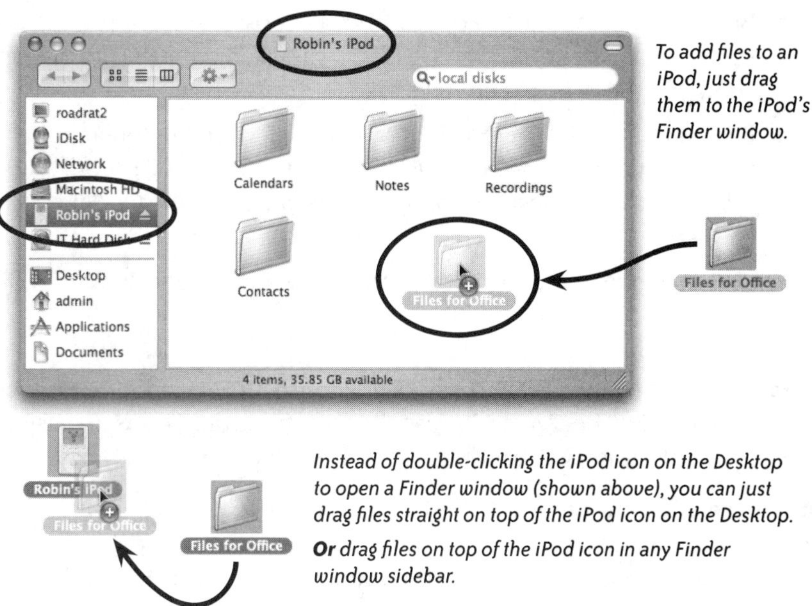

To add files to an iPod, just drag them to the iPod's Finder window.

Instead of double-clicking the iPod icon on the Desktop to open a Finder window (shown above), you can just drag files straight on top of the iPod icon on the Desktop.

Or *drag files on top of the iPod icon in any Finder window sidebar.*

Note: While the iPod is mounted as a hard disk, you can use it as a hard disk and listen to its songs through iTunes and the computer speakers, but you cannot use the iPod menu (on the iPod itself) or hear music through earphones connected to the iPod.

Create an On-The-Go playlist on the iPod

You'll notice in your iPod Playlist menu that you have an item called "On-The-Go." This is a **temporary playlist** that you can customize **directly on the iPod** without access to your computer or iTunes.

iPod's menu screen.

The On-The-Go playlist can only contain songs that are already on the iPod. ***The playlist is temporary***—the next time you connect the iPod to your computer, the playlist is deleted.

1. Turn the iPod on. It does not need to be connected to a computer.
2. On the iPod's menu screen choose "Settings," then choose "Main Menu," then select "Playlists," and make sure it is set to "On."
3. Browse your iPod music collection and choose a song or playlist that you want to add to the On-The-Go playlist. When the playlist or song shows on the iPod screen, select it.
4. Press-and-hold the "Select" button (the round spot in the middle of the scroll pad) for two seconds. When you see the playlist or song title flash three times, the song has been added to the On-The-Go playlist.
5. Repeat Step 3 to add additional playlists or songs to your On-The-Go playlist.

To access the On-the-Go playlist, choose "Playlists" from iPod's screen menu, then scroll to "On-The-Go" and press the Select button. This is an easy way to vary your playlist while traveling.

To remove all songs from the On-the-Go playlist, select the playlist on the iPod screen, then scroll to the bottom of its list of songs and choose "Clear Playlist." Click the "Select" button (the round spot in the center of the scroll pad), then in the next screen confirm your choice (choose "Cancel" or "Clear Playlist").

You may want to **create multiple On-the-Go playlists.** To do this, first *save* the existing On-the-Go playlist:

1. Select the existing On-The-Go playlist on the iPod screen.
2. Scroll to the bottom of its list of songs and choose "Save Playlist."
3. Click the iPod's Select button
4. In the next screen confirm your choice: choose "Save Playlist" again.

The songs that were in the On-the-Go playlist are now in a new playlist named "New Playlist 1," and the On-the-Go playlist is empty.

Now you can repeat the procedure: Add other songs to the On-the-Go playlist, then save that playlist. Once again, the songs are moved to a new playlist named "New Playlist 2" and the On-the-Go playlist is empty again.

The next time you connect your iPod to your computer, you'll notice that the saved playlists have been renamed "On-the-Go 1," and "On-the-Go 2," etc.

Create a playlist directly in your iPod

If you have chosen to "Manually manage songs and playlists," as described on page 121, you can create new playlists on the iPod without first creating them in iTunes.

1. Select the mounted iPod in the Source pane.
2. Click the plus button at the bottom of the Source pane to create a new, unnamed playlist.
3. Name the new playlist.
4. Drag songs or other playlists from iTunes into the new playlist. You can even drag entire playlists already on the iPod into the new playlist.

Sync Contacts and Calendars to iPod

Use iTunes to synchronize your iCal and Address Book information to an iPod. After syncing, the iPod screen shows the categories of "Calendars" and "Contacts" in its main menu. Using the iPod scroll wheel, you can select either category and access your important information while on the go.

1. Connect an iPod to your computer. iTunes opens (if that preference is set, as shown in the example at the bottom of this page) and shows the iPod in the Source pane (shown below).

2. An iPod Preferences button appears in the bottom-right corner of the window (circled above). Click the button to open the iPod pane of iTunes Preferences, shown below.

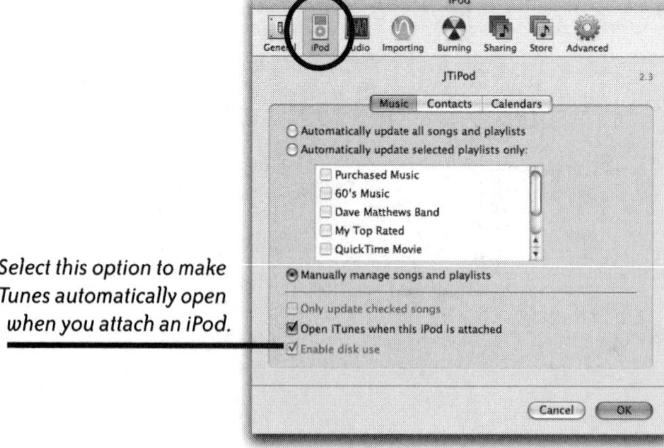

Select this option to make iTunes automatically open when you attach an iPod.

3. Click the **Contacts** button to show the Address Book options that are available. Check "Synchronize Address Book contacts" if you want to automatically update the iPod with current Address Book information whenever an iPod is attached.
4. Choose to "Synchronize *all* contacts" or to "Synchronize *selected* groups only."

   If you choose to sync selected groups only, checkmark the groups in the list that you want to sync. This list is made up of groups that you previously created in Address Book.
5. Click OK.
6. Click the **Calendars** button to show the iCal options that are available. Select "Synchronize iCal calendars" if you want to automatically update the iPod with current iCal information whenever an iPod is attached.

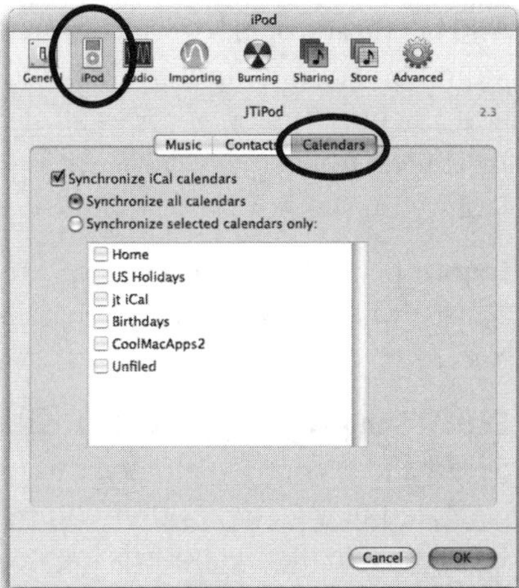

7. Choose to "Synchronize *all* calendars" or to "Synchronize *selected* calendars only."

   If you choose to sync selected calendars only, checkmark the calendars in the list that you want to sync. This list is made up of calendars that you previously created or subscribed to in iCal.

Menu Commands

Most of the commands in the iTunes menu bar are covered elsewhere in this chapter, but there are a few commands that only exist in one of the menu bar items.

You can activate most commands by clicking a button or with a keyboard shortcut, which is usually easier than using the menu bar. For instance, we never go to the File menu and choose "New Playlist"—we just click the plus sign beneath the Source pane. The menu bar is the best place to look for commands when you can't remember where or how to do something.

The following pages list the commands in each menu (except for the most self-explanatory ones) and give brief descriptions of each one.

File menu

New Playlist creates a new playlist. See page 69.

New Playlist from Selection creates a new playlist based on the songs you have selected (highlighted) in iTunes.

New Smart Playlist creates a new Smart Playlist. See page 71.

Add to Library opens a window from which you can choose songs that are stored on your computer, then add them to the iTunes Library. You can add an entire folder of songs all at once. These songs are just *referenced* by iTunes, not actually *copied* there, unless you also choose "Consolidate Library" in the Advanced menu.

Import playlists that you've exported from another computer. An imported playlist will only show songs that are already on your computer or on a connected drive.

Export Song List so you can have the same playlist on another computer. Select a playlist, then choose this command to make a copy. Copy the exported playlist to another computer, then go to the other computer and from the File menu choose "Import…." Choose "XML" from the "Format" menu. Exported playlists do not export the actual songs, just a list of the songs.

Export Library saves a copy of all your playlists in XML format. Use the copy as a backup, or copy it to another computer to be imported.

Get Info provides information for a selected song.

My Rating lets you choose 1–5 stars in a submenu.

Edit Smart Playlist lets you change the conditions of a Smart Playlist.

Show Song File opens the folder in the iTunes Music folder that contains the song file you selected in iTunes.

Show Current Song shows the current song (the one that's playing) in the iTunes window.

Burn Playlist to Disc burns a CD of the selected playlist. This is the same as clicking the "Burn Disc" button.

Create an iMix lets you publish a collection of music on the iTunes Music Store for others to enjoy.

Update iPod syncs the music on your computer to a connected iPod.

Publish Playlist to Music Store publishes a selected playlist as an iMix on the iTunes Music Store. Learn more about iMix on page 81.

Update Songs on iPod is available if you have an iPod connected and if you've selected one of the *automatic* updating options. See more about iPod on pages 120–127.

Page Setup opens a pre-printing dialog box in which you can choose settings, a printer, paper size, page orientation, and scale.

Print gives you access to templates for printing CD jewel case inserts, song lists, and album lists.

Edit menu

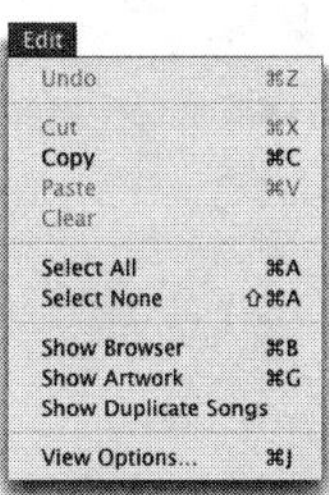

Show Browser makes the iTunes Browser pane visible. Choosing this command is the same as clicking the "Browse" button. See more about the Browser on page 79.

Show Artwork makes the Song Artwork pane visible. This command is the same as clicking the Hide/Show Song Artwork button beneath the Source pane. There's more about song artwork on page 98.

View Options lets you choose which columns of information will show in the Detail window.

Controls menu

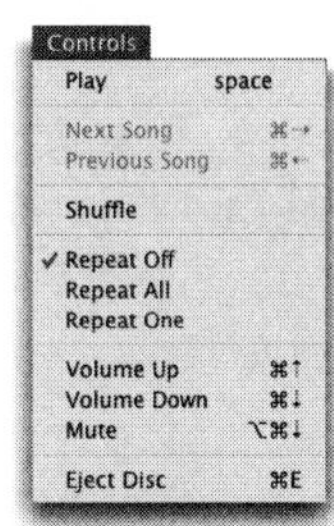

Shuffle shuffles songs in a playlist or the Library. In "Advanced" preferences, set to shuffle by song or album.

Repeat Off turns off the repeat feature. After a song plays, iTunes moves to the next song in the playlist that has a checkmark next to it.

Repeat All turns on the feature that repeats songs or playlists. When "Repeat All" is selected, the symbol on the Repeat button is blue.

Repeat One limits the repeat to just the song that's selected. When "Repeat One" is selected, the symbol on the Repeat button is blue and includes a small "1" symbol.

Mute turns the sound off. When "Mute" is selected, the little sound waves coming out of the speaker symbols that appear on either side of the volume slider disappear.

Visualizer menu

Turn Visualizer On starts the visual effects show in the iTunes window. When Visualizer is on, this command changes to "Turn Visualizer Off."

Small, Medium, Large are options for choosing how large the visual effects window will be. These settings affect the size of the display in the iTunes window and also in full-screen mode (see page 114).

Full Screen displays visual effects full-screen, hiding the iTunes window.

Advanced menu

Open Stream lets you enter the URL (web address) for an Internet radio station or other webcast. Type the URL in the "Open Stream" text field.

Convert Selection to ___ enables you to select a song and convert it to the file format shown in the menu command (MP3, in this example). The file format is determined by what you chose for "Import Using" in Importing preferences. Read more about converting files on pages 73 and 109.

Consolidate Library makes a copy of all songs that are stored in other places on your computer and puts them in the iTunes Music folder.

Get CD Track Names connects to a CD database and enters the track names of a mounted CD into the iTunes window.

Submit CD Track Names lets you submit song information for a CD if the information is not available on the CD database that iTunes uses. Select a CD, then type Command I (Get Info). Enter the CD's artist, album, and genre information. Select each song on the CD, open Get Info, then enter the song name information. Finally, select the CD again, then from the Advanced menu, choose "Submit CD Track Names."

Join CD Tracks imports two adjacent CD tracks as one. See page 103.

Deauthorize Computer disables the computer for buying music from the Music Store or for playing purchased music. To buy music from the iTunes Music Store, you must authorize the computer you order from. You can deauthorize a computer to prevent others from using your Apple Account to buy music.

Also, iTunes permits up to five computers to play purchased songs. If you want to use a particular computer to play purchased songs, but you've already authorized five computers, you can deauthorize one of them. Remember to deauthorize your computer before you sell it or give it away.

Check for Purchased Music checks to see if you have any purchased music that has not been downloaded yet.

Convert ID3 Tags corrects the information in the Song Information window when it shows incorrectly. An ID3 tag is a song's information tag (the same information you find in a song's Get Info window). If a song's title and information are garbled, it was created by a program that stores information in a different way from iTunes. Select the problem songs, then choose this command. Songs play correctly even if the ID3 tags are wrong.

Window menu

Minimize sends the iTunes window to the Dock to get it out of the way, but does not interrupt the music.

Zoom replaces the large iTunes window with a tiny, space-saving window.

Bring All to Front brings all iTunes windows to the front. This could be useful if you have lots and lots of windows open.

Help menu

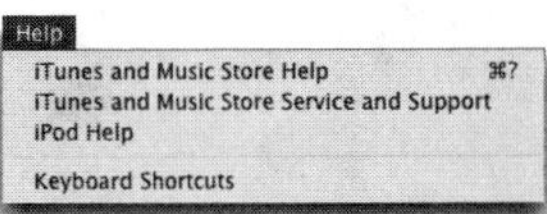

iTunes and Music Store Help contains lots of information and tips about iTunes and iTunes Music Store.

iTunes and Music Store Service and Support connects to Apple's customer service site where there's lots of information about Music Store features.

iPod Help offers tips for iPods, plus a link to the iPod support web site.

Keyboard Shortcuts shows a complete list of keyboard shortcuts for iTunes.

Favorite Keyboard Shortcuts

These are the **iTunes keyboard shortcuts** that you'll have the most fun with:

Command 1	toggles between Show Player and Hide Player
Command T	toggles Visuals on and off
Command F	toggles Visualizer full-screen mode on and off
Command DownArrow	turns the volume down
Command UpArrow	turns the volume up
LeftArrow	first tap selects the beginning of the current song; second tap selects the previous song
RightArrow	selects the next song
Option Command DownArrow	mutes the sound
Spacebar	toggles between Pause and Play

Other keyboard shortcuts:

Command N	creates a new playlist
Shift Command N	creates a new playlist from the *highlighted* songs (*not* the songs that are checked)
Command A	selects all songs in the current song list
Shift Command A	deselects all songs in the current song list
Command R	shows current song file in the Finder
Command E	ejects a CD
Command M	minimizes Player window to the Dock
Command ?	launches iTunes Help
Command Q	quits iTunes

Visualizer shortcuts:

R	changes Visualizer to a new random set of visual effects
M	cycles through Visualizer modes
N	toggles between Normal and High Contrast colors
D	resets Visualizer to the default settings
I	displays song information
F	toggles Frame Rate Display on and off
B	displays the Apple logo briefly when Visuals are turned on

iMovie

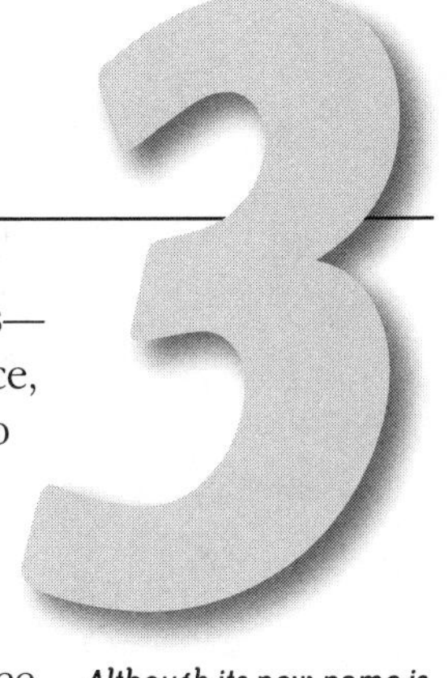

Chances are that your first home movie experiences were similar to ours—you shot some video tape, connected the camera to the TV, watched it once, then never looked at it again. In fact, we just stopped carrying our video camera with us on trips because it was big and heavy and we knew that we would never get around to looking at the footage again when we returned home.

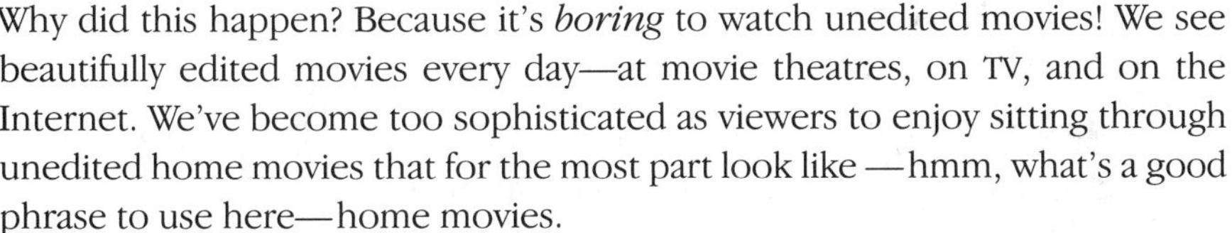

Why did this happen? Because it's *boring* to watch unedited movies! We see beautifully edited movies every day—at movie theatres, on TV, and on the Internet. We've become too sophisticated as viewers to enjoy sitting through unedited home movies that for the most part look like —hmm, what's a good phrase to use here—home movies.

Although its new name is iMovie HD, for simplicity's sake we affectionately call it iMovie in this chapter.

That's where iMovie comes in and dazzles. Get rid of the boring and repititous shots. Toss the scenes that have bad lighting. Add titles and a music soundtrack from iTunes. Create special effects and put Hollywood-style transitions between scenes. iMovie makes all of this incredibly fun and easy.

When you connect a digital video camera to your computer with a FireWire cable and launch iMovie, you're ready to create home movies that you won't mind watching again and again.

The best part is that iMovie makes it easy to share your movies with others in a variety of ways. Create small movies files that you can email or upload to a .Mac Homepage. You can even use your movie to create a professional DVD that plays on any computer or almost any DVD player.

This is the FireWire icon.

If you didn't get a **FireWire cable** with your digital video camera, check the box your Mac came in—often there is a FireWire cable in it. If you don't have a cable, buy one at your local electronics store or order it from one of the many dealers online (search for "firewire cables").

Digital video (DV) requires a lot of disk space—one minute of DV footage uses about 220 MB of hard disk space. A four-minute iMovie that contains soundtracks, transitions, and titles may use 4 to 6 *gigabytes* of disk space.

If you're serious about making iMovies or if you just can't control yourself after making your first iMovie, buy an extra, very large hard disk to use when working with video. You'll be surprised how fast you can fill a dedicated 80 GB disk when you start making movies.

Once you've seen what a difference editing can have on the audience reaction to your "home movies," you'll be inspired. If you don't have a digital video camera, consider getting one. Teamed with iMovie, even the least expensive video camera is enough to create fabulous movies that can amaze you and your friends.

The Steps of Making a Movie

Making an iMovie consists of **five basic steps.** This chapter walks you through each step.

Of course, you must first shoot some video! Keep in mind that when you shoot video, every time you start and stop the camera, iMovie interprets that as a separate movie "clip." You will be able to rearrange those clips to create a simple storyboard (a visual outline) for your movie.

Once you've got footage, these are the five basic steps you will follow:

1. Connect a camera, open an iMovie project window, and import the video.
2. Edit the clips.
3. Add clips to the Timeline.
4. Add enhancements (transitions, titles, effects, chapter markers, etc).
5. Save and share the movie in various formats.

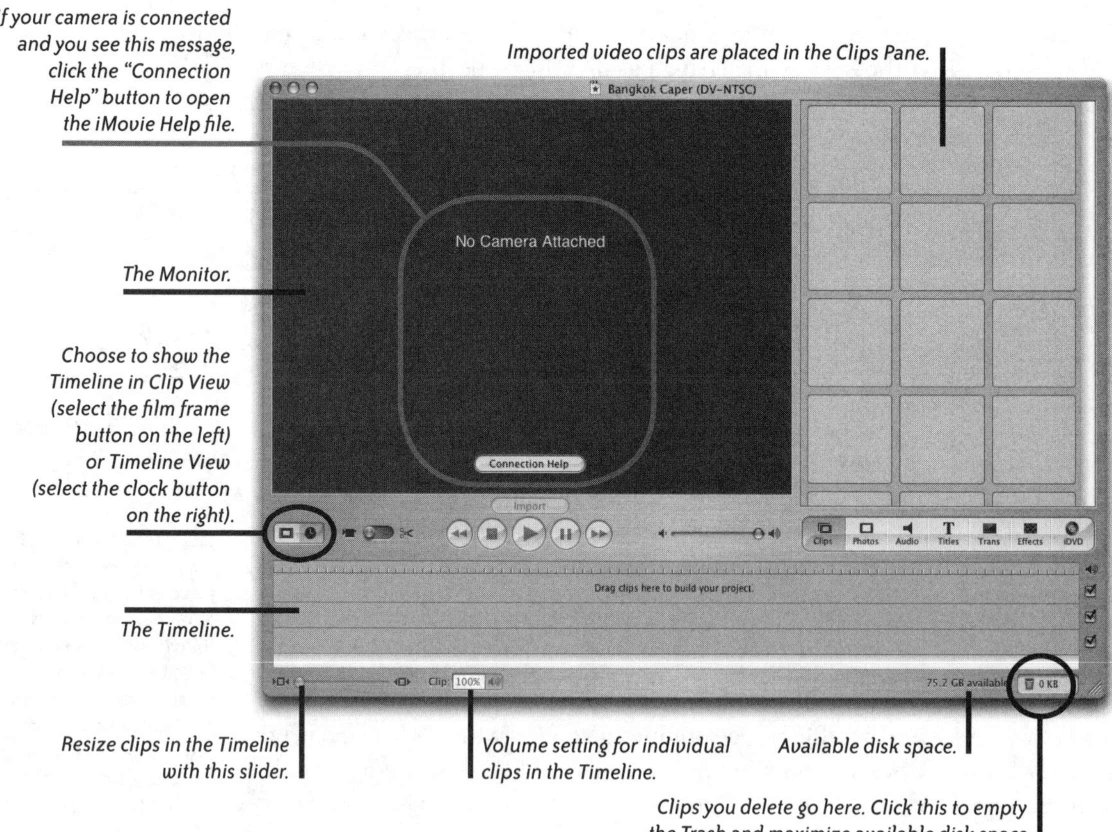

If your camera is connected and you see this message, click the "Connection Help" button to open the iMovie Help file.
Imported video clips are placed in the Clips Pane.
Bangkok Caper (DV-NTSC)
No Camera Attached
Connection Help
Import
The Monitor.
Choose to show the Timeline in Clip View (select the film frame button on the left) or Timeline View (select the clock button on the right).
Clips
Photos
Audio
Titles
Trans
Effects
iDVD
Drag clips here to build your project.
The Timeline.
Clip: 100%
75.2 GB available
0 KB
Resize clips in the Timeline with this slider.
Volume setting for individual clips in the Timeline.
Available disk space.
Clips you delete go here. Click this to empty the Trash and maximize available disk space.

Connect a video camera

Before you can import video footage, you must connect your digital video camera to your Mac. If possible, it's best to connect the video camera's AC adapter for power while you import video footage to preserve the camera's battery power. Insert a video tape in the camera that has footage on it you want to import.

A video camera FireWire cable usually is a "4-6 pin" cable with a 4-pin connector on one end and a 6-pin connector on the other end.

To connect your camera:

1. Plug the 4-pin connector end of a FireWire cable into the camera's FireWire port and then plug the 6-pin connector end into your computer's FireWire port.
2. Set your video camera to "VTR" (Video Tape Recorder) or "Play" mode (do *not* set the camera to "Record").
3. Open iMovie, if it's not already open.
4. **Turn on** the camera. After several seconds the words "Camera Connected" appear in the Monitor area, as shown below.

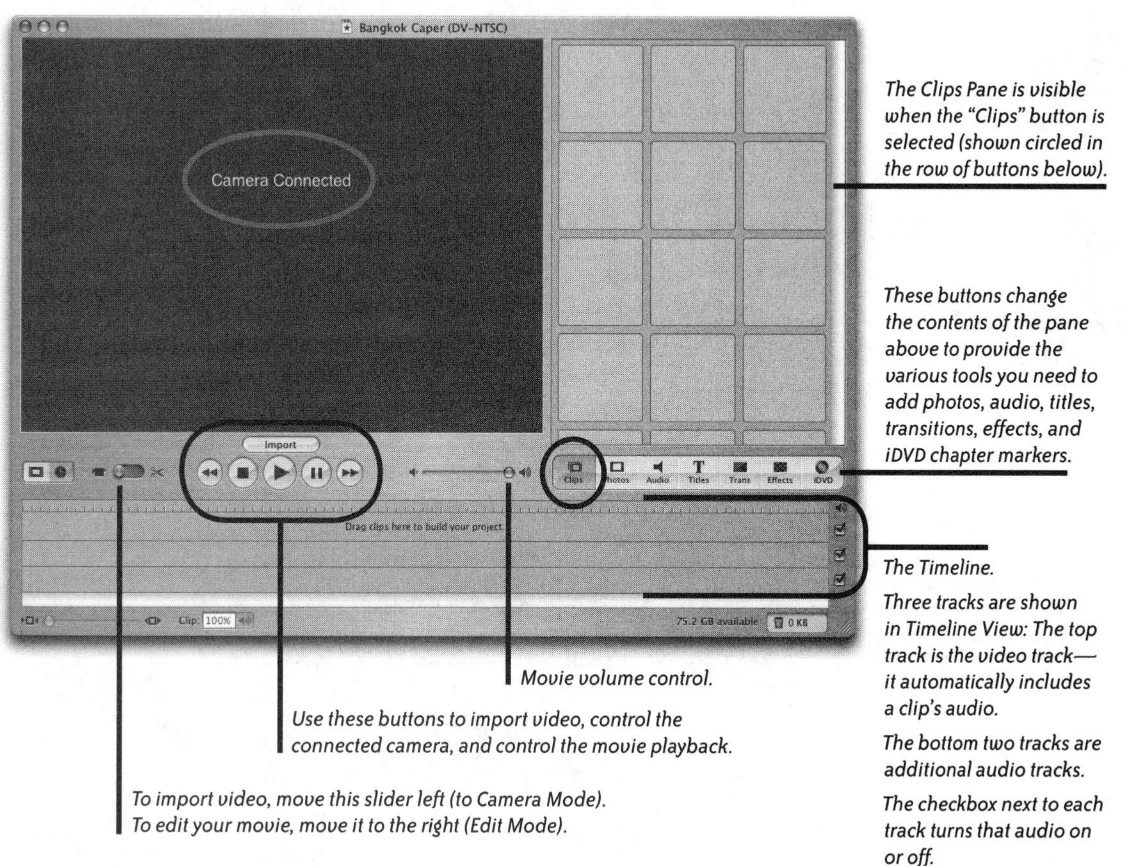

The Clips Pane is visible when the "Clips" button is selected (shown circled in the row of buttons below).

These buttons change the contents of the pane above to provide the various tools you need to add photos, audio, titles, transitions, effects, and iDVD chapter markers.

The Timeline.

Three tracks are shown in Timeline View: The top track is the video track—it automatically includes a clip's audio.

The bottom two tracks are additional audio tracks.

The checkbox next to each track turns that audio on or off.

Movie volume control.

Use these buttons to import video, control the connected camera, and control the movie playback.

To import video, move this slider left (to Camera Mode). To edit your movie, move it to the right (Edit Mode).

Create a new iMovie project

1. Open iMovie. The project selection window opens. Choose "Create a New Project" (unless you want to open a project you've already been working on, in which case click "Open an Existing Project")

See page 181.

If iMovie is already open, you won't see the project selection window shown above. Instead, go to the File menu and choose "New Project..." to open the "Create Project" window (shown below).

If you've already created a project, choose "Open Project...." Find and select the project you want to open. **Or** choose "Open Recent," then select a project you've opened recently (shown on the left).

2. In the "Create Project" window (shown below), name your project and choose the location where you want to save it. Be sure to choose a drive or partition that has plenty of unused disk space! If you make lots of movies, consider buying an external FireWire drive to use just for movie projects. Do not click "Create" yet!

We saved our project to an external FireWire drive that has lots of available storage space.

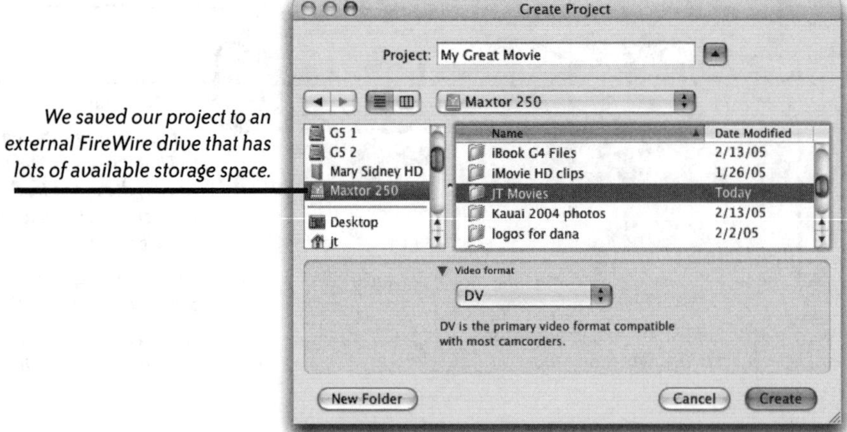

3. From the "Video format" pop-up menu, choose a video format to use:

   DV (Digital Video) is the format most video cameras use. This standard video format, the same proportion that standard TV uses, has an "aspect ratio" (proportion) of 4:3. This is most likely the format you should choose for your movie.

   DV Widescreen is the same format as DV, but it uses the widescreen aspect ratio of 16:9. Some video cameras have a setting that shoots in the 16:9 aspect ratio. If your video was shot using a widescreen setting, choose this format for your movie.

   HDV 1080i is High Definition Video that uses a vertical screen resolution of 1,080 *interlaced* scan lines. The horizontal scan lines that make up an interlaced image are divided into *even* and *odd* scan lines. Any given instant in the video actually displays only half of the image—either the even scan lines or the odd scan lines. Choose HDV 1080i only if your video camera shoots in this format.

   HDV 720p is a competing High Definition Video format that uses a vertical screen resolution of 720 *progressive* scan lines. There are fewer scan lines, but any given instant in the video displays *both* even *and* odd scan lines (referred to as *progressive*). Choose HDV 720p only if your video camera shoots in this format.

   MPEG-4 is a highly compressed video format used by many consumer video devices, such as a digital still camera. If your video footage comes from a camera that used MPEG-4 format, choose it here.

   iSight is a video format compatible with the Apple iSight video camera. Choose this format if you plan to make a movie using video clips captured with an iSight camera.

Which is better—HDV 1080i or HDV 720p?

1080i has higher resolution (more vertical scan lines), but its interlaced video is lower quality than progressive video.

720p has lower resolution (fewer vertical scan lines), but its progressive video is better quality than interlaced video.

The result is that the two technologies are comparable in quality.

4. Click the "Create" button to open a new, empty iMovie window.

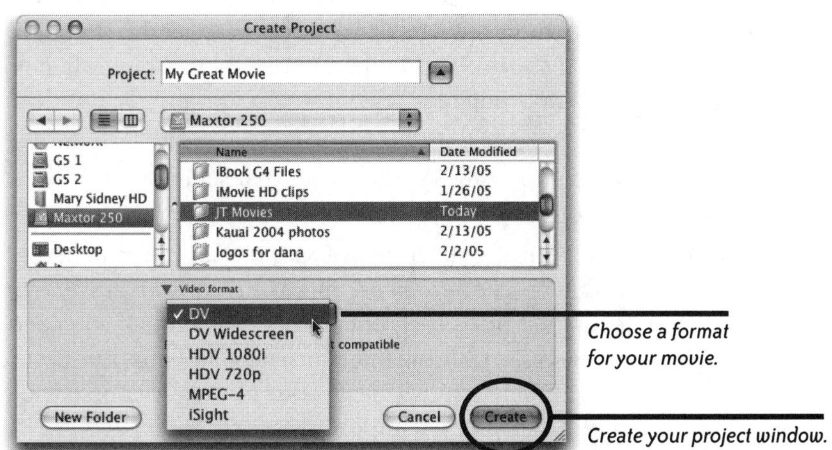

Preview the video footage in your camera

Tip: Don't forget to rewind the tape in your camera before you preview it. If the Monitor shows only a blue screen, you're looking at the unrecorded tape that comes after your last recorded scene.

1. In the iMovie window, click the Camera mode button.
2. Click the "Play" button (shown on the left) to view the video from the camera in iMovie's Monitor.

   At this point you are just *previewing* the video. iMovie does not digitize and import any video until you click the "Import" button. Use the controls below the "Import" button to control the camera. Rewind, pause, play, stop, and fast-forward to preview specific scenes.

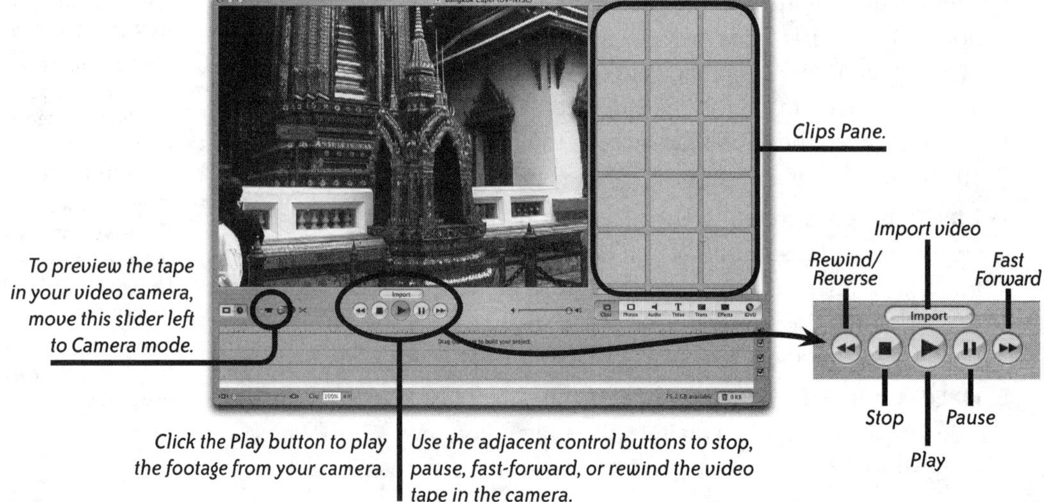

Clips Pane.
Import video
Rewind/
Reverse
Fast
Forward
Import
Stop
Pause
Play
To preview the tape
in your video camera,
move this slider left
to Camera mode.
Click the Play button to play
the footage from your camera.
Use the adjacent control buttons to stop,
pause, fast-forward, or rewind the video
tape in the camera.

Import video footage into iMovie

1. Click the "Play" button to preview the video footage in your camera.
2. When you see the scene you want to import, click the "Import" button (shown above). The "Import" button turns blue when it is selected and importing files.
3. To stop importing, click the "Import" button again. Each time you start and stop importing, iMovie places that segment of video, called a "clip," into one of the square slots in the Clips Pane.

   If you have plenty of disk space, you can just let the camera run. iMovie will detect scene changes, import the individual scenes as separate clips, and place each one in the Clips Pane. If you need to conserve disk space, preview the entire tape and import only the scenes you definitely want to use in your movie. Of course you can always delete a clip after it's imported (see the next page).

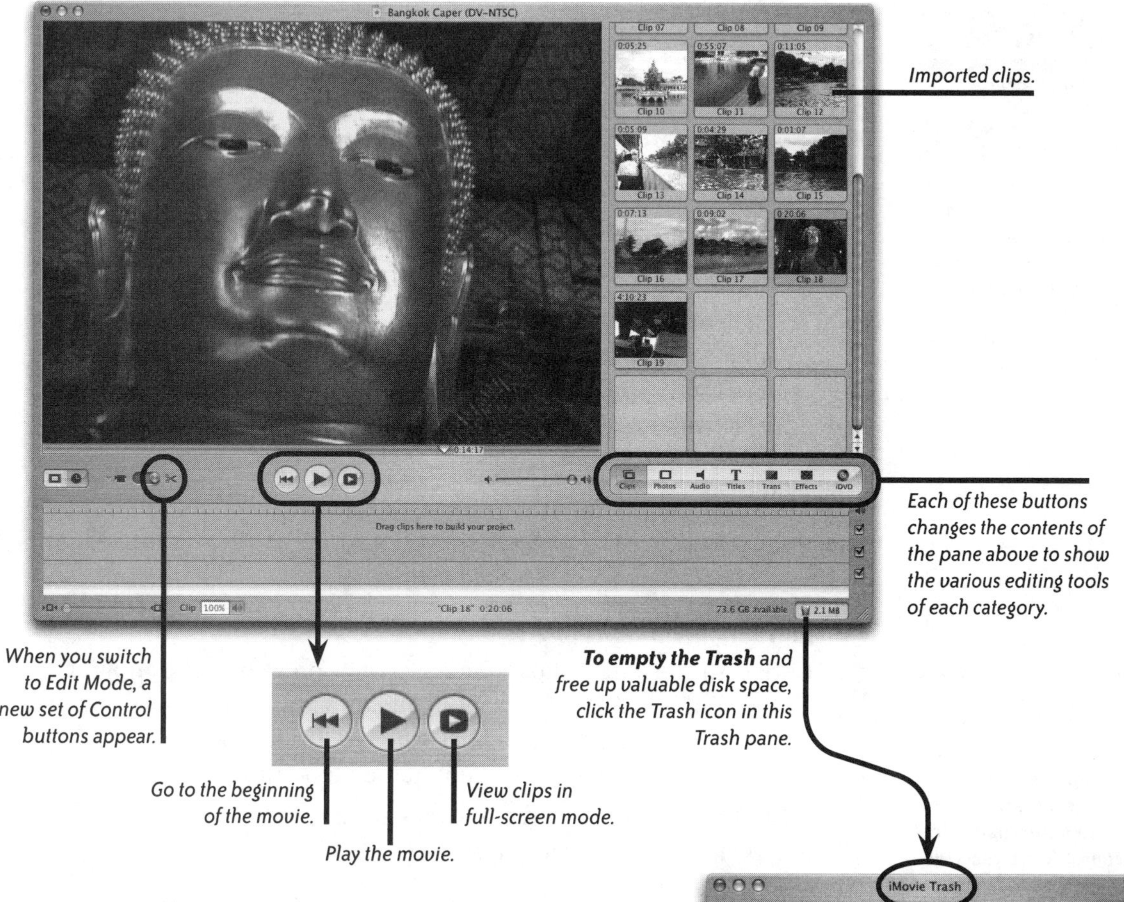

Imported clips.

Each of these buttons changes the contents of the pane above to show the various editing tools of each category.

When you switch to Edit Mode, a new set of Control buttons appear.

To empty the Trash and free up valuable disk space, click the Trash icon in this Trash pane.

Go to the beginning of the movie.

Play the movie.

View clips in full-screen mode.

Delete clips and empty the Trash

To delete a clip, select a clip in the Clips Pane (or in the Timeline), then hit the Delete key. **Or** Control-click on a clip, then choose "Clear" from the contextual menu.

As you delete unwanted clips, the number in the Trash pane gets larger, indicating that the deleted clips are going into the Trash.

Clips in the Trash take up disk space. To free up valuable disk space, you need to empty the Trash often: Click the Trash icon to open the "iMovie Trash" window. In this window you can play a clip's preview to make sure the clip is not important. You can select just the clips you want to delete, then click "Delete Selected Clips...." Or click the "Empty Trash..." button to delete all clips in the Trash.

To recover a clip from the Trash, drag it from the "iMovie Trash" window to the Clips Pane.

Press on the camera icon to see the name of the connected camera. If more than one camera is connected, choose the one you want to use from this pop-up menu.

Import live video with a video camera

You can import live video (without first recording it to tape) into iMovie with any compatible digital video camera, even an iSight camera.

1. Connect the video camera to your computer with a FireWire cable.
2. Set the video camera to "Camera" or "Record" (not "VTR" or "Play").
3. Put iMovie in Camera Mode (shown on the left).
4. Click the "Import" button in the iMovie window.

If you're using an iSight camera and can't get iMovie to recognize it, go to iChat's "Video" preferences, disable the option to "Automatically open iChat when camera is turned on," then quit iChat. The "Import" button in iMovie changes to "Record with iSight."

Edit Video Clips

Clips often contain more footage than you want to use in your movie. You can preview a clip and select just the best part of it.

To display and preview a clip:

As you drag the Playhead, you'll notice the last two digits in the time counter (next to the Playhead) go from :30 to :00. That's because the last two digits represent *frames* (not *seconds*), and digital video contains 30 frames per second.

1. Click on a clip in the Clips Pane to show its preview in the Monitor. A blue *Scrubber Bar* (representing the duration of the clip) appears below the Monitor. The Scrubber Bar contains the *Playhead,* a white triangle that indicates the current frame of the clip.
2. Click the Play button to preview the entire clip. **Or** drag the Playhead to a point in the clip you want to see.

Single-click on a clip to preview it in the Monitor.

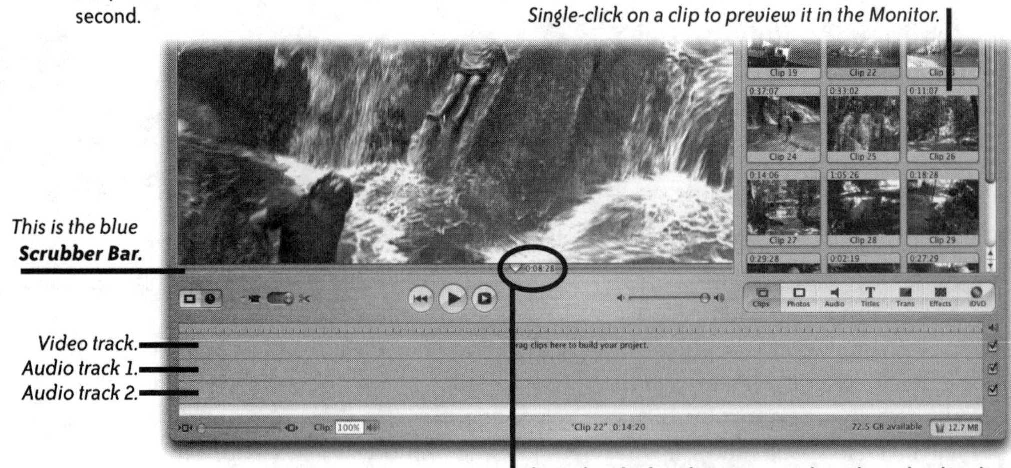

This is the blue ***Scrubber Bar.***

Video track.
Audio track 1.
Audio track 2.

This is the ***Playhead.*** *It moves to the right as the clip plays. The number next to the Playhead indicates how many minutes, seconds, and frames have elapsed in the clip. The Playhead above is positioned at 8 seconds, 28 frames.*

Trim or crop selected clips

Many clips are longer than necessary and should be **trimmed** or **cropped.**

- **Trim:** Remove *selected* video frames at the *beginning* or *end* of a clip.
- **Crop:** Remove all frames in a clip *other than* the selected frames.

Trimming and cropping video clips in iMovie is **non-destructive.** See page 144.

To trim a clip:

1. Beneath the Scrubber Bar, locate the "crop markers," two small triangles (circled, right). They become visible on the left side of the Scrubber Bar when your pointer gets close to the Scrubber Bar. Drag the crop markers (shown below) to select the part of a clip that you *want to remove.* The selected section is highlighted in yellow.
2. To remove the yellow highlighted frames, go to the Edit menu and choose "Clear." **Or** press the Delete key.

Crop markers.

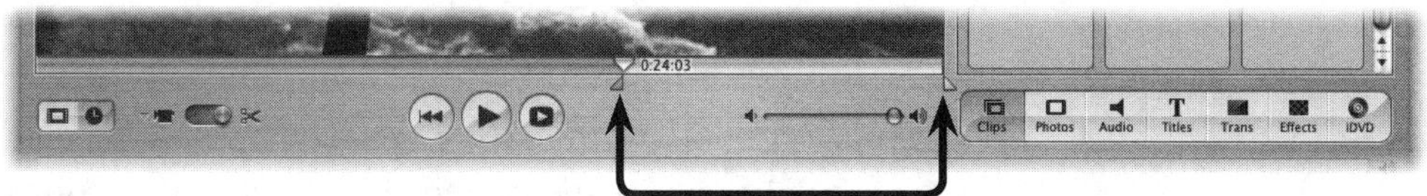

Crop markers highlight the selection of video to be trimmed. The "Clear" command removes the selected video.

To crop a clip:

1. Drag the crop markers to select a range of frames in the clip that you *want to keep.* The selected frames are highlighted in yellow.
2. To remove all of the frames that are *not* yellow highlighted (the ones on either end), go to the Edit menu and choose "Crop."

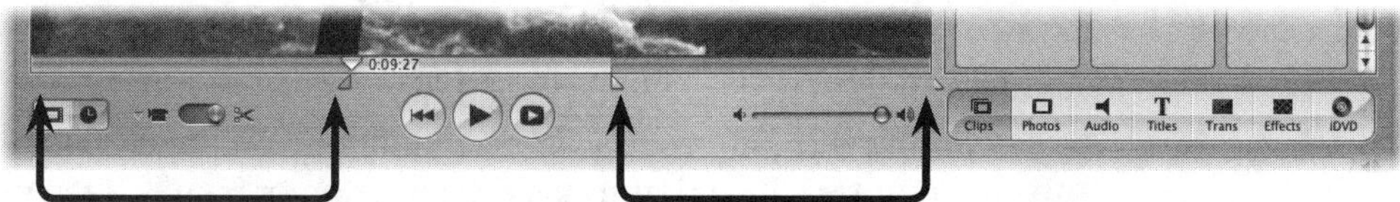

Crop markers highlight the selection of video to be cropped. The "Crop" command saves the yellow selection and removes the video on either side.

After you edit a clip to the duration you want, drag it from the Clips Pane to the video track in the **Timeline** at the bottom of the window (as explained on the following pages) so you can make a *rough cut* of your movie. A rough cut is the first stage of editing a movie in which you assemble the clips in the order you want to use them in the Timeline before you add transitions or effects. Later you can fine-tune the duration of clips with additional trimming directly in the Timeline (see pages 142–143).

Add Clips to the Timeline

A simple way to add clips to the Timeline is to just drag a clip from the Clips Pane to the Timeline. This leaves an empty space in the Clips Pane. We prefer to use the copy-and-paste technique described here so the Clips Pane always contains a full original copy of all our imported clips. When we want to grab a certain clip or just a segment of a clip, we don't have to search in the Timeline for it.

We like to keep the original clips unaltered in the Clips Pane, then **copy** and **paste** segments into the Timeline (instead of dragging trimmed or cropped clips straight from the Clips Pane to the Timeline). This makes it easy to go back to the original, unaltered clips.

To copy and paste a clip:

1. Select a clip so it appears in the Monitor.
2. Use the crop markers to select a range of frames that you want to add to the movie Timeline.
3. Press Command C to copy the video selection.
4. Click in the Timeline to select it.
5. Press Command V to paste the video selection into the Timeline:

   If a clip of video in the Timeline is selected (highlighted in blue), the new video is pasted *to the right* of that selected clip.

   If a clip is *not* selected in the Timeline, the new video is pasted at the position of the Playhead. If the Playhead happens to be in the middle of an existing clip, the pasted video splits the existing clip.

To use the Monitor to trim or crop a clip that's already in the Timeline:

After you've made a "rough cut" of your movie, you might need to fine-tune the duration of clips that are in the Timeline so you can sync with the beat of an imported soundtrack, or just to change the pacing of the movie.

1. Click on a single clip in the Timeline so it shows in the Monitor.
2. Use the crop markers beneath the Monitor's Scrubber Bar to select a range of frames in the clip.
3. To *crop* the clip (remove everything in the clip *except* the selected frames), go to the Edit menu and choose "Crop."
4. To *trim* the clip (remove the *selected* frames), use the crop markers beneath the Scrubber Bar to make a selection of frames, then press the Delete key.

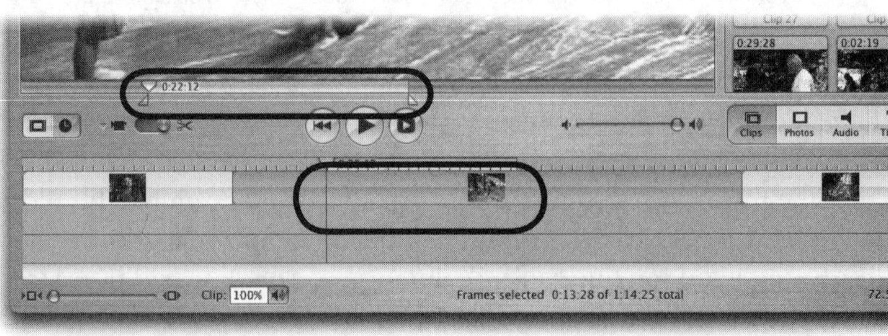

When you select a clip in the Timeline and use the crop markers to select a range of video frames in that clip, the selection is highlighted in both the Scrubber Bar and the Timeline.

To trim clips directly in the Timeline:

After you've made a rough cut of your movie, you'll may want to trim a little more footage from some of the clips in your movie. An easy way to trim a clip (remove footage from the beginning or end of the clip) is to do it directly in the Timeline: drag an *edge* of the clip towards the *center* of the clip.

Before you trim a clip in the Timeline, go to the View menu and make sure the "Show Clip Volume Levels" option is *not* selected. A clip volume level shows in the Timeline as a horizontal black line in the video track, as shown below. You *cannot* drag clip edges and trim clips in the Timeline when clip volume levels are shown.

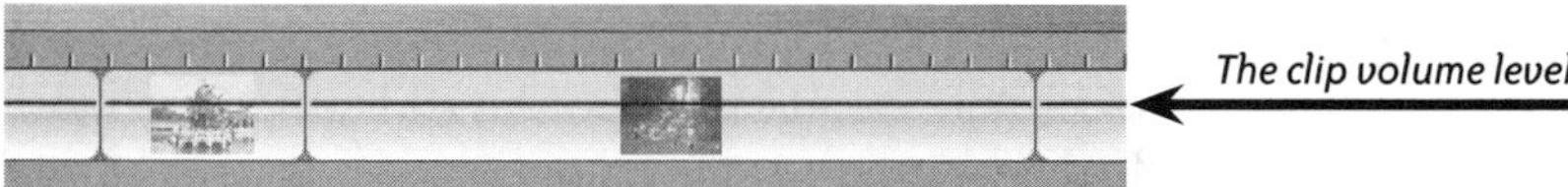

The clip volume level.

When you position your pointer over the *right edge* of a clip, the pointer turns into an arrow that indicates which direction you can drag the edge. If the arrow points left, it means you can drag to the left **to shorten the video clip.** If the arrow points left *and* right, it means the video clip was previously trimmed; you can drag the edge to the right **to recover the trimmed frames.**

When you position your pointer over the *left edge* of a clip, the pointer turns into an arrow pointing right, meaning you can **shorten the clip** by dragging the edge to the right. If the arrow also points *left,* there are hidden frames of video to the left that you can **recover** by dragging the clip's edge to the left.

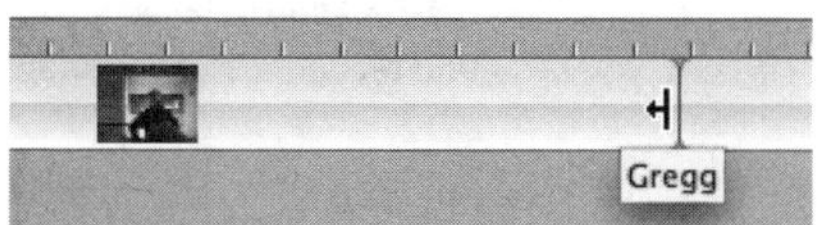

Shorten a clip in the Timeline by dragging its right edge to the left.

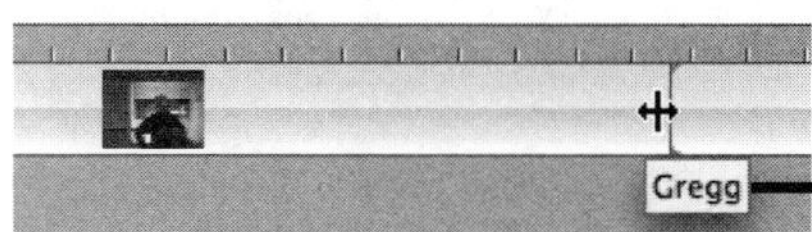

This clip can be shortened ***or*** *lengthened in the Timeline, indicated by the double-facing arrow.*

As you hover over a clip in the Timeline, a small info tag pops up to identify the clip. It disappears after about ten seconds or as soon as you move the pointer away from the clip.

Notice that complete clips (clips that haven't been trimmed or cropped) have **rounded edges** in the Timeline. When you trim frames from one or both edges, the clip corners are **square** instead of rounded.

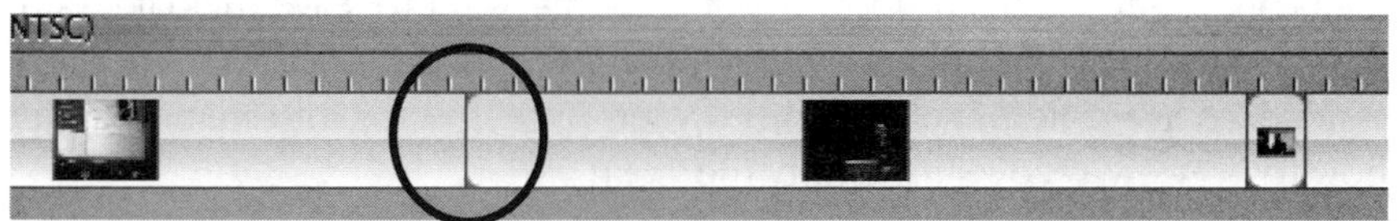

The shape of clip corners tell you if video frames have been trimmed from the clip, and which side of the clip has been trimmed.

Recover deleted footage from a cropped or trimmed clip

Because iMovie uses non-destructive editing technology, you can recover footage that has been trimmed or cropped.

▾ Select a clip. From the Advanced menu choose "Revert Clip to Original."

(If a selected clip has *not* been previously trimmed or cropped, the command "Revert to Original" is dimmed.)

If the selected clip is in the Timeline, the clip width expands to show the extended duration created by adding video frames that had been trimmed or cropped previously.

If the selected clip is in the Timeline, the duration numbers in the upper-left corner of the clip change to show the addition of recovered footage that had been trimmed or cropped.

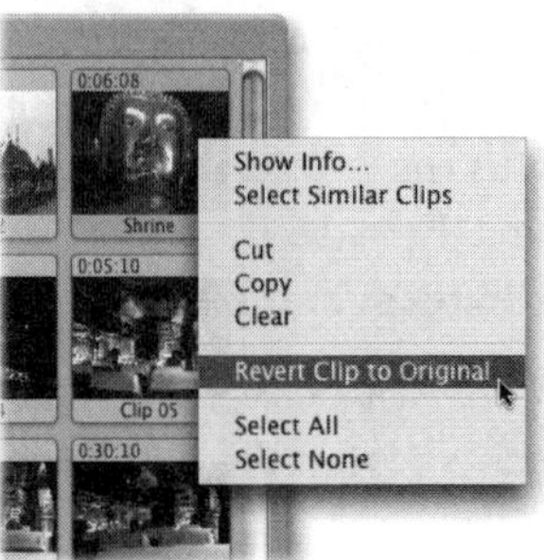

You can also Control-click on a clip in the Clips Pane to revert a clip and recover deleted footage.

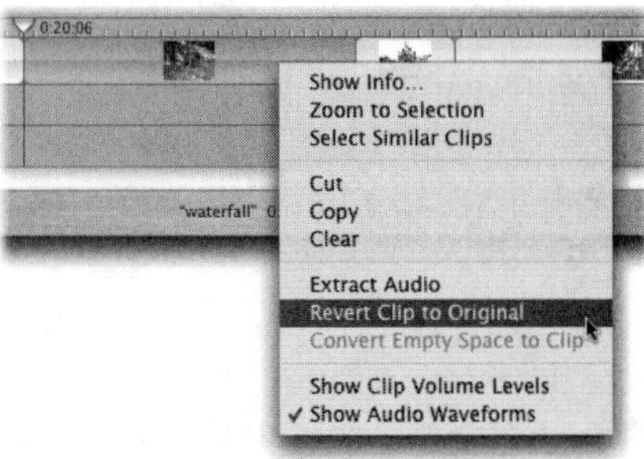

Or Control-click on a clip in the Timeline to revert a clip and recover deleted footage.

Notice the edges of the clips in the Timeline. Complete clips (untrimmed and uncropped) have round-cornered edges. When frames have been trimmed or cropped from one or both sides of a clip, the edge of that clip has square corners. See the illustration on the previous page.

Keep track of your Trash

The Trash icon in the bottom-right corner of the window tells you how much data you've deleted from your project. You may want to leave the data there in case you need to recover some of it later. Empty the Trash to make more disk space available for your project—see page 139 for information about how to preview, recover, or empty the Trash.

Choose a Timeline View

There are two editing views available in iMovie: the **Clip View** and the **Timeline View**. Both of these views show all the clips that you've added to your movie Timeline, with a few differences. When you place a clip in one of the views, it also appears in the other view. To switch between the two views, click the view buttons.

Click the left view button (the film frame icon) to show the **Clip View** (below). Clips are shown as large thumbnails, making it easy to identify clips by their content or name. In this view you can drag a clip to another position in the Timeline to rearrange the order of clips.

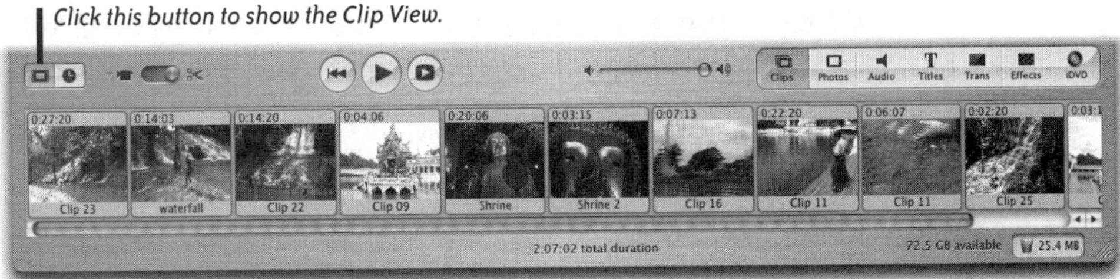

The Clip View gives a large view of clips and lets you rearrange the order of clips by dragging them to other positions in the Timeline.

Click the right view button (the clock icon) to show the **Timeline View** (below). This view is more versatile than the Clip View. It shows two audio tracks in addition to the video track. In this view you can rearrange clips, edit the volume of clips, turn a track's audio on or off, trim clips, split video clips, and more. This is the view in which most of your edtiting takes place.

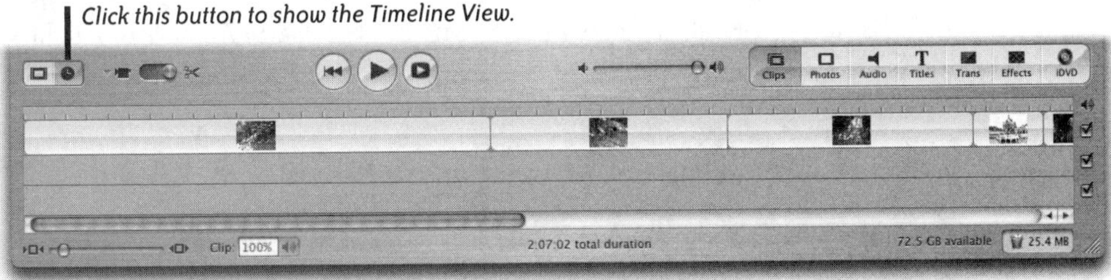

The Timeline View shows the video and audio tracks. In this view you can add audio tracks, edit the duration of audio and video clips, adjust the volume of clips, or use the checkboxes on the right side of the Timeline to mute the audio of an entire track.

About the Timeline

Use the **Timeline** to arrange the order of clips, add transitions between clips, add effects, create titles, and add extra audio to your movie. The Timeline is where you spend most of your time, so let's look at more Timeline details.

Add clips to the Timeline

- Drag clips directly from the Clips Pane to the Timeline.
- **Or** (as explained on page 142) copy clips or segments of clips and paste them into the Timeline.

  To copy and paste an entire clip from the Clips Pane, select the clip and press Command C (copy). Position the Playhead in the Timeline where you want to paste the clip, and press Command V (paste). The clip is now in the Timeline, yet still accessible in the Clips Pane.

Rearrange clips in the Timeline

1. In either Clip View or Timeline View, select a clip in the Timeline.
2. Press and drag the clip to a new position in the Timeline.

If the position to which you want to move the clip is too far down the Timeline to drag, use this procedure:

1. Select the clip you want to move.
2. Press Command X to cut it from its current position in the Timeline.
3. Drag the horizontal scroll bar to the right until you can see where you want to paste the clip you're moving.
4. Place the Playhead exactly where you want to paste the clip, then press Command V.

   If the Playhead is *in the middle* of an existing clip, the pasted clip splits the existing clip. If the Playhead is *between two clips*, all clips to the right of the Playhead move right to make room for the pasted clip.

In Timeline View (top) or Clip View (bottom), drag a clip to a new position to rearrange the order of clips in the Timeline.

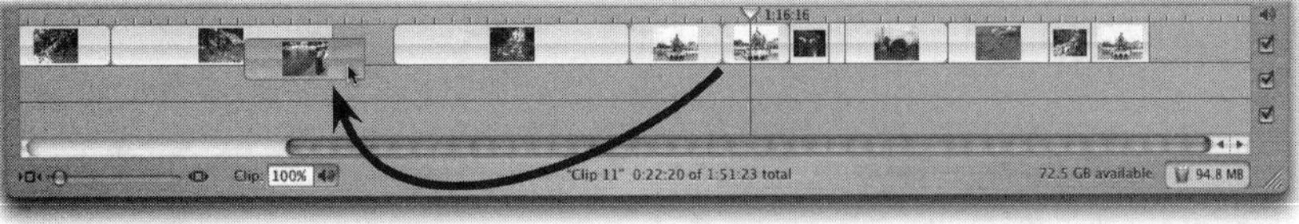

This text shows the selected clip's name, duration, and the total duration of all clips in the Timeline.

Return clips to the Clips Pane from the Timeline

You may decide to delete a clip from your movie, but want to keep it somewhere in case you change your mind. If you used the copy and paste technique described on page 142, you can just select the clip in the Timeline and press the Delete key. The original clip is still in the Clips Pane when you need it later. If you originally dragged the clip from the Clips Pane to the Timeline, it's not in the Clips Pane any more. If you delete the clip, it goes to the Trash. You can recover it from the Trash as long as you don't empty the Trash first. But you can also just drag the clip from the Timeline back up to the Clips Pane and drop it there. Now the clip is available if you decide to use it later.

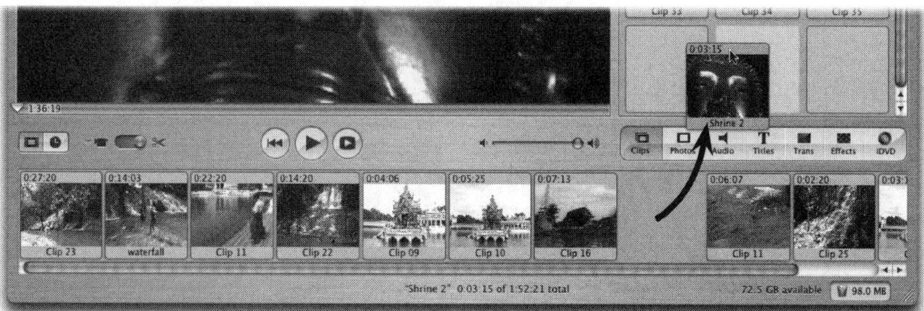

You can drag clips out of the Timeline and place them back in the Clips Pane.

This can be done in both Clip View (shown here) and Timeline View.

Use the Zoom slider to magnify clips in Timeline View

The Zoom slider resizes clips horizontally in Timeline View. When the Zoom slider is all the way to the left (the lowest zoom level), clips are squeezed horizontally so the entire movie is visible in the Timeline. When the Zoom slider is moved to the right (a magnified zoom level), the clips stretch horizontally and take more space in the Timeline. A higher zoom level can make it easier to place the Playhead exactly where you want, or to work with short clips that may appear tiny in the Timeline.

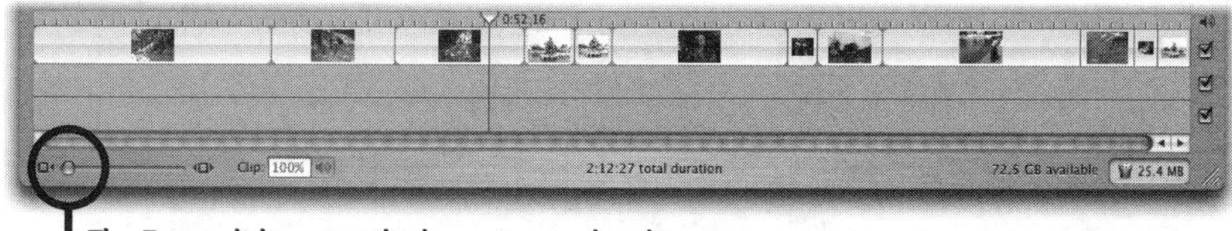

The Zoom slider set at the lowest zoom level.

At a low zoom level the scroll bar reaches all the way across the Timeline and more clips are visible in the Timeline.

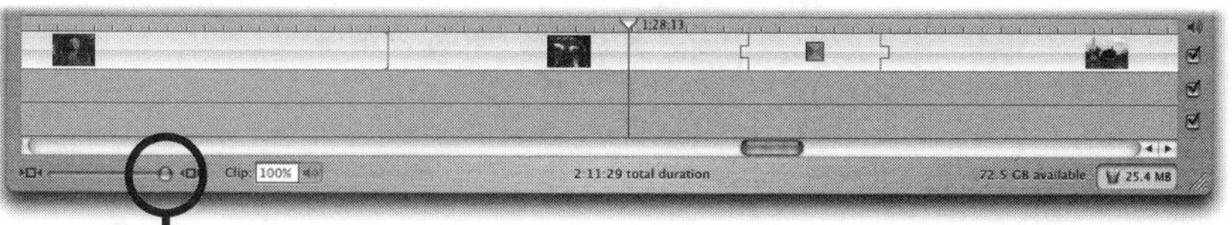

The Zoom slider set at the highest zoom level.

At higher zoom levels, the scroll bar appears smaller and you must scroll to see all of the clips that are used in the movie.

Renaming clips

When iMovie imports clips to the Clips Pane, it assigns sequential numbers as names—Clip 1, Clip 2, etc. You can rename clips so the name is more descriptive. Sometimes the thumbnail image associated with a video clip is misleading and doesn't really identify the main content of the clip. Or you may want to rename clips to reflect the order in which you plan to place them in the Timeline.

To rename a clip in the Clips Pane:

1. Click on a clip in the Clips Pane to select it. The clip's top and bottom bars turn blue to show that it is selected.
2. Click on its title in the bottom bar to highlight the text.
3. Type a new title in place of the highlighted text (shown below).

The duration of each clip is shown at the top of the clip in a 00:00:00 format (minutes:seconds:frames).

The duration of this clip is 4 minutes, 10 seconds, and 23 frames.

To rename a clip in the Clips Pane, type a new name in this area.

To rename a clip in the Timeline:

1. Double-click a clip in the Timeline to open the "Clip Info" window shown below.
2. Type a new name in the "Name" field.
3. Click the "Set" button.

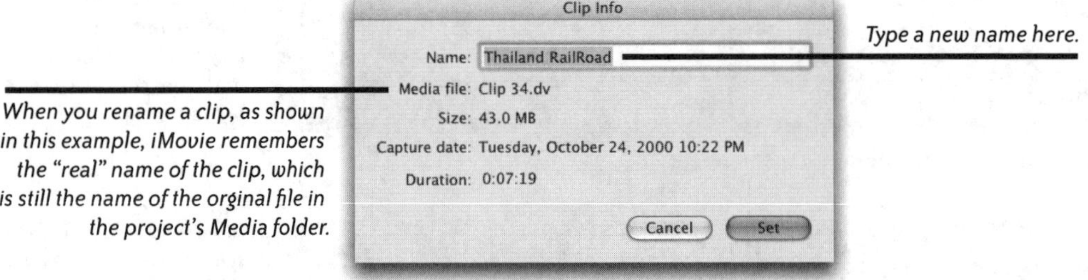

Type a new name here.

When you rename a clip, as shown in this example, iMovie remembers the "real" name of the clip, which is still the name of the orginal file in the project's Media folder.

Get information about clips

The "Clip Info" window (above) also provides other information about a clip, such as the original name (Media file), size, capture date, and duration.

Render clips

When you add transitions to a movie or add effects to clips, iMovie automatically *renders* them so you can see them. The render progress shows as a red bar moving across the bottom edge of the clip or transition.

*The red progress bar at the bottom of a **clip** shows an **effect** being rendered in Clip View.*

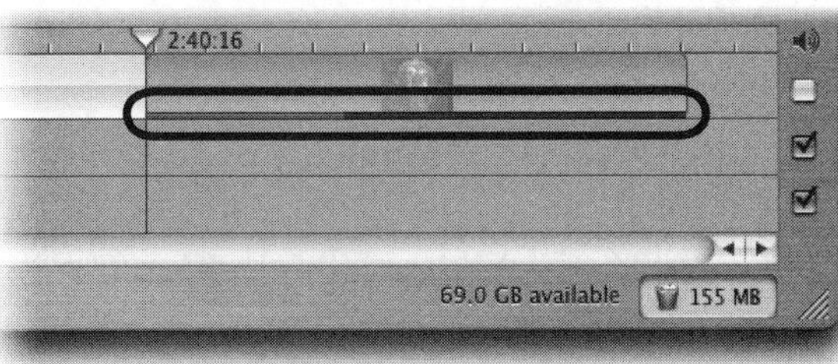

*A red progress bar at the bottom of a **clip** shows an **effect** being rendered in Timeline View.*

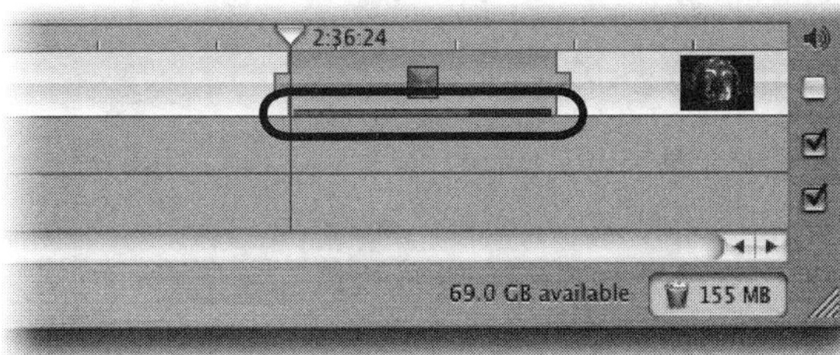

*A red progress bar at the bottom of a **transition** shows a **transition** being rendered in Timeline View.*

***Tip:* To stop a render in progress if you're in Timeline View,** press Command Period.

Some effects that need to be rendered, such as slow motion and reverse direction clips, delay the rendering until you export the movie.

Use bookmarks to mark key frames of clips

Place **bookmarks** to mark key frames in the Timeline where you want to sync an audio track with a video clip, or where you want to trim or place a clip. Press Command B to place a Bookmark at the Playhead position, **or** from the Markers menu, choose "Add Bookmark."

See page 180 for more information about bookmarks.

Try this: Place an audio track in the Timeline, then play the track. As the music plays, press Command B at the downbeat of the music. Then adjust the duration of video clips so they start and stop at bookmarks. Preview the movie and watch the scenes change to the beat of the music. Music video! It's easy and it's fun.

Preview the assembled clips

To preview your movie, move the Playhead (the white triangle, circled below) in the Timeline to the beginning of the movie, then click the Play button.

Or click the double arrow button to the left of the Play button to jump to the beginning of the movie.

Notice that if you click on a specific *clip* in the Timeline, only that clip shows and plays in the Monitor. **To load the entire movie** into the Monitor, click anywhere *except* on a clip in the Timeline (click outside of the Timeline or on empty space in one of the audio tracks). Notice that when you click somewhere other than on a specific clip, the Scrubber Bar appears to be divided into many separate segments. Each segment represents a clip in the Timeline. When you see the Scrubber Bar divided like this, it means the entire movie is selected, not just a single clip.

To preview a movie (or selected clips) in **full-screen mode,** click the button to the right of the Play button. When you preview in full-screen mode, click anywhere on the screen to quit the preview and return to the iMovie window.

When the Monitor contains an entire movie, the **Scrubber Bar** is divided into segments. Each segment is a separate clip in the movie.

Go to the **beginning** of the movie.

To preview your movie in **full-screen mode,** click here.

To preview your movie in the **Monitor,** click here.

Add Enhancements

Once you've made a rough cut of your movie that includes all the clips you want and you've arranged them in the order you want, you can start adding enhancements to make the movie look more professional. Add transitions between scenes, titles, effects, still photos with a pan-and-zoom effect, additional audio, and chapter markers that can be used later if you create a DVD.

Transitions

A **transition** is a visual effect that creates a bridge from one scene to the next. It could be a cross-dissolve, fade-out, spinning image, or any of the other transitions that are included with iMovie.

To add a transition effect between two clips:

1. Click the "Trans" button to show the Transitions Pane, shown below.
2. To preview transition effects in the small preview window, click on a transition in the list. To preview the effect full-size in the Monitor, click the "Preview" button at the top of the Transition pane.
3. Use the "Speed" slider to set the duration of the transition in seconds and frames (formatted as 00:00).
4. Select a transition, drag it to the Timeline and drop it between two clips of your choosing.

Use this control to set the direction of some transitions, such as "Push."

Preview

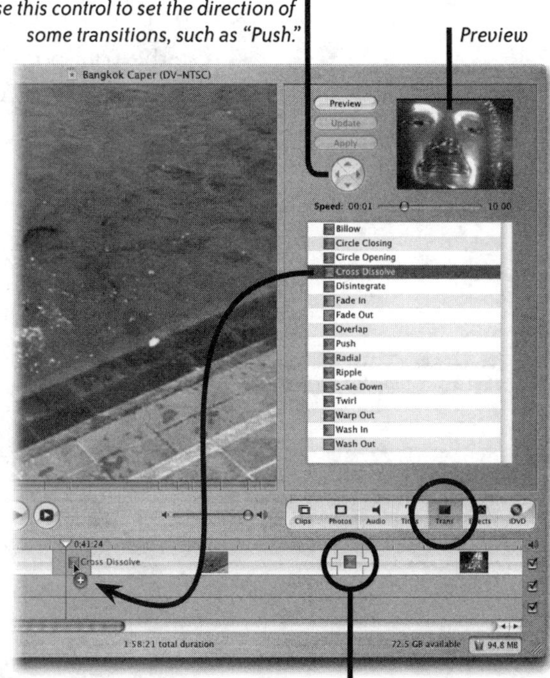

This is a transition that has been dragged from the Transitions Pane to the Timeline and rendered.

To apply a transition to multiple clips: Select multiple clips in the Timeline to which you want to apply a transition, then click the "Apply" button.

To delete a transition: Click on the transition in the Timeline, then hit the Delete key.

To change a transition: Select it in the Timeline, change the settings in the Transitions Pane, then click "Update." In the Transitions Pane, choose another transition or modify existing transition settings, then click "Apply."

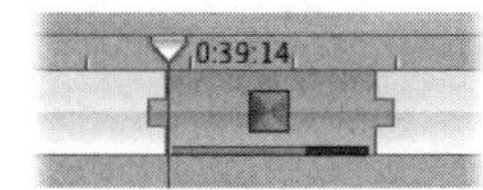

A red progress bar shows a transition being rendered.

Add titles to your movie

A **title** is text that you place in its own frame or on top of a clip. A title can show credits, act as a caption, or add comments. There are many styles of titles to choose from and you can use different typefaces, sizes, and colors.

To add titles to your movie:

1. Select a clip in the Timeline (click once on it). The clip you select shows in the thumbnail preview window when you click on a title style.
2. Click the "Titles" button to reveal the Titles pane, then select a title style.
3. Type your title text into the text fields in the Title pane.
4. Use the Font pop-up menu to select a font.
5. Use the "Size" slider to enlarge or reduce the type.
6. Click the "Color" box to choose a font color from a color palette.

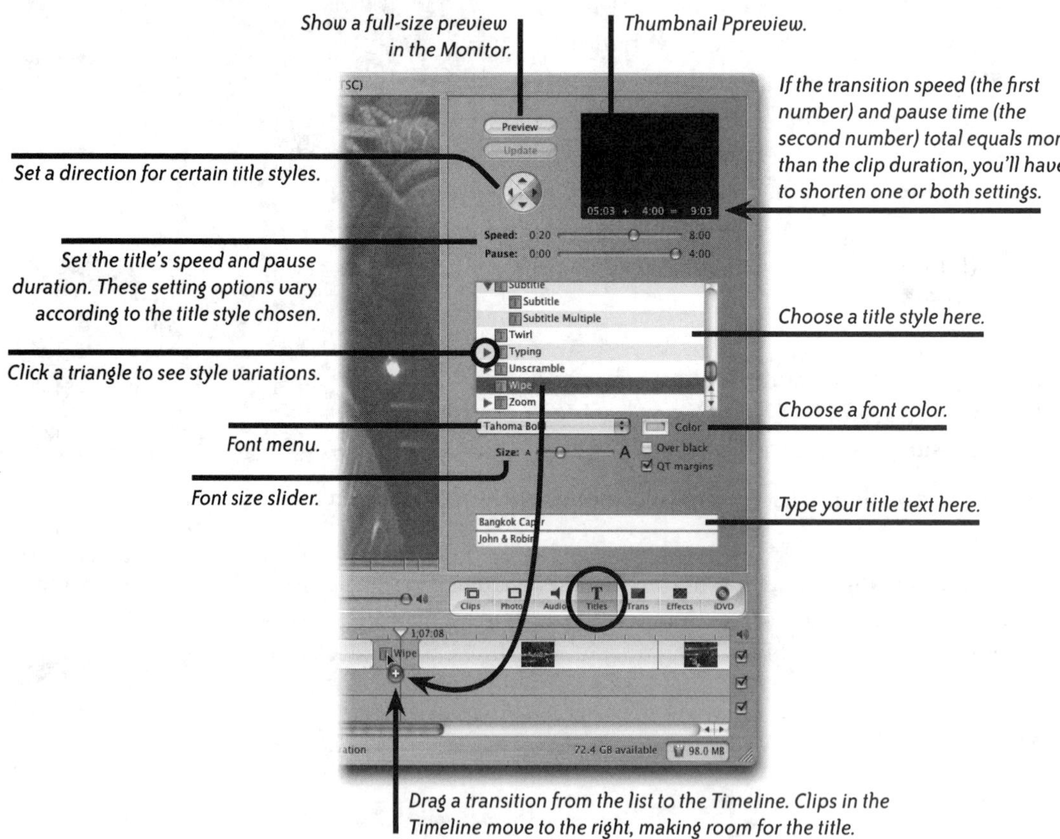
Show a full-size preview in the Monitor.
Thumbnail Ppreview.
If the transition speed (the first number) and pause time (the second number) total equals more than the clip duration, you'll have to shorten one or both settings.
Set a direction for certain title styles.
Set the title's speed and pause duration. These setting options vary according to the title style chosen.
Click a triangle to see style variations.
Choose a title style here.
Choose a font color.
Font menu.
Font size slider.
Type your title text here.
Drag a transition from the list to the Timeline. Clips in the Timeline move to the right, making room for the title.
Preview
Update
Speed:
Pause:
Subtitle
Subtitle Multiple
Twirl
Typing
Unscramble
Wipe
Zoom
Color
Over black
QT margins
Size:
Clips
Titles
Trans
Effects
iDVD
72.4 GB available
98.0 MB

7. Click the "Over black" checkbox to create a title that stands alone against a black background and does not affect other clips (other than moving them down the Timeline to make room for the added title). If you *do not* select the "Over black" checkbox, the title will be rendered on top of the clip immediately to the *right* of where you drag and drop the title in the Timeline (see Step 9).
8. If you plan to export the movie as a QuickTime file, check the "QT margins" box to allow the title to expand within the limitations of the QuickTime margins.

   If you plan to burn a DVD and show it on a television, make sure this button is *not* selected or your type may be cut off on the edges, or just leave it unchecked all the time to play it safe for any media.
9. Select a title style in the list of styles and drag it to a position in the Timeline between two clips (see the example on the previous page). All of the clips to the *right* of the dragged title move to the *right*, making room for the title.

To identify clips that have a title effect applied, switch to the Clip View of the Timeline and look for a "T" symbol at the top of a clip.

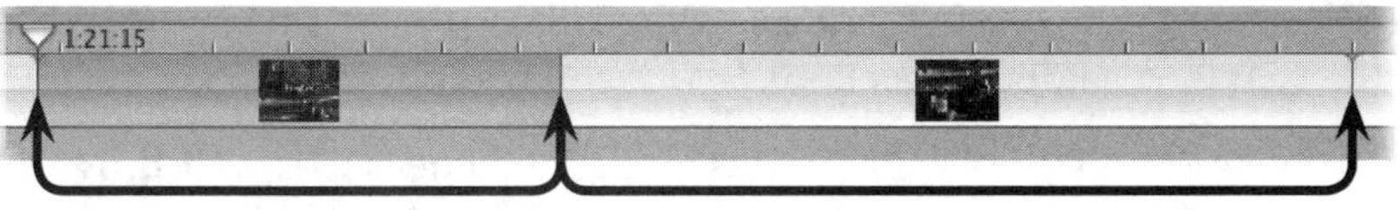

*This was originally one clip. iMovie **split** the clip to render the title over its first 8 seconds (4 seconds for the title's **speed** setting and 4 seconds for the **pause** setting).*

*This title was set to render **on top** of an existing clip ("Over black" was **not** selected in the Titles pane).*

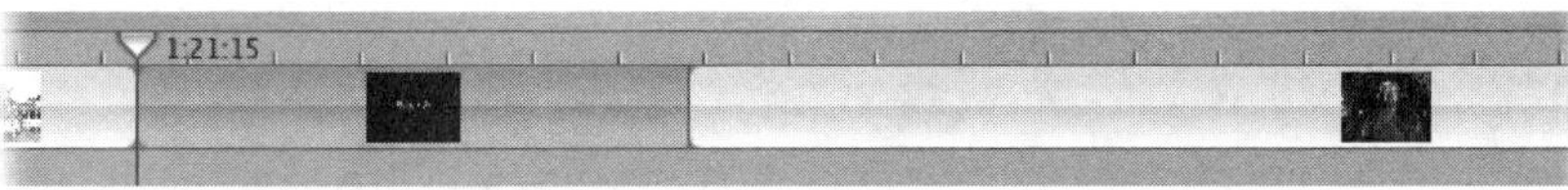

*This title was set to render as a new clip ("Over black" was **selected** in the Titles pane).*

To delete a title:

▼ Select the title clip, then hit Delete.

To modify and update a title:

▼ Select the title clip, change the title style or any of the title settings, then click the "Update" button.

Place still photos in the Timeline

There are several ways to place photos in iMovie. The easiest and most convenient method is to **click the "Photos" button.** The Photos Pane replaces the current pane to the right of the Monitor and shows the tools you'll use for selecting photos, setting a duration, and adding motion to photos.

The Photos Pane is divided into the "Ken Burns Effect" section and the iPhoto section. The iPhoto section contains all the photos that are currently stored in iPhoto. From the pop-up menu you can select the iPhoto Library or any album in iPhoto. The scrolling pane displays thumbnails of your photos.

1. Click on a photo to select it, or Command-click on multiple photos.
2. Click the "Ken Burns Effect" checkbox to activate a *pan-and-zoom effect* (see the opposite page).
3. Click the "Apply" button. Selected photos are placed at the end of the Timeline, to the right of existing clips.

To identify photos that have a Ken Burns Effect applied, switch to the Clip View of the Timeline and look for a "Play" symbol at the top of a photo clip.

You can also **drag photos** from the Photos Pane to a *precise point* in the Timeline that you choose (shown below). The current Ken Burns Effect settings, such as duration, are automatically applied to photos unless you *un*check the "Ken Burns Effect" checkbox *before* you add photos to the Timeline.

Another method for placing photos in the Timeline is to simply **drag a photo from anywhere** on your computer straight to the Timeline. The current Ken Burns Effect settings will be applied to the photo.

You can also **import photos into iMovie,** as explained on the next page.

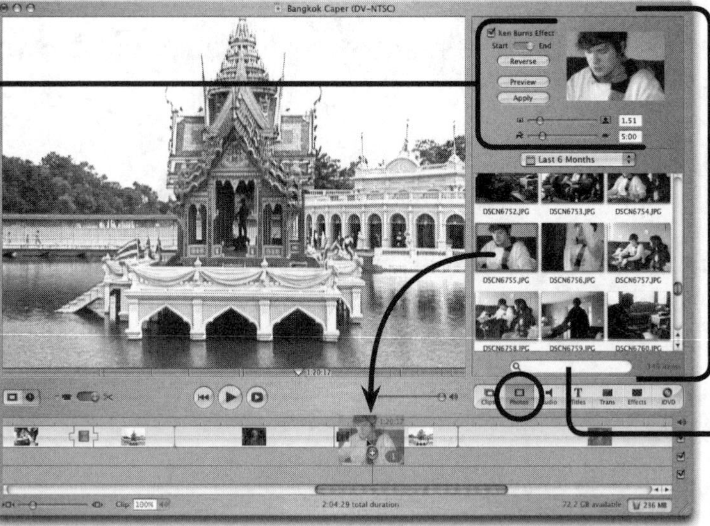

Ken Burns Effect controls, including Zoom and Duration sliders.

Photos Pane.

When you drag a photo to a position in the Timeline, existing clips move over to the right to make room for the new content.

Type here to search for photos by title.

Import still photos

You may want to use photos in your movie that are not in iPhoto. Perhaps you have a collection of scans in some other folder, or a CD of photos from someone else. You could import those photos into iPhoto to make them accessible from the Photos Pane, but you don't have to. Instead, just import them from wherever they're stored on your computer.

To import from a CD or from any location on your computer:

1. From the File menu, choose "Import...."
2. In the sheet that drops down from the iMovie title bar, locate a photo or a folder of photos that you want to import. Select a single photo, multiple photos, or an entire folder, then click "Open."

   The imported photo is placed in the Clips Pane (*not* the Photos Pane). The photo's duration is automatically set to the duration setting in the Ken Burns Effect pane. If Ken Burns Effect is turned on, the effect settings are applied to the imported photo.
3. Drag the imported photo to the desired position in the Timeline.

Tip: To quickly change the duration of a photo in the Timeline, drag the photo's edges left or right in the Timeline.

Or double-click a photo to open the "Clip Info" window (below), then type a duration in the "Duration" field, using a format of 0:00:00 (minutes:seconds:frames).

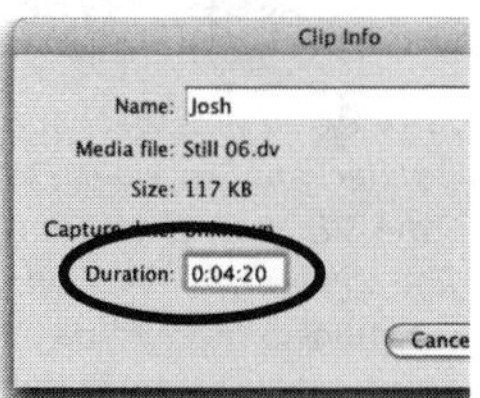

If a Ken Burns Effect is applied to the photo, use the Duration slider in the Photos Pane to change its duration.

The Ken Burns Effect: pan-and-zoom still photos

Ken Burns is a documentary filmmaker who popularized the technique of slowly panning across and zooming in or out of still photos to add motion and drama. Click the "Photos" button in the button bar to show the Photos Pane and the "Ken Burns Effect" controls.

To apply a Ken Burns effect to a still photo:

1. Click a photo in the Photos Pane to show it in the thumbnail Preview window (in the upper-right corner of the Photos Pane).
2. Click the "Start" side of the toggle button to set a *start* size and position. Drag the Duration slider (the rabbit and tortoise symbols) to set a duration for the photo.
3. Inside the thumbnail Preview window, drag the thumbnail preview to a *start* position, then adjust the Zoom slider (the top slider) to set a zoom level (magnification) to start the effect.
4. Click the "End" side of the toggle button to set a *final* size and position. Drag the Zoom slider to set a final zoom level, then drag the thumbnail preview to a final position for the end of the effect.
5. To see the effect full-size in the Monitor, click "Preview." **Or** click a photo in the Photos Pane to show it in the thumbnail Preview.
6. Drag the photo from the Photos Pane to a position in the Timeline. **Or** click "Apply" to automatically place it at the end of the Timeline.

Tip: After you set the "Start" settings for a Ken Burns Effect, Option-click the "Finish" button to automatically apply the same settings to the end of the effect.

To create a perfectly aligned and smooth horizontal or vertical pan: With the "Finish" button still selected, Shift-drag the thumbnail image left or right, up or down.

Effects

An **effect** is a visual distortion or alteration that is applied to a clip. The effect may be used for aesthetic reasons or for visual impact. A limited number of effects come with iMovie, but many more are available from third-party vendors such as Gee Three (www.GeeThree.com).

To identify clips that have an Effect applied, switch to the Clip View of the Timeline and look for an Effects symbol (a checkerboard) at the top of a clip.

To add effects to a clip in your movie:

1. Single-click a clip in the Timeline to select it.
2. Click the "Effects" button to show the Effects pane.
3. Select an effect from the Effects list.
4. Use the "Effect In" and "Effect Out" sliders to set the amount of time it takes for the effect to fade in and to fade out.
5. If there are other settings sliders below the Effects list, set those as well. Some effects have more adjustment options available than others. Click the effect in the list to see a thumbnail preview.
6. When you're satisfied with the effect, click the "Apply" button. iMovie starts rendering the effect immediately, indicated by a red progress bar that moves across the bottom of the clip.

   To stop the rendering and revert the clip to its original state, hit the Delete key.

   To remove an effect *after* it has been applied to a clip, select the clip in the Timeline, then hit the Delete key.

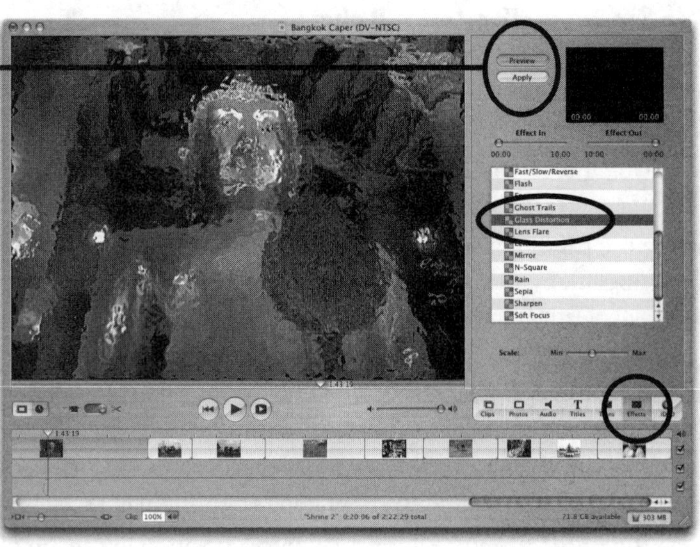

Click the "Preview" button to preview the effect full-size in the Monitor.

Click the effect name in the Effects list to see a preview in the small Preview window.

Click the "Apply" button to apply the effect to the selected clip.

Show a large preview in the Monitor.

Set the effect's adjustment sliders, then click "Apply."

Each effect has its own unique controls.

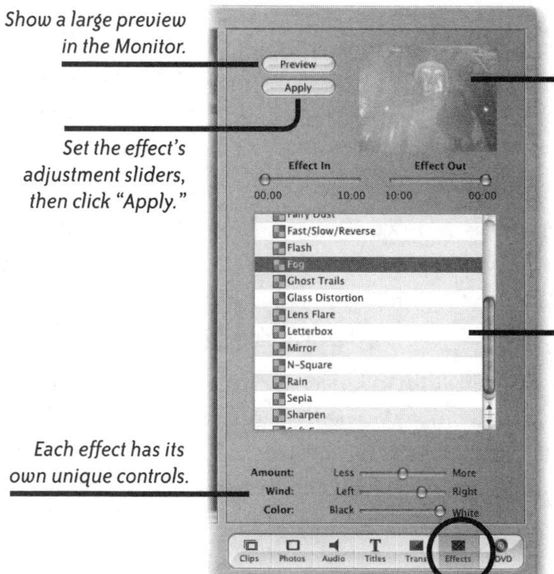

The Effects preview uses the currently selected clip in the Timeline. If no clip is selected, the preview uses the clip under the Playhead. If the Playhead is positioned between two clips, the preview uses the clip to the right of the Playhead.

Choose an effect from this list.

Tip: To apply an effect to just part of a clip, split the clip into sections, then apply an effect to just one section. Position the Playhead where you want to split the clip, then from the Edit menu, choose "Split Video Clip at Playhead." See page 176.

Some effects, such as Electricity (shown below) and Fairy Dust, let you grab the effect in the thumbnail Preview window and drag it to a new position.

The Electricity effect:
Click anywhere in the thumbnail Preview window to set the endpoint of the electric bolt.

Press-and-drag the bolt to position it anywhere in the frame.

Rotate the effect clockwise (CW) or counter-clockwise (CCW).

Audio

Audio *editing* is critically important to the perceived professionalism of your movie. When you shoot a scene, the background noise often is distracting or even unbearable. Audio editing lets you lower or mute the volume of problem clips and add a background music track or a narrative voice-over.

Even if the existing audio is fine, you can enhance the aesthetic and emotional impact of your movie just by having fun with additional soundtracks and narration clips. If you're making an instructional video, narrative voice-overs can add clarity and comprehension to your project.

Place as many **audio clips** in iMovie's two audio tracks as you need. When you record narration directly into iMovie, it's automatically placed in track 1, but you can choose to put additional imported soundtracks there also. You can drag imported audio clips to any position in an audio track. You can also drag audio clips from one audio track to another.

Audio clips can overlap on the same track or in separate tracks. When two audio clips in two different audio tracks overlap, both are audible. iMovie's advanced audio-editing features allow you to adjust and control the volume in overlapping tracks.

For instance, you can lower the volume of a background music clip while someone in a video clip is talking. Or you can fade-out the audio of a video clip as you raise the volume of a background soundtrack. The volume of each individual audio and video clip is editable. In fact, you can make multiple volume adjustments to a single clip. See "Advanced audio editing" on pages 162–163 to learn more about adjusting the volume of audio and video clips.

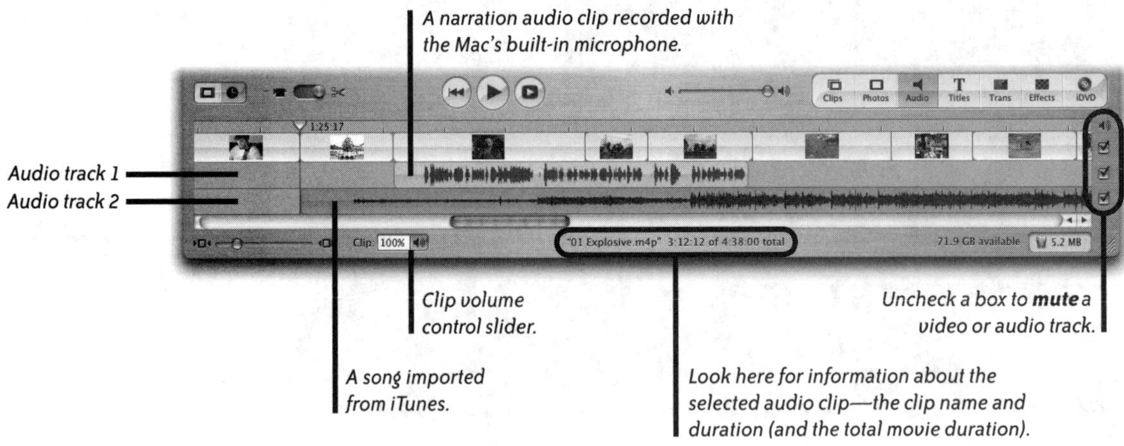
A narration audio clip recorded with the Mac's built-in microphone.
Clips
Photos
Audio
Titles
Trans
Effects
iDVD
1:25:17
Audio track 1
Audio track 2
Clip: 100%
"01 Explosive.m4p" 3:12:12 of 4:38:00 total
71.9 GB available
5.2 MB
Clip volume control slider.
Uncheck a box to **mute** a video or audio track.
A song imported from iTunes.
Look here for information about the selected audio clip—the clip name and duration (and the total movie duration).

Add audio files to your movie:

1. Click the "Audio" button to show the Audio Pane (below).
2. Position the Playhead in the Timeline where you want the audio clip to start.
3. The Audio Pane's pop-up menu lets you choose a source location: the iTunes Library, any iTunes playlist, iMovie Sound Effects, or a CD that is inserted in your CD drive (shown below-right). The source you select is displayed in the scrolling Audio Pane.
4. Click on an audio clip in the Audio Pane list to highlight it.
5. Click the "Place at Playhead" button to place the audio clip in the Timeline. **Or** drag a clip from the list of audio files to either audio track and to any position in the Timeline.

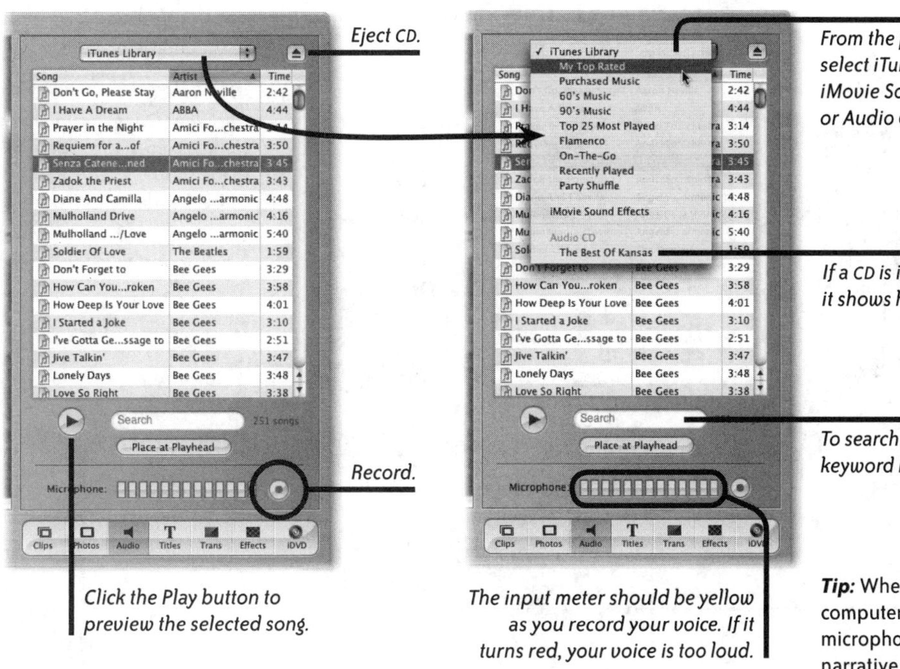

Eject CD.

From the pop-up menu, select iTunes Library, iMovie Sound Effects, or Audio CD.

If a CD is in the CD drive, it shows here.

To search for a song, type a keyword in the Search field.

Record.

Click the Play button to preview the selected song.

The input meter should be yellow as you record your voice. If it turns red, your voice is too loud.

To record a narration clip:

Narrative voice-overs are a great way to add interest to your movie. If your computer has a built-in microphone or if you've connected an external mic, click the Record button to begin recording your voice; the button's outer ring is red when recording. Click the button again to stop recording. (If the Record button is dimmed, you don't have a microphone.)

The voice clip automatically appears in the audio track 1 in the Timeline when you start talking, starting at the current Playhead position. After you finish recording, you can move the audio clip to any position in the Timeline.

Tip: When you use the computer's built-in microphone to record a narrative voice-over, the sound quality may not be acceptable to you. Try recording the narrative with your video camera, speaking straight into the video camera microphone. Then import that video clip into iMovie, place it in the Timeline, extract the audio (as explained on page 163), and delete the video clip.

To import an audio track from anywhere on your computer:

You might have audio files in various formats stored on your Mac, but not in iTunes, and therefore not accessible from the Audio Pane. You can import audio files from anywhere on your computer straight into an audio track.

1. From the File menu, choose "Import…."
2. In the Open dialog box that drops down from iMovie's title bar, locate an audio file that is stored on your computer. Select it, then click "Open." The entire audio file is placed in the lower audio track.

   If a music file name is dimmed in the Open dialog box, you can't use it in the movie because its format is one that iMovie doesn't support. Music must be in a format that works with QuickTime.

   The most common formats to work with are AIFF (Audio Interchange File Format) and MP3. You can also import WAV (Waveform, a Microsoft/IBM audio format) and AAC (Advanced Audio Coding) files.

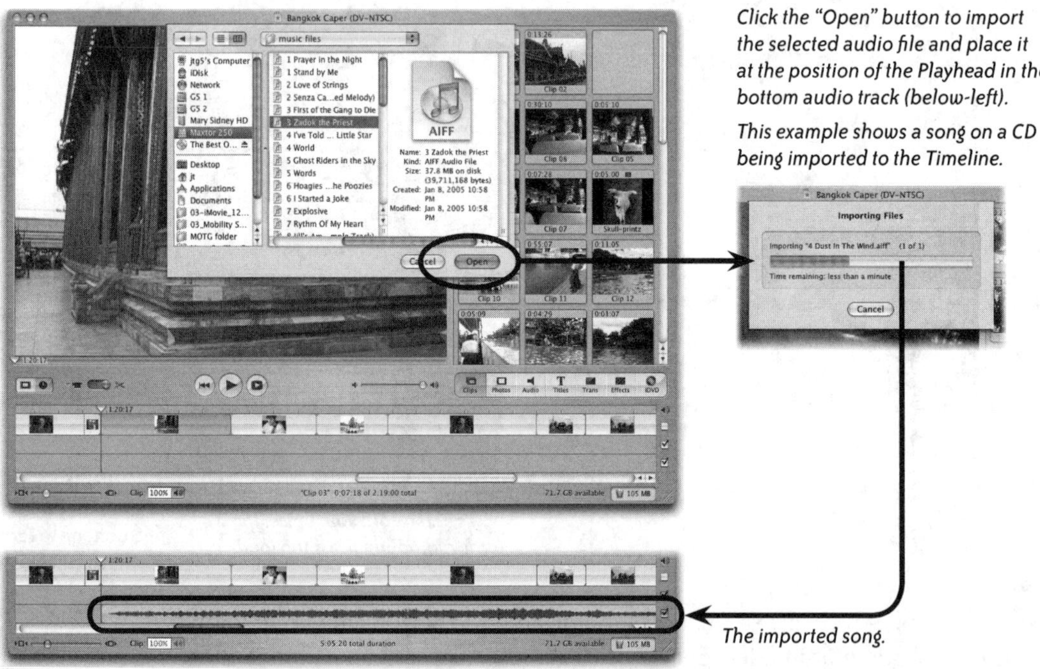

Click the "Open" button to import the selected audio file and place it at the position of the Playhead in the bottom audio track (below-left).

This example shows a song on a CD being imported to the Timeline.

The imported song.

To show the audio waveform of an audio clip (as seen here), from the View menu select "Show Audio Waveforms."

To turn off the waveform display, select the item again.

When the waveform is not shown, the audio file's name shows on the clip (shown above).

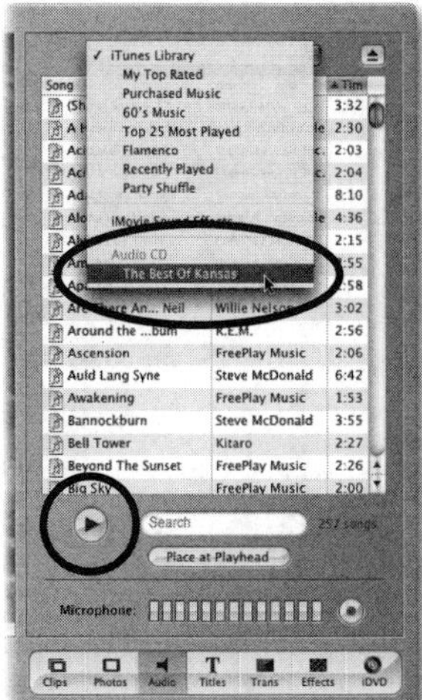

The CD title appears in the Audio Pane's pop-up menu.

To review and import a CD soundtrack:

If you want to use music from a CD, follow these steps:

1. Insert a CD into your CD drive.
2. Select the CD from the pop-up menu at the top of the Audio Pane. The CD songs show in the Audio Pane list.
3. **To review** CD songs *without* importing them, click on a song, then click the Play button (circled on the right).
4. **To import** a song, click on a song in the list.
5. In the Timeline, move the Playhead to the point you want the song to start.
6. Click the "Place at Playhead" button. **Or** drag a song from the list to a point in the Timeline where you want the song to play.

To adjust the position of an audio file in the Timeline, drag the entire clip left or right.

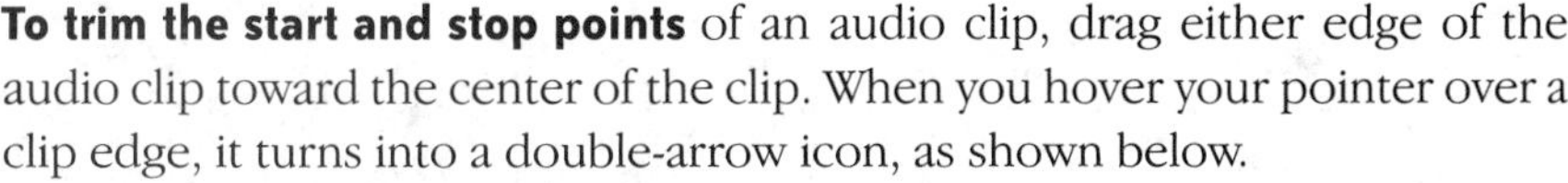

To trim the start and stop points of an audio clip, drag either edge of the audio clip toward the center of the clip. When you hover your pointer over a clip edge, it turns into a double-arrow icon, as shown below.

To fine-tune the trimming of an audio clip, select it, then use the left and right arrow keys on your keyboard: Tap an arrow key to crop the audio clip one frame for each tap. Shift-tap an arrow key to trim ten frames at a tap. **To recover cropped audio,** or use the arrow keys or just press-and-drag the clip edge outward (away from the center).

You can **drag** an audio clip from one audio track to another. This helps keep clips organized and accessible when you need to overlap audio files, such as a music track and a sound effect (shown on the next page).

You can even lay multiple audio tracks on top of each other in the same audio track and they all will be audible. Depending on the nature of the audio, you may need to adjust the individual volume levels of each clip.

As with video clips, a trimmed audio clip has square corners on the edge that has been trimmed. Untrimmed clips have round-cornered edges.

Drag an audio clip edge towards the center of the clip to trim audio from the beginning or end of the clip.

Advanced audio editing

iMovie's **advanced audio-editing features** are similar to those used in Final Cut Pro and other professional-level editing software. These features give you control over the placement and the duration of audio fade-ins and fade-outs. They let you create professional effects, such as lowering the volume of a background music track while a voice-over narrates the video, then lowering the video volume so the background music is emphasized. Very cool stuff. And easy.

From the View menu, choose "Show Clip Volume Levels." Black horizontal lines appear in every audio and video clip, indicating volume levels.

To adjust the volume of an entire clip (audio or video), select the clip, then move the clip volume control slider up or down. In the example below, the audio clip in the bottom track is selected and the volume control slider is set to 40% of the original volume. The volume slider will only affect clips (audio or video) that are *selected* (highlighted).

The clip in the bottom audio track is selected and the volume set to 40%.

To adjust the volume of multiple clips, select two or more clips, then move the clip volume control slider left or right to adjust the volume of all selected clips at once.

To set multiple volumes in a single clip, first make sure to select "Show Clip Volume Levels" in the View menu. Click anywhere on the volume level line in a clip. A *volume marker* appears on the volume level line. When the marker is *selected,* it is slightly larger and *yellow.* When it's *not selected,* it's *purple*. **Drag markers up or down** to raise or lower the volume. The percentage number (volume) next to the clip volume control slider changes as you drag. Create as many markers on the volume level line as necessary to make the changesyou want.

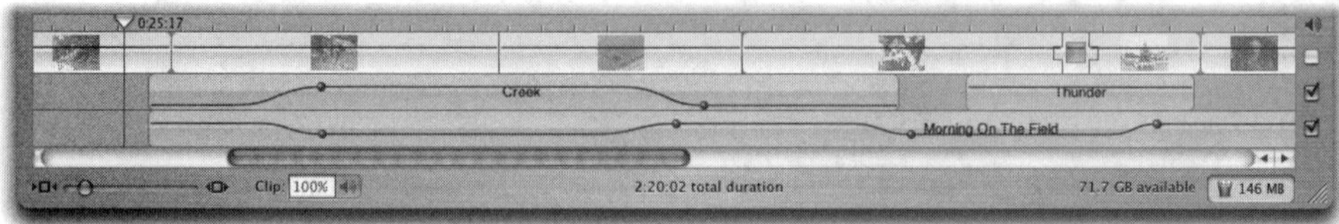

The volume in the top audio clip is set to increase as the volume in the bottom clip goes down.

When you click on or drag a volume marker, a purple square appears to the left, marking the start point of volume change. The round marker identifies the end point of volume change. Grab the purple square and move it *away* from the round marker to increase the *duration* of the volume change, making it more gradual. **Or** move it *closer* to the round marker to make the volume transition happen faster.

A selected marker is yellow.

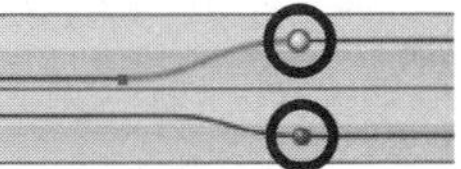

Other markers are purple.

In the example below, two audio clips are sharing the same track. The short volume line represents a short clip of sound effects ("Thunder") on top of a longer music clip ("Foreboding"). Since they are both audible, we adjusted the volume of the "Foreboding" clip to zero just in the area where the "Thunder" clip plays. We could drag the "Thunder" clip to the upper audio track to avoid confusion, but it works this way too.

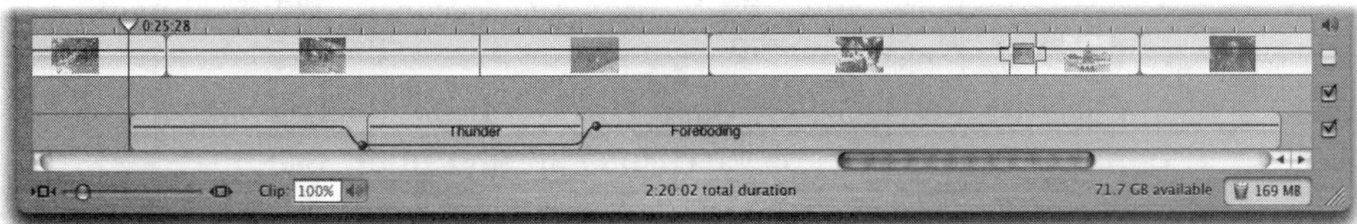

If you drag an audio clip on top of another audio clip in the same audio track, both clips are audible.

To extract audio from a video clip: You might want to use the audio from a video clip—*without* the video. Select a clip in the Timeline. From the "Advanced" menu, choose "Extract Audio." The extracted audio is automatically placed in audio track 1 (the top audio track in the Timeline). You can delete the video clip and use just the audio clip. The audio remains in the source video clip, but is muted; see below if you want to restore it.

To restore the video clip's audio, select the clip, click "Clip" volume control, then move the volume control slider from 0% to the desired volume. A volume setting of 100% restores the volume to its original state.

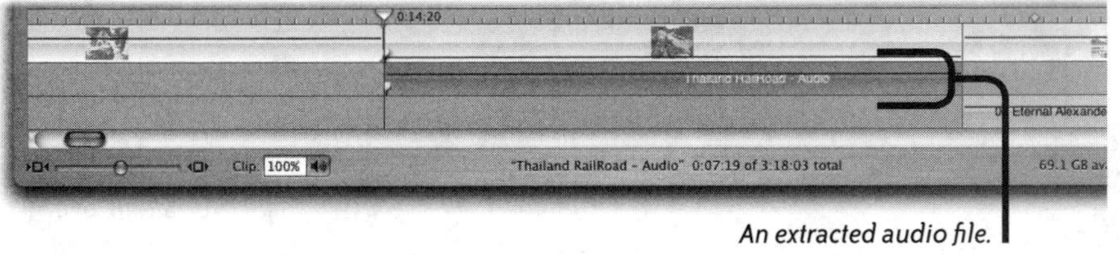

Yellow pins are placed in the audio and video clips (on the left edges) to lock the extracted audio in sync with the video.

Dragging the Playhead through a movie to preview it is called "scrubbing." **To hear audio as you scrub through your movie,** hold down the Option key as you drag the Playhead in the Timeline. This could be helpful when you need to locate a specific section of music or dialog that you want to synchronize with another clip, such as a loud musical accent or a shout.

Create chapter markers in a movie

One of the best ways to share movies is to create a DVD using Apple's iDVD software. And one of the biggest advantages of DVD is the ability to jump directly to pre-designated points in a movie, called "chapters."

Chapter markers that you create in iMovie are automatically exported with your movie when you create an iDVD project (see the next page). See Chapter 4 to learn all about the amazing iDVD application.

To add chapter markers:

1. Open an iMovie project that is completed.
2. Click the "iDVD" button in the button bar to show the iDVD Chapter Markers pane.
3. Move the Playhead in the Timeline to a position where you want to place a chapter marker.
4. Click the "Add Chapter" button in the Chapter Markers pane. A thumbnail image for the chapter appears in the pane.
5. If necessary, replace the clip name with a more meaningful chapter name. Later you can choose to let iDVD use these chapter names when it automatically creates a scene selection menu (as shown on the following page).

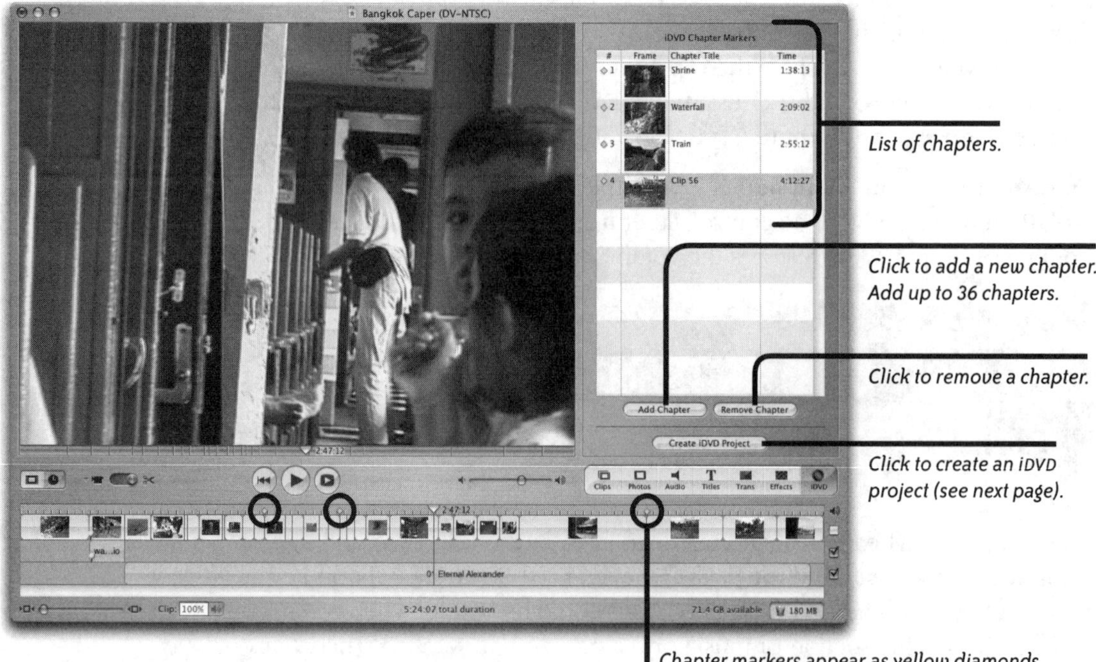

Create an iDVD Project

After you edit a movie, iDVD can immediately transform it into an iDVD project in which it creates menus and submenus automatically. An iDVD window opens, ready for you to customize the DVD design and burn the movie (or several movies) onto a blank DVD.

This is a really quick way to create a DVD project. You can add additional content to the DVD project after it opens, such as other movies, slideshows, and files. See Chapter 4 for details.

Tip: If you aren't ready to create a DVD project, but you want to **prepare your movie for iDVD,** export the movie as "Full Quality." See pages 172–173.

Later, when you open a DVD project, you can import that digital video file into iDVD.

To create an iDVD Project:

1. Open an iMovie project that is finished.
2. Click the "iDVD" button in the button bar to open the iDVD pane.
3. Click the "Create iDVD Project" button.

   You may get a message asking if you want to render certain clips. Click "Render and Proceed." After iMovie renders the necessary clips, iDVD launches.

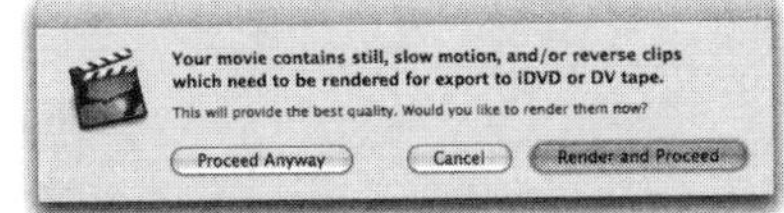

4. In the iDVD window that opens, choose a design theme from the Customize drawer, then make changes if you choose. iDVD automatically creates a main menu with two links: **Play Movie** plays the movie from the start; **Scene Selection** links to a submenu in which each chapter marker you created in iMovie is a link that jumps to that chapter.

   For this automation to work, make sure "Automatically create chapter marker submenu" is selected in the "Movies" pane of the iDVD preferences.

iDVD automatically builds a main menu (below-left), and a submenu (below-right) that contains links to the chapters you created in iMovie.

iDVD named each scene by the chapter name we assigned in iMovie. This text is editable in iDVD and can be changed at any time.

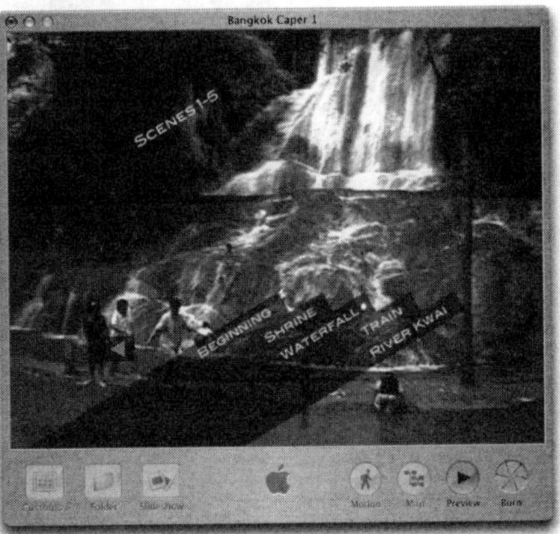

More Ways to Share a Movie

Once you've finished creating your movie, you can store it on your hard drive, but that uses a lot of disk space and the only place you can then show it is on your computer. Since iMovies are usually large, from several gigabytes on up, you can't pass them around on a Zip disk or even on a CD. To **share** your movie with others, you need to export the movie in a format that *can* be shared. iMovie is able to export a movie in a variety of formats, depending on its final intended use.

To share your movie:

1. From the File menu, choose "Share...."
2. A sheet drops down from iMovie's title bar and offers six ways to share a movie: Email, HomePage, Videocamera, iDVD, QuickTime, and Bluetooth.

   Click one of the icons at the top of the sheet to show the options available for that category. A separate sheet for each category provides its options and settings, including a description of the file that will be exported.

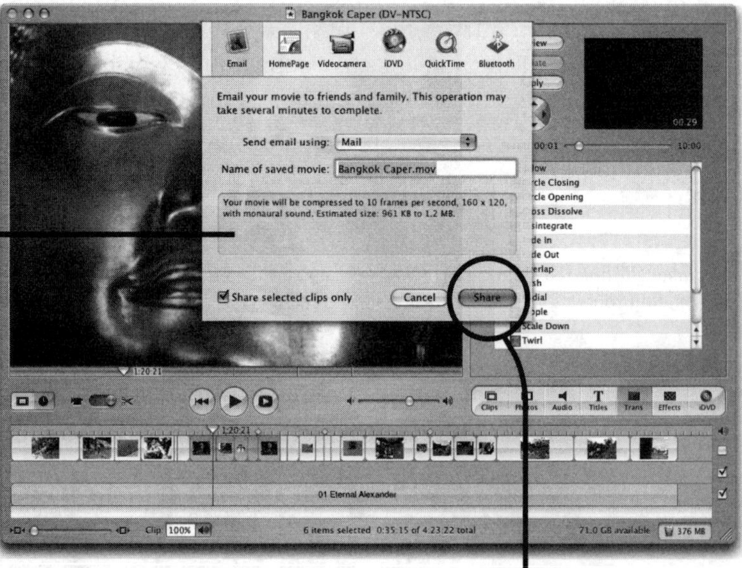

This inset pane gives a description of the file that will be created.

Look here for a description of how your movie will be compressed, and for an estimate of its exported size.

The Share settings change according to which icon you select at the top of this drop-down sheet.

Click the "Share" button to compress the movie, as shown on the next page.

Email option

Send a small movie to someone through email. iMovie will compress the movie to 10 frames per second (digital video is usually 30 frames per second) and 160 x 120 pixels with monaural sound (not stereo). Even a short and highly compressed movie makes a large file, so don't send long movies through email unless absolutely necessary.

1. Open an iMovie project.
2. From the File menu, choose "Share…." Click the "Email" icon.
3. From the "Send email using" pop-up menu, choose the name of the email program you use.
4. Type a name for the exported movie in the "Name of saved movie" text field.
5. Click the "Share" button. The chosen email application opens with the exported movie attached to a new message form (below-right).
6. Type a message, put an address in the "To" field, then send the email.

Instead of emailing an entire movie to someone, send a movie made of just a few clips: Before Step 2, above, select several clips in the Timeline. Carry on, and in the Email sharing sheet (below), make sure there is a checkmark in "Share selected clips only."

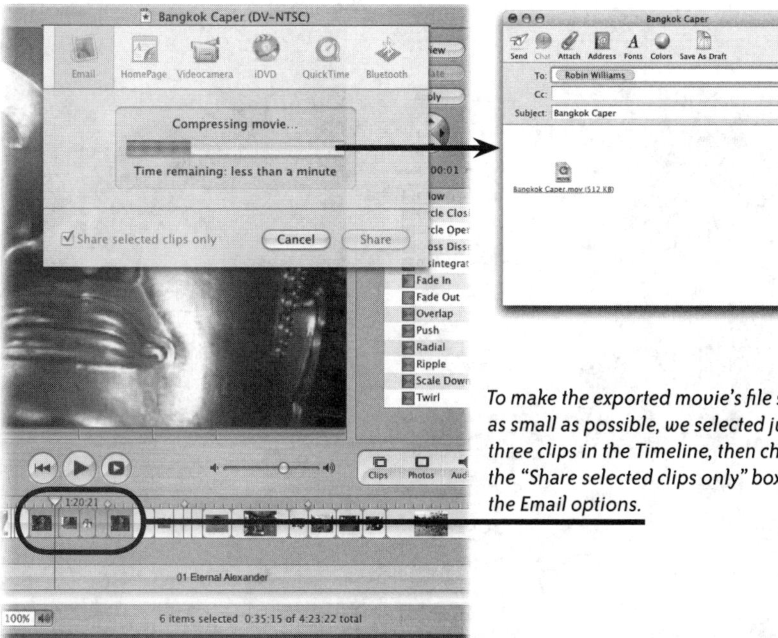

iMovie opens your email application and adds your movie as an attachment, with the movie name in the "Subject" field.

To make the exported movie's file size as small as possible, we selected just three clips in the Timeline, then checked the "Share selected clips only" box in the Email options.

HomePage option

If you have a .Mac account, you can share your movie by uploading it to your iDisk (storage space that comes with a .Mac account) and publishing it on the Internet through HomePage. See Chapter 8 to learn all the details.

iMovie automatically compresses the movie into a format necessary to play on a QuickTime Streaming Server, the type of server that's used with your .Mac account and HomePage. After compression, iMovie moves the exported movie file to the "Movie" folder on your iDisk.

1. To conserve storage space on your iDisk, you might want to export only selected clips instead of the whole movie. If so, first select several clips in the Timeline.
2. From the File menu, choose "Share...." Click "Homepage."
3. Type the name you want to use for your exported movie. Don't change the extension (.mov).
4. If your iDisk is almost full, click "Buy More Space" to log in to your .Mac account and purchase more iDisk storage space.
5. If you selected clips earlier, now click "Share selected clips only."
6. Click the "Share" button. A sheet drops down from the title bar that contains a "Compressing movie..." progress bar (left). iMovie compresses the movie, formats it to play on the web, and copies it to your iDisk on Apple's servers.

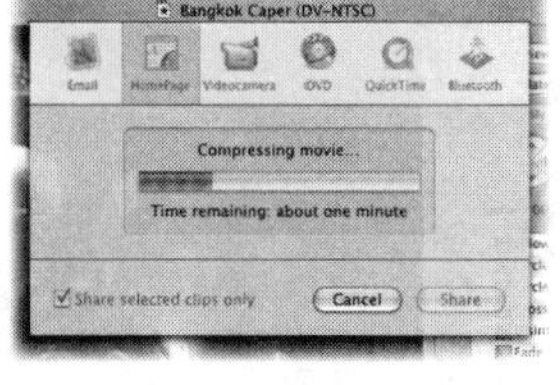

This is a description of how the file will be compressed, plus an estimate of the exported file size.

When "Share selected clips only" has a check in it, iMovie copies only the previously selected clips in the Timeline to your iDisk.

These clips are selected to share.

7. A .Mac login page opens in your web browser. Enter your member name and password, then click the "Enter" button.
8. A .Mac HomePage window opens as shown below. Choose one of the movie page themes from the templates provided to open an *editable* HomePage movie page (below-right).

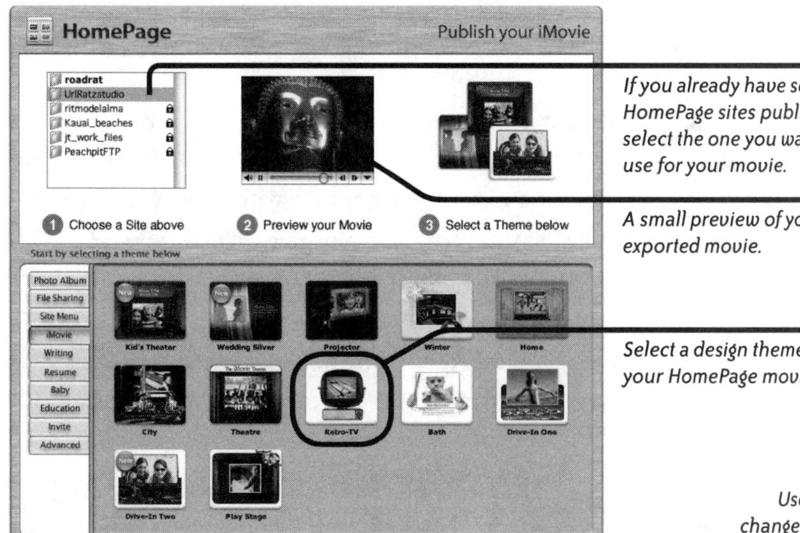

If you already have several HomePage sites published, select the one you want to use for your movie.

A small preview of your exported movie.

Select a design theme for your HomePage movie page.

Use these buttons to change themes, preview, or publish your page.

9. Edit your movie page (shown on the right) by customizing the text in the text fields.

   Click the "Preview" button to preview the page.

   To change design themes, click the "Themes" button.

   When you're satisfied with the page, click the "Publish" button.

Videocamera option

An easy way to share a movie with others is to copy the edited movie onto a tape in your video camera. You can then connect the camera to a TV and show it, or connect the camera to any computer with video editing software to show it in the preview window (it's the same as previewing raw footage). You can also connect your video camera to a VHS tape recorder and record to a VHS tape. Or you can send the tape from the camera to someone so they can play it on their own TV or computer. They can even show it on their video camera's LCD screen.

1. Put a *blank* video tape in your camera, or make sure the tape is positioned at a point where you will not record over other footage.
2. Connect the camera to your computer with a FireWire cable.
3. Put the camera in VTR mode (sometimes called VCR mode) or "Play" mode. Do not use "Record" or "Camera" mode.
4. In the iMovie File menu, choose "Share...."
5. In the "Videocamera" sheet (shown below), set how many seconds of black to record before the movie, and how many seconds of black to record after the movie.

You can choose to export only selected scenes to a video camera.

6. Click the "Share" button. If your movie contains scenes that have slow motion, fast motion, or reversed effects, iMovie will tell you that it needs to render those scenes before it can export the movie.

Your edited movie is copied to the digital video tape in your camera.

iDVD option

This sharing option opens your movie in iDVD, ready for any customization you may want to add. iDVD is Apple's amazing software for putting a collection of movies and slideshows onto a DVD that will play on your computer (if you have a supported DVD drive) and will also play on most commercial DVD players.

Sharing through iDVD opens the iDVD application and automatically creates a main DVD menu and submenus based on chapter markers that you placed in the movie. If some scenes in your movie need to be rendered because they contain an effect such as slow motion, iMovie alerts you that it needs to render those scenes before you can open the movie in iDVD.

1. Open an iMovie project.
2. From the File menu, choose "Share...."
3. Click the "iDVD" icon.
4. Click the "Share" button.
5. This opens your edited movie in iDVD. Your movie is now part of an iDVD project and is saved in your Documents folder as "your-project-name.dvdproj."

Tip: This export option immediately starts a DVD project by opening your movie in iDVD.

If you want to import your movie into a DVD project later, export the movie as "Full Quality," as explained on pages 172–173, then import the full-quality DV file into an iDVD project at some other time.

See page 165 for more information about creating a DVD project. Chapter 4 provides all the details about iDVD and how to customize your iDVD project.

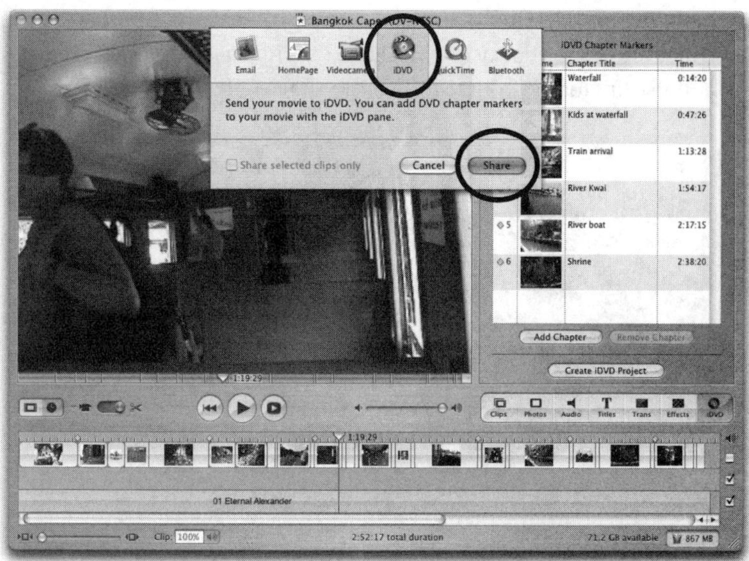

QuickTime option

QuickTime is a popular format for multimedia files. QuickTime compresses movies to make their files sizes are manageable for transport and delivery, either on the Internet or other media (such as CDs).

Email
Web
Web Streaming
✓ CD-ROM
Full Quality
Expert Settings

These are the QuickTime compression options in the pop-up menu shown below.

QuickTime provides several compression options, depending on how the movie is to be shared.

1. Open an iMovie project.
2. From the File menu, choose "Share...." Click the "iDVD" icon.
3. From the "Compress movie for" pop-up menu (circled below), select one of these compression options:

▼ **Email:** This compression option is suitable for sending a small movie to someone through email. It compresses your movie to 10 frames per second, sized to 160 x 120 pixels, with monaural sound.

If your movie is very long, even this highly compressed format will produce a file that's too large for email. A 10-second QuickTime movie with the above setting is around 200 kilobytes. To keep the movie size as small as possible, select several clips from the Timeline *before* you choose "Share..." from the File menu. Then make sure to click the "Share selected clips only" box in the drop-down sheet.

▼ **Web:** This option creates a QuickTime movie file that is 12 frames per second, 240 x 180 pixels, with medium-quality stereo sound.

▼ **Web Streaming:** Choose this compression setting to create a QuickTime file that uses the same settings as the "Web" option, but also includes "hints" to the file that enable web streaming.

Web streaming movies do not have to wait for the entire movie to download to your computer before they can play. In fact, streaming movies don't download to your computer at all. Instead, the movie starts playing after a buffer of data is received by your computer, and continues to play until the stream of data ends.

Streaming movies work on QuickTime Streaming Servers, such as the HomePage server that's included with a .Mac membership.

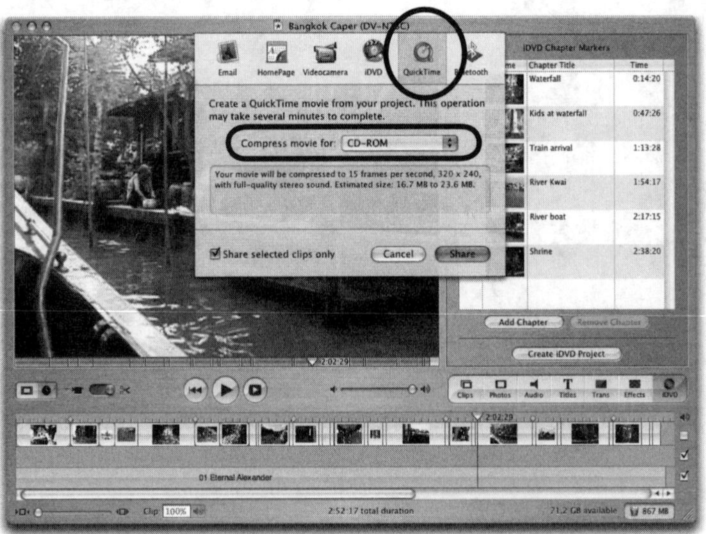

- **CD-ROM:** This option compresses your movie to half of full quality—15 frames per second, 320 x 240 pixels, and full-quality stereo sound—ideal for copying to another computer or to a CD. The final file size is approximately twice that created by "Web" or "Web Streaming" compression.
- **Full Quality:** Choose this compression option to save a QuickTime movie that is full quality—30 frames per second, 640 x 480 pixels, and full-quality stereo. The final file size is MANY times larger than the files created with the other compression schemes listed here. A *10-second* test movie file compressed as "Web" weighed in at 500 kilobytes—and 32.4 MEGAbytes when compressed as "Full Quality."
- **Expert Settings:** If you've upgraded your QuickTime software to QuickTime Pro, you can use *custom* export settings that you've set in QuickTime. QuickTime Pro enables you to edit, save, import, and export multimedia files using a large selection of file formats. You can upgrade your copy of QuickTime for $29.99 at **www.apple.com/quicktime/upgrade**.

Bangkok Caper
Audio Waveforms
Bangkok Caper
Cache
Media
Shared Movies
Email
Bangkok Caper.mov
HomePage
iDVD

When you use the Share options of "Email," "HomePage," or "iDVD," the exported file is put in a "Shared Movies" folder that iMovie creates inside the project "package."

***To open the iMovie package,** Control-click on the iMovie project icon, then choose "Show Package Contents." A Finder window opens to display the files and folders of the package.*

Bluetooth option

If you want to send a QuickTime movie to a Bluetooth-enabled device, such as a PDA or cell phone, choose this option to create a file that is low-quality but very small in file size, making it suitable to copy across the very limited bandwidth provided by Bluetooth devices. Make sure the Bluetooth device contains an application that can display movies.

1. Use Bluetooth Setup Assistant to set up your Bluetooth device.
2. Open iMovie. If you want to export only selected clips, then select those clips now.
3. From the File menu, choose "Share...." Click "Bluetooth"; see below.
4. Click the "Share" button to compress the movie. If you selected clips, check the box to "Share selected clips only."
5. In the Bluetooth Device window that opens, select a device.

Click "Share" to compress the movie and copy it to your Bluetooth device.

iMovie Preferences

Check the iMovie Preferences to see if there are any options you want to change. From the iMovie menu, choose "Preferences…."

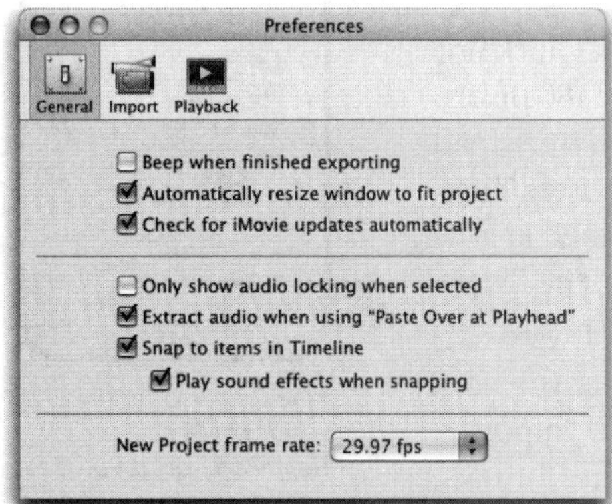

General preferences

Click "General" in the toolbar to show the General preferences pane. Click the checkbox next to items you want to select.

Beep when finished exporting: A sound alerts you that your movie has finished the export procedure.

Automatically resize window to fit project: When you create a new project (pages 136–137), you choose a video format to use. The options have different shapes and dimensions. This preference resizes iMovie's window to fit whatever format you choose (Widescreen, iSight, etc.)

Check for iMovie updates automatically: iMovie can notify you when updates are available (if you have an active Internet connection).

Only show audio locking when selected: Choose to show locked audio clips in the Timeline only when a locked audio clip is selected.

Extract audio when using "Paste Over at Playhead: This preference removes the audio in a video clip used to "paste over" an existing video clip (see page 178). To "paste over" and keep the audio with the pasted video, *uncheck* this checkbox.

Snap to items in Timeline: As you move the Playhead, Timeline snapping makes the Playhead snap to the edges of video and audio clips, chapter markers, bookmarks, silent areas in audio tracks, and the previous position of the Playhead. A yellow snap line appears under the Playhead when it snaps to an item in the Timeline. Snapping helps to precisely align audio and video.

Play sound effects when snapping: This option adds a sound effect when the Playhead snaps to an item.

New Project frame rate: Choose **29.97 fps** (frames per second) if your video camera records in the NTSC video standard (a common standard in North America and Japan). Choose **25 fps** if your video camera records in the PAL video standard (a common standard in Europe).

Import preferences

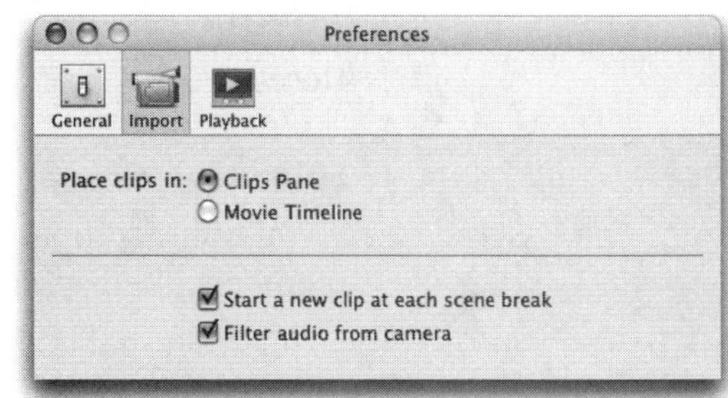

Place clips in: Choose to place new imported clips in the **Clips Pane** or directly in the **Movie Timeline.**

Start new clip at each scene break: During the import process, iMovie detects scene breaks. It automatically creates a separate clip during import for each time you started and stopped the video camera during recording. Uncheck this option if you want video from your camera to import as one continuous clip. You will still be able to click the "Import" button to stop the import at any time, manually creating a scene break.

Filter audio from camera: Filters out *some* noises that may happen during the import process. If you hear beeps or strange noises while importing video, make sure this option is selected.

Playback preferences

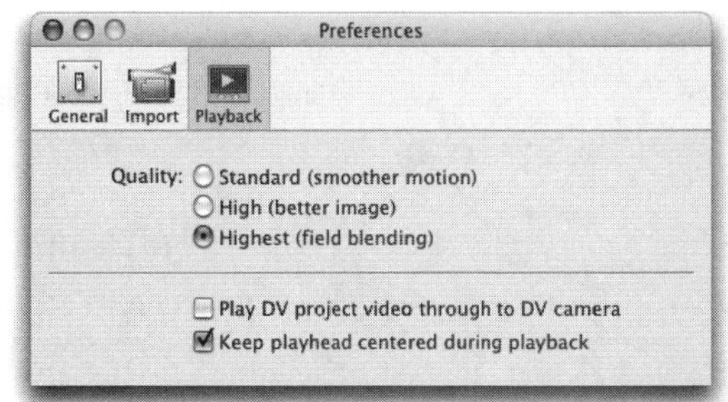

Quality: These three quality setting options affect only the computer playback quality, *not* the quality of the final exported movie.

Standard (smoother motion) is the default setting for Macs with a G3 processor, which is slower than a G4 or G5 processor.

High (better image) displays a better image on your Mac's screen if your Mac has a G4 or G5 processor.

Highest (field blending) shows the best image possible for Macs with a G4 or G5 processor. No matter what kind of processor you have, if playback is jumpy or uneven, try a lower quality setting.

Play DV project video through to DV camera: Allows you to play a movie simultaneously in iMovie *and* in your camera. Connect your camera to a TV monitor to see how your movie will look on a TV as compared to your computer screen.

Keep Playhead centered during playback: This option is meant to keep the Playhead stationary and centered in the Timeline during playback. This keeps the Playhead visible at all times as movie clips scroll by. This option requires a fast processor and is disabled unless you have a G5.

Advanced Tips

Here are a few more fun tips to make your movies even more professional.

Split video clips at the Playhead position

If you want to apply an effect to just part of a video clip, *split* the video into segments, then apply the effect to one of the segments.

Position the Playhead at the point where you want to split a clip.

The split clip.

1. Position the Playhead over a video clip where you want to start the effect (top-left), then from the Edit menu choose "Split Video Clip at Playhead." **Or** use the keyboard shortcut Command T. A vertical dividing line appears on the clip under the Playhead.

   To split the clip into more than two parts, move the Playhead to another position in the clip, then press Command T again. Another vertical line appears in this position, dividing the clip into three segments.

   Do this as many times as you want.
2. Select the clip segment to which you want to add an effect, then choose an effect from the Effects pane.

You can create some interesting visual effects by splitting video clips into multiple segments, then adding transitions between the segments.

Create a still frame

You can make a still frame (a static image) from any single frame of video in your movie. You might use the still frame as a title background for visual effect or to simulate a slideshow effect. One of our favorite techniques is to create a still frame of the last frame of a clip, then place the still frame after the clip, creating a freeze frame effect for the end of the clip. You can set the duration of the still frame to whatever length you want.

1. Select a clip in the Clips Pane or in the Timeline.
2. Position the Playhead so the frame you want is showing in the Monitor.
3. From the Edit menu, choose "Create Still Frame."
   The still image is placed in the Clips Pane.
4. Drag the new still frame to a position in the Timeline.

When you drag the edge of a clip, watch the bottom of the window to see the clip's duration change.

The default duration for a still frame is five seconds. **To change the duration,** double-click the still frame clip. In the "Clip Info" window that opens, type in a new duration. **Or** drag an edge of the clip in either direction to increase or decrease the clip duration.

Save a single frame in another format

Occasionally you'll find that you need a copy of a single frame that you can email to someone or use as a photo in any number of ways.

1. Select a clip in the Clips Pane or in the Timeline.
2. Position the Playhead so the frame you want is showing in the Monitor.
3. From the File menu, choose "Save Frame…."
4. In the Finder sheet that drops down from iMovie's title bar, name the file, select a file format from the pop-up menu (JPEG or PICT), and choose a location in which to save the file.
5. Click "Save."

Reverse a clip's direction

To reverse a clip's direction, select the clip, then from the Effects pane choose the "Fast/Slow/Reverse" Effect. Click the "Reverse Direction" checkbox in the Effects pane, then click "Apply."

Create a color clip

Create color clips to use as transitions between scenes, as backgrounds for titles or captions, as artistic elements, or to replace black color spaces between two clips.

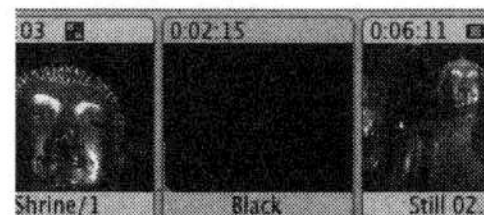

A color clip in Clip View.

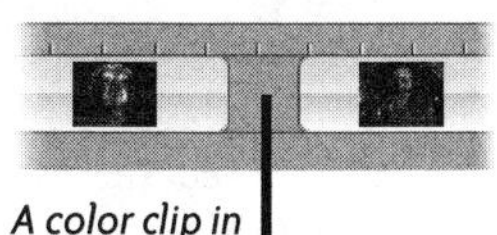

A color clip in Timeline View.

When there's an *existing* blank space between two clips in the Timeline, iMovie creates a black color clip to fill the space. This clip is visible in Clip View mode. **To replace the black with another color,** double-click the black color clip to open the "Clip Info" window, click the Color box to choose another color, then click "Set."

To create a *new* color clip: In the Timeline, drag two clips apart to create a blank space between them. iMovie automatically creates a color clip to fill the space. But the color clips are not visible in Timeline View—switch to Clip View to see and modify them.

You can use color clips as placeholders in the Timeline until you get the video footage you want for a particular scene. For instance, if you're making a music video, you may have an idea for one section of music that's 15 seconds long. Place a 15-second color clip in the spot where you need video, then edit the rest of the movie. After you've had time to record the missing scene, paste the new video in place of the color clip. This prevents clips from moving around and getting out of sync with your music soundtrack.

When you use color clips for a transition, add a "Cross Dissolve" or a "Fade In" and "Fade Out" transition to either side of the color clip to soften it.

Extract audio in paste over

You may eventually be in an editing situation where you want to **replace existing video** in the Timeline, but **keep the audio** of the original clip. For example, the original video clip may have narration you want to use, but you want to replace the video with new shots of whatever the narrator is talking about. You can replace the original video but retain its audio with a "paste over."

1. Make sure that "Extract audio when using 'Paste Over at Playhead'" is selected in iMovie's Preferences (page 174).
2. Select a video clip *you want to insert.* Use the crop markers under the Monitor to select the specific video frames that you want to paste, then press Command C to copy the selection.
3. Position the Playhead at the first frame of video *to be replaced.* If you're replacing just part of an existing video clip, use the crop markers to select the specific frames to be replaced.
4. From the Advanced menu, choose "Paste Over at Playhead." The audio of the *pasted* video is muted (set to zero), and the *original clip's audio* is placed in audio track 1, below the pasted video.

To do a Paste Over of a replacement video clip *including* the audio, *uncheck* "Extract audio when using 'Paste Over at Playhead'" in iMovie's Preferences.

The pasted video clip with its audio muted (the volume line is moved to the bottom of the clip) replaces the original video clip.

The original clip's audio is extracted and placed in audio track 1.

Music in audio track 2.

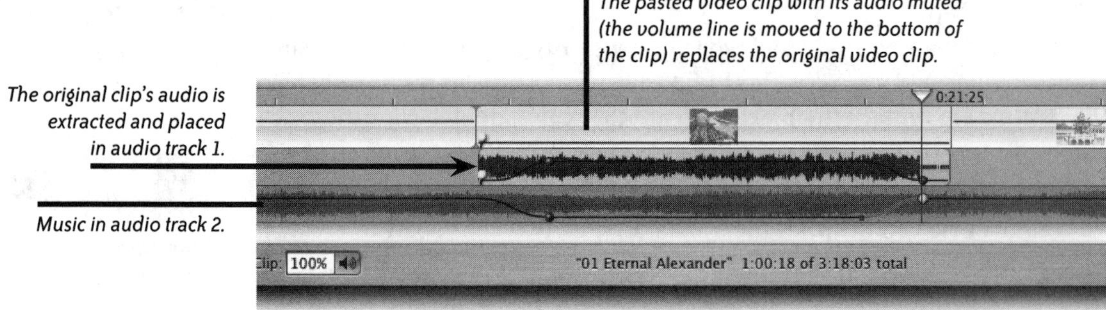

The volume of each audio track can be adjusted so the narration in track 1 fades in as the music in track 2 fades out. See pages 162–163 for more audio-editing information.

- The newly pasted video replaces an equal amount of existing video.
- Any excess video longer than the selected frame range of existing video is not pasted.
- If the pasted video is shorter than the selected frame range of video to replace, the additional frames are filled with a color clip (see the previous page).
- Pasted-over still images expand to fill the selected frame range.

Lock an audio clip to a video clip

You may have an audio clip in one of the audio tracks that you want to start playing at a certain point in a video clip. But you want to experiment by moving the video clip around in the Timeline. You can lock the audio clip to the video clip so they move together.

1. Place the Playhead at the point in a movie where you want the audio to start playing.
2. Place an audio clip in the Timeline so that it lines up with the Playhead.
3. With the audio clip selected, from the Advanced menu, choose "Lock Audio Clip at Playhead."

To unlock the clip, first select it. Then from the Advanced menu, choose "Unlock Audio Clip."

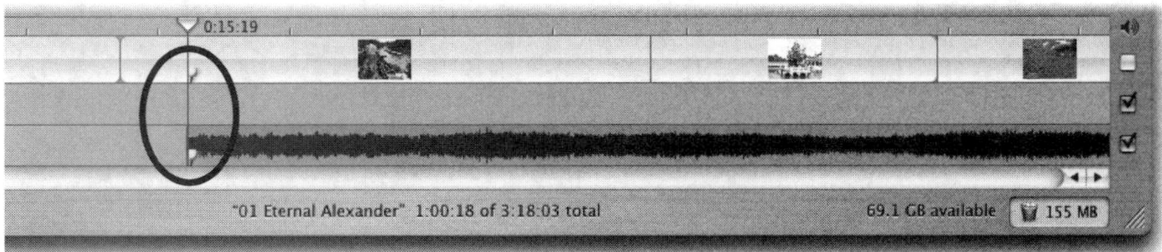

Yellow pins in the audio and video clips indicate the point at which the two clips are locked together. When you drag one of the clips, the other one will move with it.

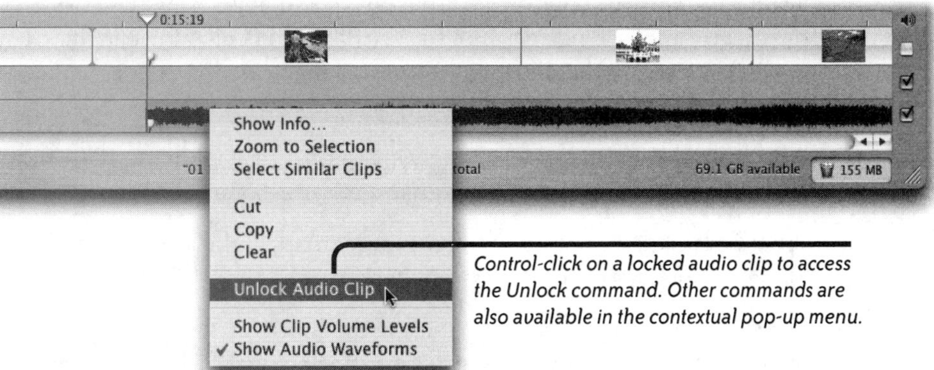

Control-click on a locked audio clip to access the Unlock command. Other commands are also available in the contextual pop-up menu.

Use contextual menus to choose commands

Many of iMovie's menu commands are available through pop-up contextual menus, as shown above. Control-click on clips in the Clips Pane, on clips or transitions in the Timeline, on audio clips, on the Monitor, or on a blank spot in the Timeline to see what commands are available at your finger tips.

Extract audio from a clip

To extract audio from a clip, select one or more video clips in the Timeline, then go to the Advanced menu and choose "Extract Audio." The extracted audio file is placed in the Timeline below the corresponding video clip. Yellow pins are automatically placed in the audio and video clips (on the left edges) to lock the extracted audio in sync with the video.

To restore audio to a clip, select the clip and change the Clip volume level (circled, below-right) to 100%.

Audio is actually still in the video clip, but muted. The audio level (a black line) in the video clip is at the bottom of the clip, which means it is set to zero (muted).

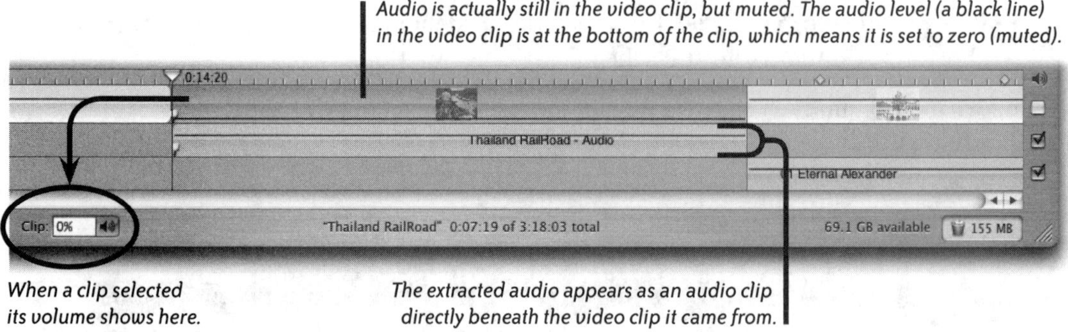

When a clip selected its volume shows here.

The extracted audio appears as an audio clip directly beneath the video clip it came from.

Use bookmarks to mark important frames

It's often helpful to mark a certain point in the Timeline so you can find it again later. Perhaps your movie contains a clip that you want to work on later, or you've found the perfect spot to add a sound effect. iMovie includes markers called **bookmarks** that you can use to mark a precise point in an audio or video clip.

Bookmarks appear in the Scrubber Bar of the Timeline as green diamonds.

Position the Playhead where you want to place a bookmark, then from the Markers menu choose "Add Bookmark." **Or** use Command B.

Press Command J to jump to the next bookmark in the Timeline. **Or** from the Markers menu, choose "Next Bookmark."

Press Command [to jump to the previous bookmark in the Timeline. **Or** from the Markers menu, choose "Previous Bookmark."

To remove a bookmark, place the Playhead on top of it. From the Markers menu, choose "Delete Bookmark."

To remove all bookmarks in the Timeline, go to the Markers menu and choose "Delete All Bookmarks…."

Bookmarks stay where you put them in the Timeline, even when you move clips or change their durations.

Make a Magic iMovie

If you want to make a movie quickly, without fussing over finely tuned editing, you can let iMovie compose the movie for you. You specify the title, transitions between scenes, and a music soundtrack. iMovie does the rest—imports the video and creates the movie. You can even choose to automatically send the finished movie to iDVD where you can create a custom designed DVD that will play on any DVD-enabled computer or almost any consumer DVD player.

1. Connect a video camera to your computer with a FireWire cable. Set the camera to "Play" (some cameras call this setting VCR or VTR).
2. Open iMovie and click "Make a Magic iMovie" in the project selection window (shown below-left). If iMovie is already open, from the File menu, choose "Make a Magic Movie…."

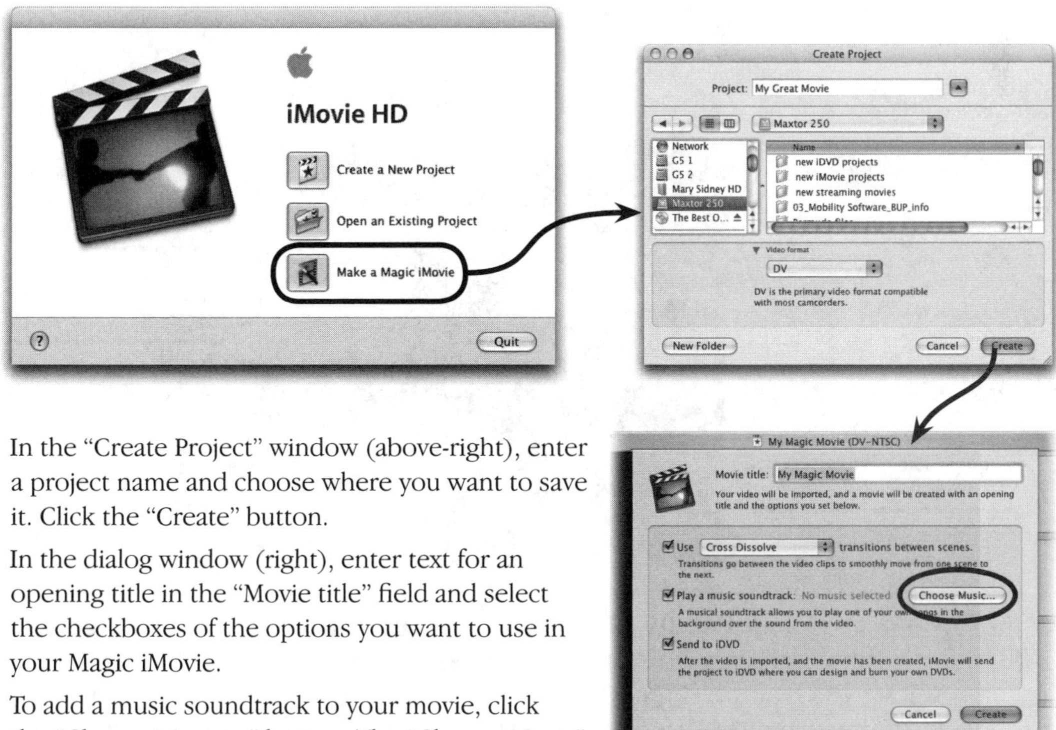

3. In the "Create Project" window (above-right), enter a project name and choose where you want to save it. Click the "Create" button.
4. In the dialog window (right), enter text for an opening title in the "Movie title" field and select the checkboxes of the options you want to use in your Magic iMovie.
5. To add a music soundtrack to your movie, click the "Choose Music…" button. The "Choose Music" window opens, shown on the following page.

—*continued*

6. Drag songs you want to add to your movie to the right side of the "Choose Music" window, set the volume, then click OK.

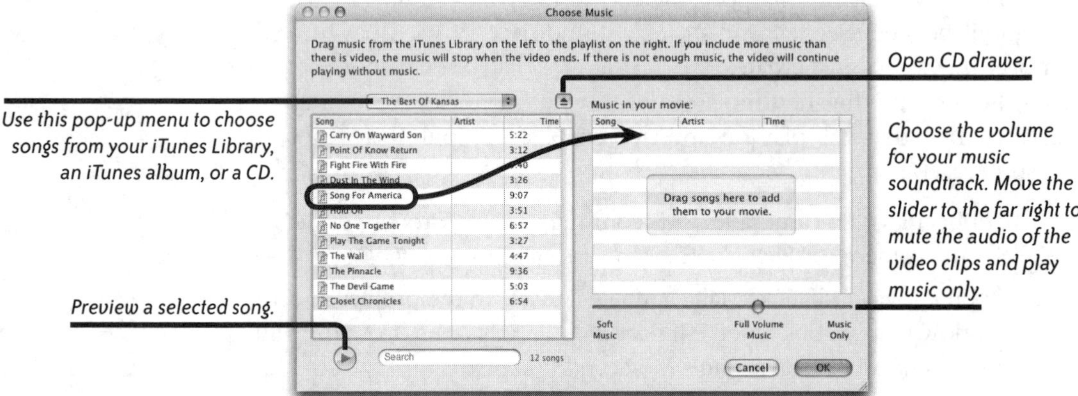

Music Only

Preview a selected song.
Open CD drawer.
Choose the volume for your music soundtrack. Move the slider to the far right to mute the audio of the video clips and play music only.

7. Click "Create." iMovie begins the process of importing video from the camera and adding transitions or music if you specified them.

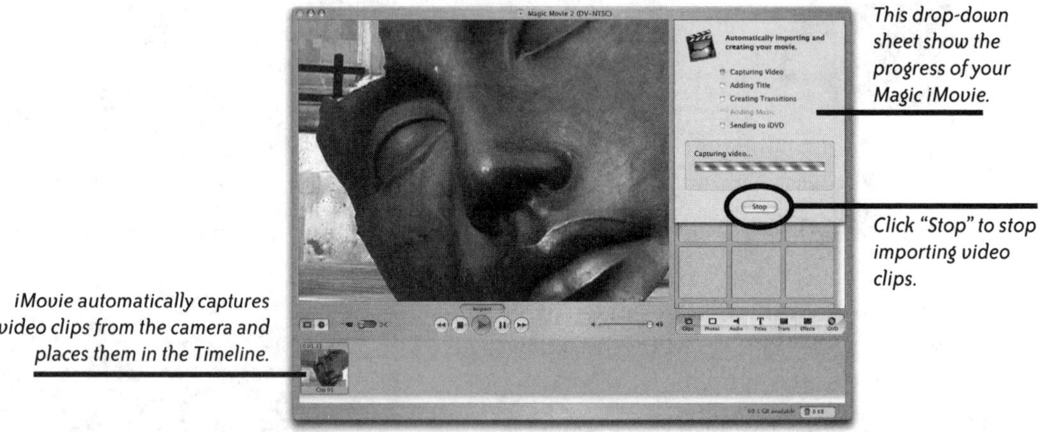

This drop-down sheet show the progress of your Magic iMovie.
Click "Stop" to stop importing video clips.
iMovie automatically captures video clips from the camera and places them in the Timeline.

Important HD information: Even though iMovie can edit HD (High Definition) movies, current DVD specifications do not support HD content, which means you can't burn an HD movie to a regular DVD. However, two new and competing DVD technologies will be available very soon—Blue-ray Disc (also known as BD) and HD-DVD (High Definition/High Density DVD). These new DVDs not only support HD video, they hold much more data (approximately 25 gigabytes for a single-layer Blue-ray Disc). Of course, this means you'll also need a new DVD player to play Blue-ray or HD-DVDs. Fortunately, the new Blue-ray/HD-DVD players will probably be designed to play both traditional and second-generation DVDs.

4

iDVD doesn't help you *edit* a movie—it *assembles* finished movies into a beautiful presentation that lets you choose which movie to play. An iDVD project can contain multiple movies and slideshows. If you used iMovie's feature of setting chapter markers to identify scenes in your movie, you can create DVD "menus" with links that let you jump straight to those scenes. Even if your original movie doesn't include chapter markers, iDVD can create some to enable navigation to specific parts of a movie.

iDVD can also create slideshows from still photos. Because iDVD is closely integrated with other iLife applications, it's easy to access iMovie, iPhoto, or iTunes from within iDVD to add movies, photos, and music for slideshows.

The same disc that plays your movies and slideshows can also deliver any other content to anyone's computer: PDF files, applications, high-resolution photos, archived files, websites, and almost anything else you want to make accessible on the disc. Since DVDs are not platform-specific, they work on any Mac or PC that has a DVD drive.

FYI: In the world of DVD design and authoring, the term "menu" refers to the DVD interface in which users click on links to play specific movies, movie scenes, and slideshows, or to show submenus that offer more content.

This chapter contains a lot of information about iDVD, but it's really as simple as this:

1. Select a menu theme.
2. Drag media files to the menu.
3. Customize your menu design.
4. Burn a disc.

What Do You Need to Make DVDs?

If your Mac has a SuperDrive (a drive that reads and writes DVDs), you can use the iDVD software to create and burn professional-looking DVDs that will play on almost any current DVD player or on any computer that can play DVDs.

Supported disc formats

You need blank discs on which to burn your project. iDVD prefers a type of "general media" disc called **DVD-R** (pronounced *DVD dash R*). iDVD is also compatible with other disc media formats:

DVD+R (*DVD plus R*) is a similar, but competing format.

DVD-RW (*DVD dash RW*) and **DVD+RW** (*DVD plus RW*), which are rewritable media.

Note: All SuperDrives (Apple's internal DVD burner) support **DVD-R** media, but older SuperDrives may not support the other media types.

You can find low prices on the Internet for large-quantity bundles of discs. One of our frequent shopping sites for DVDs (and mini DV tapes for our digital video camera) is www.TapeAndMedia.com.

iDVD allows a total of 99 movies and slideshows (in any combination) on a single DVD disc. Of course, the length of your movies, the number of images in your slideshows, and how much DVD-ROM content you want to include on the disc will affect exactly how many movies and slideshows will actually fit on your DVD.

A DVD disc officially claims to hold 4.7 GB (gigabytes) of data. But due to various factors ranging from marketing hype to variances in techniques for translating bits to gigabytes, you really have approximately 4.3 GB of space to work with, or about 90 minutes of video (including video used in motion menus). That's still a lot of data storage, especially compared to the 650–700 MB (megabytes) of storage space you get on a CD.

If you don't have a SuperDrive

Even if you don't have a SuperDrive, you can still *create,* customize, and preview an iDVD project on your Mac. But you must have a SuperDrive to burn an iDVD project to a disc. You *cannot* burn iDVD projects using a third-party, external DVD burner. You *can* build an iDVD project on a Mac that doesn't have a SuperDrive, then *archive* the project, take it to a Mac that *does* have a SuperDrive, and burn it to a DVD on that Mac. See page 216 to learn about archiving iDVD projects.

What iDVD does not do

You do not use iDVD to *create* content, but to *organize and present* content that you've already created in another application. Before you create an iDVD project, you need to have some content available, such as iMovies, QuickTime movies, or still photos with which to create a slideshow.

Make a OneStep DVD

With iDVD, you can create visually stunning, technically sophisticated DVD menus for your movies. You might spend a lot of time exploring all the design options and fine-tuning your project.

But there are times when speed is much more important than creativity. You may simply need to create a video record of an event, or perhaps a client wants to see the unedited video you shot. Or you may want to quickly create a back-up copy of important video footage. If your Mac has a SuperDrive, iDVD's **OneStep DVD** feature grabs the video in your camera and automatically creates a DVD disc that's set to *autoplay*—when the disc is inserted in a DVD player (or a computer with a DVD drive), it automatically starts playing—no menu system necessary. When playing the disc you can pause, rewind, or fast forward the video as you can with any DVD.

iDVD automatically captures video until the tape ends, **or** until after 10 seconds of no video, **or** until you click "Cancel" (circled below-right). When you click the "Cancel" button a dialog appears so you can choose to cancel the entire process or stop only the capture of additional video and contine the OneStep DVD process with the video that's already been captured.

1. Connect a video camera to your Mac using a FireWire cable.
2. Turn the camera on and set it to VTR mode (some cameras call this mode VCR or Play).
3. Load the camera with a tape you want to capture and burn to disc.
4. From the File menu in iDVD, choose "OneStep DVD." A drop-down sheet prompts you to insert a recordable DVD media (a blank disc) into the computer.
5. After you insert a blank DVD disc, a drop-down sheet appears that shows the progress during each step of creating the OneStep DVD.
6. When the last stage, "Burn, is complete, the disc ejects and a dialog appears "(shown below) that asks if you want to create another DVD.

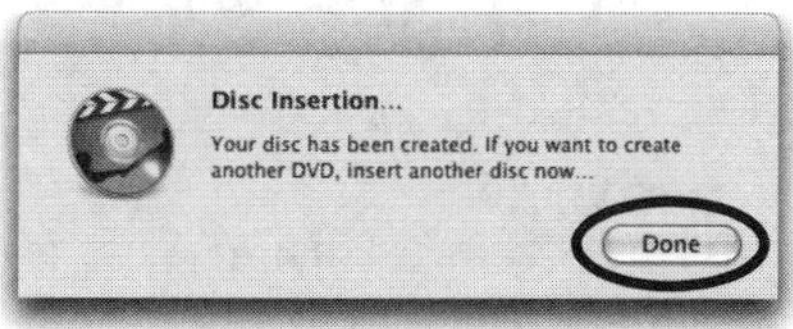

Start by Selecting a Theme

Tip: If you don't have any movie content yet, follow the tutorial that came with iDVD and use the content included in the iDVD "Tutorial" folder.

DVDs use *menus,* as explained on page 183, to provide navigation to the content on the disc. iDVD provides various **menu themes** for you to choose from. Many of them are in motion and arthus called *motion menus.* If you have a lot of content to squeeze onto a disc, you can economize disc space by using static menus instead of motion menus.

A single iDVD menu can contain a maximum of 12 "buttons" (also called "links") which connect to movies, slideshows, or to other menus. The other menus can also contain up to 12 buttons each. So a single iDVD project can contain a maximum of 99 menus.

iDVD

To open iDVD, double-click the iDVD icon in your Applications folder. **Or** single-click the iDVD icon in the Dock, if it's there.

To select a theme:

1. Open idvd. From the File menu, choose "New...."
2. In the Save As dialog box that appears, name your project. Choose the location in which you want to save it.
3. Click the "Customize" button in the bottom-left corner of the idvd window to open the Customize drawer, shown below-left.
4. Click the "Themes" button at the top of the drawer to display the possible options.
5. Choose a menu design style from the scrolling list of thumbnails.

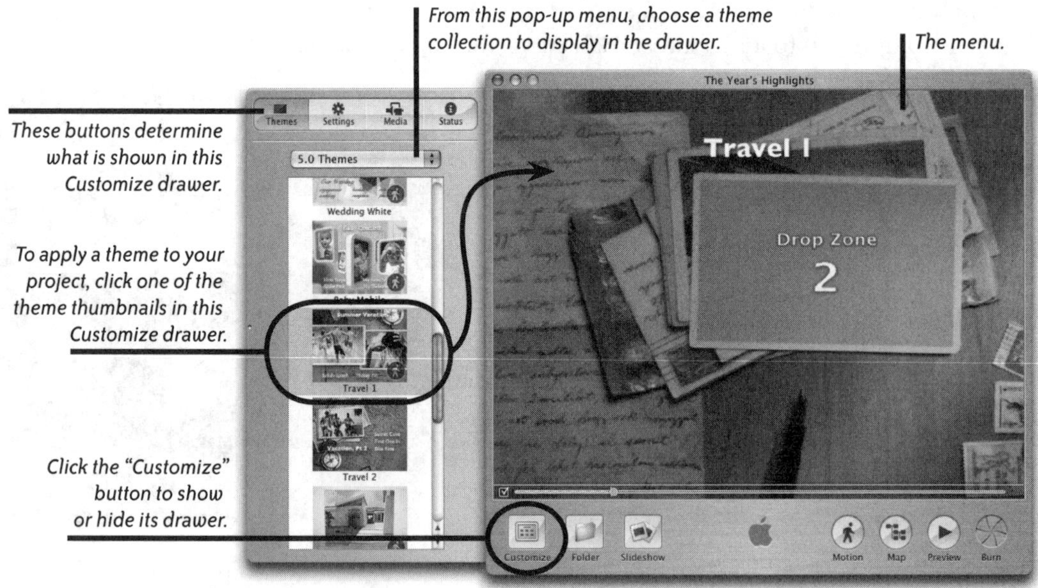
From this pop-up menu, choose a theme collection to display in the drawer.
The menu.
These buttons determine what is shown in this Customize drawer.
To apply a theme to your project, click one of the theme thumbnails in this Customize drawer.
Click the "Customize" button to show or hide its drawer.
The Year's Highlights
Themes
Settings
Media
Status
5.0 Themes
Wedding White
Travel 1
Travel 2
Travel I
Drop Zone
2
Customize
Folder
Slideshow
Motion
Map
Preview
Burn

Drop zones

Some menu themes contain **drop zones** into which you can *drag and drop* a movie, a single photo, or a folder of photos. Drop zones do not link to anything—they're just for visual effect and to make your menu more exciting and sophisticated.

If you click the "Media" button at the top of the Customize drawer, as shown below, you have access to all the photos, movies, and music on your Mac (see pages 198–200 for details). **To place a photo or movie in a drop zone,** drag a photo or movie from the Media pane (or from any Finder window) to a drop zone. A folder of photos plays as a slideshow in a drop zone.

To customize the background of a menu and retain the drop zone, Option-drag a movie, a photo, or a folder of photos on top of the *background* (*not* into the drop zone). A blue highlight appears around the window to indicate you are replacing the existing *background* image. The drop zone remains as part of the menu design.

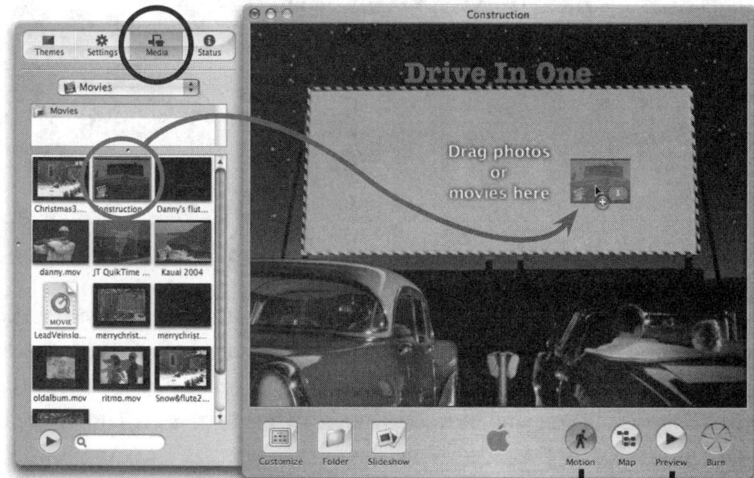

As you drag a movie to a drop zone, the drop zone highlights with a striped border.

You can turn menu motion on or off with the "Motion" button. Turn it off while editing your DVD to make iDVD more efficient, and turn it on when you're ready to preview your project or burn the final DVD.

Click this button to preview your project at any time.

To remove an item from a drop zone, just drag the item *out* of the drop zone. When the pointer turns into a little puff of smoke, let go and watch it disappear in a big puff of smoke.

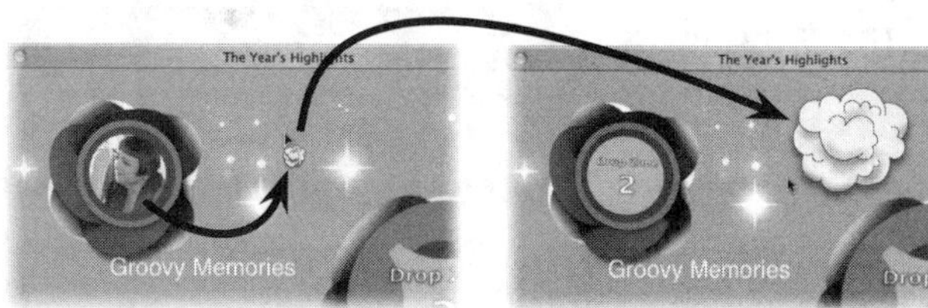

Dynamic drop zones

iDVD's collection "5.0 Themes" in the themes pop-up menu includes motion menus that contain *dynamic* drop zones—drop zones that are animated and move across the screen, adding even more visual dazzle to your menu. Menu themes with dynamic drop zones usually have *multiple drop zones* in the same menu that move into view. The theme shown here has five drop zones. You can drag a different movie or photo into each drop zone of a menu (see the following page).

A small "walking man" icon in the lower-right corner of a thumbnail indicates that theme contains motion.

It's easier to work with motion menus if the **Motion Playhead** and **Scrubber Bar** are visible. If you don't see them, go to the Advanced menu and choose "Enable Motion Playhead." Click the "Motion" button to see the menu play. The Playhead moves along the Scrubber Bar which is actually a **Timeline** like you've seen in iMovie. You can grab the Playhead and drag it to any position in the Scrubber Bar, enabling you to easily work with different drop zones.

The intro segment of a motion menu plays only one time, then continues to the looping segment which repeats over and over.

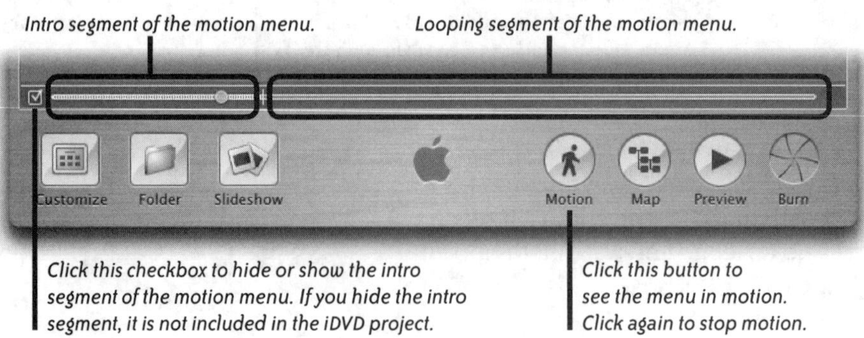

Intro segment of the motion menu.
Looping segment of the motion menu.
Customize
Folder
Slideshow
Motion
Map
Preview
Burn
Click this checkbox to hide or show the intro segment of the motion menu. If you hide the intro segment, it is not included in the iDVD project.
Click this button to see the menu in motion. Click again to stop motion.

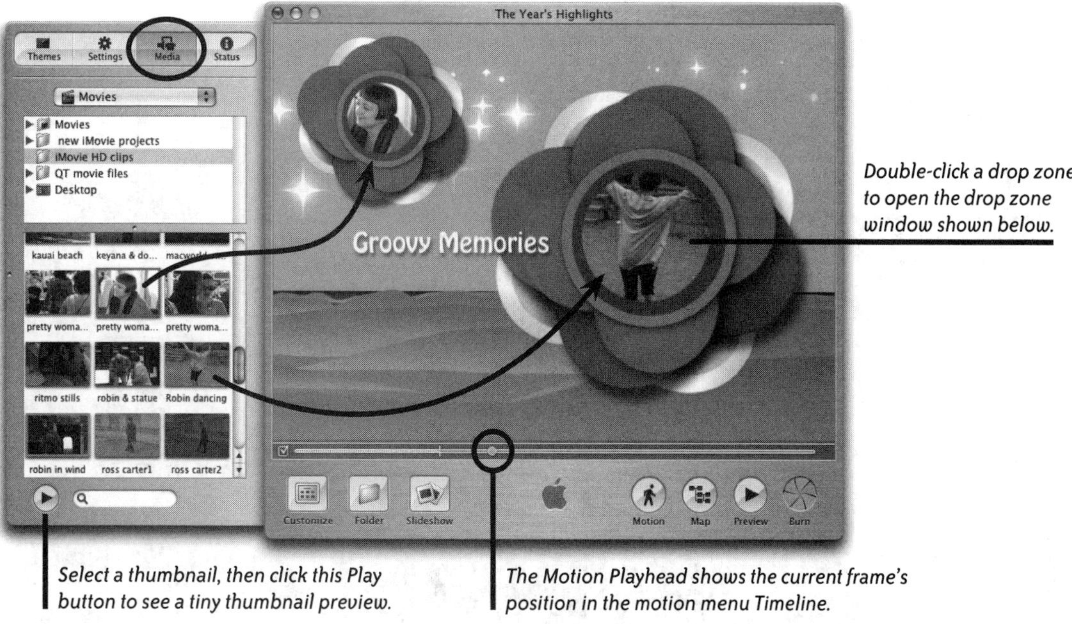

Double-click a drop zone to open the drop zone window shown below.

Select a thumbnail, then click this Play button to see a tiny thumbnail preview.

The Motion Playhead shows the current frame's position in the motion menu Timeline.

You can drop items into drop zones while the menu plays and drop zones move across the menu, but it's easier if you click the "Motion" button to stop the motion. Drag the Playhead to a position that shows the drop zone you want to work with, then drag an item into it.

Or *double-click a drop zone* to open the window shown below. All of the menu's drop zones are shown here and you can drag items to each zone.

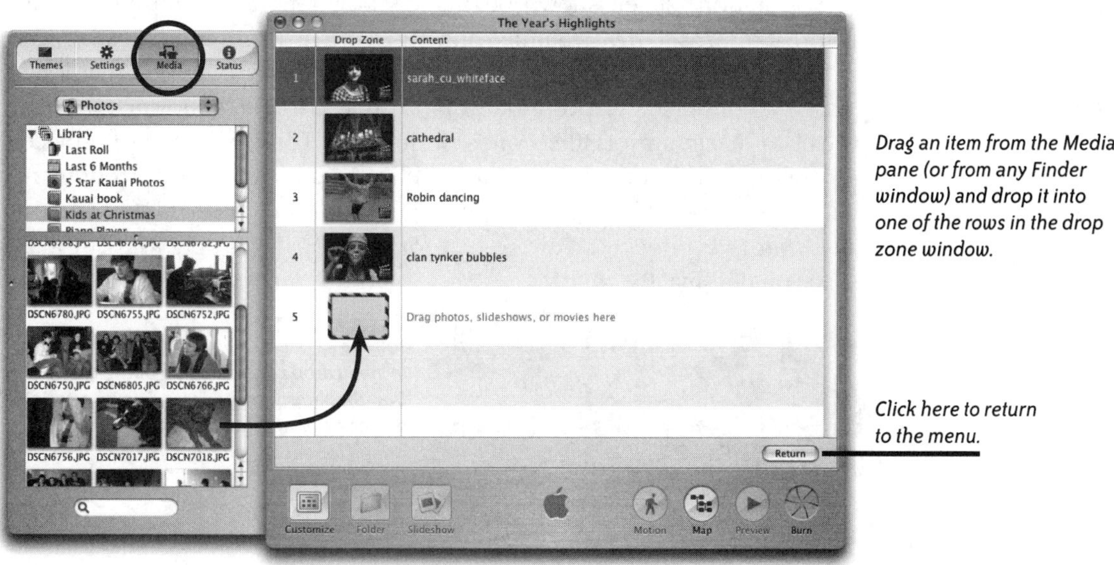

Drag an item from the Media pane (or from any Finder window) and drop it into one of the rows in the drop zone window.

Click here to return to the menu.

The Settings Pane of the Customize Drawer

You can adjust many settings of your iDVD menu. If the slide-out Customize drawer shown below isn't visible, click the "Customize" button to open it, then click the "Settings" button at the top of the drawer.

Click here to show Settings in the Customize drawer.

***Text buttons** that link to movies or slideshows are automatically created when you drag movie files or folders of photos onto the menu background. See page 194.*

Duration setting

The "Duration" slider, shown below, sets how long a motion menu plays before it returns to the beginning and repeats, a process called *looping.* The maximum loop duration allowed is 15 minutes (if your media is that long). Most DVD designers create motion loops that are much shorter than that, usually a maximum of 30 seconds in duration. Longer loops are unnecessary because most people will make a selection and leave the current menu before a 30-second loop starts repeating. If you hope to get a lot of content into your DVD project, be aware that *longer* loops take up a *lot* of storage space on the final DVD.

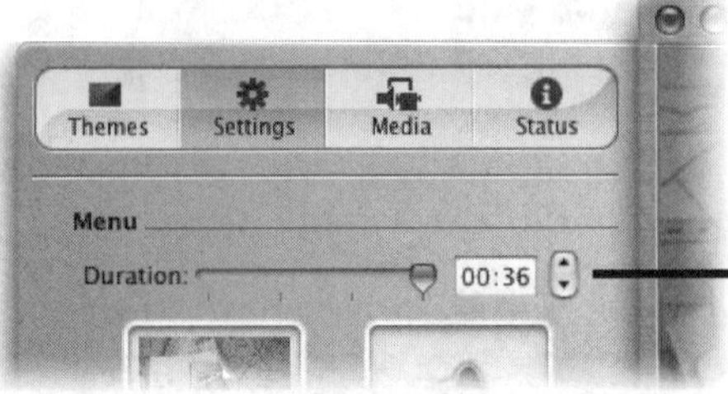

You can set the duration of movies that are in menu drop zones or menu backgrounds. Drag the slider, use the up and down arrows, or type a duration value in the text field using a format of 00:00 (minutes:seconds).

Background and audio settings

There are a couple of ways to **customize a menu background.** You can drag a photo or a movie into the "Background" well (shown to the right), **or** you can drag a photo or movie into the background area of the existing menu.

When you drag a movie file or photo into the "Background" well, any drop zone that may have been included in the selected theme is *removed.* If you want to *keep* the drop zone as part of the menu design, *Option*-drag the movie you want to use as a menu *background* to the menu area, but *not* into the drop zone area. The drop zone remains and you can drag another movie into it. iDVD composites the two movies into one amazing menu.

Some themes include a soundtrack. **To change a menu's soundtrack,** drag an audio file into the "Audio" well (shown above-right).

In the example below we selected a wedding theme from "4.0 Themes" on the Themes pane. We *Option*-dragged a movie ("pool cleaner.mov") to the menu background to preserve the drop zone area. Then we dragged another movie ("bug.mov") to the drop zone (the area with a striped border). We changed the menu's default title ("Wedding Silver One") to "Costa Rica." Finally, we dragged three movies to the menu background to automatically create text buttons that link to the three movies ("Jungles," "Monkeys," and "Resorts"). The following page explains how to customize text buttons.

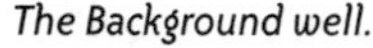

The Background well.

The Audio well.

***To mute** a menu soundtrack, click the tiny speaker icon in the bottom-right corner of the Audio well.*

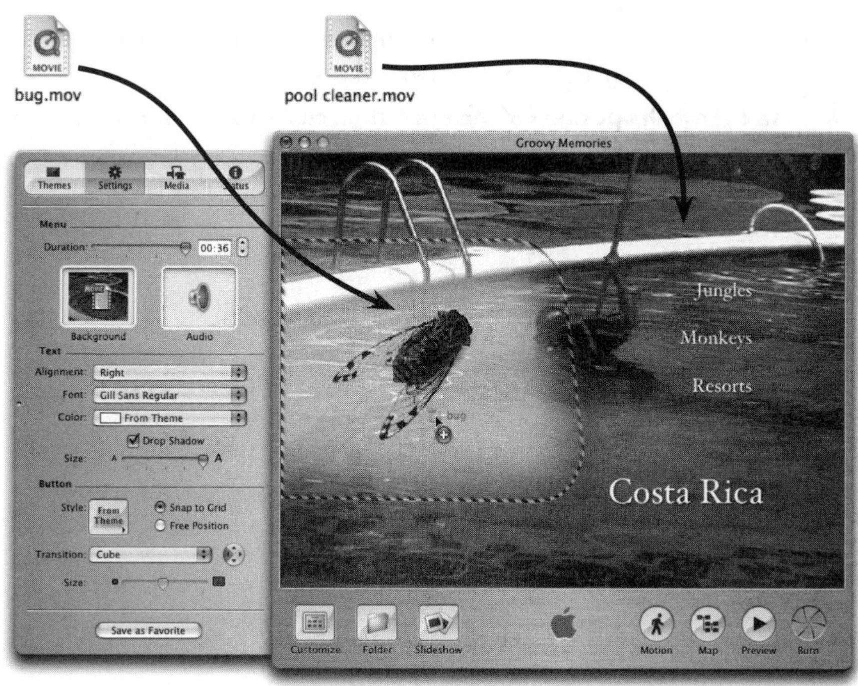

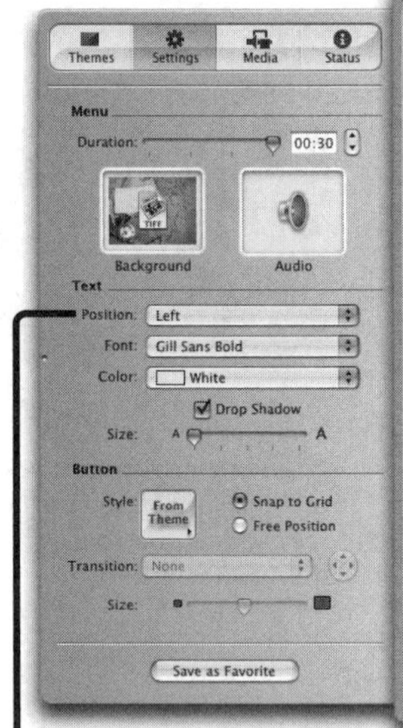

*When a **title** or **picture button** is selected, this menu becomes the "Position" menu.*

Title and Button settings

See page 194 for details about how to create buttons. Every theme includes placeholder text for a title.

To customize the title text, double-click the existing placeholder text to select it, then type a new title. **To remove the title,** choose "No Title" from the "Position" pop-up menu.

To change the title position, select the title, then choose an alignment option from the "Position" pop-up menu. **To position a title anywhere,** select the title, choose "Custom" from the "Position" pop-up menu, then drag the title anywhere in the menu.

Edit text buttons

To rename a button, single-click on the existing text, then type.

To change the size of text buttons, select a button, then drag the "Size" slider.

To change the alignment of text buttons, select a button. Click "Snap to Grid" in the "Button" section. Choose an option from the "Alignment" pop-up menu (Left, Center, or Right).

To delete a text button, select the button, then go to the Edit menu and choose "Delete."

*When a **text button** is selected, this menu becomes the "Alignment" menu.*

Edit picture buttons

To change the position of picture buttons, click "Free Position" in the "Button" section, then drag the button to any position.

To change the position of picture button captions *in relation to a button's picture,* select a button, then from the "Position" pop-up menu select one of the options.

To remove picture button captions, choose "No Text" from the "Position" pop-up menu.

To change the size of picture buttons, select a button, then drag the "Size" slider in the "Button" section.

To apply a transition to a button, select the button in the menu, then choose a transition from the "Transition" pop-up menu. See the next page for more information about transitions.

To delete a picture button, select the button, then go to the Edit menu and choose "Delete" or hit the Delete key.

Text or picure buttons: To change a button font or color, select a button. Choose a typeface from the "Font" pop-up menu. Choose a font color from the "Color" pop-up menu.

Transition settings

When you watch a DVD and click a menu button, the visual on the screen usually jumps abruptly to a movie, a slideshow, or to another menu. The "Transition" pop-up menu lets you select a transition effect to soften the jump or make it more visually interesting. Transitions can also add a touch of professional sophistication to your project.

1. Click on a menu item to select it.
2. Select a transition style from the "Transition" pop-up menu. (The menu is dim until you add buttons that link to other content.)
3. Choose a *direction* for the transition if it is directional, such as the "Cube" transition chosen below. Click one of the arrow quadrants on the direction control next to the pop-up menu.

You can apply a different transition to each button in a menu.

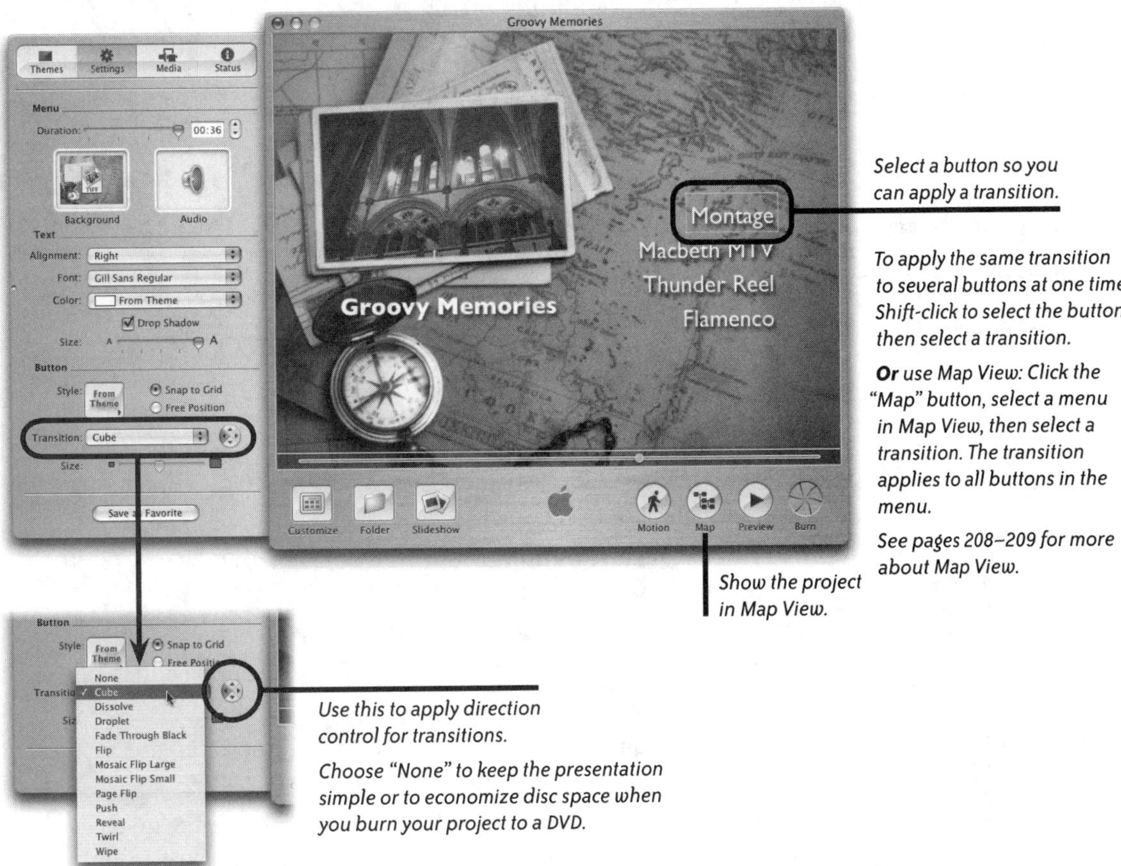

Select a button so you can apply a transition.

To apply the same transition to several buttons at one time, Shift-click to select the buttons, then select a transition.

***Or** use Map View: Click the "Map" button, select a menu in Map View, then select a transition. The transition applies to all buttons in the menu.*

See pages 208–209 for more about Map View.

Show the project in Map View.

Use this to apply direction control for transitions.

Choose "None" to keep the presentation simple or to economize disc space when you burn your project to a DVD.

How to create buttons

To create a button that links to a movie or slideshow, drag a movie file or a folder of photos from the Media pane of the Customize drawer (or from any Finder window) to the iDVD menu.

When you drag movie files (or a folder of photos) to the menu, iDVD automatically creates **text buttons** that link to the corresponding file or folder. The button names are the same as the file or folder in which they were created. You can change button names after you've added them to the menu.

*This menu is the same as shown on the previous page, except that we've selected a style of **picture button** from the "Style" pop-up menu. This picture button style automatically replaces the **text buttons** (see the previous page) and plays the linked media's video **inside** the new button. We used both of the Size sliders (Button and Text) to reduce the size of the buttons and the text.*

The Button "Style" pop-up menu.

The options in the **"Style** pop-up button (shown above in the Customize drawer) let you customize existing buttons. Click on the pop-up menu to see a graphical menu of button choices.

- To convert **picture buttons** (buttons that display a movie or photo) to **text buttons,** choose the "T" option.

  Or choose one of the other custom shapes in the pop-up to change text buttons to picture buttons or to change the appearance of a picture button.
- To show buttons as they were designed for the selected theme, choose the default, "From Theme."
- To customize the placement of buttons, select either "Snap to Grid" or "Free Position." When "Snap to Grid" is selected, choose an option from the "Alignment" or "Position" pop-up menu.

Tip: If you customize a menu by changing themes, or by changing the button style to something other than the default theme style, you may need to reposition or resize buttons in the menu to correct the alignment or to prevent buttons from overlapping.

Save a customized menu as a favorite

When you've created a custom menu that you want to use again for other menus or for other iDVD projects, click "Save as Favorite" at the bottom of the Settings pane (circled below).

In the dialog sheet that drops down, name this menu design and select the options you want.

> To make the favorite menu accessible to other users who have accounts on this computer, check the box "Shared for all users."
>
> To make the favorite available to the current user only, do not check this box.
>
> To *replace* an existing favorite, name the current favorite the same as the favorite you want to replace. Check the "Replace existing" box, then click OK.

—continued

To use a favorite, click the "Themes" button at the top of the Customize drawer, then from the pop-up menu in the Themes pane choose "Favorites." Your customized menu design now appears as a thumbnail image in the list, shown below. Click on a favorite in the Favorites list to apply its settings to the current menu. You can also see favorites, identified by a "first place ribbon" icon, when you select "All" from the pop-up menu.

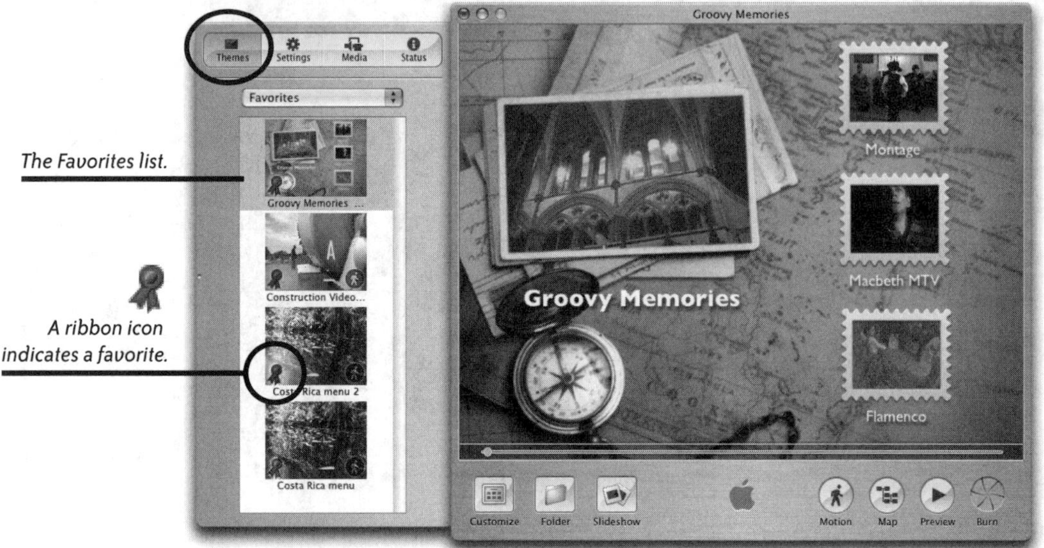

The Favorites list.

A ribbon icon indicates a favorite.

Delete a favorite

If you decide to **delete a favorite** that you've created, you must go to the Favorites folder in which favorites are stored and manually throw it away.

1. Quit idvd.
2. Find the Favorites folder where the favorite is located.

   If you selected "Shared for all users" in the "Save as Favorite" dialog sheet (shown on the previous page), the favorite is saved in a "Favorites" folder located deep within the Library folder on your *startup disk*. Look inside the Library folder for the idvd folder. Next, locate the Favorites folder. The favorites you've saved are located there. The folder path looks like this: YourStartupDisk/Library/idvd/Favorites.

   If you did not select either of the checkboxes, **or** if you selected the "Replace existing" checkbox, the favorite is saved in a Favorites folder located deep within your *Home folder*. The folder path looks like this: YourHomeFolder/Library/idvd/Favorites.
3. Drag the favorite file from the Favorites folder to the Trash.

Groovy Memories.favorite

This is what a Favorite file looks like in the Favorites folder.

Customize a motion button

A **motion button** is a small window that contains either a movie or a slideshow, and it links to another movie, slideshow, or menu. You can set the duration of a motion button movie up to 15 minutes (if the movie or slideshow is that long), and you can also set the point at which the movie in the button starts playing.

1. Click on a motion button in a menu.

   If there's not a motion button in the menu, you can create one by dragging a movie file to a menu background.
2. Click on a motion button. A "Movie" checkbox and slider appear above the button (shown below).
3. Check the "Movie" checkbox if you want the button to contain motion (play a movie or slideshow). Move the slider left or right to scrub through the movie or slideshow to the point you want the motion to start playing.
4. Uncheck the box if you want the button to contain a static image. If you uncheck the "Movie" checkbox, use the slider position to set the *poster frame*—the static image that shows in the picture button to represent the movie or slideshow.

To add motion buttons to a menu, drag movie files (or a folder of photos) from any Finder window to the menu. Or drag movies or photos from the Media pane of the Customize drawer. See the following pages for more information about the Media pane.

To change text buttons into motion buttons, select a picture button style from the "Style" pop-up menu located in the Settings pane of the Customize drawer.

You cannot have motion buttons and text buttons in the same menu.

Click this checkbox for the button to play motion.

When you use the "Duration" slider in the Settings pane to set the duration of a button, it also affects the duration of the background movie and background audio. The maximum loop duration shown on the slider is determined by the longest media clip used in the current menu.

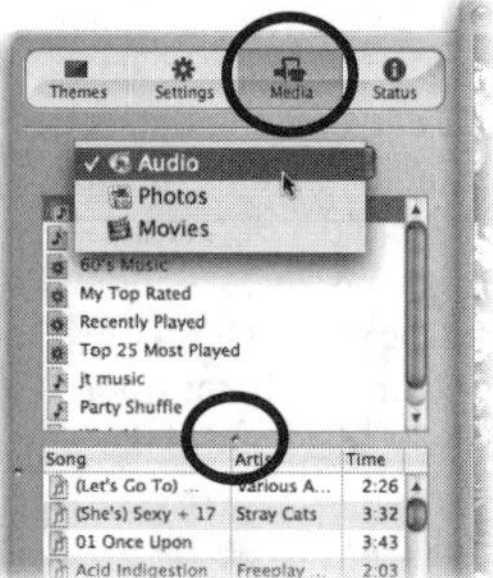

If you lower the separator bar, you'll see a list of playlists, as shown directly below, instead of a second pop-up menu.

The Media Pane of the Customize Drawer

Select the "Media" button at the top of the Customize drawer to show the Media pane. This pane shows photos, movie files, and audio files that are on your computer. Click the pop-up menu at the top of the Media pane (shown to the left) to choose the kind of media files you want to access—audio, photos, or movies.

Audio media

When you choose "Audio" from the pop-up menu in the Media pane (shown, left), a list displays the iTunes Library and all iTunes playlists. Select a playlist to show all the music files in that playlist in the lower section of the pane. Use any song you see as menu background music or slideshow music.

- **To preview a song,** select it in the list and click the Play button in the bottom-left corner of the drawer. Click the Play button again to stop. You can also double-click a song to preview it.
- **To change a menu's background music,** drag a song's icon from the Media pane onto the menu background. When a blue border highlights the menu window, let go of the icon. **Or** single-click a song name in the list, then click the "Apply" button in the bottom-right corner of the drawer.
- **To add a song to a slideshow,** double-click a slideshow button in a DVD menu to open the Slideshow editor (page 204). Then drag a song from the Media pane to the "Audio" well in the Slideshow editor. Learn more about slideshows on pages 204–207.

You can alter the Media pane to allow more space for browsing its contents: drag the dimpled separator bar up until the top panel becomes a pop-up menu, as shown above.

Photos media

Choose "Photos" from the Media pop-up menu to access all the photos in your iPhoto collection. Select any photo to use as a menu background or a button image. You can even drag an iPhoto album to the menu background to create a background slideshow.

- **To use a still image** for a menu background, drag the image from the Media pane onto the menu background. When you see a blue border highlight the edges of the menu window, let go of the image.
- **To replace the image** on a picture button, drag an image from the Media pane and drop it on top of a button in the menu.
- **To replace an existing image or a movie in a drop zone,** drag a photo from the Media pane on top of a drop zone. When you see a striped-border highlight appear around the drop zone, let go.
- **To add one or more photos to a slideshow,** open the Slideshow editor (see details on pages 204–207). Then drag a photo (or photos) from the Media pane to the Slideshow editor.
- **To add an entire slideshow,** first create an album in iPhoto that includes the photos you want to use. Then drag that iPhoto album from the Media pane to the menu. You can also drag a folder of photos from any Finder window to the menu.

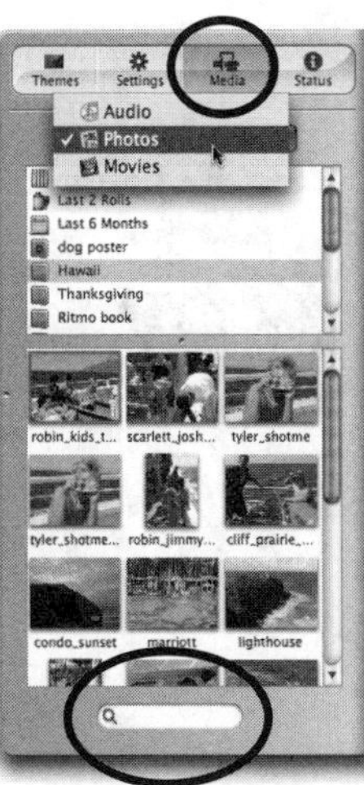

Use the Search field to find media files in a selected album, playlist, or movie folder. The lower pane changes to show only files whose name matches the letters or words you've typed in the text field.

You can drag still photos on top of existing motion buttons. You can also drag a still photo onto the menu background to create a photo background.

If you drag the Media pane's dimpled separator bar up, the contents of the upper pane—iPhoto images—are moved to a pop-up menu (shown above). To show the pop-up menu's contents in a pane again, drag the bar down.

Movies media

The Movies pane displays movie files that you can drag to menu backgrounds, buttons, or menu drop zones. iDVD automatically shows the Movies folder that's in your Home folder, but you might have other movies located in other folders or perhaps on other drives.

To show other folders that contain movies in the Movies list: Go to the iDVD application menu and choose "Preferences...." Click the "Movies" icon at the top of the preferences window. Click the "Add..." button, then choose a folder containing movie files from the Open dialog box that appears. **Or** simply drag a folder of movie clips from any Finder window to the Movies list in the Media pane.

Select a folder in this list to show its contents in the pane below.

This lower pane shows the contents of the folder selected in the list above.

To preview a movie clip in the Media pane, select it, then click this Play button. ***Or*** *double-click the movie thumbnail.*

To add a movie or a slideshow to a drop zone, drag a movie file or a folder of photos on top of a drop zone. When the drop zone highlights with a striped border, let go. If part of the image area is cut off, press-and-drag on the movie or photo to move it around inside the drop zone.

Three ways to drag a movie from the Media pane or Finder window to a menu:

- *Drag* a movie from the pane and drop it onto the menu background. The movie becomes a button that links to that movie.
- *Option-drag* a movie and drop it onto the menu background. The current background is replaced, but the drop zone remains.
- *Command-Option–drag* a movie to the menu background. The current background is replaced, and the drop zone disappears.

Create Additional Menus

A single iDVD menu can technically contain up to twelve buttons, but the design theme you choose may not be suitable for that many buttons. Or you may want to organize your content so that additional menus help to create a more effective presentation. In either case, additional menus, or **submenus,** are often an essential element in DVD design.

Create submenus

Open or create a project that has one main menu, then click the "Folder" button (circled, below-left) to create a button named "My Folder." Double-click this new button to open its new menu, into which you can drag more movies or create more slideshows. A submenu automatically contains a navigation arrow that lets users return to the previous menu.

If you've already placed a number of buttons on a menu and decide you need a submenu, you can select multiple buttons (Shift-click on the buttons), then from the Project menu choose "New Menu from Selection." iDVD replaces the selected buttons with a new button called "My Folder," which links to a new submenu containing the buttons that you selected.

The main menu.

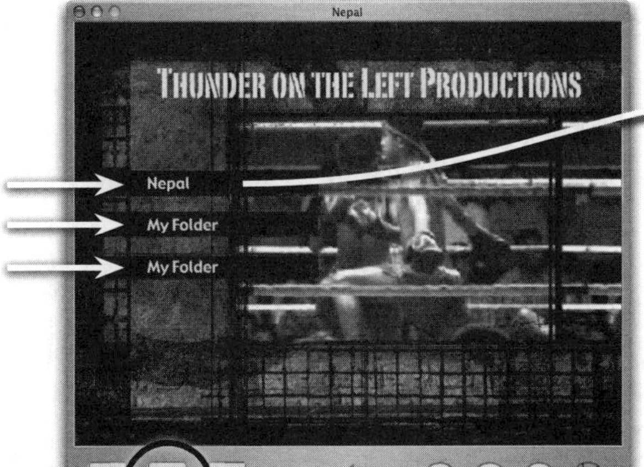

We created the three buttons in the menu above by clicking the "Folder" button at the bottom of the window. The top button's name has been changed from "My Folder" to "Nepal." Each button links to a new submenu, like the one shown to the right.

A submenu.

This submenu contains buttons that link to four different movies. We created these buttons by dragging movies from the Media pane to this submenu's background. iDVD takes care of all the design work.

Notice the "back" arrow in the lower-left corner that iDVD created.

Create a scene menu

Video-editing software, such as iMovie, lets you place **chapter markers** in a movie to mark specific scenes. If you previously set chapter markers in your movie, iDVD can automatically create **scene menus** that link to those chapter markers. iDVD can import up to 99 chapter markers for one movie.

To automatically create scene menus

1. Drag a movie containing chapter markers into an idvd menu.

   idvd automatically creates two buttons: a "Play Movie" button that plays the movie and a "Scene Selection" button that links to a new submenu. If the menu already contains one or more buttons, idvd creates a submenu that includes the "Play Movie" and "Scene Selection" buttons.

2. Double-click the "Scene Selection" button (below-left) to go to its submenu. idvd automatically created a menu that lists the chapter markers (scenes) as buttons (below-right). idvd allows a maximum of twelve buttons per menu, and some themes allow less than twelve. If there are more scenes in a movie than a menu allows, a right-facing arrow links to another menu containing more scene selection buttons.

iDVD creates as many submenus as necessary until all chapter markers in a movie have been accommodated, up to the maximum of 99 markers.

The title and text buttons were created automatically, as described above. Double-click the "Scene Selection" button to open a submenu that iDVD also created (shown on the right).

The submenu, its title, and the text buttons that link to the movie's chapter markers were all created automatically. The button names were picked up from the chapter marker names that were set in iMovie. Double-click any button to rename it.

Add Text to a Menu

A menu usually has a title, and menu buttons usually have a descriptive word or two next to them. But you may want more extensive text in a menu that provides comments, a description of the content, or any other creative use you can think of.

1. From the Project menu, choose "Add Text." Default text, also known as a text object, appears on the menu that says "Click to edit."
2. Double-click the text to select it, then type the text you want to use.
3. Click the "Customize" button to open the Customize drawer, then click the "Settings" button.
4. Use the pop-up menus in the "Text" section of the Settings pane to customize the text position, font, and color.

You can add as many text blocks as you want. In the example below, we added a second text block so we could make "ROBIN" larger than the rest of the text.

When you add a text object to a menu, by default the text style is based on the menu's *title* style. Change the font style and size in the Settings pane of the Customize drawer.

Instead of typing, you can copy text from another application, select the default text in a text object, and then paste the new text into the text object.

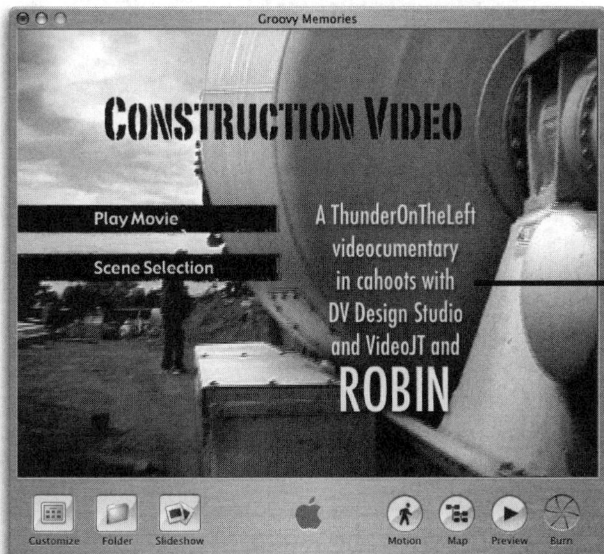

Text added to a menu.

Create a Slideshow

A DVD slideshow is a convenient and dramatic way to present your photos to friends, family, clients, or customers.

1. Click the "Media" button in the Customize drawer, then select "Photos" from the pop-up menu.
2. Select an album (folder) from the list of iPhoto albums and drag it to the menu. idvd automatically creates a button named for the album.

   Or drag a folder of photos from the Finder to the menu to create a slideshow button that is named the same as the folder of photos.

   Or click the "Slideshow" button on the bottom of the window to create an *empty* slideshow button called "My Slideshow." If you use this technique, you must use the **Slideshow editor** (shown on the next page) to add photos to the slideshow.
3. **To open the Slideshow editor,** double-click the new slideshow button that appears in the menu.
4. Use the Slideshow editor to customize your slideshow.

iDVD resizes the photos in a slideshow to 640 x 480 pixels, and converts them to a resolution of 72 ppi—official DVD specifications for slideshows.

Drag a photo album to the menu.

The "Slideshow" button creates a new and empty slideshow button in the menu.

The Slideshow editor window

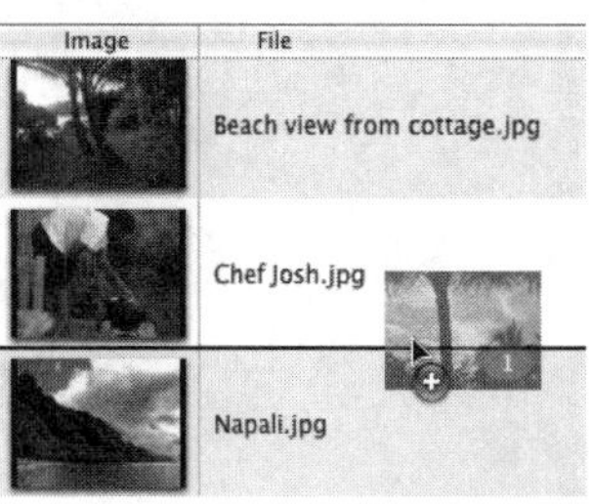

To add additional photos to a slideshow, drag an entire iPhoto album, multiple photos, or a single photo from the Photos pane (or from the Finder) to the Slideshow editor window. As you drag items to the editor window, a black line indicates where the item will be placed when you drop it (shown on the right).

To rearrange the order of photos in a slideshow, drag one or more photos up or down the list of images in the editor.

To delete photos in a slideshow, select one or more photos, then hit the Delete key.

To make a slideshow repeat, click the "Loop slideshow" checkbox.

To display Back and Next arrows during a slideshow, click the "Display navigation" checkbox. If the "Slide Duration" pop-up menu is set to "Manual," the Back and Next arrows can serve as reminders to use the DVD remote control (or the keyboard's arrow keys) to change slides.

Navigation arrows.

Add files to DVD-ROM: Click this checkbox to add the original, full-resolution photos to the final DVD. When you burn your project to a DVD, a folder containing the original photos will be on the disc, accessible for anyone who has a computer with a DVD drive. This option can also be set in the iDVD preferences (page 214).

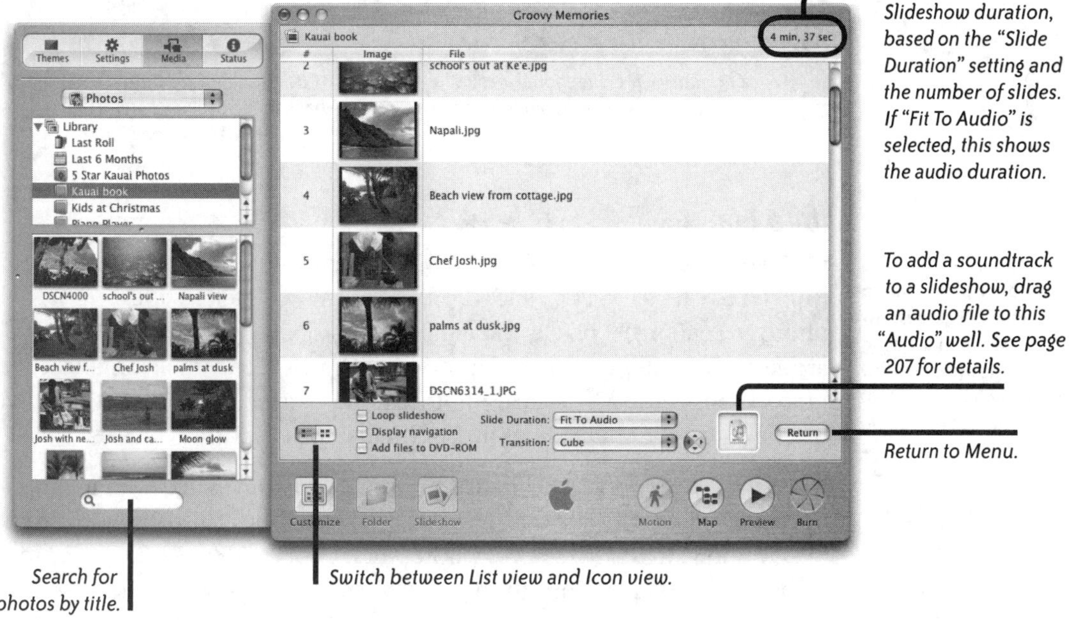

Slideshow duration, based on the "Slide Duration" setting and the number of slides. If "Fit To Audio" is selected, this shows the audio duration.

To add a soundtrack to a slideshow, drag an audio file to this "Audio" well. See page 207 for details.

Return to Menu.

Search for photos by title.

Switch between List view and Icon view.

More slideshow settings

From the **Slide Duration** pop-up menu, choose how many seconds each slide will display. Choose "Fit To Audio" if you've added audio and want the slideshow to match the duration of the selected audio track. If the audio track is shorter than the slideshow, the track repeats until the slideshow finishes.

Choose "Manual" if you want the user to advance each slide with a remote control or with the arrow keys on a computer keyboard. You cannot include audio when you choose "Manual."

From the **Transition** pop-up menu, choose a style of transition to use from one photo to the next. If the transition you select is *directional,* click one of the directional arrows on the small control (circled below) to choose in which direction the transition moves.

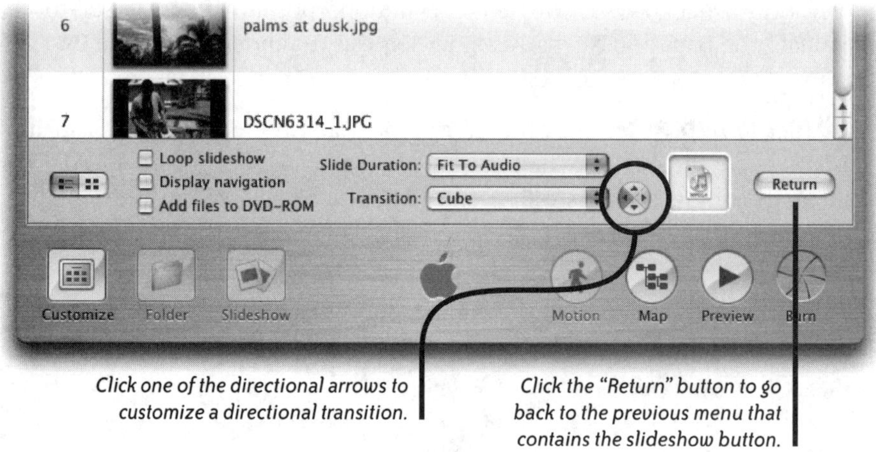

Click one of the directional arrows to customize a directional transition.

Click the "Return" button to go back to the previous menu that contains the slideshow button.

iDVD slideshow photo formats

File formats other than JPEG may not display a thumbnail preview in Slideshow editor, but should play in iDVD's slideshow preview and on the final DVD without a problem.

iDVD slideshows can use any file format supported by QuickTime, such as BMP, JPEG, GIF, PICT, PNG, and TIFF. When iDVD creates a slideshow it scales photos to 640 x 480 pixels, a standard DVD size and proportion. Photos that are not 640 x 480 will be scaled down, but will retain their original aspect ratio (proportion). A vertical photo will be resized to 480 pixels tall, with black bands on either side to fill out the 640-pixel width.

If you want your photos to fill the DVD window, use an image-editing program to crop them to 640 x 480 pixels. You can use iPhoto to crop photos to fit a DVD window: In iPhoto select a photo, then click the "Edit" button. From the "Constrain" pop-up menu, choose "4 x 3 (DVD)" as shown on the left.

Add music to a slideshow

It's amazing how much a musical soundtrack can add to the richness and enjoyment of a slideshow. iDVD's integration with iTunes makes it easy to add a soundtrack to your slideshow:

iDVD's slideshow creation is fast, easy, and convenient. It's also limited in that you can choose just one audio soundtrack and one transition style. It you want more creative control, create your slideshow in iPhoto, then export the slideshow, or choose "Send to iDVD" from iPhoto's Share menu. See pages 41–45.

1. Click the "Customize" button at the bottom of idvd's window to open the Customize drawer.
2. Click the "Media" button at the top of the drawer.
3. Choose "Audio" from the pop-up menu.

   The iTunes Library and all of your iTunes playlists appear in the upper pane of the drawer, and the lower pane shows the songs in the selected playlist.
4. Select any song and drag it from the Audio pane to the Audio well, as shown below.

   Or select a song in the Media pane, then click the "Apply" button at the bottom of the drawer (circled below).

   Or drag an audio file from anywhere on your computer and drop it in the Audio well.

To delete the audio soundtrack from a slideshow, drag the audio file's icon *out* of the Audio well.

iDVD will accept audio file formats that are compatible with QuickTime and iTunes, including AIFF, WAV, MP3, M4P, and AAC.

Map View

Map View shows a graphic representation of your iDVD project. Menus, submenus, movies, and slideshows appear as icons in a graph with navigation lines that show the connections between items. This is a great way to see the overall organization and structure of your project.

You can even build your project in this view: To add content links (buttons) to a menu, drag movies or photo albums from the Customize drawer to a menu (a folder icon). To add a submenu to a menu, select a menu icon, then click the "Folder" button at the bottom of the window. To add a slideshow button to a menu, select the menu icon, then click the "Slideshow" button.

Map View is where you can add an **autoplay** movie or slideshow. An autoplay movie automatically plays when a DVD is inserted in a player, then moves automatically to the main menu (unless you've set the autoplay to loop—see the next page). This is similar to the FBI warning screen you've seen on commercial DVDs. Although you probably don't need an FBI warning for your project, it might be fun to add a pseudo warning. Or you can find other creative ways to use the autoplay feature.

To create an autoplay movie, drag a movie or slideshow from the Media pane, or from anywhere on your computer, onto the project icon (the first item in the Map View diagram). **To remove an autoplay movie,** drag it out of the project icon.

The example below-right shows a photo album (Kauai book) dragged to the project icon in Map View to create an **autoplay slideshow.**

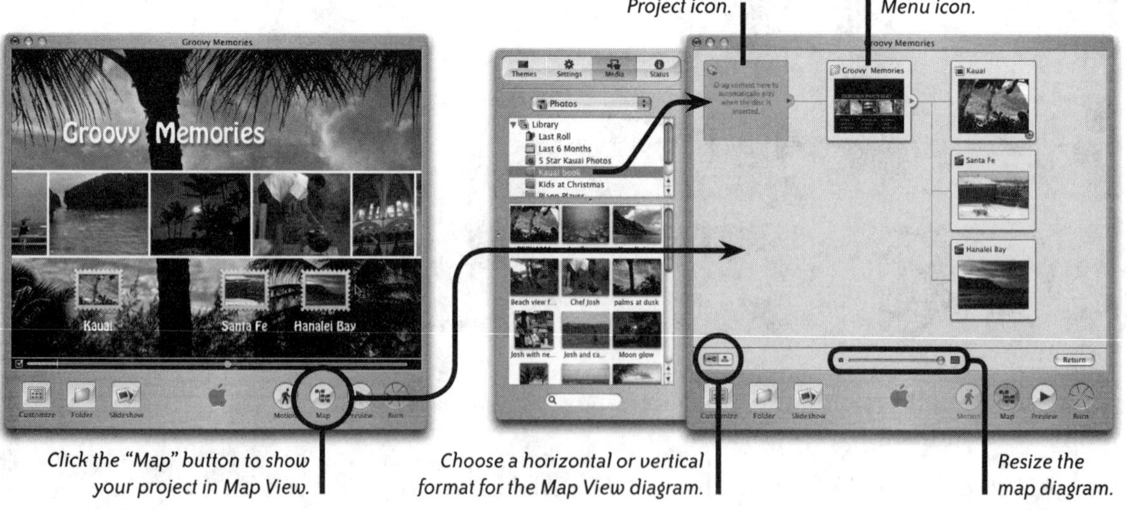

Map View makes it easy to find specific elements of a project and navigate to them, especially when the project is large and complex. From within Map View you can:

- Open a menu for editing: Double-click the menu icon.
- Open a slideshow in the Slideshow editor: Double-click the slideshow icon.
- Preview the entire project: Select the project icon, then click the "Preview" button.
- Preview a menu, movie, or slideshow: Select the item, then click the "Preview" button.
- Loop an autoplay movie, a movie, or a slideshow: Select the item's icon, then from the Advanced menu choose "Loop Movie" or "Loop Slideshow."

If your project isn't completely visible in the Map View window, drag the resize slider at the bottom of the window to the left. **Or** if you place the pointer in an empty area of the window, it turns into a little hand icon; press-and-drag the diagram and move it around inside the window.

A slideshow in Map View.

When a movie or slideshow is set to loop, it's marked with a loop icon.

A movie in Map View.

A menu in Map View.

Create a Music DVD

How about creating a music DVD with visuals for a party or special event? Or just to impress your friends.

1. Click the "Customize" button to open the Customize drawer, then click the "Themes" button.
2. Select a theme, click the "Slideshow" button, then double-click the new slideshow button to open the Slideshow editor.
3. In the Customize drawer, click the "Media" button, then choose "Audio" from the pop-up menu.
4. Drag an iTunes playlist from the Media pane to the Slideshow editor's Audio well. Set "Slide Duration" to "Fit To Audio." Click the "Loop slideshow" checkbox to make the final dvd repeat.

If you want to show photos (or graphic images of any kind) while the music plays, drag photos or a folder of photos from the Media pane (or from any Finder window), into the Slideshow editor.

You can also display just one image, such as a list of the songs playing. Create a graphic of the song list in a graphics application. Make it 640 x 480 pixels, 72 ppi, and save it as a JPEG. Drag the graphic into the Slideshow editor. The graphic will be displayed as the playlist plays.

A DVD can hold a lot of music files, but check the Status pane (page 212) to make sure you have enough room for all of the songs and pictures you may have dragged to the Slideshow editor.

Create DVD-ROM Content

In addition to menus, movies, and slideshows, DVDs can store and deliver any files from your computer, making them accessible for anyone with a DVD drive. This data storage feature is called DVD-ROM (DVD–Read Only Memory). A small business may want to include PDFs, forms, documents, maps, or other data on a disc. Or when you create a DVD slideshow, you may want to include the original, high-resolution photos on the disc for someone to use in a brochure or family album. Remember that files you add to the DVD-ROM section of a disc adds to the total space used for the rest of the project. Be sure to check the Status pane (see page 212) as you add files to ensure that everything will fit on a disc.

To put DVD-ROM content in your DVD project:

1. From the Advanced menu, choose "Edit DVD-ROM Contents...."
2. In the "DVD–ROM Contents" window that appears, click "Add Files...." Browse and select the files you want, then click the "Open" button.

   Or drag files from the Finder into the "DVD-ROM Contents" window.

You can create new folders to help organize files, change the order of folders and files, and delete items from the DVD-ROM section of the disc.

- **To create a new folder,** click the "New Folder" button at the bottom of the window. Double-click the new folder to rename it.
- **To reorganize** the DVD-ROM contents, drag the folders up or down in the list, or drag files and folders in or out of other folders.
- **To delete** an item from the DVD-ROM content, select the item, then press the Delete key on your keyboard.

To access the DVD-ROM content that's on a DVD disc:

1. Insert the disc in a DVD drive, then double-click the DVD disc icon.
2. In the window that opens, double-click the folder "DVD-ROM Contents." The folder may also have the same name as your project.
3. Drag any of the files in the DVD-ROM folder from the disc to any location on the local computer.

Preview Your iDVD Project

As you create your iDVD project, you should preview it often. First, click the "Motion" button to turn on motion menus, then click the "Preview" button to see how your final project will look.

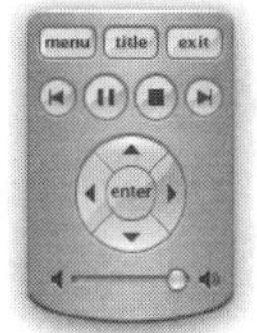

The iDVD remote control.

While in **Preview mode,** a remote control appears on the screen that lets you test the DVD as if you were using a real remote control on a consumer DVD player. **To return to editing mode,** click "Preview" again. For better efficiency, when you return to editing mode *disable* motion menus by clicking the "Motion" button at the bottom of the iDVD window.

Change the Name of a DVD

The final DVD that you burn will be named the same as your iDVD project. **To change the project name** (and thus the disc name), go to the Project menu and choose "Project Info...." Type a new name in the "Disc Name" box. Any spaces you type will be replaced with an underscore. You can use numbers, upper- and lowercase characters from A to Z, and the underscore.

Burn Your Project to a DVD

When you're satisfied with your menus and you've added all the movies, slideshows, and DVD-ROM content, it's time to render, encode, and *multiplex* all those files into the official DVD format and burn them onto a DVD. Happily, all of those complex operations happen with a click of the "Burn" button.

Multiplexing, also known as "muxing," refers to the process of assembling DVD assets into an official format that DVD players can use.

1. **Preparation:** Make sure your Energy Saver preferences are not set to make the Mac go to sleep.

   Make sure your hard disk has as least twice as much free space available as the project takes up. Check the "dvd Capacity" meter (see the following page) to check the size of the project.

   Turn on motion: Click the "Motion" button.
2. Place a blank dvd-r disc in your SuperDrive (or use other compatible media; see page 184).
3. Click the "Burn" button to open the aperture and show the Burn icon.
4. Click once again on the "Burn" icon, which is now pulsating. idvd starts rendering, encoding, multiplexing, and burning all the files and menus that are part of the dvd project.

The Status Pane of the Customize Drawer

The meters in the Status pane give information about the size of your project and the progress of background file encoding.

- **DVD Capacity:** Shows how much space your project currently requires and the maximum space available. A DVD-R can hold approximately 4.3 gigabytes, or around 90 minutes of video. Click on the text to the right of the meter to show how many *minutes* your project currently takes.
- **Motion Menus:** Shows how many minutes your motion menus take, out of an allowed maximum of 15 minutes (one gigabyte). The duration total shown includes motion menus, still menus (each still menu uses one second), transitions, and autoplay movies.
- **Tracks:** Counts how many video tracks and slideshows are used in the project. The maximum number of tracks in a project is 99.
- **Menus:** Counts how many still menus and motion menus are used in the project. A maximum number of 99 menus is allowed.
- **Background Encoding:** Shows the progress of iDVD's background file encoding that happens invisibly while you design and build your project (if you enabled background encoding in iDVD preferences).

The Encoder Settings you choose in iDVD preferences will affect how many minutes of video will fit on a disc. See the following page.

Movies that you place in an iDVD project must be encoded to a certain format that conforms to official DVD specifications.

If your computer's performance slows down due to so much intense processing, you can choose to turn off background encoding in iDVD Preferences. When you finish your project, iDVD will properly encode the files before burning the project to a disc.

Preferences

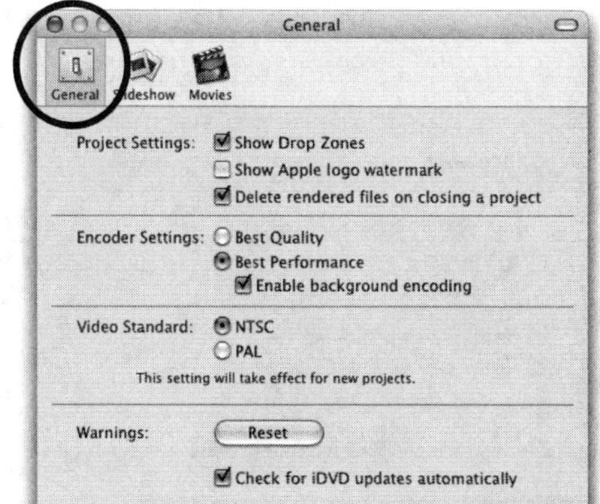

Use iDVD's preferences to customize settings for iDVD projects. From the iDVD menu, choose "Preferences...."

General preferences

Project Settings:

- **Show Drop Zones:** Check this to show the drop zones in menus.
- **Show Apple logo watermark:** This places the Apple logo in menu designs.
- **Delete rendered files on closing a project:** This will help conserve hard disk space. If you plan to burn other DVDs of the same project, *un*check this option.

Encoder Settings:

- **Best Quality:** Choose this if you want the best quality possible, **or** if you have more than 60 minutes of video. iDVD will evaluate how much video you have and produce the best quality possible for the number of minutes in the project.
- **Best Performance:** Choose this if you have less than 60 minutes of video in your project; it will burn faster, but perhaps with less quality.
- **Enable background encoding:** If you chose "Best Performance," this option allows iDVD to begin encoding your project into the MPEG-2 format required by DVD specifications. If background encoding slows down your computer, uncheck this box, and iDVD will postpone the encoding until you're ready to burn the project onto a DVD.

Video Standard:

Choose "NTSC" if your DVD will be played on a consumer DVD player in North America or Japan. A few other non-European countries also use the NTSC format. Most European and other countries use the PAL format.

NTSC uses 29.97 frames per second.

PAL uses 25 frames per second.

Warnings:

Click the "Reset" button if you've turned off certain alert messages when they appeared, but would like to see them again.

"Check for iDVD updates automatically" enables iDVD to connect to the Internet and check for available updates.

Slideshow preferences

When iDVD optimizes photos for a DVD slideshow, it converts them to a low resolution—72 ppi (pixels per inch). Check **Always add original slideshow photos to DVD-ROM** to copy all the original high-resolution photos to a folder on the DVD disc, which enables anyone to drag the photos from the disc to their own hard drive. Uncheck this option if you want to conserve space on the DVD, or if the user doesn't need access to the original, high resolution images. You can also set this option in the Slideshow editor (see page 205).

To ensure that photos won't be cropped when viewed on a television, select **Always scale slides to TV Safe area.** To see the safe area in iDVD menus, from the Advanced menu, choose "Show TV Safe Area."

An iDVD menu with the "TV Safe area" shown.

Movies preferences

These settings let you choose whether iDVD will create chapter marker submenus and where iDVD should look for movie files.

Automatically create chapter marker submenu: iMovie lets you place chapter markers in a movie. If this option is chosen, when you drag an iMovie with chapter markers to an iDVD menu, iDVD creates two menu buttons: One named "Play Movie" that plays the movie, and one named "Scene Selection" that links to a new submenu containing buttons that link to each chapter marker in the movie. If there are more than twelve chapter markers in the movie, iDVD creates another submenu containing buttons that link to the remaining chapter markers. iDVD can have a maximum of twelve buttons per menu.

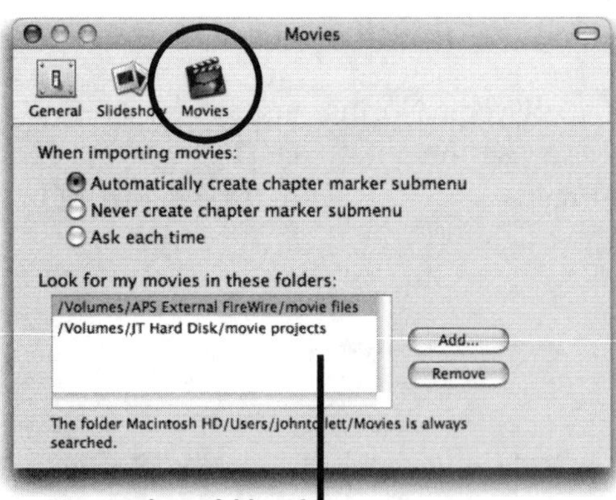

You can drag a folder of movies from anywhere on your computer to this list.

Look for my movies in these folders: iDVD automatically looks for movies in the Movies folder located in your Home folder. Because movies take up so much disk space, it probably won't take you long to realize you need an additional hard disk (or two) on which to store movies. If so, you can add those other locations for iDVD to search. Click the "Add..." button, then select any folder on any drive. Your selection will appear in the list. To remove a location from this list, select it, then click "Remove."

The Advanced Menu

The Advanced menu contains commands that can be helpful in the creation of your iDVD project.

Motion

Choosing this command is the same as clicking the "Motion" button in the iDVD window. To be efficient, turn motion *off* while working on a project. Motion should be *on* when previewing a project or burning a disc.

Hide/Show Motion Playhead

This command hides or shows the menu Scrubber Bar and Timeline described on page 188.

Show TV Safe Area

Some TVs may distort or clip the outer edges of DVD menus and movies. iDVD guide lines that show that show a "TV Safe area" can be turned on or off, as shown on the opposite page. When you design menus, make sure important elements such as text and buttons fall within the TV Safe area.

Apply Theme To Project

Choose this option to apply a selected theme to every menu in a project.

Apply Theme To Folders

Choose this option to apply a selected theme to a specific menu *and all of its submenus.* Menu icons in Map View are *folders* (shown on the right).

1. Open a menu whose theme you want to change, and at the same time change all of the menu's *submenus.*
2. In the Theme pane of the Customize drawer, click on the theme you want to use. From the Advanced menu, choose "Apply Theme to Folders." The theme is now applied to the selected menu and all of its submenus.

A menu in Map View is automatically named for its theme style, which is also the default title in the menu. When you edit the title text of the menu, the text on the Map View icon changes as well.

Loop Movie

Select a movie or slideshow in a menu or in Map View. Then from the Advanced menu, select "Loop Movie" to make the movie or slideshow repeat.

Delete Encoded Assets

Choose this command to reclaim disk space taken up by the encoded files that iDVD had to create for the final disc.

Edit DVD-ROM Contents...

Select this command to copy files of any kind to the final DVD. See page 210.

Archive Your Project

Archiving a project bundles all of the project assets together, making it easy and convenient to store complete projects or move them to another computer. You may need to move a project to a computer that has a SuperDrive so you can burn a disc, or take it to someone else's Mac so she can work on the project. When you *archive* your project, it's saved as an iDVD project (.dvdproj) that can be opened later with iDVD.

To archive an iDVD project:

1. From the File menu, choose "Archive Project."
2. In the Archive Project dialog sheet that drops down (shown below), type a name for the project and choose a location in which to save the archived file. idvd adds "Archived" to the file name.

Groovy Archived.dvdproj

An archived project icon looks like this.

3. If you've used custom themes or want to use your theme in future versions of idvd, click the box to "Include themes" to archive the themes with the project. You can uncheck this checkbox if you've used standard idvd themes.
4. Click the "Include encoded files" checkbox to avoid having to re-encode project files after they're moved to another location. If you're more interested in archiving speed and economizing hard disk space, uncheck this option.
5. Click the "Save" button.

Once your project is completely finished, you can choose to save it as a disc image (.img), a format that compresses the DVD-encoded files into a single file that's convenient for storage or transport. The following page explains how to *save as a disc image.*

Save As Disc Image

How is this process different from the "Archive Project" on the opposite page? When you *archive* a project, it remains in the iDVD format so you can open and revise it at any time. When you save as disc image, the iDVD files are converted to special DVD-specification files. These files cannot be opened and edited without special software—they can only be *played* (by a desktop or computer DVD player). The "Save As Disc Image" command does everything to create a final DVD except burn the files to a disc. The disc image that's created contains the final files that can be burned to a DVD disc. A disc image file is an easy way to copy your entire project, completely encoded, to another computer—ready to burn to a DVD. If you want to create a copy of your project that *can* be edited, you should *archive* the project as described on the previous page.

1. Open a project. From the File menu, choose "Save As Disc Image...."
2. In the "Save Disc Image As..." window that opens, type a name in the "Save As" field and select a location in which to save the file.
3. A drop-down sheet (below-left) shows the dvd creation progress. The "Burn" button in the bottom-right corner glows and rotates, but it's not going to actually burn a disc. It will, however, do everything necessary to create a dvd *except* burn the disc.
4. When the disc image has been created, the drop-down sheet (below-right) shows a "Burning Finished" message—even though a disc was not burned. Click ok.

This is an iDVD project saved as a disc image file.

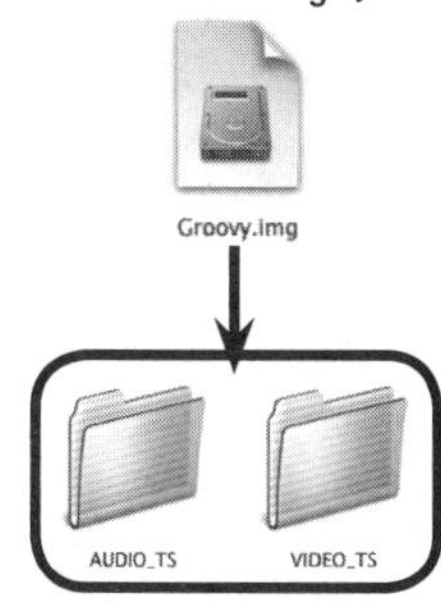

Double-click the disc image file (top) to see the contents—two folders.

The "AUDIO_TS" folder is empty, but required by DVD specifications.

The "VIDEO_TS" folder contains all of the specially encoded project files.

You can create a working DVD movie by burning these two folders to a disc.

Click "Cancel" to stop the procedure.

The animated "Burn" button makes it appear that a disc is being burned, but it's not.

You can use the **DVD Player** application (on the right) to play a DVD project that's saved as a disc image. Open DVD Player (it's in the Applications folder); a black DVD window appears. Press Command 2 to make the screen "normal" sized. Double-click the disc image to mount it and show its VIDEO_TS folder. Click on DVD Player again. The project starts to play in the DVD window.

DVD Player

If you want to play a VIDEO_TS folder that's not inside a disc image, open DVD Player. Then from the File menu, choose "Open VIDEO_TS Folder...."

In the window that opens, locate the VIDEO_TS folder you want to play, then click the "Choose" button.

iDVD Specifications, Formats, and Limitations

Most of these items are mentioned in various other places in this chapter, but it may be helpful to summarize them here, in one place.

- iDVD can use any format that QuickTime recognizes, such as JPEG, PICT, PNG, TIFF, or Photoshop.
- Photo sizes of 640 x 480 pixels work well in iDVD. Larger sizes can be used but will be resized by iDVD to 640 x 480.
- A resolution of 72 ppi is ideal, although you can use higher-resolution images and iDVD will convert them to 72 ppi.
- Images smaller than 640 x 480 pixels will be enlarged by iDVD, usually adversely affecting the image quality. If you use a large quantity of high-resolution images in a slideshow, you may notice the iDVD application acts sluggish, but the final DVD will be okay.
- Each slideshow you create can have up to 99 photos.
- In the Slideshow editor, if you set the "Slide Duration" pop-up menu to "Manual," you cannot include music with the slideshow.
- MPEG-1 files, QuickTime VR movies, and movies with sprite or Flash tracks cannot be added to an iDVD project.
- iDVD accepts audio files that are supported by QuickTime, such as AAC, MP3, M4P, AIFF, and WAV.
- Each iDVD menu is allowed a maximum of twelve buttons.
- A slideshow in a drop zone can have a maximum of thirty photos.
- iDVD projects can have a combined total of 99 tracks (movies and slideshows). Of course, that depends on the duration of the content. You're still limited to 4.3 gigabytes of storage space.
- iDVD projects can contain up to 99 menus.
- iDVD will recognize up to 99 chapter markers in a movie.
- NTSC is the video standard for North America and Japan.
PAL is the video standard for most of Europe and elsewhere.

GarageBand 5

Think of GarageBand as your own private recording studio. Even if you're not a musician and didn't even play in the high school band or sing in the church choir, you'll soon be composing and arranging music soundtracks that will amaze everyone. If you do happen to have musical talent on any level, GarageBand provides the studio of your dreams.

If you don't play a musical instrument, use the provided musical loops to compose original arrangements, then enjoy playing them in iTunes. And with the help of iDVD, iMovie, and iPhoto, you can use your musical compositions for DVD menu audio tracks, movie soundtracks, or slideshow soundtracks.

GarageBand is capable of much more than we can cover in this short chapter, but we'll get you started with the basics and enough information to make GarageBand one of your favorite, creative pastimes.

A rapidly growing collection of GarageBand web sites provides training, tech support, forums, soundtrack loops, and other music-community offerings.

One of our favorite GarageBand sites is MacJams (**www.MacJams.com**). Be sure to check out their Buyer's Guide for great advice on accessories (keyboards, microphones, and more). The site also contains tutorials, reviews, and lots of original music submitted by GarageBand users.

When GarageBand opens, a virtual keyboard appears on your Desktop, as shown below. You can use it to play notes, but you'll find other techniques easier for creating songs. We suggest you play with this keyboard to experiment with the many different instrument voices and effects available in this amazing app.

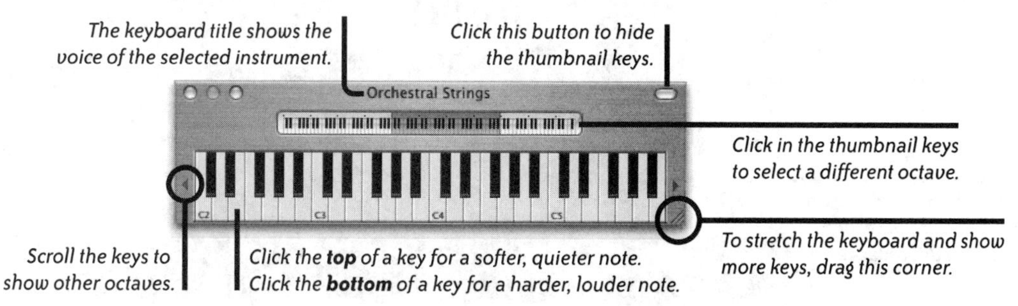

The keyboard title shows the voice of the selected instrument.
Click this button to hide the thumbnail keys.
Orchestral Strings
Click in the thumbnail keys to select a different octave.
C2
C3
C4
C5
Scroll the keys to show other octaves.
Click the top of a key for a softer, quieter note.
Click the bottom of a key for a harder, louder note.
To stretch the keyboard and show more keys, drag this corner.

You can change these settings at any time in the "Track Info" window (see page 245).

Create a New Song File

Double-click the **GarageBand** icon in your Applications folder to open it. If this is the first time you've opened GarageBand, the window shown on the left appears. Click "Create a New Project."

In the "New Project" window that opens (shown left-bottom), type a name for your project. Choose a location in which to store it from the "Where" pop-up menu. The default location is the GarageBand folder inside the Music folder that's located in your Home folder, but you can choose any location you prefer.

The bottom section of the "New Project" window contains the song's Tempo, Time, and Key settings.

Tempo is the speed of the song measured in beats per minute (bpm). You can set the tempo anywhere between 60 bpm (slow) and 240 bpm (fast).

Time, such as 4/4, defines *how many* beats (the number before the slash) will be in a single measure, and which *length* of note will have a value of *one* beat (the number after the slash). In 4/4 time the 4 after the slash stands for $^1/_4$ and indicates that *quarter notes* will equal one beat. In 2/2 time there are 2 beats per measure, and a *half note* (the 2 after the slash stands for $^1/_2$) equals one beat.

Key is the central note that determines the pitch of all other notes.

Click the "Create" button to open the GarageBand window, shown below.

Grand Piano track.

When GarageBand opens, it automatically includes a Grand Piano track, and an onscreen keyboard floats on top of the window, as shown here. You can drag the keyboard out of the way or click its red Close button.

Click one of these buttons to open the Loop Browser (next page) or the Track Editor (page 224).

The GarageBand Interface

As an easy way to get started, take a quick look at the components that make up the the GarageBand window. The next several pages provide an overview and description of the tools contained within this main window. The GarageBand concept is simple—find loops with the Loop Browser, then drag the loops from the Results list to the Timeline and arrange them in a limitless variety of ways to create original compositions.

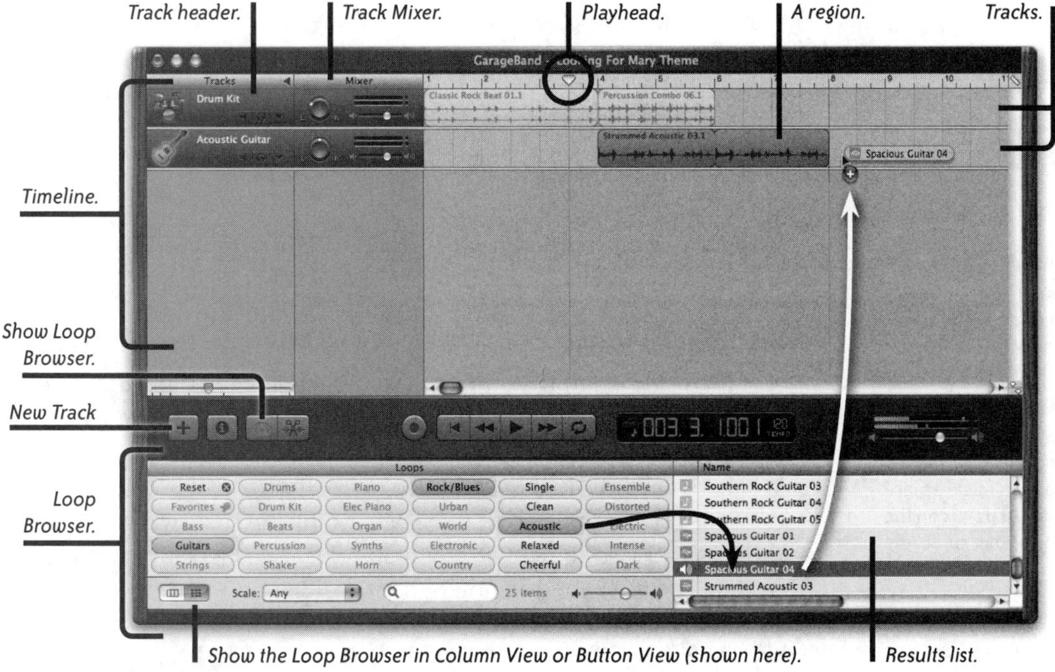

The **Playhead** indicates the current position in a track. Dragg the Playhead to the position in the track where you want to start playing a song.

When a loop resides in the Timeline, it's referred to as a ***region.***

The **Timeline** holds the various tracks that you create and provides the space in which you arrange pre-recorded loops of music into a composition.

Create **tracks** by dragging *loops* (pre-recorded clips of music) from the Loop Browser into the Timeline. You can also click the + *button* to create a new, empty track (see page 232). If you've connected a musical instrument or a microphone to your computer, you can record original music or vocals to a track (see page 248).

GarageBand uses two types of tracks: Real Instruments (recordings of real instruments) and Software Instruments (MIDI data created digitally). See pages 246–247.

A close look at tracks

__To delete a track,__ select it, then press Command Delete. __Or__ from the Track menu choose "Delete Track."

In the **Tracks column,** the *track name and icon* identify the track. A track is named for the type of instrument you initially drag into it. **To change a track name,** Command-click it and type in a new name.

The small row of buttons in the Tracks column are to *record, mute, solo, lock track,* and *volume/pan track*.

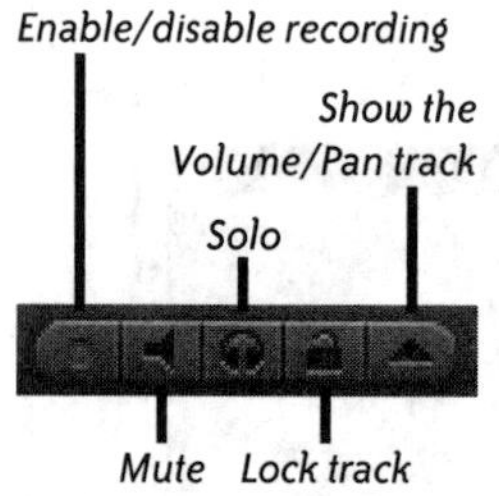

- **Record:** Click the dot icon to enable or disable recording for the track.
- **Mute:** Click the speaker icon to turn a track on or off.
- **Solo:** Click the headphones icon to mute all tracks except that one (click again to *unsolo* the track).
- **Lock track:** Click the lock icon to lock the track. Locking a track prevents editing and provides more processing power by rendering the track to the hard disk.
- **Volume and pan track:** Click the disclosure triangle button to reveal a drop-down track (shown below). Choose "Track Volume" or "Track Pan" from the pop-up menu.
  When "Track Volume" is selected, click on the horizontal gray line (the *volume curve*) to add points to the line. Drag points up or down to adjust the volume, left or right to affect the duration of a volume change.
  When "Track Pan" is selected, click on the horizontal line (the *pan curve*) to add points to the line. Drag points up or down to adjust the balance of sound between left and right speakers; drag points left or right to affect the duration of the pan.

To change the volume or pan of an entire track, use the Mixer controls in the Mixer column.

To change the volume or pan of individual loops in a track, use the volume or pan track—place and adjust points on the volume or pan curve line as shown below.

The points in a pan curve move sound more towards the right speaker (below the horizontal line) or more towards the left speaker (above the horizontal line), depending on how high or low the points are positioned.

The **Mixer column** includes a *pan control* to adjust the balance of sound between left and right speakers and a *track volume control slider* to adjust the entire track's volume. These controls are disabled if you've edited the volume or pan of individual loops in the track by adding points to the volume curve or to the pan curve, as shown on the previous page.

Above the volume control are two audio level meters, one each for left and right speakers. If the volume exceeds acceptable levels, the meter shows orange and red in the meter. The small round warning lights *(clipping indicators)* on the right of the meters turn red when audio volume is high enough to cause audio distortion, known as *clipping*. Click on the *clipping indicator* lights to turn them off.

Drag the **Zoom slider** left or right to zoom in or out of the Timeline. Drag left to show more loops in the window, or drag right to show fewer loops in greater detail.

The **Track Info** button (the letter "i") opens the selected track's "Track Info" window where you can change instrument settings and add effects to a track. See pages 243–245 for more information.

The Loop Browser

Click the **Loop Browser** button to show the Loop Browser, a collection of music loops with which you can build a song. Click one of the **Browser View** buttons in the lower-left corner of the browser to view the loops in *Button View* or *Column View:*

Loop Browser button.

- **Button View** (shown below) shows the Loop Browser as a collection of buttons representing different instruments and music styles. When you select a button, unrelated buttons are dimmed. Loops that fit the criteria of all *selected* buttons appear in the Results list.

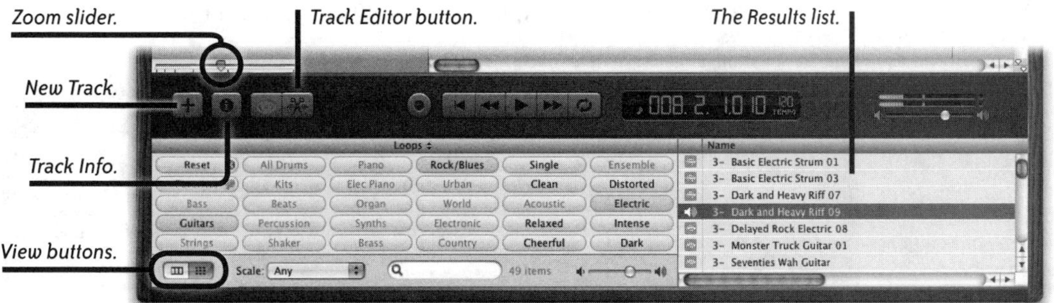

To turn off a keyword button selection in Button view, click it again.

To turn off *all* keyword button selections, click the "Reset" button in the upper-left corner.

The Loop Browser shown in Column View.

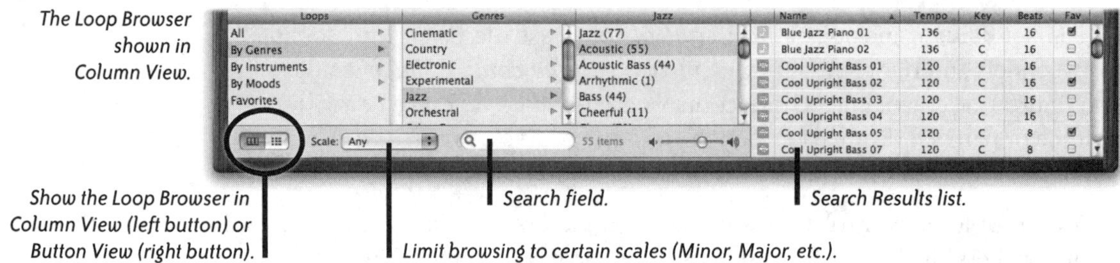

Show the Loop Browser in Column View (left button) or Button View (right button).

Limit browsing to certain scales (Minor, Major, etc.).

Search field.

Search Results list.

- **Column View** (shown above) contains a "Loops" column from which you choose a loop category, then make keyword selections from the next two columns to narrow the selection. The Results list on the right shows the loops that match your choices.

Use the **Search field** (shown above) to find certain loops quickly: Select a loop category in the first column, then type a keyword in the Search field that might appear in a loop name. Press the Return key to show found matches in the Results list.

Track Editor button.

The Track Editor

Click the **Track Editor** button (left) to open the Track Editor in place of the Loop Browser. The Track Editor lets you edit single notes and entire regions.

When a region in a *Software Instrument* track is selected in the Timeline, notes in the Track Editor are represented by gray and black horizontal bars, as shown in the example below.

- A black bar indicates a *high velocity* (louder or harder) note. Gray bars indicate *lower velocity* (quieter or softer) notes. **To change a note's velocity,** select it, then drag the "Note Velocity" slider in the Region column.
- **To change their pitch**, drag notes up or down in the Track Editor. **To change their position** in the music, drag notes left or right.

Velocity refers to how hard you press the keys on a MIDI keyboard. Different levels of pressure produce different sounds. The Desktop piano keyboard simulates velocity by detecting a click's location: Click the top of the keys for low velocity notes; click on the bottom of keys for high velocity notes.

*The Track Editor, with a **Software Instrument** track selected in the Timeline.*

Choose Graphic View (shown here) or Notation View (pages 226–227).

Zoom slider.

Align notes in the grid to the nearest beat.

- **To change a note's duration,** drag its right edge to the left or right.
- **To create a note** directly in the Track Editor, Command-click on a position in the Timeline grid. When you press the Command key the pointer turns into a pencil icon.
- **To change a region's pitch** + or – 36 semitones, in the Region column, drag the "Region Pitch" slider left or right.
- **To accurately align notes** in the grid so they match the music beat perfectly, in the "Advanced" column, click the "Align" button. The accuracy level indicated on the button (1/8, 1/16, etc.) is determined by your zoom-level setting. Drag the Zoom slider to the right to enlarge the Timeline view and increase the alignment accuracy.

When a region in a *Real Instrument* track is selected in the Timeline, the Track Editor looks a little different, as shown below.

*The Track Editor, with a **Real Instrument** track selected in the Timeline.*

*The Track Editor shows **Real Instrument** regions as waveforms (left).*

***Software Instrument** regions are shown as individual note bars in **Graphic View** (see the previous page), or as traditional music notes in **Notation View** (see pages 226–227).*

- **To change a region's pitch** + or – 12 semitones, in the Region column drag the "Region Pitch" slider left to lower the pitch, or drag right to make the pitch higher.
- **To enhance tuning,** select a Real Instrument track, then drag the "Enhance Tuning" slider left or right. Use this when you've recorded a Real Instrument that's not perfectly in tune. GarageBand moves the notes to the closest note on the chromatic scale. Click the "Limit to Key" checkbox to limit enhancements to the song's set key. Enhanced tuning is only accurate on regions that are monophonic (no chords) in Real Instrument tracks.
- **To enhance timing,** use the "Enhance Timing" slider to help improve the timing of a track or region that you recorded using a Real Instrument, such as drums, chordal instruments, and single-note instruments. To open the track you want to enhance, double-click it in the Track Editor. Drag the Timing slider to the right. From the pop-up menu below the slider, choose a note value to use as the basis for timing enhancement (¼ note, ⅛ note, etc.).

***Tip:** You can use the "Region Pitch" slider to make identical loops sound different.*

From the Track Editor you can select, then delete, copy, or move, an entire loop or sections of a loop.

- **To select an entire loop,** hover over the loop's *upper* section so the pointer turns into a **double-arrow pointer,** then click.
- **To select a fragment of a loop,** hover over the loop's *middle* section so the pointer turns into a **cross-hair pointer,** then *press-and-drag* to make a selection. Click on the selection to turn it into a separate loop that can be moved, modified, copied, etc.
- **To crop a loop,** hover near the loop's edges in the *lower* section so the pointer turns into a **single-arrow pointer,** then drag the edge.
- **To repeat a loop,** hover near the loop's right edge in the upper section so the pointer turns into a **loop pointer,** then drag.
- **To overlap another loop,** drag one loop over another. The overlapped section of the bottom loop is replaced by the top loop. To recover the overlapped section, drag the bottom left or right edge of the shortened loop. Overlapped loops adopt the key of the other loop.

The appearance and function of your pointer changes when it hovers over different sections of a loop in the Track Editor.

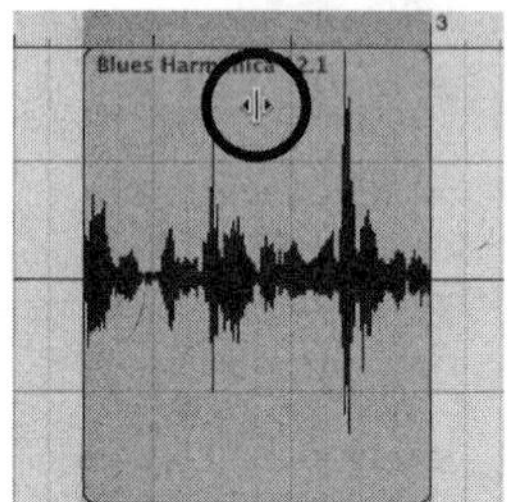

Double-arrow pointer.

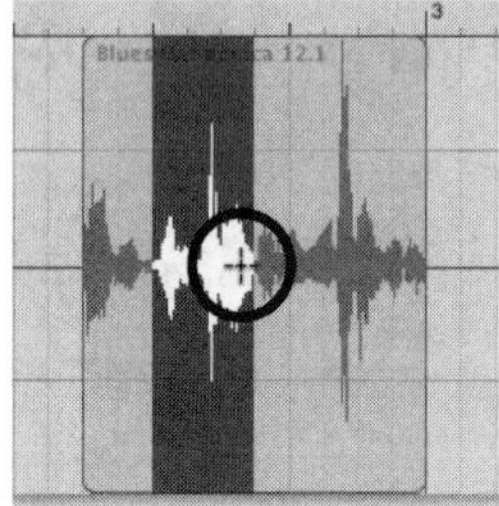

Cross-hair pointer.

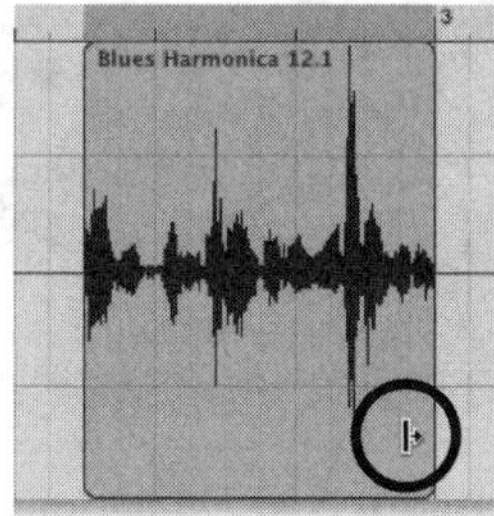

Single-arrow pointer.

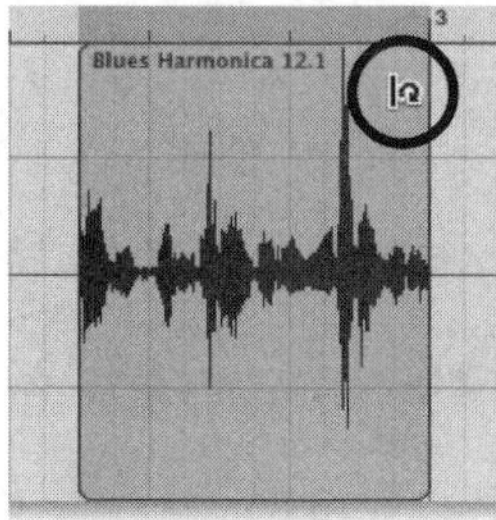

Loop pointer.

Notation View

You can show *Software Instrument regions* (loops) as traditional music notation view in the Track Editor: Double-click a Software Instrument region to open it in the Track Editor. Then click the *Notation View* button in the bottom-left corner of the GarageBand window (shown below).

Note Value button (see next page).

Notation view button.

To change a note, drag it to a different position.

While in Notation View you can edit the notes of a selected track:

- **To add a note,** Command-click in the Track Editor Timeline where you want to add a note. When you hold down the Command key, you can see a shadow of the new note.
- **To determine the value of notes you add,** click the Note Value button in the "Advanced" column (shown on the right). From the button pop-up menu, choose a note value you want to use, then Command-click in the Track Editor Timeline to add a note.

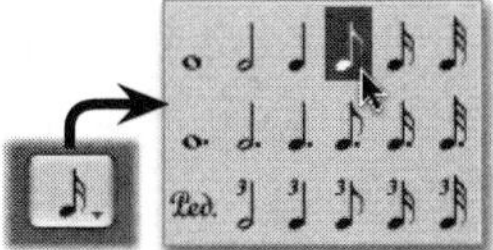

Note Value button.

- **To delete a note,** select it, then hit the Delete key.
- **To copy a note,** Option-drag the note to a new position.
- **To move a note in time,** drag it left or right. Or select the note, then use the left and right arrow keys.
- **To change a note's pitch,** drag it up or down. Or select the note, then use the up and down arrow keys. The note's new pitch plays as you you move it.
- **To change the duration of a note,** drag the right edge of the green duration bar that extends from the note, as shown to the right. The duration bar is hidden until you select a note.

The note duration bar.

- **To change the velocity of a note,** select the note, then drag the "Note Velocity" slider in the Region column.
- **To add pedal markings** (to sustain notes), Command-click where you want to add the *pedal down* symbol (the word "Ped," shown to the right), and drag to the point you want to add the *pedal up* symbol (a green asterisk). The green dashed line indicates the duration of the sustained note.

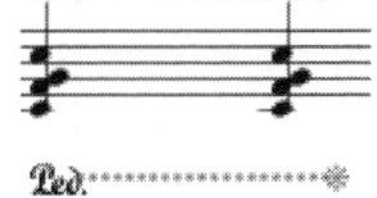

Pedal markings.

Other controls in the main GarageBand window

The Master volume slider and level meters control and monitor the output volume of the entire song.

- Drag the *Master volume slider* left or right to adjust the entire song's final output volume.
- The two *level meters* located above the volume slider show the activity of the left and right audio channels (left and right speakers). Volume levels that are too high cause sound *distortion,* also referred to as *clipping.* If clipping occurs, the small round lights to the right of the meters (called *clipping indicators*) turn red. Monitor the volume levels as you create a composition to make sure the volume stays within a safe range. If the clipping indicators turn red, lower the volume, then click the clipping indicator lights to reset them.

The clipping indicators glow red when volume settings cause audio distortion problems.

Master volume slider and level meters.

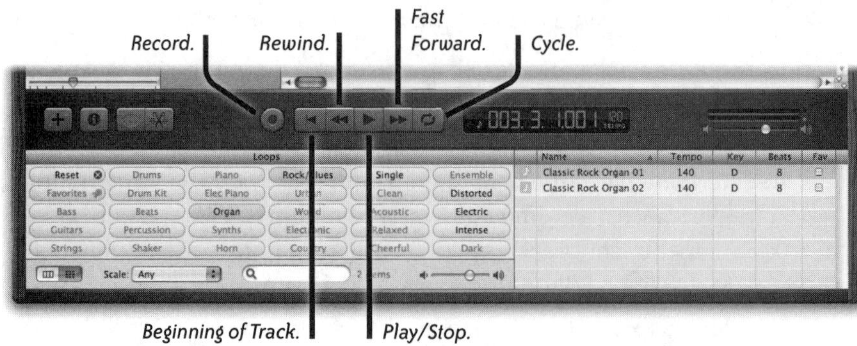

The **Transport Control** buttons, shown above, include *Record, Beginning of Track, Rewind, Play/Stop, Fast Forward,* and *Cycle* (loop).

- **Record:** Click this when you've connected a MIDI-compatible keyboard, a guitar, or a microphone and you're ready to record an original track, or if you want to record a track using the Desktop keyboard. Click the Record button again to stop recording.
- **Beginning of Track:** Click to jump the Playhead to the beginning of the track.
- **Rewind:** Click to move the Playhead back in the track one measure. Press-and-hold the Rewind button to move the Playhead back continuously.
- **Play:** Click to **start** playback of a song or cycle region. Click the Play button again to **stop** playback. You can also use the Spacebar on your keyboard to start and stop playback.
- **Fast Forward:** Click to move the Playhead forward in the track one measure. Press-and-hold the Fast Forward button to move the Playhead forward continuously.
- **Cycle:** Click to turn looping on and off. To designate a *cycle region* (a segment of the Timeline you want to loop), click the Cycle button. A *cycle region bar,* a yellow-orange area, appears at the top of the window to indicate the segment of the Timeline that will loop. Drag either edge of the bar to change the cycle region.

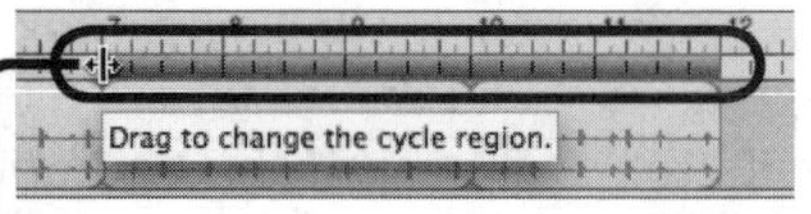

The cycle region is indicated by a yellow-orange color.

The pointer turns into a double-arrow pointer when hovering over the edge of the cycle region.

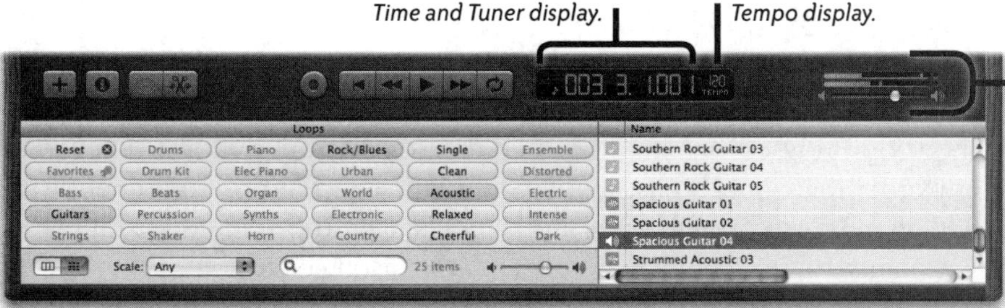

The Master volume slider and level meters. See page 227.

*The Time display above shows **musical time,** as indicated by the music note icon in the corner.*

*A music note in the corner indicates **music time.***

*A clock in the corner indicates **absolute time.***

Time display: Shows the position of the Playhead in *musical time* or *absolute time.* Musical time is shown as measures, beats, and ticks; absolute time is shown as hours, minutes, seconds, and fractions of a second. *Click on the left side* of the time display to change to absolute time (shown on the right).

To change the Playhead position from within the Time display, click on one of the numerals, then drag *vertically* up or down. You can also double-click one of the numerals in the Time display, type a value, then double-click the numeral again to set it.

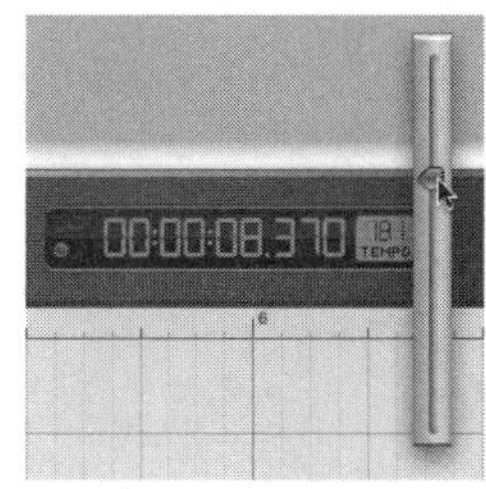

The Tempo slider pops up when you press on the Tempo area of the Time display.

Tempo display: Shows the current tempo. *To change the tempo,* press on the Tempo area of the display, then drag the pop-up Tempo slider to a new tempo. If the Time display is set to show absolute time, the Time display changes as you adjust the tempo.

Tuner display: Click the tuning fork icon in the Time display (below-right) to show the digital tuner. If you've connected a Real Instrument to the computer, such as a guitar, you can use the Tuner display to tune the instrument.

1. Select the Real Instrument track of the instrument you need to tune.
2. Click the tuning fork icon to show the Tuner display, as seen below. **Or** from the Control menu choose "Show Instrument Tuner."
3. Play a note on the instrument. The name of the note appears on the left side of the horizontal scale.
4. A green light in the center of the scale means the instrument is in tune.

   Red lights left of center indicate the instrument's pitch is flat (too low). Red lights right of center indicate the instument's pitch is sharp (too high).

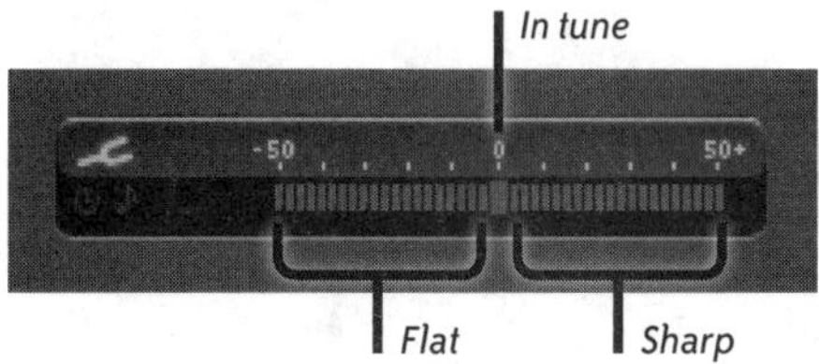

Compose Your First Song

Yes, it's possible to go from musically challenged to brilliant composer in one day or less. Possibly *much* less. Just locate some pre-recorded **loops** in the Loop Browser that you like, then drag them around in the Timeline in any order that sounds pleasing. If you want to juice it up, experiment with adding more tracks with other instruments, fade the volume in and out at key points, then add some effects or adjust existing effects.

If you haven't already created a new song file, see page 220. The following pages explain in detail how to find loops, add tracks, place loops in tracks, arrange and mix your song, then export it to an iTunes playlist.

Find loops for your song

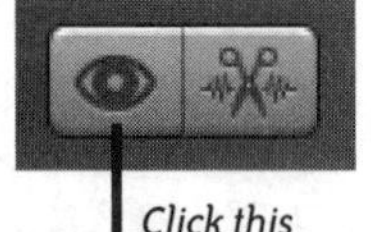

Click this button to open or close the Loop Browser.

Unless you're recording your own original music (see page 248), you'll create original compositions by placing loops of music in the Timeline. To locate the loops you want to use, use the Loop Browser.

1. Click the Loop Browser button (the eye icon) to open the Loop Browser (shown below).
2. Choose the *view* in which you prefer to browse for loops: click either the *Column View* button or the *Button View* button.
3. **To browse in Button View,** click the browser's keyword buttons to narrow your search. When you click a keyword button, other buttons that don't relate to that category are dimmed. The loops that appear in the Results list change as you click different buttons.

   To browse in Column View, select a keyword in each column to narrow your search for different types of loops (shown on page 231).
4. Loops that match the criteria of your search appear in the Results list.

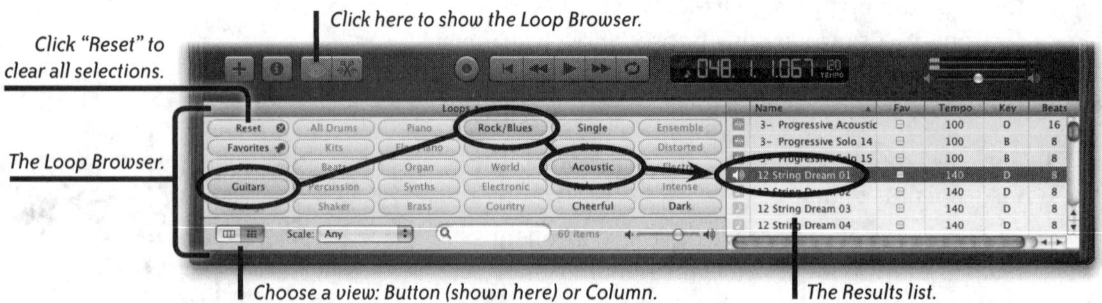

Click here to show the Loop Browser.

Click "Reset" to clear all selections.

The Loop Browser.

Choose a view: Button (shown here) or Column.

The Results list.

To deselect a button, click it again. To deselect all buttons, click the "Reset" button. Drag buttons to rearrange them; to reset buttons to their default positions, click the "Reset" button in preferences (see page 252).

Preview loops

As you browse the loop selections, you really have no idea what they really sound like unless you listen to them.

- Click a loop name or icon in the Results column to preview it. A speaker icon appears next to the loop while it plays.
- To stop the preview, click the loop name or the speaker icon.
- To adjust the preview's volume, drag the volume slider located at the bottom of the browser.
- As you browse and preview loops, you can mark your favorites for easy access later. Click a loop's "Fav" checkbox (circled below) in the Results list to mark it as a favorite. If you don't see the "Fav" column, scroll the Results list sideways until it comes into view.

  To show Favorites in Button View, click the "Favorites" button in the top-left corner of the browser.

  To show Favorites in Column View, click "Favorites" in the "Loops" column, then choose categories from the other two columns.

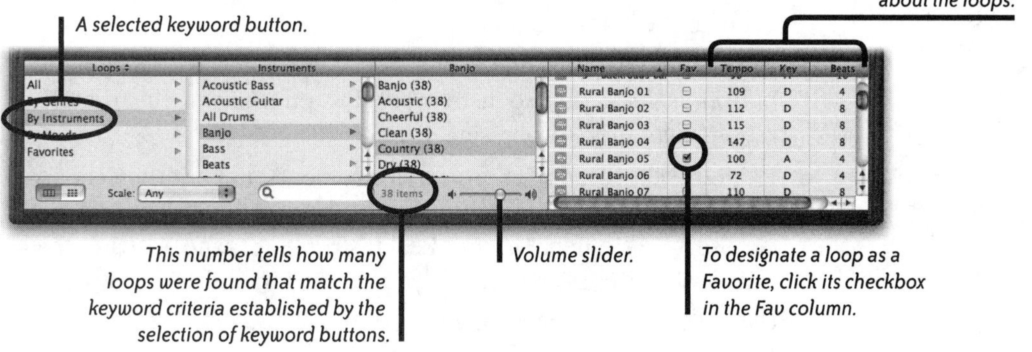

These columns provide musical information about the loops.
A selected keyword button.
This number tells how many loops were found that match the keyword criteria established by the selection of keyword buttons.
Volume slider.
To designate a loop as a Favorite, click its checkbox in the Fav column.

At this point you may notice that some loops shown in the Loop Browser are green and have a music note icon, while others are blue with a waveform icon. GarageBand includes loops of two kinds: *Software Instruments* and *Real Instruments.* See pages 246–247 for more information about using Software Instrument loops vs. Real Instrument loops.

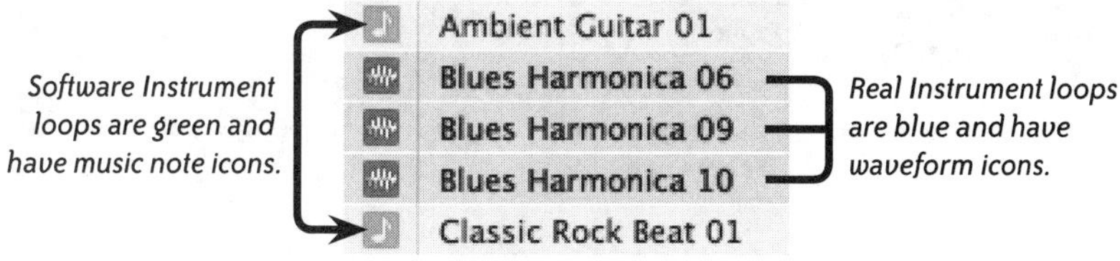

Build a song with tracks

The number of tracks you can add to a song depends on how much memory your computer has installed. A maximum of 255 Real Instrument tracks or 64 Software Instrument tracks are allowed.

GarageBand automatically sets the maximum number of tracks your computer can support without affecting performance. You can change this setting in Preferences (see page 254).

Tracks, along with loops, are GarageBand's main building blocks. As you add tracks, they're stacked on top of each other in the Timeline. This makes it possible to overlap the sound of many different instruments. You can reorganize the tracks by dragging them up and down in the list of tracks, but the order of tracks won't affect the sound.

Each track you add can hold one or more loops, referred to as *regions.* A track may contain more than one kind of instrument loop (a drum loop and a guitar loop, for example), but every loop in a track must be either a *Software Instrument* loop or a *Real Instrument* loop; Software and Real loops cannot be in the same track.

There are two basic ways to add a track to GarageBand—use the "New Track" window (shown below), or drag loops from the Loop Browser to the Timeline (shown on the following page).

Use the "New Track" window to add a new track:

When you first open GarageBand, a Grand Piano track is automatically added to the Timeline. To delete this default track (or any other track), select it, then press Command Delete.

1. From the Track menu, choose "New Track…" **or** click the plus button beneath the Tracks column.
2. In the "New Track" window that opens, click the "Real Instrument" button or the "Software Instrument" button (Software Instruments require a lot more processing power).
3. From the left column, choose an instrument category, then choose an instrument from the right column. If you plan to *record* a track, choose a "Basic Track" in the "Real Instrument" pane. A "Basic Track" has no effects applied to it, but you can add them later.
4. Click "Create." A new track is added to the Timeline.

To change the icon that appears in the header of a track, click this button and choose a new icon from the scrolling pop-up collection of instrument icons.

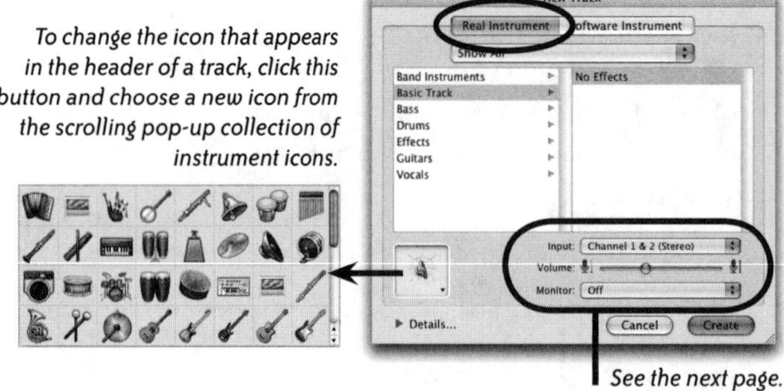

See the next page.

Input settings in the "New Track" window:

- The "Input" pop-up menu offers three *input channels.* Choose "Channel 1 & 2 (Stereo)" or one of the mono channels—"Channel 1 (Mono)" or "Channel 2 (Mono)". By default, Real Instrument loops have a "Stereo" format.
- Set the track volume with the Volume slider.
- To hear your recorded music or vocals through the speakers as you record, set "Monitor" to "On." If you have a problem with feedback, choose "Off."

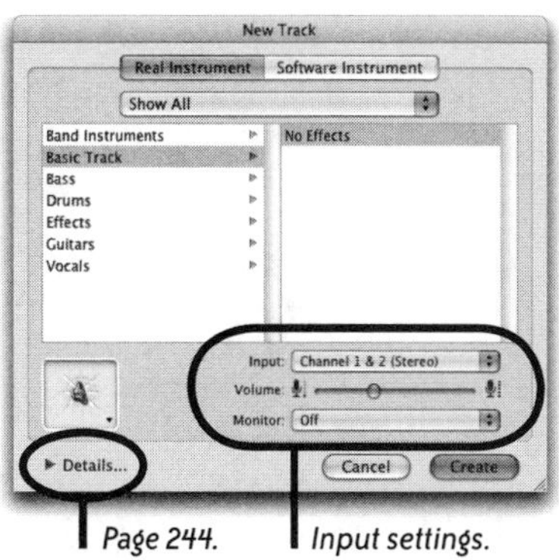

Page 244. Input settings.

Drag loops from the Loop Browser to the Timeline

The other way to create a new track is even easier:

1. Use the Loop Browser to select a loop you want to use in your song.
2. Drag the loop from the Results list of the Loop Browser and drop it into an empty area of the Timeline. Or drop it into an existing track as long as it's the same kind of loop—Real Instrument (blue) or Software Instrument (green).

As shown below, GarageBand automatically creates a track and places the loop in the track. You can choose to add effects to the track; see page 244.

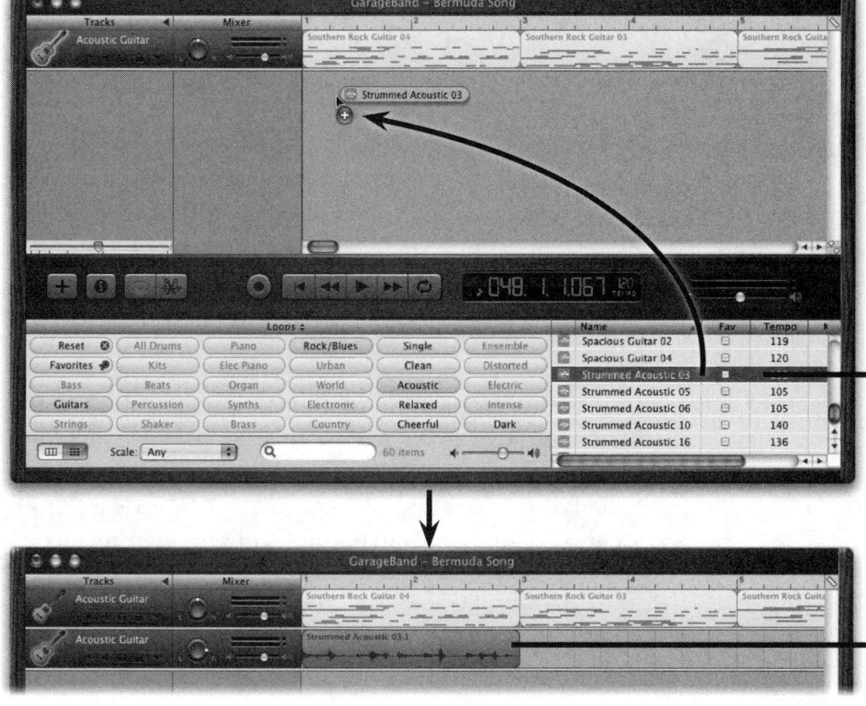

Drag a loop to the Timeline to create a new track.

The new track contains the loop that was dragged to the Timeline.

Add multiple loops to a track

Drag multiple loops to a single track to compose your song. Experiment with different loops to see how they sound next to an existing loop. Drag some loops to other tracks to see how certain instruments sound when playing at the same time. For instance, you can place a drum loop in one track, a southern rock piano in a second track, and a horn section in a third track, all playing at the same time. The example below shows what such an arrangement could look like.

As you drag a loop to the Timeline, a black vertical line appears under the loop icon to show the position of the loop's start point. Let go of the loop when the vertical line is positioned at the point you want the loop to start playing.

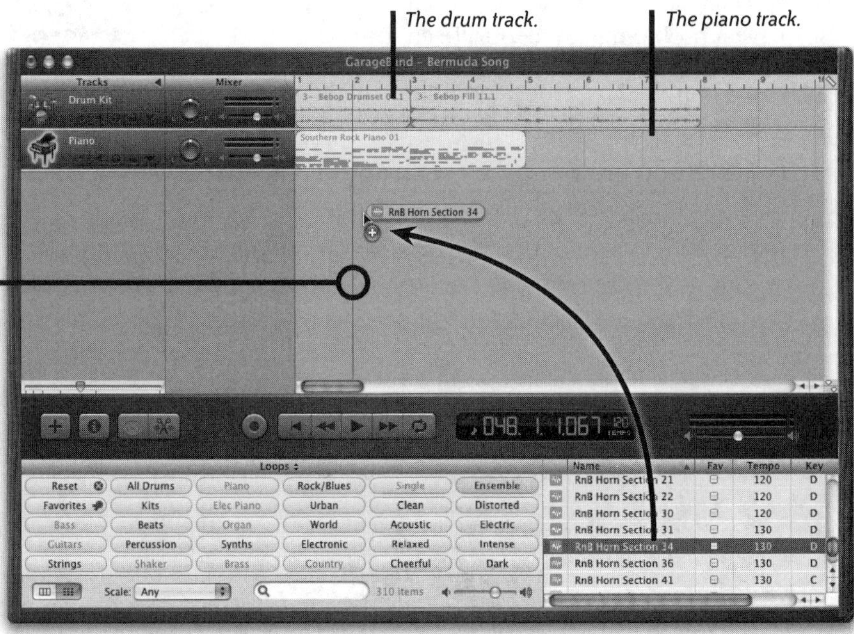

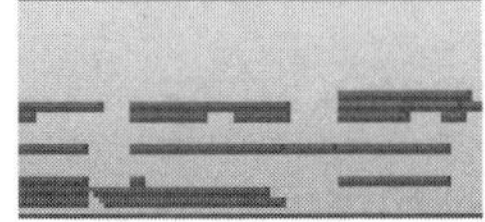

The graphic display of notes in a Software Instrument loop.

Notice above how the top track, "Drum Kit," looks different from the second track ("Piano"). The loops in the first track are *Real Instrument* loops and they appear as audio waveforms. The loop in the second track, "Southern Rock Piano," is a *Software Instrument* loop; it appears as a graphic representation of notes.

Because Software Instrument loops require more computer processing power than Real Instrument loops, you may want to consider converting some Software Instrument loops to Real Instrument loops as you add them to the Timeline, explained on the next page. See pages 246–247 to learn more about the differences between Real Instruments and Software Instruments.

Convert loops and regions

A loop or a collection of loops adjacent to each other in a track is called a **region** (learn more about regions starting on page 237). You can convert a *Software Instrument* loop or region to a *Real Instrument* loop or region. You might want to do this to reduce processing demands on your computer, since Software Instruments require more processing, or perhaps you prefer working with Real Instrument loops and waveforms in the Track Editor instead of Software Instruments and individual graphical notes.

To convert a Software Instrument loop to a Real Instrument loop:

- Drag a loop from the Loop Browser to an existing Real Instrument track (Real Instrument tracks and Real Instrument loops are *blue*).

  Or Option-drag a Software Instrument loop from the Loop Browser to an empty area in the Timeline to convert the loop and create a new Real Instrument track for it.

To convert a Software Instrument region to a Real Instrument region:

Solo

1. "Solo" a track (mute all other tracks) that contains only the region you want to convert. **To solo a track,** click the small headphones icon in the Track header; all other tracks in the project will be turned off.
2. From the File menu, choose "Export to iTunes."
3. Go to the location on your computer in which the exported song file is stored: Open your Home folder, open the Music folder, open the iTunes folder, open the iTunes Music folder, then look for a folder whose name is the same as the "Album Name" set in the "Export" pane in the GarageBand preferences (see page 254).
4. Drag the exported file (the one you located in the step above) into an existing Real Instrument track in the GarageBand Timeline.

   Or drag the file to the Timeline in an empty area beneath existing tracks to create a new Real Instrument track.

You can also **drag audio files from the Finder** to the Timeline to import them. Imported files are colored orange in the Timeline and in the Track Editor. Drag an audio file (AIFF, WAV, MP3, or AAC) from anywhere on your computer to the Timeline.

The "protected" AAC format is not supported—that includes songs purchased from the iTunes Music Store. MP3 and AAC files that you drag to the Timeline are converted to the AIFF format.

Control your Timeline view

If you **lock** the Playheads for both the Timeline and the Track Editor, the Timeline and the Track Editor display the same part of a song. When you click the *Play* button, both Playheads move to the right until they reach the middle of the Timeline, then they stop and remain stationary as the Timeline scrolls by beneath them.

If you **unlock** the Playheads, the Timeline remains stationary and the Playheads move to the right until they are out of sight. With the Playheads unlocked, you can work with one part of the song visible in the Timeline and another part of the song visible in the Track Editor.

To lock the Timeline and Track Editor Playheads, click the pair of small white triangles (circled on the left). When the two triangles are aligned, they are locked. Click on them again to unlock them.

Aligned triangles (above) indicate ***locked*** *Playheads.*

Unaligned triangles (left) indicate ***unlocked*** *Playheads.*

Playheads. *Track Editor.*

Monitor GarageBand's processing

Click the Play button and watch the Playheads as they move across the Timeline. The top triangular part of the Playhead changes color to show how much of the computer's processing power GarageBand is using.

GarageBand demands a lot of processing power and works best with newer computers that have lots of memory installed.

- White Playhead: the computer is handling the task without a problem.
- Orange Playhead: The computer is struggling to process all the digital information in real time.
- Red Playhead: GarageBand is over-taxed and may not be able to finish playing the song.

If your computer is struggling, try deleting some tracks, especially Software Instrument tracks. You can also set a lower number of maximum tracks and notes in GarageBand preferences as shown on page 254.

Arrange and modify regions in your song

A loop placed in a track is considered a **region.** You can make as many changes as you want to a region's position, duration, pitch, or sound effects without affecting the original loop. As you work on your song, "loop" refers to the original, unchanged audio clip, and "region" refers to the version of the audio clip that's in the Timeline, modified or not.

Ways to modify a region:

- **To delete a region** (loop) from a track, select it, then press Delete.

  Or select a region in a track, then press Command X.

  Or from the Edit menu, choose "Cut" or "Delete."

- **To copy a region and place it somewhere else,** select it, then press Command C, **or** from the Edit menu, choose "Copy." Select a track into which you want to paste the copied region. Position the Playhead where you want the beginning of the region to be placed. Then press Command V, **or** from the Edit menu, choose "Paste."

  Or Option-drag a region to a different position in the track or to another track. The original region stays in its position and a copy of the region is dragged to the new position.

- **Resize** a region to change its duration.

  To lengthen a region's duration, place the pointer over the top half of the region's right edge. The pointer changes to a *loop pointer.* Drag the edge to the right to lengthen the region. A duplicate of the original region shows in the new lengthened area (shown below). This is known as *looping.* The region will loop (repeat) seamlessly and smoothly. You can drag the region edge out as far as you need to make the loop repeat as many times as necessary.

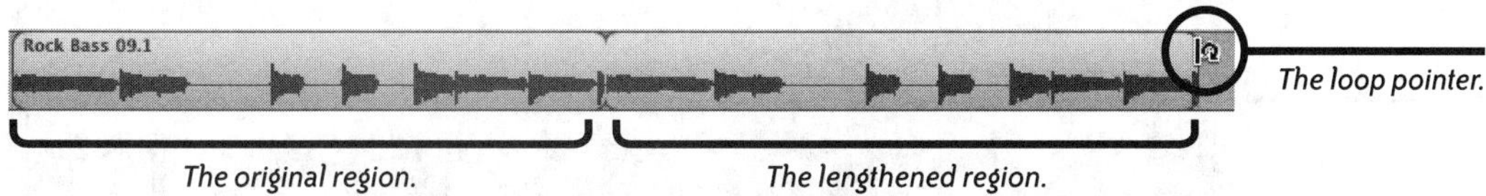

  To shorten a region's duration, place the pointer over the bottom half of the region's right edge. The pointer changes to a *resize pointer.* Drag the edge to the left to shorten the region.

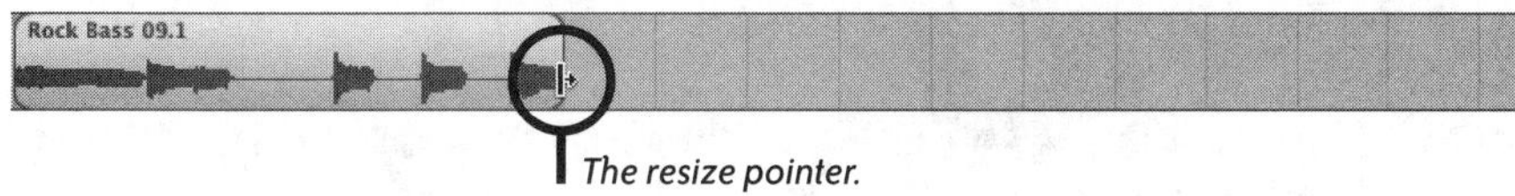

Tip: Try this technique to add interest to a track: Paste multiple copies of the same loop next to each other, then transpose each of the loops a different amount (+1, –1, +2, etc.).

- **Transpose** a region to a different key, up or down, in semitone increments. There are 12 semitones in an octave.

  Regions created with Real Instrument *loops* (blue regions) can be transposed up or down a maximum of 12 semitones.

  Regions created with Software Instrument *loops* (green regions) can be transposed up or down 36 semitones, or three octaves.

  Regions created from Real Instrument *recordings* (purple regions) cannot be transposed.

To transpose a region:

1. Click a region to select it.
2. Click the Track Editor button (the scissors icon) to open the Track Editor. The selected track is displayed in the Editor pane. **Or** you can just double-click a region in the Timeline to open it in the Track Editor.
3. In the "Region" column of the Track Editor, drag the "Region Pitch" slider left or right to lower or raise the region's key.

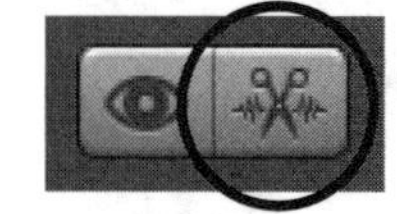

The Track Editor button.

Transposing sometimes moves an instrument out of its natural range and then it doesn't sound right. If this happens, try transposing the region up or down an entire octave (12 semitones).

The selected region.

The Track Editor button.

Click this small triangle to hide or show the "Advanced" column on the right.

Use this slider to change the pitch of a selected region.

The selected region as it appears in the Track Editor.

- **Split a region** to divide it into separated sections that can be moved, modified, copied or deleted. If you want a region to start playing somewhere in the middle, split it and delete the first section.

  Or split a region, then drag the two pieces apart in the Timeline to create a short pause between sections of the music.

  To split a region, select a region in the Timeline, then from the Edit menu choose "Split."

- **Join two or more** Software Instrument regions (green regions) to make it easy to rearrange entire sections of music. To join regions they must be adjacent to each other in the same track.

  You can also join a recorded Real Instrument region (a blue region) with another Real Instrument region, but two Real Instrument regions created from loops cannot be joined.

  1. Select the regions you want to join. To make a multiple selection, hold down the Shift key as you select regions that are adjacent in the same track.
  2. From the Edit menu, choose "Join Selected."

  Two selected regions that are to be joined.

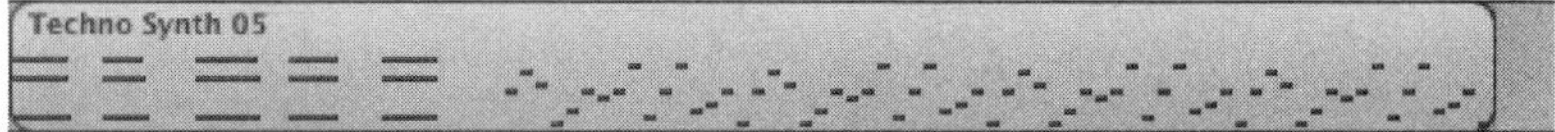

  The two regions joined as one.

  When you join a *recorded* Real Instrument region (a purple region) to another Real Instrument region (a blue region), a dialog box opens to ask if you want to create a new audio file. Click "Create" to join the regions and place them in a new Real Instrument region.

- **To Rename a region,** select the region in the Timeline, then click the Track Editor button. In the "Region" column of the Track Editor, type a new name into the "Name" field.

- **To move regions** anywhere in the Timeline, even to other tracks, drag them. If you move a region so it overlaps another region, the overlapped section of the other region will be clipped. **To recover the clipped content,** drag the bottom-right or bottom-left edge of the clip with the resize pointer, as shown on page 237.

- **To edit the individual notes** of a Software Instrument region (a green-colored region), double-click the region to open it in the Track Editor. Each note of the region is represented in the Track Editor Timeline as a rectangular bar. You can change the pitch of a note, change a note's position or duration, and add a pedal effect to sustain the note. See pages 224–227 for details.

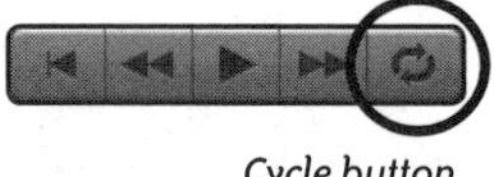
Cycle button.

- **Set a cycle region** (a region that repeats, or loops) when you want to preview a specific section of a song as you work on its arrangement or if you want to record over a specific part of a song.

  To set a cycle region, click the Cycle button (the looping arrows, circled on the left). A yellow *cycle region ruler* appears just below the beat ruler. Drag this yellow ruler to the section you want to cycle. Drag either end of the yellow ruler to adjust the region selection.

  If you don't see the yellow ruler, just press-and-drag in an empty section of the cycle ruler to set the cycle region to a new position.

  To hide the cycle region ruler, click the Cycle button again.

Drag the edges of the Cycle region ruler to mark the section you want to loop.

Beat ruler.

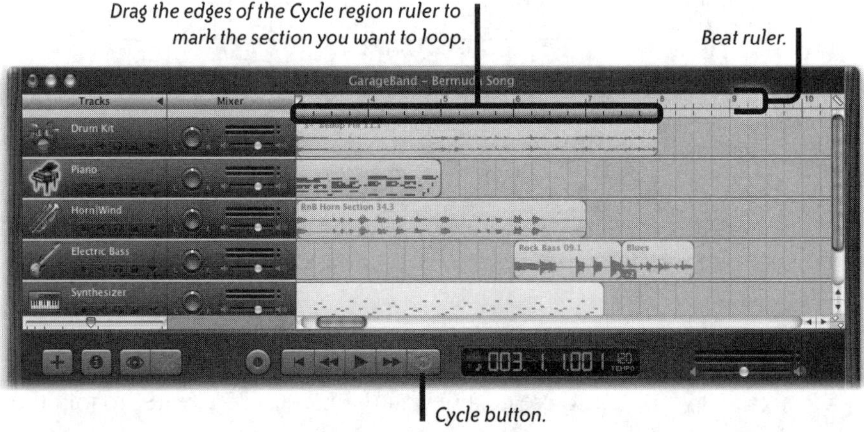

Cycle button.

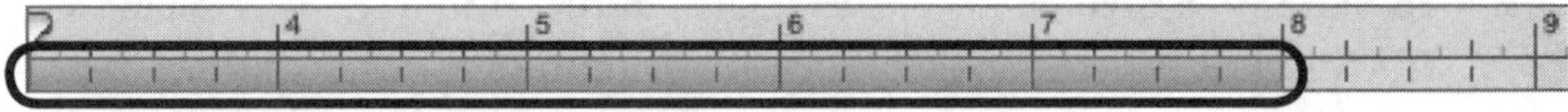

Close-up of the Cycle region ruler.

Change the grid

The GarageBand window contains two tiny ruler icons called **grid buttons.** These let you set the Timeline grid and the Track Editor grid to any of the note values shown in the grid button pop-up menus. When the grid value is set to "Automatic," the grid value changes automatically as you zoom in or out of the Timeline or Track Editor. The Triplet and Swing settings can completely change the rhythm and feel of a region. **To test the effect,** try this grid-setting experiment:

1. Place a Software Instrument loop, such as "70s Ballad Piano" in the Timeline. Select it, click the Play button, and *listen to it.*
2. Click the Track Editor button (scissors icon) to open the Track Editor.
3. Click the Track Editor's grid button and choose "1/8 Swing Heavy" from the pop-up menu.
4. Select a note in the Track Editor, then press Command A to select all the notes in the region.
5. Click the "Align" button in the "Advanced" column (shown below). The notes realign themselves to the Swing grid you selected.

Listen to the region again and notice the difference in rhythm and beat emphasis. A different grid selection won't make any difference unless you make sure to do Steps 4 and 5.

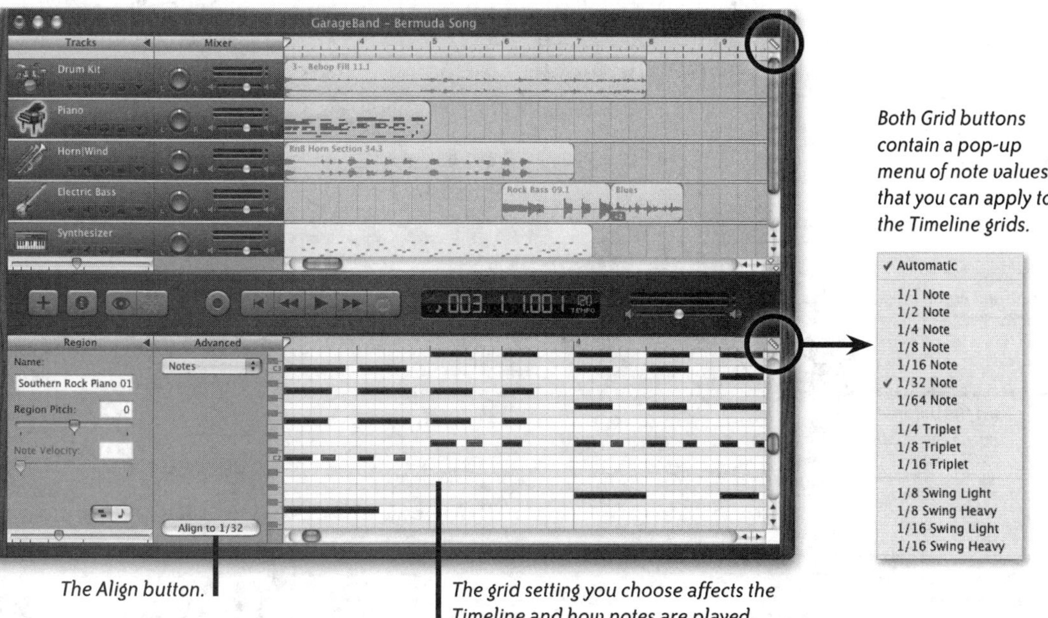

Both Grid buttons contain a pop-up menu of note values that you can apply to the Timeline grids.

The Align button.

The grid setting you choose affects the Timeline and how notes are played.

Mix Your Song

After you've created tracks, placed and edited music loops (the main building blocks of your song), you're ready to **mix** your song. Mixing a song is the process of fine-tuning the individual parts so they work together as a pleasing, cohesive whole. This usually includes adjusting the volume of tracks or regions to emphasize or downplay certain instruments or themes, changing the pan position (the balance of left and right speakers) of certain regions, and adding effects to tracks or regions to enhance sound or give it a special character.

Adjust track volume

Multiple tracks playing at the same volume level sound okay, but you can add richness and interest by setting individual volume levels for different tracks. You can also independently modify the volume of any region (loop) or any portion of a region, and control how fast the volume fades in or out.

To adjust the volume of an entire track: In the "Mixer" column, drag the volume slider left or right.

To make multiple volume adjustments to a track or region: Click the small triangle button in the "Tracks" column (shown on the left) to show the *volume/pan curve* track, then choose "Track Volume" from the pop-up menu. The horizontal line (the "curve") represents the track's volume. Click anywhere on the volume line to create control points (small colored spheres). Drag control points up or down to raise or lower the volume. Drag control points left or right to change the duration of a volume change.

Click to show or hide track volume as a volume curve track (below).

Volume curve track.

Turn the volume curve on or off.

With the volume curve turned off, track volume is determined by the volume slider in the Mixer column.

Adjust pan position

Pan control.

Pan position refers to the balance of sound between the left and right speakers and is also known as *stereo placement.*

To adjust a track's pan position, press-and-drag the white marker on the pan control to the left or right. You can also click anywhere around the dial and the white marker will jump to that position.

You can't fully appreciate and enjoy some aspects of GarageBand (like pan control) unless you have stereo headphones or stereo speakers connected to your Mac.

If a track is playing while you adjust the pan control, you can hear the sound moving from one speaker to another—if you have stereo speakers or headphones connected to your computer.

To make multiple pan adjustments to a track or region: Click the small triangle button in the "Tracks" column to show the drop-down *volume/pan curve* track, then choose "Track Pan" from the pop-up menu. The horizontal line represents the balance of sound between left and right speakers. Click on the line to create control points, then drag the points up or down to move sound more towards the left (up) or right (down) speakers. See page 222.

Add effects

To further enhance the sound of specific instruments or your entire composition, add adjustable, high-quality sound effects such as compression, echo, reverb, equalizer settings, and more.

You can apply effects to a single track, as explained here and on the following page, or to the entire song as explained on page 245.

Track Info button.

To add effects to a track:

1. Select a track in the Timeline.
2. Click the Track Info button to open the "Track Info" window. **Or** double-click a track header.

The Instrument button at the top of the Track Info window indicates whether a *Real Instrument* or *Software Instrument* has been chosen in the Timeline.

Choose an instrument category from the left pane, then choose an instrument effect from the pane on the right. Experiment—choose different instrument effects, then play the track and listen to the difference. With a track selected, experiment with different choices from both panes of the window. Also experiment with changing the tempo. You'll be amazed at what you create, even if you're musically challenged.

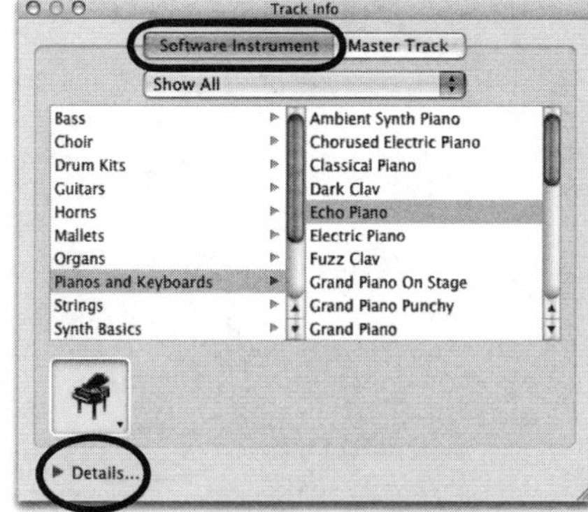

For more control, click this button and show settings for the selected instrument effect. See the next page learn more about this "Details..." button.

The **Details pane** in the bottom half of the "Track Info" window contains the settings used for the currently selected instrument in the list. You can dramatically affect the sound of instruments by changing these settings.

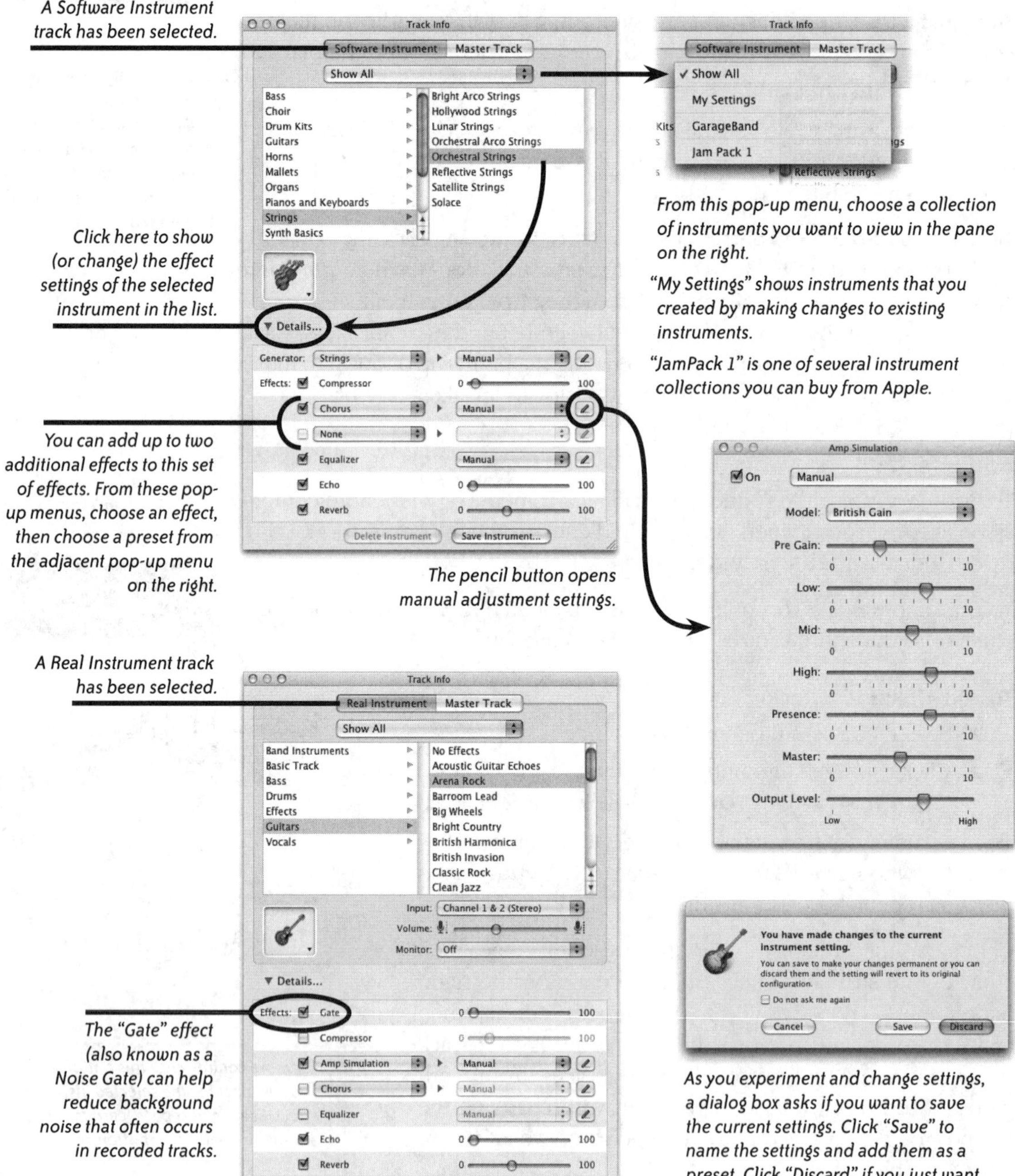

A Software Instrument track has been selected.

From this pop-up menu, choose a collection of instruments you want to view in the pane on the right.

"My Settings" shows instruments that you created by making changes to existing instruments.

"JamPack 1" is one of several instrument collections you can buy from Apple.

Click here to show (or change) the effect settings of the selected instrument in the list.

You can add up to two additional effects to this set of effects. From these pop-up menus, choose an effect, then choose a preset from the adjacent pop-up menu on the right.

The pencil button opens manual adjustment settings.

A Real Instrument track has been selected.

The "Gate" effect (also known as a Noise Gate) can help reduce background noise that often occurs in recorded tracks.

As you experiment and change settings, a dialog box asks if you want to save the current settings. Click "Save" to name the settings and add them as a preset. Click "Discard" if you just want to preview effects.

Add effects to the entire song

Click the **Master Track** button in the "Track Info" window to work with settings that affect the sound of the entire song rather than just a single track. In addition to choosing instruments and effects, you can also change the **tempo, time,** and **key** in the "Master Track" view. If a song is playing as you change settings, you can hear the effect immediately.

To change instrument and effect settings, select an instrument *category* in the left pane, then select an *instrument effect* in the right pane. Click the Play button in the main window to hear the changes as you try different settings.

The "Details" pane provides a standard set of effects, plus a pop-up menu from which you can choose one additional effect. As shown on the previous page, you can modify an effect by choosing "Manual" from the effect's adjacent pop-up menu, then click the pencil icon to open a separate window of manual adjustments.

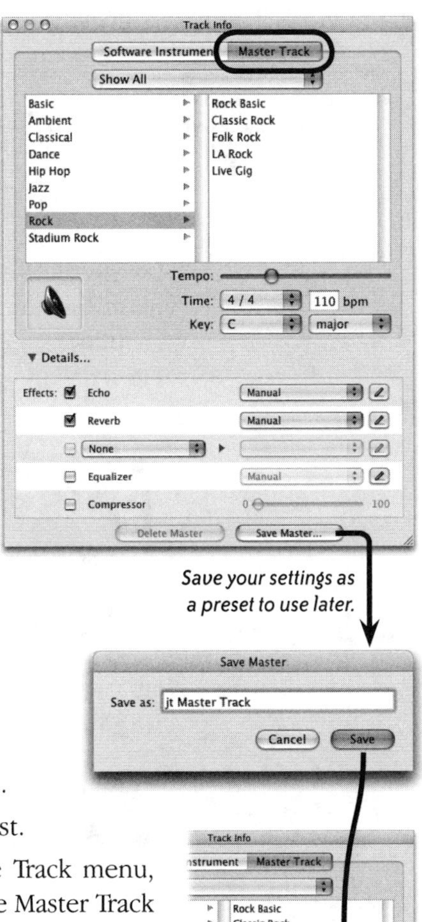

Save your settings as a preset to use later.

The saved Master Track settings are added to the list in the Track Info window.

When you make changes to the sound of a Master Track, you can **save the settings** as a preset to use later.

1. Choose the settings and effects you want.
2. Click the "Save Master..." button.
3. In the "Save Master" dialog, type a name for the settings.
4. Click "Save." The new preset appears in the Track Info list.

To hide or show the Master Track in the Timeline, from the Track menu, choose "Show Master Track" or "Hide Master Track." When the Master Track is showing, it stays positioned in front of all other tracks—if the window is full of tracks, other tracks scroll behind it.

If you turn off "Echo" and "Reverb" effects in the *Master Track* settings, they will also be disabled in the *Instrument* button settings.

The best way to learn what various effects are about is to listen to them, but here are definitions of several terms:

Compressor: Adjusts the difference between the loudest and softest parts of a song or track.

Chorus: A delay effect in which copies of the sound are played back slightly out of tune to simulate several voices or instruments.

Flanger: Similar to Chorus, but played back more out of tune.

Phaser: Adds a whooshing sound.

Real Instruments and Software Instruments

Real Instrument loops are created by recording real instruments in a studio, such as the ones included with GarageBand.

GarageBand uses two different instrument formats—Real Instruments and Software Instruments. Throughout this chapter we've scattered explanations of the differences and pointed out instances where one or the other format was used. In case you didn't start at the beginning of this chapter and read straight through, this brief summary of Real and Software Instruments will help you understand the differences and identify them in GarageBand.

Real Instruments

Real Instruments appear as both *tracks* and *loops.* Real Instrument tracks and loops are always *blue.* The volume curve that's located beneath a Real Instrument track is also blue. Blue equals *Real Instrument* format.

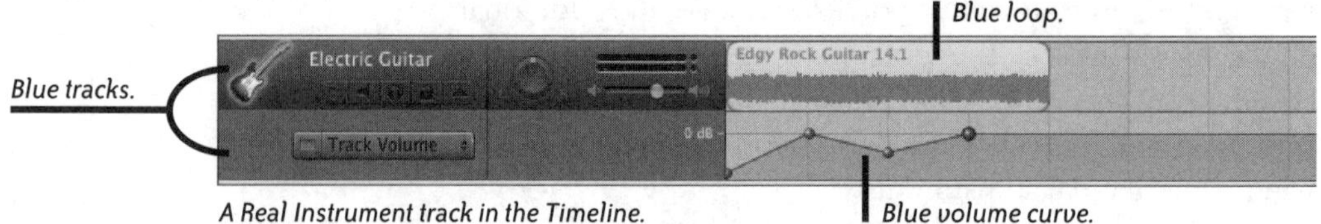

A Real Instrument track in the Timeline.

Real Instrument loops in the Loop Browser are blue and have blue waveforms. When you drag a blue loop (a Real Instrument loop) from the Loop Browser to the Timeline, it automatically creates a Real Instrument track.

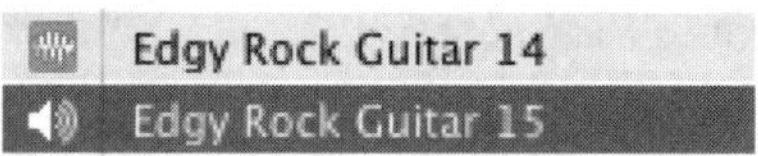

Real Instrument loops in the Loop Browser have blue shading and blue icons.

Only Real Instrument loops can be placed in Real Instrument tracks. You can place different kinds of musical instruments (drums, guitars, harmonica, etc.) in a single Real Instrument track, as long as they're all in the Real Instrument format (blue).

Since Real Instruments require less processing power during playback than Software Instruments, you may have fewer performance problems on slower computers if you use mostly Real Instrument loops.

A Real Instrument loop in the Track Editor appears as a blue waveform. In the Track Editor you can change the pitch of a Real Instrument loop, or select and transform just part of a loop.

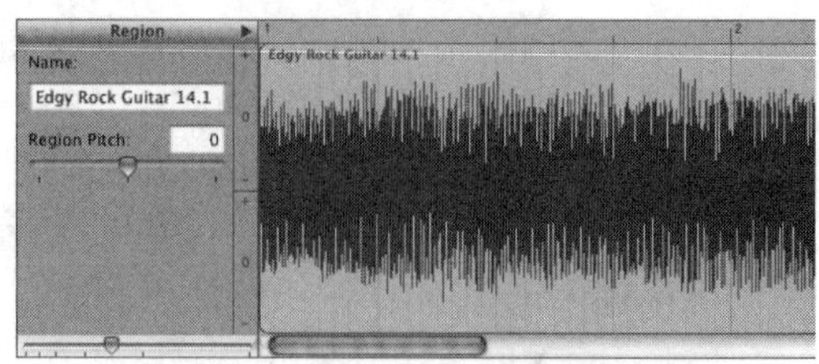

A Real Instrument loop in the Track Editor.

Software Instruments

Software Instruments appear as both *tracks* and *loops,* and are always *green.* The volume curve beneath a Software Instrument track is green, and Software Instrument loops in the Loop Browser have green music note icons and green backgrounds.

Software Instrument loops are MIDI voices (Musical Instrument Digital Interface). They are created digitally and are actually mathematical descriptions of musical sounds, which require intensive computer processing to play.

Green tracks

Green loop.

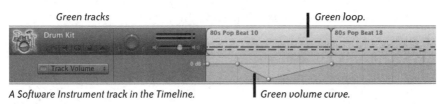

A Software Instrument track in the Timeline.

Green volume curve.

Classic Rock Beat 03
Classic Rock Beat 04

Software Instrument loops in the Loop Browser have green shading and green note icons.

A Software Instrument loop in the Graphic view of the Track Editor shows each individual note as a rectanglular shape. When the Track Editor is in Notation view, notes are shown as traditional looking notes. In the Track Editor you can fix the timing of notes, alter the rhythm by changing the grid value, change the pitch of any note, or change its velocity. From the "Display" pop-up menu you can choose to show graphic representations of notes, modulation, pitchbend, or sustain effects.

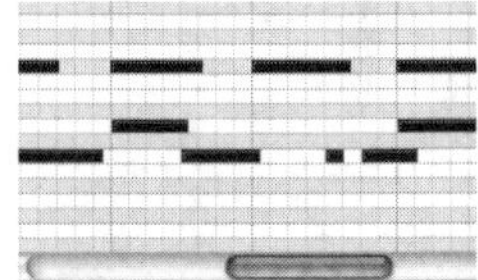

Graphic view of a Software Instrument loop in the Track Editor.

Only Software Instrument loops can be placed in Software Instrument tracks. Different musical instruments can be placed in a single Software Instrument track, as long as they're all in the Software Instrument format (green).

Notation view of a Software Instrument loop in the Track Editor.

When you work with Software Instruments, a pop-up menu in the Advanced column of the Track Editor lets you view and edit things like Modulation, Pitchbend, and Foot Pedal effects. If you have a MIDI keyboard or other musical device connected to your computer that has such controls, you can record those effects, then modify them in the Track Editor. Even if you don't have a music device connected, you can experiment with those effects—Command-click in the Track Editor to create control points.

In addition to notes, you can view (and edit) these effects in the Track Editor.

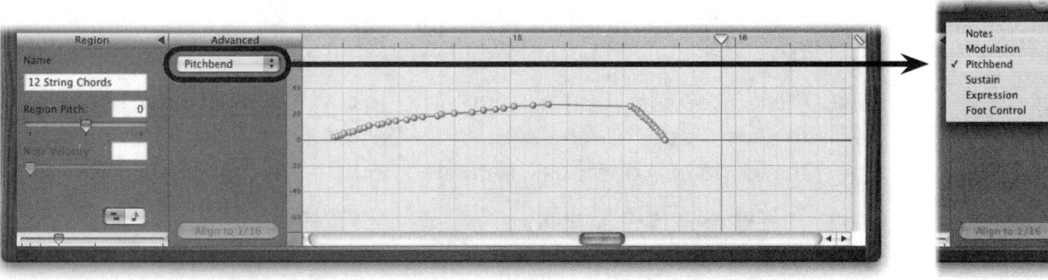

Notes
Modulation
✓ Pitchbend
Sustain
Expression
Foot Control

Record Live Instruments or Vocals

You can create totally original music by recording your own instruments or vocals. Connect a musical instrument, such as a guitar, a MIDI keyboard, or a microphone, then record straight into a GarageBand track.

Some MIDI keyboards and other instruments can plug directly into your computer. Some instruments and microphones may need to connect to an audio interface device that connects to the computer.

To connect an electric guitar, you can buy an adapter for about $20 that lets you plug directly into the computer. To connect several input devices at a time, such as a mic, a guitar, and a keyboard, consider buying a FireWire or USB audio adapter. You'll find excellent advice about these and other recording products at **MacJams.com**; click the "Buyer's Guide" link.

To record in a Real Instrument track:

1. Connect an instrument or a microphone to your computer.
2. Select an *existing* Real Instrument track in the Timeline and position the Playhead where you want to start recording.

   Or create a *new* track: Click the the plus sign, then click the "Real Instrument" button in the "New Track" window. Choose an instrument or effect from the left and right panes, then click OK.
3. Click the Record button, then play the instrument or sing into the microphone. As you record, a region that contains your music is created in the track.
4. **To stop recording,** click the Record button again.

To record in a Software Instrument track:

1. Connect a MIDI-compatible keyboard to your computer.

   Or open the onscreen music keyboard, shown here. From the Window menu, choose "Keyboard."

2. Select an *existing* Software track in the Timeline. Position the Playhead where you want to start recording.

   Or create a *new* track as described in Step 2 above.
3. Click the Record button, then play the connected keyboard or click the keys of the onscreen music keyboard. As you record, a region that contains your music is created in the track.
4. **To stop recording,** click the Record button again.

Musical Typing

If you don't have a MIDI keyboard that you can connect to your computer, you can use your computer keyboard as a music keyboard. If you're musically talented and can play keyboards, this technique might actually be a productive one. For those of us who can barely type words, musical typing is just fun experimentation. In any case, it's pretty amazing.

1. From the Window menu choose "Musical Typing."
   The "Musical Typing" window opens (shown below) and shows the computer keys that can be used to play notes and act as effects controllers.
2. Select a Software Instrument track to play.
3. Play notes using the keys on your keyboard that correspond to the keys in the "Musical Typing" window. The keys in the window highlight as you play.

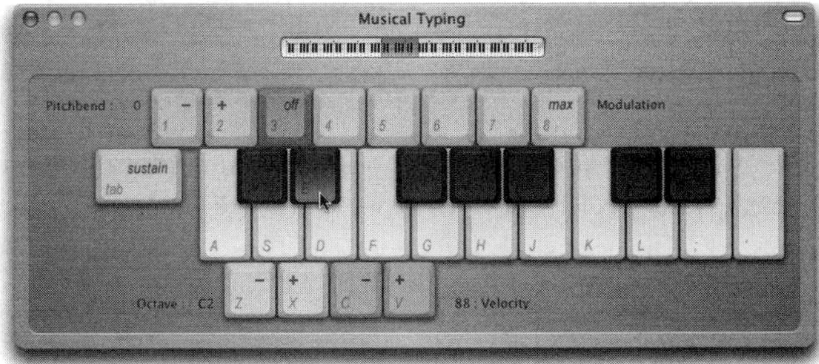

- To move the pitch up by octaves, Press Z.
- To move the pitch down by octaves, Press X.
- To raise or lower velocity, press C or V.
- Key 3 turns modulation off.
- Keys 4 through 8 change the modulation value.
- To bend the pitch down, press 1.
  To bend the pitch up, press 2.
  The pitch continues to bend as long as you hold down the key.
- The Tab key sustains notes, similar to a sustain pedal on a piano. Press the Tab key to turn sustain on and off.
- The middle row of keys on your computer keyboard play the "white keys" on a piano. The W, E, T, Y, U, O, and P keys in the top row play the piano's "black keys" (sharp and flat notes).
- To change the octave range of the keyboard, click in the thumbnail keyboard to highlight a different section of keys.

Save Your Song as an Archive

If any of your song loops get moved or deleted, GarageBand won't be able to find them when you open a song project that uses those loops. Or if you copy a song project to another computer, that computer may not have the same collection of loops that were on the first computer. To avoid any of these problems you can save your song project as an archive. When you save a song as an archive, all the loops you used in the song are saved and packaged with the archive, including any original recordings you made.

Be aware that saving as an archive increases the size of a song file. An ordinary song file (not archived) is smaller because it *references* loops rather than *contains* them. Songs that use a large number of loops can create very large archive files.

To save a song as an archive:

1. From the File menu, choose "Save as Archive."
2. In the dialog that drops down from the title bar (shown below), type a name in the "Save As" field, then choose a location from the "Where" pop-up menu.

Bermuda Song

An archived GarageBand song looks just like any other GarageBand file.

Add "archive" to the name you choose so you can later identify which file is an archive. If you choose to save the archive with the same name and in the same folder as the original song file, a dialog box appears and asks if you want to replace the existing song file with the new one.

GarageBand automatically chooses to save archived songs in the GarageBand folder that's located in your Home folder's *Music folder,* but you can choose any location you want.

Add Additional Loops to GarageBand

You can add additional loops that you've acquired from Apple (or third-party vendors) to your collection of loops in the GarageBand Loop Library. Just drag a loop or a folder of loops on top of the Loop Browser. If you've created or modified a loop in GarageBand and want to add it to the Loop Library, select it, then from the Edit menu, choose "Add To Loop Library...."

The Master Track

In addition to Real and Software Instrument tracks, GarageBand includes a **Master Track.** To show the Master Track in the Timeline, from the Track menu, choose "Show Master Track."

From the pop-up menu choose "Master Volume" or "Master Pitch."

From the pop-up menu in the Master Track header, choose "Master Volume" to show the master volume curve in the Timeline and to edit the volume of the entire song (all tracks). Click on the volume curve (the horizontal line) to add control points, then drag the control points up or down to adjust the volume. Drag control points left or right to shorten or lengthen the duration of the volume change. Click the small box on the left side of the pop-up menu to turn volume curve on or off.

To show the master pitch curve in the Timeline and change the pitch of the entire song, use the pop-up menu and choose "Master Pitch." Edit the curve the same way you edit the master volume, described above. Click the small box on the left side of the pop-up menu to turn the pitch curve on or off.

Instead of adding multiple control points to a curve, you can move the entire curve up and down to raise and lower the volume or pitch.

Export Your Song to iTunes

When your song is finished, export it to iTunes so you can share it with others in a variety of ways. Once it's in iTunes, you can burn it to CD, use it in an iPhoto slideshow, or use it as a soundtrack in iMovie. You can use it as a background audio track in an iDVD menu, or just play it along with other songs in your iTunes collection.

Exported song files are saved as AIFF files, a standard Mac audio format.

To export your song to iTunes:

1. Open GarageBand preferences, then click the "Export" button.
2. Type names in the text fields that you want iTunes to use for a new playlist that contains your song, a composer name (your name will do), and an album name. See page 254 for more information about Export preferences.
3. From the File menu, choose "Export to iTunes." Your song appears in the iTunes Library, named the same as your GarageBand song file. It also appears in the automatically created playlist that you just named.

GarageBand Preferences

The GarageBand preferences window lets you set certain behaviors and options that suit your hardware and your preferred way of working with music files.

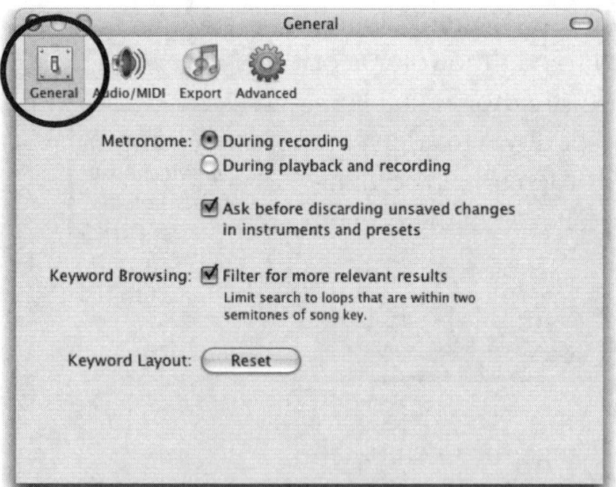

To open the preferences window, go to the GarageBand application menu and choose "Preferences...." The top of the window contains four category buttons. Click each one to see the options available for that category.

General preferences

Metronome: A metronome is a device that clicks at regular, preset intervals so a musician can keep an accurate beat as she plays music. Choose to have GarageBand's metronome play just during a live recording session, or during playback *and* live recording. **To enable the metronome,** from the Control menu at the top of your screen, choose "Metronome." A checkmark appears next to the word in the menu. To disable the metronome, select it again in the Control menu to remove the checkmark.

Ask before discarding unsaved changes in instruments and presets: When you experiment with modifications of an instrument or a preset, you can choose to have an automatic message ask if you want to save or discard the changes. If you're doing a lot of experimenting to learn what various effects sound like and don't want to keep the changes you're making, uncheck this box so you won't be bothered with messages.

Keyword Browsing: To increase the number of loops found by a keyword search in the Loop Browser, uncheck "Filter for more relevant results." Click the checkbox to limit a keyword search (such as "violin") to loops that are close (two semitones) to the key you're working in.

Keyword Layout: If you drag keyword buttons around in the Loop Browser to rearrange them and generally make a big mess, you can return them to the default layout. Just click this "Reset" button.

Audio/MIDI preferences

Audio Output: Choose the speakers you want to use for playback as you compose your song. Choose "Built-in Audio" to use your built-in computer speaker or headphones. If you have external speakers connected, you can choose them from this menu. This setting overrides the existing audio output settings in the Sound preferences pane of System Preferences.

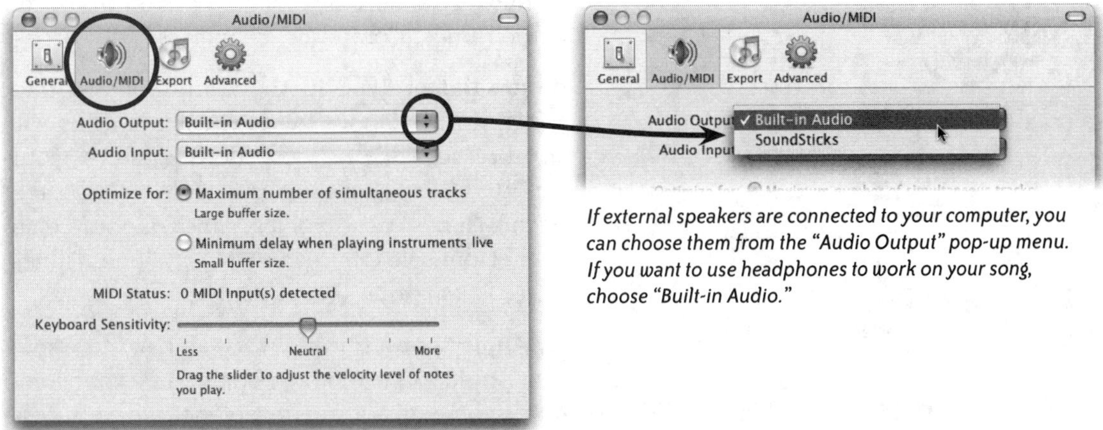

If external speakers are connected to your computer, you can choose them from the "Audio Output" pop-up menu. If you want to use headphones to work on your song, choose "Built-in Audio."

Audio Input: If you have an input device connected to your computer, such as an audio interface for MIDI keyboards or some other instrument, you can select the device from this menu. This setting overrides the existing audio input settings in the Sound preferences pane of System Preferences.

Optimize for: These settings attempt to help optimize the performance of GarageBand when recording live instruments. Choose **Maximum number of simultaneous tracks** if you don't have *latency* issues or if you have a slower computer (slower than a G5). Also try this setting when your song contains a lot of tracks.

In audio recording, ***latency*** is the delay you may hear between playing a sound and recording it on the computer. It is caused by the amount of time it takes for a real instrument sound to reach the input port and be digitally processed by the computer.

If you do have *latency* problems while playing/recording your musical instrument, choose **Minimum delay when playing instruments live** to set a small buffer size. This setting uses more of the computer's processing power to speed up the processing of audio input signals and may affect overall performance on slower computers.

MIDI Status: Shows how many MIDI devices are connected to the computer.

Keyboard Sensitivity: Drag the slider to set the amount of velocity (hardness or loudness) a note will have when you play the on-screen keyboard. To display the keyboard, from the Window menu at the top of your screen, choose "Keyboard."

Export preferences

Enter the information that you want to appear in iTunes when you finish your song and export it to iTunes (explained on page 251).

iTunes Playlist: iTunes creates a new playlist in which to organize your exported GarageBand songs. Type a name for the playlist.

Composer Name: Type a name you want to appear in the iTunes "Composer" column.

Album Name: Type in the name you want to appear in the iTunes "Album" column. This will also be the name of the folder that stores your exported GarageBand songs. The folder is located in the iTunes Music folder, which is located in your Home folder (Home/Music/iTunes/iTunes Music Folder/Your Album Name).

My Apple Loops: Choose who can have access to your Apple loops. If other people share your computer, you may not want everyone to have access to your collection of loops, especially if you've added extra collections, such as Apple's JamPack series or other third-party collections available online.

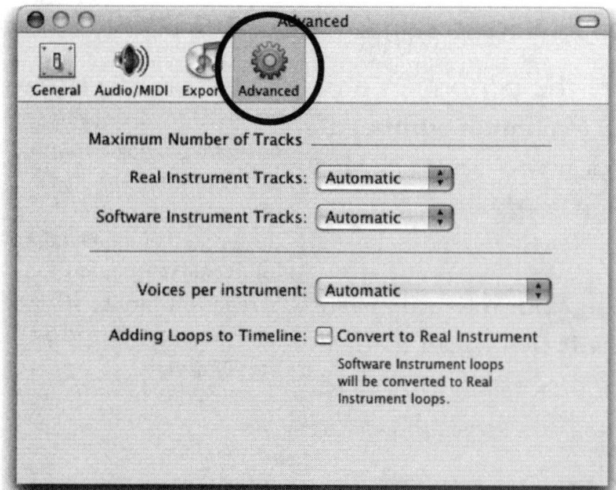

Advanced preferences

Maximum Number of Tracks: Select how many Real Instrument tracks and Software Instrument tracks are allowed in a song. Select "Automatic" to let GarageBand choose the best number based on your computer's speed and how much RAM is installed.

From the **Voices per instrument** pop-up menu, select how many notes a Software Instrument can play at one time. If you select "Automatic," GarageBand chooses the best number based on your computer's speed and amount of RAM.

Adding Loops to Timeline: Check **Convert to Real Instrument** if you want Software Instrument loops to automatically convert to Real Instrument loops when dragged to the Timeline. If you don't select this checkbox, you can still convert a Software Instrument to a Real Instrument: Option-drag it to an empty area in the Timeline, beneath existing tracks. **Or** drag it to an existing Real Instrument track.

Section two

.Mac apps

.Mac (pronounced "dot Mac") is a collection of tools and services that are available when you subscribe to a one-year .Mac membership for $99.95. A .Mac membership includes 250 megabytes of combined email and iDisk storage. There's also a .Mac Family Pack available ($179.95/year) that includes one full .Mac membership with a combined 250 megabytes of email and iDisk storage, four .Mac sub-accounts with 100 megabytes of combined email and iDisk storage, and a shared iDisk folder for you and your family. For most people, the value of a .Mac membership far exceeds the price tag.

The software and services included in a .Mac membership are explained in this section: An **email account** with "mac.com" address; **webMail** for access to your email account and Address Book from any Mac or PC in the world; .Mac **Bookmarks** for accessing your favorite web sites from any computer; **iDisk** storage, 250 megabytes of email and personal storage space on Apple's servers; **HomePage,** web-based software for creating and publishing web pages; **iSync** to synchronize Address Book and iCal calendar information between multiple computers; **Backup** software to archive important files to your computer, to removable discs, or to your iDisk; **iCards** (electronic greeting cards) using your own photos; and more. Membership also gives you access to a members-only technical support service, free software, and other perks.

Go to www.mac.com and click "Join Now." Or sign up for a sixty-day free trial, complete with an email address, to help you decide if you should join.

iDisk

6

When you become a .Mac member, you have instant access to your **iDisk**—250 megabytes of personal storage (including email storage) on Apple's servers. You can upgrade your iDisk storage capacity at any time (for a fee), up to 1 gigabyte (1,024 megabytes).

Your .Mac account relies on iDisk to make its best features a reality: web pages, backup protection of important files, synchronization of address books with your Mac, customized iCards, online calendars, slideshow screensavers, and whatever else Apple's innovative imagination may offer in the future.

You may want to use your iDisk to store files in a safe, remote location as personal backups or to store important files so you can retrieve them from any other location. Any files stored on your iDisk are accessible by you or (if you choose) a guest at any time, from almost any computer (Mac or PC).

Sharing files with others is effortless using iDisk Utility, a free download from Mac.com. Just set permissions and give someone your .Mac name and password to allow them to upload or download files to your Public folder. iDisk Utility also makes it easy to monitor your iDisk space, access other .Mac members' Public folders, or purchase additional storage space.

Put iDisk on Your Desktop

When you sign up for a .Mac account, you automatically get 250 megabytes of hard disk space on a computer at Apple. This storage space is called your **iDisk.** You can "mount" your iDisk so it appears on your Desktop just like any other hard disk, then copy files between your Mac and the iDisk—you are really copying files from your Mac to Apple's computer (or vice versa). Once files are on your iDisk (on the Apple computer), you can access them from anywhere in the world.

To open your iDisk:

If you don't see the Go menu, you are not at the Finder—just click on any blank space you see of the Desktop and that will take you to the Finder.

1. If you haven't already connected to the Internet, do so now.
2. From the Go menu in the Finder, choose "iDisk," and then choose "My iDisk" from the submenu, as shown below.

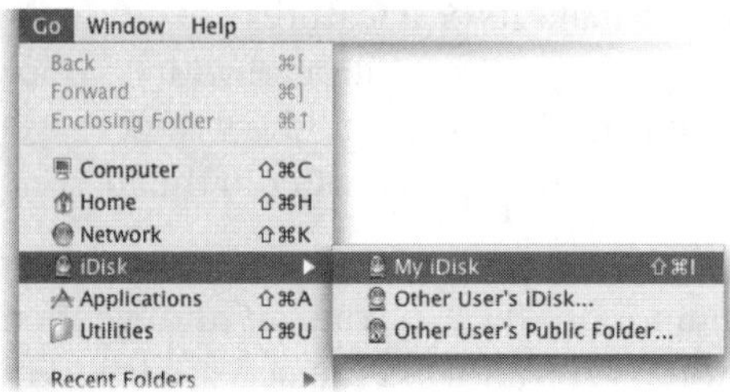

If you've *never* logged in to your .Mac account before: The Mac will ask you to enter your member name and password before you can mount your iDisk.

After the first time you log in to your .Mac account: When you choose "My iDisk" from the Go menu, a window opens that displays your iDisk, as shown below. Amazing. Don't get confused with these folders *that are named exactly the same as the folders in the Home folder* on your computer. The icon in the iDisk title bar (the crystal ball) indicates you're looking at folders on Apple's servers.

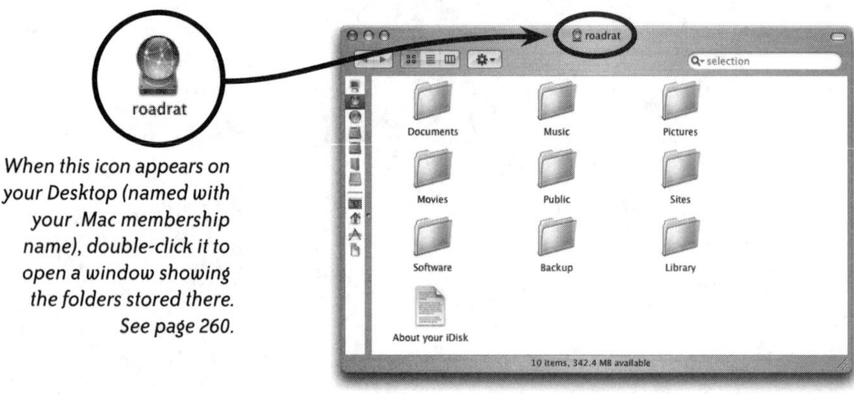

When this icon appears on your Desktop (named with your .Mac membership name), double-click it to open a window showing the folders stored there. *See page 260.*

How does your Mac know which iDisk to open?

How does your Mac know which iDisk is yours? After you set up an account, your member name and password appear in the .Mac System Preferences. Click the "System Preferences" icon in your Dock, then click the ".Mac" icon. You can see below the .Mac member name and password.

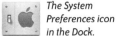

The System Preferences icon in the Dock.

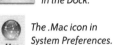

The .Mac icon in System Preferences.

If you have more than one .Mac account, you can go to a different account: Change the member name and password in this .Mac preference pane. In the Finder, when you choose "My iDisk" in the Go menu, it opens the account that is entered here.

Here's an even quicker way to access a different iDisk without changing your .Mac preferences: At the Finder, choose "iDisk" from the Go menu; then choose "Other User's iDisk..." in the submenu (see previous page).

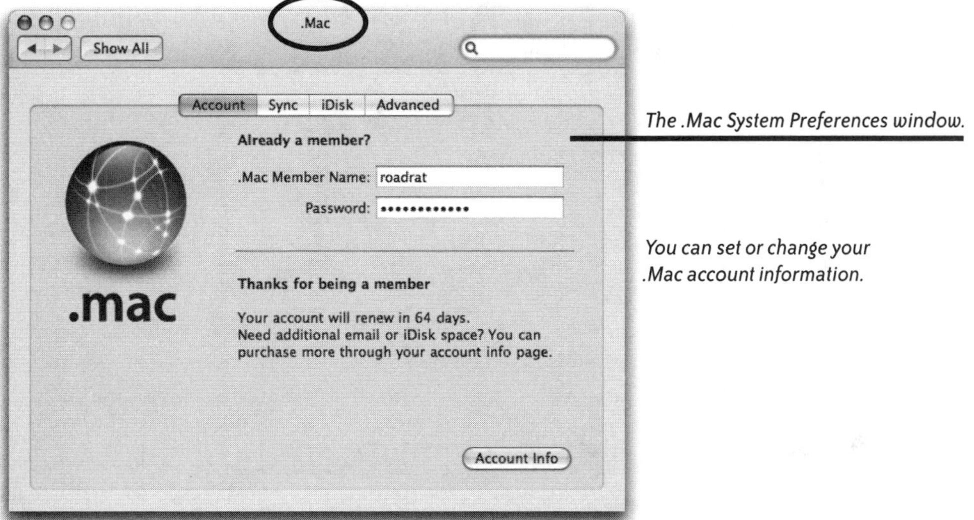

The .Mac System Preferences window.

You can set or change your .Mac account information.

Other ways to open your iDisk

- **Click the iDisk icon in a Finder window Sidebar** (shown to the right). An iDisk icon appears in the Sidebar of all Finder windows, giving you quick access to your iDisk at all times.

  If the iDisk icon does not appear in the Sidebar: From the Finder menu, choose "Preferences…." Click the "Sidebar" icon. Make sure that "iDisk" has a check next to it.

- **Use iDisk Utility,** explained on page 263–264.

iDisk Contents

When you double-click the **iDisk** icon on your Desktop to open its **window,** you're actually looking at files and folders that are on Apple's server. This explains why the window is sometimes slow to open (especially if you're using a telephone modem to connect instead of broadband).

An iDisk window is shown below. The folders you see are actually on one of Apple's computers. The icon in the title bar is one visual clue that you're *not* looking at folders in your own Home folder on a local computer. Another clue is the highlighted iDisk icon in the Sidebar, indicating the location of the files and folders in the main window.

All of your iDisk folders are **private** and accessible only to you (or someone who knows your password), except the folder called "Public."

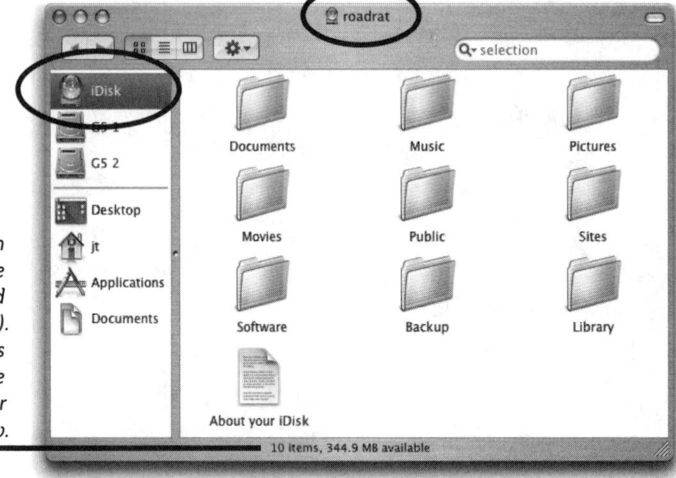

This example shows an iDisk whose storage space has been upgraded (see page 264). The status bar shows more space available (344.9 MB) than your iDisk window may show.

Documents folder: Drag into this folder any kind of document that you want to store and make available to yourself over the Internet. This folder is private and only you have access to it.

Music folder: Drag music files and playlists to this private iDisk folder so you can have access to them from anywhere in the world.

Pictures folder: Drag individual photos or a folder of photos that you plan to use in a HomePage web site into this iDisk Pictures folder so you'll have access to them when you're building the web page.

Movies folder: Drag movies that you might use in a HomePage web site into this iDisk Movies folder so you'll have access to them when you're building the web page.

Public folder: Put files and folders here that you want to make accessible for other people. Unless you set up password protection (see page 264), *other people who have your .Mac member name can access files that you drag to your iDisk Public folder.* You can open any one else's Public folder that doesn't use password protection if you have that person's .Mac member name.

Sites folder: The Sites folder stores any web pages that you've created using HomePage. You can also store sites that were created with any other web authoring software.

Software folder: The Software folder contains free software provided to you by Apple. If you see anything you want in these folders, drag it to your Desktop. The content of this folder does not count against your iDisk storage space allotment.

Backup folder: When you use **Backup,** Apple's software for .Mac members, this is where the archived files are put. See Chapter 10 to learn about Backup.

Library folder: The Library folder contains application support files. Anything that needs to be in this folder will automatically be placed there. Don't drag files into or out of this folder.

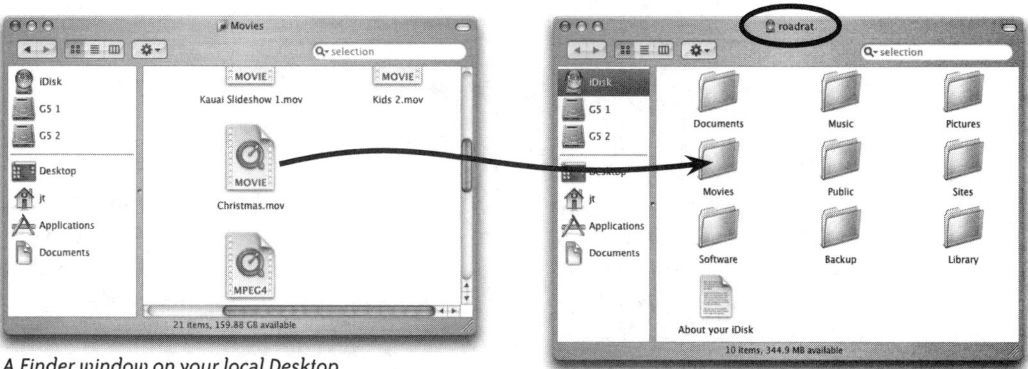

A Finder window on your local Desktop.

To copy files TO your iDisk, *drag files or folders from your computer to the appropriate folder in the iDisk window. In this example, I dragged a movie file to the Movies folder on my iDisk.*

To copy a file FROM your iDisk, *drag it from the iDisk window to your Desktop or to any folder on your computer.*

It's Easy to Get Confused!

When you open your iDisk, you may notice that it looks almost exactly like your Home window. You can tell it's your iDisk, though, because of the name of the window and the icon in the title bar, as shown on the previous pages.

But as soon as you open any folder on your iDisk, the iDisk icon in the title bar disappears, and you can no longer tell if the Movies folder you opened is the Movies folder on Apple's server or your own folder on your hard disk!

This is how you can check: Hold down the Command key and click on the title bar of any window. A window is actually a folder that shows the files and folders stored in it. A drop down *path menu* tells you where the folder is stored.

Command-click on a window's title bar to see a pop-up ***path menu.***

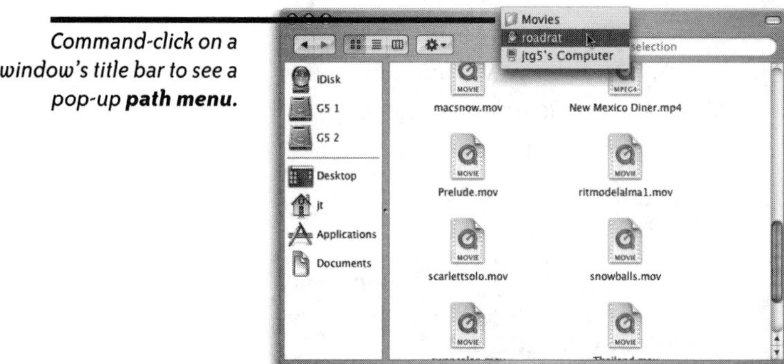

Save Directly to Your iDisk

You can save any document directly to your iDisk. From the document's File menu, choose "Save As...." From the sheet that slides down, choose your iDisk as the volume you want to save to, then choose the Documents folder from the iDisk (as shown below). Type a name for the file, then click "Save."

Save documents in iDisk's "Documents" folder.

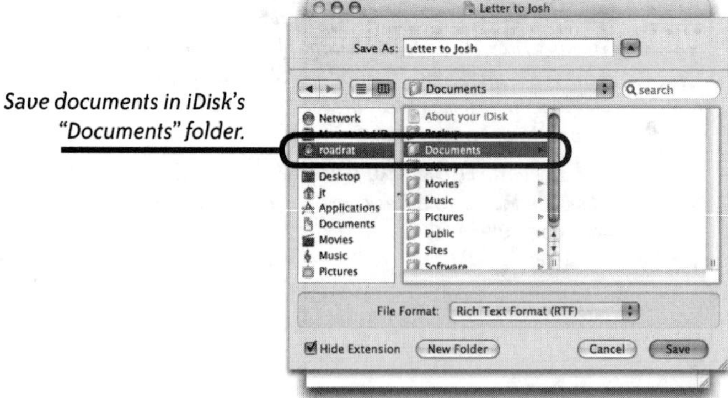

Manage Your iDisk with iDisk Utility

iDisk Utility

The **iDisk Utility** is the easiest way possible to manage your iDisk.The software is free, even if you don't have a .Mac account—but the software is not fully functional unless you have a .Mac membership. With iDisk Utility you can open your other accounts without changing your .Mac settings, you can set access privileges for your iDisk, password protection for your Public folder, monitor your iDisk storage capacity, add extra storage to your iDisk, and open other .Mac members' Public folders.

To download iDisk Utility from the .Mac web site:

1. Go to www.mac.com.
2. Click the "iDisk" icon in the web page sidebar, then from the iDisk page click on "iDisk Downloads" (shown to the right).
3. On the "Download iDisk Utility" page, click the "iDisk_Utility.dmg" link to download the installer. Double-click the installer package (iDisk_Utility.pkg, shown on the right) and follow the instructions in the installer window. iDisk Utility is installed in the Utilities folder (located in your Applications folder).
4. Double-click the iDisk Utility icon in the Utilities folder. The iDisk Utility window opens, as shown below.

iDisk Downloads

iDisk_Utility.pkg

To open a Public Folder, either yours or another member's:

1. Open iDisk Utility (see above for downloading and installing).
2. Click "Open Public Folder," then enter your .Mac member name or another member's name in the text field. Click "Open."

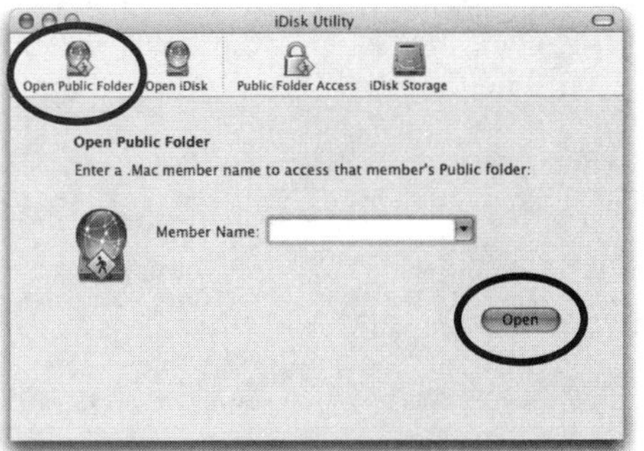

*This is the "Open Public Folder" pane. It gives access to a .Mac member's **Public Folder** only.*

*To access **all** of the folders on your iDisk, click the "Open iDisk" button in the iDisk Utility toolbar (explained on the following page).*

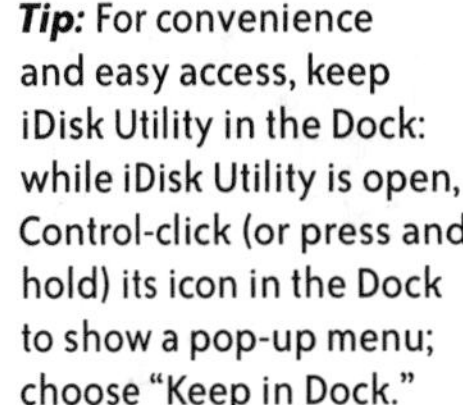

Tip: For convenience and easy access, keep iDisk Utility in the Dock: while iDisk Utility is open, Control-click (or press and hold) its icon in the Dock to show a pop-up menu; choose "Keep in Dock."

3. An icon representing your other account (or another member's Public folder) appears on your Desktop, as shown on the right. Double-click this icon to open that Public folder so you can access the files stored there.

dearrobin

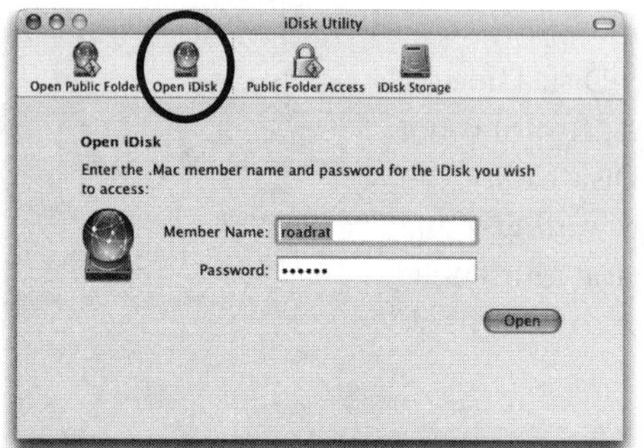

To access an entire iDisk:

In the iDisk Utility toolbar, click the "Open iDisk" icon to access an entire iDisk for which you have a member name and password. This can be another .Mac membership of yours, or it can be someone else's.

Type in a member name and password, then click the "Open" button.

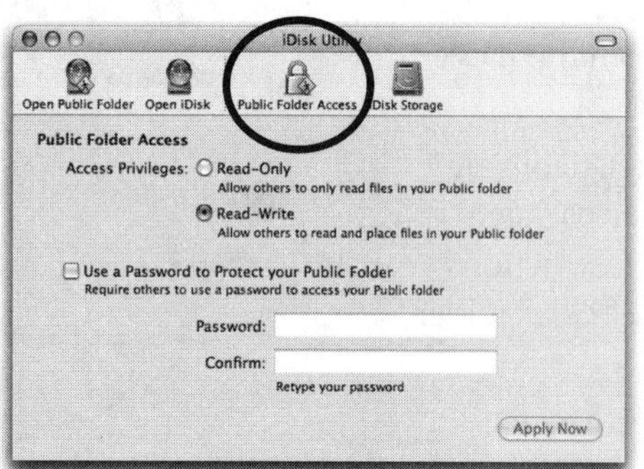

To set access privileges or password protection:

Click the "Public Folder Access" icon to set access privileges or password protection for your Public folder. To allow others to upload files to your iDisk—click the "Read-Write" button. You should then add a password—click the checkbox for "Use a Password to Protect your Public Folder." Type a password in the fields, then click "Apply Now."

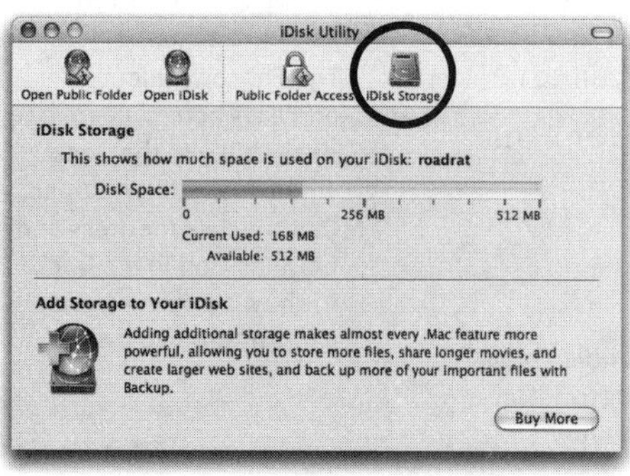

To monitor your iDisk Storage:

Click the "iDisk Storage" icon to see how much .Mac storage space you're using and how much you have available. Click the "Buy More" button to see available options and prices and to purchase more iDisk storage.

Tip: If you need to access an iDisk from a machine running **Windows XP,** download the free **iDisk Utility for Windows XP.** Installation instructions are included with the download.

You'll find it in the iDisk section of Mac.com.

iDisk Storage Settings

A .Mac account includes combined email and iDisk storage of 250 MB on Apple's servers. The total amount of storage is automatically divided evenly between email and iDisk when you start your account, but you can change that ratio if you need more email storage or more iDisk storage. To set this and other .Mac settings, open .Mac Preferences.

To change your iDisk storage settings:

1. Open System Preferences and click the .Mac icon.

The .Mac icon in System Preferences.

2. In the .Mac pane of System Preferences (shown below), click the "Sign In" tab. If you're already a .Mac member, type in your member name and password. If you want to become a member or just learn more about .Mac membership, click the "Learn More" button.

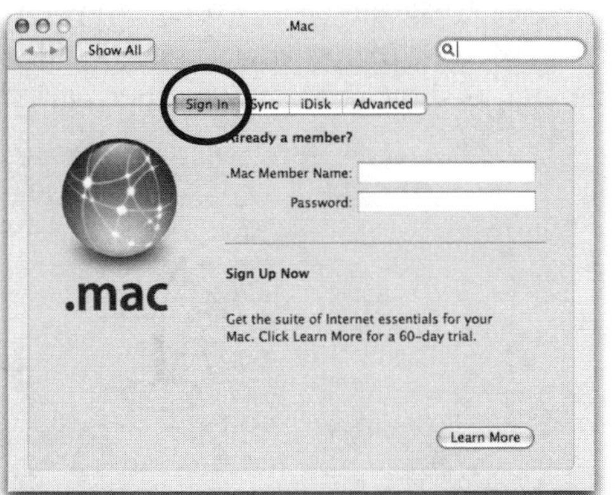

If you've previously entered a member name and password, the "Sign In" button says "Account." Skip to Step 3.

3. After you sign in, the "Sign In" tab turns into the "Account" tab and the window displays the Account pane. Click the "Account Info" button to open a .Mac web page that contains your account info.

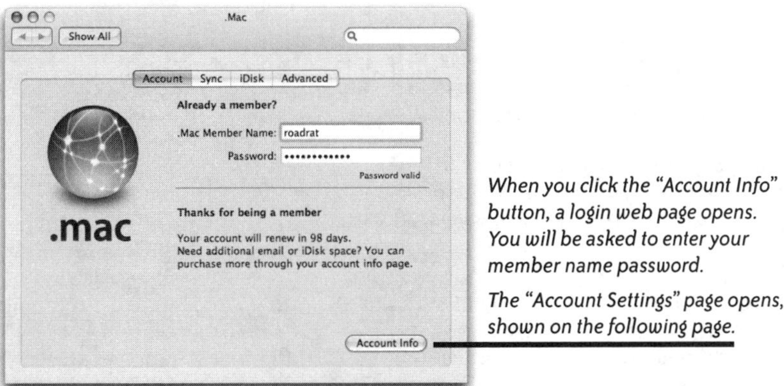

When you click the "Account Info" button, a login web page opens. You will be asked to enter your member name password.

The "Account Settings" page opens, shown on the following page.

4. On the "Account Settings" web page, click the "Storage Settings" button (below) to show the storage management tools.

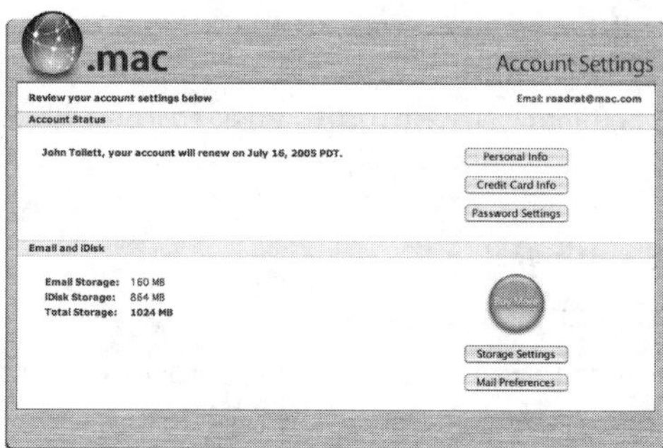

5. The graph below shows the distribution of your .Mac account storage space divided between email storage and iDisk storage. If you want to change the 50–50 default setting (below-left), choose a different ratio from the pop-up menu, as shown on the right, then click "Save."

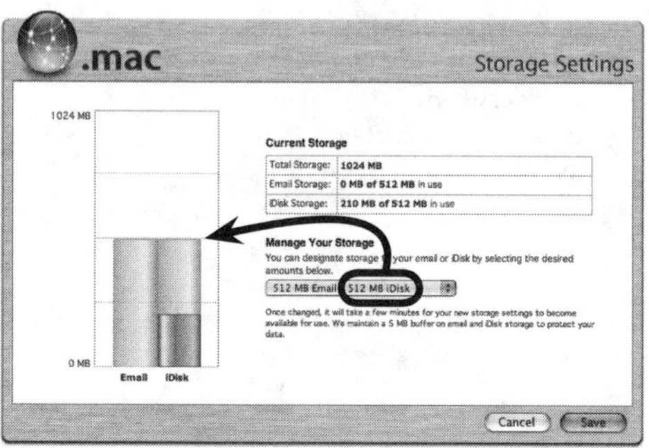

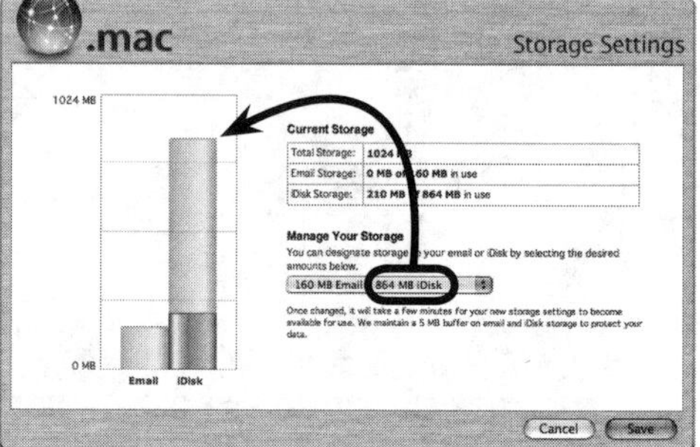

iDisk Preferences

Click the iDisk tab of .Mac preferences to show your iDisk preferences.

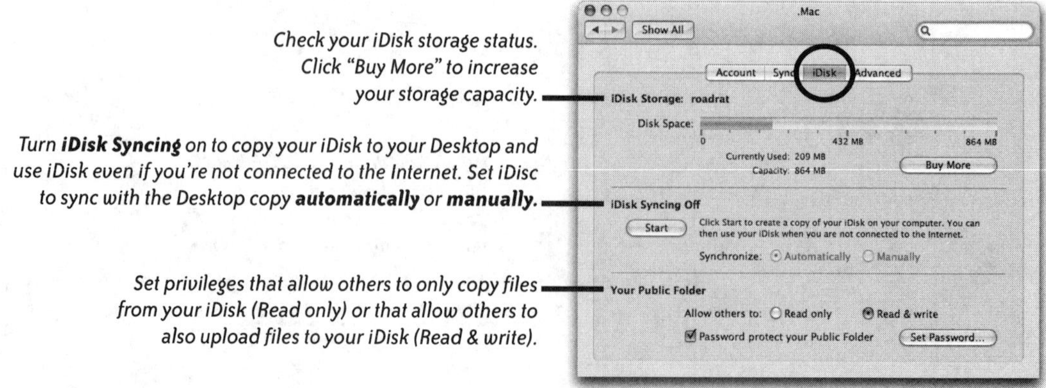

7 iCards

If you've never had the urge to send an email postcard to friends, **iCards** could change your attitude. This ever-changing collection of beautiful, eye-catching images is a notch or three above what you usually get from online greeting card services. A great-looking card with a postmark captures attention more effectively than a plain old email message. You can even use one of your own photos that you've copied to your iDisk, instead of a photo from the iCard Image Library.

Because iCards are such a great way to announce events, HomePage uses it to announce newly created web sites. You can also use your .Mac Address Book for quick-click iCard addressing.

So start uploading your favorite photos to the Pictures folder in your iDisk. If you haven't signed up for a .Mac account yet, you're missing a lot of *fun.* And it's a great way to keep in touch without a lot of writing.

This sidebar appears on the .Mac page.

Send an iCard

Anyone can send **iCards** to friends and family, even without a .Mac membership. But to send an iCard *using your own photo,* you do need a .Mac membership. An iCard is simply an electronic postcard you can send to anyone on any computer. iCard is far better than most Internet postcards for two reasons: The quality of the graphics is superior, and iCards are sent straight to the recipient instead of requiring a visit to a web page to "pick up" a card.

To send an iCard from the iCard Image Library:

1. Go to **www.mac.com** and click "iCards" in the sidebar (shown on the left). Or click "iCards" in the page's navigation bar (shown below).

2. On the iCards welcome page, shown below, click on a specific iCard thumbnail or one of the many iCard categories to display more card options. Once you click a card thumbnail, it opens a full-sized, editable version of the card (next page).

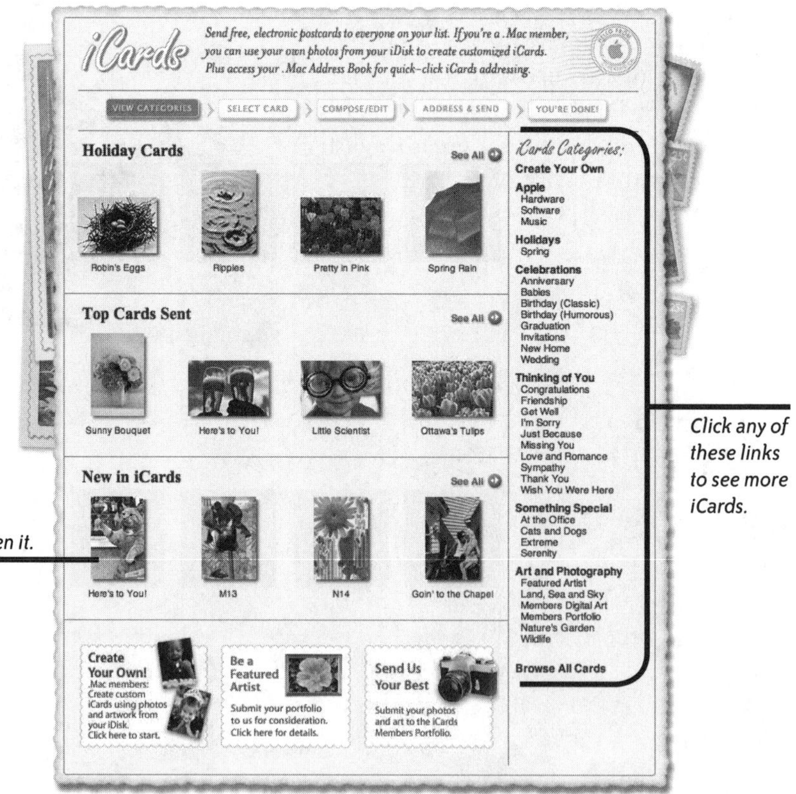

Click an iCard to open it.

Click any of these links to see more iCards.

3. On the editable iCard page that opens (shown to the right), select a type style and write a message. Click "Continue."
4. The next page previews your card and lets you address the card to as many recipients as you like.

   If you're logged into your .Mac account already, your name and email address are automatically placed in the name and email fields. You can override these and type in a different name and return address.

   If you want to receive a copy of the iCard, check the box to "Send myself a copy."

   To protect the privacy of multiple recipients, hide their email addresses: Check the box to "Hide distribution list."

   Enter a recipient's email address in the address field. To add multiple addresses, separate each address with a comma.

   Or choose a recipient from the "Choose a Quick Address" pop-up menu.

   Or click the "Address Book" button (circled on the right) to access your .Mac Address Book list, shown on the next page. Put a checkmark next to the addresses you want placed in iCard's address field. See Chapter 9 to learn more about the .Mac Address Book and Quick Addresses.

   —continued

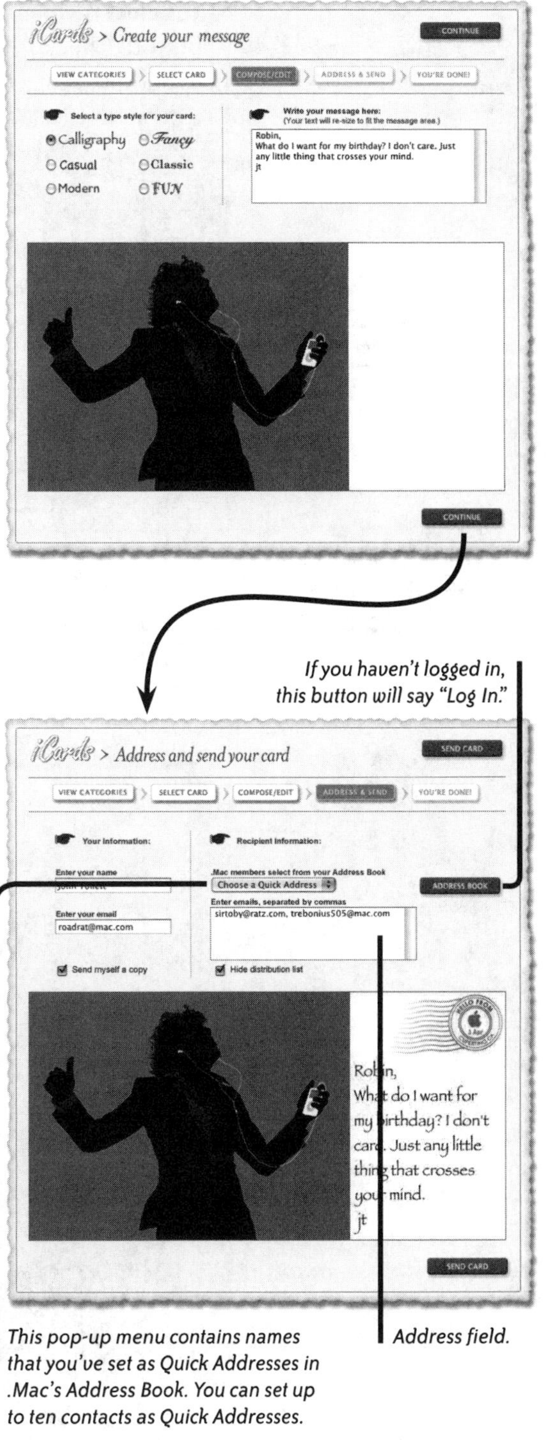

If you haven't logged in, this button will say "Log In."

This pop-up menu contains names that you've set as Quick Addresses in .Mac's Address Book. You can set up to ten contacts as Quick Addresses.

Address field.

To select recipients from your Address Book, click the "Address Book" button. Check the box next to the name of the recipient(s) you want to add. Use the scroll buttons to scroll up or down the list, or type a name in the search field to find a specific name or address. Click "Return to Card" when you have selected all the recipients you want.

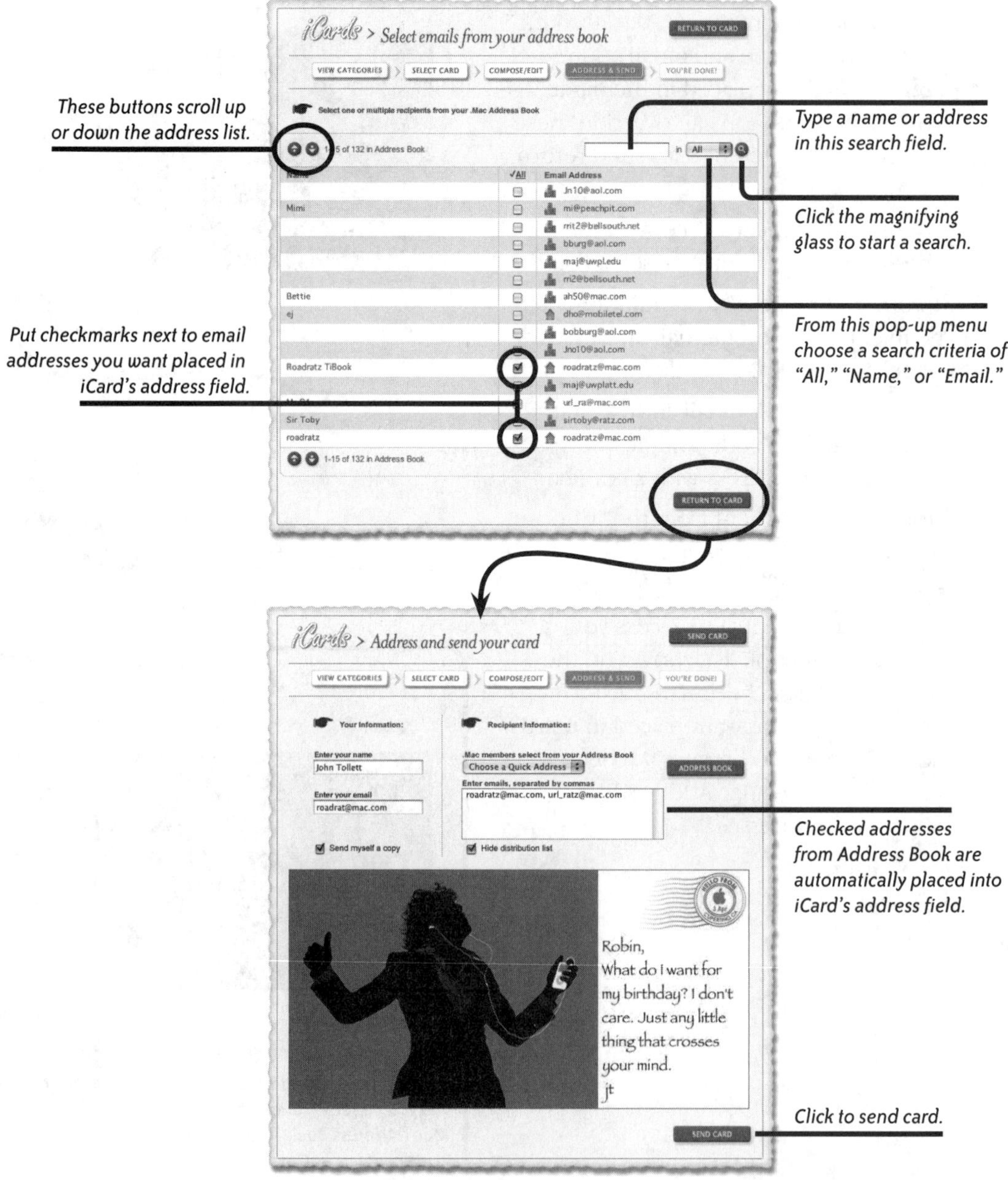
These buttons scroll up or down the address list.
Type a name or address in this search field.
Click the magnifying glass to start a search.
From this pop-up menu choose a search criteria of "All," "Name," or "Email."
Put checkmarks next to email addresses you want placed in iCard's address field.
iCards > Select emails from your address book
RETURN TO CARD
iCards > Address and send your card
SEND CARD
Checked addresses from Address Book are automatically placed into iCard's address field.
Robin,
What do I want for my birthday? I don't care. Just any little thing that crosses your mind.
jt
Click to send card.

5. Click one of the "Send Card" buttons (in the top-right or bottom-right corner of the page).
6. A "Congratulations" web page opens (shown below), with the options to "Send Same Card" to someone else, "Return to Category" to choose another photo or "Return to iCards Main" to go to the main iCards menu. Once you see the "Congratulations" page, it means your iCard has been successfully sent.

Create Your Own iCard

Tip: Before you upload photos to the Pictures folder on your iDisk, convert the photos to a resolution of 72 ppi (pixels per inch) and maximum dimensions of 640 pixels wide and 480 pixels tall to keep image sizes and upload times reasonable.

Apple's iCard images are beautiful, but you probably have photos of your own that you'd like to use. It's easy—first copy some photos to the Pictures folder on your iDisk. See Chapter 6 to learn how to do that.

To create your own iCard:

1. On the iCards welcome page, click "Create Your Own" to open the "Select an image" page shown at the bottom of this page.

2. Choose a photo or a folder of photos from the Pictures list (shown below). If the photo you want to use is in a sub-folder, click on the folder to show its contents in this list.
3. Click on a photo name to view it in the preview pane, as shown on the next page. When you see the picture you want, click "Select This Image."

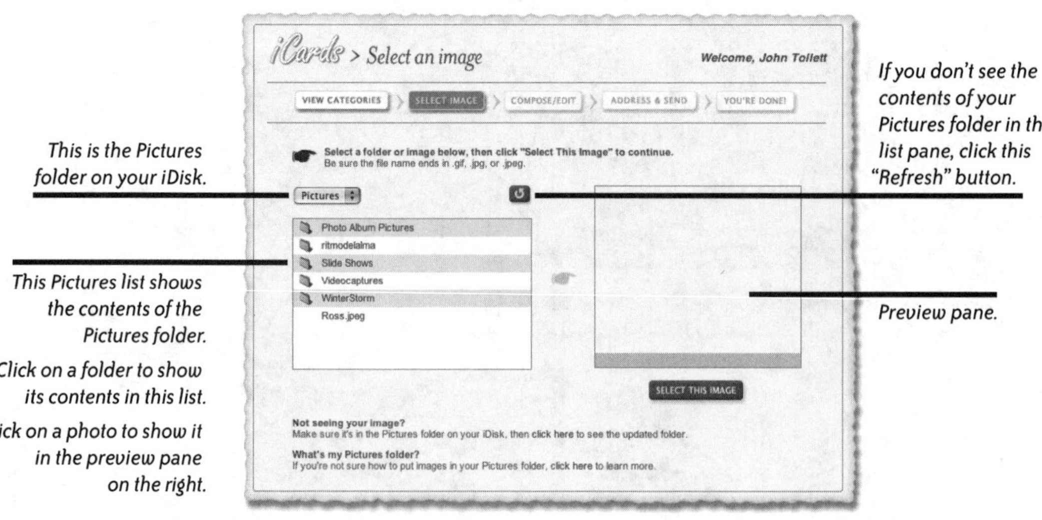

This is the Pictures folder on your iDisk.

This Pictures list shows the contents of the Pictures folder.

Click on a folder to show its contents in this list.

Click on a photo to show it in the preview pane on the right.

If you don't see the contents of your Pictures folder in the list pane, click this "Refresh" button.

Preview pane.

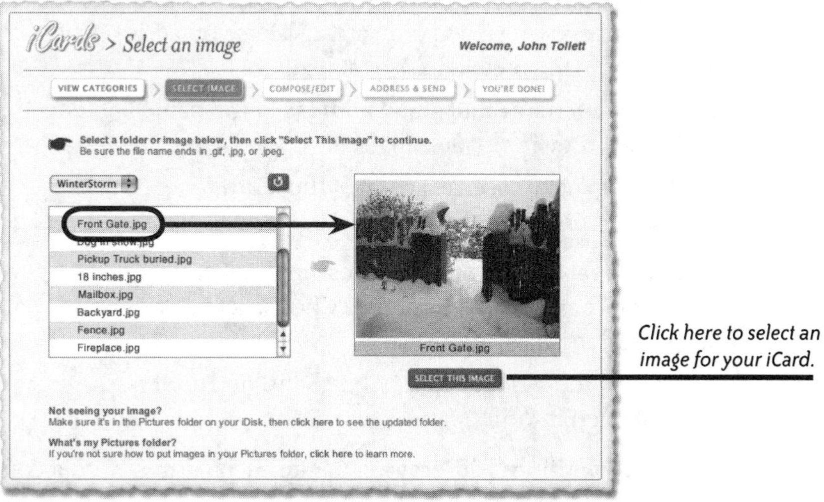

4. In the "Create your message" page (below), select a type style, then type your message in the text field.
5. To trim your photo to fit the dimensions of an iCard, check the box shown below. If you don't like the results, uncheck the box.
6. Click "Continue."

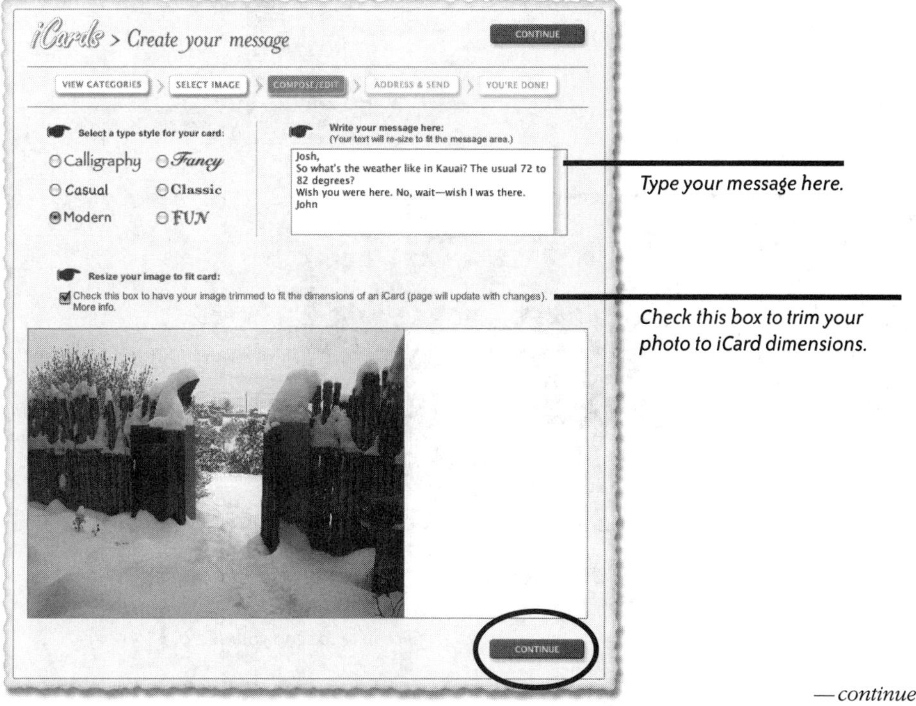

—continued

7. The next page previews your card and lets you address the card to as many recipients as you like.

   Enter your name and email address in the name and email fields if they're not automatically placed there.

   If you want to receive a copy of the iCard, check "Send myself a copy."

   Enter a recipient's email address in the text box.
   Or select an address from the "Choose a Quick Address" pop-up menu.

   Or click the "Address Book" button to find addresses contained in your .Mac Address Book.

   To add multiple addresses, separate each address with a comma.

8. Click "Send Card" in the bottom-right corner of the page.

   In the "Congratulations" page that opens, choose to "Send Same Card" to someone else, "Return to Category" to create another card, or "Return to iCards Main" to start over (see page 268).

Click here to go back and make changes to your card.

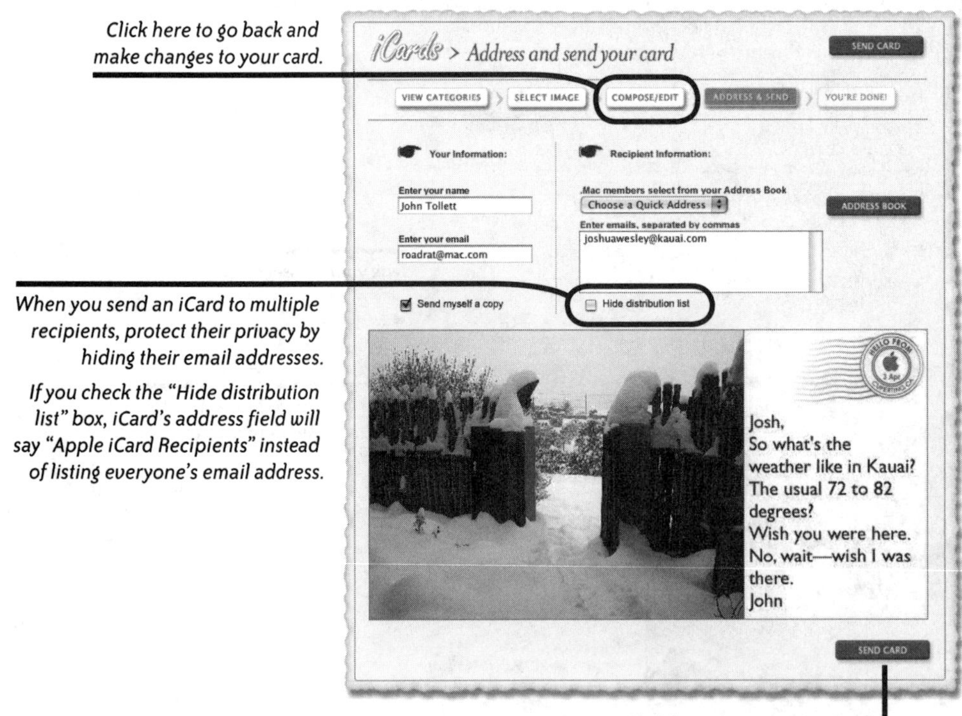

When you send an iCard to multiple recipients, protect their privacy by hiding their email addresses.

If you check the "Hide distribution list" box, iCard's address field will say "Apple iCard Recipients" instead of listing everyone's email address.

Click here to send your iCard.

HomePage 8

While some people complain that a .Mac account costs $99.95 a year, this one feature alone, **HomePage,** is worth many times more than the price tag. The wide variety of templates that come with HomePage are among the best-looking template-based solutions you'll find anywhere. Being able to publish photos or streaming QuickTime movies on a great-looking page within minutes is not just convenient—it's amazing. And fun.

The iPhoto and iMovie chapters provide details on how to create HomePage photo albums and movie pages from within those applications. This chapter explains how to create photo albums, movie pages, and lots of other types of documents by going straight to the HomePage section of the .Mac web site. You can use Apple's beautifully designed templates to create documents such as newsletters, résumés, announcements, file-sharing pages, and invitations.

While using HomePage templates is really fast and easy, you're not limited to using them. You can use HomePage to host non-commercial web sites that you've created with any web-authoring software.

If you travel with a laptop, HomePage is an easy and fun way to send photos, newsletters, or even movies back home so you can share your adventures as they happen.

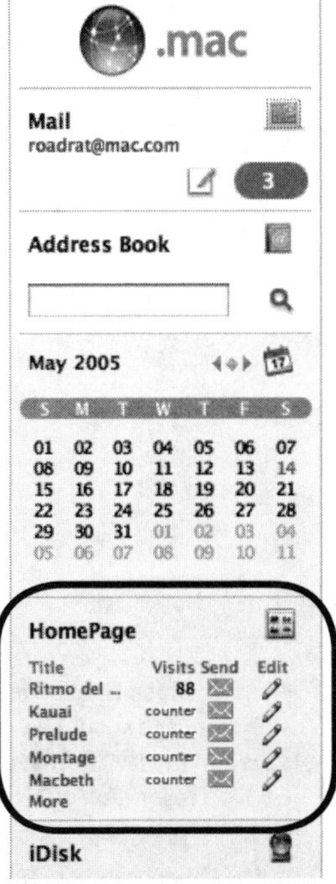

The HomePage link on the .Mac web page lists your HomePage sites. Click one to go there.

Add Photos, QuickTime Movies, and HTML Files to iDisk

HomePage gets all the photos, movies, and HTML files from three folders *on your iDisk:* the Pictures folder, Movies folder, and Sites folder. That means, of course, that before you start a project in HomePage, you must first copy the photos, movies, or HTML files you want to use to these folders on your iDisk.

- Log in to your iDisk (see Chapter 6) and drag individual photos or an entire folder of photos from your hard disk to the **Pictures** folder on your iDisk.
- Drag QuickTime movies to the **Movies** folder on your iDisk.
- If you plan to use external HTML files (created in an HTML editing program) on your HomePage, drag those HTML files to the **Sites** folder on your iDisk (see pages 290–291).

Use images from Apple's Image Library

HomePage provides access to Apple's Image Library in case you don't have pictures of your own to use. If you need a photo while building a site on the following pages, you can select one from iDisk's **Image Library** folder.

1. When a HomePage template contains an empty photo cell, click "Choose" to open the "Choose a file" page (shown below).
2. Select the "Image Library" folder in the first column. Select a *category* folder from the next column, then choose an image from the last column.
3. Click "Choose." The selected image appears in the template's photo cell.

To add your own photos or movies to a HomePage template, use this same procedure and choose a movie or photo from the Movies or Pictures folder. Make sure you've copied movies or photos to these iDisk folders, as explained in Chapter 6, so they will be accessible from HomePage.

Tip: Photos to be used in HomePage should be saved in the JPEG format with a resolution of 72 pixels per inch.

To keep image sizes and download times reasonable, use maximum image dimensions of 640 pixels wide and 480 pixels tall.

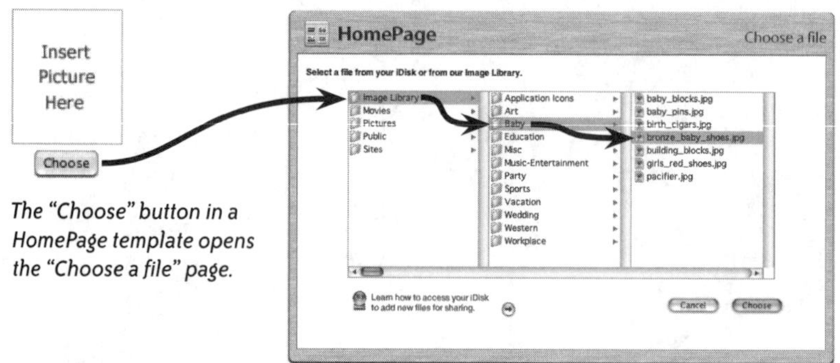

The "Choose" button in a HomePage template opens the "Choose a file" page.

Build a Web Site with HomePage

With **HomePage** you can easily create and publish a single web page, an entire web site, or several sites. Choose from a variety of themes that are designed to display photo albums, QuickTime movies, résumés, invitations, external HTML files, and more.

1. Go to the .Mac web page **(www.mac.com)**. In the page's sidebar, click the "HomePage" icon (shown circled on the right). Or click "HomePage" in the .Mac navigation bar (shown below).

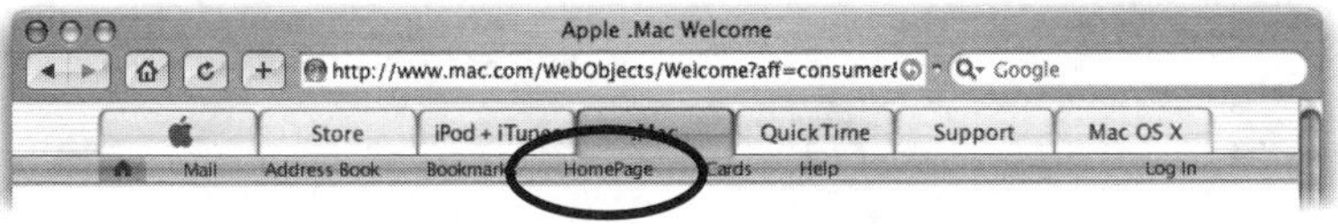

2. Log in to your account. Enter your member name and password as shown below, then click "Enter."

3. If you're not already logged in, you'll see a page like the one on the right. Click one of the category tabs on the left that seems to be a good fit with the type of web site you want to create. Depending on the category you choose, different design themes display on the right. Click one of the design theme thumbnails.

   If you've already created one or more web pages, the HomePage (after you log in) looks like the example on page 280. It provides tools to add, delete, or edit pages.

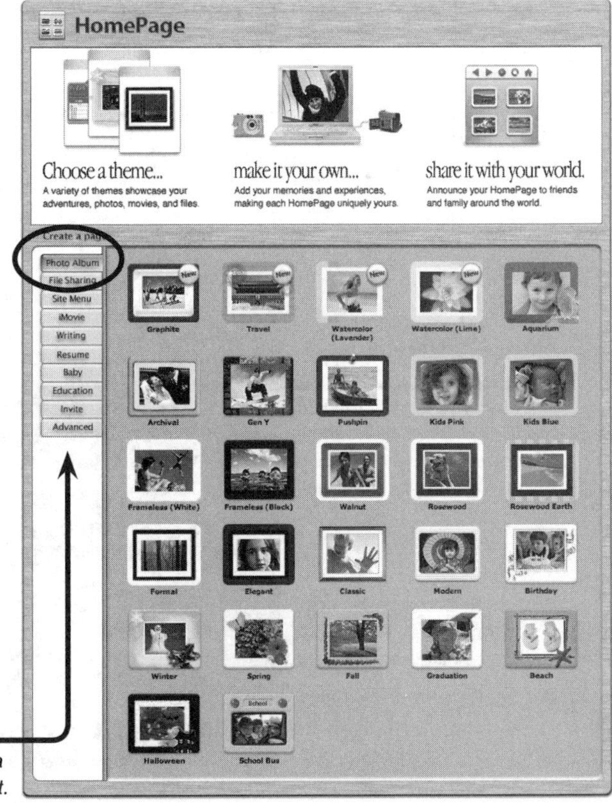

Choose a web site category, then choose a design theme from the thumbnails on the right.

3. If you choose a design theme from the "Photo Album" category, the "Choose a folder" window opens and shows the photos in the Pictures folder *of your iDisk.* Choose a folder of photos to place in your new HomePage photo album, then click the "Choose" button.

   If no folders or photos are showing, it means you have not yet copied any from your computer to the Pictures folder on your iDisk. See Chapter 6 (iDisk), or click the small arrow button beneath the columns to learn how to access your iDisk.

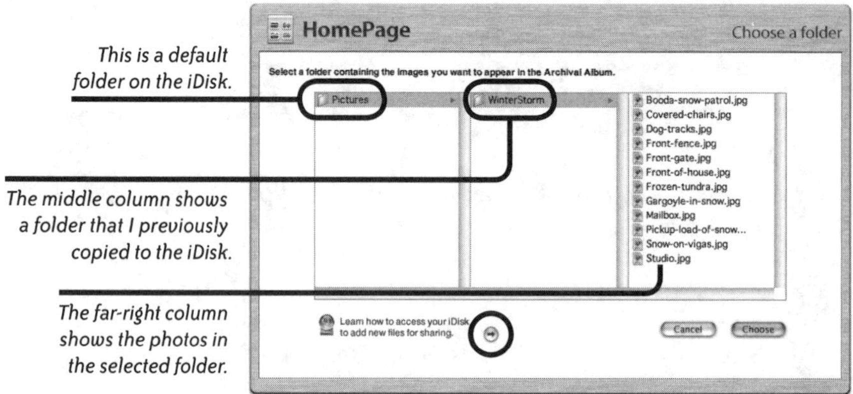

4. An editable page based on your theme choice opens (shown below). Type a headline, title, and captions in the HomePage text fields. To rearrange the photos, drag them to new positions on the page.

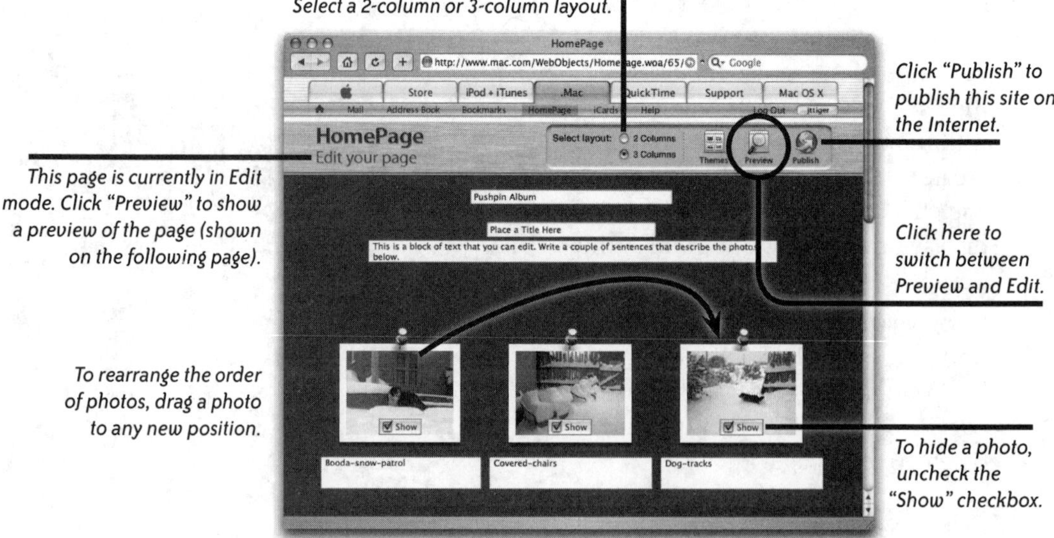

5. Click the Preview button to see what the site will look like on the Internet (shown below). If you need to make changes, click "Edit" and make the changes. When you're satisfied with how the page looks, click "Publish" (shown on the opposite page).
6. The "Congratulations" page opens to give you the web address of your new site.

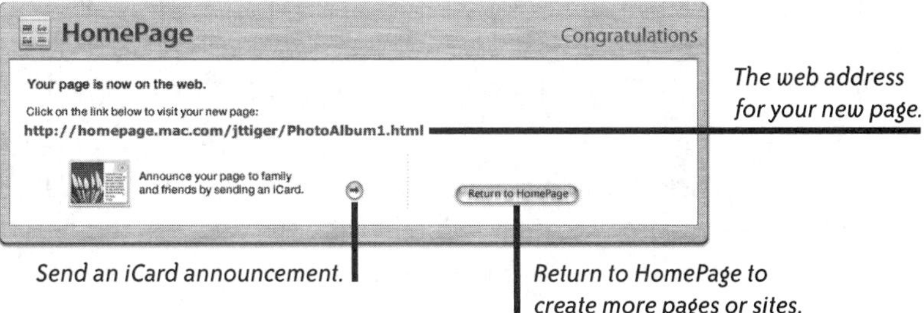

The web address for your new page.

Send an iCard announcement.

Return to HomePage to create more pages or sites.

7. In the window shown above: Click the web address to open your new photo album web site. Click the iCard image (or the tiny arrow) to send an announcement of your new site. Click "Return to HomePage" to make changes or to manage the site (see the following page). Your new web page looks something like the one shown here, depending on the design theme you chose.

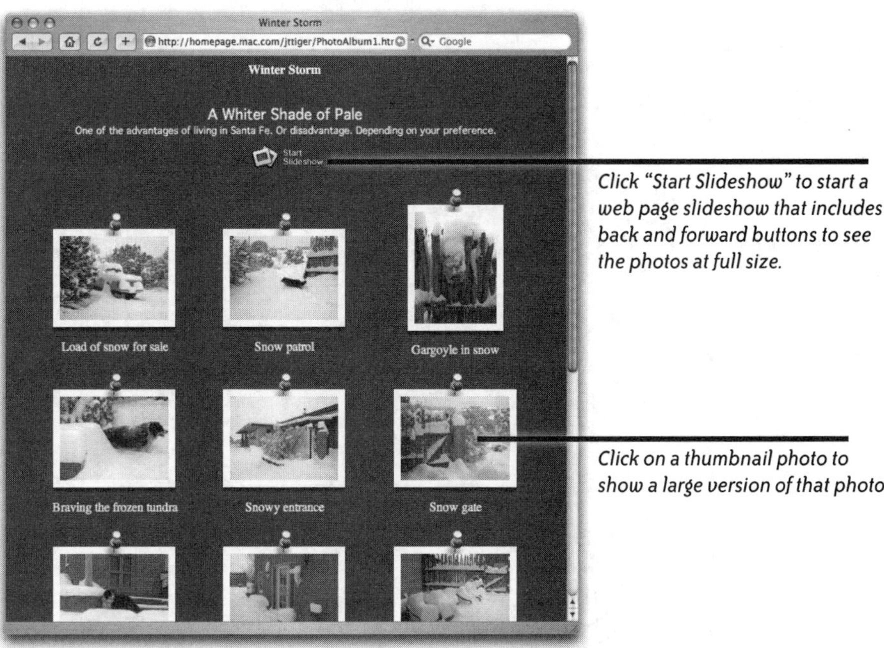

Click "Start Slideshow" to start a web page slideshow that includes back and forward buttons to see the photos at full size.

Click on a thumbnail photo to show a large version of that photo.

—continued

8. Return to HomePage and you'll see it looks different now, as shown below. The introduction graphics at the top of the page (see page 277) have been replaced by site management tools. The Photo Album we just created is listed in the "Pages" column. You can learn more about HomePage site management on page 289.

You'll certainly want to add more pages to your site, as explained in the rest of this chapter. When you've created just one page (or photo album in this case), it's considered a site. As you add pages to the site, HomePage creates text links at the top of every page that link to the other pages of the site.

If you want to create another site—one that's made up of a different collection of pages—click the arrow button labeled "Add another site." Pages that you add to the new site will not contain links to the pages in the original site. See page 288 for details about adding another site.

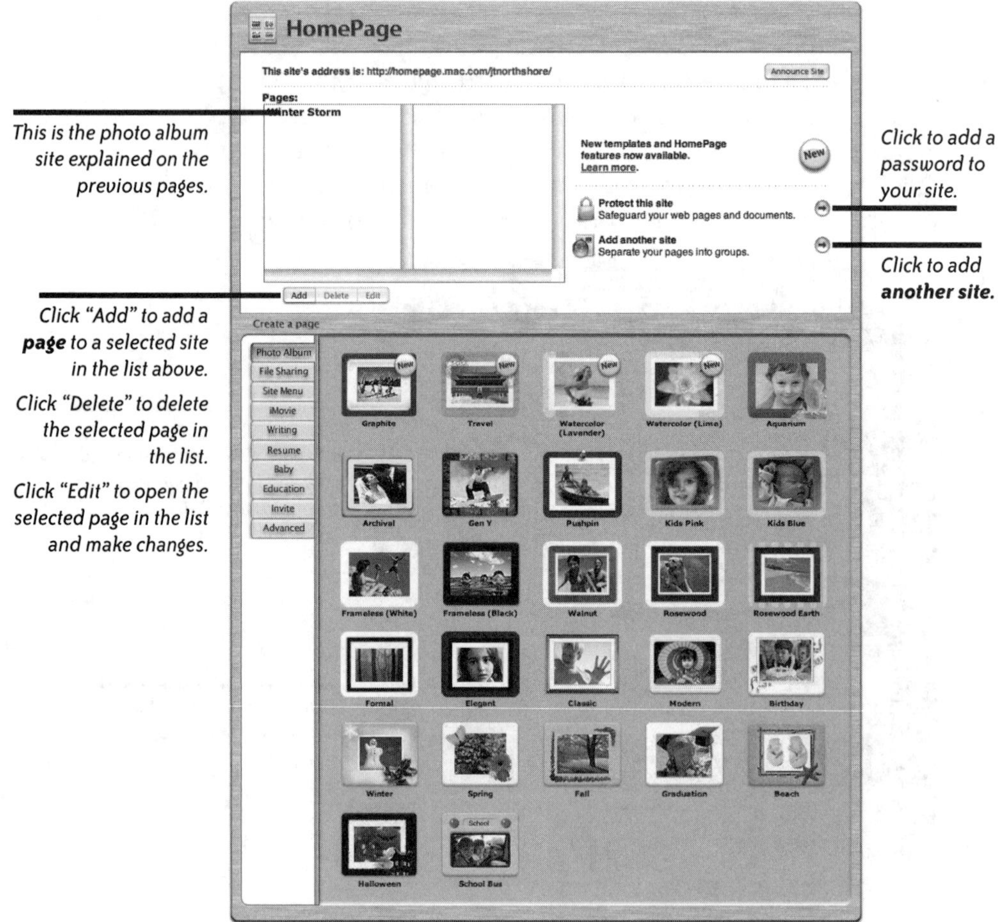

This is the photo album site explained on the previous pages.

*Click "Add" to add a **page** to a selected site in the list above.*

Click "Delete" to delete the selected page in the list.

Click "Edit" to open the selected page in the list and make changes.

Click to add a password to your site.

*Click to add **another site.***

Add another page

Let's add a web page with a QuickTime movie. Make sure you've already copied a QuickTime movie to the Movies folder on your iDisk. See Chapter 3 for information about editing a movie and exporting it as a streaming QuickTime file for the Internet.

1. Click the "Add" button beneath the "Pages" column (shown on the previous page). In the "Select a theme" page that opens, click the iMovie tab, then select a design theme.

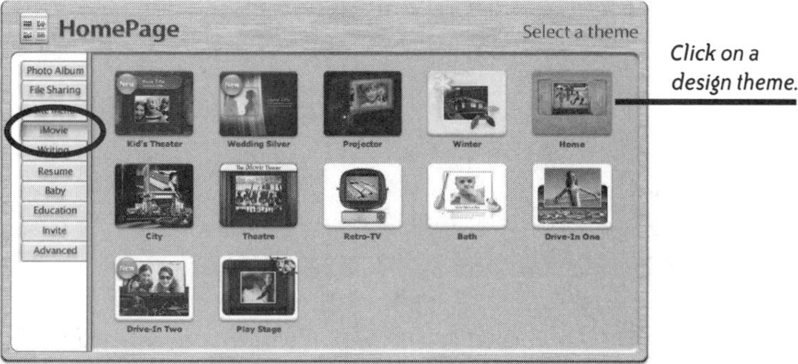

Click on a design theme.

2. Customize the text in the theme's text boxes, then click the "Choose" button below the QuickTime window to open the "Choose a file" page, shown on the following page.

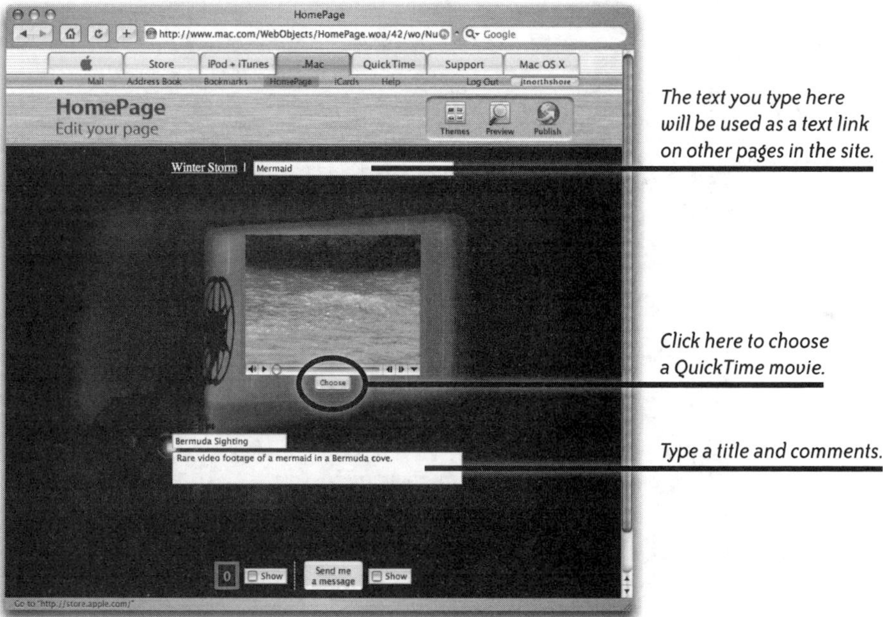

The text you type here will be used as a text link on other pages in the site.

Click here to choose a QuickTime movie.

Type a title and comments.

—continued

3. From the "Choose a file" window, select a QuickTime movie that has been copied to the Movies folder on your iDisk. Click "Choose" to place the selected movie on the iMovie page, as shown below.

A preview of the selected QuickTime movie.

These folders are on your iDisk. Select a folder to see its contents in the next column.

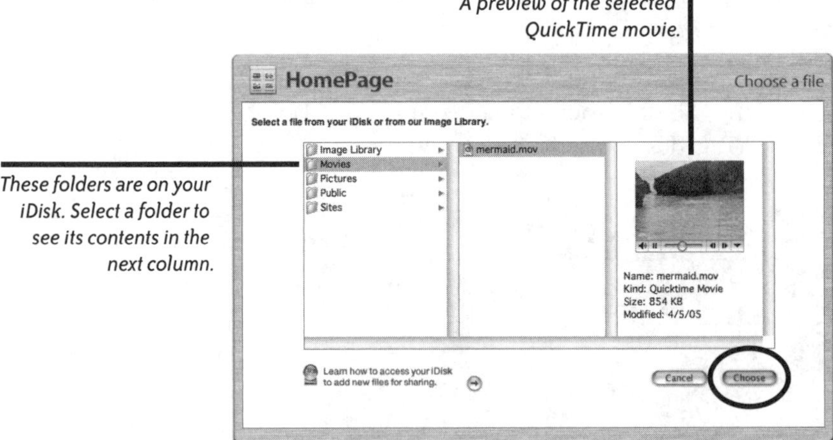

4. After the QuickTime movie is selected, a window opens (below). You can make additional changes here, or click the "Publish" icon to publish the page on the Internet.

Click "Preview" to see what the page will look like when it's published.

Click here to publish this page on the web.

Every time you add a new page, a link to that page is added to every page in the site.

Your movie previews here.

Select a checkbox to place a visit counter or a message button on the page.

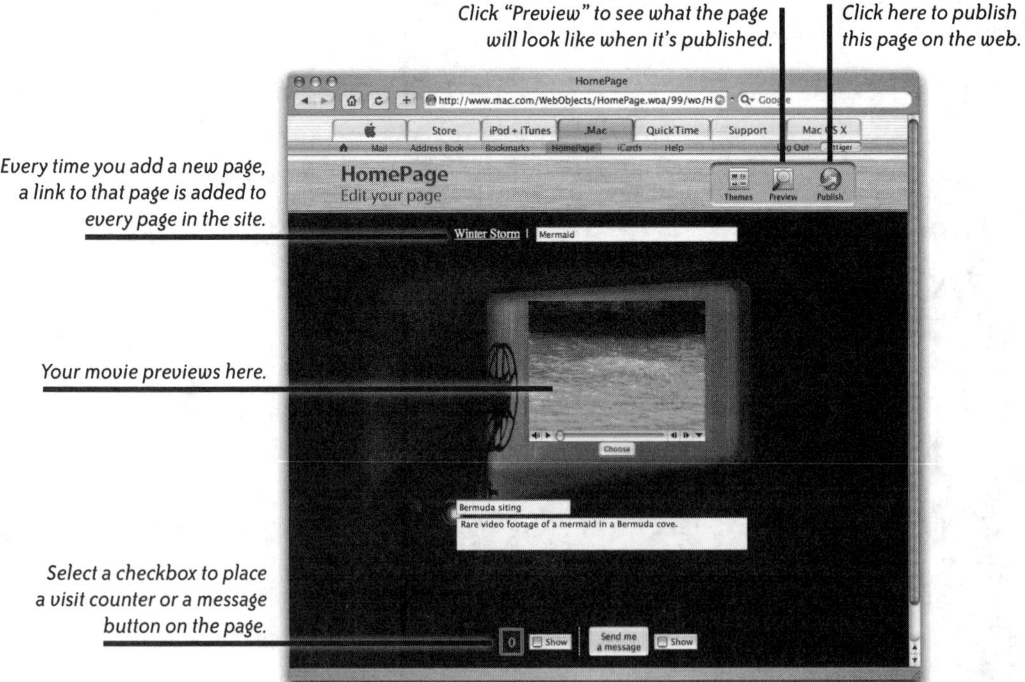

5. When you click "Publish," a dialog box opens asking you whether you want to visit the new page or return to HomePage.
6. Return to HomePage and notice the new page has been added to the list in the "Pages" column (below). **To determine which page is the first page of the site,** drag a page name to the top of the list. Bold text indicates the first page a visitor will see.

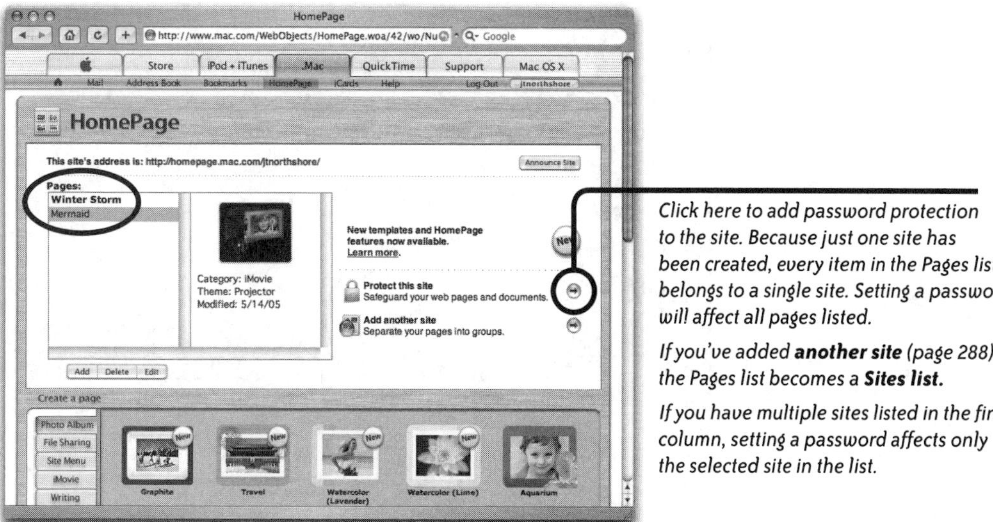

Click here to add password protection to the site. Because just one site has been created, every item in the Pages list belongs to a single site. Setting a password will affect all pages listed.

*If you've added **another site** (page 288), the Pages list becomes a **Sites list.***

If you have multiple sites listed in the first column, setting a password affects only the selected site in the list.

Add password protection to a site

Enable password protection to restrict who can visit your site.

1. Select a page or a site in the HomePage list.
2. Click the small arrow button next to the padlock icon, circled above.
3. In the window that opens (below), click the "On" checkbox.

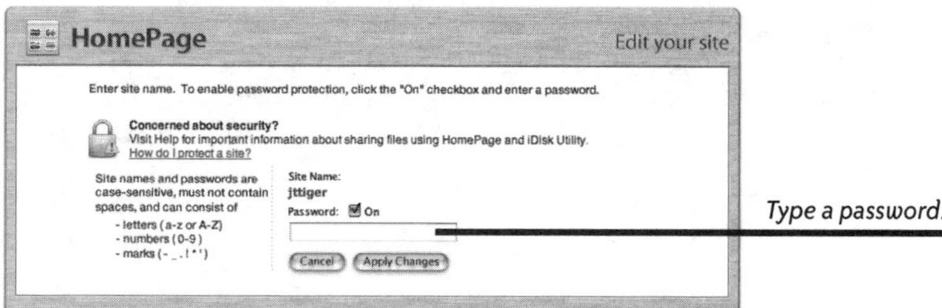

Type a password.

4. Type a password in the text field, following the guidelines listed in the window.
5. Click "Apply Changes."

Create a Site Menu

After you've made a couple of individual pages, you can create a **Site Menu** page. The Site Menu page contains a link to each page of the current site (photo albums, movie pages, invitations, etc.). It provides an overview of the entire site's content. Sounds complex? No, it's incredibly easy.

1. In the main HomePage window, click the "Site Menu" tab (shown below).
2. Select one of the themes (circled below) to open the "Edit your page" window shown on the opposite page.

   Each link on the page contains a thumbnail image or movie that links to a separate page containing the actual movie, photo album, or other content.

   In this example, the two existing pages are considered a "site." See page 288 to learn how to add *more* sites.

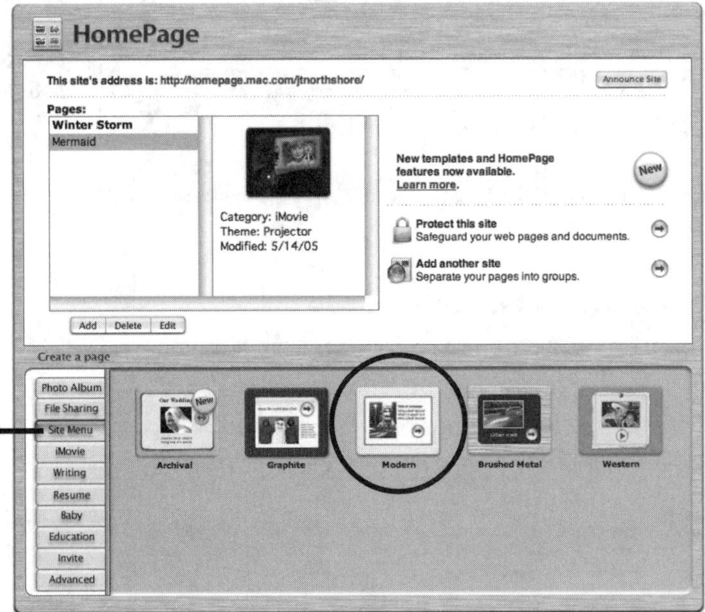

Click the "Site Menu" tab, then select a design theme from the thumbnails on the right.

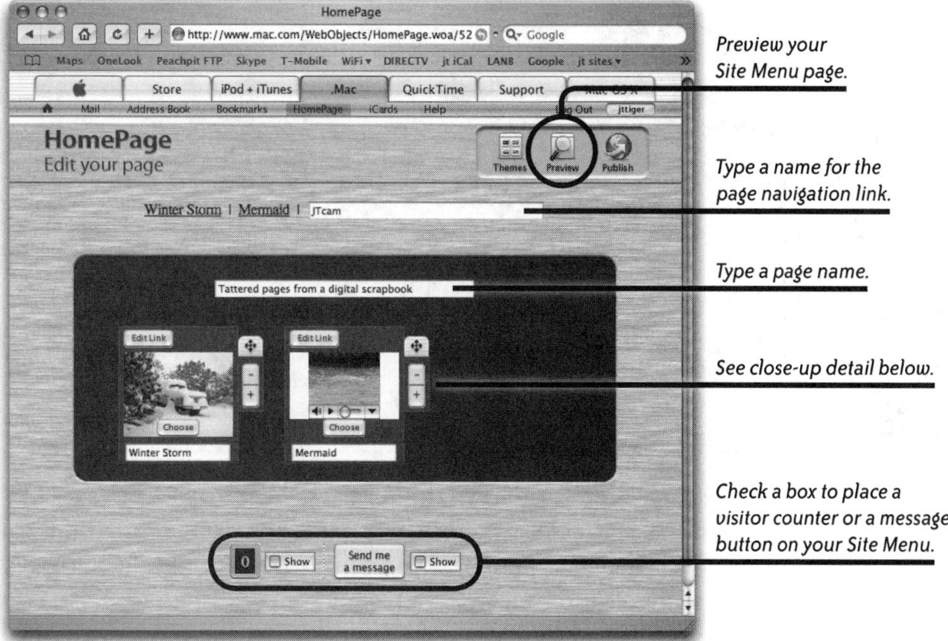

page navigation link.

See close-up detail below.
Check a box to place a

button on your Site Menu.

3. Type your own customized text in the text fields.
4. **To add more links,** click the plus button. The Site Menu above has just two links because two pages existed when the Site Menu was created.

   After you create more pages for the site, you can add them to the Site Menu: Click the plus button to place an empty link (shown below) on the page.

   Click the "Choose" button to select a movie or photo to place as a thumbnail in the link window (see the next page).

   Click the "Edit Link" button to choose a new page you want to link to (see the next page).

   To delete a link from the Site Menu, click the minus button

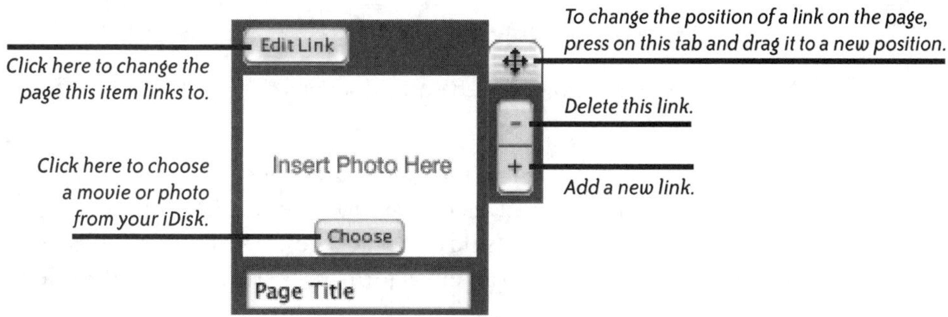

Click here to change the
page this item links to.
Click here to choose
a movie or photo
from your iDisk.
Edit Link
Insert Photo Here
Choose
Page Title
To change the position of a link on the page,
press on this tab and drag it to a new position.
Delete this link.
Add a new link.

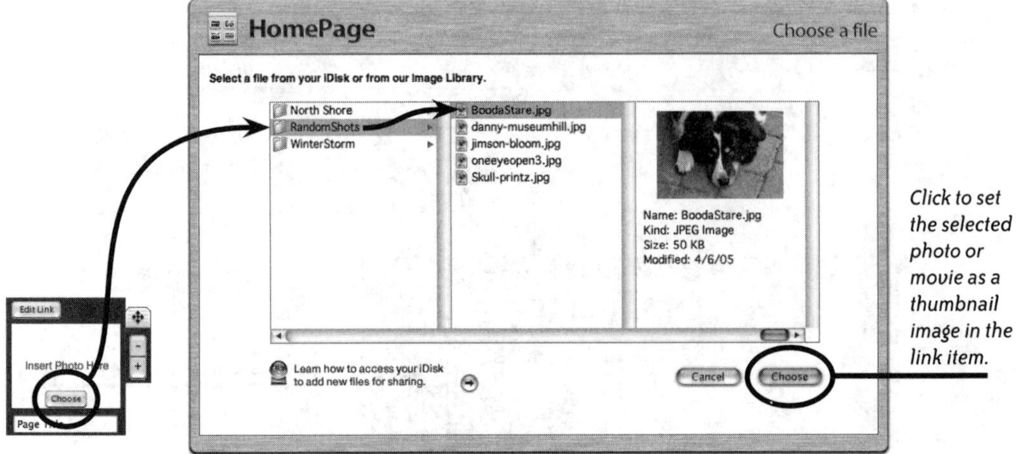

When you click "Choose" on a HomePage template, the "Choose a file" page opens so you can select a photo or a movie to place in the thumbnail area of the link. The left column, above, shows folders of photos that have been copied to the Pictures folder on an iDisk.

We used the "RandomShots" folder to create a new page (a photo album), and now we're selecting a photo from it to place in the new link as a thumbnail image (below-left). Next, as shown below, we're ready to tell the photo item to link to the new photo album.

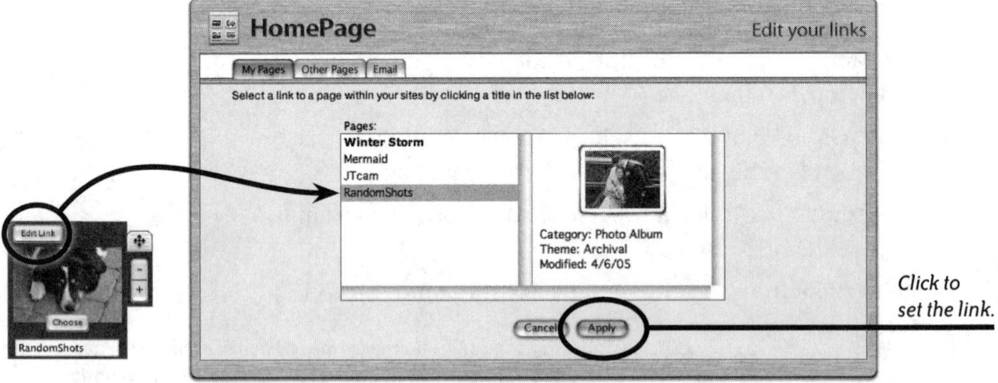

As you can see, the link (far-left) now contains the photo we selected in the example above.

When you click "Edit Link," the "Edit your links" page opens so you can choose a page from the Pages column to have this item link to. To link the item to an external site (outside of HomePage), click the "Other Pages" tab at the top. To link the item to an email form, click the "Email" tab at the top.

5. You should set the Site Menu page as the first page of the site. Since it has links and thumbnail images for all the pages of the site, it makes sense that it should be the first page you see.

   Click the "HomePage" link in the top-left corner to open the main HomePage window (shown below).

6. Locate the name of the site menu page in the "Pages" column, then drag the name to the top of the list. The name will change to bold type, indicating it is now the first page, also known as the start page.

7. To publish the page, click the "Edit" button beneath the "Pages" column, then click the "Publish" icon on the "Edit" page that opens. After the site is published, you can come back to this main HomePage window at any time and change the start page.

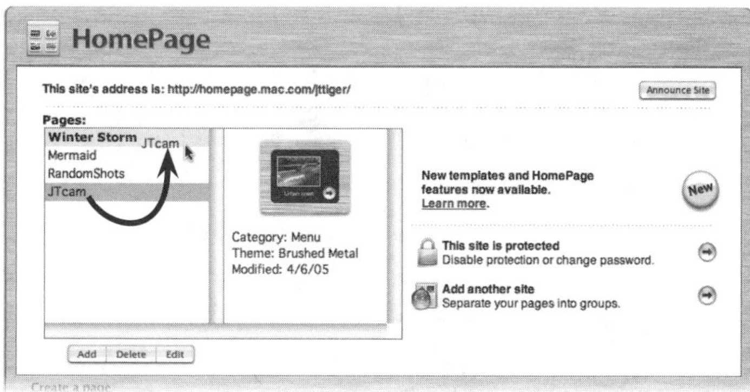

Drag the Site Menu page to the top of the list to make it the start page.

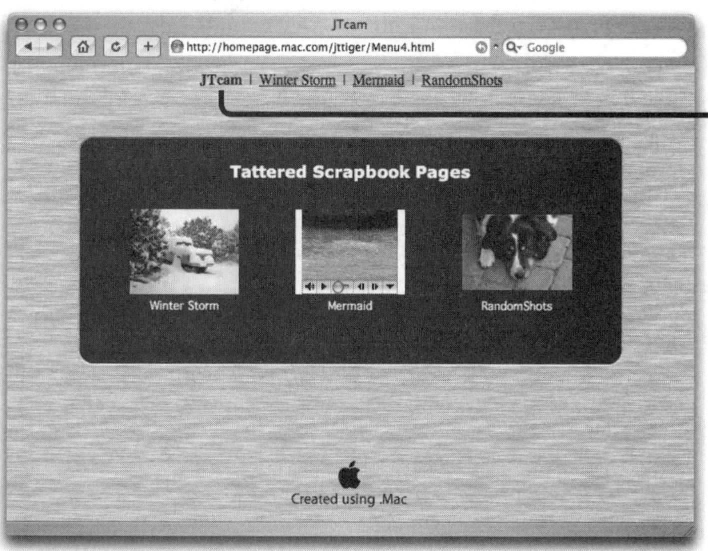

The Site Menu page as it appears on the web. Notice that HomePage has moved the JTcam link (the Site Menu page) to the first link in the list.

Create Another Site

You can add a variety of unrelated pages to your site, but it's much better to organize your pages into related groups, called sites. When you create a new site, HomePage changes to show both a "Sites" column and a "Pages" column, as shown below.

To create a new site:

1. Go to HomePage.
2. Click the small arrow button next to "Add another site."

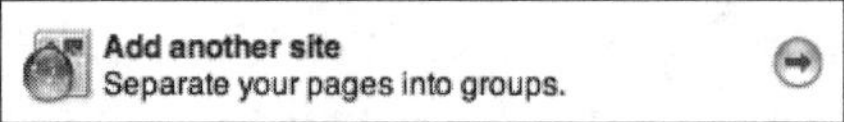

3. Enter a site name in the "Create a site" window. To include password protection, check the "On" box.
4. Click "Create Site."

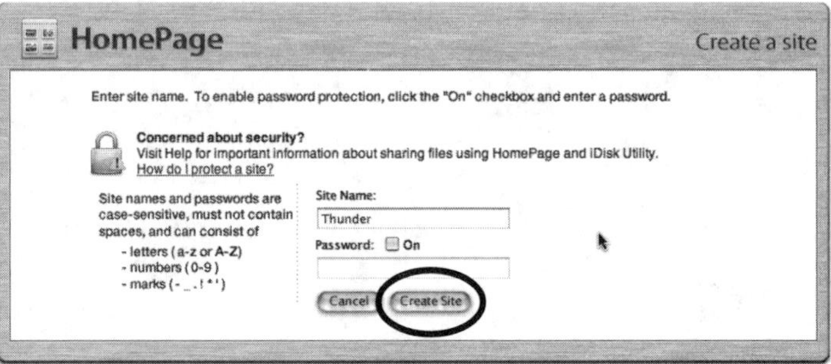

5. The top section of HomePage now includes a "Sites" column in addition to the "Pages" column, as shown below.
6. **To add pages** to the new site, select the site name, then click the "Add" button under the "Pages" column (see page 280).

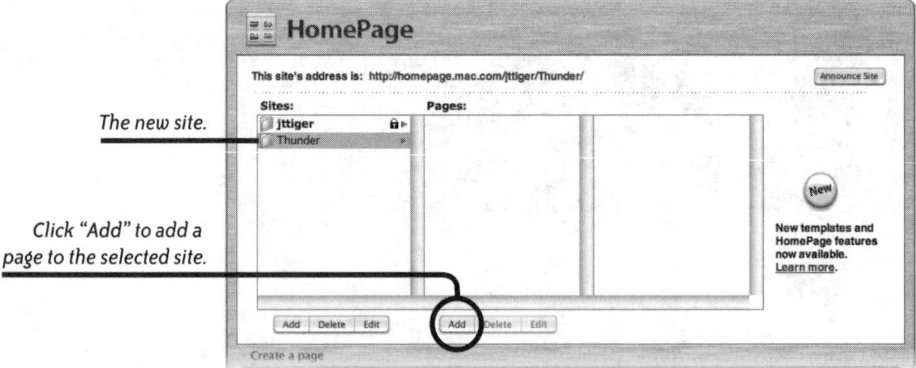

Site management

HomePage makes it easy to manage your sites. Use the buttons beneath the "Sites" column and the "Pages" column to add, delete, and edit pages or sites. Change themes or page designs whenever you want. Rearrange the order of pages in a site, or move pages from one site to another site.

- **To add pages** to a site, select the site name, then click the "Add" button under the "Pages" column. As you create new pages, the page names are added to the list in the "Pages" column.
- **To delete pages** from a site, select the page name, then click the "Delete" button beneath the "Pages" column.
- **To move pages** from one site to another, select a page in the "Pages" list and drag it to a site folder in the "Sites" list.
- **To add new sites,** click the "Add" button beneath the "Sites" column, as explained on the previous page.
- **To delete a site,** select its name in the "Sites" column, then click the "Delete" button beneath the "Sites" column.
- **To add, change, or remove a password** for a site, select it in the "Sites" column, then click the "Edit" button beneath the "Sites" column.

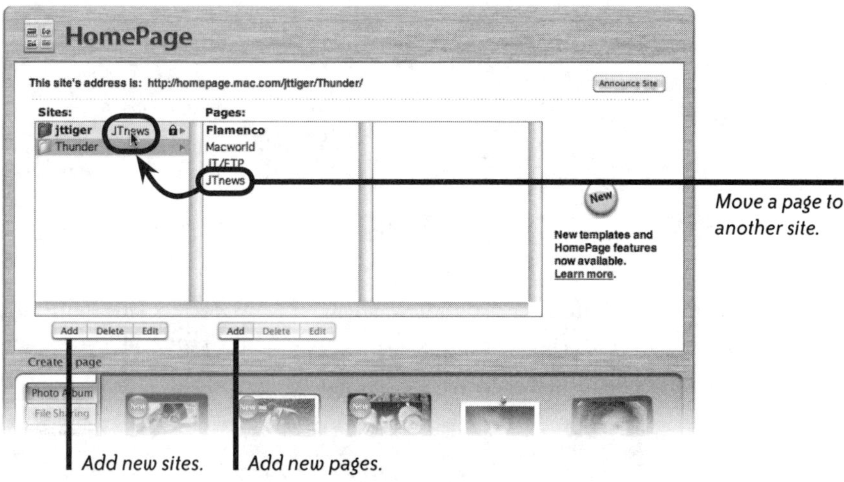

When the "Thunder" site (above) is selected in the "Sites" column, all the pages associated with that site are shown in the "Pages" column. This example shows how you can drag a page from its current location (in the "Thunder" site) to another site (the "jttiger" site).

Add External HTML Pages with HomePage

HTML (HyperText Markup Language) is a code that's used to create web pages.

Up until now, HomePage has been writing all the HTML code for you. But you can also use external HTML files, web sites you've created in an editing program such as Dreamweaver, GoLive, BBEdit, etc.

The iDisk icon.

To add external HTML files for use in HomePage:

1. Open your iDisk. From the Go menu at the top of your screen, choose "iDisk," then from the submenu, choose "My iDisk." The iDisk icon appears on your Desktop. Double-click to open it.
2. Drag a folder of HTML files that you created (including subfolders) into the **Sites** folder of your iDisk. Make sure the folder name does not include any spaces.
3. Add a new site to HomePage for the files you just copied to iDisk. In the HomePage window, click the small arrow button to the right of "Add another site" (circled below).

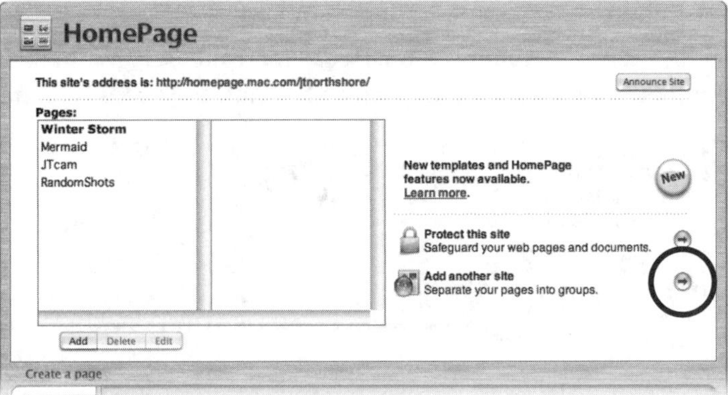

4. In the "Create a site" window, shown below, type a site name that matches exactly the name of the folder you dragged to your iDisk. Then click "Create Site."

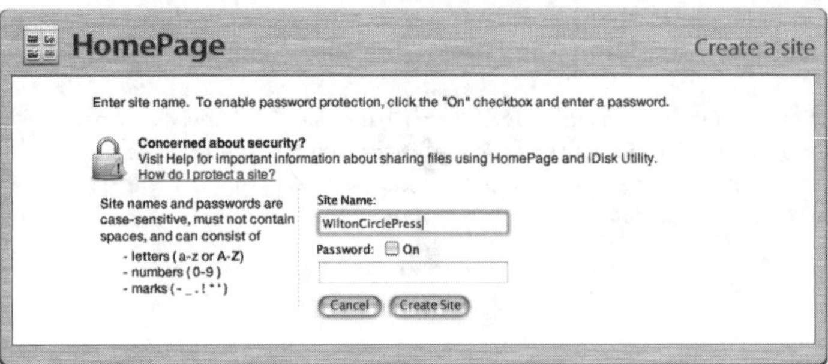

To add password protection, check the "On" box, then type a password, following the guidelines listed in the window.

5. The new site ("WiltonCirclePress," in this example) appears in the "Site" column. At the top of the page, your new site's address is listed. Click the address to see the site on the Internet.

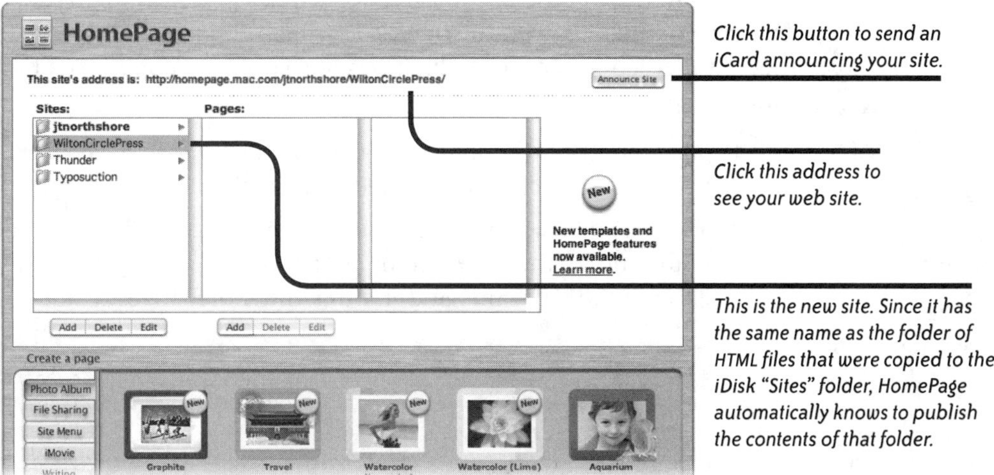

Click this button to send an iCard announcing your site.

Click this address to see your web site.

This is the new site. Since it has the same name as the folder of HTML files that were copied to the iDisk "Sites" folder, HomePage automatically knows to publish the contents of that folder.

Anyone can now access the entire web site using the address listed at the top of your HomePage window. The number and size of externally created sites is limited only by the amount of iDisk storage available in your .Mac account.

6. Announce your site to others: Click the "Announce Site" button. In the window that opens, choose an iCard, type a message, add recipients, then click "Send iCard."

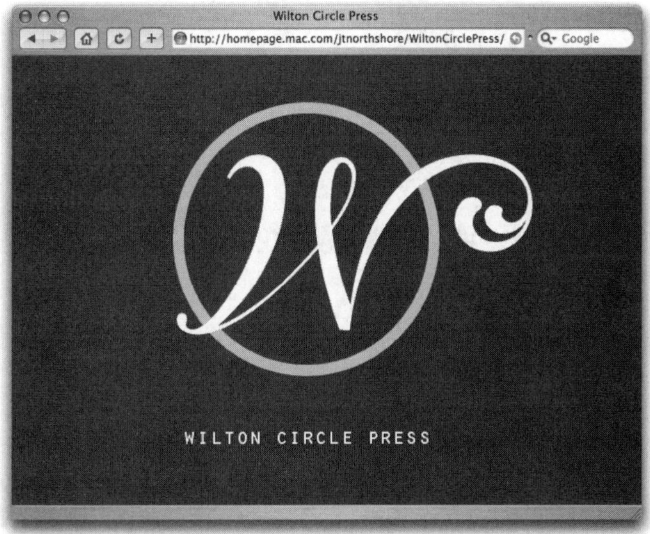

The web site as it appears on the World Wide Web.

Create a File-Sharing Page

One of the page types that HomePage can create is a *file-sharing* page. When you have photos, movies, or any other kind of files that you want to make available to others, you can put them on a file-sharing page; anyone on any computer can go to your file-sharing web page and download your files at their convenience. To limit access to certain people, set a password for the site.

1. Sign in to the .Mac site with your member name and password. On the .Mac page, click the HomePage link (shown to the left).
2. You can add a new site for your file-sharing page (click the "Add" button under the "Sites" column), or you can add a page to an existing site (click the "Add" button under the "Pages" column).

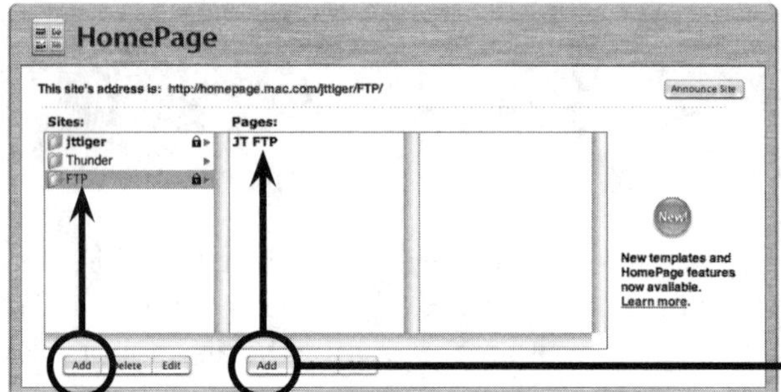

File-sharing sites are known as FTP (File Transfer Protocol) sites.

*We created a new **site** and added password protection, then created a new **page**.*

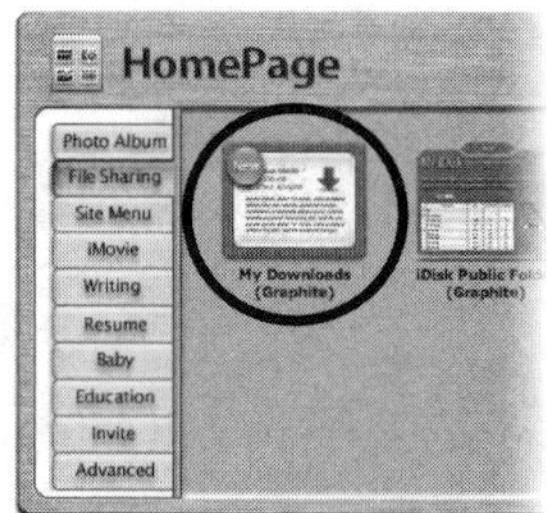

3. When you click the "Add" button, the theme window opens (shown to the left). Click the "File Sharing" tab, then pick a design from the template thumbnails.
4. Customize the text in the text fields. Then click "Choose file" to select files from your iDisk that you want to make accessible on your file-sharing page. Click the plus button (+) to add additional items to the page. The buttons and controls on the page behave the same as the links shown on page 285.
5. Click the "Preview" button to check your work, then click "Publish." A "Congratulations" window opens and gives you the web address of the new file-sharing page.

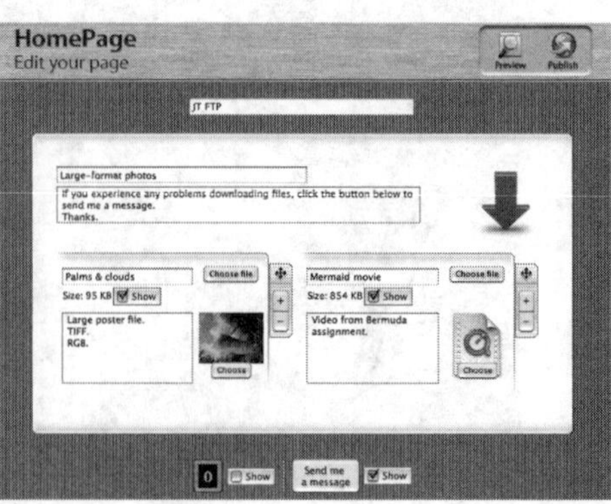

Tip: To upgrade your iDisk storage or to check your .Mac account status, click the "Account" icon on the .Mac web page (circled above).

.Mac webMail 9

Your .Mac account includes **webMail,** a feature that lets you check your email or send email from any computer with an Internet connection anywhere in the world. You can check your .Mac email account, or set up .Mac webMail to check another POP email account you might have.

As a .Mac member, you can buy additional *email-only* accounts that include 50 MB each of email storage space. Email-only accounts don't include many of the standard .Mac features such as iDisk, HomePage, Backup, and Bookmarks. But that's probably why they call it email-*only.* Each email-only account costs just $10 per year. Not a bad deal if you need extra accounts.

The official name for .Mac mail is "Mail," but in this chapter we refer to it as webMail to avoid confusing it with the mail application on your computer named "Mail."

To add one or more email-only accounts to your .Mac membership, go to **www.mac.com** and click the "Account" link in the page's sidebar. In the Account page that opens, click the big green "Buy More" button. If your current .Mac membership is due to renew in less than a year, your email-only account cost is pro-rated to charge only for the time remaining on your current membership.

.Mac webMail's **Address Book** gives you online access to all of your contacts from any computer when you use iSync (Chapter 11) to synchronize the Address Book information on your computer with your .Mac Address Book.

.Mac webMail uses an Internet standard called IMAP (Internet Mail Access Protocol). IMAP mail servers manage and store copies of your mail on a remote server so you can access it from any computer in the world. You can choose to also keep copies of email messages and folders on your own computer. IMAP is a good choice if you need to check your mail from many different computers.

The other most common type of mail server uses an Internet standard called POP (Post Office Protocol). POP servers usually erase your email from their hard disks as soon as you've picked it up (copied it to your computer). POP is a good choice if you always use the same computer to manage your email.

.Mac webMail

When you sign up for a .Mac account, you get a .Mac **webMail** account with 125 megabytes of storage space for your email messages. The advantage of webMail is that you can check your mail in any of your email accounts from any web browser on any computer, anywhere in the world.

Start using .Mac webMail:

After you log in, the sidebar on the .Mac page shows your webMail account and how many email messages are in your inbox.

1. Go to the .Mac web site at **www.mac.com,** then click the "Mail" icon in the sidebar (shown to the left), **or** click the "Mail" link in the top navigation bar (circled below).
2. Log in to your .Mac account with your member name and password.

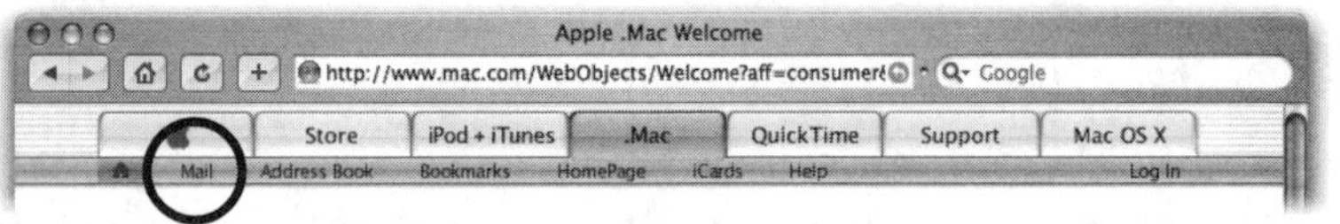

3. Your personal webMail page opens, as shown below.

   From this web page and other linked pages you can perform all your email tasks just like at home, even if you happen to be in Kathmandu.

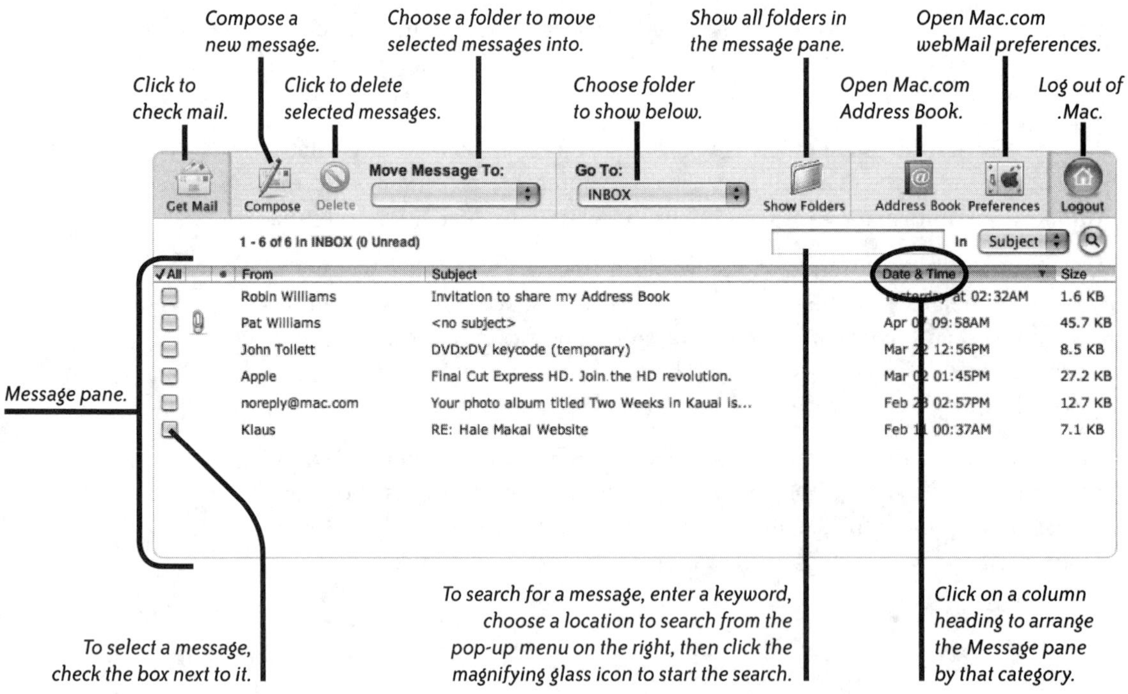

Get your Mail and Read It

1. Click "Get Mail" in the toolbar. Messages open in the "Inbox" message pane.
2. Single-click on a message in the list to open it in your browser.

Compose and Send a Message

1. Click the "Compose" icon in the toolbar to write a new message.
2. Type an email address in the "To" field.

   To send the same message to more than one person, type their addresses in the same field with a comma after each email address. **Or** put one or more addresses in the "Cc" (Carbon copy) field.
3. Type a subject that will not be confused for junk mail! For instance, don't use "Hi!" or "Sorry I missed you." Type a subject that will make it clear to the recipient what your message is about, that it pertains specifically to that person, or that it is certainly from you.

Click here to save an unfinished message as a draft. Later you can open the Drafts folder, finish the letter, and send it.

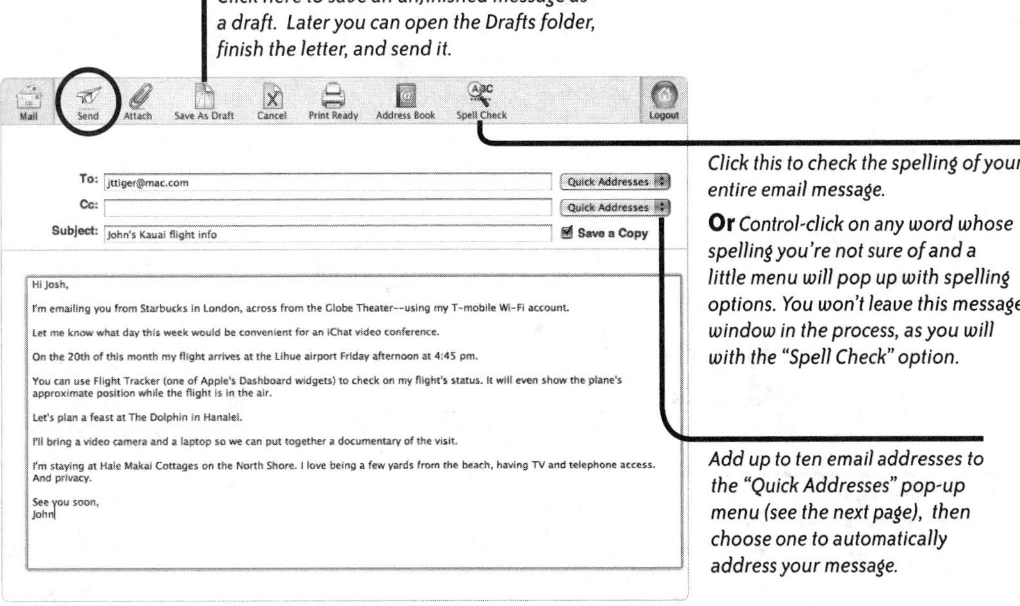

Click this to check the spelling of your entire email message.

***Or** Control-click on any word whose spelling you're not sure of and a little menu will pop up with spelling options. You won't leave this message window in the process, as you will with the "Spell Check" option.*

Add up to ten email addresses to the "Quick Addresses" pop-up menu (see the next page), then choose one to automatically address your message.

4. To check your spelling, click the "Spell Check" icon in the toolbar. It will find misspelled words and offer alternative spellings in multiple languages. When you're finished, click the "Edit" button to return to the message window.
5. Click the "Send" icon in the toolbar.

Use Address Book

The **Address Book** found in webMail is similar to the Address Book on your hard disk (as discussed in Chapter 16). You can synchronize the information in Address Book on your hard disk with .Mac's Address Book. (see page 298). There are two different ways to access your Address Book information in webMail. Each method provides different options.

Open Address Book from the navigation bar

Look carefully and you'll notice there are two links to Address Book on the .Mac Mail page. Click the "Address Book" link in the navigation bar (below-left) to open webMail's Address Book (shown at the bottom of this page).

The "Address Book" link in the navigation bar is available no matter which page of Mac.com you're working in. Click this link, checkmark one or more addresses in the Address Book window (below), then click the "Compose" button. An email form opens, addressed to the people you selected.

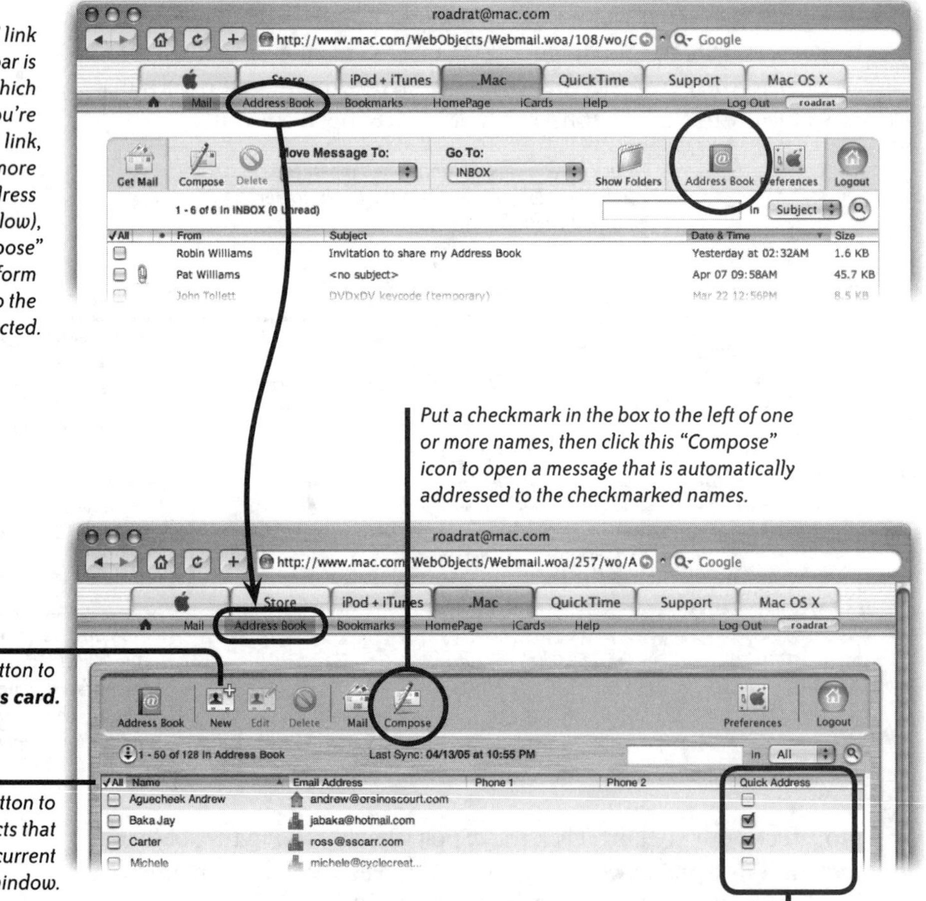

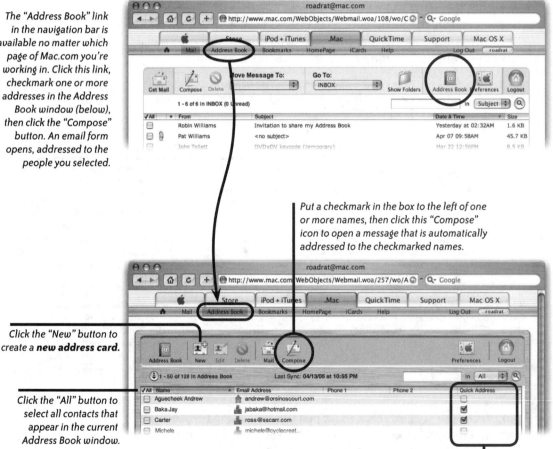

Put a checkmark in the box to the left of one or more names, then click this "Compose" icon to open a message that is automatically addressed to the checkmarked names.

Click the "New" button to create a ***new address card.***

Click the "All" button to select all contacts that appear in the current Address Book window.

The email addresses you checkmark in this column are added to the ***Quick Addresses*** *pop-up menus on webMail's new message form (shown at the top of the next page).*

Open Address Book from the toolbar

Click the "Compose" icon in Mail's toolbar (shown on the right) to open a Compose Message pane (below). Click the Address Book icon in the toolbar to open another Mail pane that contains your Address Book information, plus "Destination" pop-up menus from which you can choose a field to which a person's email address is added.

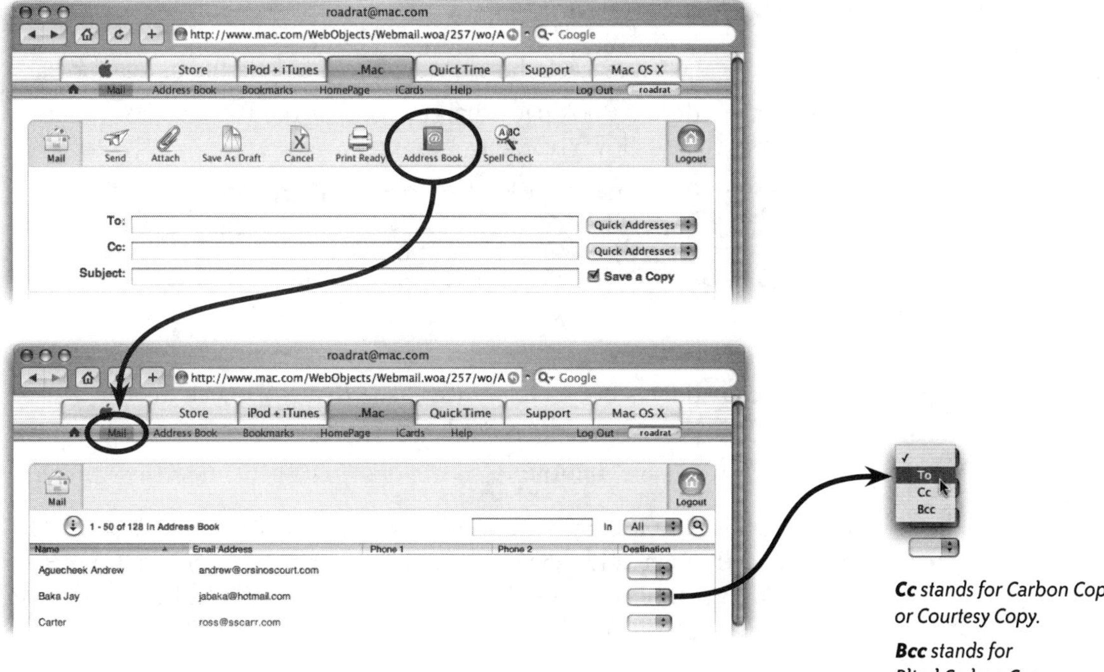

***Cc** stands for Carbon Copy or Courtesy Copy.*

***Bcc** stands for Blind Carbon Copy.*

*Addresses you put in the Bcc field are **invisible** to other recipients of the message.*

In the "Destination" column, choose the address field you want that person's address to be in (To, Cc, or Bcc). At the bottom of the pane, click the "Apply" button to return to the Compose Message pane. webMail automatically enters the recipients' email addresses into the various address fields that you designated.

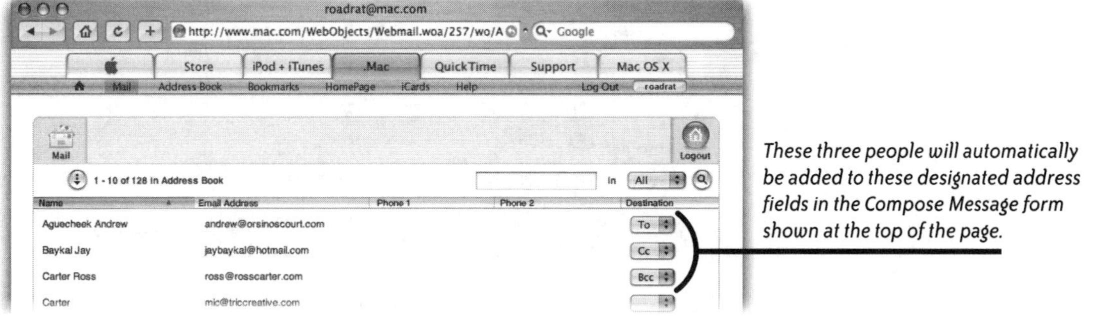

These three people will automatically be added to these designated address fields in the Compose Message form shown at the top of the page.

Synchronize .Mac's Address Book with your Mac's Address Book

Using **iSync,** another feature of a .Mac account, you can synchronize the Address Book information on your hard disk to the Mac.com webMail Address Book so you always have access to current contact information, no matter where you are. See Chapter 11 for details about iSync.

To set up syncing for webMail's Address Book:

Go to the Mac.com site, click the "Mail" link, and log in to your account.

1. In the Mail pane, click the "Address Book" icon in the navigation bar.
2. In the Address Book pane that opens, click the Preferences icon in the toolbar (shown below).

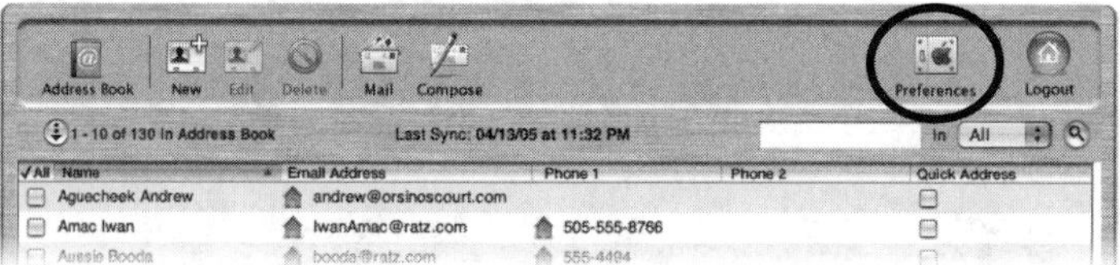

3. In the Address Book Preferences pane (below), check the box to "Turn on .Mac Address Book Synchronization."
4. Click the "Save" button.

The next time you use iSync, your Address Book information will be synced and updated. If you add new contacts while using .Mac Address Book, the contact information will be added to your computer's Address Book the next time you use iSync.

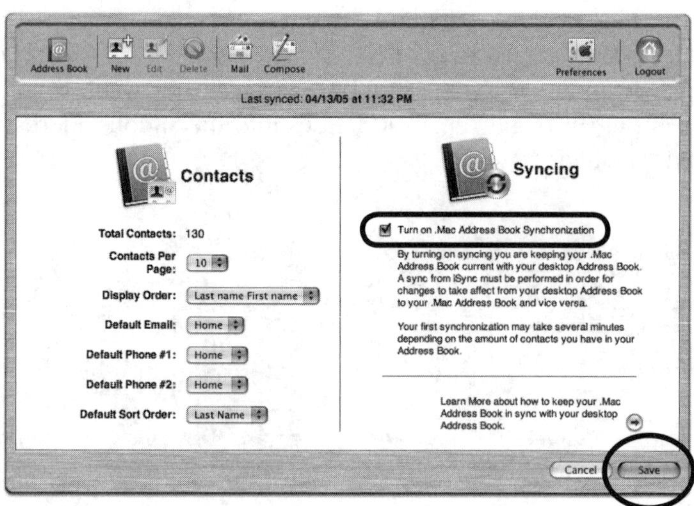

Set .Mac Address Book preferences

The Address Book Preferences window (shown below) contains pop-up menus that let you set some .Mac Address Book behaviors. Make selections from the pop-up menus, then click "Save."

Contacts Per Page: Choose how many contacts can be seen at once in the Address Book pane.

Display Order: Choose how to show contact names—first name first, or last name first. This does not affect the Sort Order (explained below).

Default Email: When a contact has more than one email address entered in Address Book, choose which one to show.

Default Phone #1 and **Default Phone #2:** When a contact has more than one phone number entered in Address Book, choose which one to show.

Default Sort Order: Choose to alphabetize contacts based on Last Name, First Name, or email address.

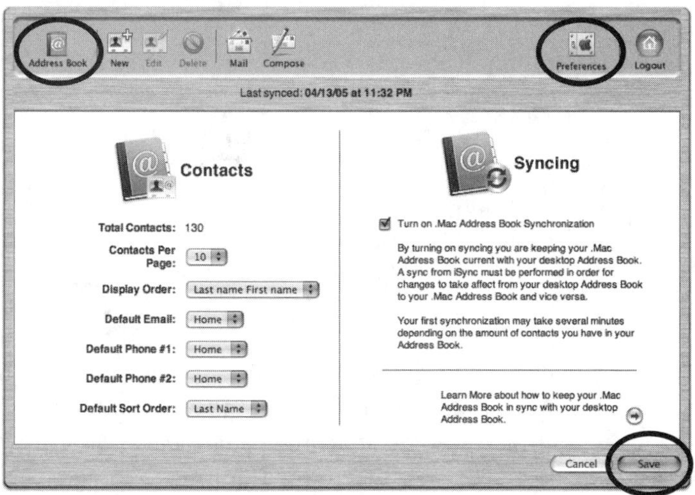

Attach a File to a Message

1. To attach a file to your message, click "Compose" in the webMail toolbar (left) to open the Compose Message pane. Click the "Attach" icon (below) in the Compose Message pane's toolbar to open the Attachment page.

2. Click the "Choose File" button (below-left). From the drop-down sheet, locate a file you want to attach, then click the "Choose" button.

When you click the "Choose File" button on the Attachment page (below), a sheet drops down from the browser's title bar.

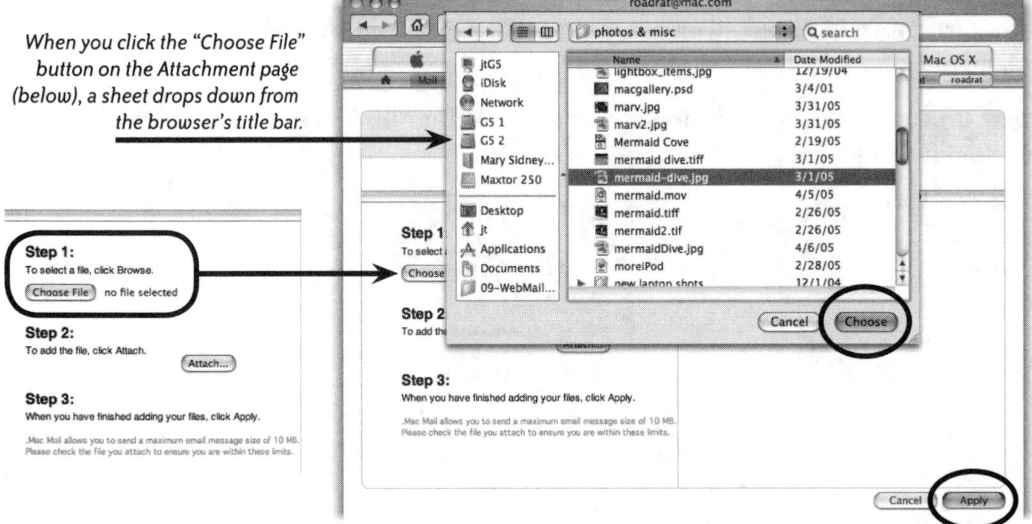

3. Click the "Attach..." button (below) to add the selected file to the "Attached Files" column. Repeat the process to add additional files. When you're finished adding attachments to the list, click the "Apply" button (shown above) to return to the Compose Message pane.

To remove an attached file, select it, then click "Remove."

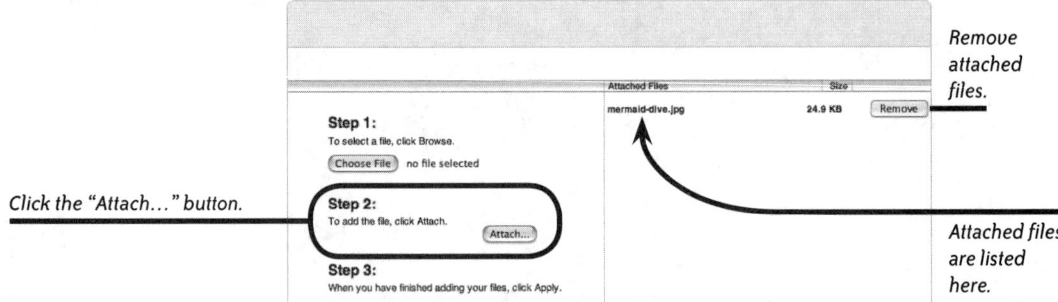

Click the "Attach..." button.

Remove attached files.

Attached files are listed here.

4. Your message header now shows a list of attached files. Address the email, type your email message, then click "Send."

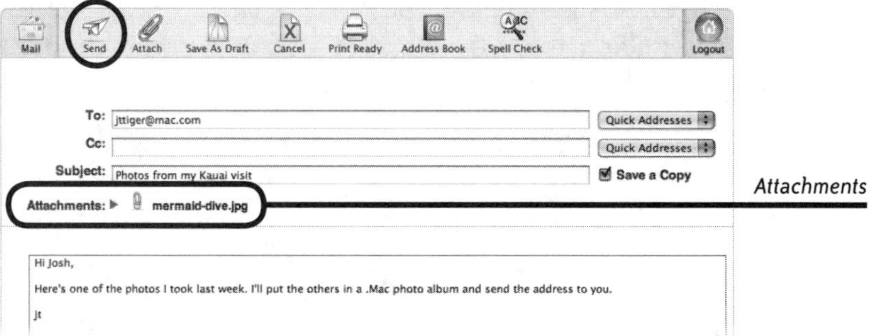

5. When the recipient gets your message, attachments are listed in the email header. If the attachment is an image or a one-page PDF, it is displayed in the body of the message.

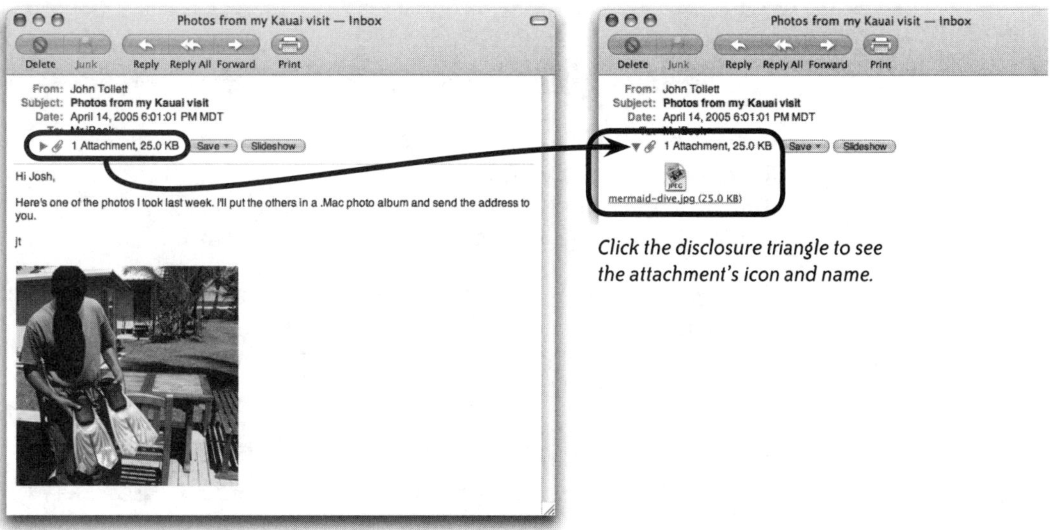

Click the disclosure triangle to see the attachment's icon and name.

The "Go To" Menu

The "Go To" pop-up menu in the .Mac webMail toolbar lets you choose which folder's content to display in the message pane, such as INBOX, Deleted Messages, or Sent Messages. If you've set the option in Mail preferences to "Check Other POP Mail" (explained on page 306), you can open your other POP email accounts from this menu.

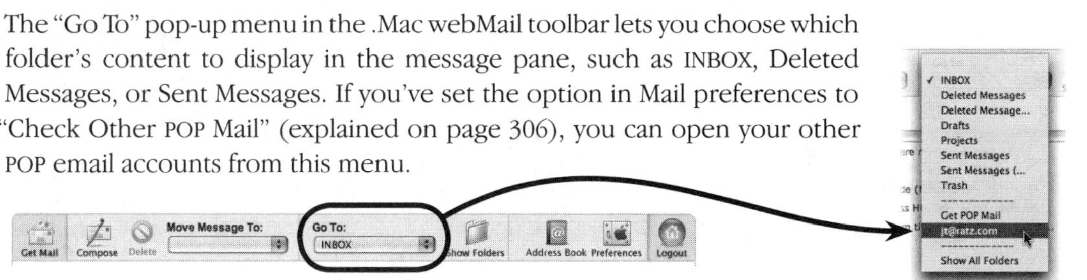

Make New Folders for Organizing Mail

If you get a lot of mail, it's good to create **extra folders** so you can organize your messages. As shown below, you can click checkboxes to select one or more messages; from the "Move Message To" pop-up menu, choose a folder into which you want to move the selected messages.

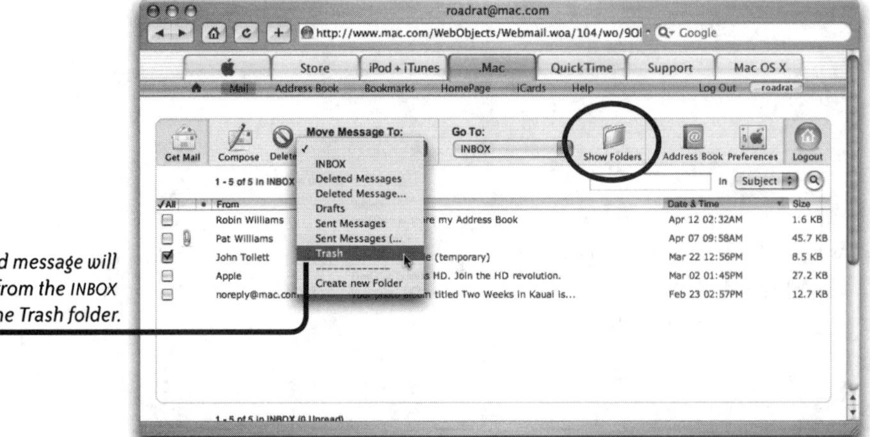

The selected message will disappear from the INBOX and move to the Trash folder.

To make new folders, choose "Create new Folder" from the "Move Message To" pop-up menu. **Or** click the "Show Folders" icon in the toolbar (circled above) to open the Folders page shown below. You can also choose "Show All Folders" from the "Go To" pop-up menu.

When webMail is in "Show All Folders" view, the toolbar includes icons to make new folders, empty selected folders, rename, or delete folders. To get back to the main Mail window, click the "Mail" icon in the toolbar.

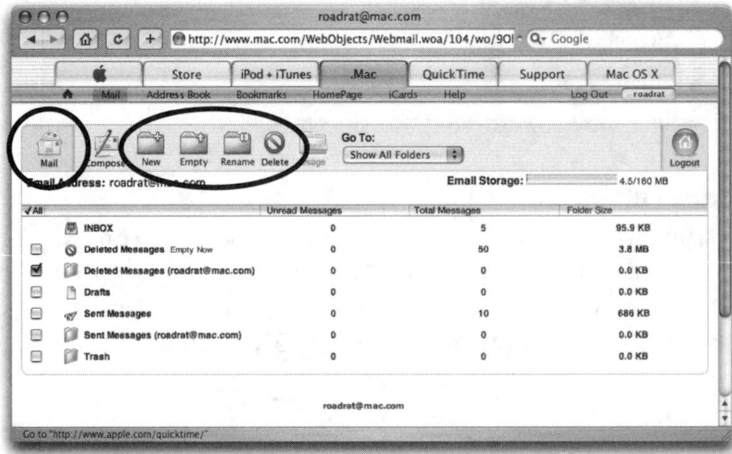

Set webMail Preferences

On the .Mac webMail page, click the "Preferences" icon in the toolbar to open the preferences page as shown below. The various options are categorized by the three buttons at the top of the page: "Viewing," "Composing," and "Account."

Viewing preferences

Time Zone: Select a time zone from the pop-up menu. This setting affects the information that appears in the "Date & Time" column of the Mail pane. You can choose to show email arrival times based on your local time or another time zone.

Messages Per Page: Choose how many messages appear at a time on a Mail page. If you get a lot of junk mail, choose a higher number so you can delete more messages at once.

Show "All Headers" Option: Select this checkbox to put a "Show All Headers" button in the top-right corner of the Mail pane (circled below). Click the button to show additional email header information in a message—a lot of technical information that you probably don't need or want to know. To return to the usual abbreviated header information, click the button again, which has changed to say "Hide All Headers."

After you complete your "Viewing" settings, click the **Save** button.

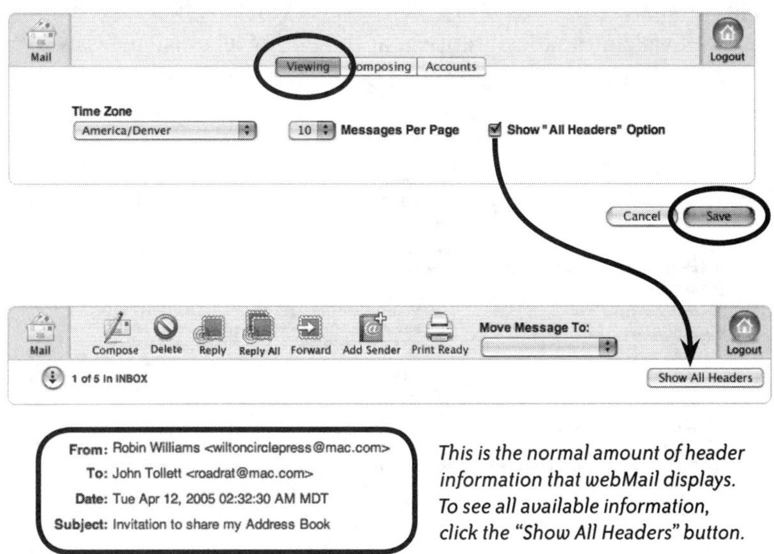

This is the normal amount of header information that webMail displays. To see all available information, click the "Show All Headers" button.

Composing preferences

Include Original Message in Reply: When you reply to an email message by clicking the "Reply" button, this option makes a copy of the original message and places it in your reply. This can help remind the recipient what the previous correspondence was about.

Add Bcc Header: This adds a Blind carbon copy (Bcc) field to the address section of a new message. The email addresses in a Bcc field are hidden from all recipients.

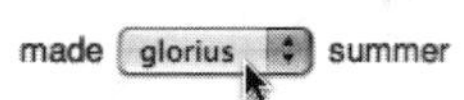

Place the pointer over a mispelled word (underlined with a red dotted line) to show a popup menu of alternate spellings.

Check spelling as I send: webMail checks for misspelled words when you click the "Send" button and lets you correct them before the email is sent.

Save Sent Messages To: Choose a folder in which messages you *send* will be saved automatically.

Move Deleted Messages To: Choose a folder in which *deleted* messages will be stored automatically.

From (Your Name): Type the name you want automatically placed in the "From" field of emails that you send.

Photo: This automatically puts an image of your choice in every message you send. If the photo area is blank, the button beneath it says "Choose"; click that button to add a photo. A window opens in which you can choose a photo file.

Signature: An email "signature" is whatever you type into the edit box shown below. It will automatically appear at the end of all email messages you send from this account. A signature can be contact information, a favorite quote, or anything you like.

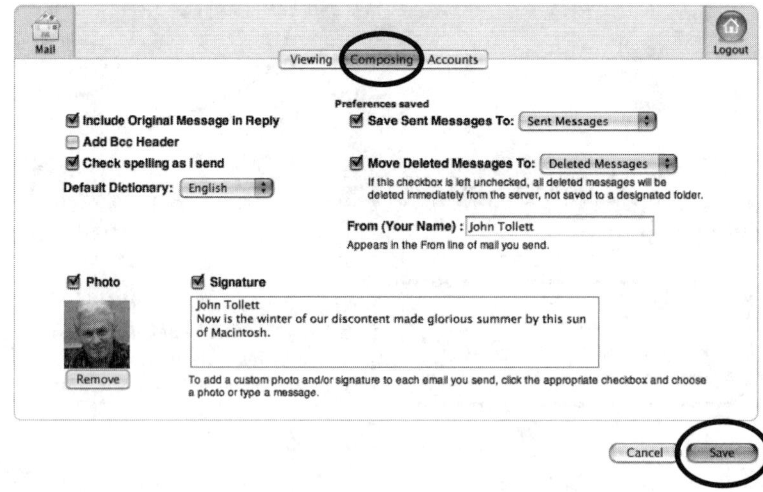

Account preferences

Email Aliases: This is a really neat feature. An email *alias* is a pretend email address. Messages to an alias address arrive in your main .Mac email account, but your real email address remains private. For instance, let's say you want to buy something online but you fear they will sell your email to every spammer on the face of the planet and you'll get hundreds junk mails a day. Use an alias address instead; after your order arrives, deactivate (don't delete) the alias until next time you need it. While it's deactivated, you won't receive any mail at that address.

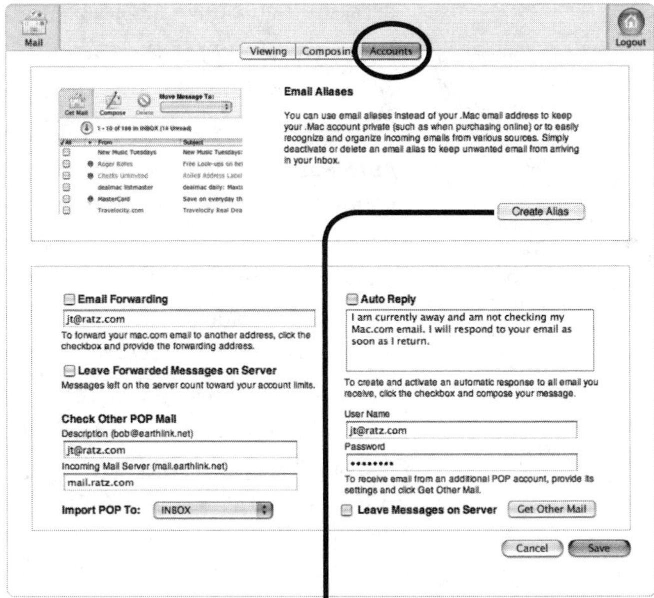

To make a new alias, *click here to open the Alias pane shown on the left.*

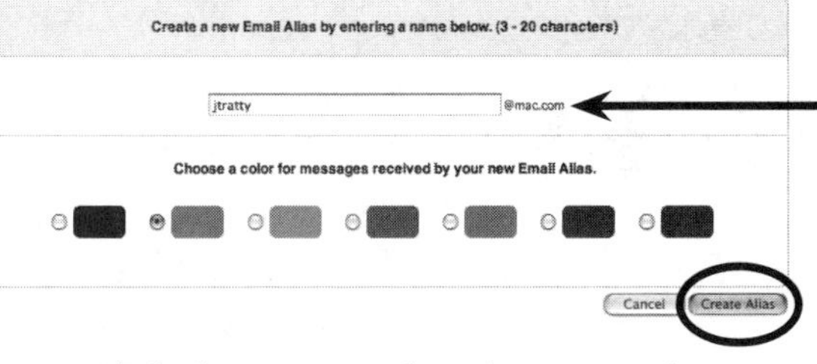

1. Click the "Create Alias" button in the Accounts pane of Mail Preferences (top-right example) to open the pane shown above.
2. Type an alias name you want to use in the text field. Choose a color swatch to color-code messages that come in to the alias address. Click the "Create Aliases" button to open the "Email Aliases" pane.
3. Click the radio button next to an alias to select it (if you've created more than one alias, all are listed here). Click the "Edit" button to open the pane shown on the right. Click one of the radio buttons to make the selected alias "Active" or "Inactive."

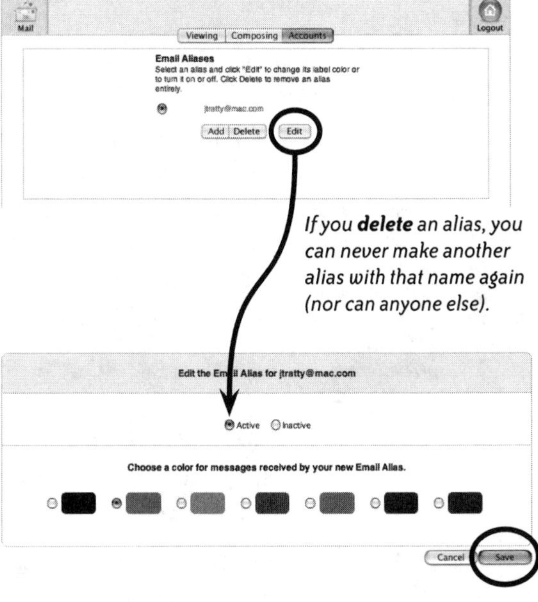

*If you **delete** an alias, you can never make another alias with that name again (nor can anyone else).*

Email Forwarding: Designate an email address to which your mail for this account is automatically forwarded.

A .Mac membership provides 250 MB of storage space, divided into 125 MB for email storage and 125 MB for iDisk storage.

You can change the ratio of email and iDisk storage in the .Mac pane of System Preferences (see pages 255–256).

Leave Forwarded Messages on Server: Any messages you have forwarded will be stored on the .Mac server so you can access them later from this account. These messages count toward your 125 MB email storage limit.

Auto Reply: If you can't check your email for a period of time, say while you're on vacation, check this option and type the response you want people to get when they send you email.

Check Other POP Mail: Lets you check one other POP email account from your .Mac webMail account (see page 438 for a description of a POP account; .Mac webMail is IMAP by default).

Enter the POP email address you want to access through .Mac webMail, its corresponding incoming mail server address, the account user name, and the account password. You can get this information from your email provider if you don't know it. Or if this is an email address you use regularly, you probably have this information already in the account preferences settings of the email program you normally use (such as Mail).

To access your POP mail from the Mail pane, select the account name from the "Go To" menu in the toolbar.

Import POP to: If you are going to bring in mail from a POP account, first make yourself a new folder with the name of that account (see page 302). Then **before you import,** choose that folder name from this menu. All of the mail from your POP account will be put in the new folder, separated from the mail in your .Mac account. You don't have to do this, but it's a good way to organize and sort messages by email account.

After you've created a new folder for importing POP email, the folder name appears in this menu in the Accounts Preferences pane (see the top of the previous page).

Leave Messages on Server: Check this if you want the POP mail server to store messages for access later; otherwise once you check the mail, messages are copied to your computer and erased on the POP server.

Get Other Mail: Click this to get mail from your POP email account immediately (not your .Mac webMail account).

Backup 10

Sooner or later, every computer user learns (usually the hard way) the wisdom of regularly backing up important files. It's a simple concept, but most of us suffer from a human operating system bug called "optimism." We think our data is safe. Instead, we should assume the worst is going to happen—corrupted files, theft, fire, lost files, accidentally trashed files, mistakenly overwritten files—and prepare accordingly.

A Mac.com membership includes **Backup,** your personal software to effortlessly backup the files you can't afford to lose. You can backup to removable media, such as CDs and DVDs, to your iDisk, to a FireWire or USB disk drive, or to all of these for extra security and peace of mind.

Some files are too large to fit on iDisk, a CD, or even a DVD. Backup can break large files apart and use multiple discs to create a backup copy. When you need to restore such files, Backup rejoins them on your hard disk.

Important Note about Backups

If you have very important files, **don't rely on one backup.** Make at least two, and store them in different locations. People have had their offices broken into and all of the computers stolen, plus all the backup disks. A fire has the same result. So make at least two backups and send one to your mother or your bank vault or your east-coast office.

Download and Install Backup

Before you can start using Backup, you must first **download** it from Apple's Mac.com web site.

1. Go to the Mac.com web site (www.mac.com) and click the "Backup" icon (the red umbrella) in the web page's sidebar.
2. Log in using your Mac.com membership name and password.
3. From the "Backup" page that opens, click the "Download Backup 2" icon (shown below-left) to open another page that contains three columns of downloadable files. In the third column, click the download icon to the right of the Backup name in the list (show below-right). Finally, the "Download Backup" page opens (below).

Tip: Turn off Energy Saver before you use Backup. If your computer goes to sleep, it might interrupt the backup process.

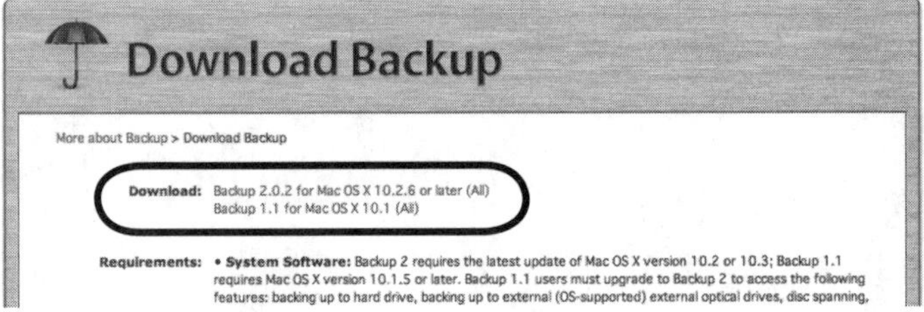

4. Click the Download *link* for the version of Backup that is compatible with your version of Mac OS X (circled above).
5. After downloading is finished, install the software as usual (double-click the .dmg or .pkg file and follow the directions).
6. Find the "Backup" icon in the Applications folder, then double-click it to open the "Backup" window, as shown on the next page.

The Backup Window

The main **Backup window** is where you select files to backup. In addition to the QuickPick options that are listed here, you can add other files or folders to the list.

- From the **pop-up menu,** choose the location to which you want to save backed-up files. **Or** choose to "Restore" backed-up files and copy them to your hard disk.
- The **QuickPick** items in the "Items" column (package icons) are *groups* of files that are all backed up at once.
- When you choose "Back up to iDisk" in the pop-up menu, a **status bar** shows how much space on your iDisk is used (dark green shading), how much space will be used after you backup the currently selected files (light green shading), and how much total space is available (white shading).
- Items that are *checkmarked* in the **Back Up** column will be backed up when you click the "Backup Now" button, or when a backup is scheduled.

Tip: The pop-up menu allows you to choose to save files to your iDisk, an external drive, or a removable CD or DVD (DVD option is only available on Macs with a DVD-writeable drive built in or attached).

When **Back up to iDisk** is selected, the *iTunes QuickPick package* includes only *playlists,* due to the limited storage space that is available with iDisk storage.

When **Back up to CD/DVD** or **Back up to Drive** is selected, the *iTunes QuickPick package* includes the entire *Library* of song files.

The *disc spanning* technology that Backup uses to copy large files to multiple discs means you have virtually unlimited backup storage.

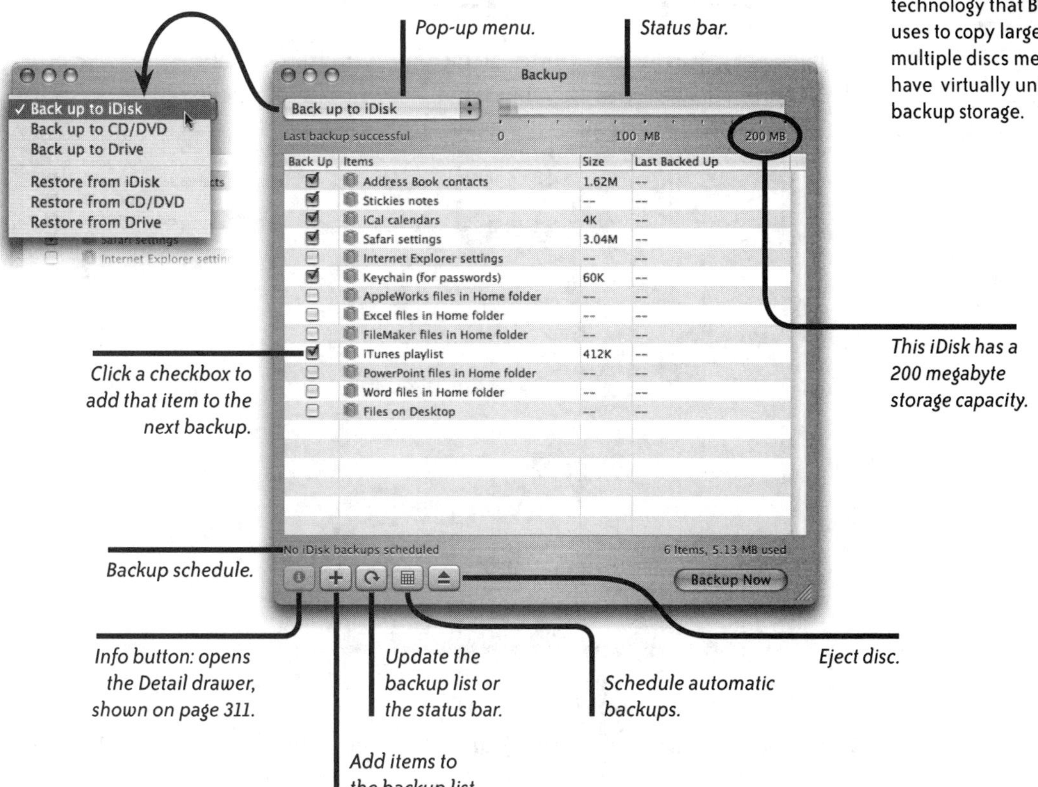

Add Items to the Backup List

Tip: To add items to the backup list from remote locations such as CDs, DVDs, or your local network, copy the items to your hard disk first.

The easiest way to **add files or folders** to the backup list is to *drag* them to the "Backup" window. You're not actually copying the files yet, just creating a list of the files you want to backup.

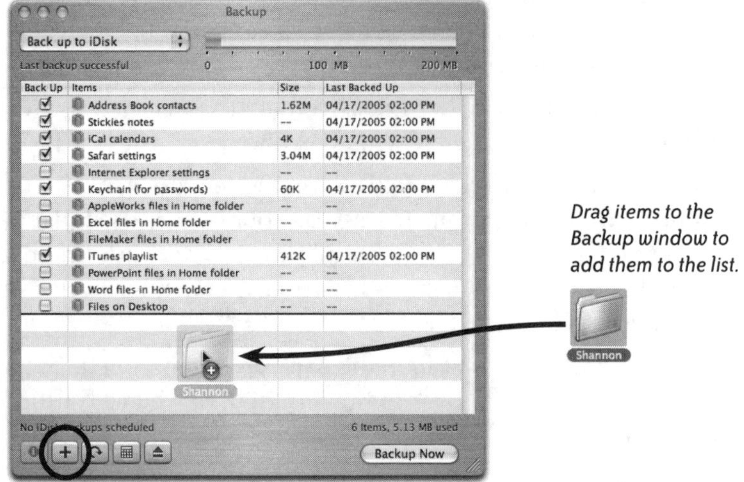

Drag items to the Backup window to add them to the list.

Tip: When an alert symbol appears next to an item in the backup list, Backup can't find the original item. You may have renamed, moved, or deleted it.

Or click the "Add items" button (the plus sign, circled above) so a Finder sheet slides down from the title bar (shown below). Locate a file or folder you want to add to the list, then click "Choose."

Note: Applications cannot be added to the backup list.

Delete items from the backup list

To remove an item from the backup list, select a file, then press the Delete key. QuickPick items (the package icons) cannot be removed.

The Details Drawer

To open the **Details drawer,** select a file or folder in the backup list, then click the Info button (shown on the right). **Or** you can double-click an item in the Backup list. The Details drawer slides open to show information about your selection. If you selected a **folder,** the drawer shows the contents of the folder and any subfolders that may be present. If you selected a *QuickPick* item (one with an icon that looks like a little package), the drawer shows the contents of the QuickPick package.

The Info button.

Exclude items from a backup

To exclude an item in the backup list from being backed up, uncheck its checkbox.

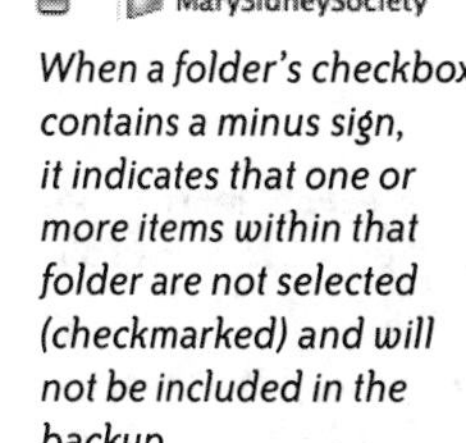

When a folder's checkbox contains a minus sign, it indicates that one or more items within that folder are not selected (checkmarked) and will not be included in the backup.

To exclude an item from being backed up that is *within a folder*:

1. Select a folder in the "Items" column, as shown below.
2. Click the Info button to open the Details drawer.
3. The Details drawer shows a list of the items in the selected folder. *Uncheck* the items you don't want to include in the backup.

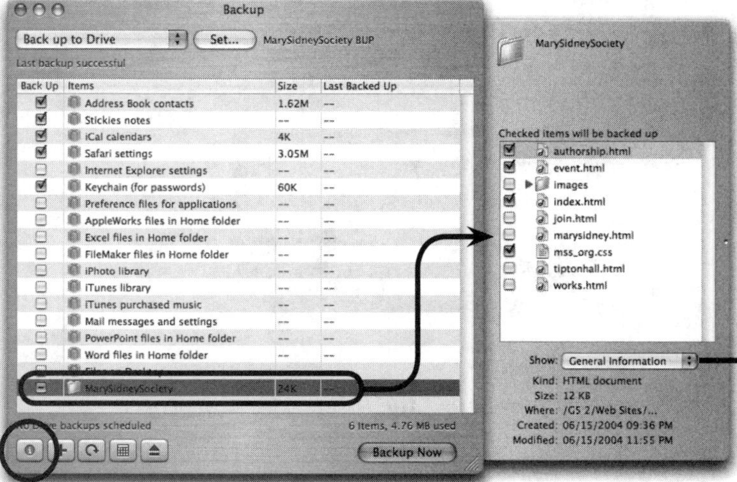

From this pop-up menu, choose to show "General Information" or "Backup Information" in the area below.

To show the contents of a selected (highlighted) item in the list, click this "Info" button.

Backup to Your iDisk

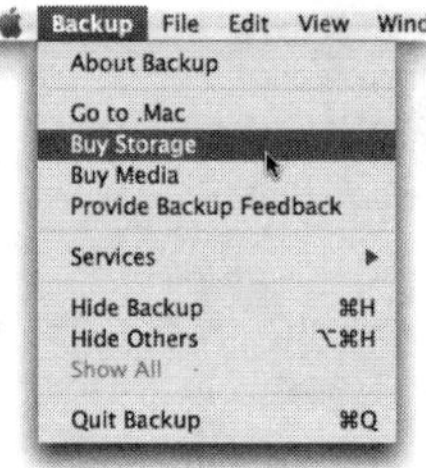

When you're ready to backup files, you can choose your **iDisk** location to save files into, depending on how much space is available. If there's not enough room on your iDisk, the empty area of the status bar is colored red. If you need more storage, from the Backup application menu (left) choose "Buy Storage." Your browser will open to a .Mac upgrade page where you can log in and order up to 1,024 megabytes (one gigabyte) of storage.

The best reason to backup files to your iDisk is so you can access them from anywhere in the world. Everything will go into a folder called "Backup."

1. From the pop-up menu, choose **Back up to iDisk** to save your files to the Backup folder on your iDisk.
2. Select the items in the list you want to backup.

To select all items in the backup list, from the Edit menu choose "Select All."

To check all checkboxes in the backup list, from the Edit menu choose "Check All."

To uncheck all items in the backup list, from the Edit menu choose "Uncheck All."

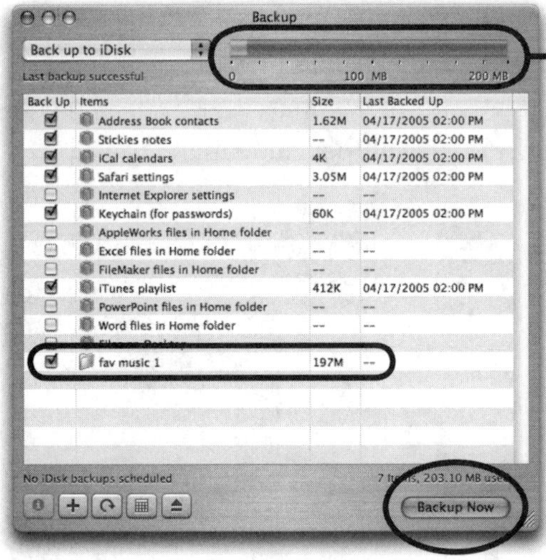

The available iDisk space is shaded red because the checkmarked music folder in the backup list is too large to fit.

3. Click "Backup Now."
4. A "Backup" window shows the progress of the process as files upload to your iDisk.

Backup to a Disk Drive

Backup allows you to backup your files to any internal or external hard disk drive connected to your Mac, including USB and FireWire devices. Backing up to a hard disk is the fastest way to archive large amounts of data. Your storage capacity is only limited by the size of the disk you backup to.

Tip: It's a good idea to backup your data to a different disk drive than the one it's on because many data-loss disasters happen to an entire disk at one time.

1. From the pop-up menu, choose **Back up to Drive.**

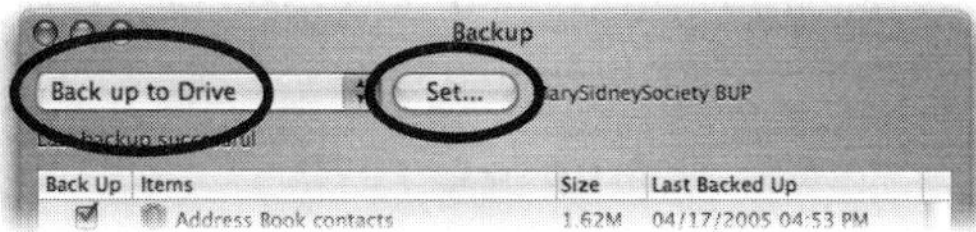

2. Checkmark items in the backup list that you want to back up.
3. Click the "Set" button (above) to specify a backup location. A sheet slides down (right) prompting you to *create* a new backup file, or chooose to *open* an existing backup.

   The backup file you create (or open) is a special file (shown on the right)—not just a folder of copies of files. To open a Backup file, use Backup's *Restore* function (page 316).

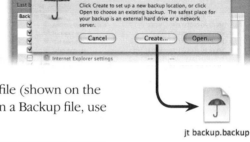

jt backup.backup

4. If you click the "Create" button, a drop-down sheet prompts you to choose a location for your backup file (below-left). Type a name for the backup file in the "Save As" field. Click "Create" (below-right) to continue.

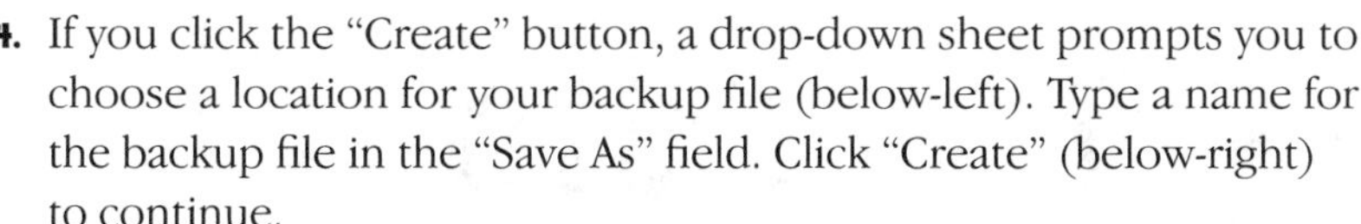

5. Click "Backup Now" to start the process.

The Backup file's name.

Backup to a CD or DVD

Tip: Backup lets you order blank CDs or DVDs and have them delivered to your door:

From Backup's application menu, choose "Buy Media." A .Mac web page will open in which you can log in to your .Mac account and order CD or DVD discs.

Also, compare prices with **www.SuperMediaStore.com.** But make sure you buy discs that are compatible with your system.

You must have an internal CD-RW drive or a SuperDrive to use this option.

Backing up files to optical discs (CD or DVD) instead of your iDisk or hard drive makes sense if you need additional backups or if you don't have an extra disk drive. You might not have access to an Internet connection and your iDisk, or your iDisk may not have enough space to hold all your backups. CDs are a good alternative. DVDs (if you have a SuperDrive) are even better since they hold much more data than a CD.

1. From the pop-up menu, choose **Back up to CD/DVD.**
2. Select the items in the list that you want to archive.

3. The "Est. Required Discs" in the bottom-left corner of Backup's window (below) shows how many CDs or DVDs are required to backup the selected items.
4. Click "Backup Now."

This is just an estimate! Have extra discs available, just in case.

5. Insert a blank CD or DVD into the drive.
6. In the window that opens (right), name your backup, then click the "Begin Backup" button.
7. At the prompt, insert a disc and click "Burn" in the "Burn Disc" window. If multiple discs are needed, Backup tells you when to insert another disc.
8. When Backup is finished, a window opens to informs you that "Your backup has been completed successfully."
9. Click OK.

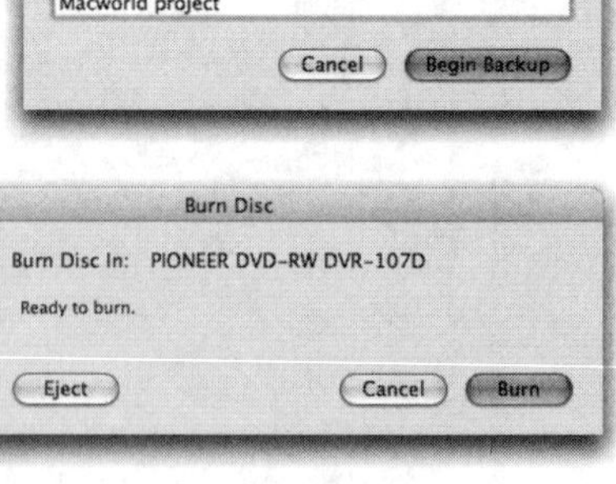

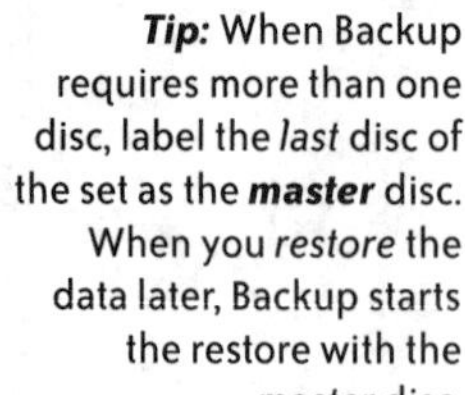

Tip: When Backup requires more than one disc, label the *last* disc of the set as the ***master*** disc. When you *restore* the data later, Backup starts the restore with the *master* disc.

Schedule Your Backups

You can schedule **automatic backups** of files to your iDisk or attached disk drive. Of course, your disk drive must be turned on, or you must be connected to the Internet for scheduled backup to your iDisk.

1. From Backup's pop-up menu, choose **Back up to iDisk** or **Back up to Drive,** depending on which device you want to schedule.
2. Click the "Schedule" button (circled) to open the Schedule sheet, shown to the right.
3. Choose the schedule settings you want.
4. Click OK.

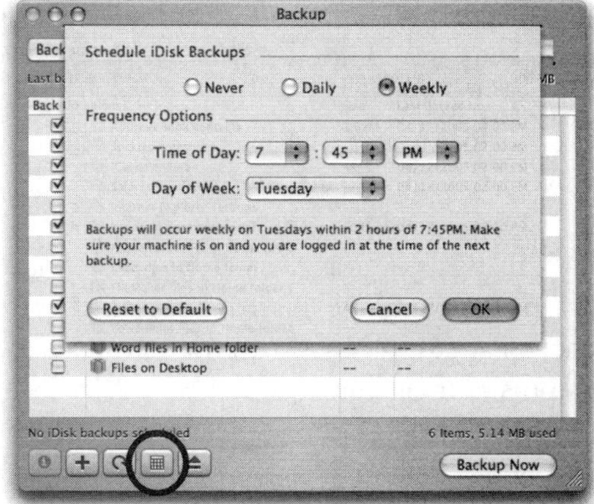

Remove Items or Clear Your iDisk

You cannot go to your iDisk and remove files directly, but you can use Backup to remove selected items. For your other disks, however, you cannot throw away individual items.

To remove a backed-up item from your iDisk:

1. Open Backup.
2. From the pop-up menu, choose "Restore from iDisk."
3. In the window, checkmark the item you want to remove.
4. From the Edit menu, choose "Remove from List."

To clear the iDisk Backup folder of all content, from the pop-up menu choose "Restore from iDisk." Then from the Edit menu, choose "Clear iDisk Backup Folder."

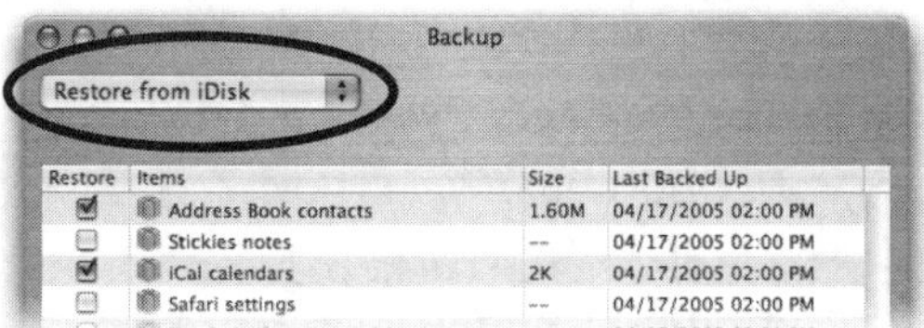

Restore Files from an iDisk

To copy backed-up files from your iDisk back to your computer:

1. From the pop-up menu, select "Restore from iDisk."
2. In the "Restore" window, choose items in the list to restore.
3. Click "Restore Now."

When QuickPick items are restored, they automatically replace the identical items on your computer. If you restore Address Book contacts, the backup version that's on iDisk replaces whatever contacts you have in Address Book on your computer. Before Backup replaces your local data, an alert opens so you can choose to "Replace" the data, "Skip" the replacement of data, or "Show" the location of the data about to be replaced. Instead of making this decision for every item (your Address Book might have hundreds of entries—and the item names are not recognizable, as shown below), checkmark "Apply to All" so you only have to click a button once to apply the command to all items.

*Huh?
Checkmark "Apply to All," then click "Replace."*

Restore Files from a Disk Drive

To copy backed-up files from a backup drive to your computer:

1. From the pop-up menu, select "Restore from Drive."
2. Click the "Set" button to locate the backup you want to restore from and the drive that it's located on.
3. In the "Restore" window, choose items in the list to restore.
4. Click "Restore Now."

Restore Files from a CD or DVD

To copy backed-up files from a CD or DVD back to your hard disk:

1. From the pop-up menu, select "Restore from CD/DVD."
2. Backup will ask for the master disc of the backup. Insert it (the master disc is the last disc burned during a backup).
3. In the "Restore" window, choose items in the list to restore.
4. Click "Restore Now."

iSync

iSync is an easy and convenient way to keep your iCal calendars and your Address Book information synchronized between multiple Macs. You can synchronize your Safari bookmarks so that multiple computers all have the same ones. When your bookmarks are synchronized, you have access to them from any computer in the world—just log in to your .Mac account (see Chapter 12, Bookmarks). You can also synchronize your Keychain information, Mail accounts, and Mail Rules, Signatures, and Smart Mailboxes. This makes it possible to quickly set up an additional (or new) computer with your existing information—just use iSync to copy the .Mac version of your information to the new computer. When you use iSync, you also have a valuable backup of your information in your .Mac account in case you somehow lose this data or experience a disaster of some sort.

To synchronize multiple computers requires a .Mac membership because each computer you synchronize compares its Address Book, iCal, and Safari bookmarks information to the copy that's stored on the .Mac server. A free 60-day .Mac trial membership is available—visit **www.mac.com** to sign up. If you don't have a .Mac membership, you can still use iSync to synchronize your Address Book and iCal information with a Bluetooth-enabled phone or a Palm OS device. A Palm OS device is any PDA (Personal Digital Assistant) that uses the Palm operating system.

Some people are intimidated by the word *synchronization* and never get around to using iSync. But it's easy and it's incredibly useful. As explained on the following pages, just sign in, choose the information you want to sync, then click "Sync Now."

Sync Your Main Mac to the .Mac Server

When you iSync your contacts, calendars, and bookmarks, etc., copies of your files are put on the .Mac synchronization server. You can also choose to put copies of your Keychain passwords, Mail accounts, Mail Rules, Mail Signatures, and Smart Mailboxes on the .Mac server. The .Mac copy of your information can then be copied (synced) to another Mac. If you have more than one computer, this is a great way to keep duplicate copies of your information on each computer.

1. Open the System Preferences: Either click its icon in the Dock, or go to the Apple menu and choose "Preferences…."
2. Click the ".Mac" icon (circled on the left).
3. Click the "Account" button (circled below). If you have a .Mac membership, type in your .Mac member name and password.

   Once you've signed in, your Mac is registered to the .Mac synchronization server. It uses the computer name that you set in the Sharing pane of System Preferences. Information that you choose to sync (see the following page) gets copied to the .Mac server. Then other Macs can sign in and sync to the same server, a procedure called Mac-to-Mac syncing (see page 321).

To register more than one computer to a .Mac account, *sign in* to the account from each individual computer. All computers registered to a specific .Mac account are listed in the "Advanced" pane of .Mac preferences (page 322).

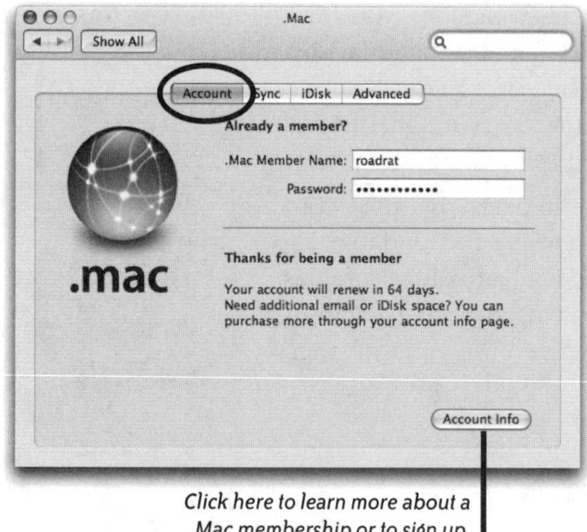

Click here to learn more about a .Mac membership or to sign up.

4. Click the "Sync" button (circled below) to show the Sync pane.
5. Click the "Synchronize with .Mac" checkbox, then from the pop-up menu set how often you want your computer to sync the selected files. If you choose "Automatically," iSync will sync whenever a change is made to the selected file type. If you choose "Manually," iSync will wait until you click the "Sync Now" button.
6. In the list of icons, select the files you want to sync, then click the "Sync Now" button.

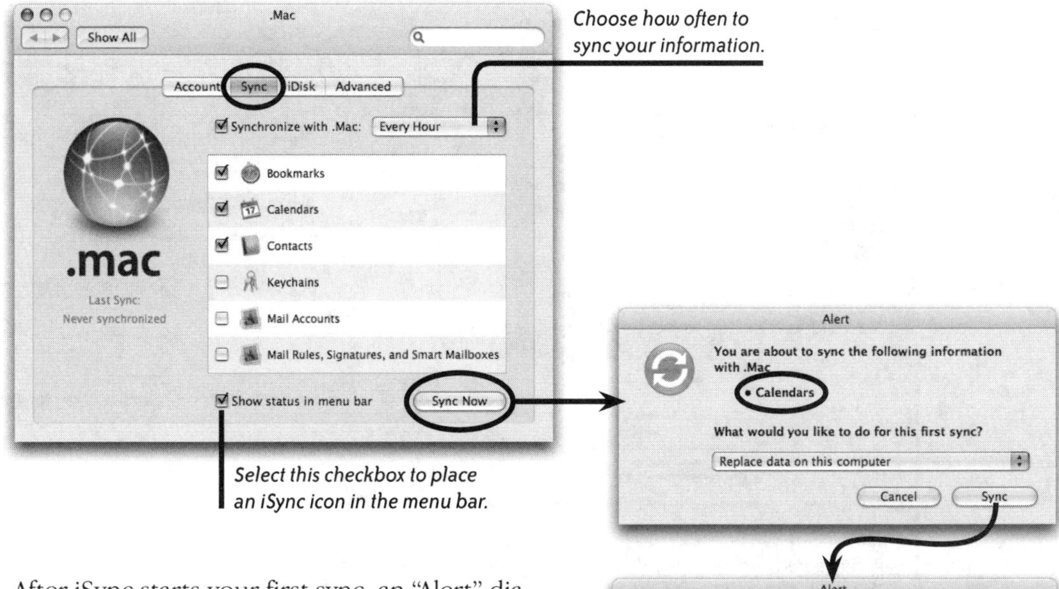

Choose how often to sync your information.

Select this checkbox to place an iSync icon in the menu bar.

7. After iSync starts your first sync, an "Alert" dialog opens (shown on the right) for each of the selected file categories. From the pop-up menu, choose how you want iSync to handle the data:

   Replace data on .Mac. This selection copies the data on your Mac to the .Mac server. This is the option you want to choose when you sync for the first time.

   Merge data on this computer and .Mac. If there's existing data on the .Mac server, merge it with the data on your Mac.

   Replace data on this computer. If there's existing data on the .Mac server, it will replace the data on your Mac.
8. Click the "Sync" button.

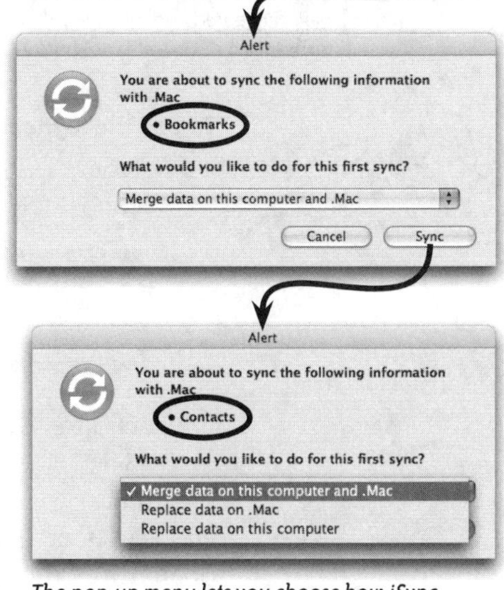

The pop-up menu lets you choose how iSync handles the first synchronization of each item.

Show iSync status in the menu bar

You can make iSync even more accessible if you put the iSync icon in the menu bar where you can click the icon to open an iSync pop-up menu.

To make the iSync icon appear in the menu bar:

- Click the "Show status in menu bar" checkbox in the iSync pane of .Mac Preferences (circled below-left).
- **Or** open iSync Preferences (from the iSync application menu choose "Preferences…") then click the "Show status in menu bar" checkbox (circled below-right).

Sync pane of the .Mac preferences window.

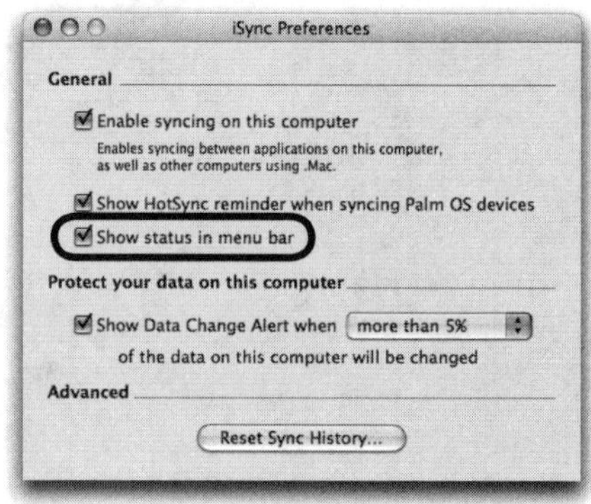

When syncing is in progress, this progress bar is animated and the "Sync Now" button turns into the "Cancel Sync" button.

To use the iSync menu:

- From the iSync drop-down menu in the menu bar (shown below), choose "Sync Now" or "Open .Mac Sync Preferences…."

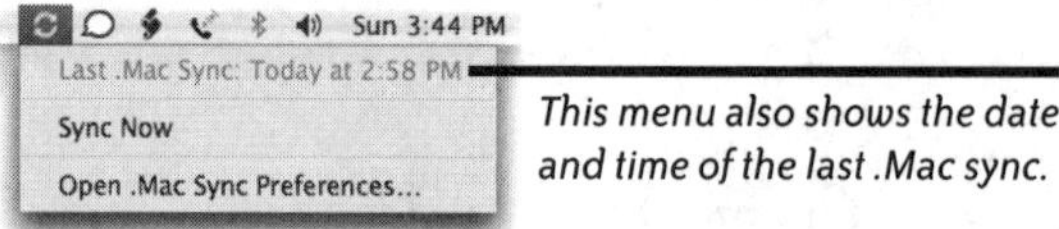

This menu also shows the date and time of the last .Mac sync.

If you choose "Sync Now," iSync syncs your files using the current settings in the Sync pane of .Mac preferences (below-left), but without opening the preferences window. If you want to check the sync settings or change them, choose "Open .Mac Sync Preferences…" and the preferences window will open before the sync operation begins.

Sync Your Mac to Another Mac

Many of us work on two or more computers—perhaps one at the office and one at home, or you may have multiple computers in one office or home. To synchronize all the computers so you have the same information everywhere you go, perform a **Mac-to-Mac synchronization.** This procedure is exactly the same as a Mac-to-*.Mac* sync, except that you sign in to the same .Mac server with a different computer (a Mac of course).

1. Make sure you've already synced your main Mac to the .Mac server, as described on the previous pages.
2. On a different computer, open the .Mac preferences (in the System Preferences window, click the ".Mac" icon"). In the Account pane, sign in with the member name and password of the .Mac account whose info you want to sync to (see page 318).
3. Click the "Sync" button to show the Sync pane (shown on the previous page). Put a checkmark next to items you want to sync.
4. Click "Sync Now."

If iSync finds a conflict between a file on the .Mac server and the matching file on your computer, "Conflict Resolver" (shown below) opens. Click "Review Later" to put "Review Conflicts Now…" in iSync's status menu for later access. Click "Review Now" to show the conflicting files. Click the pane that contains the information you want to use in the sync, then click "Done." In the sheet that drops down, choose "Sync Later" or "Sync Now."

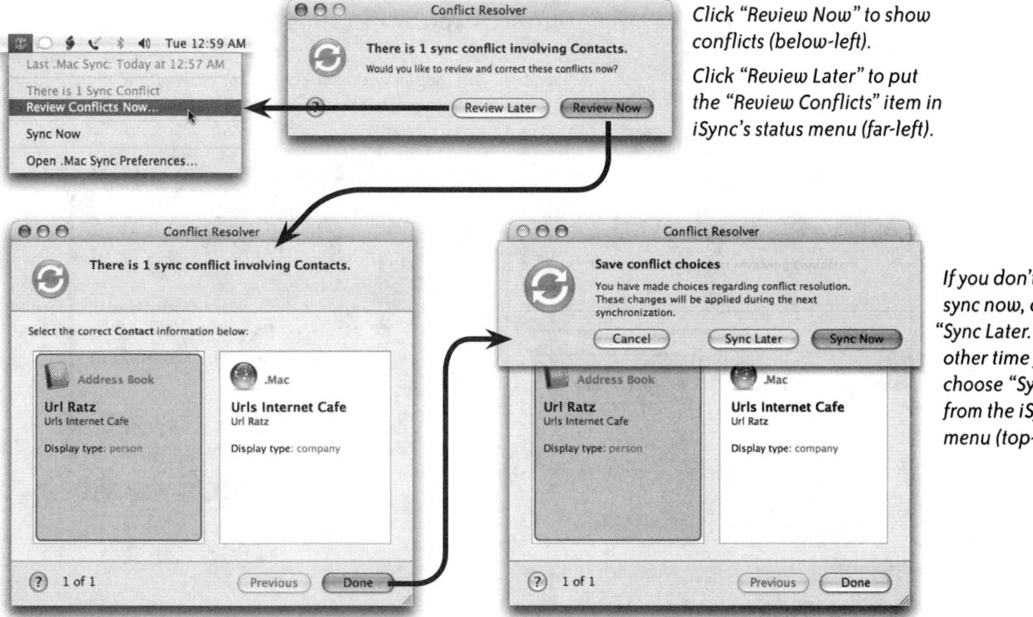

Click "Review Now" to show conflicts (below-left).

Click "Review Later" to put the "Review Conflicts" item in iSync's status menu (far-left).

If you don't want to sync now, choose "Sync Later." At some other time you can choose "Sync Now" from the iSync status menu (top-left).

The Advanced Pane

The "Advanced" pane of .Mac preferences lists all of the computers that are registered to sync with the current .Mac account. Page 321 explains how to register multiple computers to sync with a single .Mac account.

To *unregister* a computer, select the computer name in the list, then click the "Unregister" button.

Click "Reset Sync Data..." to reveal a drop-down sheet of controls that lets you choose the applications whose information you want to reset. You can also choose in which direction you want the reset data to sync—you can either replace the data on the .Mac server with the data on your computer, or you can replace the data on your computer with the .Mac data.

- In the sheet that drops down, choose which sync data you want to reset. The pop-up menu option "All Sync Info" includes *all* data for applications that are currently checkmarked in the Sync pane of .Mac preferences. Each checkmarked application appears in the pop-up menu as a separate item. If you want to replace data of just *one* of the checkmarked apps, select the app from this pop-up menu.
- Click the left arrow button to replace the data on your computer with .Mac data.
- Click the right arrow button to replace existing .Mac data with the data on your computer. The "Replace" pop-up menu contains the applications that are checked in the Sync pane of .Mac preferences.
- Click the "Replace" button (circled below-right).

The "Replace" pop-up menu contains applications that are selected in the Sync pane of .Mac preferences.

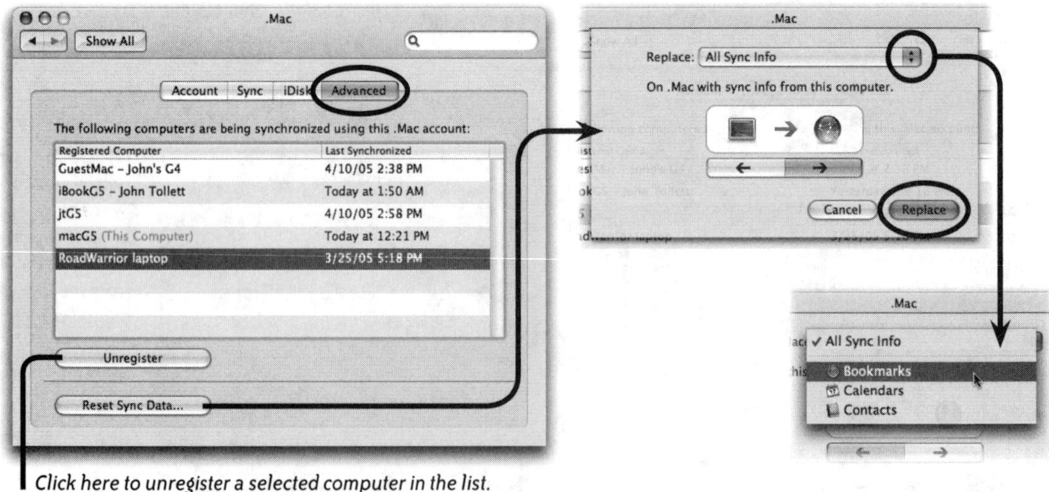

Click here to unregister a selected computer in the list.

iSync Preferences

You can enable or disable syncing and set certain behaviors.

1. Open iSync. It's in your Applications folder. From the iSync menu, choose "Preferences...."
2. In the iSync Preferences (below-left), check the options you want to enable.

Enable syncing on this computer: This allows the process to happen. It enables syncing of the applications listed in the Sync pane of .Mac preferences (page 319).

Show status in menu bar provides access from the menu bar (below) to iSync's status, sync commands, and to the .Mac preferences Sync pane where you choose the applications you want to sync.

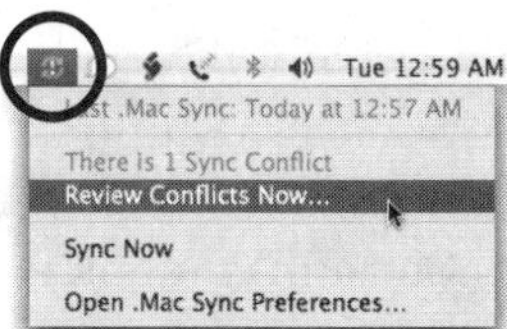

iSync status in the menu bar.

The exclamation point in the menu bar icon indicates a sync conflict (page 321).

Show Data Change Alert: This pop-up menu lets you set an alert when iSync is about to change more than a certain pre-set percentage of your information. The alert will give you a chance to cancel or allow the sync.

Reset Sync History: Resets the sync history, but does not delete any data. The next time you sync, iSync behaves as if syncing for the first time, asking if you want to merge or replace information (as shown on page 319).

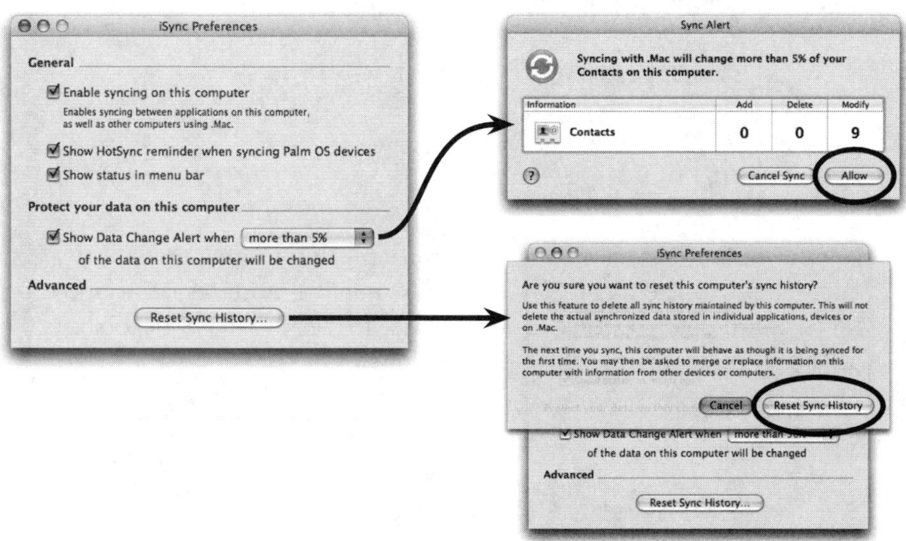

Add Devices and Synchronize

iSync also enables you to synchronize your contact and calendar information to other devices:

- **Palm OS devices** such as Palm Tungsten and Zire, the Handspring Treo, the palmOne Visor, and the Sony Clié models.
- **Bluetooth-enabled phones,** such as the models offered by Sony Ericsson, Nokia, Motorola, and Siemens. Motorola also makes USB phones that are compatible with iSync. Also, most USB mobile phones can be synced using iSync.

Add a Bluetooth phone to iSync

Bluetooth devices have to be *paired* with your computer, using Bluetooth Setup Assistant, and they must be in *discoverable* mode. Some Bluetooth devices are automatically in discoverable mode.

To add a USB phone to iSync, use Steps 4–8.

1. Make sure that both your computer and your mobile phone have Bluetooth installed and that it is turned on.
2. Open System Preferences, then click the "Bluetooth" icon.
3. In the "Devices" pane of Bluetooth preferences, click "Set up new device..." to open the Bluetooth Setup Assistant. Follow the step-by-step instructions to *pair* your phone and computer.
4. Open iSync (double-click the iSync icon in the Applications folder). iSync appears on your Desktop, shown below.

5. From the Devices menu, choose "Add Device...."

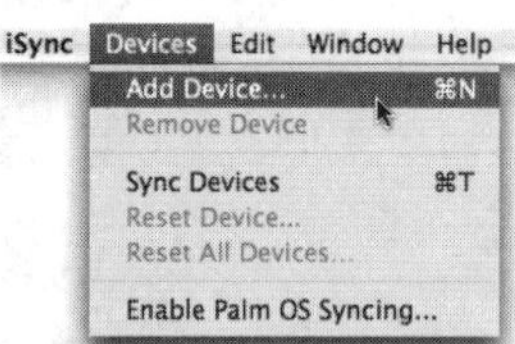

6. iSync automatically finds any Bluetooth device within range (approximately 32 feet) and displays it in the "Add Device" window shown below. Double-click the device to add it to the iSync toolbar.

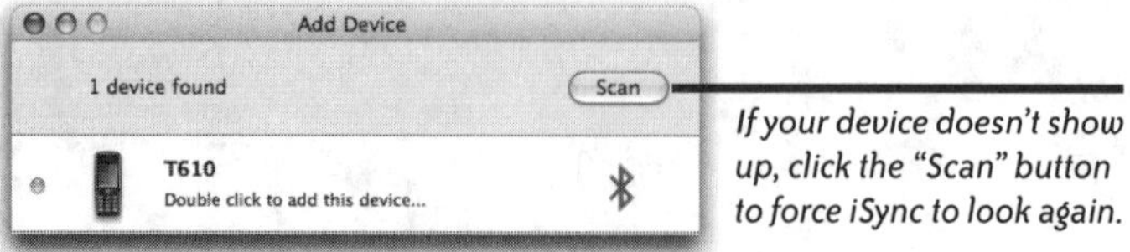

If your device doesn't show up, click the "Scan" button to force iSync to look again.

7. In the iSync drawer that opens (shown below), put checkmarks next to the items you want to enable. Choose the contacts and calendars you want to synchronize.
8. Click "Sync Devices" in the iSync toolbar. The iSync drawer closes and a synchronization bar shows the progress.

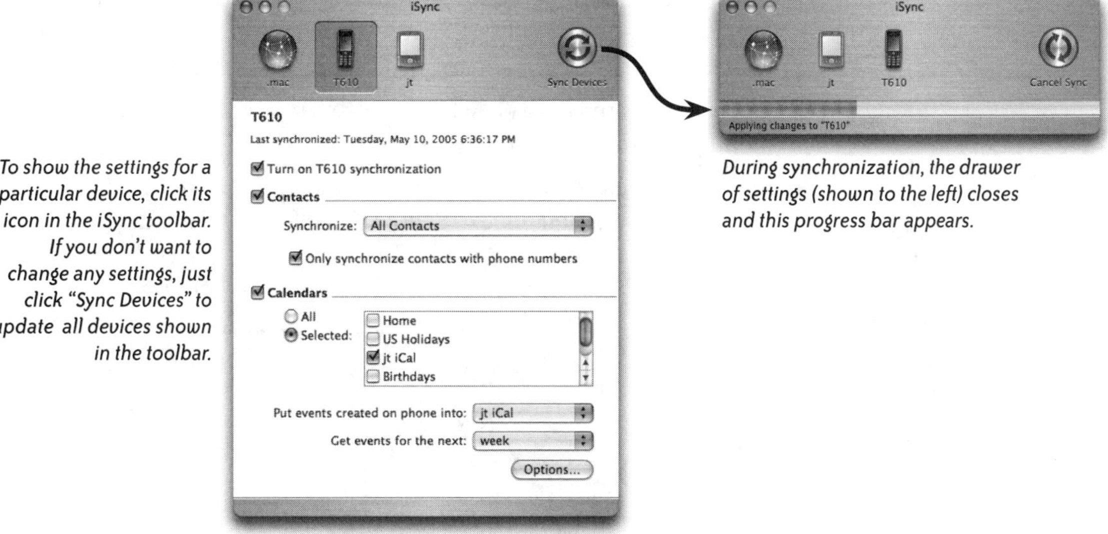

To show the settings for a particular device, click its icon in the iSync toolbar. If you don't want to change any settings, just click "Sync Devices" to update all devices shown in the toolbar.

During synchronization, the drawer of settings (shown to the left) closes and this progress bar appears.

Reset a device

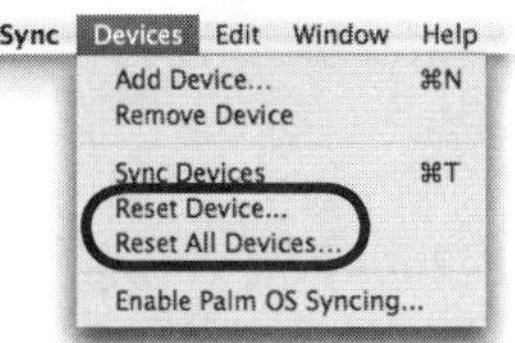

On a device, you can reset (replace) all of the contact and calendar information with the existing information on your computer: From the Devices menu, choose "Reset Device...." Click the "Reset" button in the alert window that opens (below-left). If you have more than one device showing in iSync's toolbar, the reset applies to the *currently selected device.*

To reset all connected devices at once, choose "Reset All Devices..." from the Devices menu. If you're sure you want to replace *all* the information on *all* your devices, click the "Reset" button in the alert window (below-right).

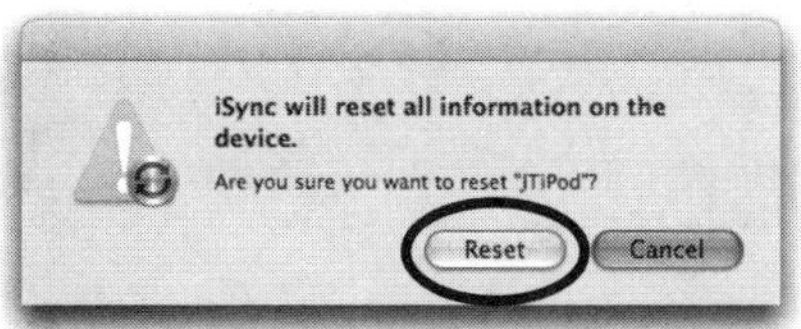

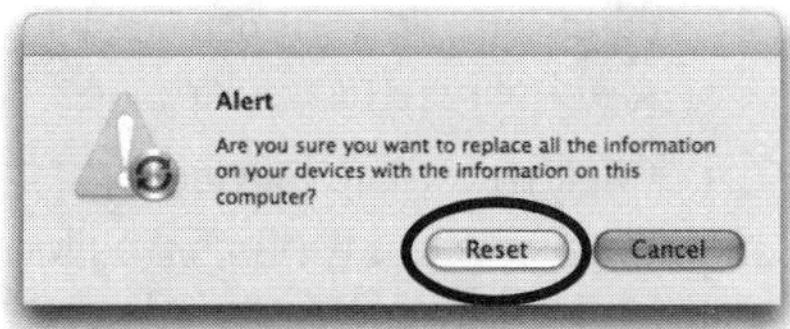

Add a Palm OS device to iSync

To sync a Palm OS device with a computer, make sure the latest versions of Palm Desktop and iSync Palm Conduit are installed (**www.palmsource.com** and **www.apple.com/isync/download**). Connect your Palm device to your computer.

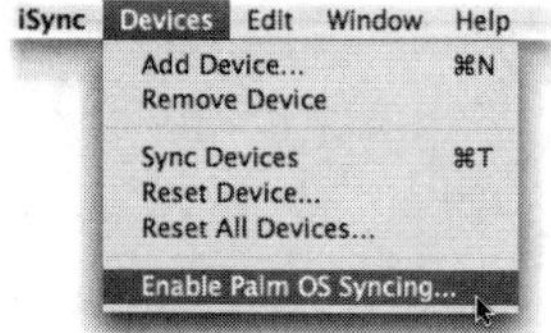

1. Open iSync. From the Devices menu choose "Enable Palm OS Syncing…" (shown to the left). An alert tells you to open the Palm Conduit Settings shown below. To do that, follow the next steps.
2. Open your Palm HotSync Manager software, then from the HotSync menu, choose "Conduit Settings."
3. In the "Conduit Settings" window, double-click "iSync Conduit" (shown below), then check "Enable iSync for this Palm device."

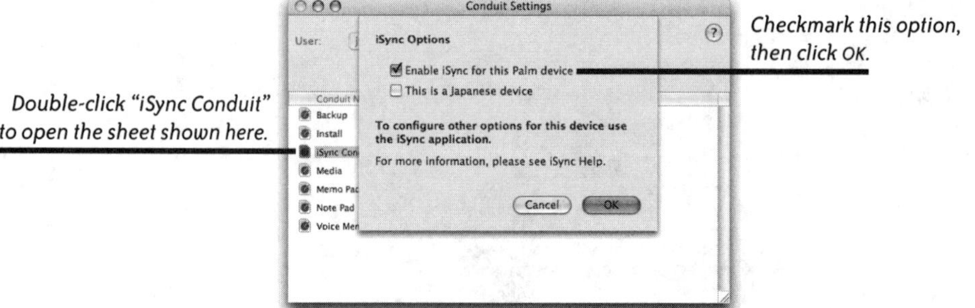

Double-click "iSync Conduit" to open the sheet shown here.

Checkmark this option, then click OK.

4. Click OK and quit HotSync Manager.
5. In iSync, from the Devices menu, choose "Add Device…." iSync detects the Palm device and adds it to the iSync toolbar.
6. Click the Palm device icon in the toolbar. In the iSync drawer that opens (shown to the right), put checkmarks next to the items you want to enable. Choose the contacts and calendars you want to synchronize to your device.
7. Click the "Sync Devices" button in the toolbar. An alert appears and instructs you to click the HotSync button on your Palm device cradle. For future syncs, just press the HotSync button on the Palm cradle.

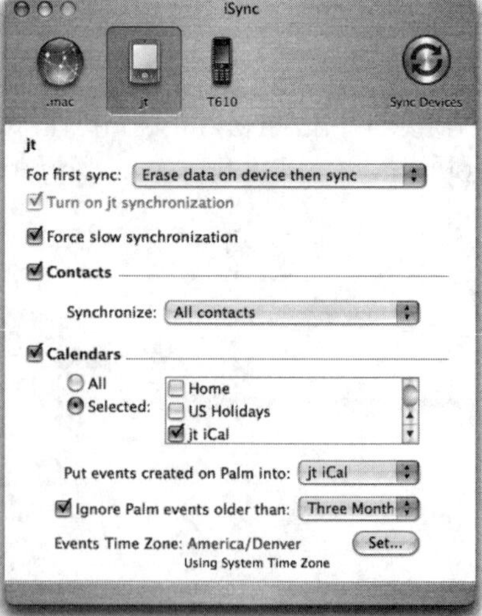

To close the iSync drawer, click the highlighted button in the toolbar.

.Mac Bookmarks

12

For most of us, browsing the Internet is more than entertainment. It's a news, research, teaching, training, communication, and shopping tool that we can't get along without. One of the most useful techniques of our online activities is the ability to bookmark web sites, allowing us at any time to instantly jump back to a page of information that we need—as long as we're sitting at our own computer at home or at the office. Or if we happen to have our laptop with us.

If you have a .Mac membership, you can use iSync to sync your Safari bookmarks to the .Mac synchronization server and have total access to all of your valuable links no matter where in the world you are, and no matter what computer you're using.

Knowing this is possible, you may want to start bookmarking web pages now in anticipation of future trips. You can bookmark restaurants, activities, or maps well in advance of your trip. Later, from an Internet cafe or from a laptop in your hotel room, pull up your .Mac bookmarks and finalize your plans. If you're on business, you can access your business-related bookmarks from an office down the hall, from a client's computer, or from another country.

The following pages explain how to sync your Safari bookmarks and access them with your .Mac account.

Sync your Safari Bookmarks

In order to use .Mac Bookmarks, you need to sync your existing Safari bookmarks to your .Mac account. Before you do this, it might be helpful to do a little bit of housekeeping and organization of your bookmarks. It's not absolutely necessary—but now's a good time to throw out bookmarks that you never use or that are outdated and don't link to anything. You should also organize the bookmarks into folders so it's easy to find them. Because some web pages are difficult to categorize, you might want to create some generic folders that have names such as "Favs," "Work," or even "Organize Later." The less messy your bookmark organization is, the easier it is to find the bookmark you want.

Sync your bookmarks with .Mac:

1. Turn on .Mac synchronzation in iSync: open System Preferences and click the .Mac icon. In the .Mac preferences window (below) sign in with your .Mac member name and password.

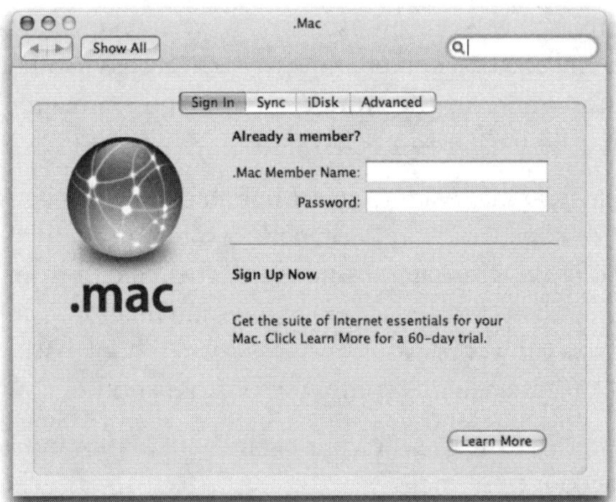

2. Click the "Sync" tab to open the Sync pane shown below.
3. Click the "Synchronize with .Mac" checkbox. From the pop-up menu choose to sync manually (whenever you want), hourly, daily, etc.

Turn on .Mac synchronization.

4. Click the "Advanced" tab to open the Advanced pane (below) and register your computer with the .Mac synchronization server. Select your computer in the list, then click the "Register this Computer" button. If the selected computer is already registered, the button says "Unregister."

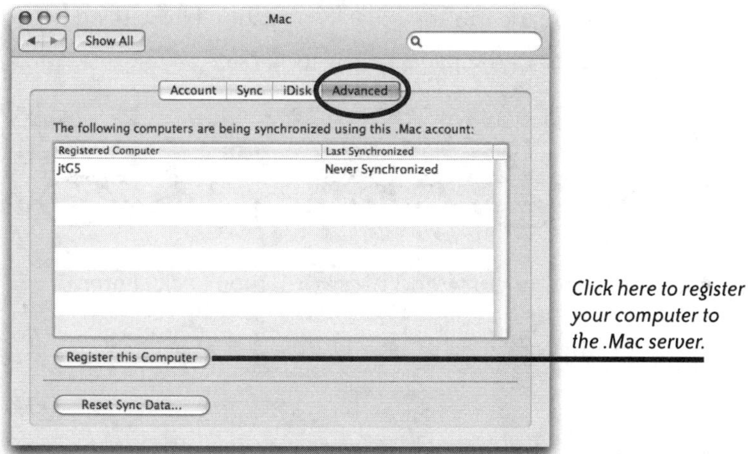

Click here to register your computer to the .Mac server.

5. In the Sync pane (below), click the "Bookmarks" checkbox (and any of the other items you want to sync with .Mac's server.
6. Click the "Sync Now" button. All of your Safari bookmarks are copied to the .Mac server.
7. Go to the .Mac web site to access your .Mac bookmarks (next page).

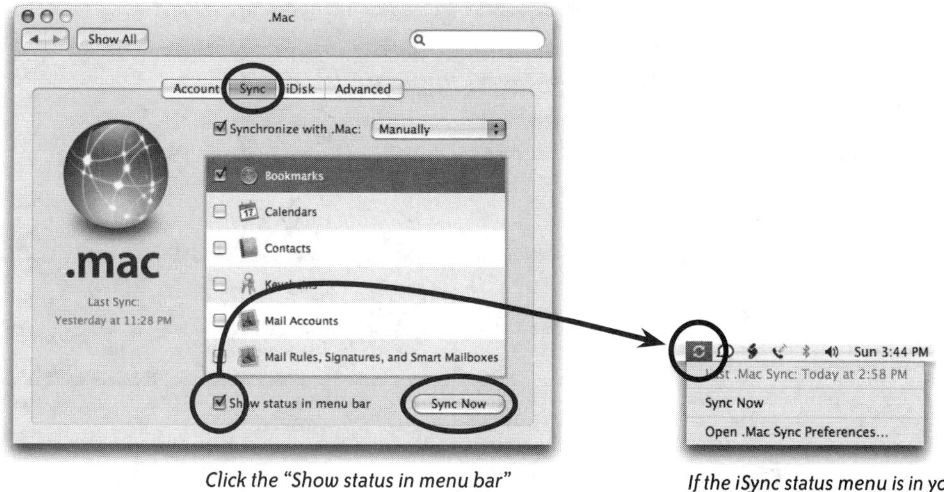

Click the "Show status in menu bar" checkbox to put the iSync pop-up menu in the menu bar, as shown on the right.

If the iSync status menu is in your menu bar, you can open .Mac Sync Preferences from its pop-up menu.

Access Your Bookmarks

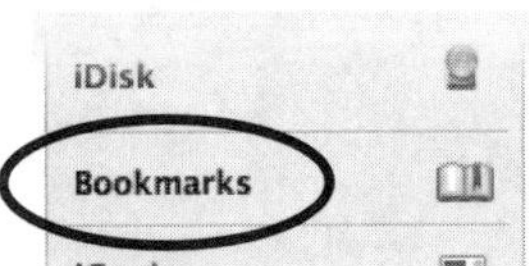

1. Go to www.mac.com, then do *one* of the following to open the .Mac log in page:
   - In the .Mac Welcome page that opens, click the "Bookmarks" icon in the sidebar (circled on the left).
   - Click "Bookmarks" in the page's navigation bar (circled below).
   - Click "Log In" in the page's navigation bar.

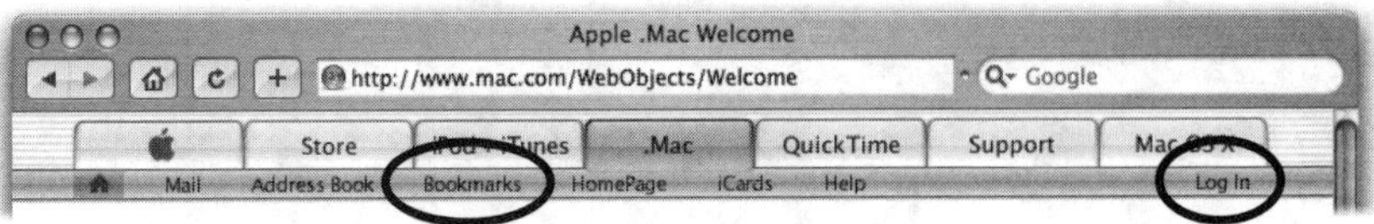

2. Type your member name and password, then click "Enter."

3. A window opens to alert you that your bookmarks will be synced. Click "Sync Now." The Safari bookmarks on your computer are copied to the .Mac server.

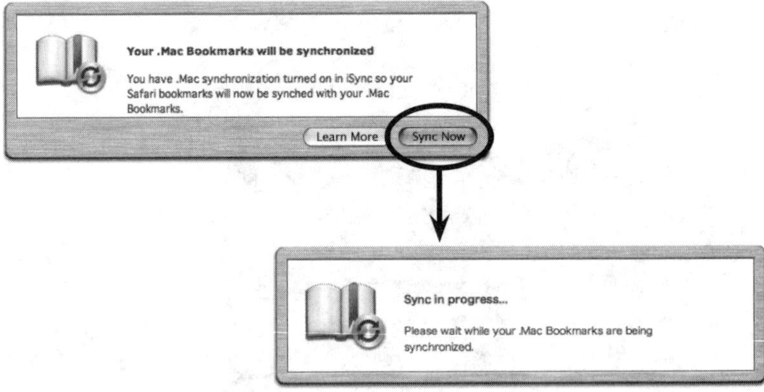

4. When the synchronization is finished, a page opens with "Welcome to .Mac Bookmarks." Click the "Open Bookmarks" button.

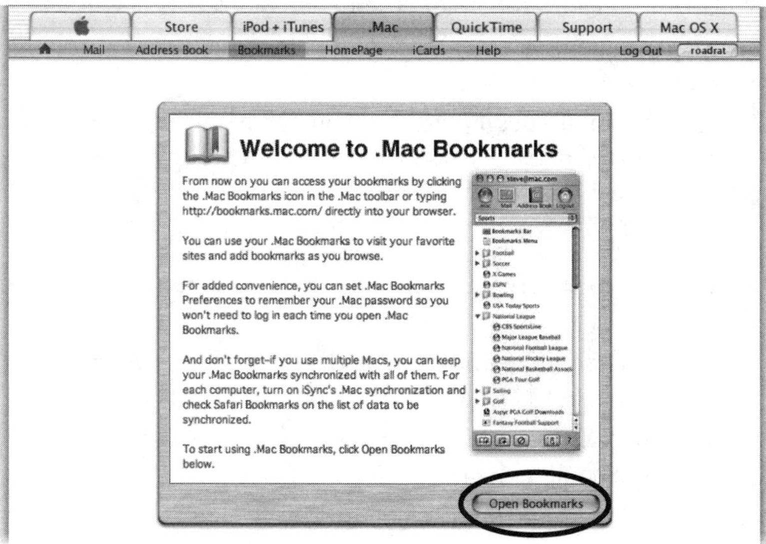

5. The .Mac Bookmarks window that opens contains a copy of your bookmarks, organized the same as on your computer.
   - From the Bookmarks pop-up menu, choose a particular collection (a folder) of bookmarks to display, such as "Bookmarks Bar," shown below-left. Or choose "All Collections," shown below-right.
   - Click on a Bookmark link (the Internet globe symbol) to open it in your browser.
   - Click on a folder to show the Bookmarks contained within it.

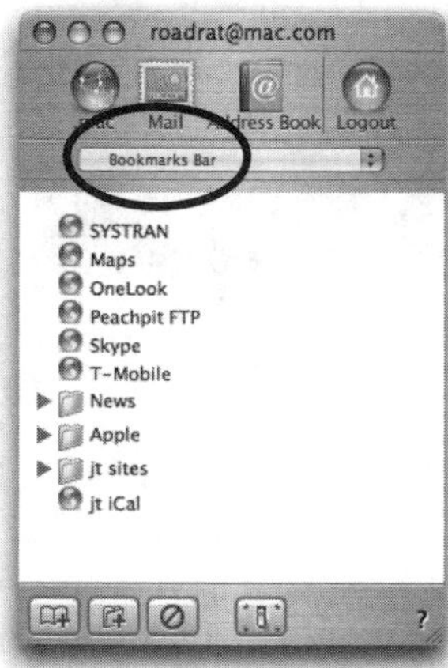

Click the question mark to open .Mac Bookmarks Help Files.

Managing .Mac Bookmarks

With the Bookmarks window open on the Desktop, you can add or delete bookmarks, or create a new folder to organize bookmarks.

Add bookmarks

When you're at another computer and you find a web site that you want to bookmark, don't scribble the address on a piece of scrap paper that you'll lose—bookmark it.

1. Open .Mac Bookmarks (as explained on the previous pages).
2. Click the bookmark-plus button (circled below-left). A new pane slides up into view (below-right).
3. Type a name for the bookmark and its address in the text fields. You don't have to include "http://" as part of the address.
4. From the "Add Bookmark To" pop-up menu, choose a folder to put the bookmark in.
5. Click the "Add" button (circled below-right).
6. Click the bookmark-plus button again to close the pane.

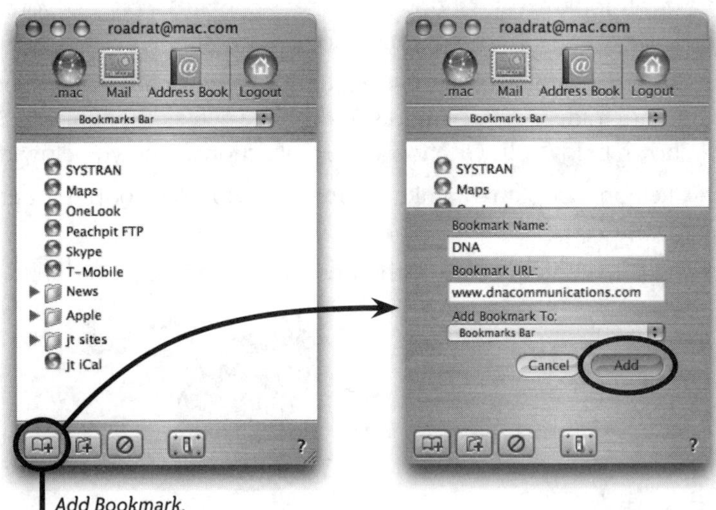

Add Bookmark.

Add folders

You may want to add a new folder to keep your new bookmarks organized.

1. Click the folder-plus button (circled below-left). A new pane slides up into view (below-right).
2. Type a name for the folder in the text field. From the pop-up menu choose a folder to put the new folder in.
3. Click the "Add" button. The new folder now appears in the pop-up menu when choosing a folder for bookmarks or folders.
4. Click the folder-plus button again to close the pane.

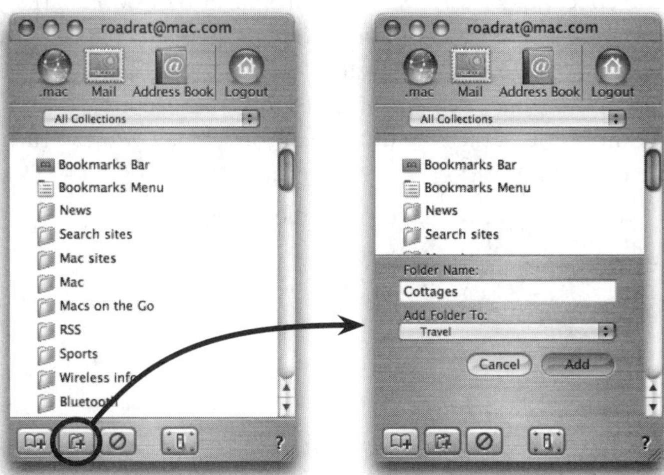

Delete bookmarks

To delete a bookmark:

1. From the pop-up menu at the top of the window, choose the folder that contain the bookmark you want to delete.
2. Click the *square* "not" button (circled below-right). A gray X is placed next to every item in the list.
3. Click the X next to the bookmark or folder you want to delete.
4. Click "Delete" (circled to the right) to delete the selected bookmark.
5. Click the square "not" button again to clear all of the Xs.

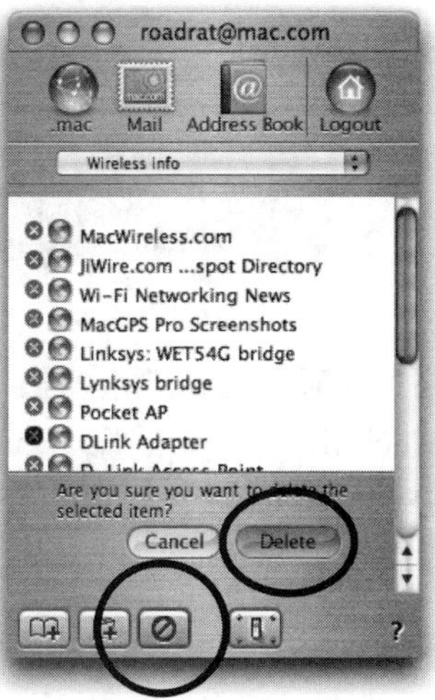

Bookmark Preferences

Click the light switch button to open the Bookmark Preferences.

- Click one of the radio buttons to "Always open pages in a new browser window" or to "Always open pages in the same browser window."
- From the "Default folder to open" pop-up menu, choose the folder of bookmarks that's open when you go to .Mac Bookmarks.
- From the "Language" pop-up menu, choose the language in which web sites display.
- Click the checkbox to turn .Mac synchronization of Bookmarks on or off. If you're at another computer and making changes to your .Mac bookmarks, you may not want these changes copied to the other computer that's synchronized to the .Mac account. Even if the other computer is set to synchronize automatically, you can turn it off here to avoid the sync.
- Click "Save" after you've made your selections.

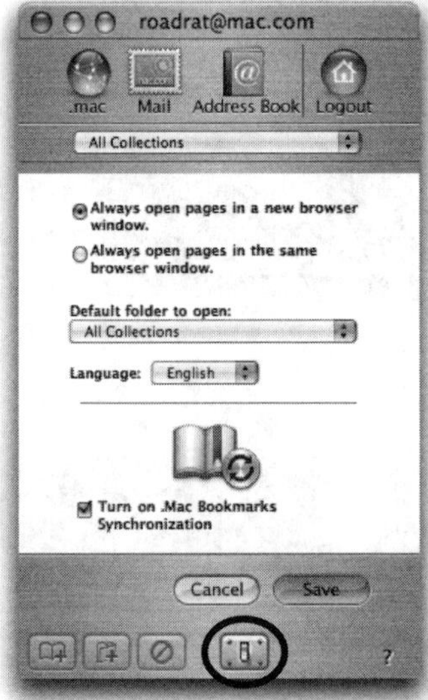

The .Mac Bookmarks Toolbar

Click the icons in the toolbar to open the .Mac home page, the .Mac Mail page (Webmail), or the .Mac Address Book page. Click the "Logout" icon to quit .Mac Bookmarks and close its window.

Section three

Mac OS X apps

The applications in this section are productivity applications that were designed specifically to run on the latest version of the computer world's state-of-the-art operating system, Mac OS X. The following chapters explore the applications that let you efficiently organize, create, and manage email, contact information, calendars, and to-do lists: **Mail, Address Book,** and **iCal.**

Mac OS X also includes communication applications that make it convenient, efficient, and fun to be productive: **iChat AV** provides instant messaging in text, audio, and video formats for keeping communication lines open with family, friends, and associates. **Bonjour** makes file-sharing and communication on a local network effortless. **Safari,** Apple's custom-built web browser, offers top browsing speed and cutting-edge features such as Private Browsing and RSS news feeds.

While other Mac applications inspire creativity, these Mac OS X apps enhance the efficiency and productivity of your ever-expanding digital lifestyle.

iCal

iCal is a personal calendar, an organizer, and a scheduler built around the idea that you need more than one calendar to manage the different aspects of your life. You can create as many specialized calendars as you want: one for work, one for family, another for school, etc. You can choose to display just one calendar at a time, all calendars, or any selection of calendars.

Use iCal's **To Do list** to prioritize and manage your busy day, week, or month. Add an **event,** such as a party, to iCal and let iCal email invitations to selected people in your Address Book. iCal can **notify** you of upcoming events and appointments with an alarm sound, email alert, or display a notification. And iCal's **search** feature let you easily find any event or To Do item that you've added to your calendar.

If you travel a lot you'll like iCal's **time zone** features that let you set everything to another time zone, or just specific events.

You can even **publish** your own calendar online so you (or friends, family, or coworkers) can check it from any computer, anywhere in the world. The number of calendars you create is limited only by the amount of free disk space on your computer. All sorts of iCal calendars are available online that you can subscribe to—many organizations, bands, and entertainment companies are posting iCalendars on their web sites.

iCal does all this and more with style and simplicity. Your Mac even makes it fun to be organized!

The iCal Window

iCal's window provides access to all calendars, views, events, and To Do lists. Color-coding makes it easy to glance at multiple calendars in the window and instantly see if there are any overlapping events. Each person in your family can have their own color-coded calendar. And you can create separate calendars for special projects, events, or interests.

Your list of calendars

The upper-left pane of the iCal window shows the **Calendars** list. The list contains calendars that you've created or to which you've subscribed. You can select any calendar in the list to show just that calendar's information (check its checkbox) in the main View pane. Select multiple calendars to show them simultaneously in iCal (check any or all of the checkboxes).

When you click an event, all events in that calendar are brought forward and shown in full-strength color. Events that belong to non-selected calendars are dimmed and transparent.

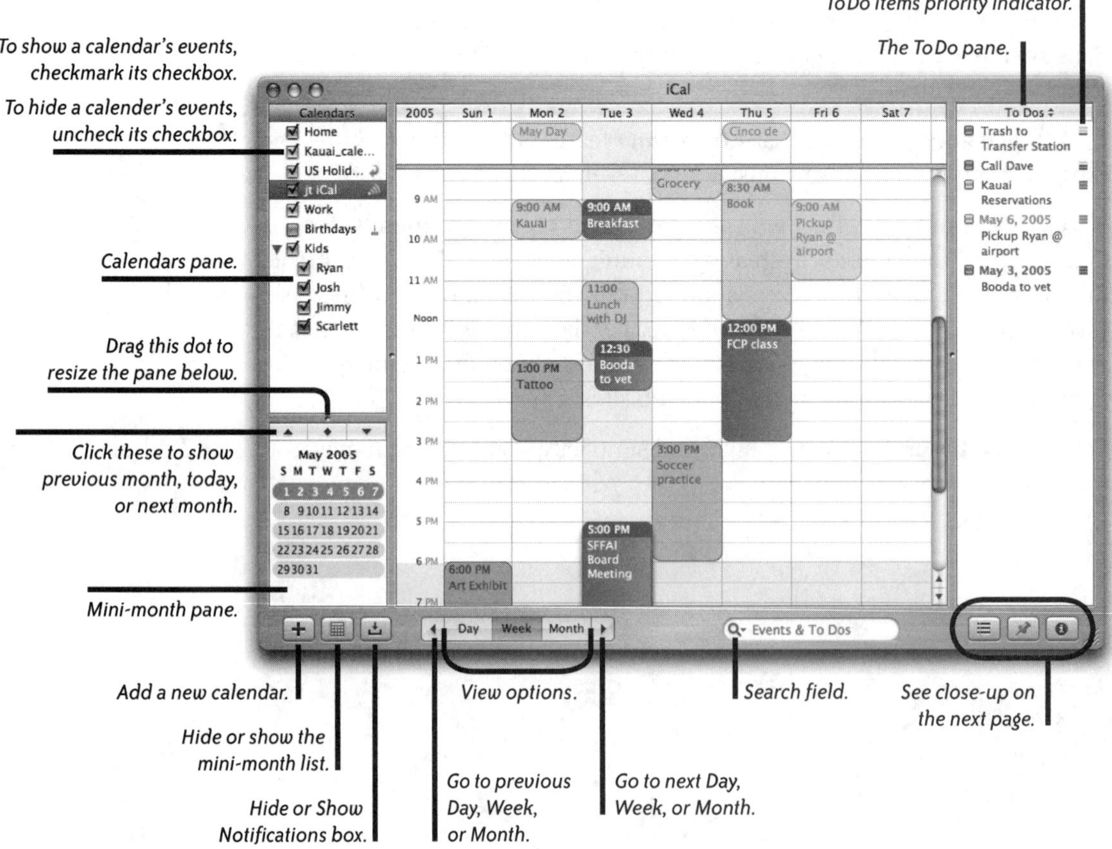

ToDo items priority indicator.
The ToDo pane.
To show a calendar's events, checkmark its checkbox.
To hide a calender's events, uncheck its checkbox.
Calendars pane.
Drag this dot to resize the pane below.
Click these to show previous month, today, or next month.
Mini-month pane.
Add a new calendar.
Hide or show the mini-month list.
Hide or Show Notifications box.
View options.
Go to previous Day, Week, or Month.
Go to next Day, Week, or Month.
Search field.
See close-up on the next page.

This is a closeup of the **hide-and-show buttons** located in the bottom-right corner of iCal's window.

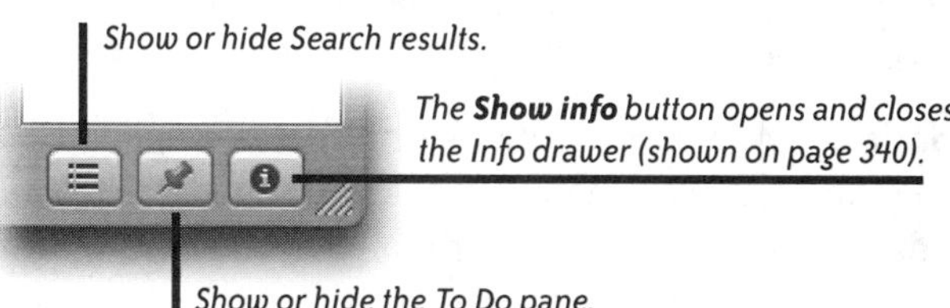

To change the number of days that display in the weekly calendar view, press Command Option <any number from 1 through 7> (e.g., Command Option 3 shows three days instead of seven days). **Or** change the "Days per week" setting in iCal Preferences.

Choose a calendar view

The appearance of the main View pane changes according to which view option you choose: Day, Week, or Month.

- **To choose a view,** click one of the View buttons at the bottom of the iCal window (shown on the right).
- **To go to the *previous* or *next* day, week, or month** in any view, click the small triangles on either side of the View buttons.

Day Week Month

Previous *Next*

The mini-month pane

The mini-month pane lets you jump to any day, week, or month of any year.

- **To display a particular month** in iCal's main View pane, select the month you want to see in the mini-month list.
- **To scroll forward or backward in time through the mini-month calendars,** click the up or down triangle located at the top of the mini-month list.

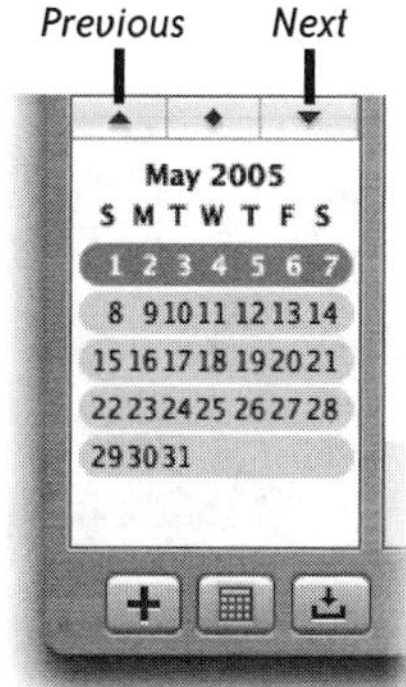

Return to today's date

There are several easy ways **to get back to the current date** after jumping to future dates in iCal. Do one of the following:

- In the mini-month pane, click the diamond-shaped symbol at the top of the list (between the up and down triangles).
- **Or** from the View menu, choose "Go to Today."
- **Or** press Command T.

The Notifications box

The Notifications box lets you know when you've received email with an iCal invitation to an event, or an email reply to an iCal event invitation that you sent. When the iCal icon in your Dock shows a red circle with a number in it, go check the iCal Notifications box. See page 349 for details.

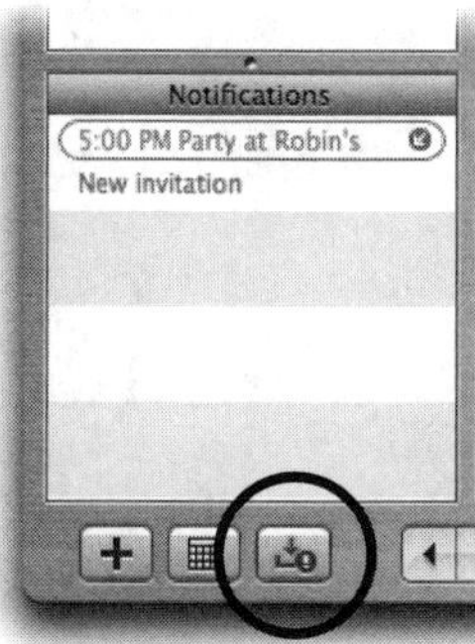

Hide or Show the Notifications box.

Create a New Calendar

Keep track of the schedules of selected family, friends, or colleagues. If you share a user account on your Mac with other family members, you can view their individual calendars in iCal.

Untitled

To create a new calendar, click the New Calendar button (the "plus" sign) in the bottom-left corner, and type a name for the new untitled caledar (left). Click the new calendar in the Calendars list, then click the Info button to open the Info drawer. Choose a color for the calendar from the pop-up color menu found in the top-right corner of the Info drawer (shown below).

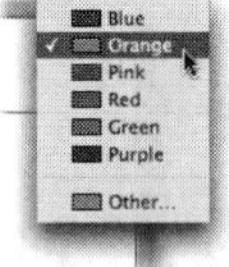

To change the color of a calendar, select the calendar (click once on its name) in the Calendars list, click the Show Info button, then choose a color from the pop-up menu in the Info drawer (shown below and left).

To change a calendar name, double-click the name in the Calendars list, then type a new name.

Create a Calendar Group

Organize calendars by grouping similar calendars together, as shown below with the "Kids" group. If several people use your computer, each person could have a separate group for all of their personal calendars.

From the File menu, choose "New Calendar Group." Name the new group in the Calendars list, then drag individual calendars into the group by dropping them on top of the new group name. You can also create a new calendar group by Shift-clicking the New Calendar button (shown on the left).

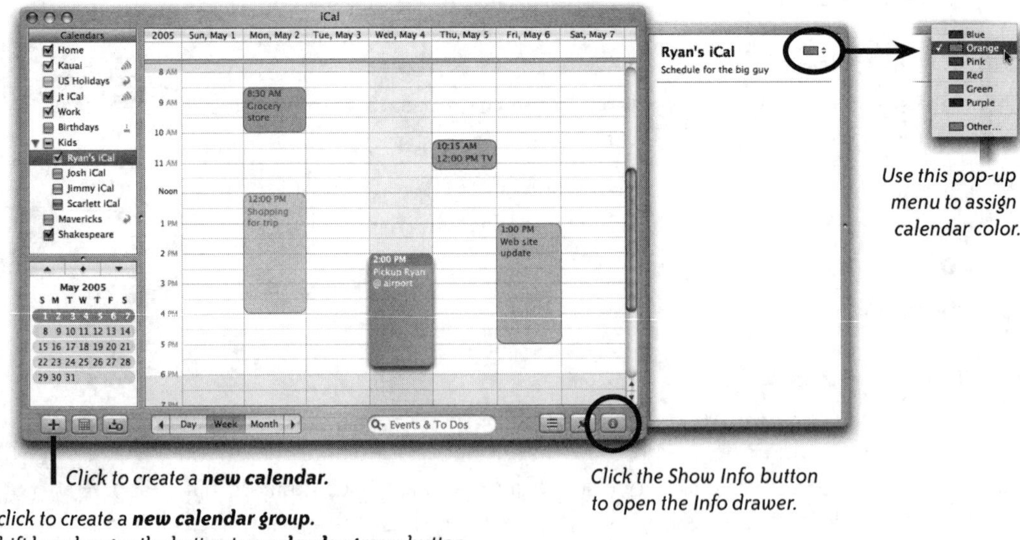

Use this pop-up menu to assign calendar color.

*Click to create a **new calendar.***

Click the Show Info button to open the Info drawer.

*Shift-click to create a **new calendar group.** The Shift key changes the button to a **calendar group** button.*

Create a New Event

Items that you enter into a calendar are called **events.** An event can be an appointment, a party, a reminder, an all-day class, or a week-long seminar. Or anything else that's in your schedule.

To create an event:

1. Select one of the calendars in the Calendars list. If none of the existing calendars seem appropriate for the new event you want to add, create a new calendar as explained on the previous page.
2. In the View pane, press-and-drag vertically in the time slot in which you want to place an event.

   Or double-click the time slot where you want to place a new event. After you create the event, you can drag it to any position in the calendar. You can also drag an event's edge to change its duration.

   Or click once in a time slot, then from the File menu choose "New Event."
3. When you create a new event, the text "New Event" is already selected, so all you have to do is type a description or name for the event.

   Or click the Show Info button to open the Info drawer (shown on the right), then click on the text at the top of the drawer and type a description. Any thing you type here appears in the event block in the calendar, and vice versa.
4. Set the other options in the drawer:

   To **repeat** this event in the calendar, click the repeat pop-up button (the small double-arrows) to open a menu containing recurrence choices.

   You can invite **attendees** to an event (see page 346).

   To switch the event to another **calendar,** click the calendar pop-up button (the small double-arrows) and assign the event to another calendar.

   To set an **alarm** for the event, click the alarm pop-up button (the small double-arrows).

   If the event has a web site, enter the address here so you can access it with a click.

Click the small double-arrow button to open pop-up menus.

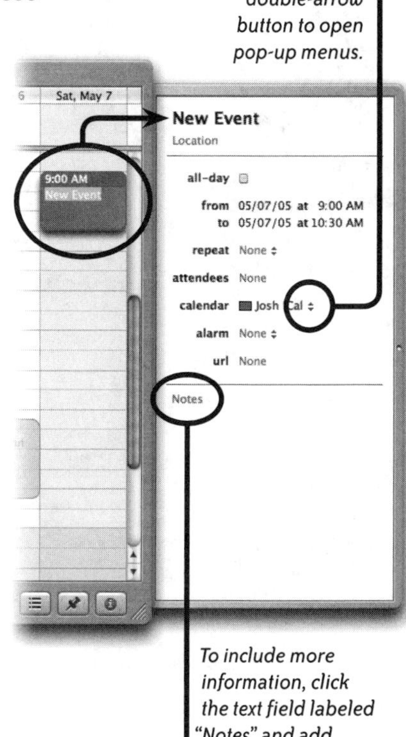

To include more information, click the text field labeled "Notes" and add your own text.

Create an all-day event or a multi-day event

All-day and **multi-day events** are represented by rounded rectangles that stretch the width of the event duration. In Day or Week view, they appear in a row at the top of the calendar in order to leave more room for other items in the main window and to avoid overlapping events in the main calendar area.

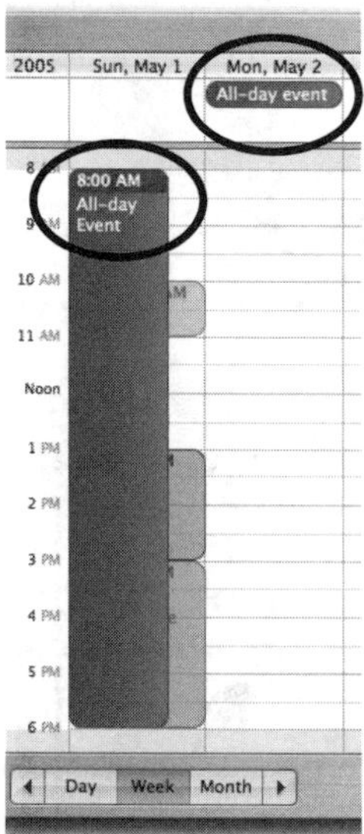

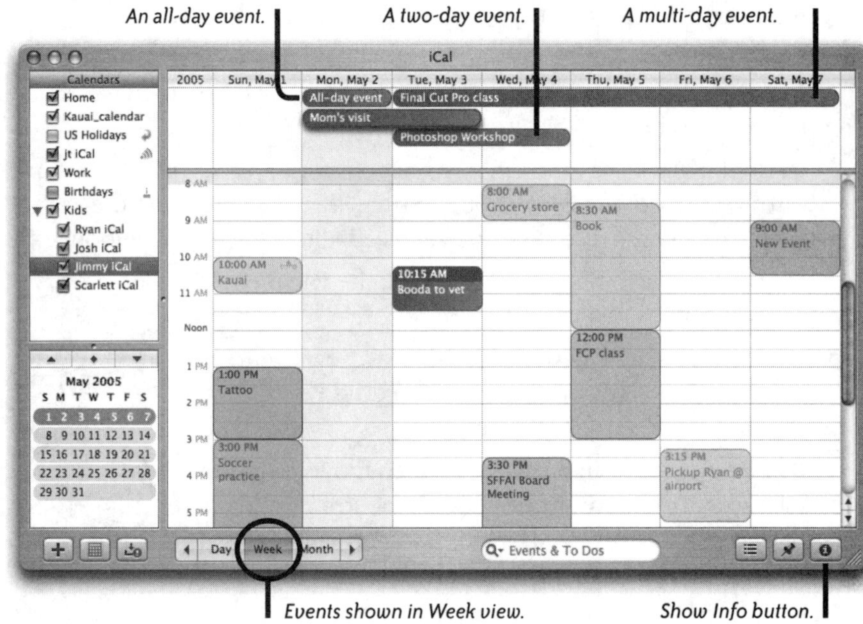

In the left column above, an all-day event has been created by dragging the event's bottom edge down to an all day duration. This technique crowds other items in the calendar.

In the right column, the same event has been designated as an all-day event in the Info drawer. This technique moves the all-day event to the top, out of the way of other events.

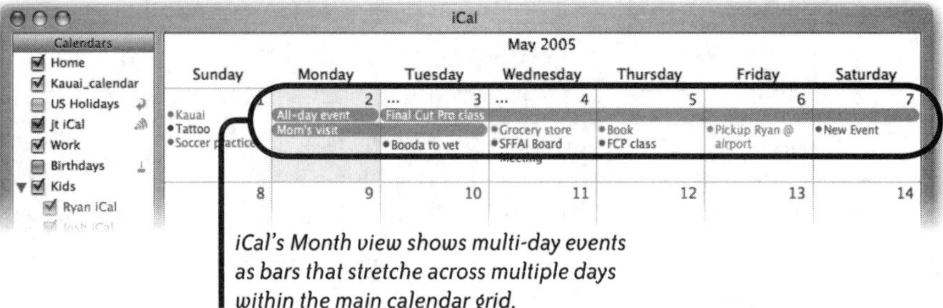

iCal's Month view shows multi-day events as bars that stretche across multiple days within the main calendar grid.

To create an all-day event:

1. Create a new event in iCal. **Or** select an existing event that you want to change to an all-day event.
2. Click the Show Info button to open the Info drawer (shown on the right).
3. Click the "all-day" checkbox.
4. Press the Return key to apply the setting.

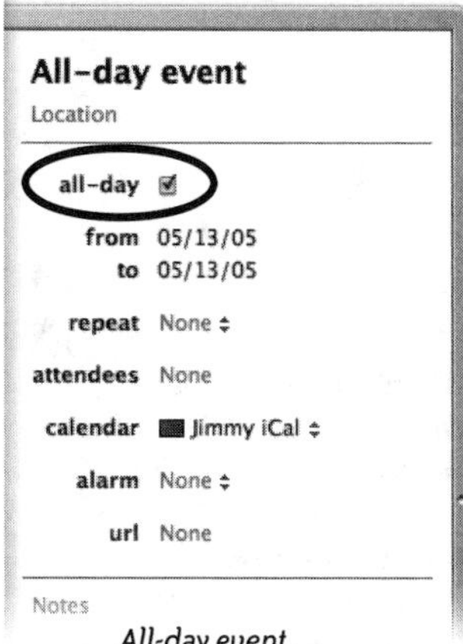

All-day event.

To create a multi-day event:

1. Create a new event in iCal. **Or** select an existing event that you want to change to a multi-day event.
2. Click the Show Info button to open the Info drawer.
3. Click the "all-day" checkbox.
4. Click the "from" and "to" values to set the event dates: Click the day, month, or year value, then press the Up or Down arrow on your keyboard to change the value. Or type a value to replace the highlighted value.
5. Press the Return key to apply the settings.

   In Month view you can also drag an event's edge to span across the days you want to include.

   In Week view you can drag an existing event to the all-day space at the top of the calendar, then drag the event's edge to include multiple days.

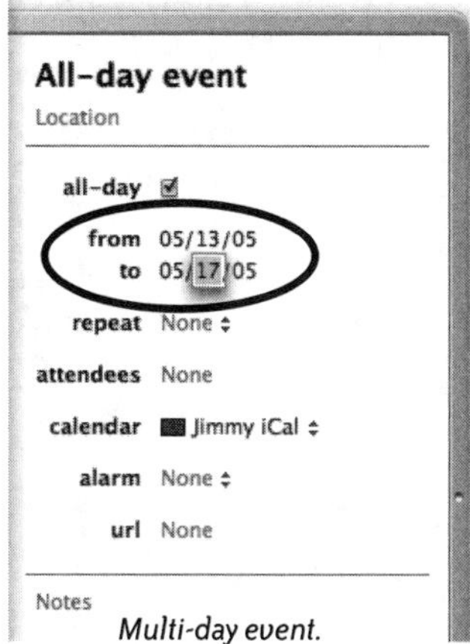

Multi-day event.

To create recurring events:

1. Click an event in iCal to select it.
2. Click the Show Info button to open the Info drawer.
3. Click the "repeat" pop-up menu (shown on the right). Choose one of the repeat options in the pop-up menu.
4. Select "Custom" from the pop-up menu if you want to make additional settings in the window shown below.

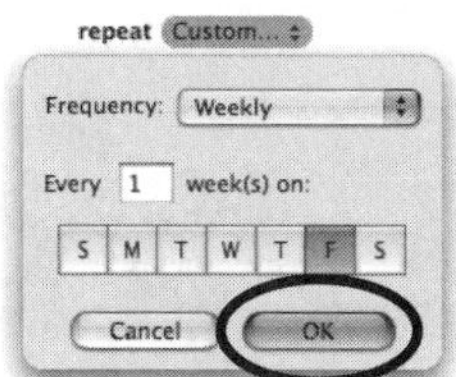

These settings are available when you select "Custom..." from the "repeat" pop-up menu.

5. Click OK (above) to apply your settings.

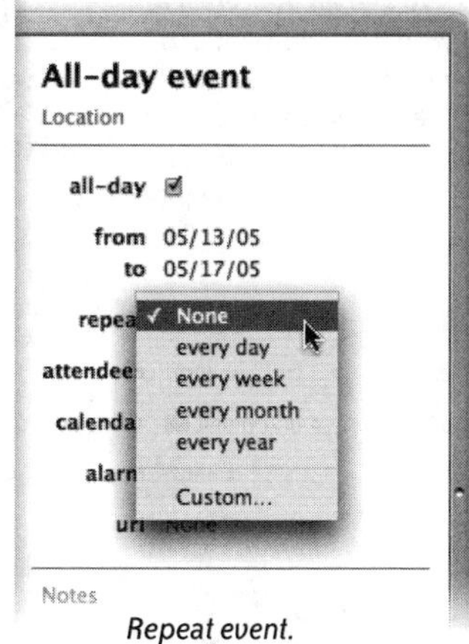

Repeat event.

iCal provides a visual indication of **schedule conflicts.** The example below shows three calendar items with overlapping times. If the items belong to *different* calendars (from the Calendars list), the color coding will indicate to which calendar an item belongs.

All-day and multiple-day events.

*iCal's **Week view** overlaps conflicting events. Click on an event to bring it to the foreground.*

***To reschedule an event to another time,** just drag the event to any position in the calendar grid.*

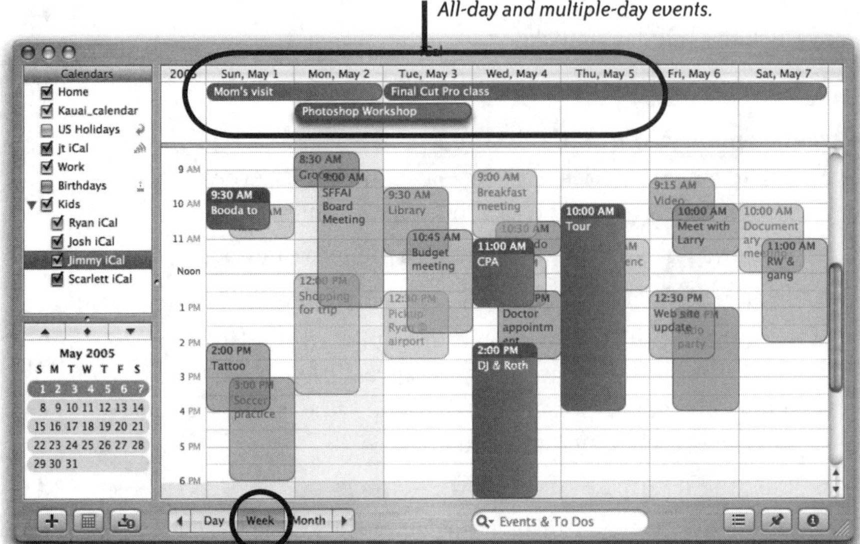

*This is how **Day view** shows different events that are scheduled in overlapping time slots.*

***To see an overview of your appointments,** use the **Week** view. Switch to **Day** view to see a more detailed, less cluttered calendar.*

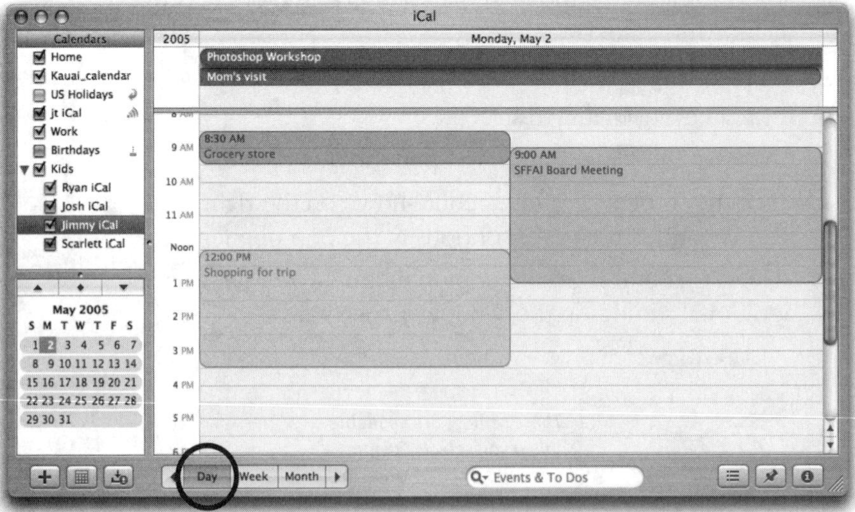

Delete an event

To manually delete an event, select it, then press the Delete key on your keyboard. To delete multiple events at once, Shift-select two or more events, then press Delete. **Or** from the Edit menu, choose Delete.

To automatically delete events that have passed:

1. From the iCal menu, choose "Preferences…," then click the "Advanced" button (shown below).
2. Check "Delete events" (circled below).

   An alert dialog opens to warn you that setting this option will automatically delete events older than 60 days (or whatever number of days you decide to use), and asks if you're sure you want to do this. Click "Yes" to delete old events.

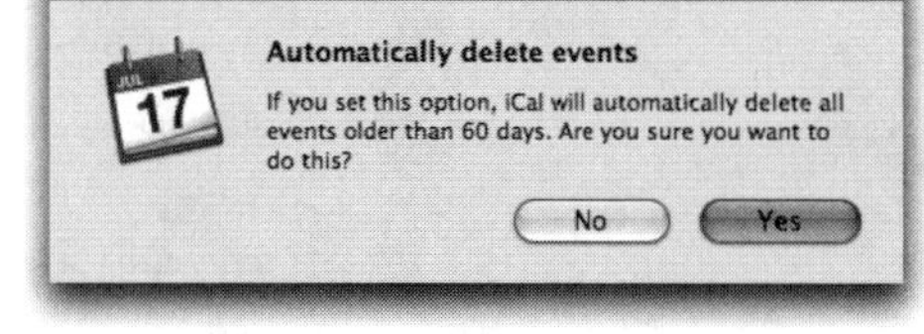

3. Type a number in the text field to set how many days will pass after events before iCal automatically deletes them.

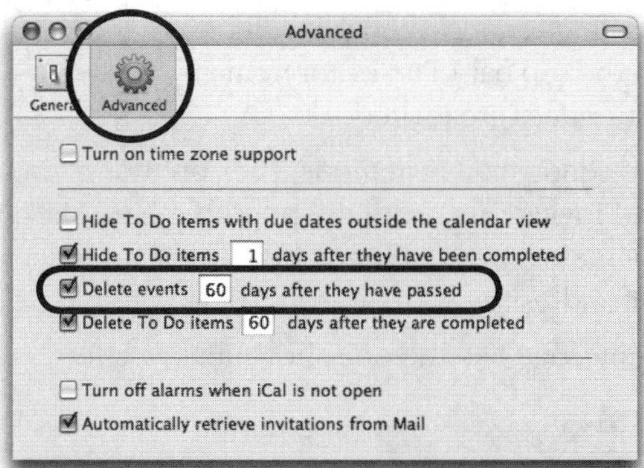

Backup Your iCal Data

The setting above keeps iCal from becoming cluttered with old events. However, if you want to keep a record of schedules, appointments, and events, you can uncheck the "Delete events" checkbox and let iCal permanently store your information.

iCal - 4/22/05.icbu

When you choose "Back up Database" from the File menu, you can save dated backups to a backup folder. Later you can revert to any previous version of the database.

But there are several better ways to keep a backup of your iCal database:

- From the File menu choose "Back up Database…." At a later date, if necessary, choose "Revert to Database Backup" from the File menu.
- Or use Backup (see Chapter 10).
- Or use iSync (see Chapter 11).

It's a good idea to use all three of these techniques.

Invite Attendees to an Event

Tip: If you have more than one email account, you can specify which account is the default: Open the Mail preferences and click the Accounts icon. The account name at the top of the list is the default. To change it, drag another account name to the top of the list.

iCal uses Mail and your Address Book to invite people to an event (if you have more than one account, Mail uses the *default* email account).

To invite someone to an event:

1. Select an iCal event, then click the Show Info button.
2. In the Info drawer, click next to the "attendees" label and enter the name of a person to invite. As you type, iCal lists matching names from Address Book in a pop-up menu. Choose the name you want, or continue typing a name.

   Or click on the "attendees" label and select "Open Address Book" from the pop-up menu (left). When Address Book opens, drag a contact's vCard from the Address Book window and drop it on top of the attendees label. A small "attendee" icon (circled on the right) appears in the top bar of an event item when one or more attendees are invited.

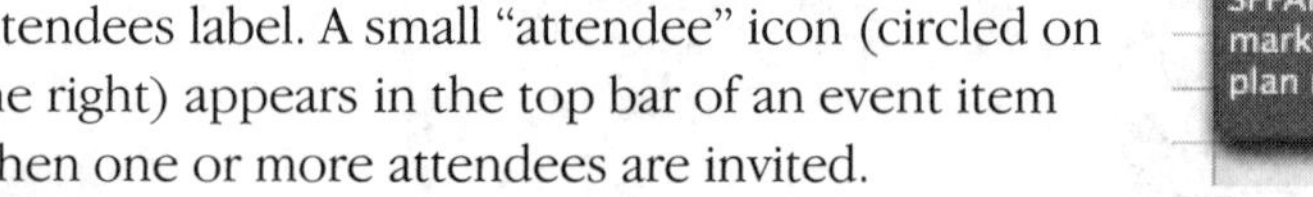

Recipients that have iCal, or some other calendar application that can read .ics files (the Open Source iCal format), get an .ics invitation attached to an email invitation.

3. When you're ready to send email invitations, click on the "attendees" label and select "Send Invitations" from the pop-up menu. Mail automatically sends email messages to all the people in the attendees list (if they have an email address in Address Book).
4. The recipient gets a message like the one shown below-left.

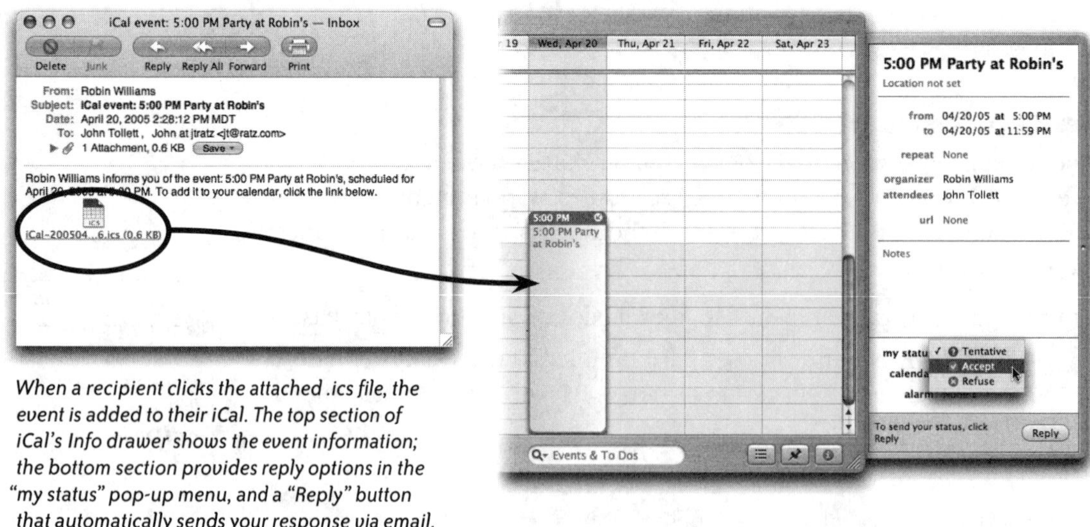

When a recipient clicks the attached .ics file, the event is added to their iCal. The top section of iCal's Info drawer shows the event information; the bottom section provides reply options in the "my status" pop-up menu, and a "Reply" button that automatically sends your response via email.

5. When the recipient chooses "Accept" in the "my status" pop-up menu and clicks the "Reply" button, you receive an email like the one shown on the right. Click the .ics attachment to update iCal with the "Accept" response. The "attendees" item in the Info drawer shows a small status icon (below) next to each attendee (Tentative, Accept, or Refuse).

attendees ary Sidney
ob Williams

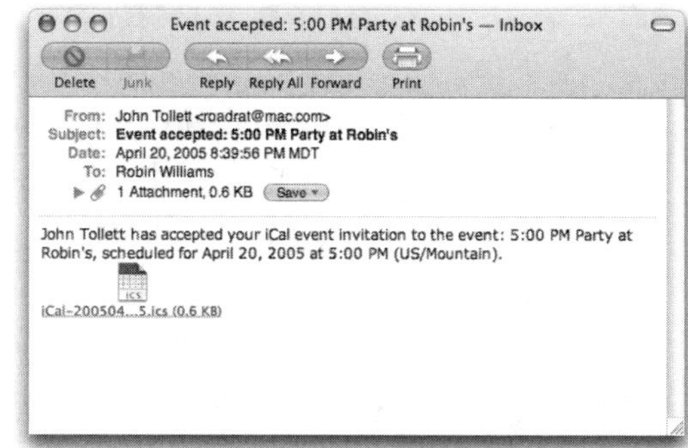

Move an event

To move an event to another day or time, drag the event to a new location in the calendar window. If the date is not visible in your current view, change to another view. For instance, in Month view you can drag an event anywhere in the month.

Change these values to move events around.

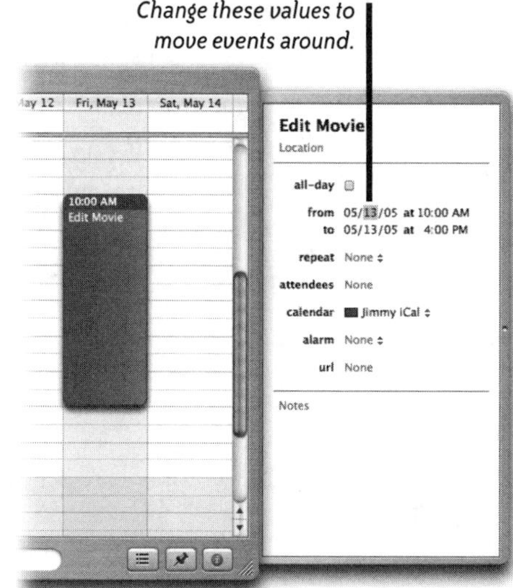

To move an event to another month or year:

1. Single-click the event to select it.
2. Click the Show Info button to open the Event Info drawer.
3. Change the date and time information to the new event date. Click the month, day, or year field to select it, then type in a new value, or use the Up and Down arrow keys to change the value. The event item moves around in the grid as you change the date or time.

To move an event to another calendar:

When you move an event to a different calendar, nothing changes except the color of the item in the calendar grid.

- **Either** Control-click the event, then choose a calendar from the pop-up menu that appears, as shown below. The event will change to the color associated with the other calendar category.
- **Or** select an event, click the Show Info button, then choose a calendar from the "calendar" pop-up menu in the Info drawer.

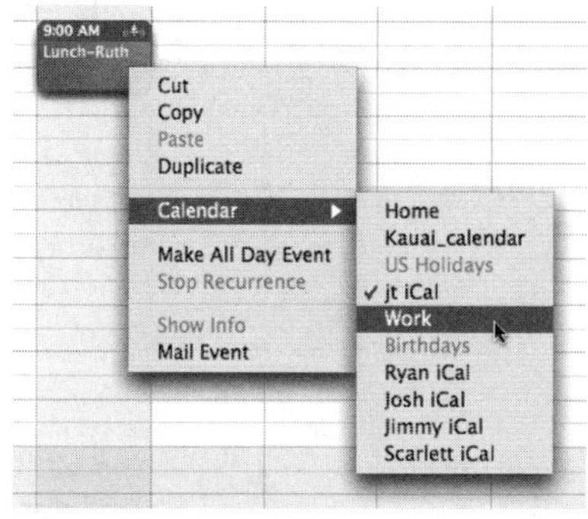

Control-click an event to open its contextual menu.

Click the double-arrows to open a pop-up menu.

Set an iCal alarm

There's no need to worry that you'll forget an important event in your calendar. iCal can notify you of upcoming events with different alarm types, even if the iCal application is not open.

To set an Event alarm:

This icon on a calendar event indicates that an alarm is set for the event.

1. Click on an iCal event to select it, then click the Show Info button to open the Event Info drawer.
2. Click to the right of the "alarm" label (where it says "none") and from the pop-up menu choose an alarm option.
3. Depending on the alarm type you choose, set the other options that appear in the alarm field (sound effect, email address, etc).
4. Enter the number of minutes, hours, or days before or after an event that you want to be notified.

   If you choose the "Message" alarm, the alarm clock window shown below opens at the set time.

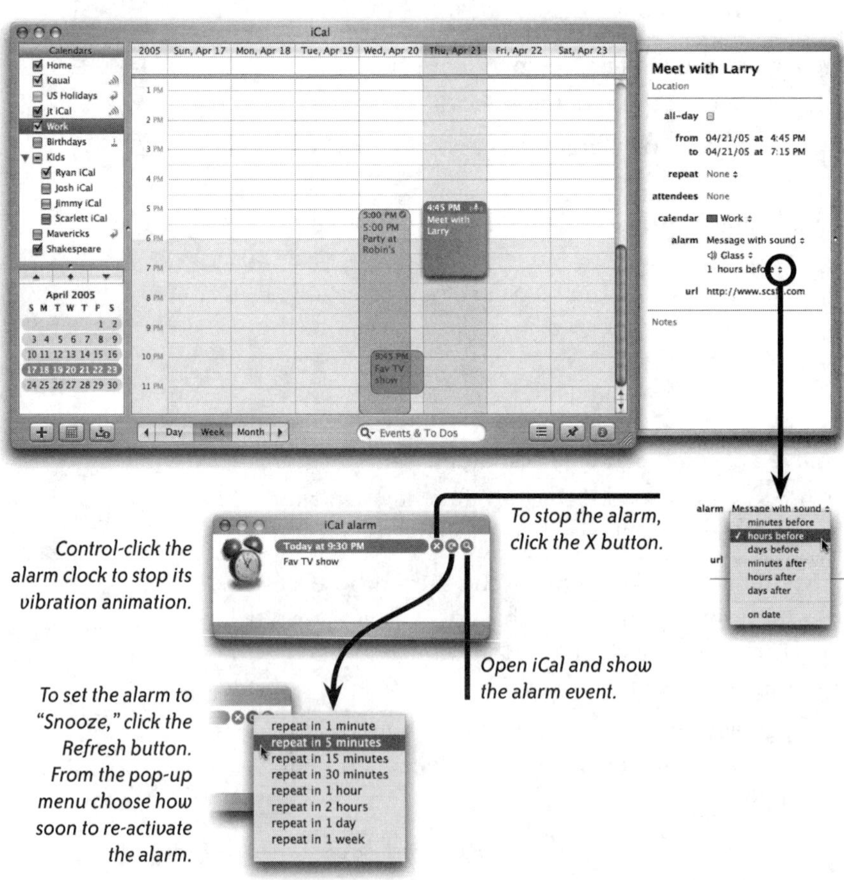

Control-click the alarm clock to stop its vibration animation.

To stop the alarm, click the X button.

Open iCal and show the alarm event.

To set the alarm to "Snooze," click the Refresh button. From the pop-up menu choose how soon to re-activate the alarm.

The Notifications box

Whenever someone sends you an event invitation from iCal, or when someone replies to an iCal invitation that you sent, the Notifications box lets you know that an iCal-originated email has arrived. When a notice arrives, the iCal icon in the Dock adds a red circle containing the number of notices received (shown on the right). In the iCal window, the Notifications button includes a red circle containing an exclamation mark.

The red circle added to the iCal icon in the Dock means there's a notice in the iCal Notifications box.

When an email invitation is received, iCal adds the event to your calendar and adds detailed event information, if available, to the Info drawer (shown below.) At the bottom of the drawer, the "my status" pop-up menu lets you set a reply of "Tentative," "Accept," or "Refuse." Click "Reply" to have iCal send your reply via email.

Choose a response from the pop-up menu, then click "Reply." An email is automatically sent with your response, the invitation notice is removed from the Notifications box, and the event (which was previously colored gray) is assigned the current calendar color. You can re-assign the event to any other calendar—from the "calendar" pop-up menu in the Info drawer, choose another calendar.

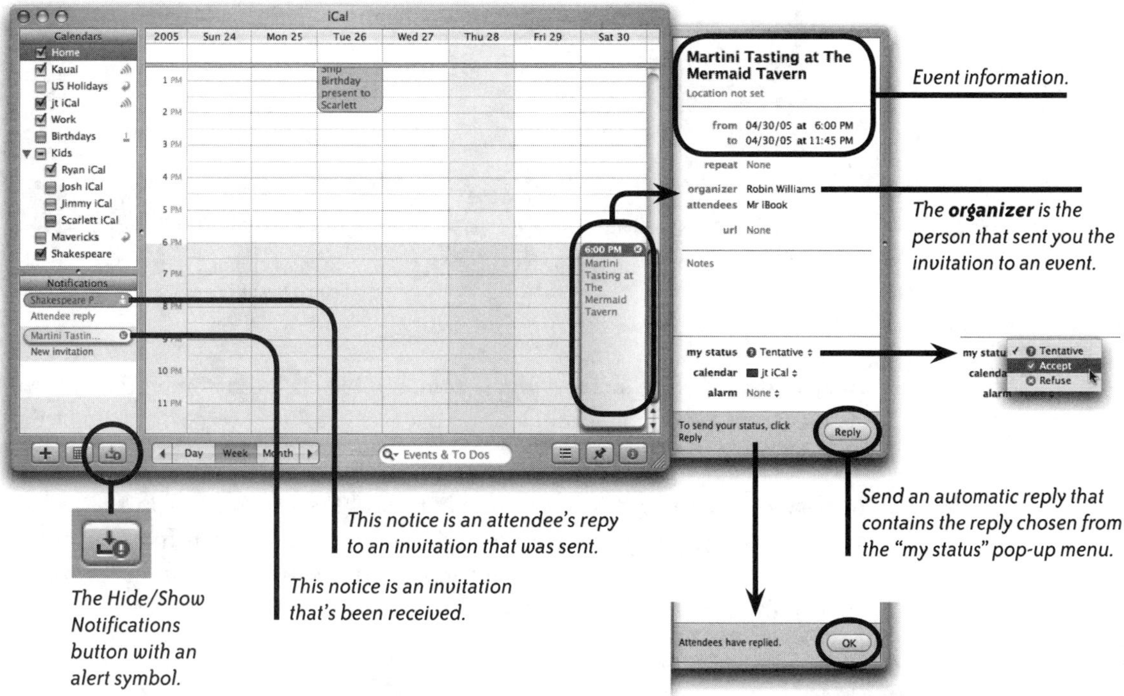

Event information.

*The **organizer** is the person that sent you the invitation to an event.*

Send an automatic reply that contains the reply chosen from the "my status" pop-up menu.

This notice is an attendee's repy to an invitation that was sent.

This notice is an invitation that's been received.

The Hide/Show Notifications button with an alert symbol.

When attendees have replied, click OK to get rid of the red alert symbol in the Dock icon and in the Notifications button.

iCal Search

Use iCal's **search** feature to locate any event in any calendar.

To search for an event:

1. In the text entry field at the bottom of the calendar, type a keyword or phrase. All possible matches to your text entry will appear in the Search Results pane. The list of possible matches is narrowed as you continue to type.
2. When you finish typing, click the item you want. iCal shows the selected item in the Calendar View pane.

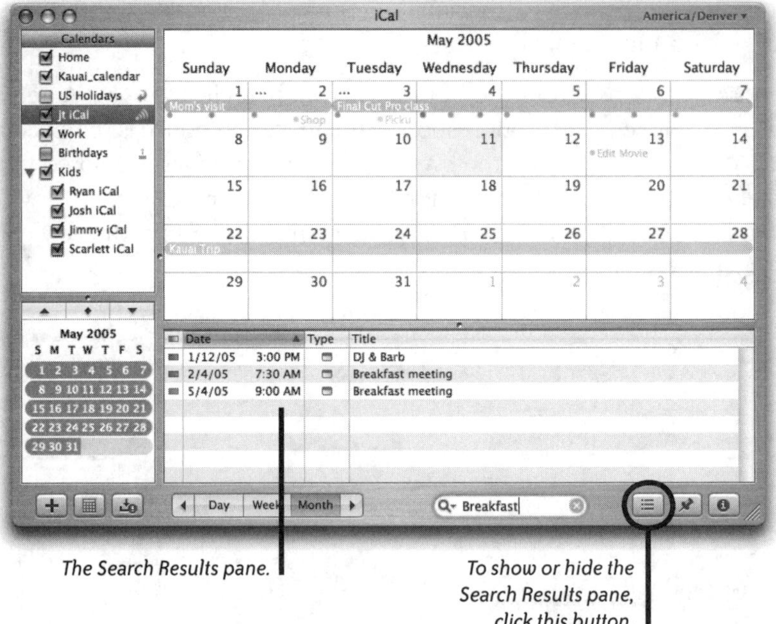

To open the Info drawer for a found item, double-click the item in the Search Results pane. **Or** double-click the title bar of the found event in the calendar grid of the main View pane.

To change the information for an event, double-click the text in the event item, then type your changes. **Or** click an event to select it, then click the Show Info button to open the Info drawer. Make changes to the text in the drawer, then press Return.

Search by category

Narrow your search by choosing a specific category. Click the small triangle (shown on the right) next to the magnifying glass in the Search field to open a pop-up menu of options (shown below). Select the category you want to use, then type a keyword in the Search field.

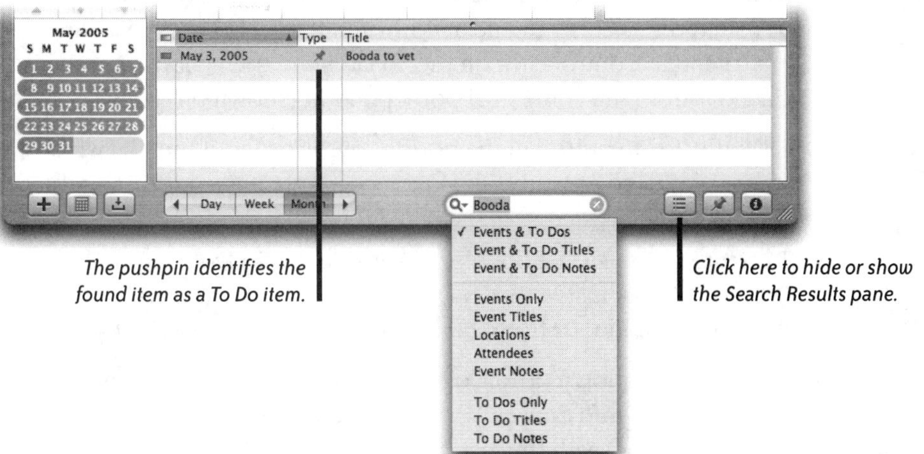

Booda.

The example below shows a search for "Booda" (I can't remember when Booda's vet appointment was scheduled). iCal found the information as a To Do item, indicated by the pushpin in the "Type" column of the Search Results pane. A double click on the search result opens the Info drawer and shows all available information.

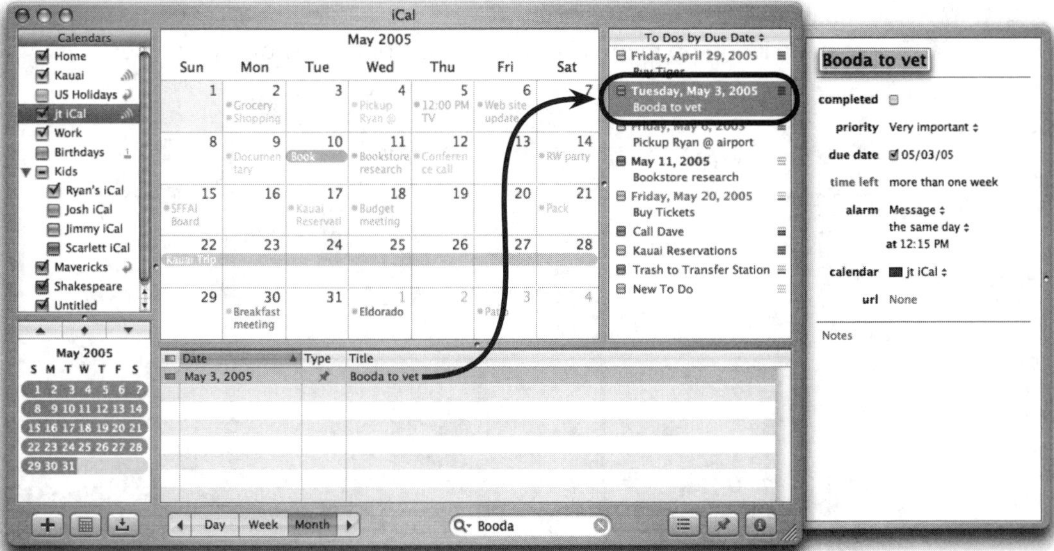

Create a To Do List

Use iCal to keep a reminder list of things you need to do.

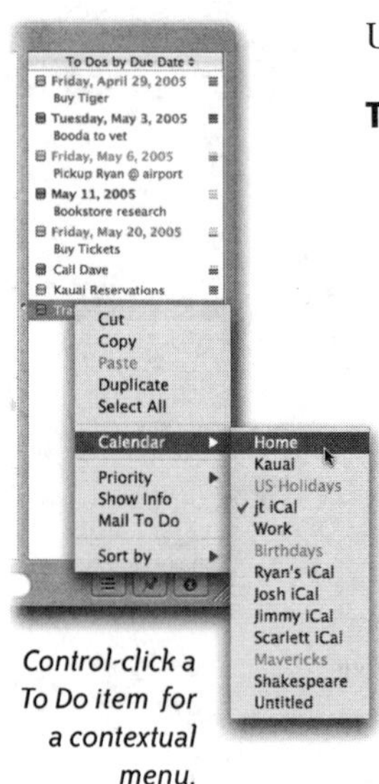

Control-click a To Do item for a contextual menu.

To create a To Do list:

1. Select a calendar in the Calendars list.

   Note: When you create a To Do item, it is automatically color-coded to match the *selected* calendar. To switch the To Do item to a different calendar, Control-click on the To Do item, then choose another calendar from the contextual pop-up menu (shown on the left).

2. Click the To Do button in the bottom-right corner of the iCal window (the pushpin) to open the To Do pane. *To resize the pane,* drag the tiny dot on the left edge of the panel (circled below).
3. To create a new To Do, double-click inside the To Do pane. **Or** Control-click inside the To Do pane and select "New To Do" from the pop-up menu. **Or** from the File menu choose "New To Do."
4. To add information to a To Do item, select it in the To Do pane, then open the Info drawer. You can set a priority, set a due date, set an alarm, or swith the task to another calendar.
5. In the bottom section you can type a description, notes, comments, direction, instructions, or anything you need for the task.

You can set an alarm for a To Do item if it has a ***due date*** set.

After a To Do task is completed, click its checkbox in the To Do pane to mark it as completed. **Or** click its checkbox in the Info drawer.

You can select **view options** for the To Do list. Click the To Do pane's title bar to open a pop-up menu and select a view option (shown on the left).

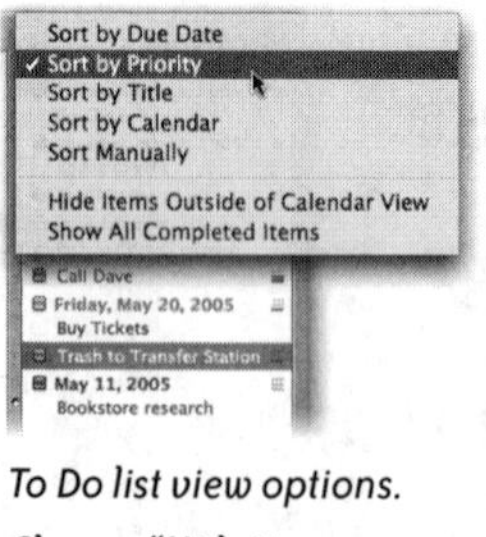

To Do list view options.

*Choose "Hide items Outside of Calendar View" to hide To Do items that have **due dates** that are not shown in the current Calendar view.*

To Do items that don't have due dates assigned are always shown.

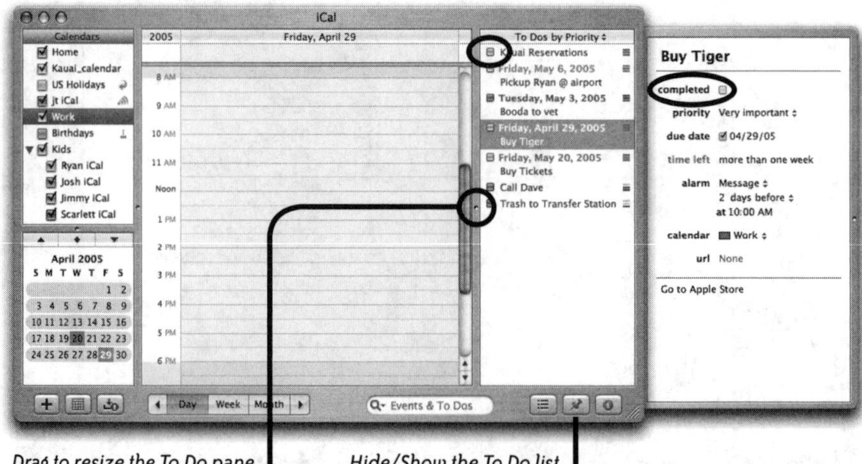

Drag to resize the To Do pane. *Hide/Show the To Do list.*

Rate the priority of To Do items

You can **assign priorities** to To Do items, rating them as "Very Important," "Important," or "Not Important."

A "Very Important" item is marked with a small icon of three horizontal bars; an "Important" item has two horizontal bars; a "Not Important" item has one horizontal bar. Multiple items with the same priority are listed alphabetically within that priority group.

1. Click a To Do item to select it.
2. Click the Show Info button to open the Info drawer (shown on the right).
3. From the "priority" pop-up menu choose a priority.

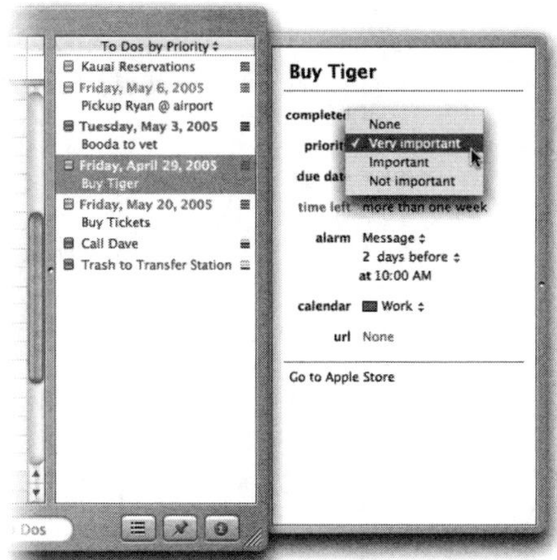

A To Do item's priority is indicated by the number of horizontal bars in the icon next to it.

Click directly on the icon to change the number of bars and the priority rating.

If all three bars are dimmed, a priority has not been assigned.

The To Do Info drawer

The To Do Info drawer also has several other uses. You can:

- Make editing changes to a task's description.
- Check off a task as "completed." You can also do this in the To Do pane by clicking the checkbox next to a task.
- Set a "due date" that will appear above the task in the To Do pane.
- Switch a selected To Do item to a different calendar (from the "calendar" pop-up menu, choose a different calendar).
- Assign a URL (a web site address) to accompany the To Do item.
- Type a lengthy task description that is too long to show in the To Do pane.

Print a To Do list

When you print a calendar, you can include the To Do list to be printed (see page 364).

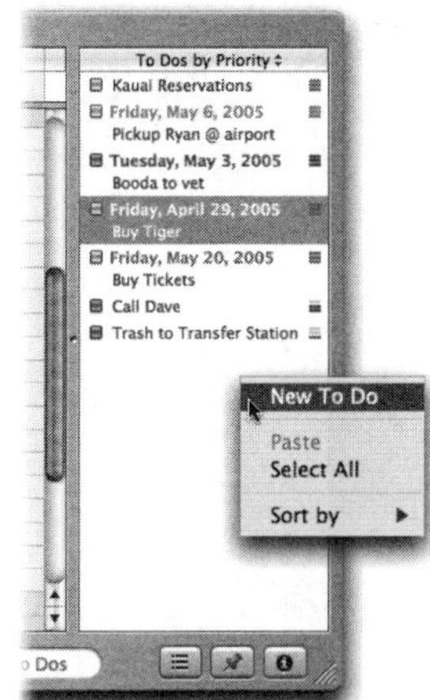

You can also access some of the view options for the To Do pane by Control-clicking inside the pane and choosing "Sort by" from the pop-up menu.

Hide or show various To Do lists

To Do items from different calendars all share the same To Do list. They are color-coded to match the calendar to which they belong. When you hide a calendar (uncheck its box in the Calendars list), all of the To Do items associated with that calendar are also hidden. If you have a lot of items in your To Do list, hiding some of them can make finding others easier. But you can always use the powerful search feature described on pages 350–351.

iCal Preferences

To customize the appearance of iCal calendars and some of their settings, use the iCal Preferences. From the iCal application menu, choose "Preferences…" to open the Preferences window (shown below).

General Preferences:

1. Click the "General" icon in the Preferences toolbar.
2. From the **Days per week** pop-up menu, choose how many days a calender shows. From the **Start week on** pop-up menu, choose the day of the week you want to start a calendar.
3. From the **Day starts at** pop-up menu, choose the first hour that's shown on a calendar. From the **Day ends at** pop-up menu, choose the last hour shown on a calendar. From the **Show** pop-up menu, choose how many hours are shown at a time in a calendar (in Day or Week view).

"Show time in month view" adds the event's start time to a calendar.

4. Checkmark **Show time in month view** to include an event time when shown in Month view (shown on the left, above).
5. Checkmark **Show Birthdays calendar** to add a Birthdays calendar to the Calendar list. Address Book contacts that include a birthday are automatically added to this calendar. A great feature for those of us who have a bad track record for remembering birthdays.

A birthday event (with a birthday cake and candle) shown in Week view.

6. Select **Synchronize my calendars with other computers using .Mac** to enable syncing. Click the ".Mac…" button to start the sync process.

   If you have a .Mac membership, you can synchronize iCal to your .Mac account to keep a current copy of all calendars available. To set up another Mac with your iCal info, just use iSync to sync your calendars to the new computer. See Chapter 11 for details about syncing and iSync.

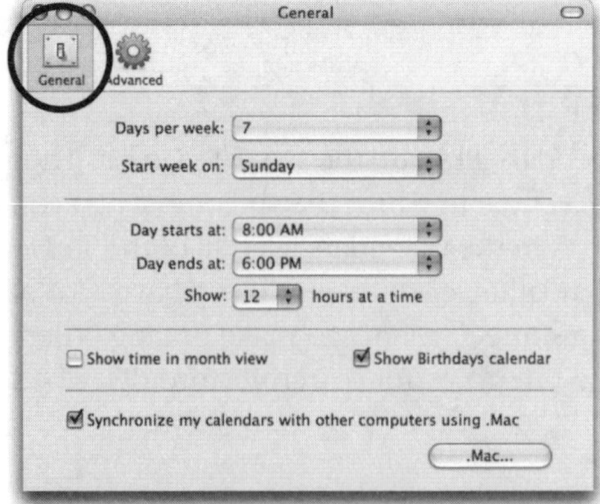

Advanced Preferences:

1. Click the "Advanced" icon in the Preferences toolbar.
2. **Turn on time zone support** lets you change calendar time zones in two different ways—for an individual event, or for iCal in general. Learn more about setting iCal time zones pages 362–363.
3. **Hide To Do items with due dates outside the calendar view** limits the number of items in the To Do list by not showing items that have been assigned a *due date* that's not visible in the current window.
4. **Hide To Do items_days after they have been completed.** Choose how many days you want to pass before To Do items are hidden. Don't checkmark this option if you want old To Do items to always show.
5. **Delete events_days after they have passed.** Choose how many days you want to pass before iCal deletes old events.
6. **Delete To Do items_days after they are completed.** Choose how many days you want to pass before completed To Do items are deleted.
7. **Turn off alarms when iCal is not open.** If you share a computer, you may not want your alarms to bother other users. Otherwise it's helpful to have alarms work, even when iCal is closed.
8. **Automatically retrieve invitations from Mail.** Choose this option so iCal's notifications feature will work when you send or receive invitations. See page 349.

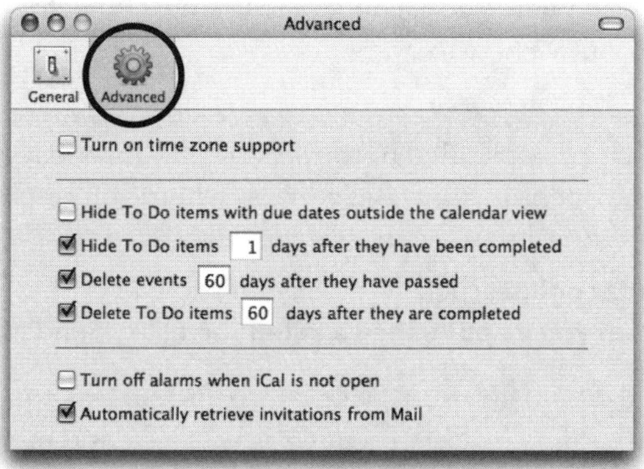

Publish an iCal Calendar

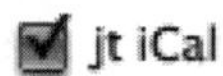

*A **broadcast** symbol in the Calendars list indicates a published calendar.*

To publish a calendar, you must be connected to the Internet.

If you want to **make your calendar available to others on the Internet,** you can *publish* it. Anyone can view published calendars from any computer in the world using a web browser.

To publish your calendar:

1. Select a calendar in the Calendars list that you want to publish.
2. From the Calendar menu in the top menu bar, choose "Publish...." A sheet slides down into view (shown below).

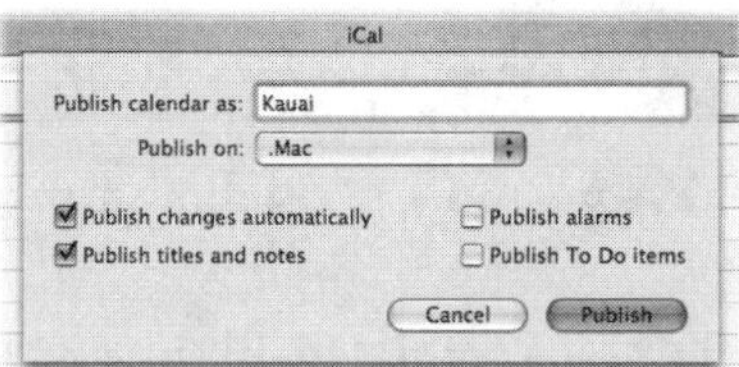

3. Type a name for your published calendar and select the checkboxes to publish changes automatically and to choose which calendar items to publish. Select an option from the "Publish on" pop-up menu:
   - Choose ".Mac" to publish your calendar to the Apple server provided with your .Mac account.
   - Choose "a Private Server" if you plan to publish to a WebDAV server other than your .Mac account. See the next page for more information about WebDAV servers.
4. Click the "Publish" button.
5. When your calendar has uploaded to the server, the "Calendar Published" window opens to show the address where you or others can go to view or subscribe to that particular calendar.

   To see your calendar online, click "Visit Page" (below-left).
   To notify others that you've published a calendar, click "Send Mail."

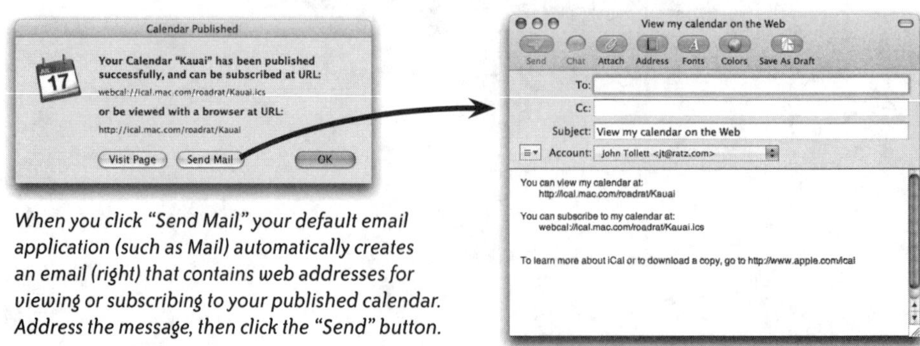

When you click "Send Mail," your default email application (such as Mail) automatically creates an email (right) that contains web addresses for viewing or subscribing to your published calendar. Address the message, then click the "Send" button.

Publish to a private server

To add password protection to a published calendar, you need to publish to a WebDAV server that supports password protection. Choose "Publish on: a Private Server" in iCal's Publish Calendar sheet. This option displays text fields for entering a WebDAV server address and for setting a login name and password. Checkmark the options you want to use, such as "Publish changes automatically" and "Publish titles and notes."

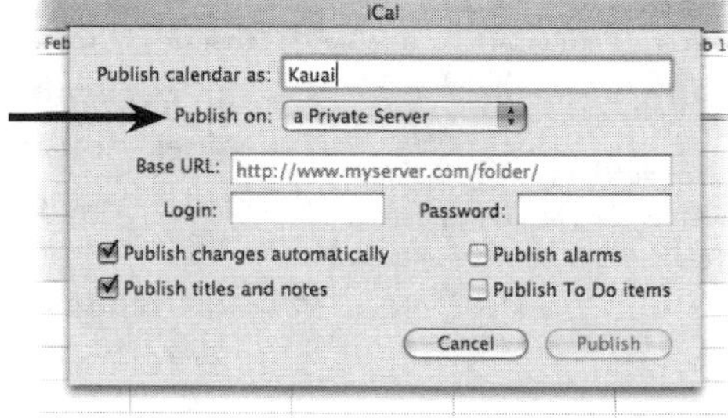

WebDAV (Web Distributed Authoring and Versioning) servers enable sharing of calendars that have been created using the industry-standard .ics format.

For an alternative to publishing calendars on the .Mac site, check iCal Exchange at www.icalx.com. iCal Exchange offers free iCalendar publishing to its own WebDAV server.

Make changes to a published calendar

You can update a published calendar in several ways.

- Select a calendar from the Calendars list, then from the Calendar menu choose "Refresh."
- **Or** select a calendar from the Calendars list, then from the Calendar menu choose "Publish." Give the calendar the exact same name as the existing published one. This new, updated calendar will replace the old one.
- **Or** select a calendar from the Calendars list, then click the Show Info button. Click next to the "auto-publish" field in the Info drawer and select "after each change" from the pop-up menu (shown right).
- **Or** when you first publish a calendar, set iCal to automatically update changes: From the Calendar menu at the top of your screen, choose "Publish," then select "Publish changes automatically" in the Publish Calendar sheet (see the top of the previous page). If you have a full-time Internet connection, iCal **automatically** uploads the changes. (If you don't have a full-time connection, *don't* choose this option; instead, dial up and publish changes when necessary.)

Unpublish an iCal calendar

If you decide **to unpublish a published calendar,** it's easy to do: Make sure you're connected to the Internet. Select a published calendar in the Calendars list, then from the Calendar menu choose "Unpublish."

You still have the original copy of the calendar on your computer, but it's no longer available for viewing by others.

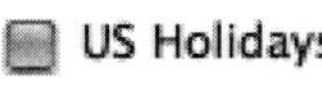

*A **Subscribe** symbol in the Calendars list indicates a calendar to which you've subscribed.*

Subscribe to iCal Calendars

You can **subscribe to calendars** that have been published by family, friends, colleagues, or total strangers. You do not have to have a .Mac account to subscribe to a calendar that's hosted on .Mac or other WebDAV servers.

To subscribe to any iCal calendar:

1. From the Calendar menu at the top of your screen, choose "Subscribe...."
2. In the sheet that appears, enter the calendar URL (web address) that was given to you or that you may have received in an email from the publisher of the calendar, then click the "Subscribe" button.

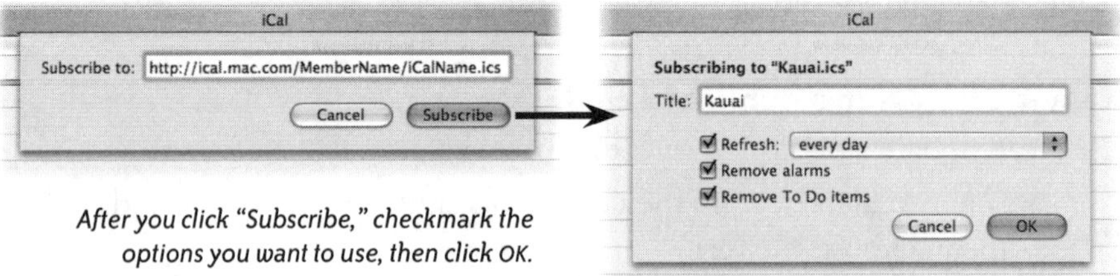

After you click "Subscribe," checkmark the options you want to use, then click OK.

Or if you know the web address of a site that offers iCalendars for subscription (such as **http://apple.com/ical/library**), use your browser to visit the site and click one of the available calendar links. A sheet opens with that link entered in the "Subscribe to:" field (below-left).

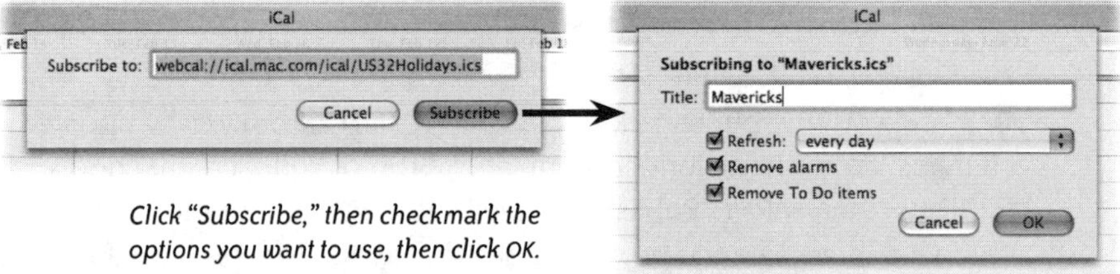

Click "Subscribe," then checkmark the options you want to use, then click OK.

3. If subscription to the calendar requires a password, an "Authentication" dialog window opens. Enter the required user name and password, then click OK to continue.

4. The subscribed calendar appears in your Calendars list. Click it's checkbox show it in the main viewing area.

Other calendars available for subscription

In addition to subscribing to the calendars of friends, family, and colleagues, there are many special-interest calendars available online to which you can subscribe. It's quite amazing—there are public calendars that list special events, sports teams, school calendars, religious events, movies, television, and many more. Visit these sites to see some of the possibilities: From the Calendar menu choose "Find Shared Calendars...." to visit **www.apple.com/ical/library,** Apple's web site of published caledars. Visit **www.iCalshare.com** to choose from a large collection of published calendars.

Refresh calendars

To make sure that you **see the most current version** of a subscribed calendar, you can manually *refresh* it. Refresh downloads the current calendar from the server, ensuring that you have the latest published information. If you don't have a full-time connection, make sure you dial up to connect to the Internet before you choose to refresh.

1. Select a subscribed calendar in the Calendars list.
2. From the Calendar menu at the top of your screen, choose "Refresh."

When you first subscribe to a calendar, you can set up an automatic schedule that determines how often the subscribed calendar is updated:

1. From the Calendar menu, choose "Subscribe...."
2. Click the "Refresh" checkbox, then from that pop-up menu, choose a time interval (every 15 minutes, every hour, every day, or every week) to set how often your computer downloads a new version of the subscribed calendar.

This automatic refresh technique is very convenient if you have a full-time Internet connection. If you have a dial-up connection iCal will alert you when it's trying to connect to the Internet, so you'll probably want to set the refresh schedule for every day or every week instead of every 15 minutes or every hour.

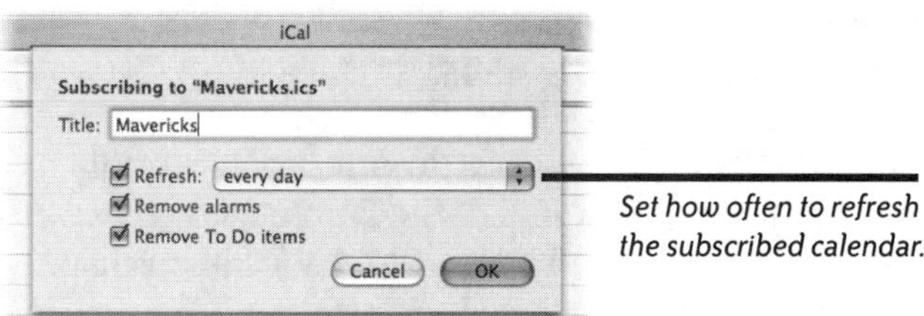

Set how often to refresh the subscribed calendar.

Import Calendars

An iCal file is actually a text file format (.ics) that can be sent as an email attachment. iCal can import other iCal files or vCal files (vCal is an older calendar data format) that you may have received from someone.

To import a calendar file:

1. From the File menu, choose "Import..." to open the Import window, shown below.
2. Click the "Import" button to open the "iCal: Import" Finder window. Locate and select the calendar file you want to import.
3. Click "Import" to place the calendar in iCal's Calendars list. Click the imported calendar's checkbox to show it in iCal's window.

   Or simply drag a calendar file (an iCal file or a vCal file) from the Finder to the Calendars list in the iCal window.

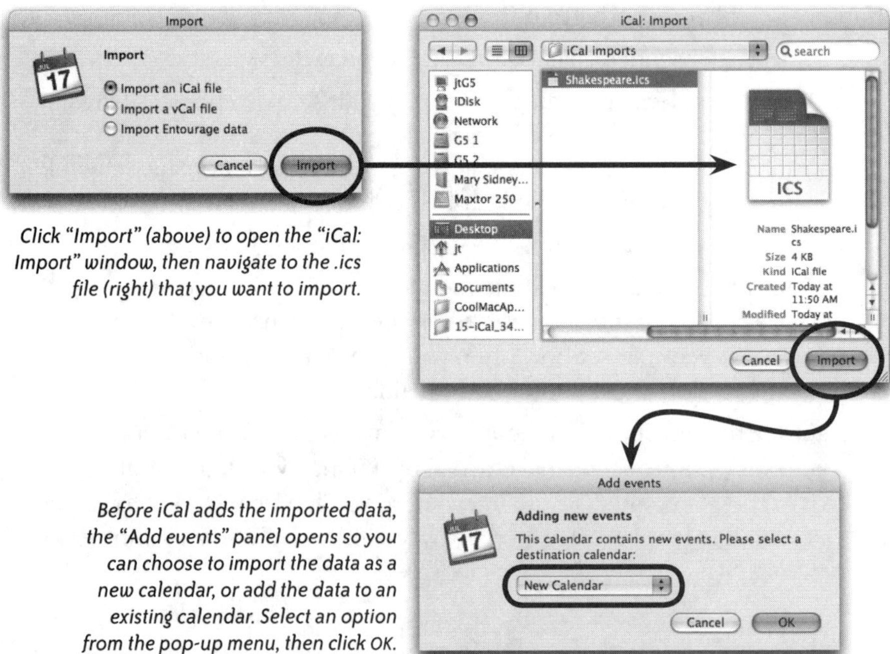

Click "Import" (above) to open the "iCal: Import" window, then navigate to the .ics file (right) that you want to import.

Before iCal adds the imported data, the "Add events" panel opens so you can choose to import the data as a new calendar, or add the data to an existing calendar. Select an option from the pop-up menu, then click OK.

If you plan to import Microsoft Entourage events, make sure the events are set for the same time zone as your iCal. If the Entourage events are set for a different time zone, their scheduled times may change. If this happens, drag the imported Entourage events to the correct time slots, or change your iCal time zone setting to match the original Entourage events' time zone. See the following page to learn about resetting iCal's time zone.

Export Calendars

You can export a calendar as an ".ics" file, a standard calendar format. The exported .ics file can then be imported by iCal on another computer, attached to an email and sent to someone else to import into their iCal, or imported into another device such as a Palm device or iPod.

To export a calendar:

1. Select a calendar in the Calendars list.
2. From the File menu, choose "Export…" to open the export sheet shown below.
3. Type a name for the exported calendar in the "Save As:" field.
4. From the "Where:" pop-up menu, choose a location to save the exported .ics file.
5. Click "Export."

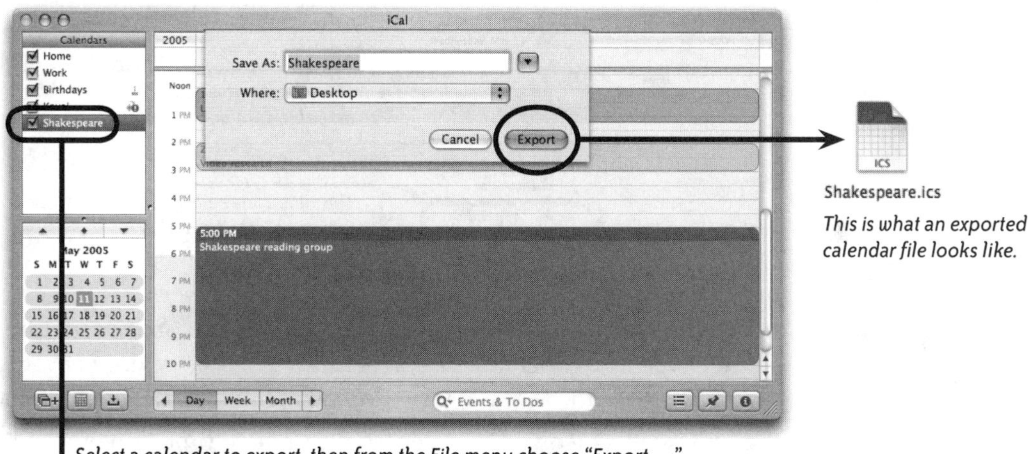

Shakespeare.ics

This is what an exported calendar file looks like.

Select a calendar to export, then from the File menu choose "Export…."

Change iCal's Time Zone Setting

iCal uses the time zone setting in your Date and Time System Preferences to set the time zone for your calendars. You can *change the time zone setting for iCal,* **or** you can change the time zone setting for *a single event,* without changing your computer's System Preference settings.

If, for instance, you create an iCal event to call someone at a certain time in another time zone, you can set that event to the other person's time zone. iCal automatically moves the event forward or back in time in your calendar to compensate for the time zone difference.

Or, if you take a trip and want to change all calendars and events in iCal to your current time zone, you can do that with a click or two.

Change the time zone setting for iCal

1. Open iCal Preferences and select "Turn on time zone support" (see page 355) so the time zone setting appears in the top-right corner of the iCal window, and also in the Info drawer (circled below).

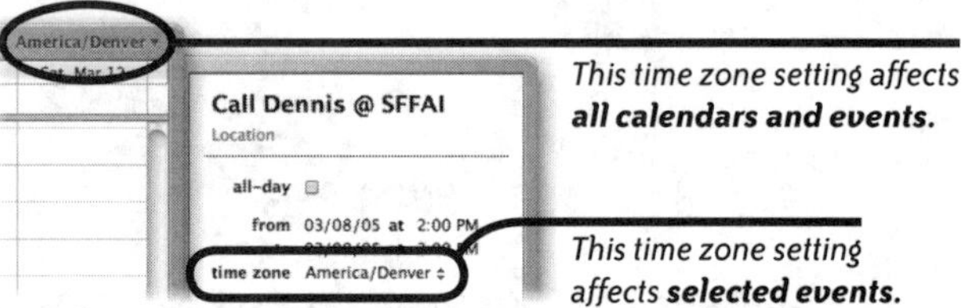

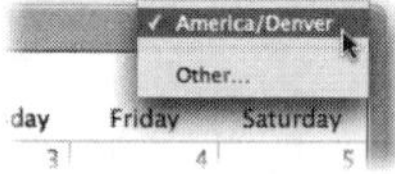

2. Click the time zone text *in the upper-right corner* (above) of iCal's main window to open the pop-up menu shown on the left. Choose "Other..." to open the map sheet shown below. Select a new time zone—use the "Closest City" pop-up menu or click a map location.
3. Click OK. Once you've selected alternative time zones, they remain in the time zone pop-up menu.

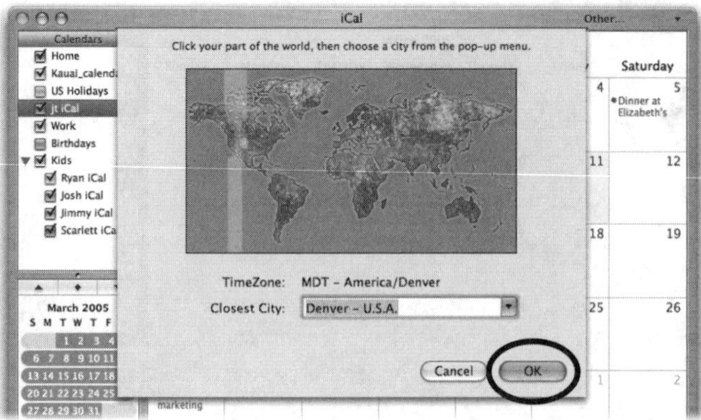

Change the time zone setting for an event

1. Open iCal Preferences and select "Turn on time zone support" (see page 355) so the time zone setting appears in the Info drawer (circled below-left).

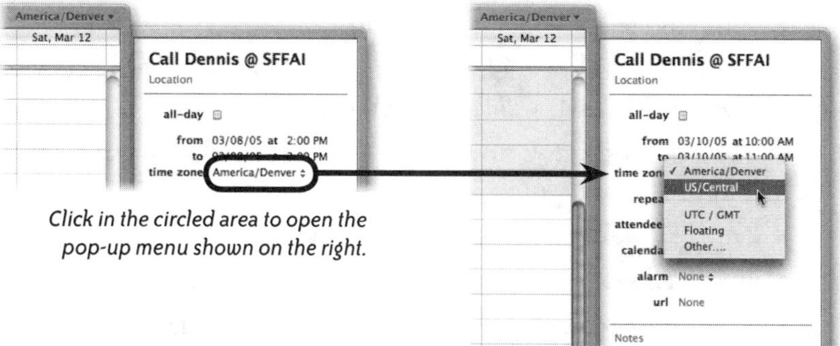

Click in the circled area to open the pop-up menu shown on the right.

2. Select an *event* in your calendar. Open the Info drawer—click the Show Info button, or just double-click an event to select it *and* open the drawer.
3. In the Info drawer click to the right of the *time zone* label (the text and small double-arrows) and choose one of the options in the pop-up menu (shown above-right).

   If you previously selected other time zones, they remain listed in the top section of the pop-up menu.

   UTC / GMT sets the time zone to Universal Time/Greenwich Mean Time—standards used as a basis for calculating time throughout most of the world.

   Choose **Floating** if you want to create events that stay at the same time, no matter what time zone you're in. For instance, a lunch event scheduled for noon will always appear in the noon time slot, no matter where you are or if you've changed the iCal time zone (as explained on the previous page) or the time zone setting in Date and Time System Preferences.

   Select **Other...** to show a small world map in the drawer, as shown on the right. Click a time zone in the map to open a pop-up menu of cities in that time zone. Select a city, then click the OK button in the bottom-right corner of the map.

An event's time zone setting affects its location on the calendar. If the iCal time zone is set to San Francisco and you create a lunch event and change its time zone to Paris, the event will move nine hours back in the iCal window.

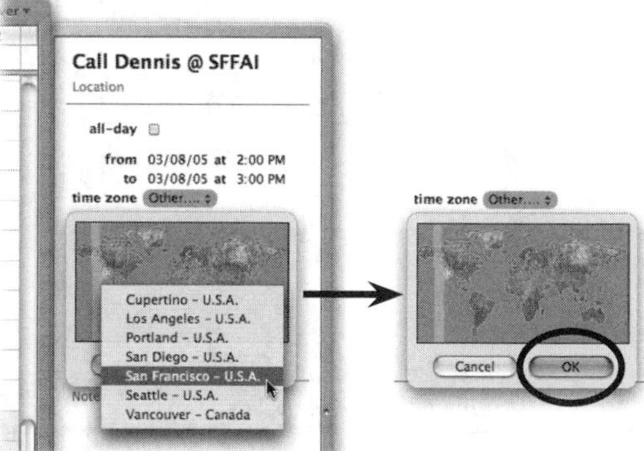

Print Your iCal Calendar

No matter how convenient the digital lifestyle may be, sometimes you need an old-fashioned paper printout. **To print a calendar:**

1. Select the calendar in the Calendars list that you want to print.
2. From the File menu, choose "Print…."
3. The Print window (below) opens. The left side shows a preview of how the calendar will look when printed.
4. From the **View** pop-up menu, choose the view you want to print—Day, Week, or Month.
5. From the **Paper** pop-up menu, choose a paper size to print on.
6. In the **Time range** section, choose a start and stop date.
7. In the **Calendars** section, checkmark the calendars whose events you want to include.
8. In the **Options** section, checkmark the items you want to include in the printing. The **Options** section changes slightly depending on the view you've selected in the "View" pop-up menu. Month view is shown below. The next page shows the Options section when Day view and Week view are selected.

   In the Options section shown below, "Calendar Keys" refers to the color legend in the top-right corner of the document. Checkmark "Black and White" if you want to print in black and white.
9. Pick a **text size** from the "Text size" pop-up menu. Choose Big, Medium, or Small. If your calendar is very crowded, choose small.
10. Click "Continue" to open a standard Print dialog box.

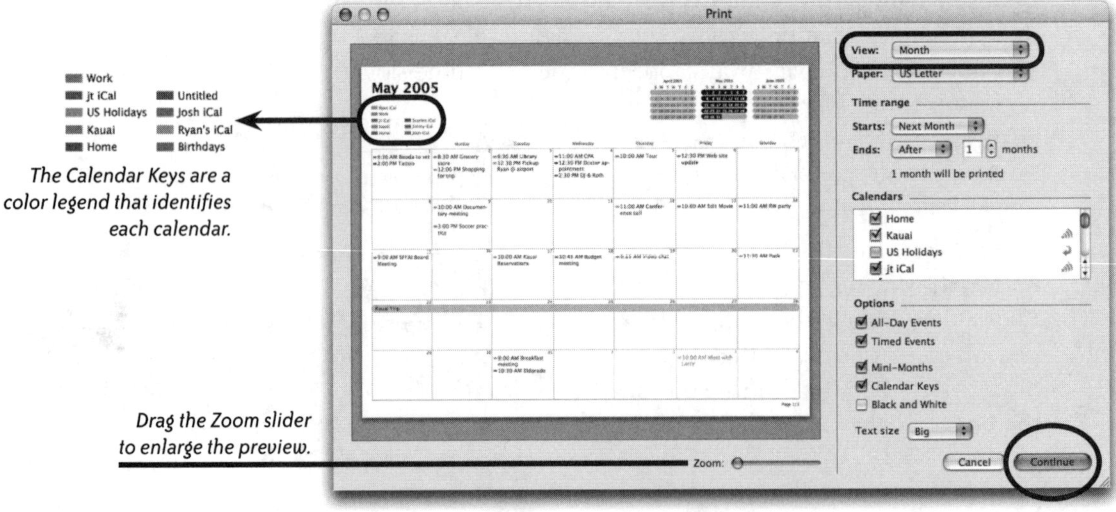

The Calendar Keys are a color legend that identifies each calendar.

Drag the Zoom slider to enlarge the preview.

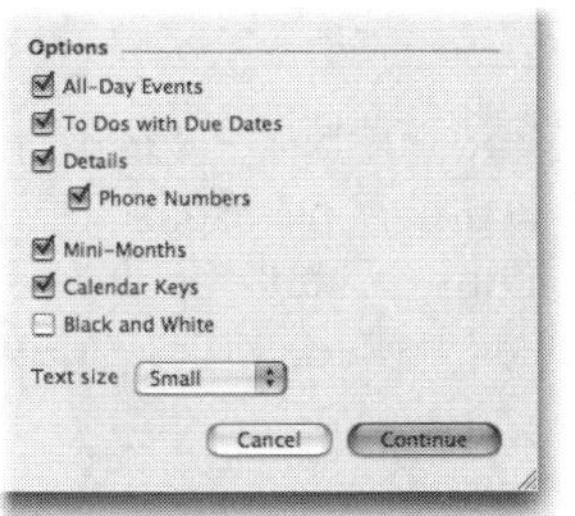

*Print options available in **Day** view.*

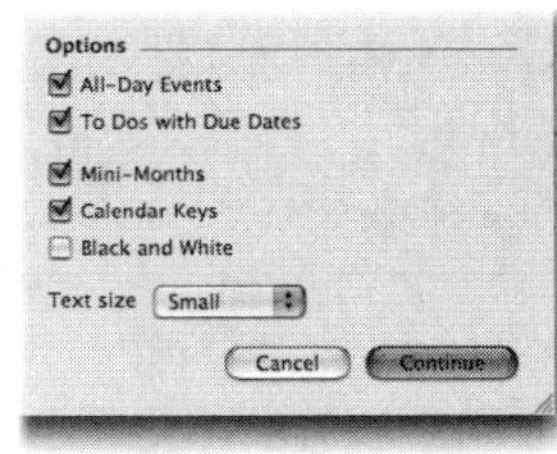

*Print options available in **Week** view.*

11. In the Print dialog box, select a printer and presets from the pop-up menus. Also select how many copies of the calendar to print.
12. Click the “Print” button.

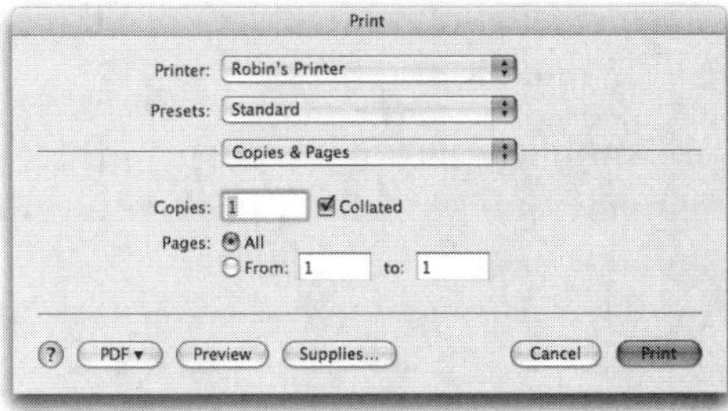

Save your iCal calendar as a PDF

An easy way to share your calendar is to save it as a PDF, the file format that almost anyone can open.

iCal_5/1/05-5/7/05.pdf

A calendar PDF file.

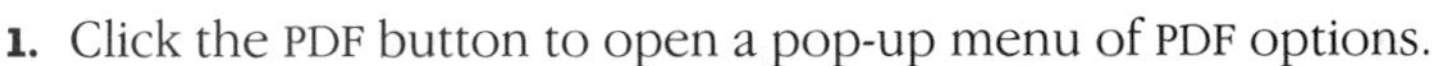

1. Click the PDF button to open a pop-up menu of PDF options.

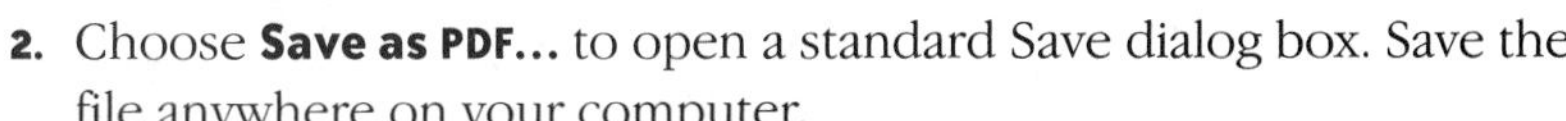

2. Choose **Save as PDF...** to open a standard Save dialog box. Save the file anywhere on your computer.

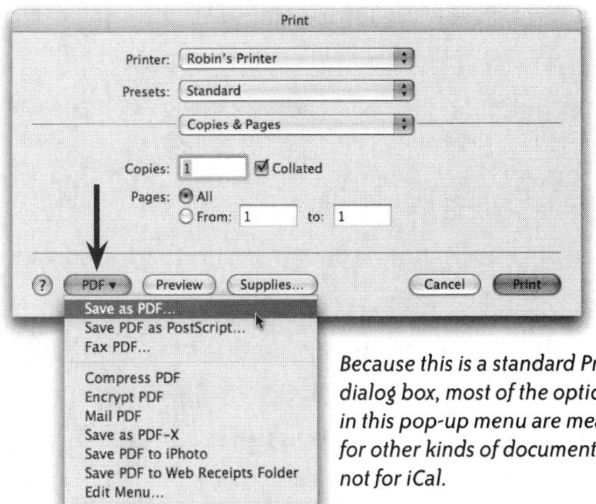

Because this is a standard Print dialog box, most of the options in this pop-up menu are meant for other kinds of documents, not for iCal.

iCal Symbols and Icons

Small symbols and icons sometimes appear in the title bar of iCal events, and also in the Notifications box. This is iCal's way of providing visual clues for you about the event. A quick glance at these tiny icons can tell you which events have an alarm set, which events have attendees invited, which events have received responses from attendees, and more.

The **people** icon means you've added one or more people to the attendees list in the iCal drawer, but you haven't sent the invitations yet.

An **exclamation point** next to the people icon means the event *needs updating.* You've made changes to the event but haven't notified the attendees.

An **ellipsis** next to the people icon means you've received mixed responses from attendees—Accept, Refuse, or Tentative.

A **checkmark** next to the people icon means all of the people invited to the event have "accepted" the invitation. A checkmark by itself means the one person invited has accepted.

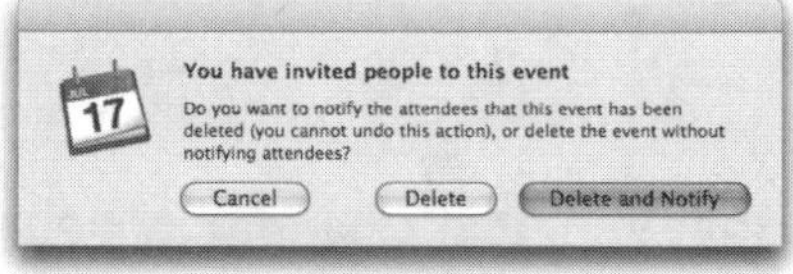

A **circle with a line though it** means "cancelled." When you delete an event to which people have been invited, the window on the right opens so you can notify the attendees that the event is cancelled. Or choose to just delete.

A **diagonal upward arrow** in the title bar of an event means iCal has sent invitations to the event, but none of the invitees have replied.

A **diagonal downward arrow** in an event's title bar means an incoming email message has arrived—either a response to an event invitation you sent, a new invitation from someone else, or an updated invitation from someone else.

A **notepad** means that comments have been added to the event's Notes field in the Info drawer.

An **alarm bell** means one or more alarms have been set for the event.

Multiple small boxes means the event has been set (in the Info drawer) as a "recurring" event.

A question mark means the invitees response is *tentative,* or undecided.

An **X** means declined. If the "x" is next to an attendee name in the Info drawer, it means that person has declined. If the "x" is in the event's title bar, it means that all invitees have declined.

Safari RSS 14

The World Wide Web is easier to browse, thanks to **Safari RSS,** Apple's web browser. The RSS (Really Simple Syndication) technology that is now available on many web sites provides news stories and articles in the form of headlines and brief summaries that link full-length versions on various web sites. Safari includes a collection of RSS feeds, but you can choose which RSS feeds you want, and you can add others whenever you want. RSS feeds make it easy to quickly browse lots of information, then click a story that interests you to see the full details. You can view RSS feeds directly in the Safari window without needing to open a separate RSS reader.

Safari also includes many other advanced features that make exploring the Internet easier, more productive, and more secure:

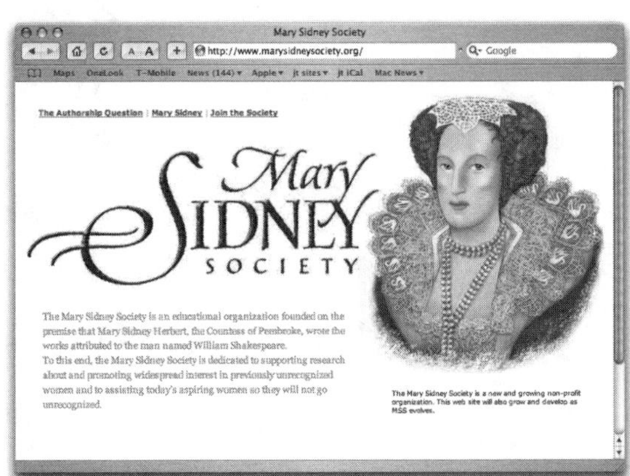

- Turn on private browsing when you use someone else's computer to prevent Safari from storing any information about you or the sites you visit.
- Email a web page to others, complete with links and graphics.
- Save a web page as an archive for viewing later.
- Turn on parental controls for your child's user account to limit web access to your authorized web sites listed in the Bookmarks bar.
- View PDFs directly in Safari without opening another application.
- Search Bookmarks and History to find web pages you need.
- Import bookmarks you've created in other browsers.

All of this plus search features that add more power and versatility than ever makes Safari more than just a browser—it's a super browser!

The Safari Interface

The Safari browser interface is elegantly designed to provide maximum functionality and minimum visual distraction. The example below shows the main elements that make up the Safari interface.

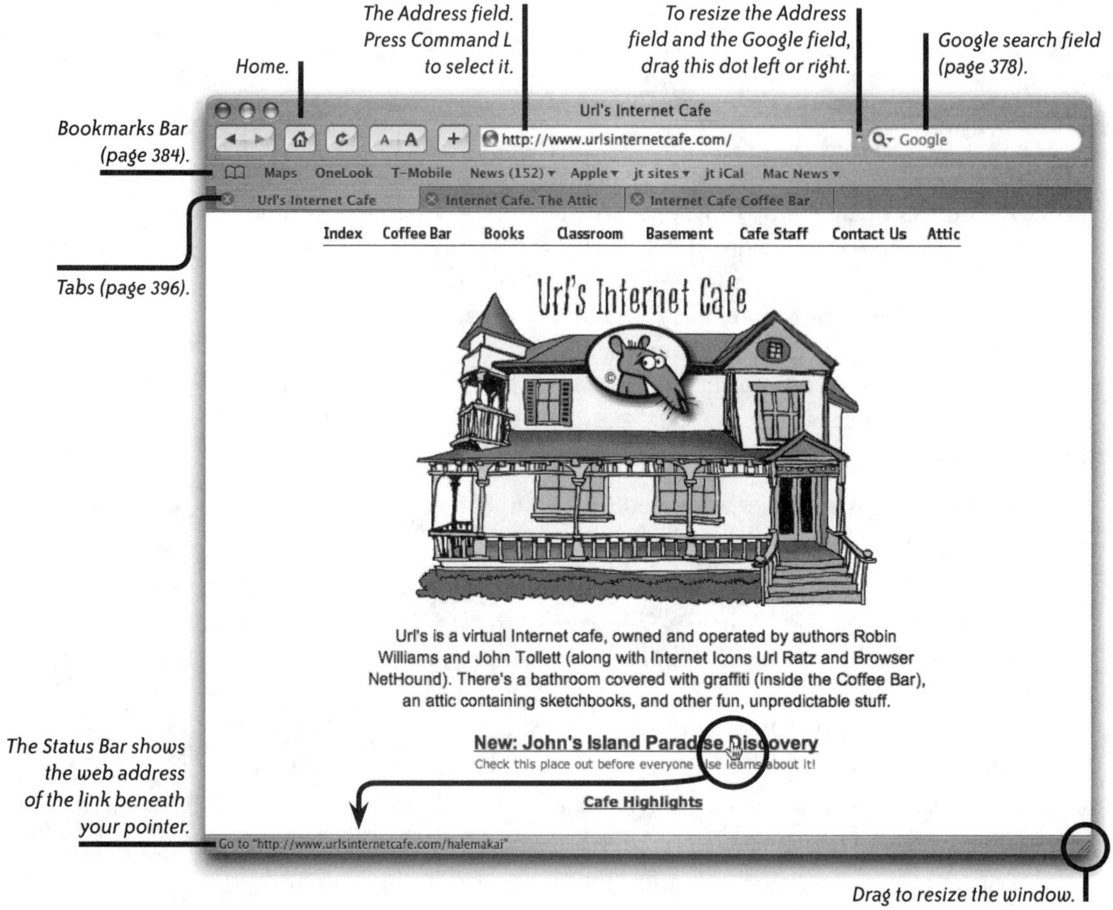

Home.

The Address field. Press Command L to select it.

To resize the Address field and the Google field, drag this dot left or right.

Google search field (page 378).

Bookmarks Bar (page 384).

Tabs (page 396).

The Status Bar shows the web address of the link beneath your pointer.

Drag to resize the window.

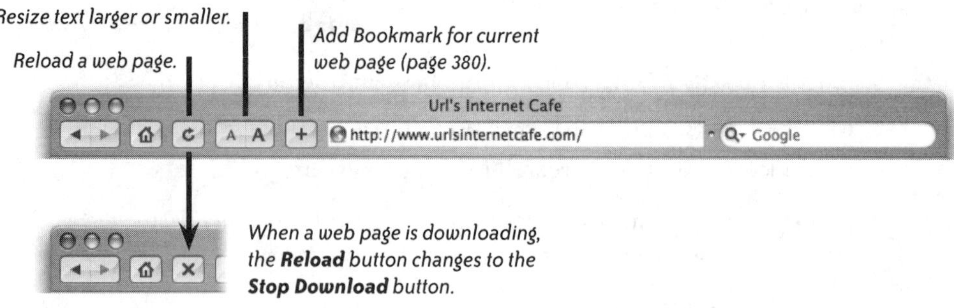
Resize text larger or smaller.
Reload a web page.
Add Bookmark for current web page (page 380).
Url's Internet Cafe
http://www.urlsinternetcafe.com/
Google
When a web page is downloading, the **Reload** button changes to the **Stop Download** button.

Customize Safari's Address Bar

From the View menu you can choose which icons and text fields to show in Safari's Address Bar (toolbar). This menu also lets you choose to hide or show the Address Bar, the Bookmarks Bar, and the Status Bar.

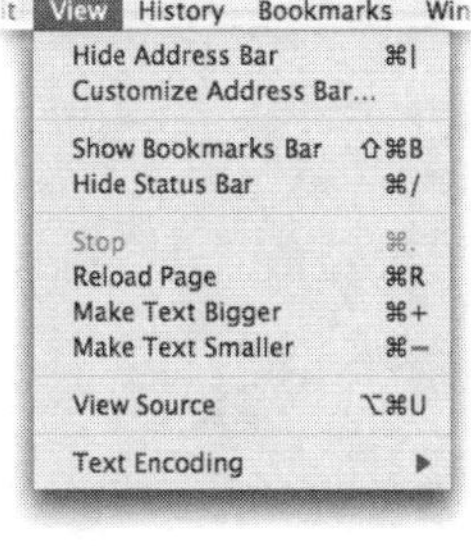

1. From the View menu choose "Customize Address Bar..." (shown on the right).
2. A sheet drops down from the browser title bar that contains the various buttons and fields that are available. Drag any item you want to the Address Bar. Continue to press while you drag the button to the desired position in the Address Bar—other buttons move out of the way when the drag gets close to them, making room for the new item. If you made changes and want to return the Address Bar to its original state, drag the default set as a unit to the Address Bar.
3. Click the "Done" button.
4. To remove an item from the Address Bar, Command-drag it to the Desktop.

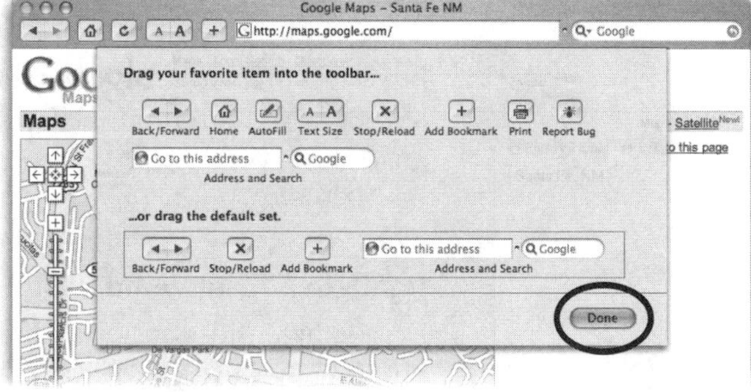

Some sites are so beautiful (such as this astrophotography site) that you just don't want to see extra clutter like the Bookmarks Bar. A quick Command Shift B gets rid of it. If you're making a presentation that involves showing a web page, you might even want to hide the Address Bar and the Status Bar.

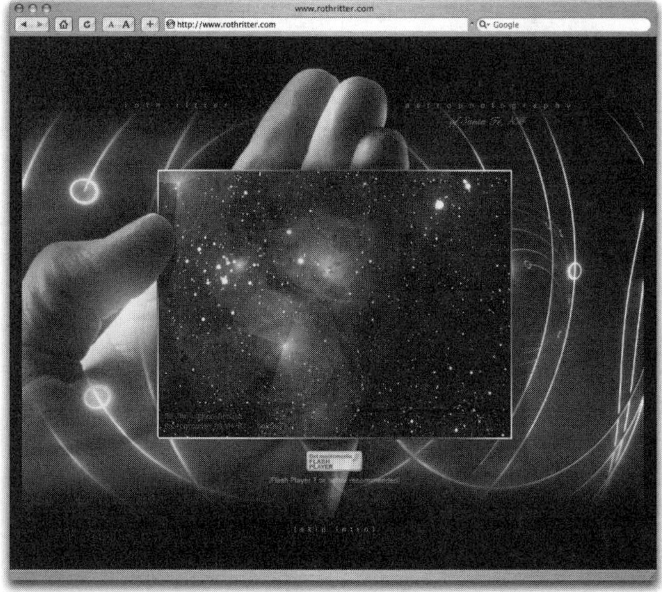

Quick Tips

Here are just a few quick tips for getting around in Safari quickly and easily.

Scrolling tips

To scroll around a web page, click in the web page then use the **arrow keys** to go up, down, or sideways.

To scroll farther, press Option and the arrow keys.

To scroll *down* a full window screen at a time, tap the Spacebar.

To scroll *up* a full window screen at a time, press Shift Spacebar.

Bigger or smaller text on the web page

Many web pages allow you to resize the page's text. **To make text bigger,** press Command +. **To make text smaller,** press Command –. **Or,** if the Text Size button is present in Safari's toolbar (shown on the left), click the large A or small A button. To place this Text Size button in the toolbar, choose "Customize Address Bar..." in the View menu.

Death to pop-up windows!

Do you hate those annoying little advertisement windows that pop up without your permission? Press **Command K** to prevent their appearance. **Or,** from the Safari application menu choose "Block Pop-Up Windows." If you decide you *want* pop-up ads (sudden burst of maniacal laughter), press Command K again to allow them.

Web address tips

If a web address ends in **.com**, all you need to type in the Address field is the main name, such as **apple, toyota,** or **NFL,** then hit Return.

As you type a web address, previous and similar addresses appear in a pop-up menu below the Address field. When you see the correct address appear, stop typing, then use the DownArrow key to select the address you want. When it's highlighted, hit the Return key to enter it.

To select a single word in a web address so you can replace it, double-click the word. Much easier than trying to press-and-drag across that tiny word in the tiny Address field to select it!

View a link's location in the Status Bar

If the **Status Bar** in Safari is showing, you can position your mouse over a link (don't click), and the address of the link appears in the Status Bar, as shown below.

To show the Status Bar, go to the View menu and choose "Show Status Bar," *or* press Command \. (The backslash is right above the Return key.)

Links tips

Sometimes you want to open several links at once without closing the page that's open.

- **To open an additional link,** Command-click on the link. If tabbed browsing is turned *off* (in Safari Preferences), the link opens in a new window. If tabbed browsing is turned *on,* the click creates a new tab in the Tab Bar.
- **To open a link in a new window that is *behind* the current window,** Command Shift click on it.

To show a menu of link options, as shown on the right, Control-click on a link. Or right-click if you have a two-button mouse.

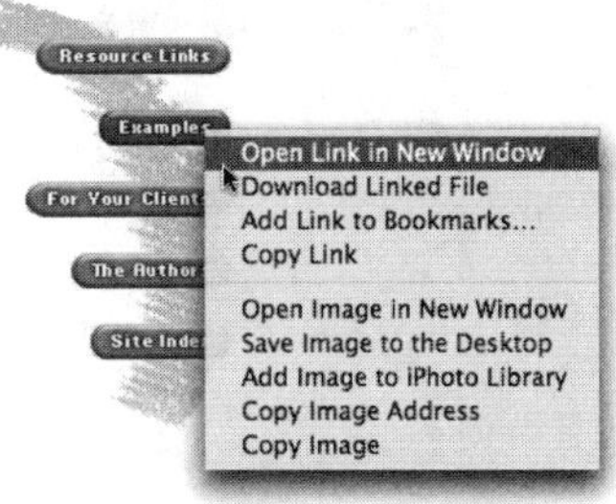

Archive a web page

At some point you may want to archive a web page on your computer, complete with text, images, and other content so you can browse the page later, even if you're not connected to the Internet. If you are connected, the links on the page are fully functional.

To open an archived file, double-click it or drop it on top of the Safari application icon.

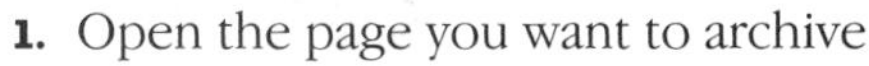

1. Open the page you want to archive.
2. From the File menu choose "Save As...," or press Command S.
3. In the Save As sheet (shown on the right), choose "Web Archive" from the Format pop-up menu.
4. Click the "Save" button.

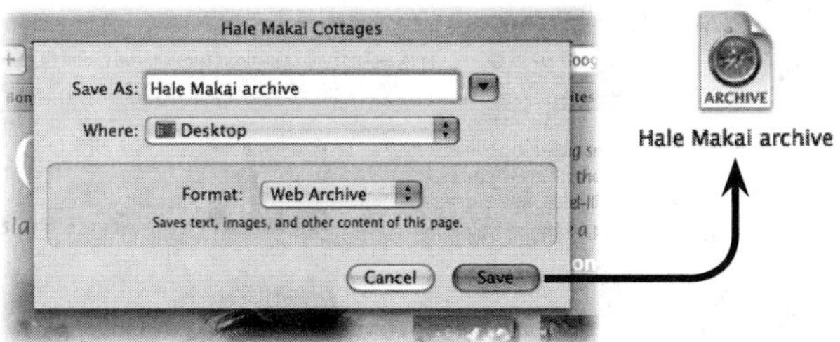

Email a web link or a web page

When you want to send a web link to a friend or associate, you can do it in several different ways.

To email an entire web page to someone:

In Safari, open the web page you want to send.

1. From the File menu choose "Mail Contents of This Page." The web page opens in a new email message window, complete with graphics and working links.
2. Address the message and click the "Send" button. The recipient will see any edits you made, but unchanged links will work and the original web site is not affected.

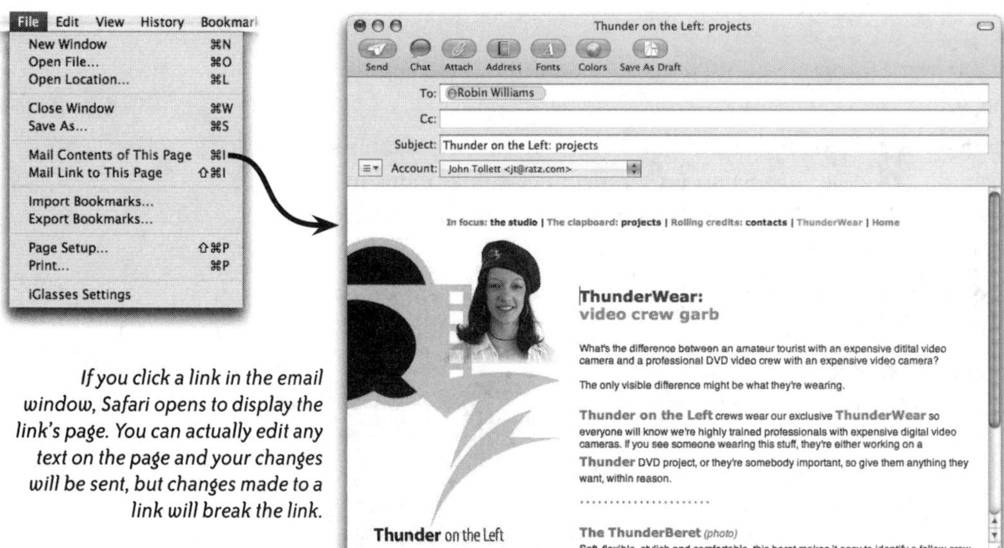

If you click a link in the email window, Safari opens to display the link's page. You can actually edit any text on the page and your changes will be sent, but changes made to a link will break the link.

To email a web link someone:

1. In Safari, open the web page you want to send.
2. From the File menu choose "Mail Link to This Page." A new email message form opens that contains a text link for the web address.

Another way to add a web address to email is to drag the web address icon in Safari's Address Bar into the email message window.

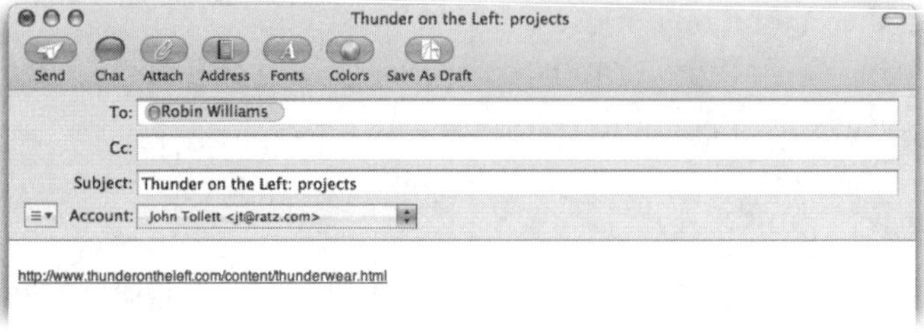

Create a Web Location file for any text link

A **Web Location** file is a small file that will open your browser (if it isn't already) and go to that web page. The advantage of a Web Location file over a bookmark is that you don't have to open Safari and look for a bookmark—just double-click a Web Location file icon and it automatically opens Safari and goes straight to that page.

Drag a link (above) from Safari to the Desktop. When you drop the file on the Desktop, it changes appearance, as shown below.

To make a Web Location file, just drag a link off of a web page and drop it on the Desktop. You can also create a Web Location file by dragging a site's web address icon (the small icon that's in the Address field) to the Desktop.

Open a Web Location icon

Once you've made a Web Location icon there are several things you can do with it.

Put the Web Location file in the Dock. Drag it to the right side of the dividing line (on the side where the Trash basket is). When you click on this icon in the Dock, that web page will open in a new, separate browser window—it won't replace any existing browser windows that are already open.

A Web Location file in the Dock.

Open the link's web page in a new and separate window. Double-click a Web Location icon on the Desktop or in a folder. Single-click one that's in the Dock.

Open the link's web page in a window that's already open on your screen. Drag the Web Location file icon and drop it in the middle of a Safari window (*not* in the Address field). The new web page will *replace* the existing one.

Send links to others. You can send a folder of Web Location files to others (via email, Bonjour, iChat, etc.) so they can have easy access to selected sites that you want to share.

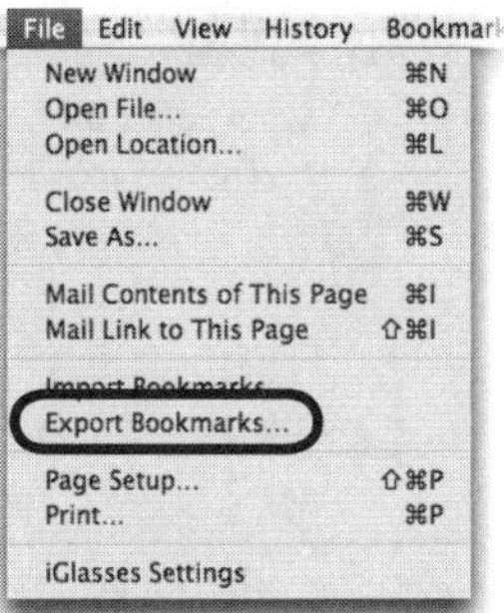

You could also *export* Safari bookmarks (from the File menu choose "Export Bookmarks...") and send the exported file, but it creates a file that contains *all* of your bookmarks—much more information than you may want to share.

Private Browsing

If you share a computer with others, Private Browsing adds a new level of privacy and protection of your personal information. Ordinarily, when you browse web sites, the browser keeps a record (a history file) of the web pages you opened. If you entered a password to enter a secure site, or if you shop online, some of that personal information may be stored and available for someone to find. When you turn on Private Browsing, Safari stops storing certain information for you, such as information you entered on a web page, usernames, passwords, even credit card numbers.

When Private Browsing is turned on:

- Web pages you visit are not added to the History list.
- Downloaded items are automatically removed from the Downloads window.
- AutoFill information isn't saved, including names and passwords.
- Searches entered in the Google search field are not added to the search field's pop-up menu.
- Cookies that were downloaded during web page visits are automatically deleted when Private Browsing is turned off.

The Safari menu is where you can turn on options for Private Browsing, Reset Safari, and Empty Cache.

To turn on Private Browsing:

1. Select the Safari window for which you want to turn on Private Browsing.
2. From the Safari menu choose "Private Browsing." A checkmark appears next to the item to indicate it's turned on. To turn off Private Browsing, choose the item again to remove the checkmark.

If you turn on Private Browsing *after* you've started browsing, the History menu retains the web pages that you visited before you turned on Private Browsing, but does not add currently visited pages to the list.

When you finish browsing, close the Safari window you used to prevent someone from using the Back button to trace your steps.

Other privacy tips:

- To manually clear the History of its list of visited web page, from the History menu choose "Clear History."
- To manually clear the Safari cache of stored temporary information, from the Safari menu choose "Empty Cache...."
- To do both of the above, plus clear the Downloads window, remove cookies, remove any AutoFill text, and clear Google search entries, from the Safari menu choose "Reset Safari...."

Parental Controls

There are thousands of web sites out there that you don't want your children to see. Unfortunately, those sites are easy to find, sometimes by accident. You can set up a new user account for your children, then turn on *parental controls* for that account. Only the web sites chosen by you and listed in the Bookmarks Bar can be visited by the user. Other sites require your authorization to be added to the Bookmarks Bar.

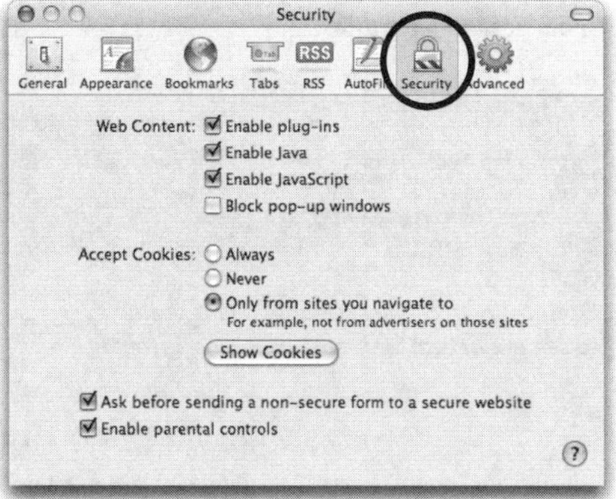

To activate Parental Controls:

1. Create a new user account for your child: Open System Preferences and choose "Accounts" (click the plus sign beneath the Accounts pane.
2. Log in as the new user, then open Safari.
3. From the Safari menu choose "Preferences...," then click the "Security" icon in the Preferences toolbar. Temporarily, make sure "Enable parental controls" is *not* selected so you can make changes to the Bookmarks Bar.
4. Remove all items from the Bookmarks Bar, then visit the sites that you want to make available, and add them as bookmarks to the Bookmarks Bar.
5. After adding bookmarks for acceptable sites, go back to the Security pane of Safari Preferences and select "Enable parental controls." An "Authenticate" dialog box opens so you can enter your administrator name and password.

The web sites listed in your child's Bookmarks Bar are now available. If a child clicks a link that connects to another site outside of the approved site, the window shown on the right opens. When the "Add Web site" button is clicked, an "Authenticate" dialog box opens so you can enter an administrator name and password.

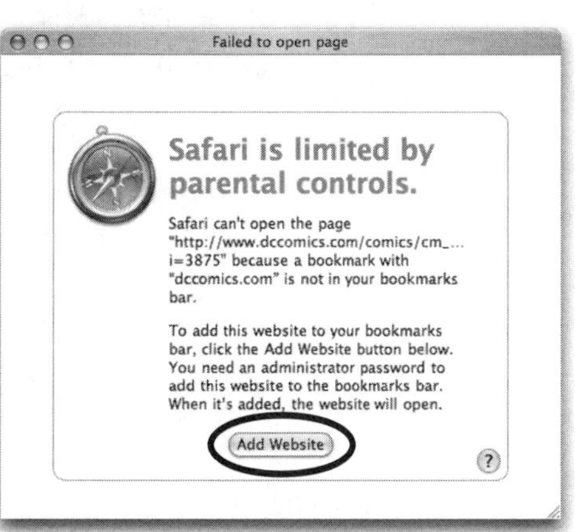

Parental controls affect only Safari. So don't be surprised if the little rascal tries to download another browser. If you have administrative privileges, you can also set up parental controls for "Finder & System" (to specify the applications a user can open) in the "Accounts" pane of System Preferences.

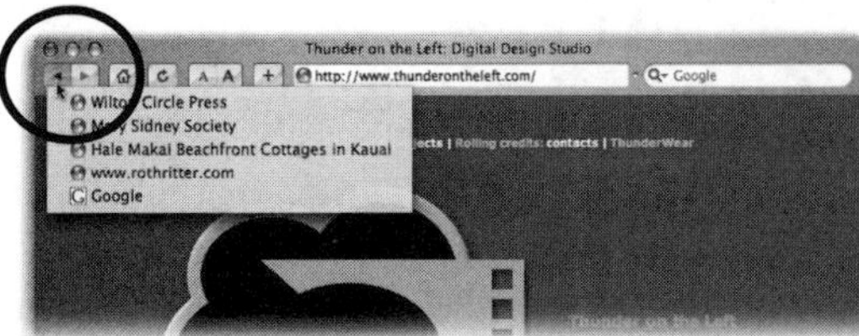

*Press on the Back or Forward button to show a pop-up menu of the web pages you've visited, showing **web page titles.***

Safari Navigation

As you may already know, you can *press* on the Back or Forward button to show a menu of the web sites you've already visited since you opened the browser. Choose a site in the list to open it in Safari.

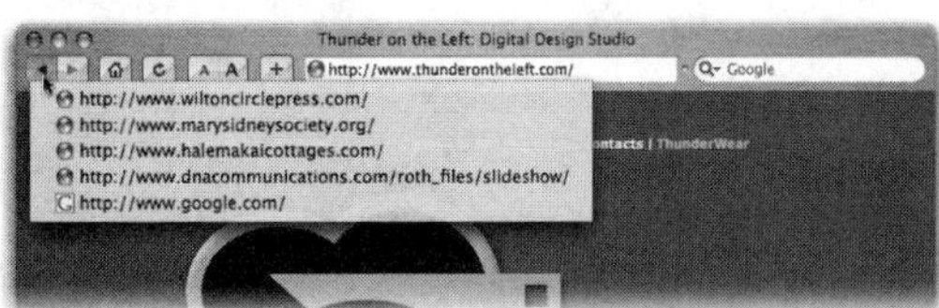

*Option-press on the Back or Forward button to see the **actual web addresses** in the menu.*

But did you know that if you hold the Option key down while you press on either the Back or Forward button, the pop-up menu **shows the actual web addresses** of the pages you've visited?

Access web sites from the Address Book menu

If your **Address Book** (see Chapter 16) info contains web site addresses, you can access those web sites directly from the Bookmarks Bar. The next page explains how to put the Address Book menu in the Bookmarks Bar.

People in your Address Book whose contact information includes a web address appear in Safari's Address Book menu.

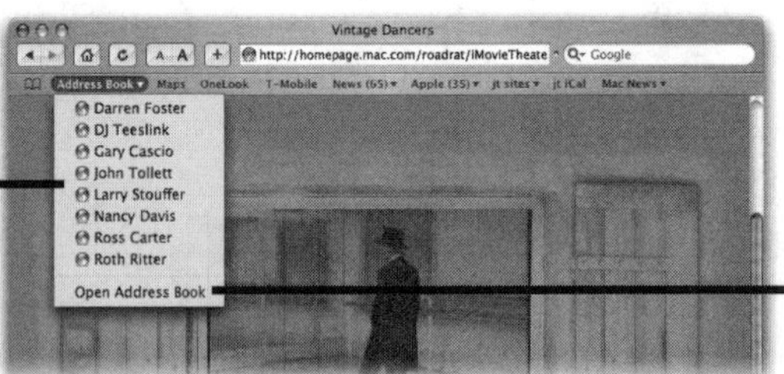

To add the current web page to a contact's info in Address Book, choose "Open Address Book," select a contact, then drag the web address icon from Safari to the "home page" field in Address Book (see page 377).

Choose a site from the History menu.

To choose from a list of the sites you visited within the past week, click the History menu. If you had Private Browsing turned on (see page 374), the History menu contains no visited sites.

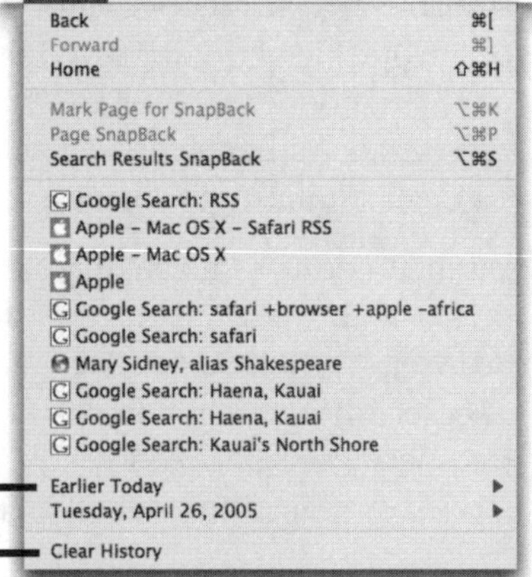

The History menu shows the ten most recent web site visits.

Sites visited earlier (up to a week ago) are shown in pop-up submenus.

Delete all sites from this menu.

To put the Address Book menu in your Bookmarks Bar:

1. Open the Safari Preferences (go to the Safari menu and choose "Preferences…").
2. Click the "Bookmarks" button in the toolbar to open the pane shown below.
3. After "Bookmarks Bar:" checkmark "Include Address Book."

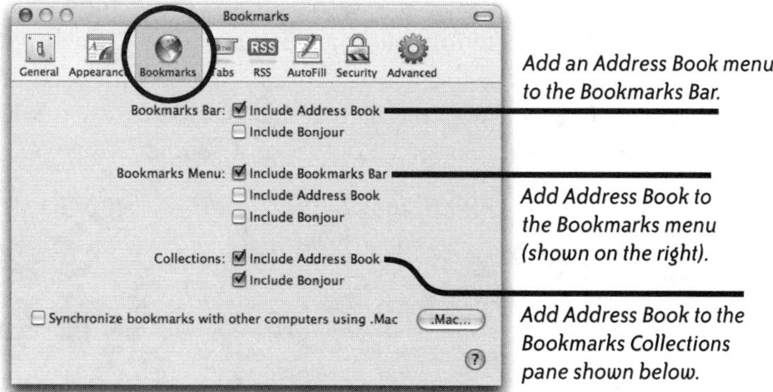

Add an Address Book menu to the Bookmarks Bar.

Add Address Book to the Bookmarks menu (shown on the right).

Add Address Book to the Bookmarks Collections pane shown below.

When you choose "Address Book" in the Bookmarks menu, a submenu shows links to web sites that you entered in Address Book.

Click this open book icon in the Bookmarks bar to show the Bookmarks Library.

If the contact information in your Address Book doesn't contain a web address field (called "home page" in Address Book), you can add one.

1. Open Address Book and select a contact.
2. Click the "Edit" button.
3. From the Card menu choose "Add Field," and from the submenu choose "URL" (Uniform Resource Locator—the technical term for a web address). The "home page" item appears in the Address Book contact information. Type a web address, then click the "Edit" button to set the changes.

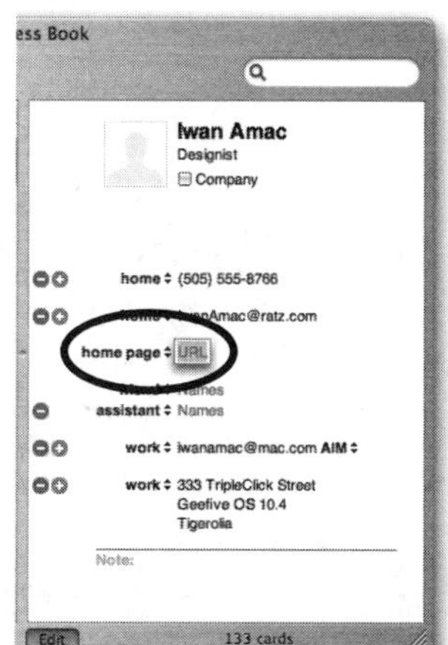

You can also drag the web address icon from Safari's address bar into this "home page" field.

Safari's Google Search

If you don't see the Google search field in your toolbar, go to the View menu and choose "Customize Address Bar…"

If you've ever used **Google** as your search engine, you know how amazing it is. Because it's so great, Apple has included it in your Safari toolbar. Use it just as you would if you went directly to the **Google.com** site. Here are a few extra tips for searching (these tips apply to any search tool, actually).

Limit your search for best results

- Put quotation marks around words that should be searched together, as one term. With quotation marks around a phrase, Google will find only those pages where the words in quotes are next to each other. The image search below found 58 matches without using quotation marks. With quotation marks, Google found 38 matches.

Type a search term in this search field.

Click the X to clear the search field.

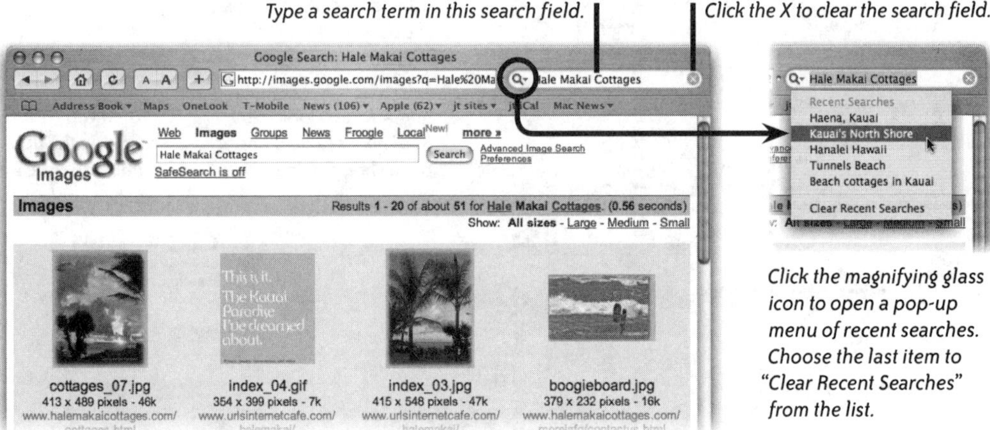

Click the magnifying glass icon to open a pop-up menu of recent searches. Choose the last item to "Clear Recent Searches" from the list.

Limit your search even more

Use *Boolean operators* to limit your search. Put a + sign in front of any word or phrase (in quotation marks) that you want to make sure Google finds; put a – sign in front of any word that you do not want included in the search results. Do not put a space after the + or –.

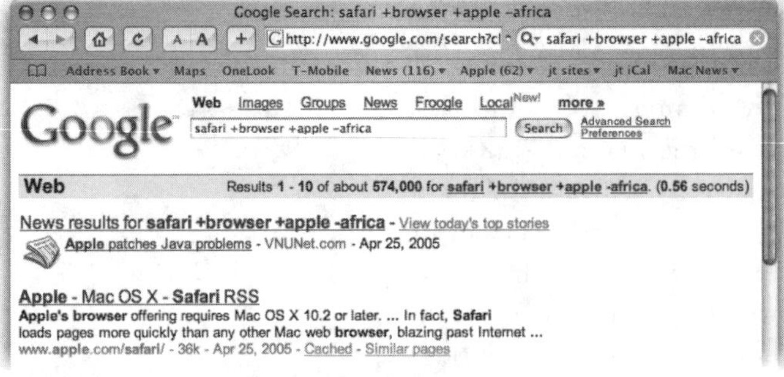

*A search for **safari +browser +apple –africa** gave "only" 574,000 results.*

*A search for **safari** gave 33,200,000 results.*

Safari search tips

- Select a word or phrase on any web page, then Control-click on that word. A **contextual menu** opens with the options to "Search in Spotlight, Search in Google, or Look Up in Dictionary." Spotlight is the powerful new search feature built in to Tiger (Mac OS X v10.4).

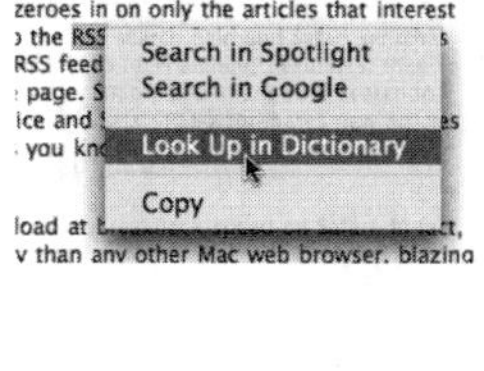

- When you want to search for a keyword or phrase on a long, lengthy web page, press Command F to open the "Find" dialog. Type the keyword you're looking for, then press the "Next" button. The first occurance of the keyword that's visible in the Safari window is highlighted. Keep clicking "Next" to find other occurences.

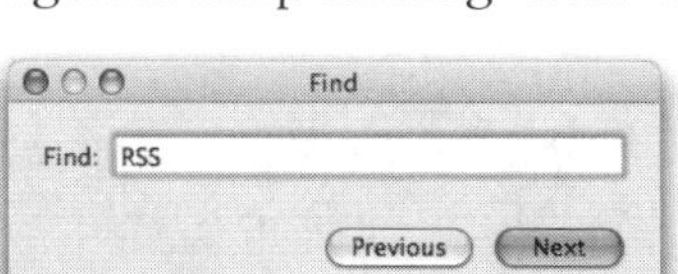

Bookmarks Search

If you've accumulated a ton of bookmarks, you'll love Safari's Bookmark search. Especially if you haven't kept them organized in folders.

Tip: If more than one person uses your computer, or if you have visitors or grandkids using it, set up another user. Then nobody can mess with your bookmarks—each user will have his own set of Safari bookmarks.

1. Click the Bookmarks button (the open book icon in the Bookmarks Bar) to open the Collections pane (on the left side of the window) and the results pane (on the right side).
2. Click the magnifying glass icon in the search field at the bottom of the window. From the pop-up menu, choose to search in the selected collection (folder), or "In All Collections."
3. Type a keyword in the search field. The results pane shows matching bookmarks.

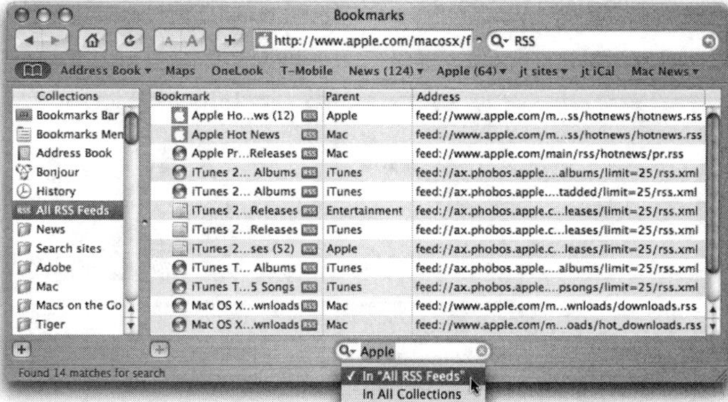

History Search

The Collections pane includes a "History" collection of web sites you've visited recently. Select the "History" collection, then from the Search field's pop-up menu, choose "In History." Type a keyword in the search field to find matching bookmarks.

Click this icon to show or hide the Bookmarks Library.

Bookmarks

Make a **bookmark** of a page that you want to return to anytime in the future; this bookmark will then be available in the Bookmarks Menu at the top of your screen. Just choose that page from the menu to go directly to it. Bookmarks are the handiest features of any browser.

The biggest problem with bookmarks is they are *so* handy you end up making hundreds of them, and then it can be difficult to find the one you want (which defeats the purpose of a bookmark in the first place). Safari makes it easy to bookmark a page and keep bookmarks organized at the same time.

To bookmark a web page:

1. Go to the web page that you want to bookmark.
2. Click the **+** button (Add Bookmark) in the toolbar, if it's there. If the **+** isn't there, you can customize your Safari toolbar to add it (from the View menu, choose "Customize Address Bar....").

   Or press Command D.

   Or from the Bookmarks Menu choose "Add Bookmark...."
3. A sheet drops down from the title bar of the window, as shown below. This sheet offers the opportunity to **change the name of the bookmark**—sometimes the default name is too long.

   From the pop-up menu in the sheet, choose where to **store this bookmark.** You can choose an existing Collections folder, *or* the main Bookmarks Menu, *or* the Bookmarks Bar (the thin bar beneath the toolbar, shown below).
4. Click the "Add" button.

Tip: To add a page to the Bookmarks Menu ***without*** displaying the drop-down sheet asking you to rename and file it, press **Command Shift D.**

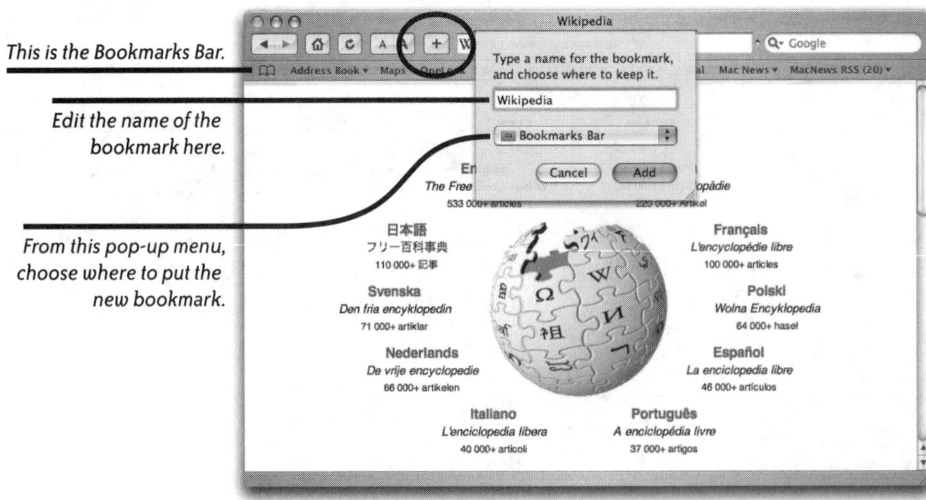

The Bookmarks Library

Below you see the **Bookmarks Library.** On the left side is the **Collections pane,** which holds your entire assortment of bookmarks. You can choose to put only your favorite bookmarks in the Bookmarks Menu Collection to keep the menu short, sweet, and useful instead of two yards long and difficult to wade through. **To open the Bookmarks Library,** click the *open book* icon in the Bookmarks Bar. If the Bookmarks Bar isn't visible, press Command Shift B. **Or** from the View menu choose "Show Bookmarks Bar."

Hide or show the Bookmarks Library.

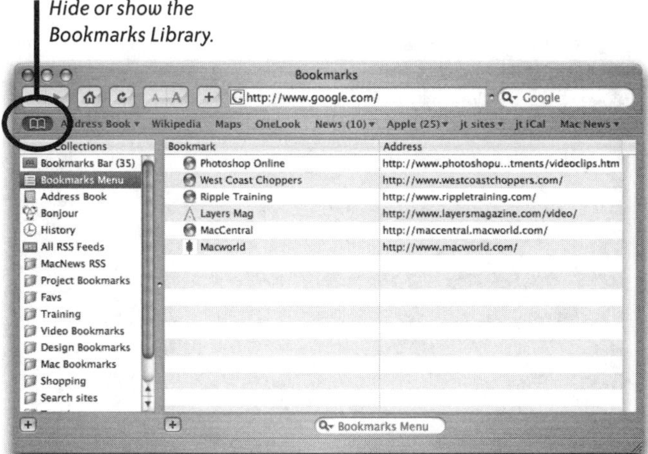

The "Bookmarks Menu" is selected. The Results pane on the right displays all the bookmarks stored in the Bookmarks Menu.

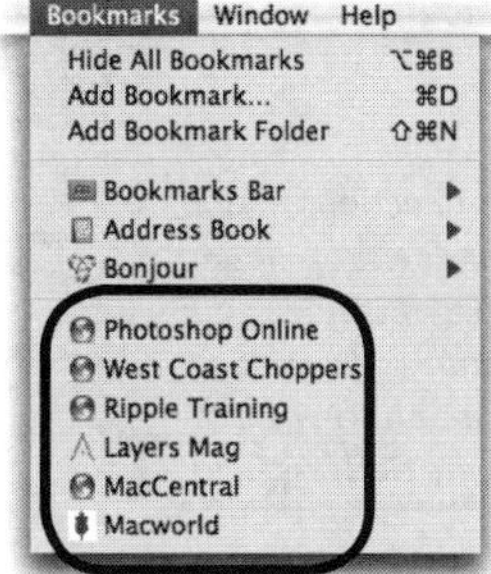

The Bookmarks that were placed in the Bookmarks Menu Collection now appear in the Bookmarks Menu.

The items in the Collections pane are:

Bookmarks Bar: Items in the Bookmarks Bar Collection (the folder in the Collections pane) appear in the bar itself. It can be a folder of bookmarks (a Collection), or a single bookmark.

Bookmarks Menu: Bookmarks or Collections in this folder appear in the Bookmarks Menu at the top of your screen, as shown above-right.

Address Book: If you've added a web site address to any Address Book contacts, the address appears here.

Bonjour: Web sites for printers, routers, webcams, or administrative sites on your network automatically appear here.

History: Every web page you have visited for the past week is automatically added to this collection—unless you've turned on Private Browsing.

All RSS Feeds: This Collection contains all RSS bookmarks.

Various bookmarks and folders: These are items that you've added.

Organize your bookmarks

You can create as many folders as you like and store as many bookmarks in those folders as you like. You can choose to put an entire folder of bookmarks into the Bookmarks Bar Collection—or any other Collection.

To make a new folder in the Collections pane:

1. Click the **+** sign at the bottom of the Collections pane.
2. The new folder appears and is ready for you to name it, as shown below—just type.

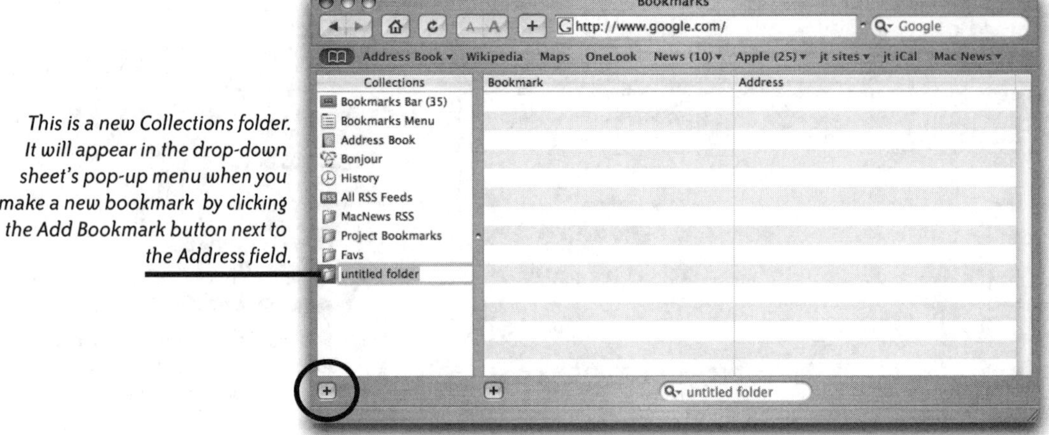

This is a new Collections folder. It will appear in the drop-down sheet's pop-up menu when you make a new bookmark by clicking the Add Bookmark button next to the Address field.

To put a new *bookmark* in the new folder in the Collections pane:

1. Make a new bookmark (described on page 380).
2. In the sheet that drops down, press on the pop-up menu and you'll see the new folder you just made. Choose it and the new bookmark is stored inside that folder.

To move an *existing* bookmark into a new folder in the Collections pane:

1. Click on any other collection in the Collections pane, such as History, Bookmarks Menu, or any other folder. The existing bookmarks that are stored in that collection appear on the right.
2. Drag a bookmark from the *right* side of the window and drop it into the new folder in the Collections pane, as shown at the top of the opposite page.

To move a *copy* of an existing bookmark, Option-drag it to another folder.

To move a bookmark or folder that's buried deep inside an existing Collection to a folder that's deep inside another Collection:

1. Open the Bookmarks Library so you can see the folder into which you want to move a bookmark or another folder (below-left).
2. Open a *new* Safari window (from the File menu, choose "New Window") shown below-right, then open its Bookmarks Library.
3. In the new Safari window, find the bookmark or folder you want to move, then drag it into the other folder.

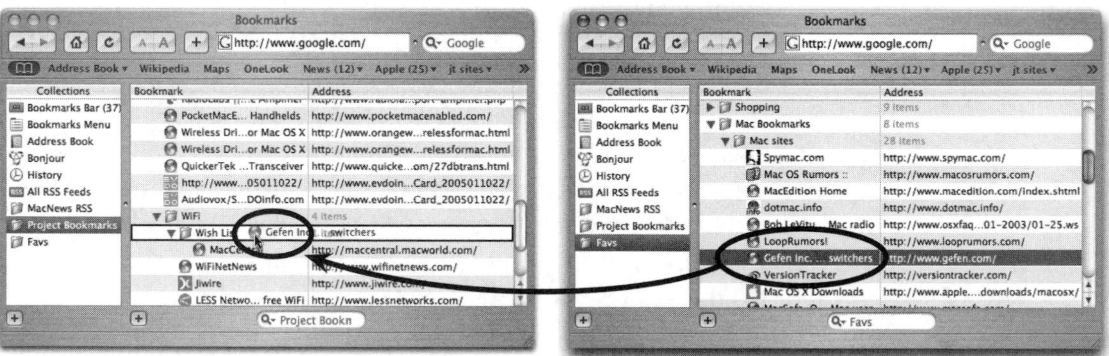

You can drag Collections or bookmarks between two Safari windows.

To make a new folder inside an existing collection:

1. Select a collection in the Collections pane, such as "Bookmarks Menu." Any bookmarks and folders stored in the Bookmarks Menu collection will appear in the Bookmarks Menu at the top of the screen.
2. On the *right* side of the window, click the **+** sign (Create New Bookmarks Folder) at the bottom of the Results pane. This will make a new, untitled folder on the *right* side, which means it is stored inside the selected collection.
3. Make new bookmarks and choose this folder to store them in. **Or** drag existing bookmarks from the same collection into this folder. **Or** drag bookmarks or Collections from the Collections pane into the new folder.

The Bookmarks Bar

The **Bookmarks Bar** is a convenient place for your most visited web sites. You can put entire Collections in the Bookmarks Bar as well as individual links.

To add a bookmark to the Bookmarks Bar:

If the Bookmarks Bar is not showing in your browser window, press Command B.

- **Either:** When you are at the page you want to bookmark, **drag the tiny icon** in the Address field and drop it on the Bookmarks Bar.
- **Or:** Press Command D to open a drop-down sheet like the one shown on page 380. Edit the bookmark so its name is short, then from the pop-up menu in the sheet, choose "Bookmarks Bar."

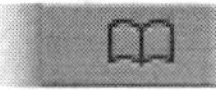

- **Or:** Open the Bookmarks Library. Click the *open book* icon on the far left side of the Bookmarks Bar(shown on the left). Select a Collection in the Collections pane that contains a bookmark you want in the Bookmarks Bar. Drag the bookmark from the right side of the window to the "Bookmarks Bar" collection on the left.

  This will *move* the bookmark from the existing collection to the Bar. **To put a *copy* in the Bar**, Option-drag.

A tiny triangle next to an item in the Bookmarks Bar means the item is a folder that contains multiple bookmarks.

Click the item to open a pop-up menu of that folder's bookmarks.

- **Or:** Open the Bookmarks Library. Find a bookmark in any collection. From the right side of the window, drag the bookmark directly into the Bookmarks Bar itself (as opposed to the Collections pane on the left). This will also put the bookmark into the Bookmarks Bar Collection. Option-drag to put a *copy* in the Bookmarks Bar.
- **Or:** Open the Bookmarks Library. Drag any **folder** from the Collections pane on the left and drop it directly in the Bookmarks Bar *or* into the Bookmarks Bar Collection.

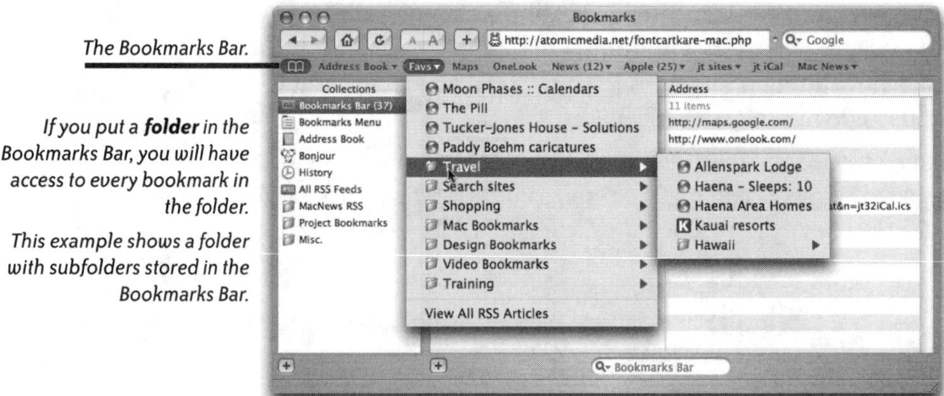

The Bookmarks Bar.

*If you put a **folder** in the Bookmarks Bar, you will have access to every bookmark in the folder.*

This example shows a folder with subfolders stored in the Bookmarks Bar.

To rearrange bookmarks in the Bookmarks Bar, Command-drag the bookmark items left or right in the Bar.

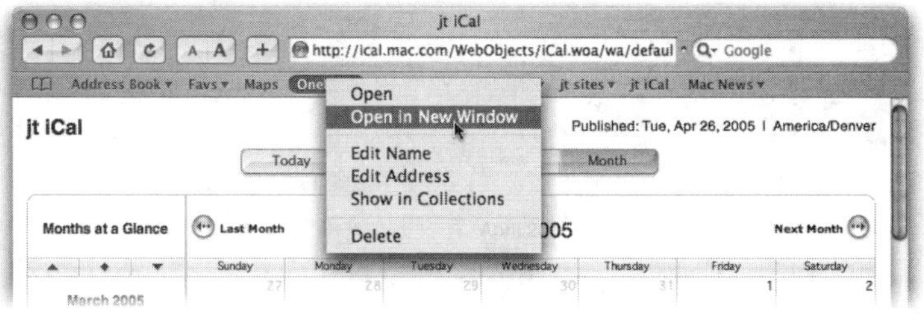

*Control-click on any bookmark in the Bookmarks Bar to open a pop-up menu from which you can **edit** the name or address, **delete** the bookmark, or **open** it in a new, separate window.*

To *remove* a bookmark from the Bookmarks Bar:

- Drag the bookmark off the top of the bar (not sideways or down). **Important note:** This will ***delete*** the bookmark, not just remove it from the Bookmarks Bar! If you drag a folder off the Bookmarks Bar, *it will delete every bookmark in that folder!*
- **To remove an individual bookmark** from the Bookmarks Bar and still **keep the bookmark,** open the Bookmarks Library. Select the Bookmarks Bar Collection on the left, then drag the bookmark you want to remove and drop it into any other collection.
- **To remove a folder of bookmarks from the Bookmarks Bar,** open the Bookmarks Library, select the Bookmarks Bar Collection in the Collections pane, drag the folder from the right side of the window, and drop it into the Collections pane on the left (or into a Collections folder on the left).

The History menu

The History menu keeps track of every web site you've visited for the past week: Use the History menu or the Bookmarks Library, as shown below. Click any History page to go back to that page. After about a week, the pages you've visited disappear from the History menu.

To clear all the pages out at once whenever you feel like it, go to the History menu and choose "Clear History." **Or** in the Bookmarks Library, select the "History" Collection, click in the pane on the right, press Command A to select all, then hit the Delete key.

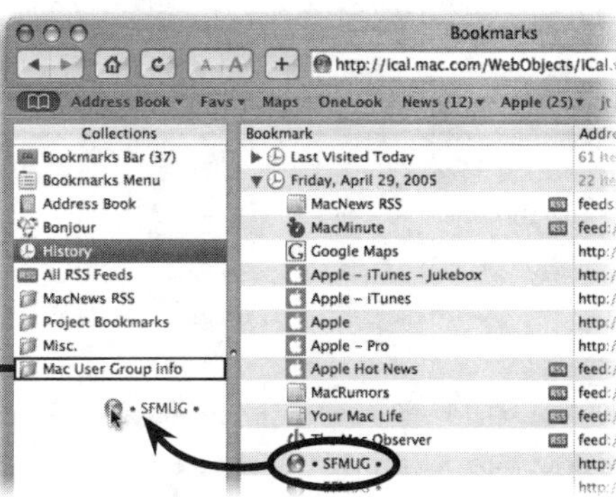

To save any History page as a permanent bookmark, *drag it from the right side of the Bookmarks Library and drop it into a folder in the Collections pane.*

Import bookmarks from other browsers

If you've been using Internet Explorer, Netscape Navigator, or Mozilla as your browser, their bookmarks are automatically imported the first time you open Safari. You'll find them in the Collections pane, labeled as "imported" bookmarks. At least, that's the way it's supposed to work. If your other browser bookmarks didn't get imported, or if later you want to import bookmarks from another browser, it's still pretty easy.

1. From Safari's File menu, choose "Import Bookmarks…" to open the "Import Bookmarks" window.
2. Click "Applications" in the Sidebar, then find the browser whose bookmarks you want to import. If that browser's icon is dimmed and not accessible, as shown below, use this window to navigate to the folder that contains the browser's bookmarks.

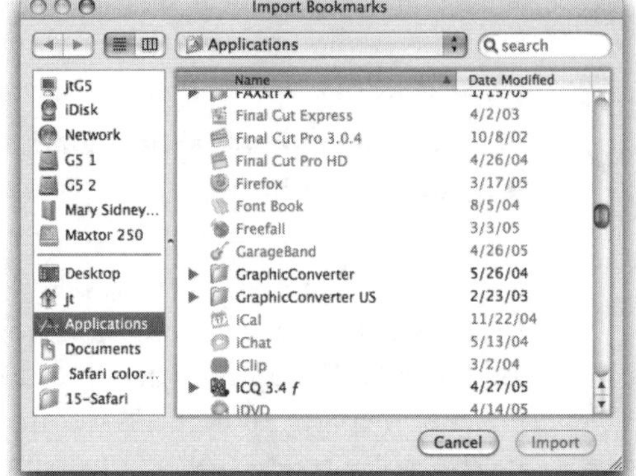

The example below is in Column view so you can see clearly the path to the bookmarks file.

- Click your Home Folder icon in the Sidebar ("jt" in this case).
- Open the "Library" folder, then open "Application Support," then open the browser folder you want. Keep digging until you find the sub-folder that contains a "bookmarks.html" file. Select it and click the "Import" button.

The Column view gives a clear picture of the path to a file.

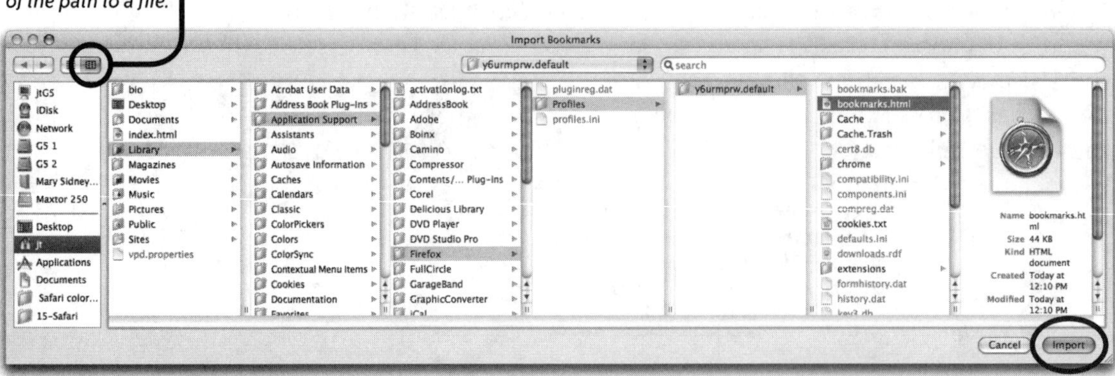

The highlighted items show the path to the "bookmarks.html" file.

Another way to import bookmarks from another browser is to first use the other browser's "export" command. Open the other browser to see if its File menu contains an "Export Bookmarks" command. If so, choose it and save the exported file to the Desktop (or anywhere on your computer). The exported file is named "bookmarks.html" (shown on the right). Then, from Safari, choose "Import Bookmarks…" and choose the exported file. The newly imported bookmarks appear as a Collections folder in the Collections pane, named "imported" and includes the import date ("imported 5/1/05" for instance—shown below).

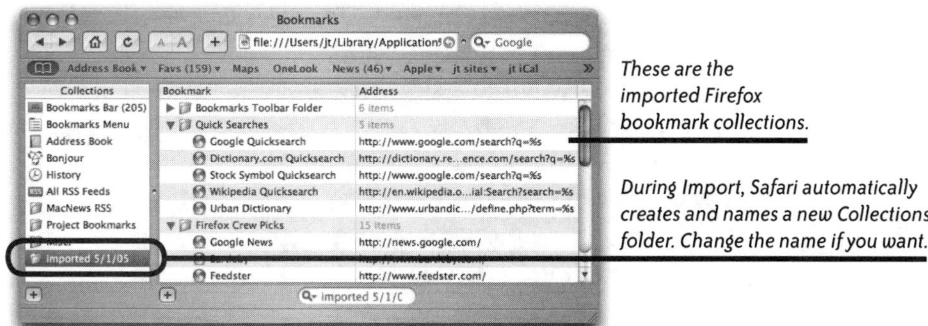

These are the imported Firefox bookmark collections.
During Import, Safari automatically creates and names a new Collections folder. Change the name if you want.

One more way to import bookmarks is to *drag-and-drop*.

1. Find the browser's bookmarks file in the same sub-folder of the "Applications Support" folder shown on the previous page.
2. Drag the "bookmarks.html" file on top of the Safari application icon in the Dock to open an HTML file of bookmark links (below-right) in a new Safari window.
3. Create a new folder in the Collections pane ("Firefox Bookmarks" in this example) and make sure it's selected.
4. Drag links from the HTML page (below right) to the Bookmarks Library (below left).

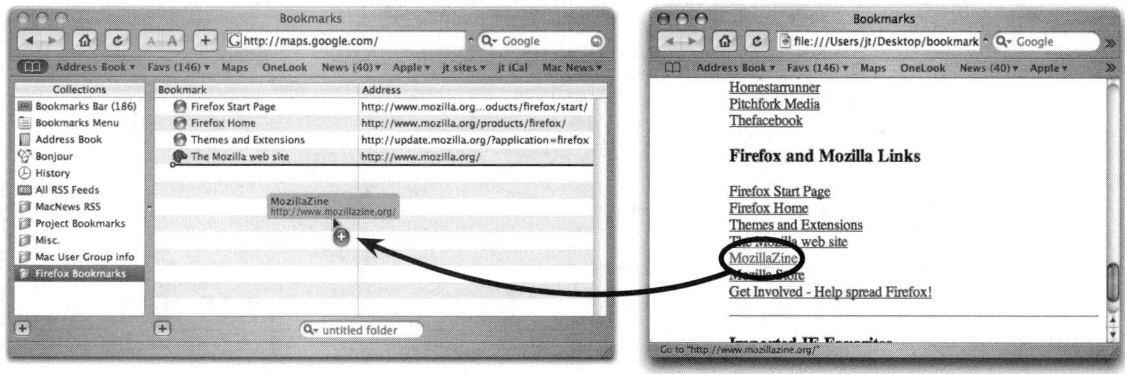

RSS—Information at a Glance

The web technology known as RSS (Really Simple Syndication) is proving to be extremely popular with people who want to browse a lot of information quickly and easily. Before Safari RSS, it was necessary to download a separate application that could collect and read RSS feeds. Now it's just built in to Safari and easier than ever. And, as usual, because the Mac is doing it, it's going to get even bigger.

Major news organizations, special interest sites, and personal weblogs offer headlines and story summaries as RSS news feeds. Safari includes a collection of RSS news feeds to get you started. You can quickly browse through RSS headlines and summaries, rather than visiting dozens of web sites looking for the latest news. If you see a story that interests you, a single click jumps you right to the story's web page.

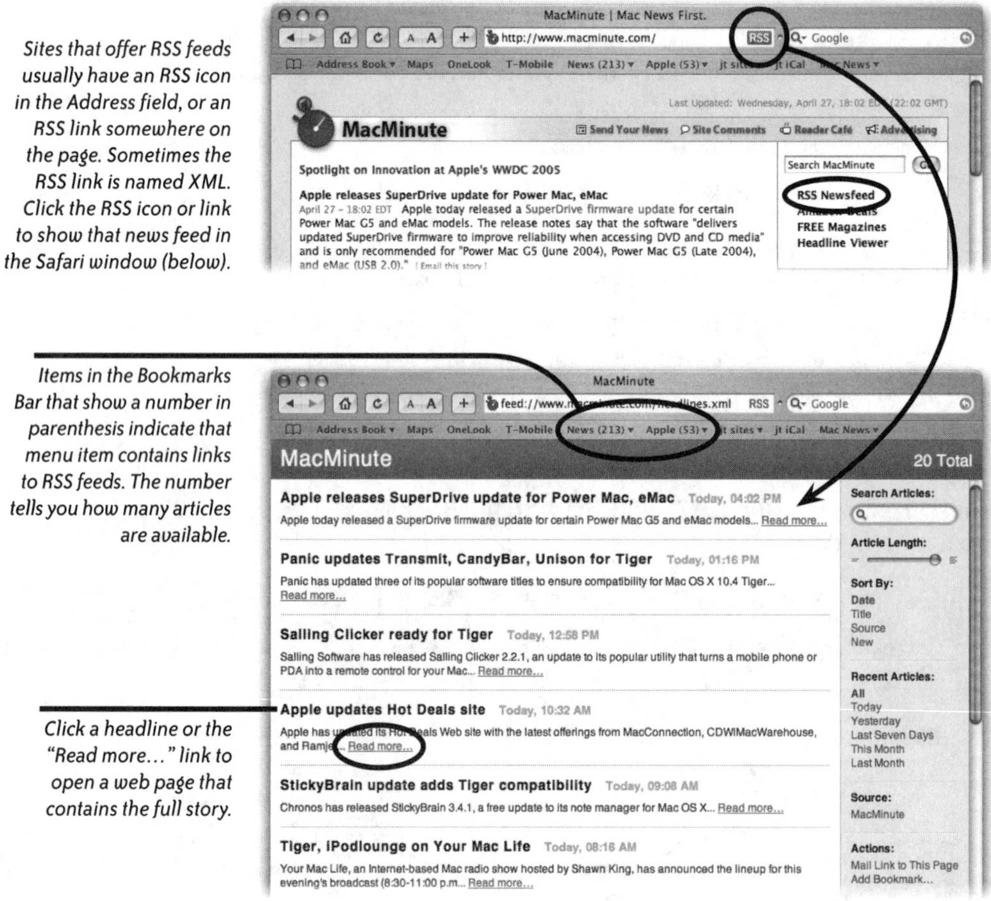

Sites that offer RSS feeds usually have an RSS icon in the Address field, or an RSS link somewhere on the page. Sometimes the RSS link is named XML. Click the RSS icon or link to show that news feed in the Safari window (below).

Items in the Bookmarks Bar that show a number in parenthesis indicate that menu item contains links to RSS feeds. The number tells you how many articles are available.

Click a headline or the "Read more..." link to open a web page that contains the full story.

Open RSS feeds from the Bookmarks Bar

Safari's Bookmarks Bar includes a couple of menus that already contain bookmarks to RSS feeds so you can see how they work. Click on the "News" item or the "Apple" item to open its pop-up menu. The bookmarks in the menu that have a "page" icon and a number in parenthesis connect to news feeds. The number tells you how many *new* articles are available since you last opened that news feed page. In the example below, after we open the "Apple Hot News (2)" page, the "(2)" disappears and the Bookmarks Bar menu changes to "Apple (57)." Of course, since news feeds are coming in all the time, this number changes often.

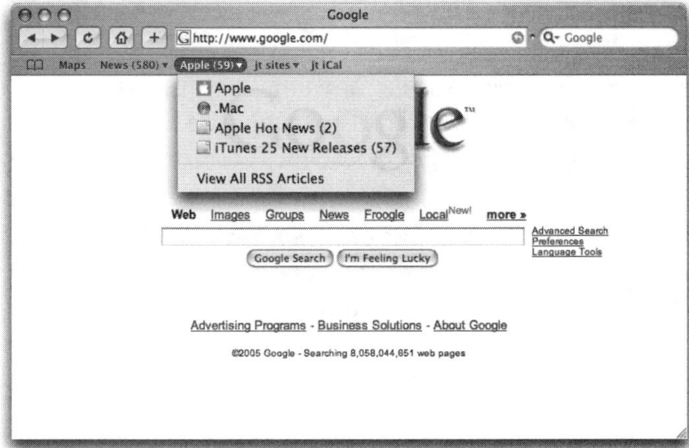

View all RSS articles

When a Bookmarks Bar menu contains RSS feeds, the last item in the pop-up menu is "View All RSS Articles," as shown above. Choose it to open all RSS stories that are available from that menu in one page.

To prevent the list of articles from a news feed from gettng too large and unwieldly, go to Safari's RSS Preferences and set how often to remove articles. The RSS pane of Safari Preferences also provides a "Remove Now" button. See details about RSS Preferences on page 393.

Bookmark favorite RSS feeds

You can create your own RSS Collections. A Collection is really just a folder in Safari's Collections pane. Click the *open book* icon in the Bookmarks Bar to show the Bookmarks Library—a window that includes the Collections pane on the left and a large pane on the right showing the bookmarks contained in the *selected* Collection.

Tip: Bookmark an RSS page to automatically receive new articles from that news feed.

1. Create a new folder in the Collections pane (click the *plus* button below the pane) and name it something that reflects the type of news feeds you plan to add to your new Collection—such as "MacNews RSS." Or you may want to collect a diverse group of news feeds and name it "RSS Favs" or "Daily News."
2. In Safari, go to a web site that contains RSS news feeds. Click the RSS icon in the Address field (left, top) to open the site's RSS page. If the web site has an RSS link or an XML link somewhere on its page, you can click that instead. An RSS page of headlines and article summaries opens, shown below.

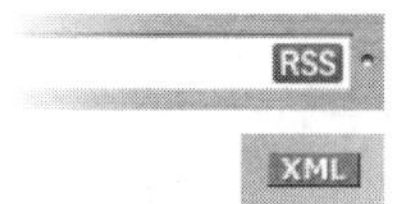

XML (Extensible Markup Language) is similar to RSS.

3. Click the Add Bookmark button (the *plus sign* circled below) to open the Bookmark sheet. Name the bookmark, then from the pop-up menu choose the folder you just created. Or choose any other folder in pop-up menu that you want to use.

*Instead of clicking an RSS link (which opens an RSS page) you can **Control-click** an RSS link. From the pop-up menu choose "Add Link to Bookmarks...." The Bookmarks sheet shown on the right opens.*

4. If you'd like for this new Collection to appear in Safari's Bookmarks Bar, open the Bookmarks Library (click the *open book* icon circled on the right).

   Click the "Bookmarks Bar" Collection in the Collections pane (highlighted at the top of the Collections list) to show its contents on the right. Drag your new Collection folder to the pane on the right.

   Now your Collection appears in the Bookmarks Bar.

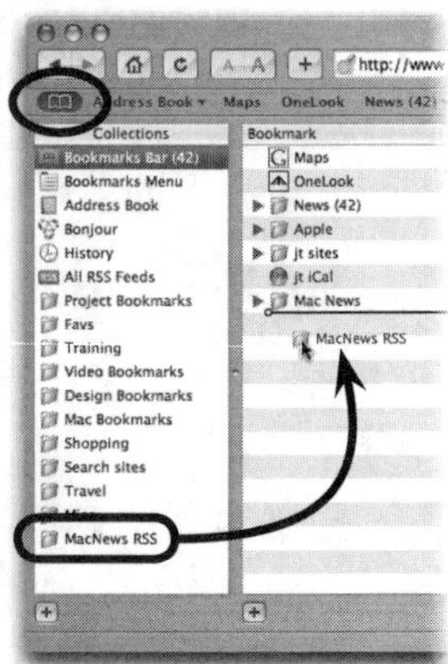

Customize the RSS information display

When you go to an RSS news feed page, Safari adds a column on the right containing controls and options that let you display the information in a way that works best for you.

- Search the articles on an RSS page. Type a keyword or phrase in the **Search Articles** field. As you type, the article list shows only articles whose headline or text contain the words you're typing.
- If you want to see more or less of an article summary, you can adjust it here. Drag the **Article Length** slider left to see less summary text, to the right to see more. Drag all the way left to show only headlines. The maximum amount of text that can be shown varies for different RSS sites, depending on how many news feeds are being displayed.
- Sort the articles on the page by selecting one of the items in the **Sort By** category.
- From the **Recent Articles** category, choose how recent you want the displayed articles to be.
- The **Source** item tells you where the news feeds are coming from. Click the source name to jump to that web site.
- In the **Actions** category, click "Mail Link to This Page" to send an email to someone with this RSS address automatically placed in the message. If you haven't yet bookmarked this RSS page, the "Actions" item also contains an "Add Bookmark…" link (shown below-right). Click "Add Bookmark…" to open the drop-down sheet shown on the previous page.

New articles have organge-colored dates (you can set the color used for new articles in Safari Preferences). Older articles, or articles you've read, have gray-colored dates.

A Bookmark link is added to the "Actions" items if the page has not been bookmarked.

View all RSS feeds

To see all RSS feeds, the name of the Collection a feed is stored in, and its web address, open the Bookmarks Library (shown below).

1. Click the Bookmarks icon in the Bookmarks Bar (circled below). If the Bookmarks Bar is not showing, from the View menu choose "Show Bookmarks Bar." **Or** from the Bookmarks menu choose "Show All Bookmarks."
2. In the Collections pane, select "All RSS Feeds." All of your RSS feeds are shown in the results pane on the right. The first column ("Bookmark") shows the Bookmark name for the feed. The second column ("Parent") shows the Parent name, the name of the Collection (the folder) that a feed is in. The third column ("Address") gives the full web address of the RSS news feed.

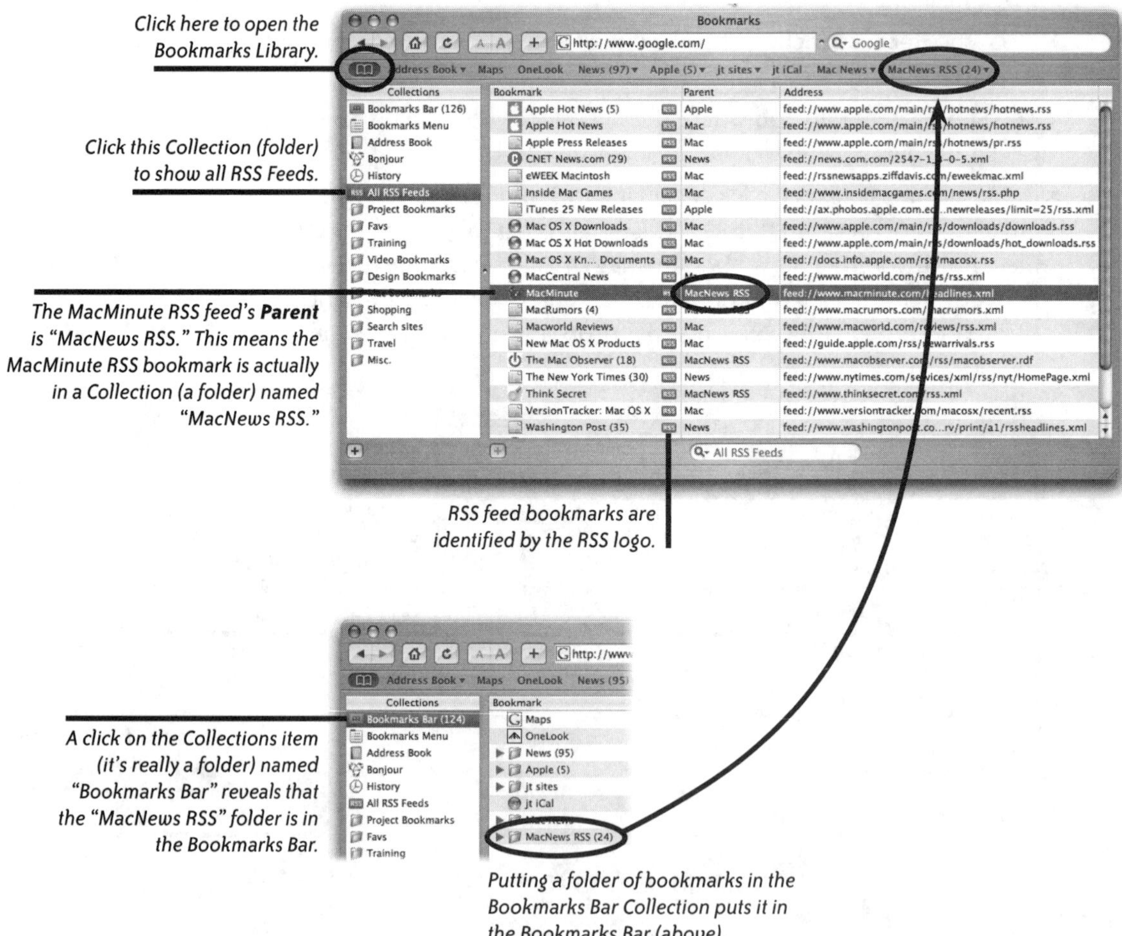

Click here to open the Bookmarks Library.
Click this Collection (folder) to show all RSS Feeds.
The MacMinute RSS feed's **Parent** is "MacNews RSS." This means the MacMinute RSS bookmark is actually in a Collection (a folder) named "MacNews RSS."
RSS feed bookmarks are identified by the RSS logo.
A click on the Collections item (it's really a folder) named "Bookmarks Bar" reveals that the "MacNews RSS" folder is in the Bookmarks Bar.
Putting a folder of bookmarks in the Bookmarks Bar Collection puts it in the Bookmarks Bar (above).

RSS preferences

Safari's Preferences includes special settings just for RSS. From the Safari menu, choose "Preferences...." Click the "RSS" button in the Preferences toolbar to open the window shown below.

- **Default RSS Reader:** Choose Safari unless you've installed some other RSS reader that you prefer. Any other RSS readers that are installed appear in the pop-up menu.
- **Automatically update articles in:** Choose if you want to automatically update RSS feeds that you have in the Bookmarks Bar or the Bookmarks menu.

- **Check for updates:** From the pop-up menu, choose how often you want rss feeds to automatically update. Choose "Never" if you want to update manually.
- **Color new articles:** Choose a color from the pop-up menu to alert you that an article is new. If you don't like any of the color choices, choose "Other..." to open a color swatch palette and create just the color you want.
- **Remove articles:** From the pop-up menu choose how long before older articles are deleted.
- **Remove Now.** Click the "Remove Now" button to immediately delete all RSS articles.

Turn RSS headlines into a Screen Saver

Tired of the usual pretty picture screen savers? Let the current headlines animate across your screen for a screen saver.

1. In System Preferences, click the "Desktop & Screen Saver" icon.
2. Click the "Screen Saver" button, then from the pane on the left, choose "RSS Visualizer."
3. Click the "Options..." button to choose which RSS feed is used to display headlines in the screen saver.

Amazingly cool—try it!

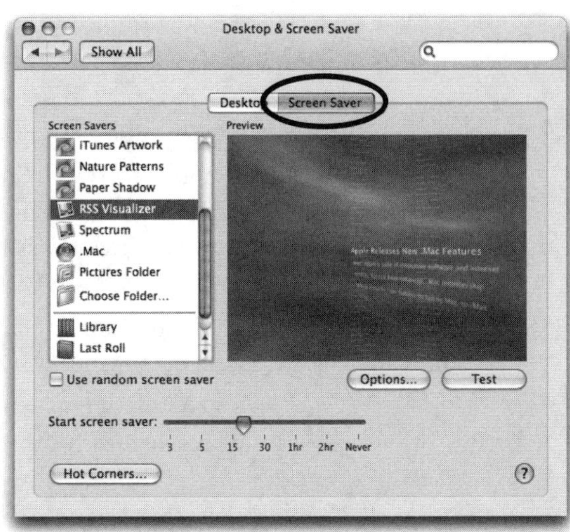

This is the SnapBack button you'll often see in the Address field or in the Google field.

SnapBack

The **SnapBack** button is a great feature. How often have you gone to a page you enjoyed, wandered off the path into the wilderness of the Internet, then tried to find that original page again? SnapBack can take you right back to where you started, no matter how many pages you visited in-between.

These are the ways to use SnapBack:

1. **In the Google search field:** When you do a search in Google, the search results page is marked as the SnapBack page. If you then wander through four or five other pages, the SnapBack button in the Google field takes you back to that *first* page of search results.

You won't see the SnapBack button in the Google search field until you clink a link that takes you to another page.

As soon as you leave a SnapBack page (the search results page above-top), the SnapBack button appears. It will stay there, linked to the SnapBack page, until you set new SnapBack page by entering a new web address in the Address field, click a bookmark, or choose a page from the History menu.

If you open different windows to use Google, the SnapBack button in each window will return you to the search results for that window.

If a link opens in a *new* window, you lose the SnapBack because it belongs with the original window.

2. **In the Address field:** When you type a new URL (web address) in the Address field, SnapBack is applied to that page.

3. **Choose a bookmark:** When you click a bookmark, that page gets marked as a SnapBack page.
4. **Choose a page from the History menu:** When you choose a visited page listed in the History menu, it's marked as a SnapBack page.
5. **Open a new window:** When you open a new Safari window, that page becomes a SnapBack page.
6. **Assign SnapBack to a page from the History menu:** You can mark any page that's open in Safari as the SnapBack page. From the History menu choose "Mark Page for SnapBack."

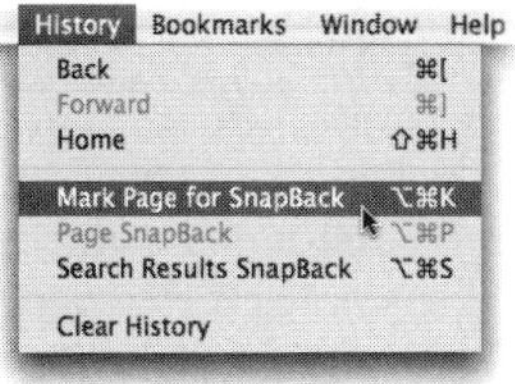

Mark any page as a SnapBack page.

Use Auto-Click to open RSS bookmarks in a single tab

If you have a combination of regular bookmarks and RSS feed bookmarks in a Bookmarks Bar folder, as shown circled on the right, you may want to enable Auto-Click Tabbed Browsing so that regular sites in the folder appear as tabs in the Bookmarks Bar, and all RSS feeds are put in a single tab (below-right).

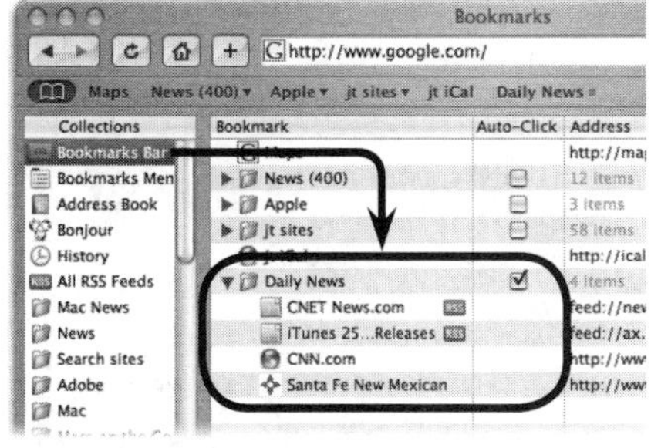

1. In the Tabs pane of Safari Preferences, choose "Enable Tabbed Browsing."

2. In the Bookmarks Library, check the box next to the folder for which you want to enable Auto-Click.
3. The Bookmarks item in the Bookmarks Bar now shows a tiny square next to it (instead of a tiny triangle) to indicate that it's an Auto-Click item.

A small square indicates that Auto-Click is enabled.

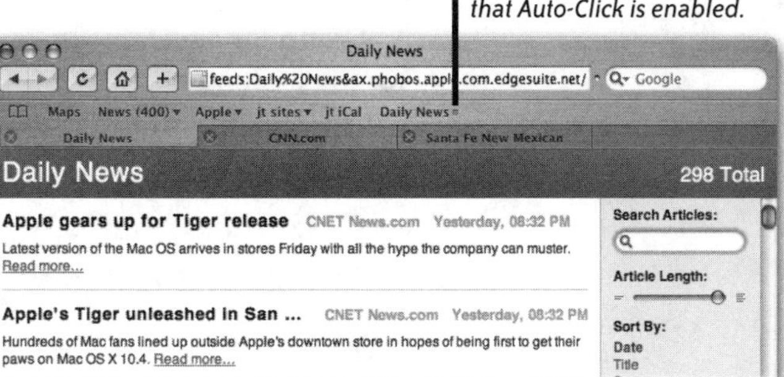

Tabbed Browsing

Safari has a feature you can turn on or off called **Tabbed Browsing.** When Tabbed Browsing is turned on (in Safari Preferences; see the next page), you can choose to have a number of pages open in the same window instead of separate windows; each page is accessible by clicking a tab, as shown below. One advantage of Tabbed Browsing is that pages can load in the background while you peruse other pages.

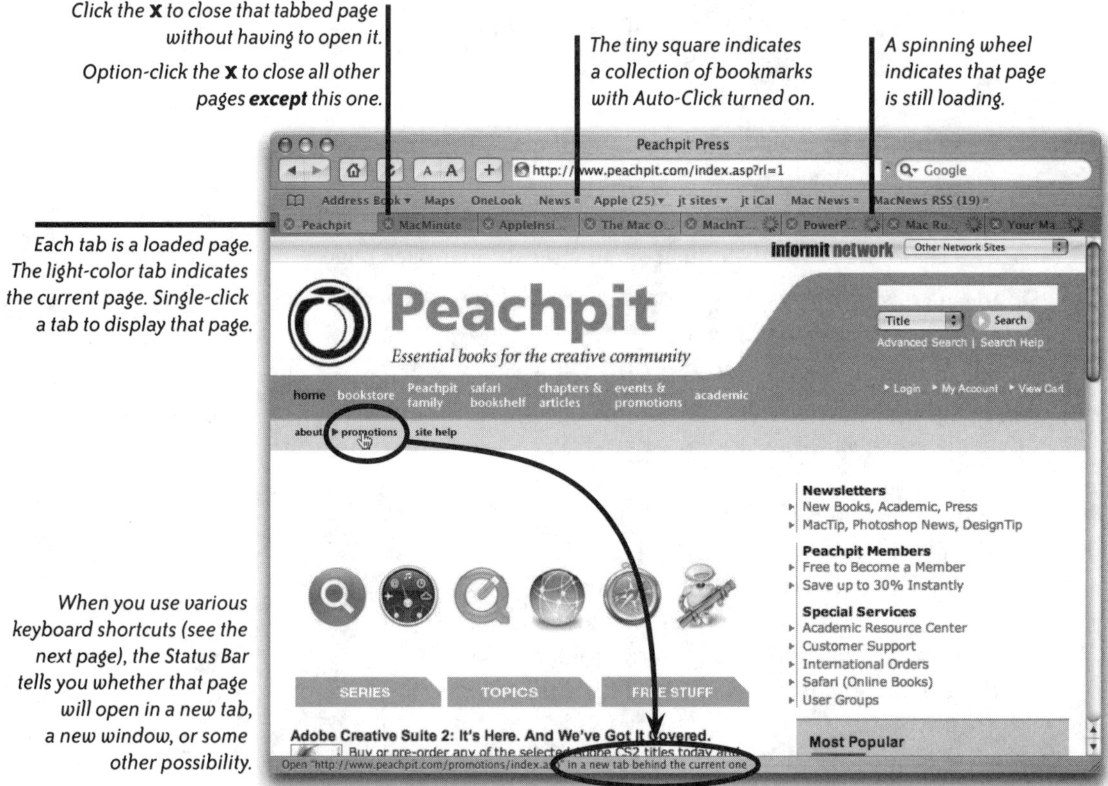

Click the **X** to close that tabbed page without having to open it.
Option-click the **X** to close all other pages **except** this one.
The tiny square indicates a collection of bookmarks with Auto-Click turned on.
A spinning wheel indicates that page is still loading.
Each tab is a loaded page. The light-color tab indicates the current page. Single-click a tab to display that page.
When you use various keyboard shortcuts (see the next page), the Status Bar tells you whether that page will open in a new tab, a new window, or some other possibility.
Peachpit Press
Peachpit
Essential books for the creative community
Open "http://www.peachpit.com/promotions/index.asp" in a new tab behind the current one

When you click on a link, the new page that opens **replaces** the one you are currently looking at—it does not automatically create a new tabbed page. Command-click a link to open it in a new tab (a new tab is added to the Bookmarks Bar).

If you have enabled Tabbed Browsing, and you want to open a link in a new Safari window instead of a tab, press Command Option click. Also see the tips on page 399.

Preferences for Tabbed Browsing

Go to the Safari menu and choose "Preferences...." Click the "Tabs" button so you can turn on Tabbed Browsing and make some choices about how to work with it. Notice in the preferences windows below that the keyboard shortcuts change depending on whether or not you choose the option to "Select new tabs as they are created."

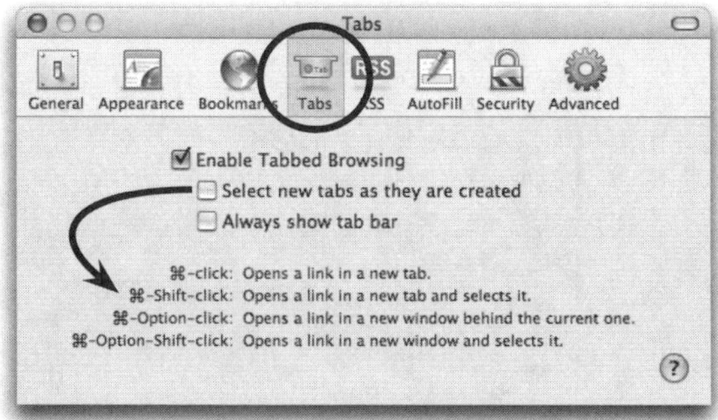

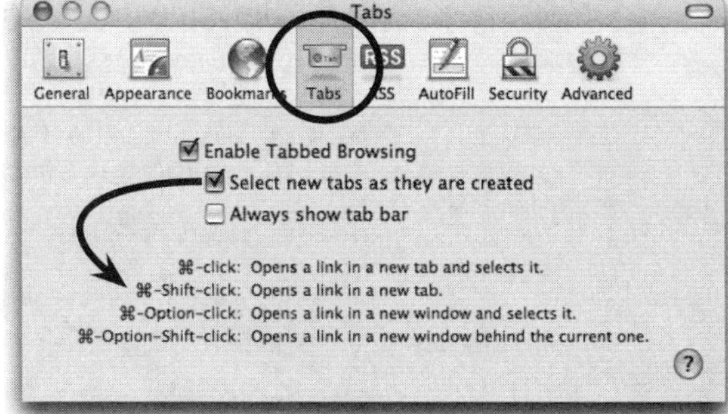

- **Enable Tabbed Browsing:** This turns the feature on or off.
- **Select new tabs as they are created:** With this checked, as soon as you create a tabbed page (Command-click on a link), Safari will display that window instead of hiding it in the row of tabs.
- **Always show Tab bar:** This makes the Tab bar visible whether or not you have a tabbed page open.

  If this is unchecked, the Tab bar appears only when you have more than one page chosen as a tabbed page or when you click on a *folder* in your Bookmarks Bar that is set to open as tabbed pages.

  If this is checked, the Tab bar is always visible in your window, even if there is only one tab in which all your pages open, as shown below.

If you choose to always show the Tab bar, you will always see at least one tab.

Every page (except Auto-Click enabled pages) will open in this one tab.

Learn about Auto-Click on the next page.

The Auto-Click feature

If you have a slow dial-up connection, it's not a good idea to open a lot of links with Auto-Click because your connection will have to go to every page (in a tab) and load it.

If you have put Collections (folders) of bookmarks in your Bookmarks Bar, you can set them to **Auto-Click.** This means when you single-click on an Auto-Click item in the Bookmarks Bar, every bookmarked page in that collection will open as a tab in the tab bar.

You will know if a Collection has been set to Auto-Click because the tiny triangle you would normally see next to a collection in the Bookmarks Bar changes to a tiny square.

Command-click any single bookmark in the Bookmarks Bar (or on a web page) to open that link in a new tab.

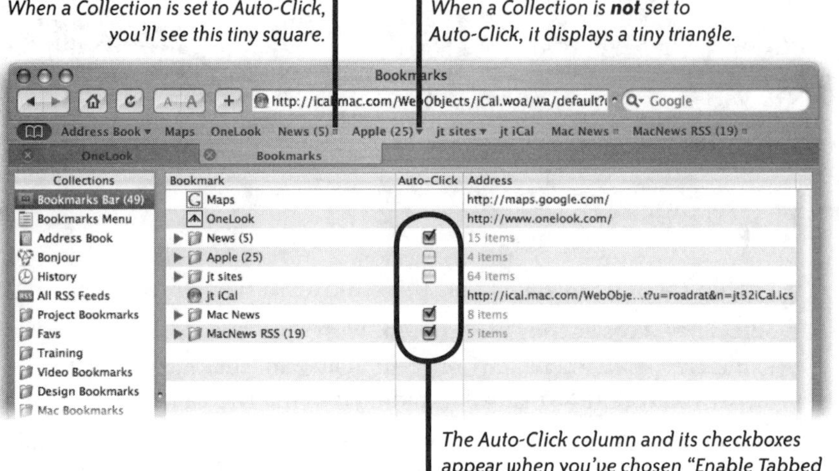

When a Collection is set to Auto-Click, you'll see this tiny square.

*When a Collection is **not** set to Auto-Click, it displays a tiny triangle.*

The Auto-Click column and its checkboxes appear when you've chosen "Enable Tabbed Browsing" in the Tabs pane of Safari Preferences.

To set a Collection (a folder of bookmarks) to Auto-Click:

1. Make sure you have enabled "Tabbed Browsing" in the Safari preferences, as described on the previous page.
2. Click the *open book* icon in the Bookmarks Bar to open the Bookmarks Library. (If the Bookmarks Bar is not showing, press Command B to make it visible, or choose "Bookmarks Bar" from the View menu.)
3. If you don't have a folder of bookmarks, create one: Click the Plus button beneath the Collections pane, name the Collection, Click the Bookmarks Bar item in the Collections pane, then drag the new Collection folder into the pane on the right.
4. In the Collections pane on the left, single-click "Bookmarks Bar." This will display, on the right, all the links you have put into your Bookmarks Bar, as shown above.
5. Only folders have checkboxes in the Auto-Click column. Simply click a checkbox to turn on Auto-Click for that Collection.

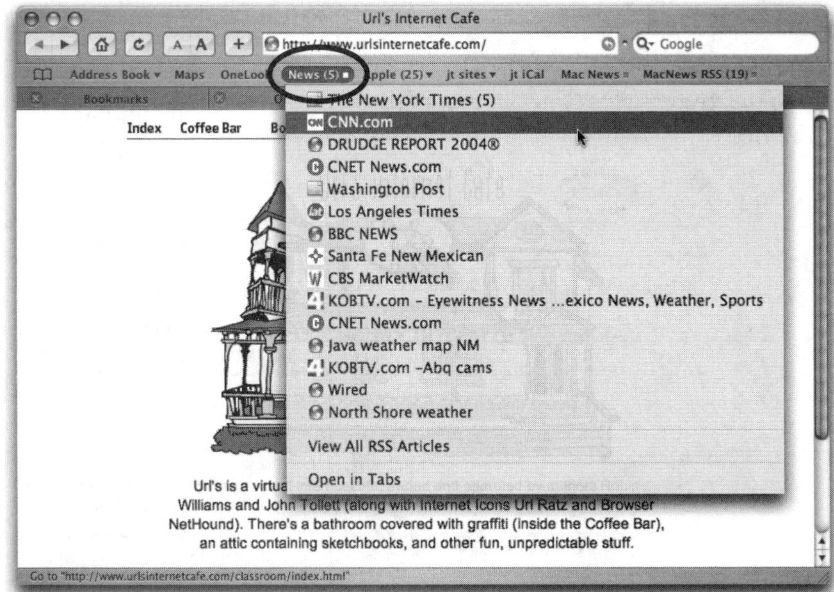

To open just one bookmark *in a Collection that is set to Auto-Click,* ***Option-click*** *the item in the Bookmarks Bar to open a pop-up menu of the individual bookmarks in the Collection.*

Tabbed Browsing tips

- You can Control-click (or right-click) any Collection in the Bookmarks Library (click the *open book* icon in the Bookmarks Bar) to open a pop-up menu and choose "Open in Tabs."
- If Tabbed Browsing is enabled, when you click on links in other applications, such as in an email program or on a PDF, that link will open in a new tab in the existing window.
- To open a new page in a new tab, press Command T, then type the URL in the Address field that appears. **Or** go to the File menu and choose "New Tab."
- If you choose a page from your Bookmarks or History list, the page opens in whatever tab is showing on your screen. If you want it to open in its own tab, first press Command T, *then* choose the page.
- Each tab has its own memory for the Back and Forward buttons. This means you can go to any number of pages in each tabbed window and go Back and Forward through those pages.
- To close a tab, click its Close button (the "x" in the tab).
- To open the web page in a tab and close all other tabs, Option-click the Close button in the tab you want to remain open.

Safari Preferences

Most preferences for Safari are self-explanatory. Click a button in the toolbar to open the preferences pane for that particular item. Each preference pane is identified by its highlighted button and by the name in the title bar.

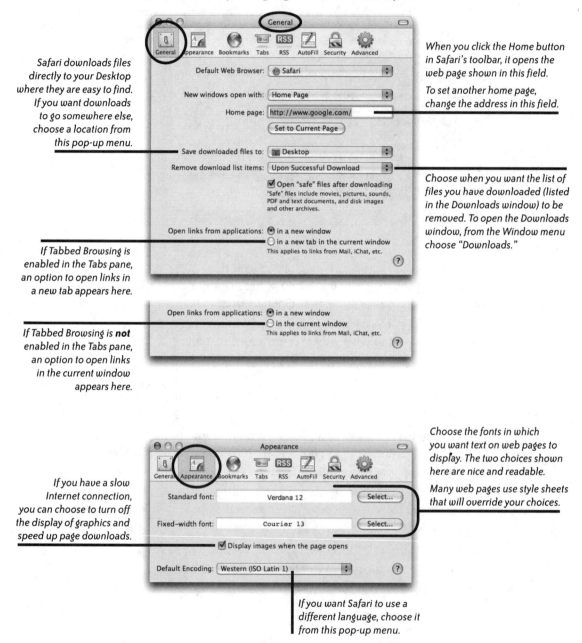

Safari downloads files directly to your Desktop where they are easy to find. If you want downloads to go somewhere else, choose a location from this pop-up menu.

General
General
Appearance
Bookmarks
Tabs
RSS
AutoFill
Security
Advanced
Default Web Browser:
Safari
New windows open with:
Home Page
Home page:
http://www.google.com/
Set to Current Page
Save downloaded files to:
Desktop
Remove download list items:
Upon Successful Download
Open "safe" files after downloading
"Safe" files include movies, pictures, sounds, PDF and text documents, and disk images and other archives.
Open links from applications:
in a new window
in a new tab in the current window
This applies to links from Mail, iChat, etc.

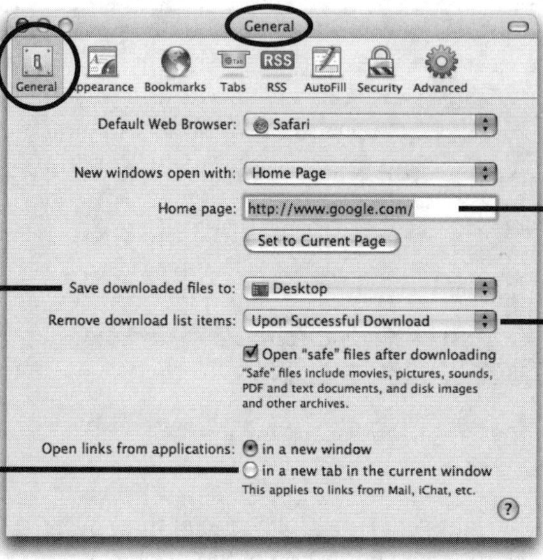

When you click the Home button in Safari's toolbar, it opens the web page shown in this field.

To set another home page, change the address in this field.

Choose when you want the list of files you have downloaded (listed in the Downloads window) to be removed. To open the Downloads window, from the Window menu choose "Downloads."

If Tabbed Browsing is enabled in the Tabs pane, an option to open links in a new tab appears here.

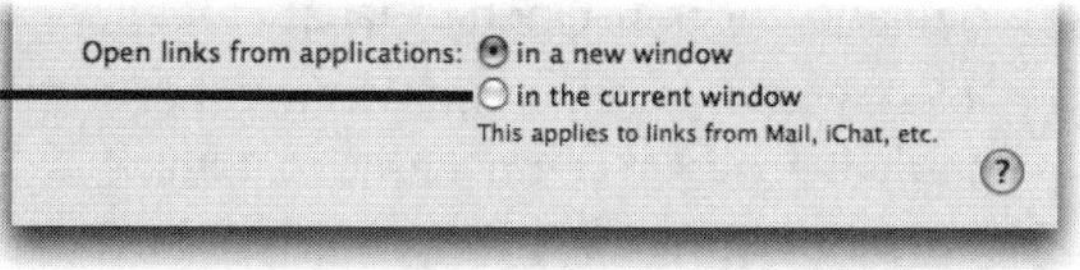

Open links from applications:
in a new window
in the current window
This applies to links from Mail, iChat, etc.

If Tabbed Browsing is ***not*** *enabled in the Tabs pane, an option to open links in the current window appears here.*

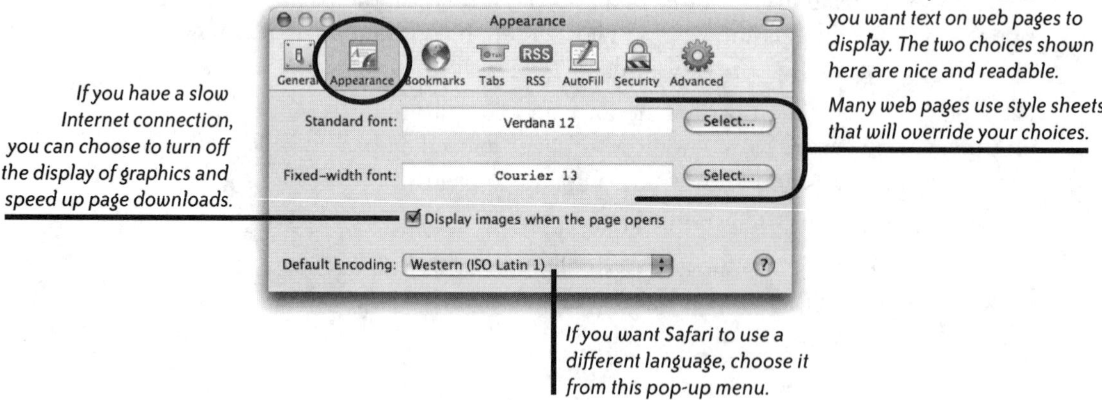

Choose the fonts in which you want text on web pages to display. The two choices shown here are nice and readable.

Many web pages use style sheets that will override your choices.

If you have a slow Internet connection, you can choose to turn off the display of graphics and speed up page downloads.

Appearance
General
Appearance
Bookmarks
Tabs
RSS
AutoFill
Security
Advanced
Standard font:
Verdana 12
Select...
Fixed-width font:
Courier 13
Select...
Display images when the page opens
Default Encoding:
Western (ISO Latin 1)

If you want Safari to use a different language, choose it from this pop-up menu.

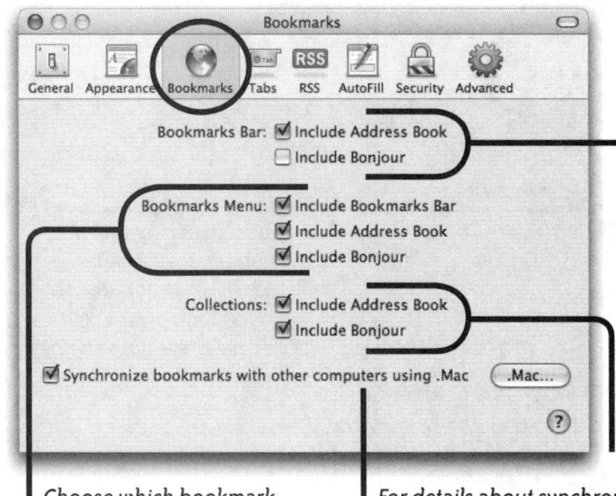

Address Book and Bonjour in the Bookmarks Bar.

When you choose to put bookmarks from these items in the Bookmarks Bar (shown above), web addresses from your Address Book appear in the Address Book pop-up menu and web addresses on your local network (for printers, routers, or webcam setup and administration) appear in the Bonjour pop-up menu.

Bonjour automatically discovers and configures network connections. See Chapter 17 to learn about Bonjour.

Choose whether or not to include Address Book or Bonjour as Collections in the Collections pane of the Bookmarks Library.

Choose which bookmark items you want to appear in the Bookmarks menu (in the menu bar at the top of your screen).

For details about synchronizing your bookmarks with your .Mac account, see Chapter 11, iSync.

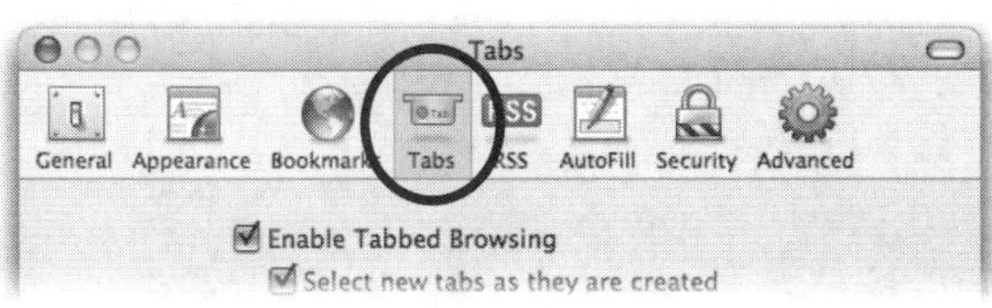

The Tabs preferences are explained on page 397.

The RSS preferences are explained on page 393.

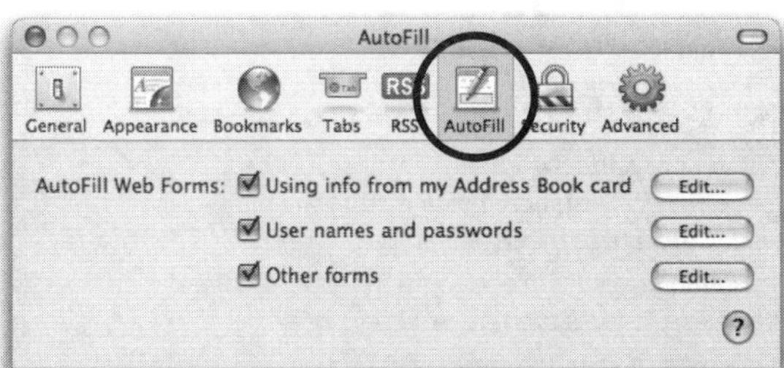

***AutoFill** automatically fills out web page forms using the personal contact information from your Address Book.*

*Click the **Edit buttons** to edit the information in your Address Book card, or to delete any web sites that you have told Safari to AutoFill.*

*If you choose "User names and passwords" and later fill out a form on a web page, Safari asks if you want AutoFill to remember this information for you. You can choose "Never for this Website," "Not Now," or "Yes." If you choose "Yes," the **next** time you go to that site, Safari fills in the name and password. Only choose this option if no one else uses your computer!*

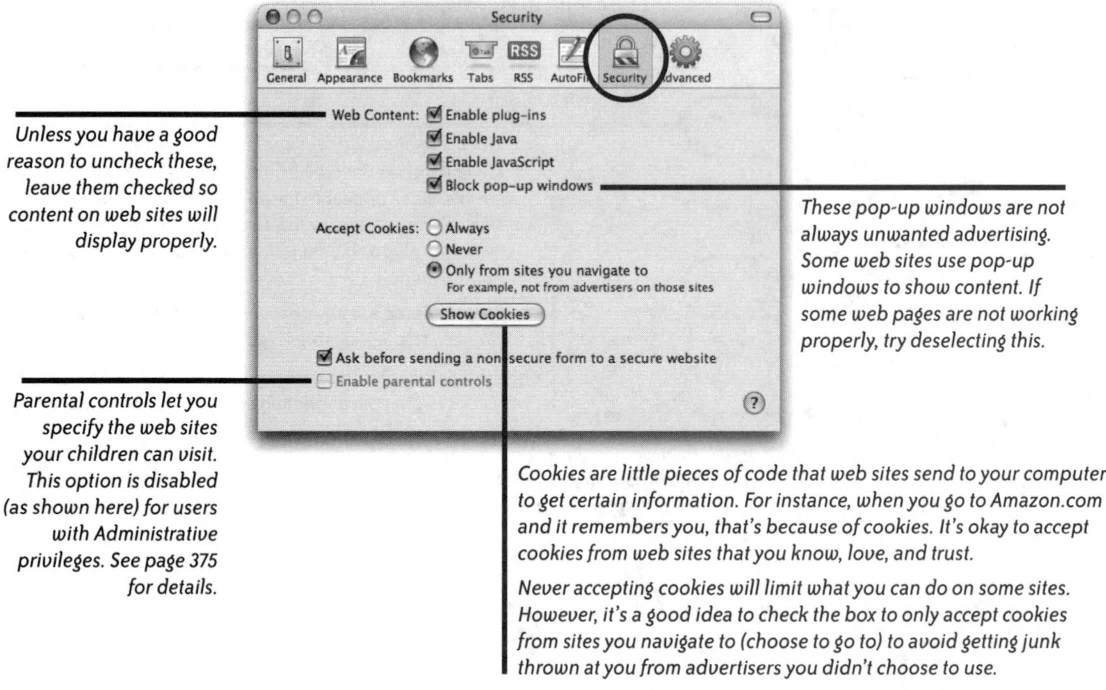

Unless you have a good reason to uncheck these, leave them checked so content on web sites will display properly.

These pop-up windows are not always unwanted advertising. Some web sites use pop-up windows to show content. If some web pages are not working properly, try deselecting this.

Parental controls let you specify the web sites your children can visit. This option is disabled (as shown here) for users with Administrative privileges. See page 375 for details.

Cookies are little pieces of code that web sites send to your computer to get certain information. For instance, when you go to Amazon.com and it remembers you, that's because of cookies. It's okay to accept cookies from web sites that you know, love, and trust.

Never accepting cookies will limit what you can do on some sites. However, it's a good idea to check the box to only accept cookies from sites you navigate to (choose to go to) to avoid getting junk thrown at you from advertisers you didn't choose to use.

__Universal Access__ can help people who have physical difficulties with web pages.

This option will try to make all text larger on the screen.

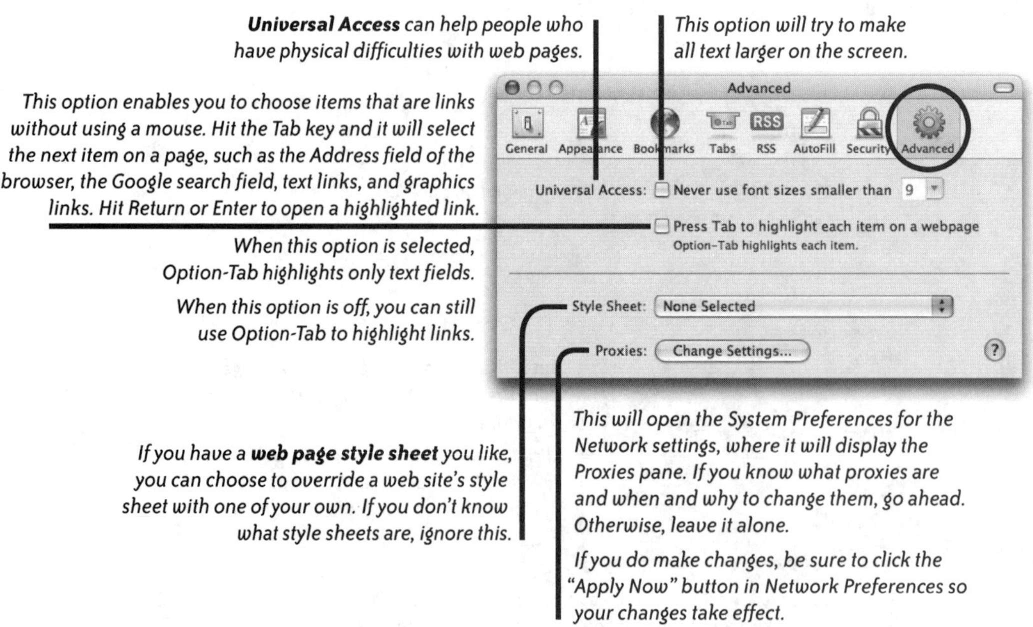

This option enables you to choose items that are links without using a mouse. Hit the Tab key and it will select the next item on a page, such as the Address field of the browser, the Google search field, text links, and graphics links. Hit Return or Enter to open a highlighted link.

When this option is selected, Option-Tab highlights only text fields.

When this option is off, you can still use Option-Tab to highlight links.

If you have a __web page style sheet__ you like, you can choose to override a web site's style sheet with one of your own. If you don't know what style sheets are, ignore this.

This will open the System Preferences for the Network settings, where it will display the Proxies pane. If you know what proxies are and when and why to change them, go ahead. Otherwise, leave it alone.

If you do make changes, be sure to click the "Apply Now" button in Network Preferences so your changes take effect.

Print a Web Page

Printing a web page is like printing any other document, but there are a couple of special Safari settings you'll find useful.

To print a web page:

1. Select "Print..." from the File menu. A sheet drops down from Safari's title bar (shown below).
2. The bottom pop-up menu is by default set on "Copies & Pages." Type in the number of copies you want to print.

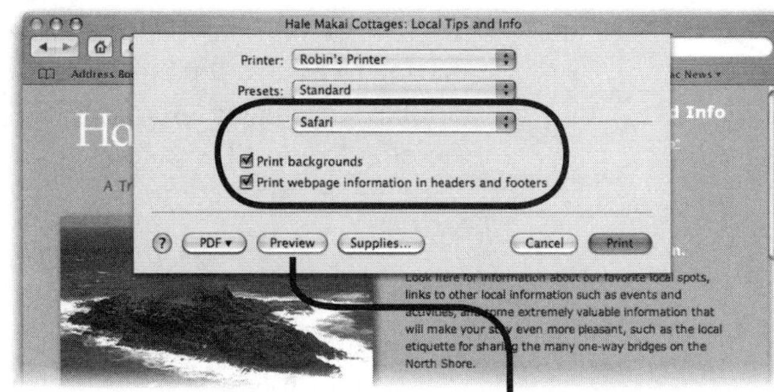

Click "Preview" to see how the page will look when printed.

When the preview PDF opens, click the "Soft Proof" checkbox to simulate how the page will look when printed by the selected printer (color or grayscale).

3. From the "Copies & Pages" pop-up menu, choose "Safari." A couple of nice options are hidden here.
4. Deselect "Print backgrounds" if the web page has a complex background that could slow down printing or make the page text difficult to read. Turning off this option can also conserve your printer's ink or toner.
5. Select "Print webpage information in headers and footers" to add the web page address, page title, date, and time to the printed document. Very helpful later when you want to know where this page came from, or how long ago it was printed.
6. Click the "Print" button.

Save PDF in Receipts Folder

When you buy something online, do you have to turn on the printer and wait for it to warm up so you can print that page that says "Print this page for your records?" Instead of *printing* a web receipt when you buy something online, just save it as a PDF that's automatically placed in a "Web Recepts" folder in your Documents folder.

1. In the Print drop-down sheet (shown right), click the PDF button to open a pop-up menu.
2. From the pop-up menu choose "Save PDF to Web Receipts Folder."
3. Click the "Print" button.

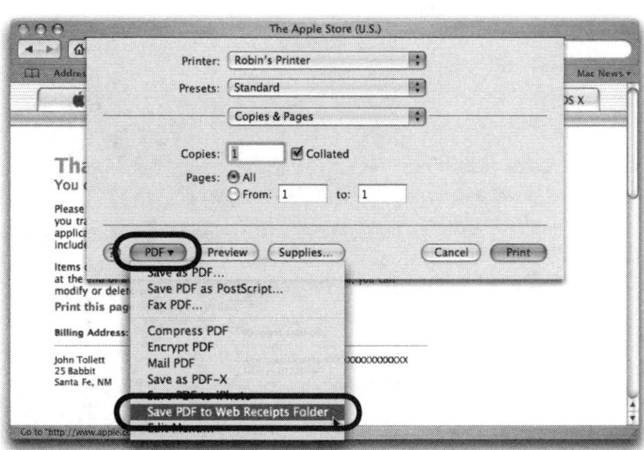

View PDFs Directly in Safari

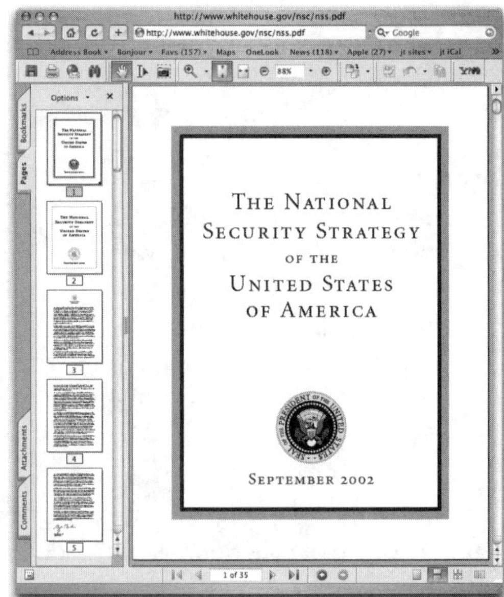

Now when you click a PDF file in Safari, the file opens directly in the Safari without having to open a separate application, such as Adobe Acrobat Reader. The Safari window provides controls and tools for viewing the file.

- Hover the pointer over a tool to see a pop-up description of that tool.
- Control-click on the PDF toolbar to add or remove tools.
- Control-click on a PDF page for more options.

Add a Web Page Image to iPhoto

Safari makes it easy to place web page photos (or graphics) in iPhoto. Since you wouldn't dream of doing anything with images that would violate copyrights, here's how you can do it.

1. Control-click on a web page image to open a contextual menu.
2. From the pop-up menu choose "Add Image to iPhoto Library." iPhoto opens automatically and imports the photo.

As you can see, the contextual pop-up menu also provides other choices of things you can do with a web page image.

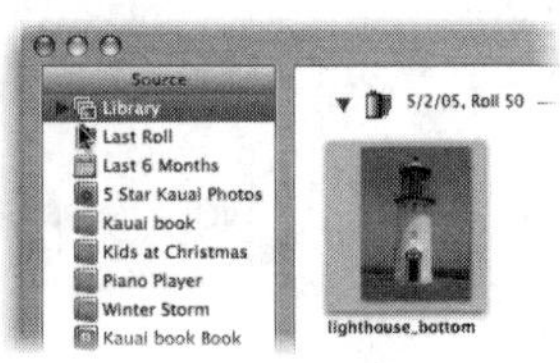

The iPhoto window.

Mail

15

With Mail you can write, send, and receive email messages. Mail also has many useful tools for organizing, formatting, searching, and filtering email.

The **basic** things you will be doing in **Mail** are checking messages, replying to messages, and composing new messages. On these first few pages are directions for how to do just that. If you haven't created an email account yet so you can use Mail, jump ahead to pages 439–443 to learn how to create accounts.

You must have an Internet connection already set up, and you must have **already set up your email service** with your .Mac membership or with any other email provider. If you haven't set up a .Mac account yet, and you want one (you don't have to have one), go to www.mac.com and sign up for a .Mac membership.

The Viewer Window

Mail opens up to the **Viewer window,** shown below. If you open Mail and don't see this window, press Command Option N. **Or** go to the File menu and choose "New Viewer Window."

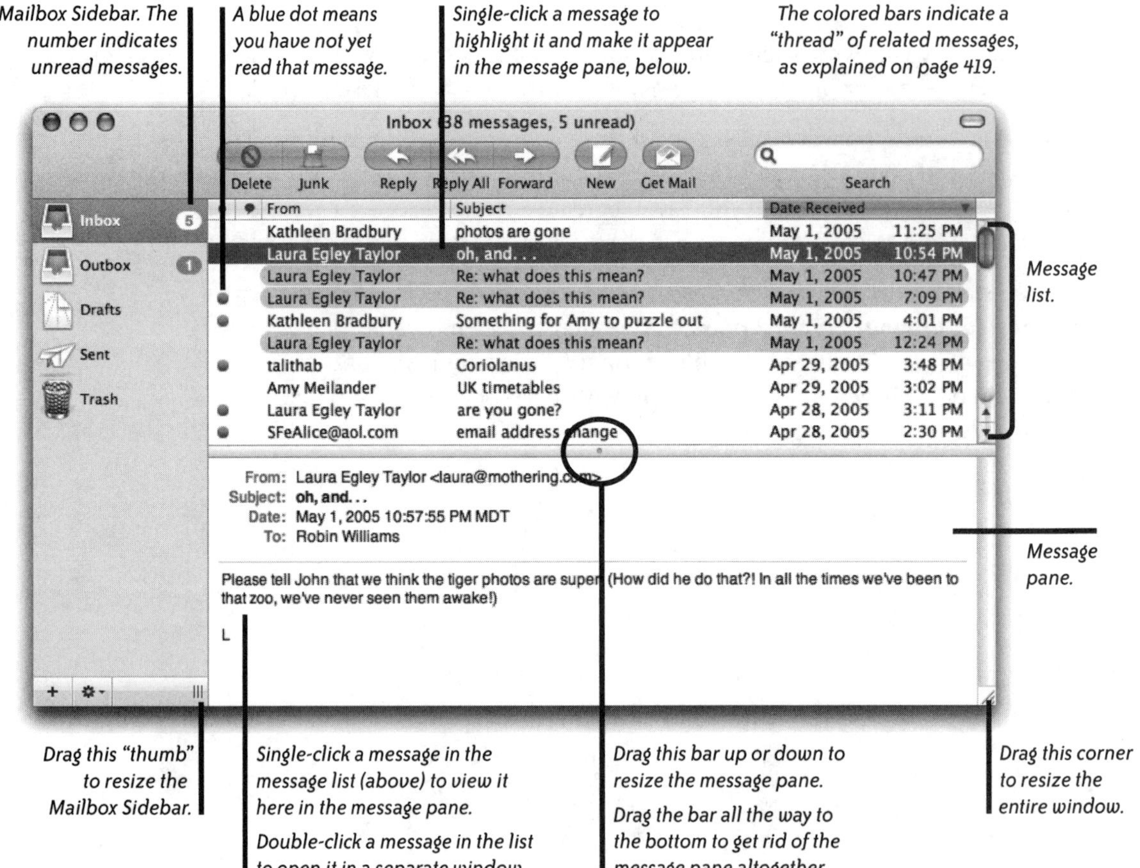

Basic Features of Mail

Here are the basic features of using Mail.

Read a message

If the message pane is visible, as shown on the opposite page, just **single-click** any email message in the list in the top portion of the Viewer window. The email opens in the message pane. Resize the pane if necessary, or use the scroll bar to see the rest of the message.

If the message pane is not visible, or if you want to open the email in its own separate window, **double-click** any email message in the list.

Why to hide the message pane

Sometimes you may want to delete email messages without having to read them first, but if the message pane is visible, the message pops up in that pane the instant you select a message, before you can delete it. To solve this problem, *press* on the tiny dot in the dividing bar (circled on the opposite page) and drag the bar *all the way to the bottom.* When the message pane is hidden, you can single-click to select any message, then click the Delete button. **To read a message,** double-click it.

Have your mail read out loud to you

Select the entire letter (press Command A) *or* press-and-drag the mouse over the text you want read out loud. Control-click (or right-click if you have a two-button mouse) anywhere in the message to open a contextual menu, slide down to "Speech," and choose "Start Speaking." Mail will read your letter out loud using the default computer voice chosen in the Speech system preferences. **To make it stop speaking,** Control-click again and choose "Stop Speaking."

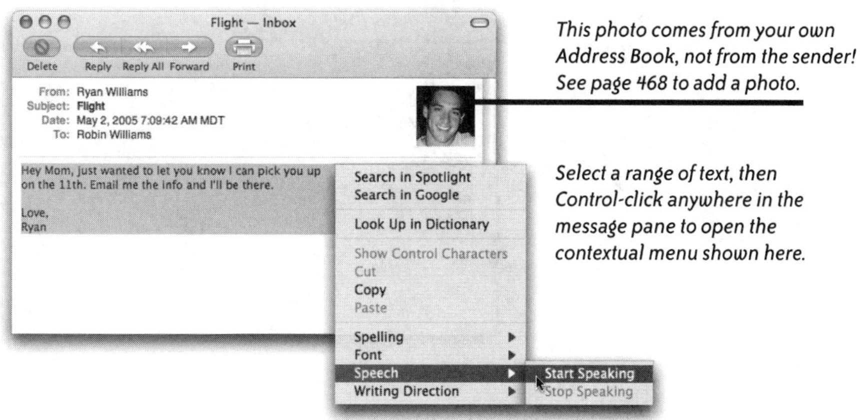

This photo comes from your own Address Book, not from the sender! See page 468 to add a photo.

Select a range of text, then Control-click anywhere in the message pane to open the contextual menu shown here.

Write and send a NEW message

1. Click "New" in the toolbar to open a "New Message" window, as shown below.
2. Click in the "To" area (called a *field*) and type an email address. You can type more than one address in here; just type a comma after each address.

   An email address must have an @ symbol followed by a *domain name,* such as "ratz.com," "aol.com," "comcast.net," etc.

   If the person you are sending email to is in your Address Book or Previous Recipients list (which you'll find in the Window menu), Mail replaces the *email address* with that person's *name* as soon as you type it. This is called a "Smart Address." If you prefer to see the actual address, see page 410 to change the preference.

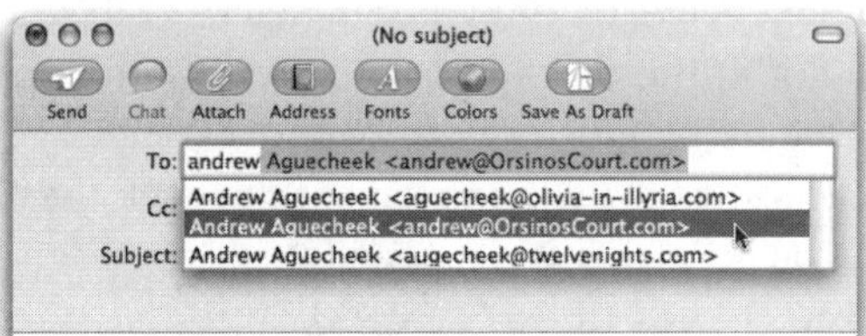

To change or edit that name, Control-click (or right-click) on the name and a little menu pops up (as shown below); choose the action you want to take. If the recipient is in your Address Book and has more than one email address, the pop-up menu also shows all available email addresses; choose the address you want to use.

3. **To send a copy** of this same letter to someone, click in the "Cc" field and type an address. You can type more than one address, separated by commas. All recipients will know these people are Cc'd.
4. Click in the "Subject" field and type a *personalized* message description so the recipient knows your message is not junk mail. Avoid using phrases that spammers use, such as "Hi," "I missed you," or "We need to talk." Provide some clue that makes it clear you know the recipient!

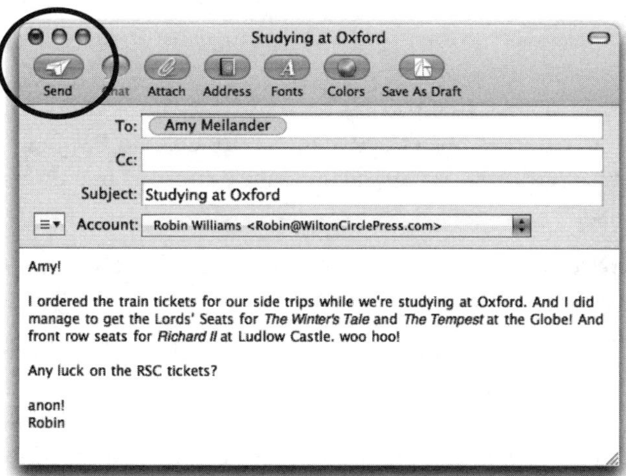

Tip: If you can't apply formatting to the selected text, such as bold, italic, or color, perhaps your mail is set up as "Plain Text." To change the setting so you can apply formatting, go to the Format menu and choose "Make Rich Text."

5. Click in the empty message pane and type a message.
6. Connect to the Internet if you're not already connected.
7. Click the "Send" icon in the toolbar (shown to the right and circled, above).

   A copy of the sent message is stored in the "Sent" folder in the Mailbox Sidebar.

Use Smart Addresses

As noted on page 408, a Smart Address is what appears when you type someone's email address that is stored in your Address Book or in your Previous Recipients list (found in the Window menu).

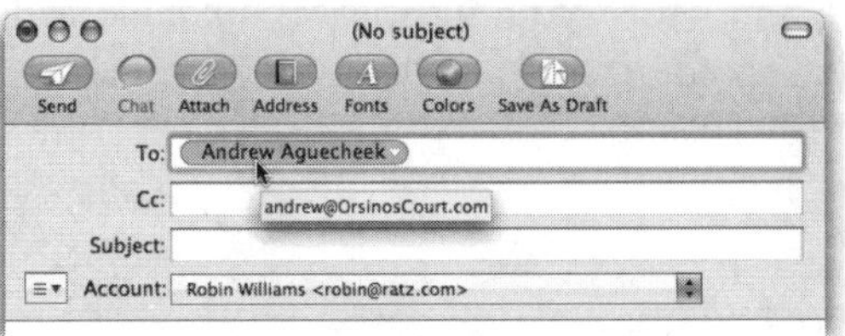

Hover the pointer over a Smart Address to see the email address associated with it.

laura@mothering.com

This is what a Smart Address file looks like on the Desktop.

A Smart Address is an "object" that you can drag and drop into other locations. You can drag a Smart Address object between the To, Cc, and Bcc fields. You can also drag a Smart Address to an email message pane, to a text document, or to your Desktop.

Double-click a Smart Address that's on your Desktop to open a new email message window addressed to that recipient.

To turn off Smart Addresses so you see the actual email adresses, go to the Mail menu and choose "Preferences...." In the "Viewing" pane, uncheck the box to "Use Smart Addresses." The great thing is the address itself is still an object that you can drag and drop into other places, as described above.

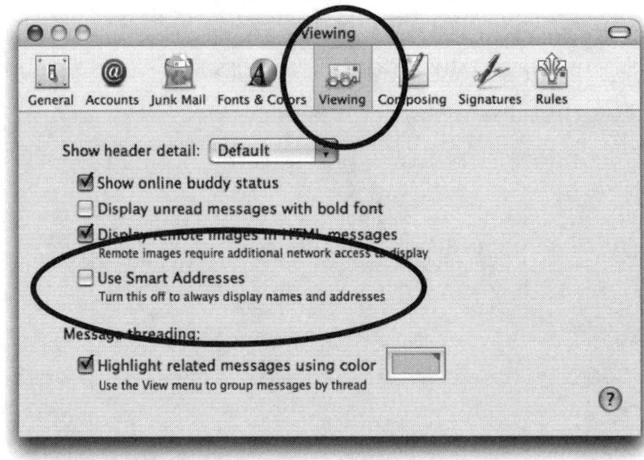

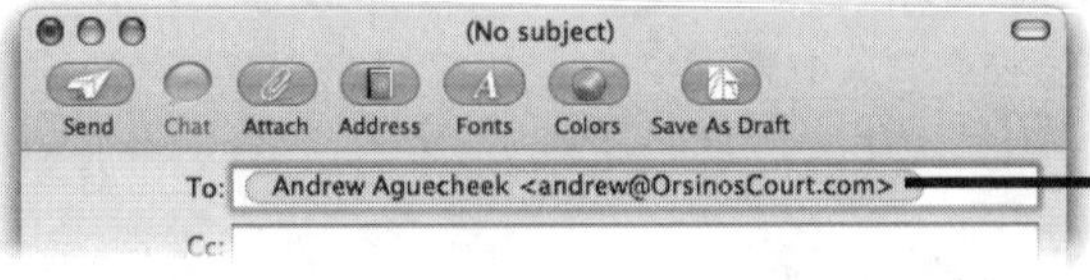

Even with Smart Addresses turned off, as shown here, you can drag this address to another field or to your Desktop.

Use the Address Pane to address messages

To address a message using the Address Pane: Click the "New" button to open a new message window. In the toolbar, click the "Address" icon to open a limited version of your Address Book, called the Address Pane. Double-click a name or Group in your list to address your message to that person.

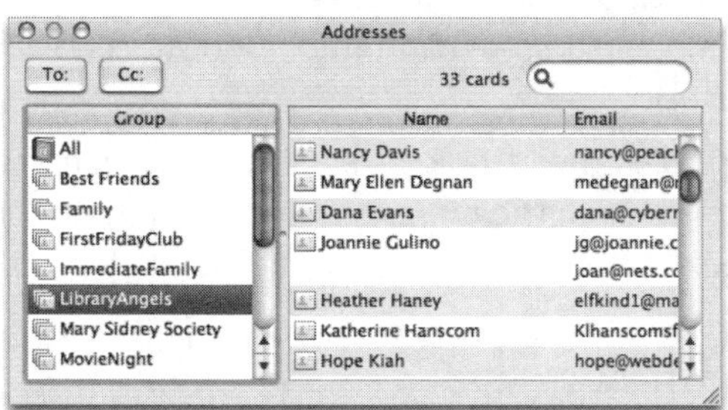

To send the same message to more than one person, hold down the Command key and *single*-click on names in the Address Pane; then let go of the Command key and click the "To" button. Or you can just double-click on each person's name and they will be added one at a time.

To add the Address Pane icon to the Mail toolbar so you don't have to open a new message first, customize the toolbar as explained on page 436.

Save a draft

To save a message as a draft: To finish a message later, click "Save As Draft" in the toolbar, or press Command S. The message will be saved in the Drafts folder within your Mailbox Sidebar. You will only see this button when you're writing a new message.

Actually, Mail **automatically** creates a draft for you whenever you're writing a lengthy letter—in case something happens and your computer goes down, you won't lose the entire letter. But to make sure, press Command S regularly, as you would in any document.

To open the draft ("restore" it) later for editing, select the "Drafts" icon in the Mailbox Sidebar, then double-click the desired draft in the list.

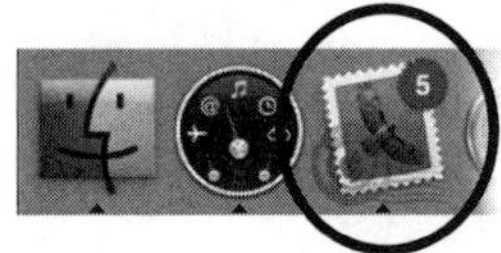

Check for messages

1. Connect to the Internet if you're not already connected.
2. Click once on the Mail icon in the Dock to open Mail.
3. Click the "Get Mail" icon in Mail's toolbar.

   Next to the Inbox in the Mailbox Sidebar (and in the Dock, as shown top-left) you might see a number in bold—that number indicates how many unread messages are in your Inbox.
4. Your messages will appear in the Message List. Single-click a message subject to display its contents in the message pane. Or double-click a message subject to open the message in its own window.

Reply to the sender of a message

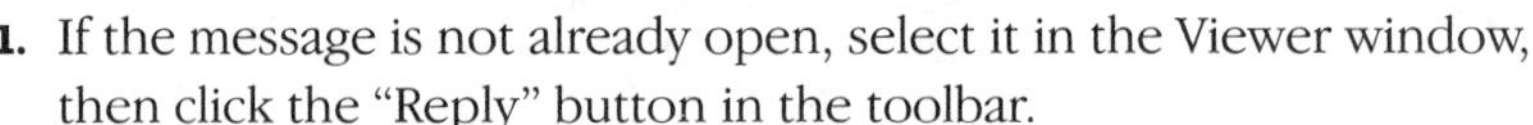

1. If the message is not already open, select it in the Viewer window, then click the "Reply" button in the toolbar.

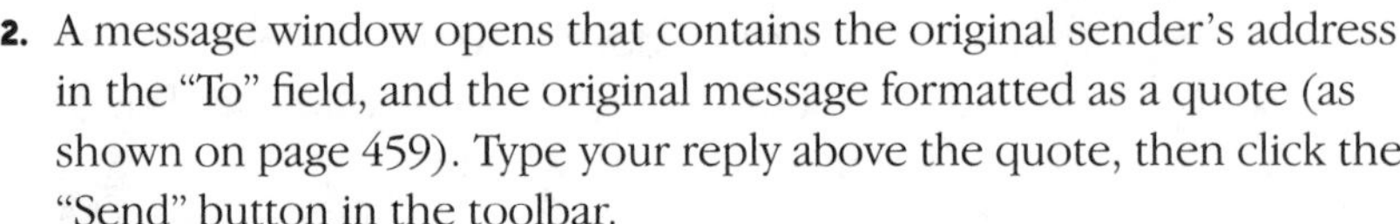

2. A message window opens that contains the original sender's address in the "To" field, and the original message formatted as a quote (as shown on page 459). Type your reply above the quote, then click the "Send" button in the toolbar.

   Great tip: If you *select* a portion of the text *before* you click "Reply," just that portion of text will be copied into the new email message!

Reply to ALL recipients of a message

Mail that you receive may have been sent to multiple recipients, either directly as a Carbon copy (Cc) (or "Courtesy copy" since it's no longer on carbon paper), or secretly as a Blind carbon copy (Bcc). You can choose to reply to all recipients with one email (the reply will *not* include anyone in the hidden Bcc list).

1. If the message is not already open, select the message in the Viewer window, then click the "Reply All" button in the toolbar.
2. Type your reply above the original quoted message, then click the "Send" button in the toolbar.

Forward a message

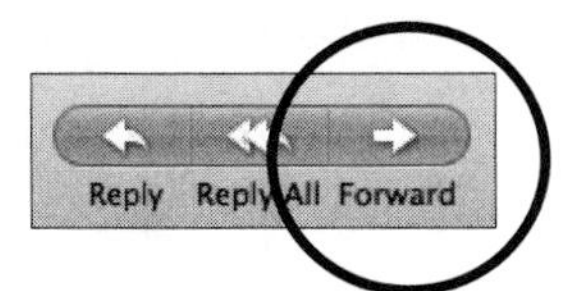

1. Select or open a message in the Viewer window, then click the "Forward" button in the toolbar.
2. Type any comments above the original quoted message, then click the "Send" button in the toolbar. *PLEASE remove all the names and addresses of everyone else in the forwarded list before you send it!*

Send a Bcc (blind courtesy copy)

Any email address you put in the Bcc field will not be seen by any other recipients. That is, you might want to send a message to a co-worker, but you want your boss to be aware of the issue and the response. So you create a Bcc field and put your boss's email address in it. The co-worker does not know your boss received a copy of the message.

When the co-worker replies, however, the reply does *not* go to anyone who was in the Bcc field of *your* message.

1. Address and write your message as usual.
2. From the View menu, choose "Bcc Address Field." This puts a new field in the address area. Any address(es) you type in this field will *not* be seen by anyone whose address is in the "To" or "Cc" field.

   To remove the Bcc field, just go back to the View menu and choose "Bcc Address Field" again.

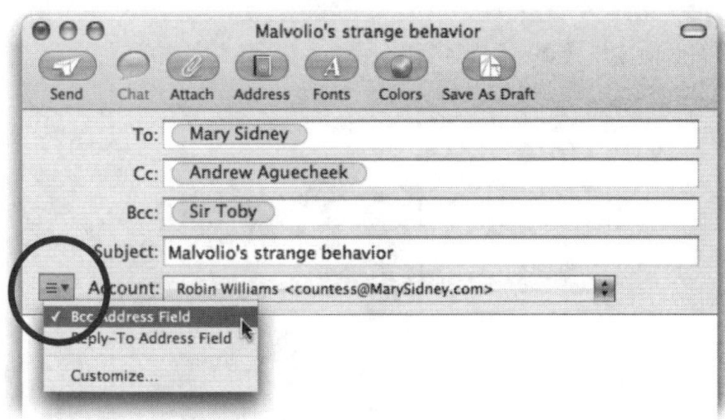

You can also use the Action button to add the Bcc field. Just click on the Action button and choose the option.

In this example, Mary Sidney gets the direct message.

Andrew Aguecheek gets a copy of the message, and Mary can tell because she will see that Cc on her message.

Neither Mary nor Andrew will know that Sir Toby also received a copy of the message because his address is in the Bcc field.

Attach a file

1. Click the "New" button to open a new message window.
2. From the File menu, choose "Attach File...."

   Or single-click the "Attach" button in the toolbar (if it's not in the toolbar, you can add it—see page 436).
3. The Open dialog box appears. Find the file you wish to attach.
4. Single-click on that file in the dialog box, then click "Choose File." (See page 457 for a tip on attachments for Windows users.)

Another way to attach a file: You can also drag a file's icon from wherever it is on your Mac and drop it in the message window. This means you need to go to the Desktop and either arrange an open window to the side of your screen or drag the file you want to attach out of its folder and let it sit on the Desktop. When you are in Mail, drag the file into the message window to attach it, as shown below.

Adjust the image: Once an image file is in the message window, a status bar appears at the bottom of the message, as shown below-right. You can choose to send the image actual size or smaller; click on the menu and choose.

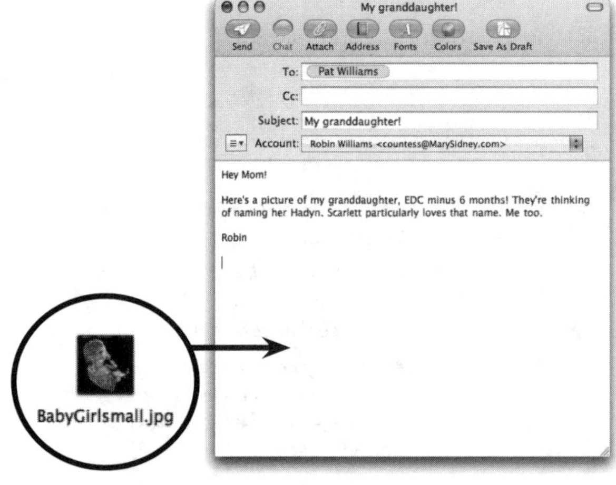

This is the image I want to send. I put it on my Desktop.

Then I opened Mail and wrote my message. Now I can just drag the image and drop it directly in the message, as shown above.

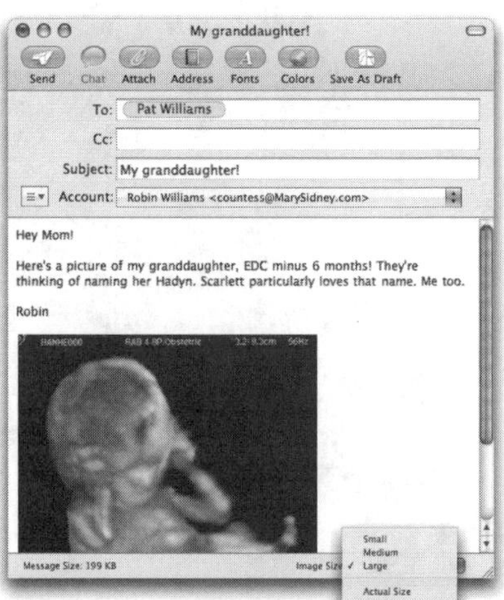

*This is what the attachment looks like in the message area. If your attachment is not an image, you'll see a file icon with a link. The recipient can usually just double-click on the image to open it **or** drag it to the Desktop first and then open it.*

To remove an attachment from your message before sending it, select the attachment in the message window (click once on it). Press the Delete key.

Tips about attachments

You can't open every file that someone sends you. Nor can your recipients open every file you send them. A file has to open within an application; if someone created a file in an application you don't have, you can't open it. For instance, someone who uses a PC might send you a file with an *extension* (the extra letters at the end of a file name) of ".pps," as in "lecture.pps." Well, this is probably a Microsoft PowerPoint file and it can only open in the application Microsoft Powerpoint; if you don't have that installed, the file can't open when you double-click on it.

Files that can travel pretty safely and are almost guaranteed that everyone can open them are PDFs, JPGs, and TXT (text) files. Other than those, you should check with your recipients to see if they can open the kinds of files you want to send.

Photographs from your digital camera are almost always in the JPG format, so you can usually safely send those without any problem.

View an attachment someone has sent you

1. Your email message tells you how many attachments are included. You'll see a "Save" button and a "Slideshow" button.
2. If you single-click the "Save" button, the Save As dialog box opens and you can choose where you want to save the files. **BUT** if you *press* (don't *click*) on the "Save" button, you get a menu where you can choose which of the individual files to save. **Or** choose the option to save all of the images directly into iPhoto!

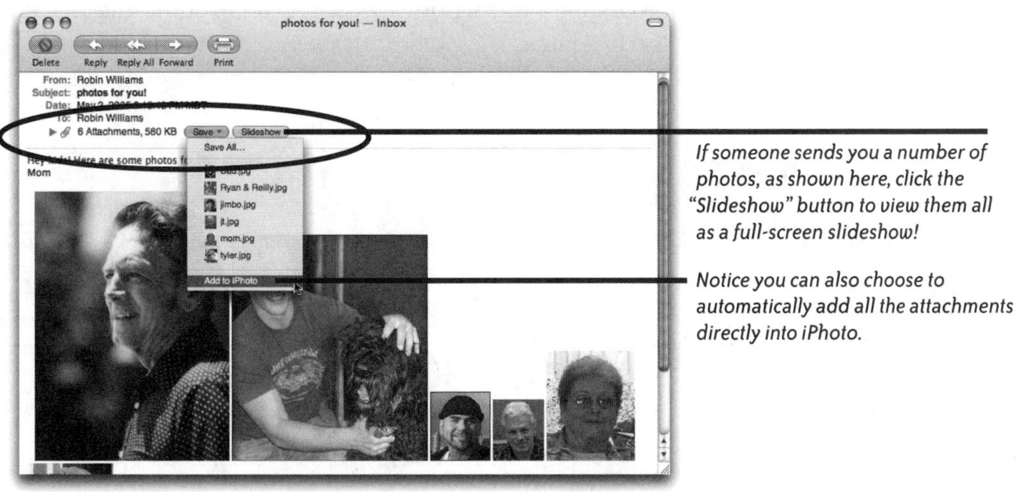

If someone sends you a number of photos, as shown here, click the "Slideshow" button to view them all as a full-screen slideshow!

Notice you can also choose to automatically add all the attachments directly into iPhoto.

Message List

The **message list** displays all messages in the currently selected Mailbox. The list is divided into several columns. The message list provides different organizations and views of a list, depending on which *column* is selected and whether or not you choose to *organize by thread.*

The columns of information

In addition to the columns that automatically appear in your Viewer window, you can choose to show a number of other columns: From the View menu, slide down to "Columns," then **show** or **hide** any column—just check it or uncheck it from the View menu list.

The function of most columns is obvious—the ones that aren't so obvious are explained on the following pages.

To rearrange (sort) the list according to the column heading, single-click the heading at the top of a column. The column heading that is blue is the one that items are currently arranged by. For instance, I like to keep my email organized by date received with the newest email at the top of the list, as shown below. But sometimes I want to find an old email from a particular *person,* so I click the "From" column to alphabetize the names; then I can quickly skim through the collection of email from each person.

To move columns, position the pointer over a column heading, then press-and-drag the column left or right. As you drag a column on top of another column, the column underneath moves over to leave an empty area for you. When you let go, the column snaps into the new position.

To change the column widths, position the pointer over the gray dividing line in the column headings. The pointer turns into a two-headed arrow, as circled below. With that cursor, press-and-drag the column edge left or right.

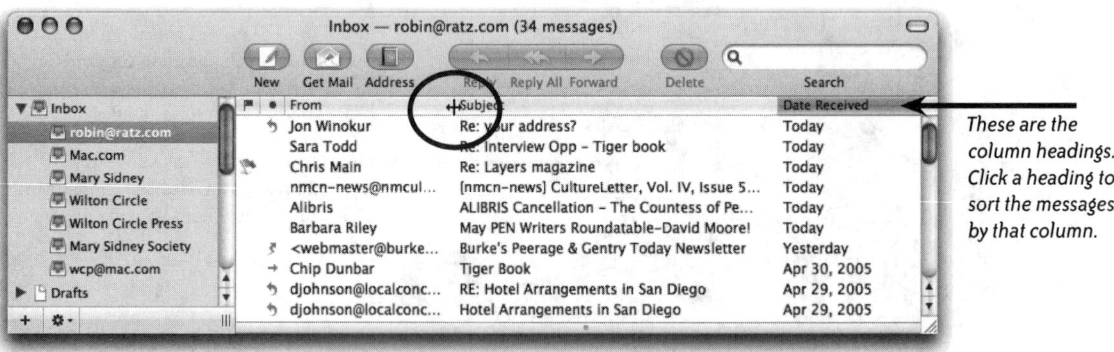

These are the column headings. Click a heading to sort the messages by that column.

Message Status column (●): This column displays different icons to indicate if you've read the message, replied to it, forwarded it, or redirected it. These icons show up automatically when one of those actions takes place.

Click the message status column heading (●) to group similar categories, such as unread or returned messages, together in the list. Click again in the column heading to reverse the order of the list.

Message status **icons** provide visual clues about the messages.

- Blue orb: Message has not been read.
- Curved arrow: Message was replied to.
- Right arrow: Message was forwarded (see page 413).
- Crooked arrow: Message was redirected (see page 437).

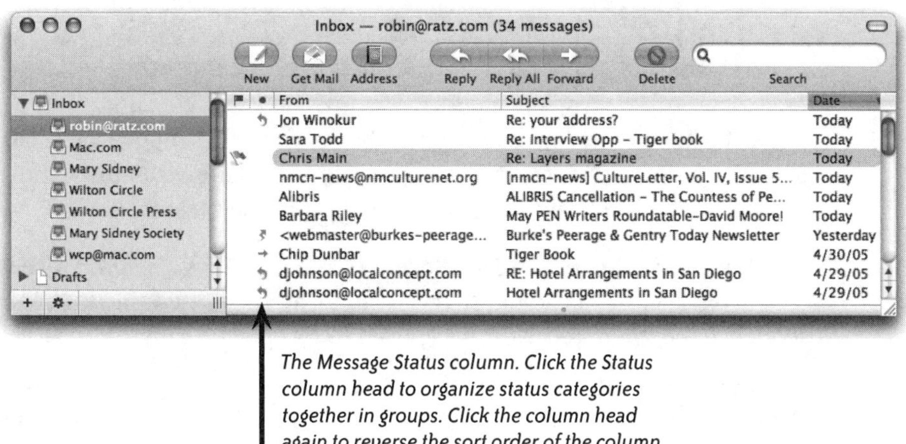

The Message Status column. Click the Status column head to organize status categories together in groups. Click the column head again to reverse the sort order of the column.

You can also manually mark an email that you've already read as "unread." Use this as a reminder to go back and read a message again or to make a message stand out: Select one or more messages, then from the Message menu, choose "Mark," then choose "As Unread." The blue orb will reappear next to the message.

The following columns may or may not be showing. To hide or show them, go to the View menu and use the "Columns" option. Or Control-click in any column heading to get the contextual menu of column options.

Number column: In a series of email exchanges, it may be useful to know in what order messages were received. The Number column keeps track of the order for you. Click the **#** symbol in the column heading to arrange messages by order. Click again in the column heading to reverse the order of the list.

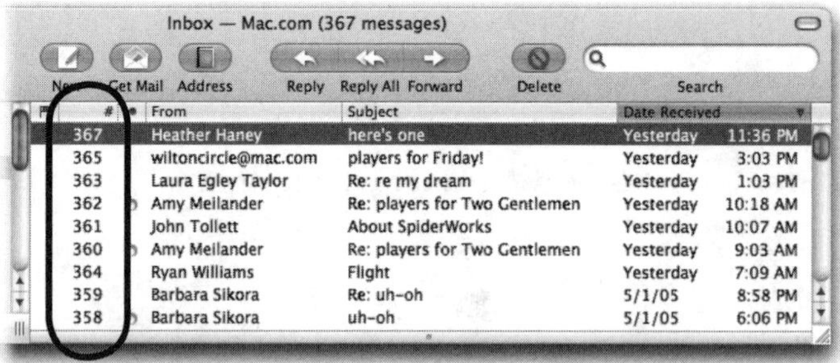

Subject column: The Subject column shows what the sender typed into the Subject header of their email message. Click the column heading to show the subjects in alphabetical order; click again to reverse the order of the list.

Date Received column: The Date Received column shows when you received a message. Click the heading of the column to show messages in the time sequence they were received; click again to reverse the order of the list.

Flags column: Mark a message as flagged when you want it to stand out in the list or if you want to temporarily tag a group of related messages. **To see all your flagged files** in a list, click the "Flag" column heading; all flagged messages will move to the top of the list. Click the heading again to reverse the order and put flagged messages at the bottom of the list.

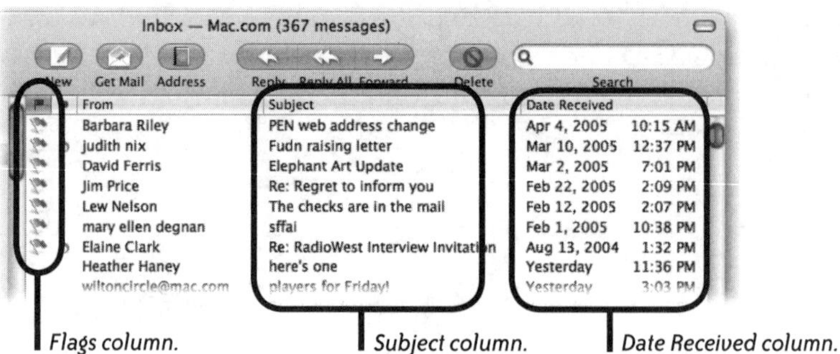

Flags column. *Subject column.* *Date Received column.*

View message threads

A group of *related* messages and replies are called **message threads.** If you reply to an email whose subject field is labeled "Dogfood," the default subject field is labeled "Re: Dogfood." Mail identifies messages that have identical subject fields (and sometimes related subject matter) as being in the *same thread* and highlights *all* of the messages in a thread when any related message is selected, as shown on page 406. You can turn off this highlighting or change the highlight color in preferences (see page 447).

To group all messages in threads together, from the View menu choose "Organize by Thread." All related messages are now grouped together and highlighted in the message list, as shown below. This is a convenient and easy way to find all the correspondence related to a particular subject.

All of the messages in a thread are *highlighted* when you select any related message. **To select** (not just *highlight*) **every message thread** (or just the next one), go to the View menu and use the "Select" command.

To expand a selected thread and *show* all its related messages, single-click the small disclosure triangle to the left of a message thread. Click that triangle again to **collapse** the thread and *hide* the related messages.

To expand all threads: From the View menu, choose "Expand All Threads."

To collapse all threads: From the View menu, choose "Collapse All Threads."

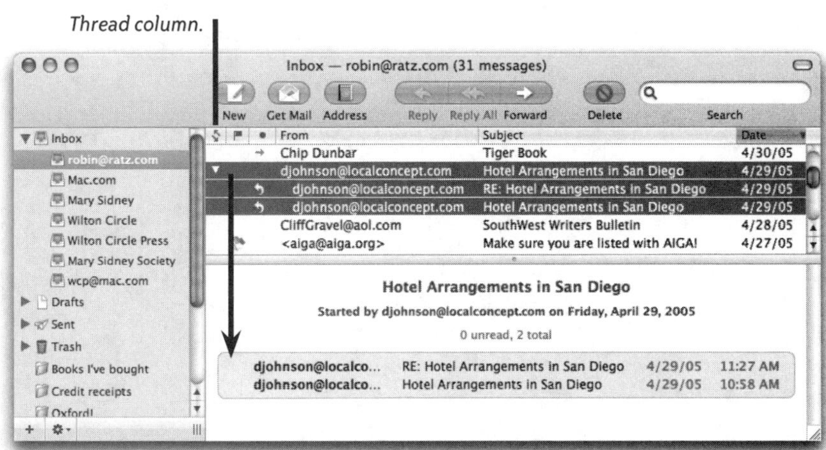

When you choose "Organize by Thread" from the View menu, each thread is grouped together.

If your message pane is showing, as above, you can select any message in the thread group and a list of the related messages appears in the pane.

Buddy Availability column: If you have a Buddy List set up in iChat (see Chapter 17) and if this feature is turned on in Mail preferences (see page 447), this column displays a green orb when a Buddy is online. If he is online but idle (perhaps his computer has gone to sleep), you'll see a yellow orb.

When you see that a Buddy is online, you can double-click the green "Chat" orb to open a new iChat instant message window and start a chat with him.

Or customize the toolbar (see page 436) to include a Chat button, as shown below. Select an *online* Buddy in the message list, then click the "Chat" button to open iChat and start an instant message.

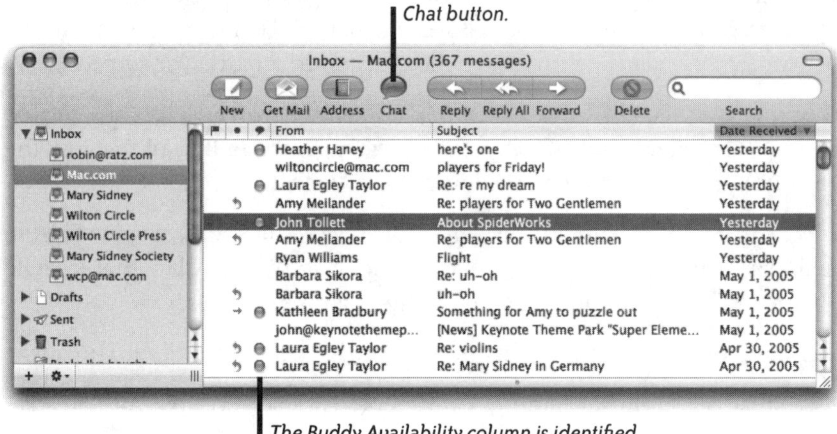

The Buddy Availability column is identified by a speech balloon icon in the heading.

Mailbox Sidebar

The **Mailbox Sidebar** is on the left side of the Viewer window.

Icons in the Sidebar

Here is an explanation of the various **icons** you might see in your Mailbox Sidebar. As you make and delete folders and change your preferences, your arrangement of icons in the Sidebar will change, so don't worry if you don't see all of these or if you see more than I have listed here.

- The **bold number** in a circle is the number of unread messages in that folder. If you have only one email account or if the Inbox is "closed," the Inbox displays the **total** number of messages in all accounts. If you open the Inbox, each account shows you how many messages are in that particular account.
- Click *one* of the individual account names to see the message list for just that selected account.
- If you have many email accounts and want to check for messages from several of them at once, Command-click the account names to make a multiple selection, then click the "Get Mail" button.

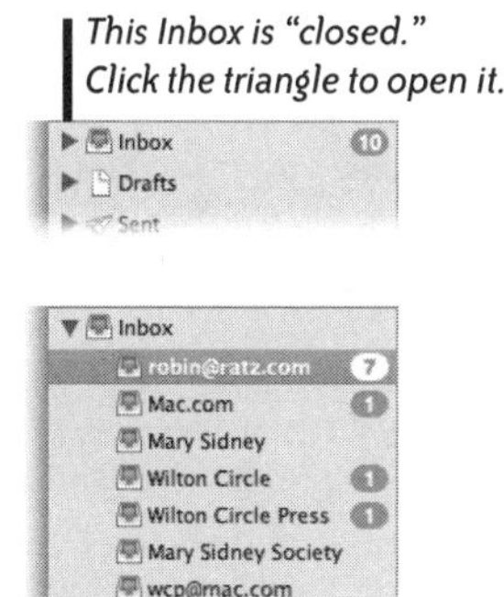

This Inbox is "closed." Click the triangle to open it.

—continued

Inbox: At the top of the Sidebar you can tell if you have received any email, as described on the previous page. Messages contained in these "Inboxes" are stored on your computer if they are POP accounts; for IMAP accounts, you can choose for them to be stored on your Mac or not; see page 441.

Out box: Stores messages temporarily while waiting to be sent. If you're not connected to the Internet at the moment (you're working "offline" or your connection is down), messages you send are stored in the "Out" box until an online connection is established.

Drafts folder: Stores unfinished messages that you're composing. If you have multiple Mail accounts set up, you'll have separate "Drafts" folders for each account. The messages in the "Drafts" folders are stored on your computer.

Sent folder: Contains copies of messages that you sent to other people. If you've set up multiple email accounts, you'll have a separate "Sent" folder for each account. The messages in the "Sent" folders are stored on your computer.

Trash folder: Contains messages you have deleted. If you have multiple accounts, you'll have a separate "Trash" folder for each of your accounts. Messages in these Trash folders are stored on your computer—they are not *really* thrown away until you choose to empty the Trash.

Use the Mail preferences to set up your Trash **to empty automatically** at certain times: In the Accounts pane, select an account name, then click the "Mailbox Behaviors" button and make your Trash choice.

If you do not set up Mail to empty the Trash at certain times, make sure to **empty all your Trash mailboxes** occasionally. If you have an IMAP account (like Mac.com), you must empty your Trash or your mailbox on the IMAP server may get too full and you won't get any more mail.

To empty all messages in the Trash, select the topmost Trash icon in the Mailbox Sidebar. From the Mailbox menu, choose "Erase Deleted Messages," then from the submenu choose "In All Accounts" (or press Command K). You can also select a specific account in this submenu (if you have more than one) to empty only trashed messages from that account.

Junk folder: This Junk folder is automatically created when you change the Junk Mail mode from "Training" to "Automatic" in the Mail menu (as explained on pages 431–435). It stores messages that have been identified by Mail as junk mail. The number in parentheses tells you how many junk messages have not been read.

On My Mac: You can create *custom folders* (called *mailboxes*) for storing and organizing your messages. When you create new folders/mailboxes, you have a choice of whether to store them "On My Mac," which is the computer you're working on, or on Apple's servers using your .Mac account (as explained below).

You can drag email messages into these mailboxes to organize them. Using Rules, you can make certain messages automatically organize themselves into these mailboxes. **All messages in these mailboxes are stored on your computer.**

To learn all about new folders, see the following four pages. To learn how to filter incoming messages into the folders, see pages 453–455.

Although these folders are not labeled "On My Mac," they are all stored on your hard disk.

Internet icon: If you choose to make a new folder/mailbox on your **.Mac account,** which you can do right from your desktop computer, the blue crystal ball appears in the Sidebar. The crystal ball indicates the Internet. **The .Mac mailboxes are stored on Apple's server, as well as all the files inside the mailboxes,** and you can access the contents from anywhere on the Internet.

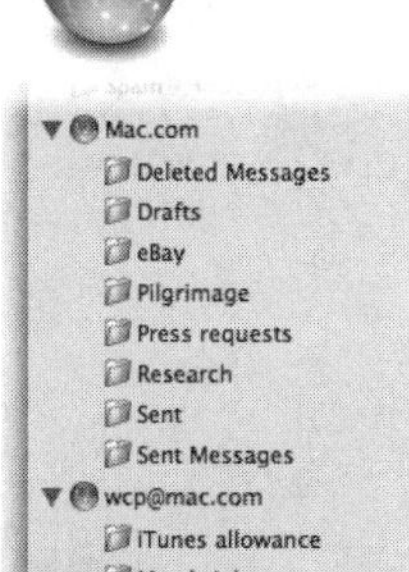

I have two .Mac accounts.

Any folders in this section also appear in your .Mac webMail, as described in Chapter 9. Any folders you make in your .Mac webMail account will appear here in Mail. Messages in this account are stored on Apple's servers in your email allotment.

You can drag other messages from any account into these folders and into any other folders you create in your .Mac account. Then you'll have access to the messages in this Mailbox from any computer in the world—just open any browser, go to **www.mac.com,** click the "Mail" icon, and sign in.

In the Mail preferences, you can set up Rules (see pages 453–455) that tell certain types of email to go into certain folders, including these .Mac folders so those messages will be available online.

If you delete all of the folders in this mailbox, the entire mailbox and the crystal ball will disappear.

If you want it back, make a new mailbox as described on the following page. Or go to **www.mac.com,** log in to Mail, make a new folder online, and it will appear here in Mail on your Mac. Amazing.

Make New Mailboxes (Folders)

You can make as many mailboxes/folders as you like in which to sort your different types of mail. You can use the Rules feature to have incoming mail automatically placed into certain mailboxes (as described on pages 453–455). And you can create Smart Mailboxes that will also sort all of your mail, even if it came in last year; see pages 428–429.

Here are a couple of different ways to make new mailboxes.

To make a new mailbox (folder):

1. From the Mailbox menu, choose "New…."
2. Choose where you want this new mailbox located:

   On My Mac: This puts the folder on your hard disk. All messages in folders on your Mac are stored on your computer.

   Mac.com: If you have a .Mac account, as explained on page 255, your account name will be listed in this pop-up menu. All messages in Mac.com folders are actually stored on Apple's servers, which means you can read anything in these folders from any browser anywhere in the world. In the Mailbox Sidebar, these folders will be under a blue magic globe icon, as shown to the left.

3. Name the mailbox and click OK.

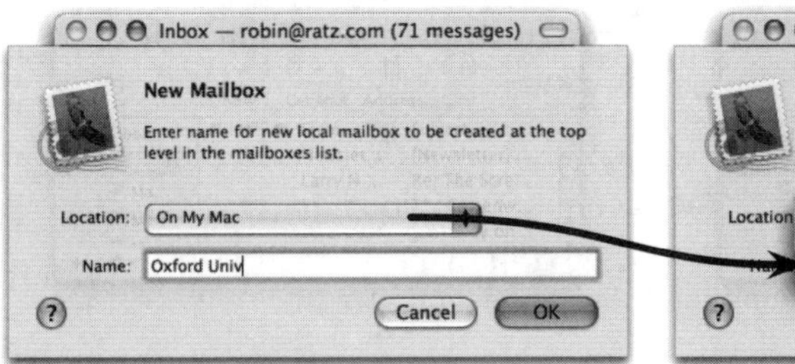

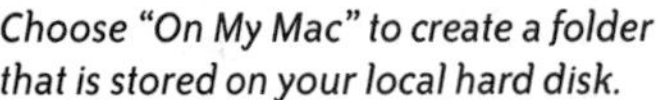
Choose "On My Mac" to create a folder that is stored on your local hard disk.

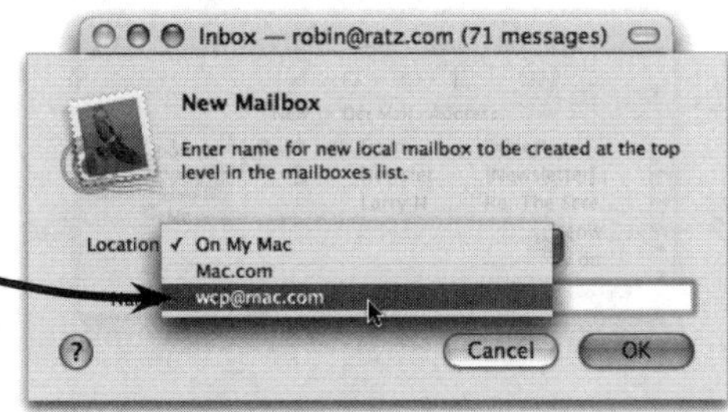

Or choose to create a folder on Apple's computers in your .Mac webMail account. These folders will also appear in Mail on your Mac.

Tip: You can create a folder within a folder in this dialog box: Type the name of the first folder, type a slash, then type the name of the folder you want *inside* the first one. For instance, Clients/Acme Inc.

Notice in the examples on the opposite page, the new mailbox will be created at the top level. You can also **create a mailbox inside an existing mailbox:**

1. Click once on an existing folder in the Mailbox Sidebar. Then . . .

   Either: Click the "New Mailbox" button at the bottom of the Sidebar (shown to the right).

   Or Control-click on that folder and choose "New. . . ."

2. The dialog box shown on the opposite page will appear with a message that this new mailbox will be created "as a child of" the selected folder.

3. Click OK. The "parent" folder will have a disclosure triangle next to it to indicate there is a "child" folder/mailbox inside.

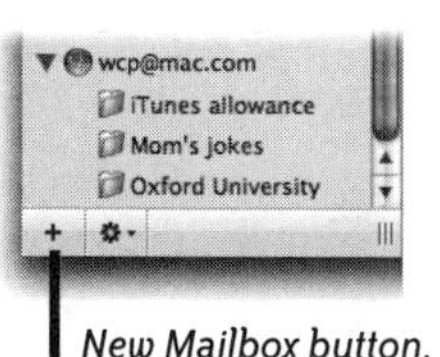

New Mailbox button.

Delete or rename existing mailboxes

You can always rename mailboxes or delete them altogether. Keep in mind that *when you delete a mailbox, you delete all the messages stored within it.*

1. In the Mailbox Sidebar, single-click to select the mailbox you want to rename or delete.
2. Go to the Mailbox menu and choose either "Rename…" or "Delete…," **or** Control-click on the mailbox you want to rename or delete.
3. In the dialog box that appears, rename the mailbox or click the "Delete" button.

Smart Mailboxes are different—if you delete a Smart Mailbox, it DOES NOT delete any of the messages that were in it. See pages 428–429.

The easiest thing to do is Control-click (or right-click) on the mailbox.

Word search through Spotlight, Google, or the Dictionary

This is a very fun feature. Select any word or phrase in any email message. Control-click on it (or right-click) and you get a contextual menu that lets you send that phrase to Google as a web search! Or choose "Search in Spotlight" to search your computer for all other references to the selected word or phrase. Or look it up in the Dictionary, which opens the same Dictionary you might use in Dashboard. I love this feature. It works on web pages and in TextEdit, too.

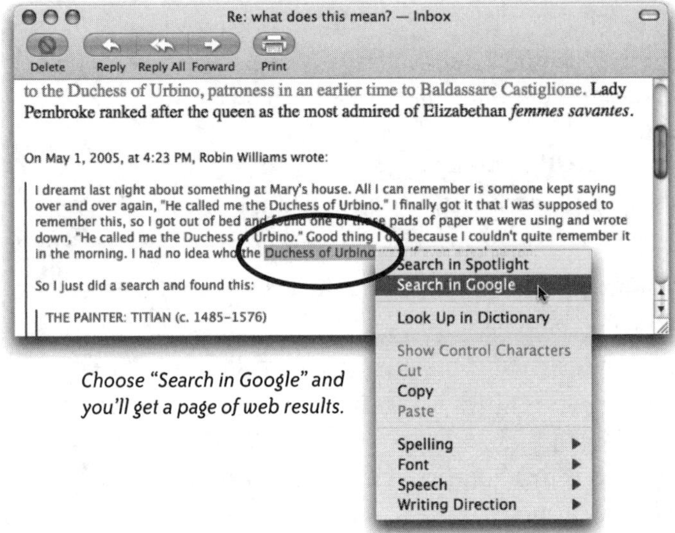

Choose "Search in Google" and you'll get a page of web results.

Mail Search

You can search a specific account, an individual mailbox/folder, or all mailboxes/accounts at once. You can limit the search to the individual fields From, To, or Subject, or have it search the "Entire Message," which includes all the fields *plus* the message body.

To search a *specific* account or folder, single-click an account or folder in the Mailbox Sidebar, then click in the Search field. Type a search term in the Search field.

As you type, the search starts immediately. The more letters you type, the fewer results will match and will be displayed in the Viewer window.

As soon as you start to type, what we call the "search bar" appears directly under the toolbar, as shown below. **Be sure to check this bar—**it tells you exactly what was searched. It's not always what you requested! For instance, you might have selected a particular account, but Mail searched "All Mailboxes" instead, even though you see the name of your selection in the search bar. **To limit the existing search** to just the account you previously selected, click the account or mailbox name in the search bar.

To search *multiple* folders and mailboxes, Command-click items in the Mailbox Sidebar to search, then follow the process above.

To search *all* mailboxes, type something in the Search field. When the search bar appears, click "All Mailboxes."

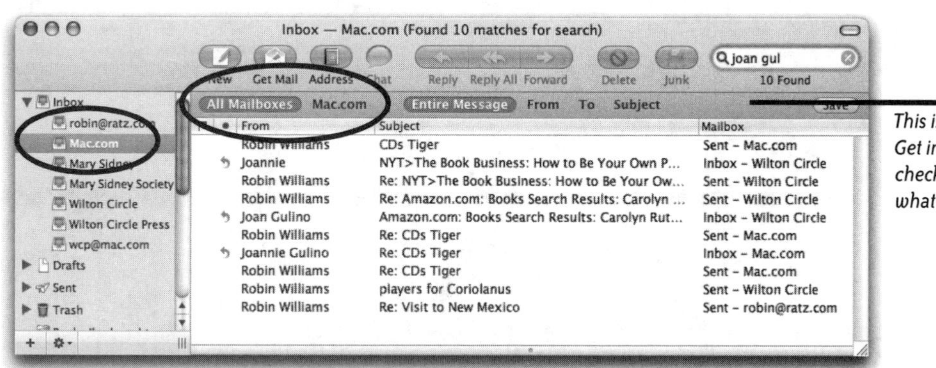

*This is the **search bar.** Get in the habit of checking to see exactly what it searched.*

The Viewer window shows the search results. The far-right column tells you which account a selected message is in.

Smart Mailboxes

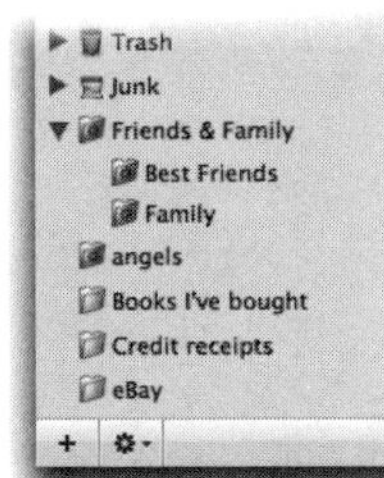

*A **Smart Folder** is an organizational tool in which to store groups of **Smart Mailboxes.** In this example, "Friends & Family" is a Smart Folder.*

You can see the special icons that indicate the other three Smart Mailboxes.

Using the Mail search described on the previous page, you can save a search and turn it into a Smart Mailbox. The Smart Mailbox checks every incoming message *and* every message you've already received for items that match the search criteria.

A Smart Mailbox is different from making a rule in that a rule only checks incoming messages and filters them at that one point. A Smart Mailbox includes all email you've ever received, as well as messages you've sent and even those in the Trash. And it updates itself automatically.

There are two ways to create a Smart Mailbox—one, through a search, and the other, through choosing criteria.

To create a Smart Mailbox from a search:

1. Do a search as explained on the previous page.
2. Make sure you have chosen the location and search fields you want in the search bar.
3. Click the "Save" button at the end of the search bar (if you don't see it, open your window a little wider).

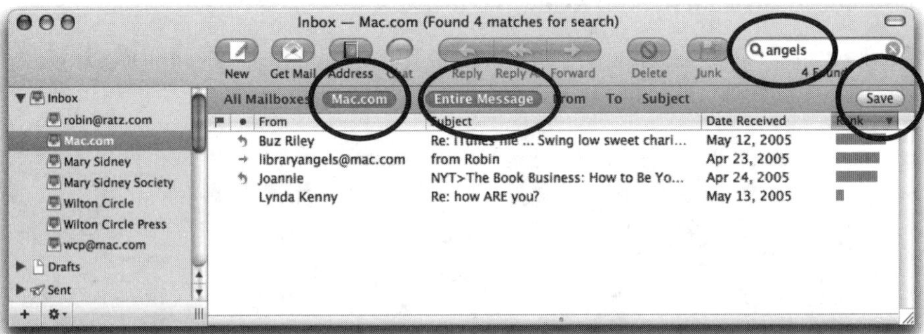

4. In the sheet that drops down, name the Smart Mailbox. Verify the parameters, as shown below, then click OK.

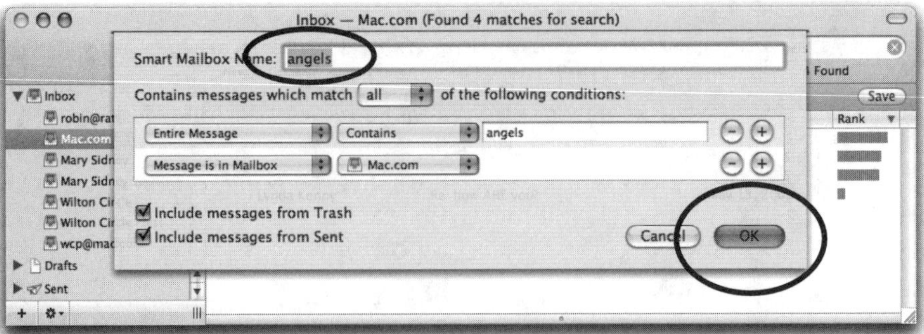

To create a Smart Mailbox Folder:

This is just an organizational folder in which to store other Smart Mailboxes, as shown on the opposite page. From the Edit menu, choose "New Smart Mailbox Folder…." Name it, then click OK.

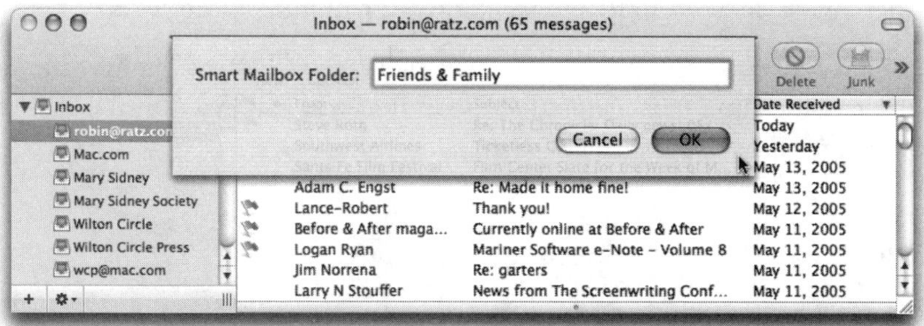

To create a Smart Mailbox by choosing criteria:

1. From the Edit menu or from the Action menu, choose "New Smart Mailbox…."

   If you want the new Smart Mailbox to be stored inside an existing Smart Folder, Control-click on the Smart Folder and choose "New Smart Mailbox…."

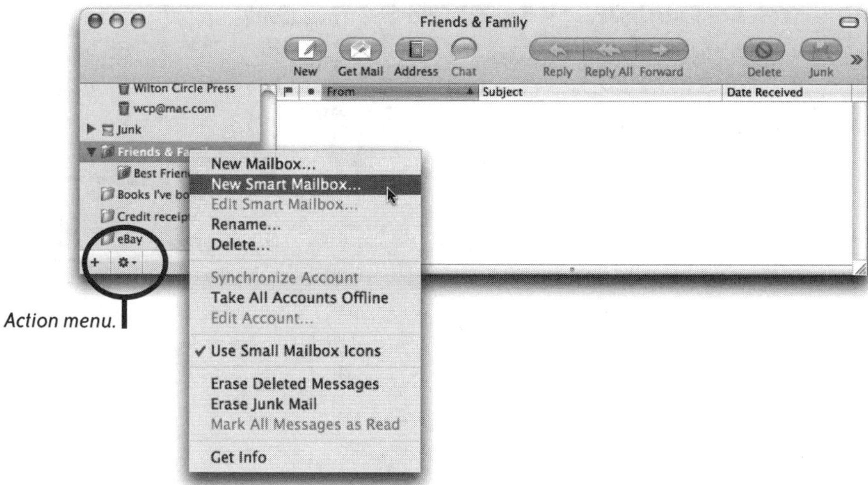

If you delete a Smart Mailbox, it does not delete any of the messages stored inside.

2. In the sheet that drops down, as shown on the opposite page, set up your parameters. Choose an option in the first menu, then see how the next two menus/fields change. Click the + sign to add more parameters; the – sign to delete a parameter.
3. Name the Smart Mailbox, click OK, and watch the results!

Dang—there is no parameter to find messages that have been addressed "To" a certain address. I was hoping to make a Smart Mailbox that would filter all mail addressed to my .Mac aliases.

Contextual Menus

Mail makes extensive use of **contextual menus:** Control-click on a message, the toolbar, or an item in the Mailbox Sidebar to open a pop-up menu that offers various commands, as shown below. If you have a two-button mouse, right-click on an item to show a contextual menu.

Using contextual menus is just a convenient way to access menu commands—there is nothing in a contextual menu that you can't find in the main menu bar across the top of your screen.

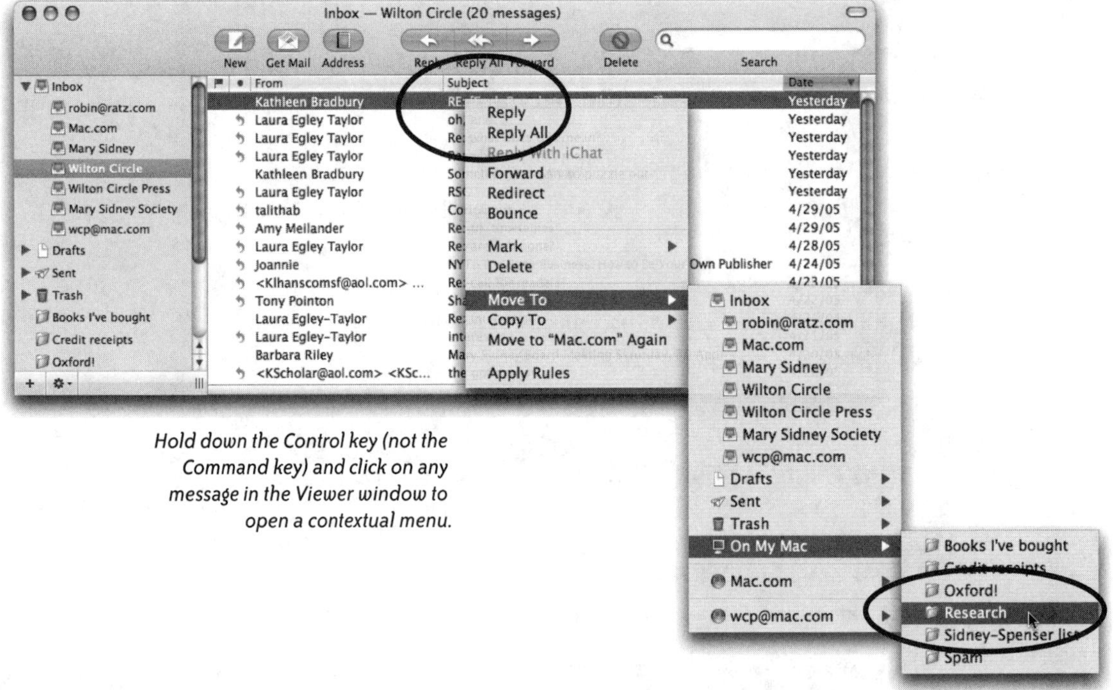

Hold down the Control key (not the Command key) and click on any message in the Viewer window to open a contextual menu.

Junk Mail Filter!

Okay, this can be really incredible. You can set Mail so it **automatically deletes junk mail without you ever having to see it.** Or if you are a little more cautious, you can have all the junk mail sent to a folder where you can check through it in case something you want accidentally ended up in the junk pile.

Although I must admit, our experience has been that it used to work really well and now it has some serious issues. Like sometimes it throws away every single piece of mail we get. So you might want to turn on "Training" and see how it works, then work your way up to automatically deleting email only if it's behaving itself.

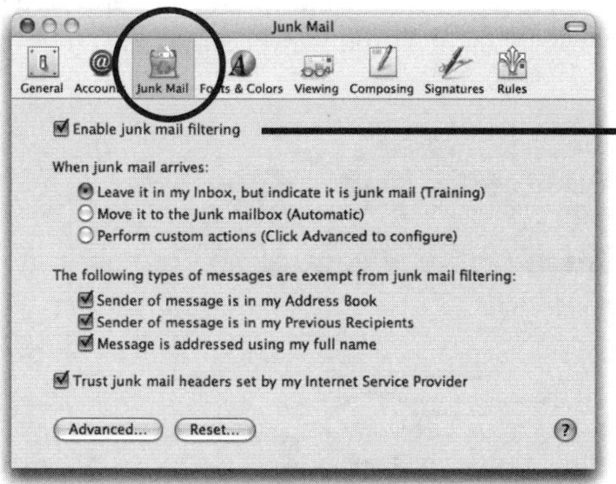

To turn the Junk Mail feature on or off:

1. Go to the Mail menu and choose "Preferences...."
2. Click the "Junk Mail" icon.
3. Check or uncheck the box "Enable junk mail filtering."

Mail automatically analyzes incoming messages and identifies what it thinks is **junk mail** by highlighting the message in brown. If your "Flags" column is showing, you'll see a junk mail icon (a brown mail bag) in that column.

To make the Flags column visible, from the View menu choose "Columns," then from the submenu choose "Flags."

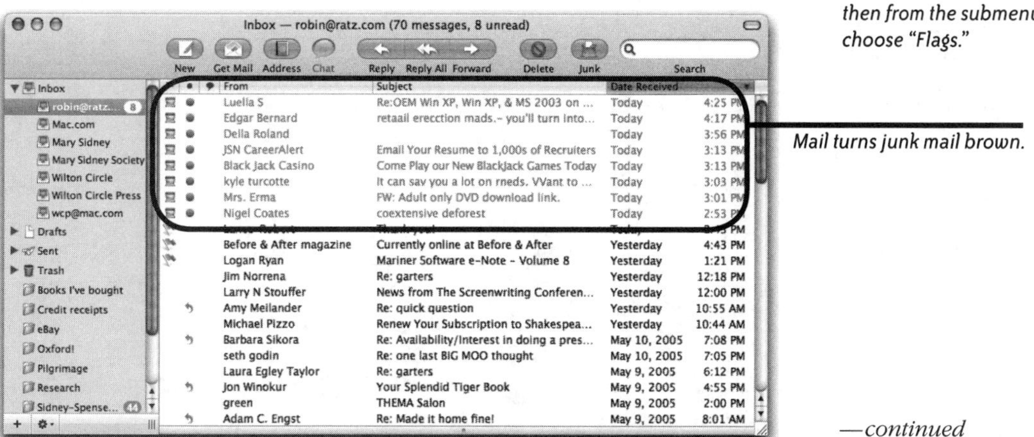

Mail turns junk mail brown.

—continued

Set up your window

First of all, make sure your Viewer window is set up as shown below. This has nothing to do with the junk filter, but it will prevent the following from happening: When you single-click on a junk message to delete it, the message appears in the bottom pane. This does two things—it displays the message, which sometimes can take valuable time and is oftentimes offensive, and it sends back a message to the despicable junk mailer confirming that this is a valid email address, which means you'll get more email from them and they'll sell your address to other evil junkheads (also known as spammers)! So you don't want to give them the satisfaction of even *opening* junk mail.

Get rid of the bottom pane, as explained below, and when you want to **read a message,** *double-click* the message name in the Viewer and it will open in its own window.

When both panes are showing, as in this example, the entire email appears in the bottom pane when you click on a message—even if you want to delete it.

***To prevent this,** drag this bar all the way to the bottom.*

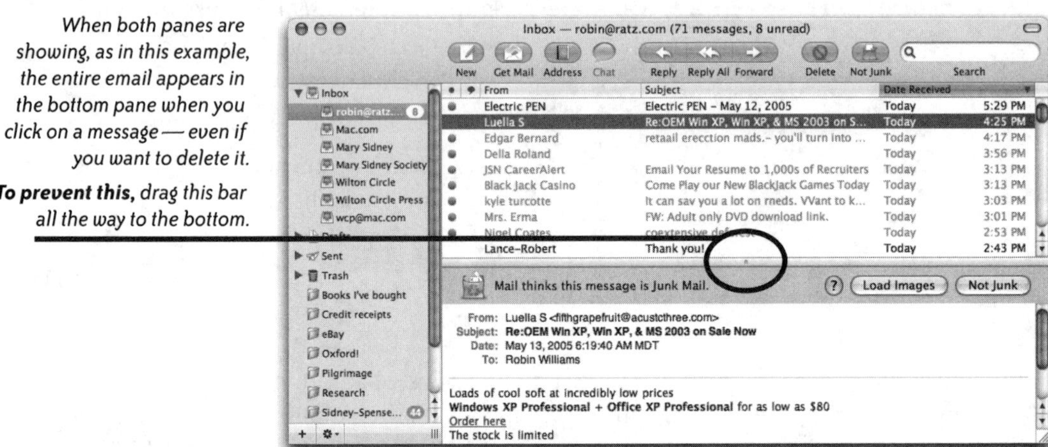

When the bottom pane is gone, you can select one, several, or all email messages and delete them (hit the Delete key) without having to open them first.

***To read a message,** double-click it and a separate window will open.*

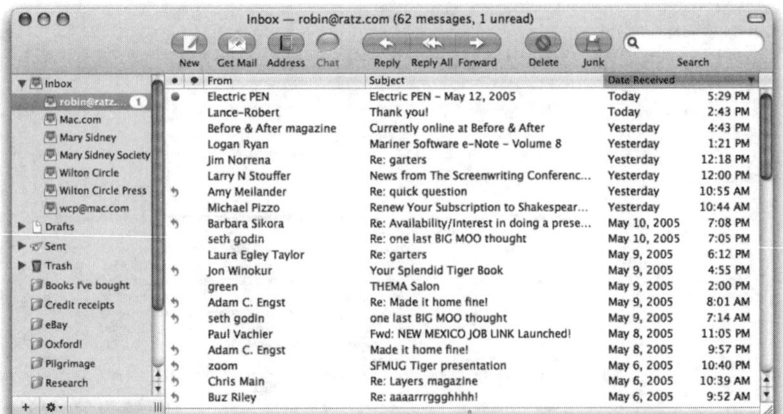

Train Mail to find junk more accurately

You can **train Mail to be more accurate** in identifying junk:

1. From the Mail menu, choose "Preferences...."
2. Check the box to "Enable Junk Mail filtering."
3. From the options titled "When Junk Mail arrives," choose "Leave it in my Inbox, but indicate it is Junk Mail (Training)."

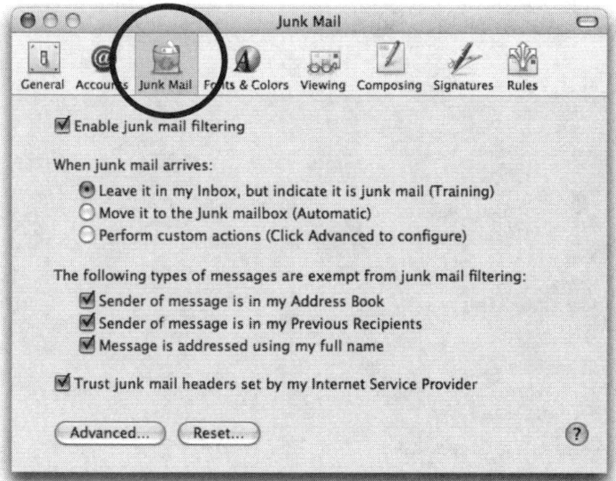

4. When you receive a new email message, check to see if Mail has correctly identified it.
   - If the new message is **unwanted junk mail, but Mail did not mark it** as such: Single-click the message, then click the "Junk" icon in the toolbar to mark it as junk mail.

     Or from the Message menu, choose "Mark," then from the submenu choose "As Junk Mail."

     Or press Command Shift J.

   - **If Mail *incorrectly* identifies** a message as junk mail, correct it: Select the message incorrectly marked and notice the "Junk" icon in the toolbar has changed to "Not Junk." Click the "Not Junk" icon to correctly identify the message.

5. Continue training Mail in this way for a couple of weeks, or until most incoming messages seem to be correctly identified.

—continued

When you're ready to **let Mail automatically handle junk mail,** go to the Mail preferences, click the "Junk Mail" button, then choose "Move it to the Junk mailbox (Automatic)." Mail will create a Junk mailbox (in the Mailbox Sidebar) to store all your unwanted mail. You might want to occasionally review the messages in this mailbox to make sure mail is being correctly identified.

If you would like to **adjust the junk mail settings yourself,** choose the option to "Perform custom actions (Click Advanced to configure)." Then click the "Advanced" button at the bottom of the window.

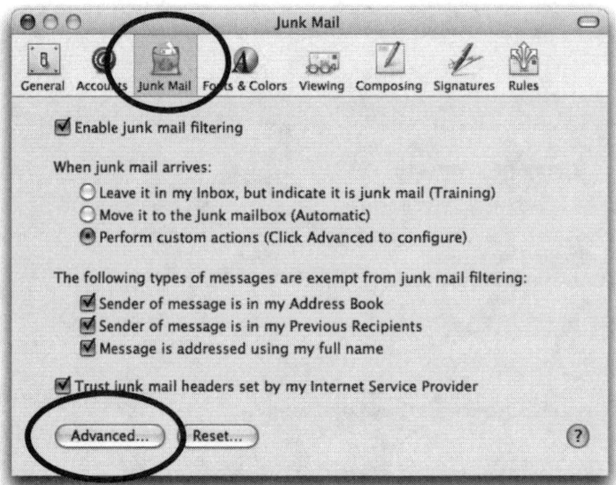

When you click the "Advanced..." button, a sheet drops down, as shown below. This shows you the rules that Mail is using to filter out the junk mail. If you find it's too restrictive or not restrictive enough, you can change these. See pages 453–455 for more details about rules.

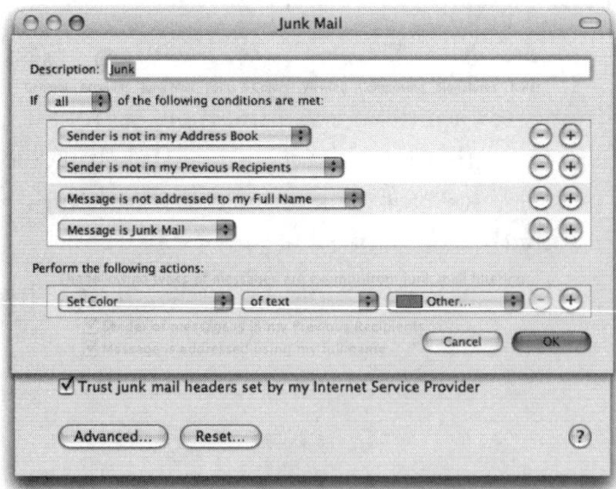

Instantly delete junk mail

When you're satisfied that Mail is accurately finding junk mail, you may want to change your setting so **Junk mail is instantly deleted.** Be careful with this! If you choose this option, you will never see the mail, nor can you undo the action or find it in any "Trash" mailbox—it's gone. And good riddance.

For more details about making Rules, see pages 453–455.

To delete junk mail before it ever appears in your box:

1. From the Mail menu, choose "Preferences...." Click the "Junk Mail" button.
2. As shown on the opposite page, put a check in the box to "Enable junk mail filtering."
3. Click the button to "Perform custom actions (Click Advanced to configure)."
4. Click the "Advanced..." button. You'll see the sheet shown below.

Tip: If you buy airline tickets online, the email confirmation might be considered spam and thus deleted. I set up a special rule (see pages 453–455) that allows mail from places like Southwest or Virgin to stay in my inbox.

5. Click on the bottom menu, the one that probably says "Set Color," as shown on the opposite page. Choose "Delete Message." Now any mail that fulfills those conditions will be instantly deleted.

Remember, you have to be very confident that you're not getting any real mail mixed up in your junk mail! (Personally, if something gets accidentally labeled as junk and disappears, that's too bad—it's not worth it to me to sort through hundreds of pieces of junk mail to see if there's one good message. Sorry.)

The Toolbar

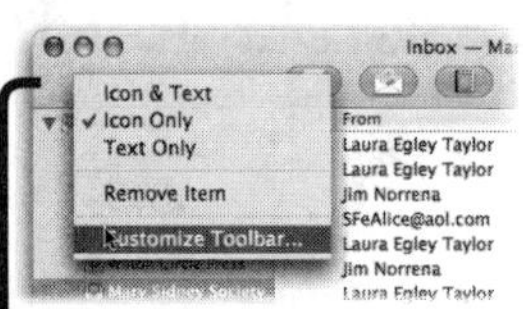

Control-click on the toolbar to open this contextual menu.

The buttons in the Mail **toolbar** are duplicates of some of the commands that are available in the menu bar at the top of your monitor. You can customize the Mail toolbar just like you customize the one in Finder windows.

To add additional tool buttons to the toolbar, go to the View menu and choose "Customize Toolbar…." **Or** Control-click in the lower two/thirds of the toolbar, then choose "Customize Toolbar…" from the contextual menu that opens.

A sheet of buttons slides down from the toolbar; the buttons represent various functions, as shown below. Drag any of these icons to the toolbar, then click "Done."

To remove a button or spacer from the toolbar at any time, Command-drag it off the bar. To remove a button while the "Customize Toolbar" sheet is visible, just drag it off.

To rearrange a button or a spacer, Command-drag it to another position.

Click this button to hide or show the toolbar.

Command-click this button at any time to switch the toolbar between different views of your icons.

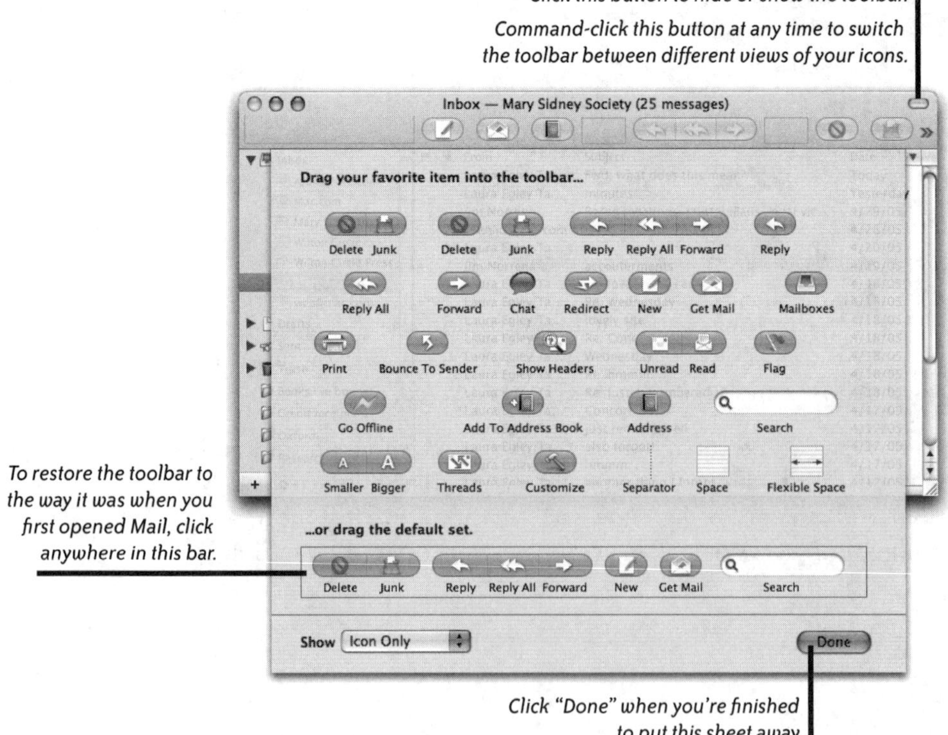

To restore the toolbar to the way it was when you first opened Mail, click anywhere in this bar.

Click "Done" when you're finished to put this sheet away.

Bounce to Sender

Bounce To Sender is meant to discourage unwanted email: Select an unwanted message, then from the Message menu, choose "Bounce To Sender." The sender receives a reply that says your email address is invalid and the message was not delivered; the recipient cannot tell if the message has been read. The unwanted message is moved to your Trash folder. Unfortunately, this does not work for most junk email because spam return addresses are usually fake (to prevent spammers' lives from being threatened).

To put this button in your toolbar, see the opposite page.

Redirect

Redirect is similar to "Forward," except that redirected mail shows the *original* sender's name in the "From" column instead of yours, and shows the time the message was originally composed. When you redirect mail, your name is at the top of the message so the new recipient knows you received the message and redirected it. To put this button in your toolbar, see the opposite page.

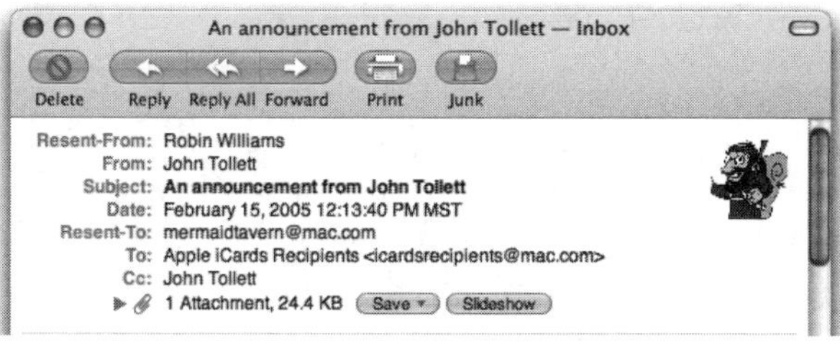

Go Offline

If you have a dial-up Internet connection, you probably don't want to stay online while you answer and compose email. You can log on to get your mail, then **go offline** (disconnect). Read your mail and write answers; Mail will save each composed message in your Drafts folder. When you're ready, go online again and send the finished messages. To put this button in your toolbar, see the opposite page.

IMAP vs. POP

Apple's Mail program can handle three types of incoming mail "protocol": **IMAP** and **POP** (or POP3, to be specific), and **Exchange.** A protocol is a particular set of standards having to do with communications between computers. You can set up IMAP or POP accounts in Mail; see the following pages.

Email from a POP account is stored "locally," which means on your hard disk.

POP3 (Post Office Protocol 3) is a protocol in which the server automatically downloads the mail to your computer when you check mail, then *deletes* the mail from the server. With POP you cannot read mail until it has been downloaded to your computer. POP works best for users who always use one computer on which the email files are stored and managed.

You can choose to leave your mail on the POP server after it has been downloaded to your Mac (see page 441), but check with your service provider before you do that—it might annoy them to have all of your email clogging up space on their server.

Email from an IMAP account is stored on a remote server (although you can keep copies on your hard disk).

IMAP (Internet Message Access Protocol) is a protocol that receives and *holds* email on a server for a certain amount of time, typically thirty days. IMAP allows you to view email before deciding whether or not to download it to your computer.

One advantage of IMAP is that you can manage your email from multiple computers because the email files are kept on the IMAP server for storage and manipulation; this means you can check your mail on a computer while you're on holiday in Istanbul, and when you come home, you'll still have the same messages available at home that you read in Istanbul.

Another advantage is that you can choose *not* to download emails that have large attachments or email from people you don't want to hear from. You can wait until it's convenient, until you know who an attachment is from, or you can just delete unwanted or unsolicited email and attachments before they ever get to your computer.

When you sign up for a Mac.com email service through .Mac, you're assigned a 125-megabyte mailbox on Apple's IMAP mail server. All unread messages within an account, *even deleted messages,* are stored on Apple's server. If you have more than 125 megabytes of mail and attachments, people will not be able to send you any more email at that account until you clear it out. See Section 2 for more information about .Mac accounts.

Exchange is an option for you if your company uses the Microsoft Exchange server and your administrator has configured it for IMAP access. You'll have to talk to your system administrator for details on setting this up!

Set up a New Account or Edit an Existing Account

Use **Mail preferences** to create new mail accounts, edit existing accounts, and customize Mail's behavior. You may have more than one email account in your life. For instance, you might have one that is strictly for business, one for friends and family, one for your lover, and one for your research. Mail can manage them all for you, even if they are all on different servers.

To open Preferences and get the Accounts pane:

1. From the Mail menu, choose "Preferences...," then click **Accounts.**
2. The **Accounts** list will show all the email accounts you've created.

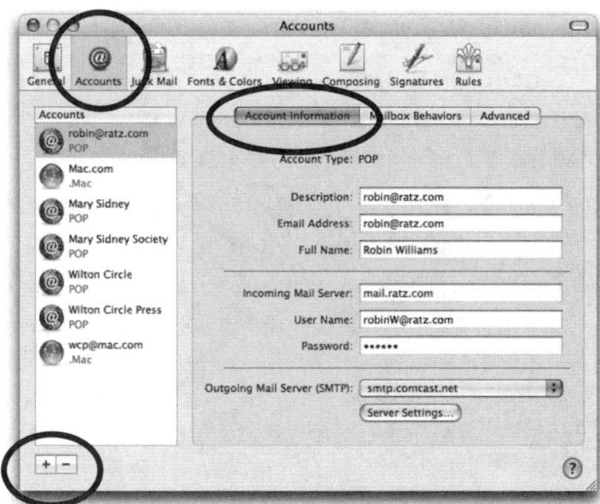

To remove an account, *select its name in the Accounts pane, then click the* **–** *sign. Or instead, you could make an account inactive; use the "Advanced" pane.*

To edit an existing account, single-click the account in the list, then see the following pages for detailed descriptions of the options.

To create a new account, click the **+** button at the bottom of the Accounts pane. You'll see the sheet shown below.

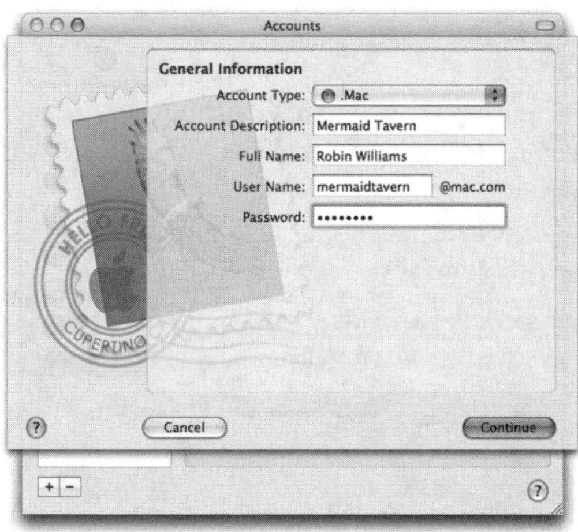

—continued

3. **Account Type** pop-up menu: Choose ".Mac" if you're setting up an email account that you created at the Mac.com website.

   If you're setting up an account that comes from some other service provider, they can tell you if they use POP or IMAP (most likely POP).

4. In the **Account Description** field, type a name that will identify this account in the Mailbox Sidebar. You can name it anything—"Lover Boy," "Research Mailing List," "earthlink," etc.

5. Enter your **Full Name.** This is what will identify you to recipients.

6. For a **POP** account, you need to enter your email address. Include the @ symbol and the domain name ("ratz.com," "typosuction.com," etc.)

7. If you're setting up a **.Mac** account, **User Name** and **Password** are the same ones you chose when you signed up for your account. You should have received an email from Apple verifying this information.

   If you're setting up a **POP** account, your **User Name** and **Password** may have been assigned by your provider, or they may have been chosen by you. *These are not necessarily the same user ID and password that you use to access your email.* If necessary, ask your provider for the user ID and password information for your account.

8. **Incoming Mail Server:** If your account type is **.Mac,** the host name is automatically filled in with "mail.mac.com."

   If you're setting up another account type, such as a **POP** account, the mail service provider can tell you what name to use. Tell them you need the "incoming" mail server name, also known as the "POP address." (It's probably something like "mail.domainname.com," where "domainname" is the name in your email address, such as mail.ratz.com.)

My friend Joannie made up a great mnemonic for SMTP: Send Money To Person.

9. **Outgoing Mail Server:** No matter where your email account *comes* from, the outgoing mail server (the SMTP Host) for every account is always the one you're paying money to for your Internet service—it's your Internet Service Provider's name, such as "mail.providername.com" because that's how your email is going *out.* Mac.com is *not* the SMTP host for your Mac.com account. (Well, technically it can work, but you'll have fewer problems if you don't use it.)

   If "smtp.provider.com" or "mail.provider.com" don't work, call your provider and ask them what the SMTP Host is called.

When that process is finished and you once again see the Accounts pane, click the **Mailbox Behaviors** tab of the window. The items in this tab change depending on whether you're creating an IMAP account (such as .Mac) or a POP account (most others).

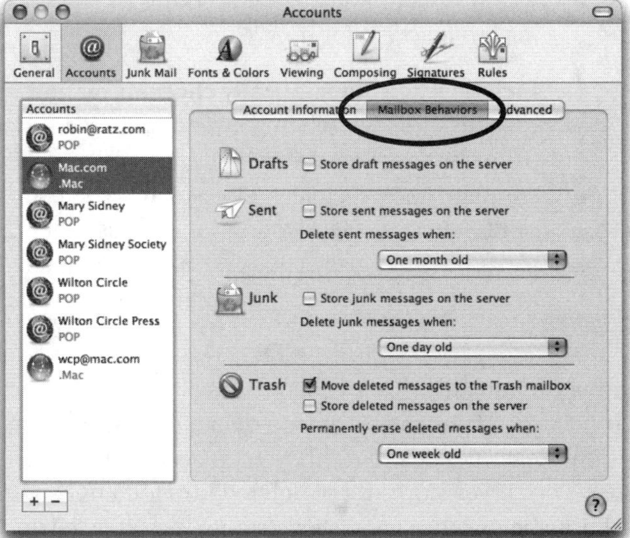

These are the IMAP options. The advantage to storing items on the server is that you can access them from anywhere in the world; they're not stored on your computer.

If you have a .Mac email acount, you can go to www.mac.com and log into your account on any computer that has a browser and an Internet connection.

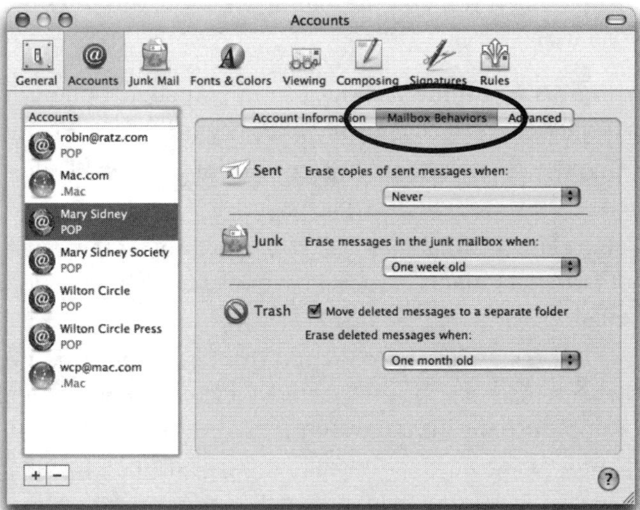

These are the POP options. These refer to the messages that are in the Mail program and stored on your Mac, not on a remote server.

—*continued*

See the opposite page for the POP options.

If you're creating an IMAP or .MAC account, the following options are shown in the Advanced pane:

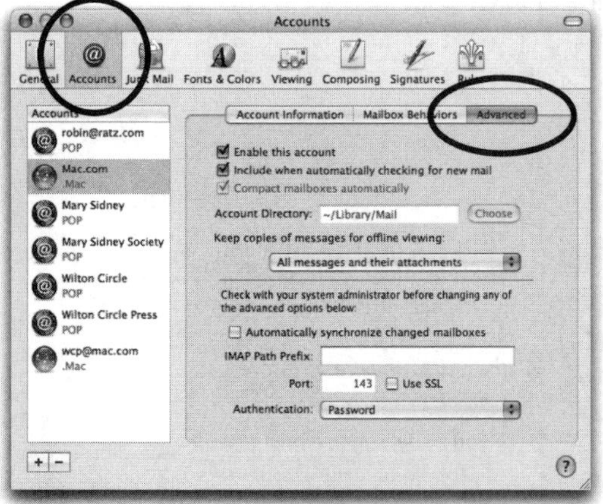

Enable this account: Check to make the account active. Uncheck it to make the account **inactive,** which does not delete the account—it just tells Mail to ignore it for now.

Include when automatically checking for new mail: UNcheck this box when you want to prevent Mail from checking email at this address. This is useful if you have several email addresses and you choose not to check some accounts as often as others. You can always manually check for messages in any account—use the "Get New Mail" option in the Mailboxes menu.

Compact mailboxes automatically: "Compacting" a mailbox is the same as deleting trashed messages. When you select and delete messages on an IMAP server, they don't really get deleted—they get placed in a "Deleted" folder on the server. The server stores these deleted files for a user-specified length of time before they are erased. Apple doesn't give you a choice about this with your .Mac email account—the files you delete will be erased immediately when you quit the Mail application; this frees up your email space on their server.

Keep copies of messages for offline viewing: This menu offers options for copying email messages from an IMAP server onto your own Mac.

"All messages and their attachments" will copy all of your email, plus any attachments you were sent, to your hard disk.

"All messages, but omit attachments" will copy the body of the email messages, but not attachments. You will have to choose to download any attachments.

"Only messages I've read" will only copy and store messages if you've read them. You can mark a letter as "Unread" or "Read" whether you really have or not—use the Message menu.

"Don't keep copies of any messages" will not copy any of your mail to your hard disk. This option provides you with extra security and privacy if other people have access to your computer. If you choose this option, be aware that some IMAP servers will eventually erase messages that have been stored for a user-specified length of time (thirty days, generally), whether you've read them or not.

If you're creating a POP account, the following options are shown in the Advanced tab:

See the opposite page for the IMAP options.

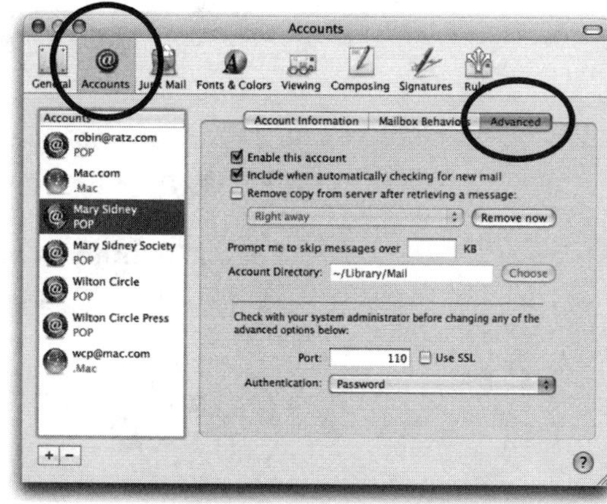

Enable this account: Check to make the account active. Uncheck it to make the account **inactive,** which does not delete the account—it just tells Mail to ignore it for now.

Include when automatically checking for new mail: UNcheck this box to prevent Mail from checking email at this address. This is useful if you have several accounts and you choose not to check some email as often as others. You can always manually check for messages in any account—use the "Get New Mail" option in the Mailboxes menu.

Remove copy from server after retrieving a message: POP servers prefer that you choose the option to delete a message from the server as soon as it is downloaded to your Mac. Uncheck it only when you need to temporarily keep a copy of your mail on the server. In the pop-up menu you'll find several options for lengths of time to store messages.

Prompt me to skip messages over __ KB: When checking for mail, you can choose to skip over messages that are larger than you want to receive. This can eliminate unsolicited attachments. Enter the maximum file size that you'll permit Mail to download. A typical text email message with no attachments is about 1 to 10 KB (kilobytes). Messages in HTML format (the fancy ones with nice type and graphics) might be 30 to 60 KB.

All done?

When all the "Accounts" preferences are set, click the red Close button (or click any other icon in the toolbar). A sheet drops down and asks if you want to save the changes. Your new account appears in the Mailbox Sidebar, under the "Inbox" icon. If you don't see it, perhaps the Inbox is closed up—single-click the disclosure triangle to display the accounts, as shown below.

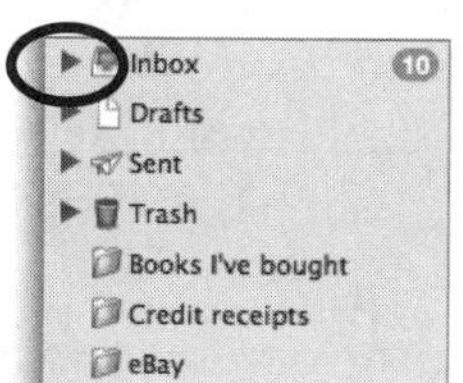

This Inbox is closed; notice the triangle is pointing to the right. Click the triangle.

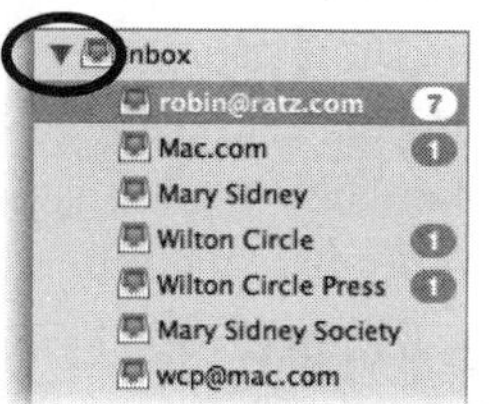

With the triangle pointing down, the accounts are displayed.

Mail Preferences

As usual in a Mac application, you have a lot of preferences to set up Mail to suit how you work.

General

In this preference pane, tell other applications to use Mail for email links and when to check for new messages.

To open Preferences and get the General pane:

- From the Mail menu, choose "Preferences...," then click **General.**

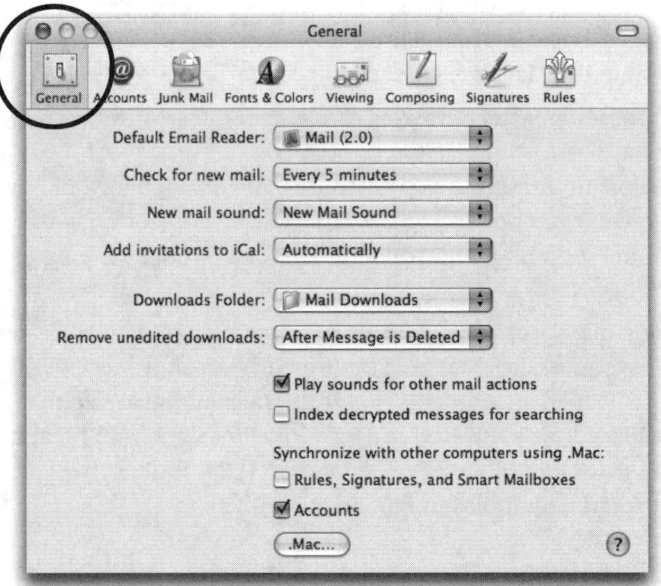

Default Email Reader: Choose "Mail" in this menu so when you go to a web page or a PDF and click an email link, it will open a pre-addressed email compose window for you.

Check for new mail: Set how often you want to check for new mail. This only works if Mail is open (if the triangle is under its icon in the Dock). If you don't have a full-time, always-on connection to the Internet (such as DSL or cable modem), you'll probably want to select "Manually" from this pop-up menu to avoid having your modem dialing and trying to connect when you least expect it.

New mail sound: Choose various sounds (or "None") to alert you when new mail appears in your Inbox. If you create various rules that filter your mail, you can have different sounds for each of the rules so you know exactly when junk mail has been deleted, a letter from your lover has arrived, or mail for your family has gone into the Family mailbox; see pages 453–455.

Add invitations to iCal: When a Mac user sends you an iCal invitation via email, this option tells Mail to automatically send it over to your iCal. You'll see the invitation in the Notifications pane and an event will be automatically created. You can respond to the person either through Mail or through iCal. The other option in this menu is "Never."

Downloads folder: When an email message to you includes an attachment and you open that attachment to view it, Mail temporarily stores the attachment in this "Mail Downloads" folder (it's in your user Library folder). If you do not manually save an attachment, then the attachment is deleted when you delete the email message it came in.

Remove unedited downloads: Read about the "Downloads folder," directly above. This option tells Mail when to delete those temporarily stored attachments. The default is to delete them "After Message is Deleted," but you can choose "When Mail Quits" or "Never." This does not affect any attachments you have saved into folders of your choice.

Play sounds for other mail actions: Plays the sound of an airplane taking off when mail has been sent, and plays other tiny sounds when it checked for mail and there wasn't any, or when there was a problem fetching mail.

Index decrypted messages for searching: If you know what encryption is and you're using it, this will add encrypted messages to Mail's database of files it has indexed for searching.

Synchronize with other computers using .Mac: If you like to synchronize your files between Macs, as explained in detail in Chapter 11, check either or both of these boxes.

Fonts & Colors

Select **fonts, font sizes,** and **text colors** for various parts of your messages.

To open Preferences and get the Fonts & Colors pane:

- From the Mail menu, choose "Preferences...," then click **Fonts & Colors.**

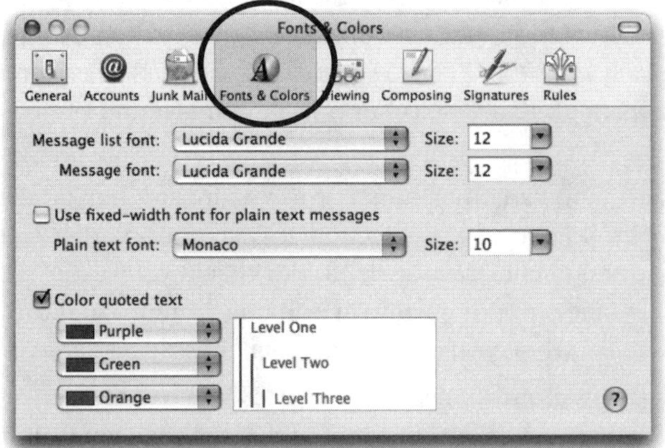

Choose default font sizes.

Message list font is the font used in the list of messages on your Mac.

Message font is the font in which you will type your email messages. If you choose a font that your recipients do not have installed on their computers, this font you choose will turn into their default fonts.

Use fixed-width font for plain text messages: When you choose to receive or write messages in "plain text," which is totally without formatting or other typefaces, this is the pop-up menu of fonts that are suitable.

Color quoted text: Email replies often contain quotes from previous emails. Color coding and indenting the quotes helps visually organize the message in a hierarchy of responses. To apply color to quoted messages, check the box, then choose colors. See the example on page 459.

Viewing

The **Viewing** preferences affect the information you see in the main Viewer window and in the body of email messages.

To open Preferences and get the Viewing pane:

- From the Mail menu, choose "Preferences...," then click **Viewing.**

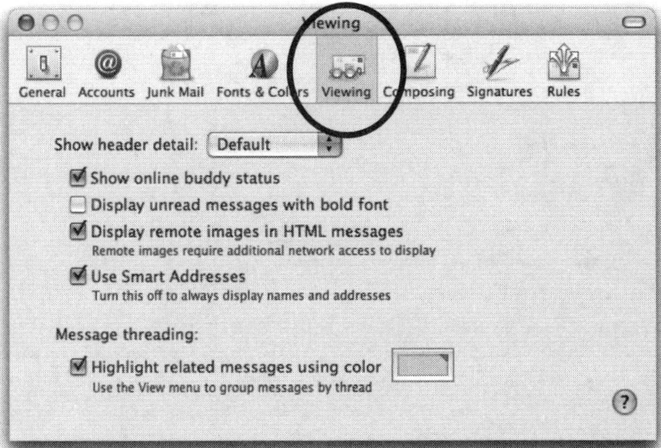

Show header detail: This menu lets you choose how much, if any, header information (all that to/from/date stuff) shows at the top of emails. This can be handy when you want to check for fraudulent emails, like those from scumbags pretending to need your eBay account information: Choose to show "All" headers and look for suspicious data, like a return address that is different from the one that appears in your Inbox.

Choose "Custom..." to customize what information appears in the headers. "Default" means the simple, basic stuff you usually see.

Display unread messages with bold font: This makes every unread message appear in your Viewer window in a bold font so it is very clear which ones you haven't read yet.

Display remote images in HTML messages: HTML messages are those fancy ones that look like web pages with graphics and links. Some junk mailers use these to embed graphics that have to be downloaded from a remote server. When you open this junk mail, the server can tell the junk mailer your computer's address, that your email address is working, and even what time of day you opened the message. To protect your privacy, you can uncheck this box. Keep in mind this will make legitimate HTML messages difficult to read because you won't see any graphics.

Highlight related messages using color: For an explanation of message threading, please see page 419.

Composing

The **Composing** pane applies to email messages as you write them.

To open Preferences and get the Composing pane:

- From the Mail menu, choose "Preferences…," then click **Composing.**

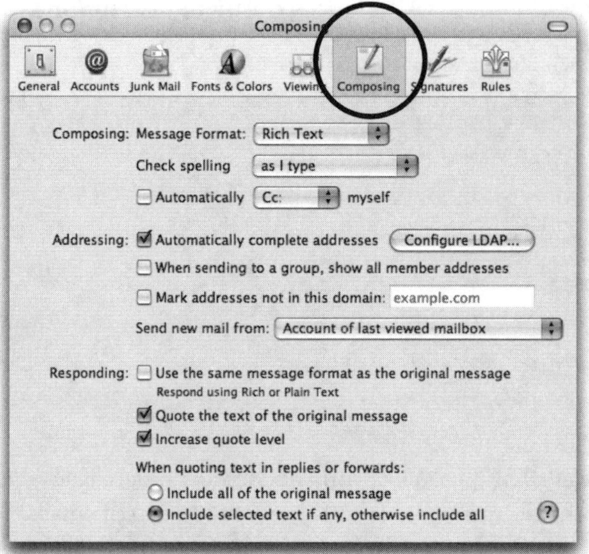

Format: "Rich Text" allows you to stylize messages with fonts and formatting, but not everyone will be able to see these features, depending on their computers and mail programs. The other option in this pop-up menu, "Plain Text," can be seen by everyone but does not show any color and style formatting. Choose the format you'll use most often; you can change individual messages to the other format when necessary (choose it from the Format menu in the main menu bar).

Check spelling as I type: Check this to catch spelling errors immediately. When Mail doesn't recognize a word, it underlines the word with a dotted red line. If you need help with the correct spelling, Control-click on a misspelled word and you'll get a pop-up menu with alternative spellings to choose from. Or from the Edit menu choose "Spelling," then choose "Spelling…" from the submenu.

You can choose "when I click Send," in which case as soon as you click the Send button, Mail runs a spell check. If there are spelling errors, the message won't go out until you've had a chance to fix them.

You can also choose to "never" spell check automatically.

Automatically Cc myself to send a copy of outgoing messages to yourself. From this same menu you can also choose **Automatically Bcc myself** to send yourself a copy without the recipient knowing it.

Automatically complete addresses: As you type a few letters in the "To" field, Mail will add the rest of the address for you. If there is more than one match, you'll get a list to choose from. If the correct one is the one in the Address field, just hit Return. If you get a list of possible addresses, use the DownArrow to move down the list, selecting each one; hit Return or Enter when the proper address is chosen.

If you hate it that the email address automatically completes itself, uncheck this box.

When sending to a group, show all member addresses: When you send a message to a Group (a mailing list, as explained on pages 470–473), Mail displays everyone's address in every message. Unless you have a specific reason to do this, UNcheck this box so the actual addresses are hidden.

Mark addresses not in this domain: If you work in a large company or a school with an internal mail system, you might want to notify yourself when you are about to send email outside of your own domain. If so, check this box and enter your internal domain in the field. The "domain" is the part of an email address after the @ symbol. For instance, "mac.com" is a domain.

Send new mail from: If you have more than one email account, or if you use aliases with your Mac.com account, each address will be listed in this menu. Choose which one you want to use as a default return address. You can always choose one from the menu in an outgoing message.

The other options in this pane are self-explanatory. It's a good idea to **quote the text of the original message** so the person you are responding to knows what you're talking about. **Increase quote level** makes each successive response a different color and indented a little more, as shown on page 459.

I love the option to **Include selected text if any, otherwise include all**. This means you can select just a few words or lines in a message that someone sends you; when you click "Reply," the message you send back includes only the text you selected.

Signatures

A **signature** is a blurb of prepared information about you or your company that can be added to the end of a message either manually or automatically. You can create different signatures that include different types of information and images. For instance, in addition to a signature for personal mail that may include your address and phone number, you may want to create a different business signature that doesn't include personal information.

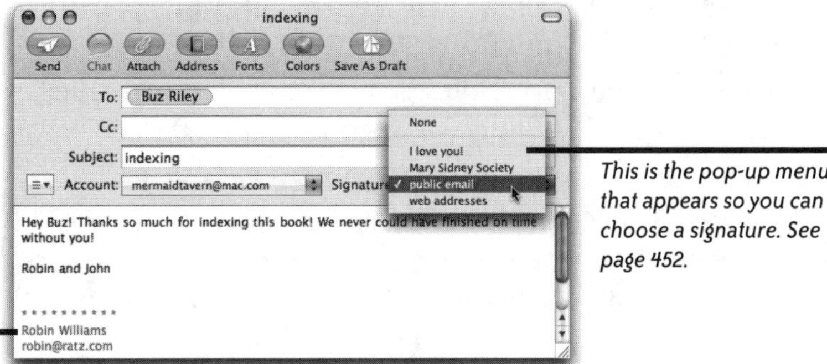

This is what a signature looks like in the email message.

This is the pop-up menu that appears so you can choose a signature. *See page 452.*

To open Preferences and get the Signatures pane:

- From the Mail menu, choose "Preferences...," then click **Signatures.**

To create a signature, first select either "All Signatures" or select a particular email account. No matter where you initially create the signature, you can always drag it to any other account.

In the middle pane, click the **+** sign. A new signature label appears in the middle pane; rename it something identifiable.

In the right-hand pane, enter the text you want to use as a signature. Add any extra Returns that you want to appear before the signature.

To add a photograph or graphic image to your signature, drag it into the right-hand pane. The image format should be JPEG (.jpg). If your message is going to another Mac, other formats will work, such as TIFF, PICT, or PNG, but JPEG is still the recommended format.

To change the font, size, and color, go to the Format menu at the top of the screen and choose "Show Fonts" and "Show Colors." Select the text and apply fonts, sizes, and colors as usual.

Always match my default message font will make sure your signature matches the text in your message. However, if you have chosen a font, size, or color for your signature, *un*check this box so your formatting choices appear in the message. You can check or uncheck this option for each individual signature.

To apply a signature to an account, drag it from the middle pane and drop it on the account name in the left-hand pane, as shown below. You can drag any signature to any number of accounts.

Drag an image and drop it into this signature pane.

Place signature above quoted text: This puts your signature at the end of *your message,* not at the end of all the quoted information that might be in the letter. This is a good thing.

To create a new signature that's similar to an existing signature, select the signature you want to use as a model, then click the **+** button. This duplicate now shows up in the list of signatures; edit its name and text.

—continued

To choose a default signature, select an account name in the far-left pane. Then select a signature in the "Choose Signature" pop-up menu. This one will be used in all messages from that account *unless* you override it from the pop-up menu (discussed below) when you're composing a new email.

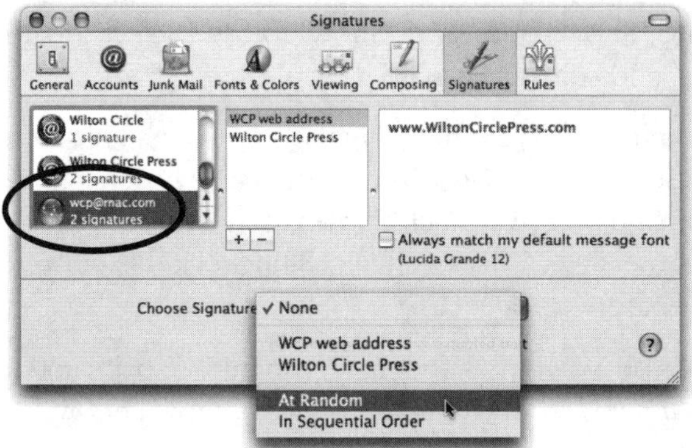

To put a signature on an email message, you can do several things. Just above, we told you how to choose a signature as a default for a particular email account. But you can override that in any message. To do this easily, you need to display your accounts and your signatures on compose messages:

1. Open a new message.
2. Click on the Action menu and choose "Customize...."
3. In the expanded window that appears, shown below, put a checkmark in the boxes next to "Account" and "Signature." Click OK.

Now you will have menus with which to select an account to use as a return address. And for each account, you can choose the signature to use. See the example of the signature menu on page 450.

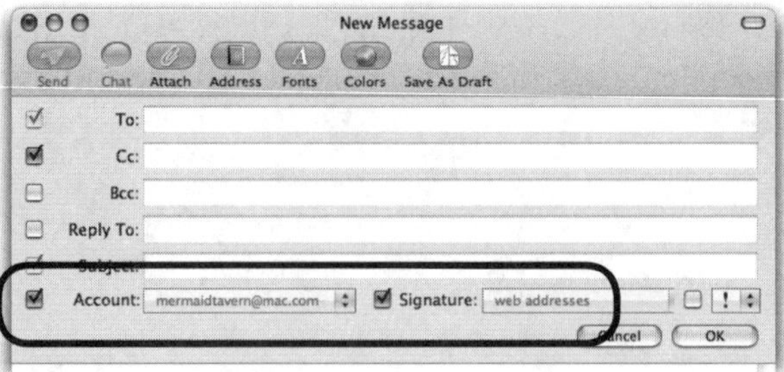

Rules

Use **Rules** to manage and organize your messages automatically. Rules act as filters that sift through your messages as they come in and put them in their proper mailboxes, delete them, forward them, or follow other actions, according to your directions. You might belong to a mailing list about pack rats, so you can have every email that comes in from that mailing list automatically delivered to the PackRat mailbox. Or you might want to delete every email with a subject that contains the words "mortgage," "enlargement," "babes," "hot," "insurance," or other obvious junk-mail words.

To open Preferences and get the Rules pane:

- From the Mail menu, choose "Preferences...," then click **Rules.**

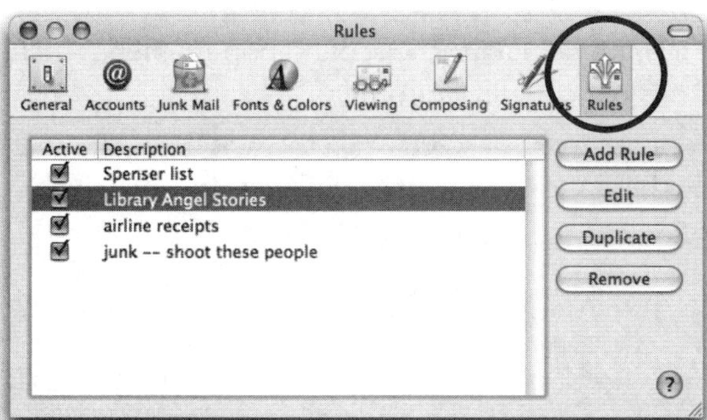

A rule called "News from Apple" is probably already in your list. It highlights email from Apple with a color. Feel free to delete it if you like—all that will happen is your news messages from Apple will not be highlighted in blue.

To create a new Rule:

1. Click the "Add Rule" button. You'll get the dialog box shown below (except yours isn't filled in yet).

—continued

2. The **Description** field contains a default name, such as "Rule #1." Change this name to something that describes your intended rule. In the example below, I want to keep track of messages about a little book I'm working on, so I want messages relating to that to go into the "Library Angels" folder (mailbox) I created.

3. In the **following conditions** section, specify which elements of an email message are to be searched and what the subject of the search will be.

   The first pop-up menu contains types of message **headers** that usually are included with an incoming message, such as To, From, Subject, etc., *or* you can choose to find text in the body of the message.

   Then choose a "modifier" from the second pop-up menu, such as "Contains," "Does not contain," or others.

   Type an appropriate word or words into the text field. The rule below will search for messages whose "Subject" field "Contains" the word "angels."

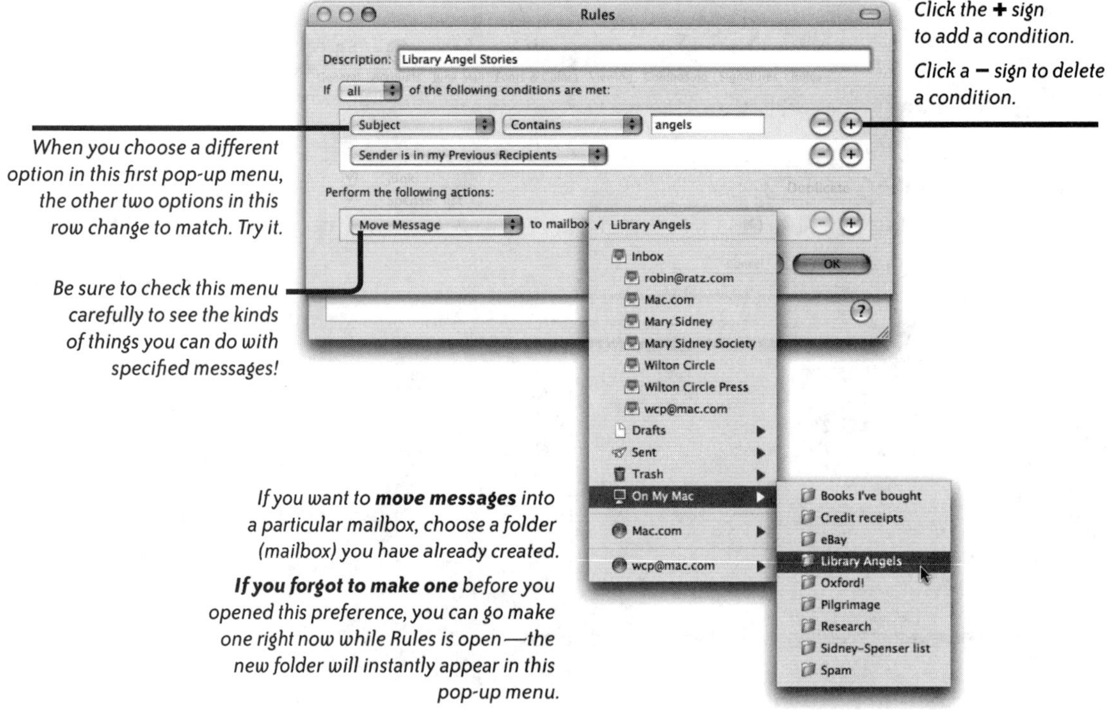

Click the + sign to add a condition.

Click a – sign to delete a condition.

When you choose a different option in this first pop-up menu, the other two options in this row change to match. Try it.

Be sure to check this menu carefully to see the kinds of things you can do with specified messages!

*If you want to **move messages** into a particular mailbox, choose a folder (mailbox) you have already created.*

***If you forgot to make one** before you opened this preference, you can go make one right now while Rules is open—the new folder will instantly appear in this pop-up menu.*

4. **Perform the following actions:** Determines what actions will be applied to messages that match the criteria you specified. You can check as many or as few of these actions as you like.
5. **OK:** Click OK and the rule is made. All incoming mail will now be searched and sorted using the criteria you just created.

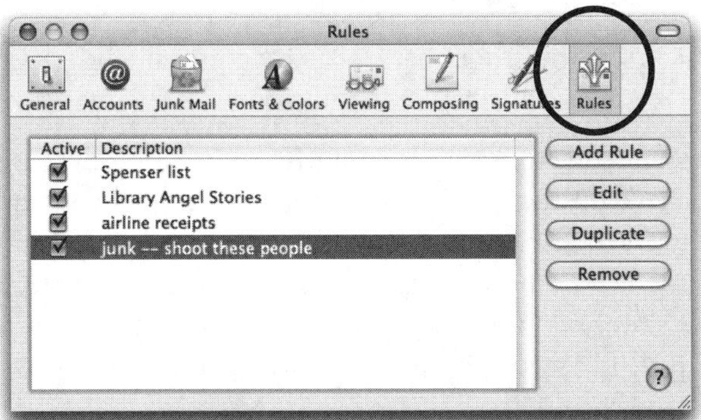

Tip: If you won't be able to respond to your mail for a while, set up an **autoresponder** that will automatically return a message saying you are away and will respond later:

Choose "If sender is in my Address Book," and "Reply to message," then click the button to enter your message. You might say something like, "Thank you for your email. When I return from the Amazon on October 27, I will answer your lovely message."

Or **forward** all of your own email to yourself at another address.

Rules are listed in an order and will be applied in that order. **Change the priority order** by dragging a rule to another position in the list.

To edit a rule, select it in the list, then click the "Edit" button, *or* double-click the rule name in the list.

Duplicate a rule if you want to create a new rule that is similar to an existing one. Select an existing rule in the list, click "Duplicate," then select and edit that new rule.

To remove a rule, select it in the rule list, then click the "Remove" button or press the "Delete" key on your keyboard.

Instead of removing a rule that might have taken some time to create, you can make it **inactive:** Uncheck the box in the **Active** column. When you want to use the rule again, it's still there and can be activated.

Rules affect new messages that are received *after* a rule was created. **To apply rules to messages you've already received,** select the messages in the main Viewer window. From the "Message" menu, choose "Apply Rules." **Or** Control-click on one of the selected messages and choose "Apply Rules" from the pop-up menu.

Menu Commands

Following are some of the items in the **menus** that aren't explained elsewhere.

File menu

New Viewer Window: If you've closed the main Viewer window and realize that you need it back, use this command, or press Command Option N.

Save Attachment: Open any message that has attachments included. Choose "Save Attachment..." and you can choose where you want the files saved.

Import Mailboxes: Mail can import the mailboxes of many popular email applications. If you have custom mailboxes already set up in another email application, from the File menu, choose "Import Mailboxes...." Select one of the email clients in the list, then click the right arrow button for instructions. Mail will open a directory window so you can navigate to the appropriate mailbox file and import it. You might also want to try using the AppleScript "Import Addresses"; see page 460.

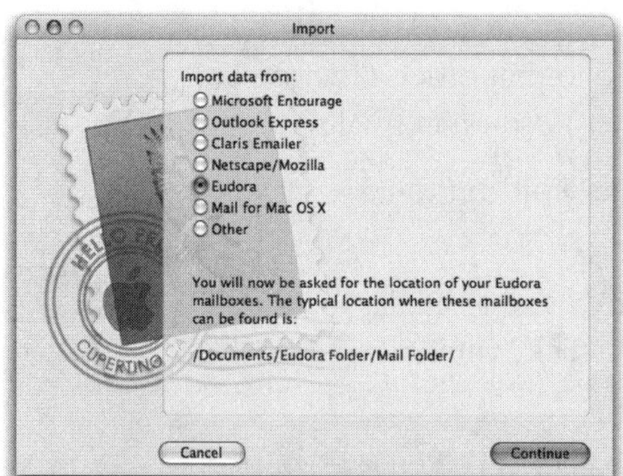

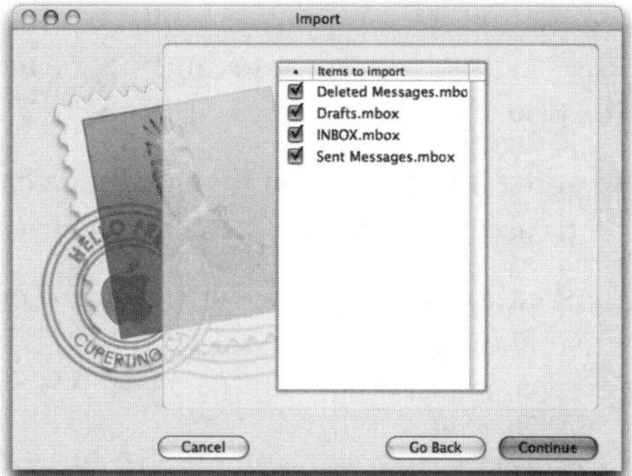

To print an email message: Double-click a message to open it. Click the "Print" icon in the open message's toolbar to open the Print dialog box. **Or** select a message in the Message List pane, go to the File menu and choose "Print...." Make the appropriate selections and click "Print."

To print multiple email messages: From the Message List, select multiple messages. From the File menu, choose "Print...." All selected messages, including header information, will print out in continuous fashion—it will not print a separate page for each message.

Edit menu

Paste As Quotation: Use this command when you want to paste text copied from another document into an email message as a quotation. In Mail, a quotation is styled with indentation, a vertical bar, and a user-specified color, as explained on page 459.

Paste and Match Style: This is a great feature. When you copy and paste text from another message or another document, it drops in with its own font and size which usually doesn't match your chosen font in the message you're writing. But if you copy text and then choose this command, the text pastes in using the font and size that is already in your message.

Paste as HTML: If you copy text from, say, a web page, you might want to paste it in with its formatting attached, which is built into the HTML code. Copy the text from a web page, then use this command. The font, color, size, alignment, and even active links will appear in your email message.

Append Selected Messages: This adds an entire email message you have received onto the end of a new message you compose. Compose your message, then go to the Viewer window, select the email message you want to append, and choose this command from the Edit menu.

Attachments: The option to **Include Original Attachments in Reply** does just what it says—when you reply, any photos or other files that came to you will be sent back to that person. Only do this if you have a reason to do so. **Always Send Windows Friendly Attachments** tries to make sure your attachments can be read by people using Windows machines. However, this can mess up files for Mac users, so only use it if you need it for every file you send. You can always choose to make **individual files** Windows friendly: Use the Attach button so you get the Open dialog box. At the bottom of that dialog box is a checkbox to "Send Windows Friendly Attachments." This will apply only to the attachment you select.

View menu

Display Selected Messages Only: Select messages (Command-click to select more than one), then choose this option so *only* those messages will be visible in the Message List. To show all of the messages again, go back to the View menu and choose "Display All Messages."

Mailbox menu

Go Online, Go Offline, Online Status: If you have a dial-up account that ties up your phone line while you're connected to the Internet, you can "Go Offline." This disconnects you from the Internet, but leaves Mail open. Before you go offline, transfer any messages you want to read to another folder (just drag them over and drop them in). Then go offline, read your mail, compose messages, print them, etc. Messages you compose while offline are stored in the Outbox in the Mailbox Sidebar, where you can open and edit them. When you're ready to send mail, from the Mailbox menu, choose "Online Status" and then select either an individual account to take online, or "Go Online" in general.

Get New Mail: If you have more than one account in Mail, go to this menu to selectively check the mail in just a single account.

Rebuild: If messages come in garbled or with some strange font, try using the Rebuild command. If your hard disk is really full, clear some room before you try this because it needs hard disk space to do its rebuilding.

Window menu

Activity Viewer: To the right of the Inbox icons you might see revolving wheels when connecting to a remote server to send or receive mail. If you want to see the actual activity represented by the wheels, go to the Window menu and choose **Activity Viewer.** The window shown below appears and you can see what's going on as Mail connects.

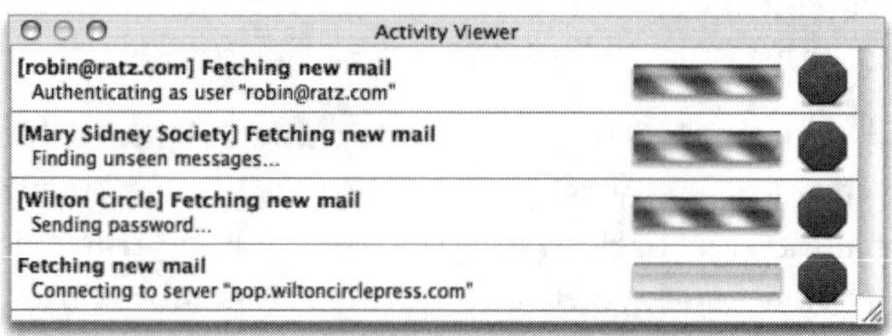

Click any "stop sign" to stop that particular activity.

Format menu

In the Format menu, under "Style," there is a command to make the selected text **Bigger.** The menu says the keyboard shortcut is Command +, but that doesn't work—use **Shift Command +**.

Make Plain Text changes messages from "Rich Text" format to "Plain Text" format, which will strip out all of the formatting, different fonts, colors, etc. If the message is already in Plain Text, this command appears as "Make Rich Text." This will *not* restore any formatting that was removed.

Quote Level: To format text as a Mail-style quote or to increase the existing quote level, click within a line of text, choose "Quote Level," and then choose "Increase." Choose the command again to further increase the quote level, as shown below. Of course, choose "Decrease" to take the text back towards normal.

The operation is much easier and faster if you learn the keyboard shortcuts: Click within the appropriate text, then type Command **'** (that's the typewriter apostrophe, just to the left of the Return key) to increase the quote level, or type Option Command **'** to decrease the quote level.

You can choose the colors for the quoted sections in the Fonts & Colors preferences; see page 446.

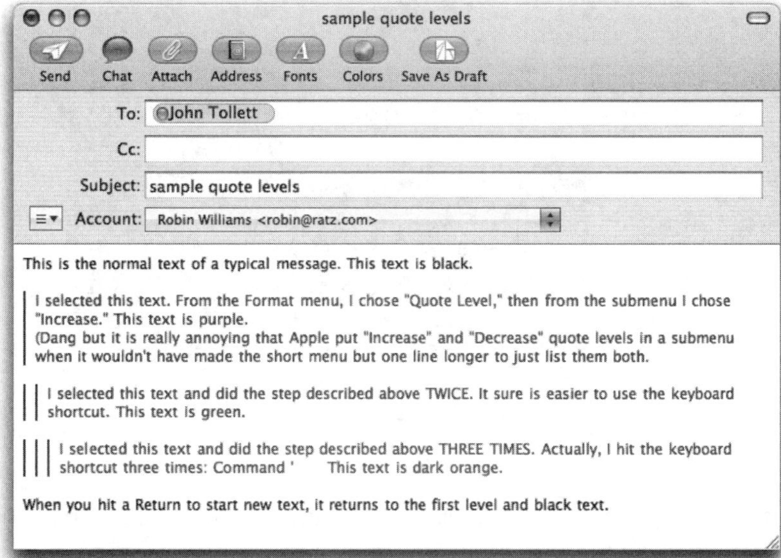

Each of these quoted sections has been increased one more level than the one above it.

Scripts menu

An **AppleScript** is a small piece of code that makes something happen. If you know how to write scripts or how to use Automator, you can do all kinds of great things. Mail provides you with a list of several useful and useless scripts in the Scripts menu (which doesn't actually say "Scripts" in the menu bar but has a little icon that looks like a parchment scroll).

If you are accustomed to using the script and noticed that the Scripts menu is no longer in the menu bar, don't worry—you can add it. Open the Applications folder, then open the AppleScripts folder, then double-click on the AppleScript Utility to open it. In the window, check the box to "Show Script Menu in menu bar." Quit the utility.

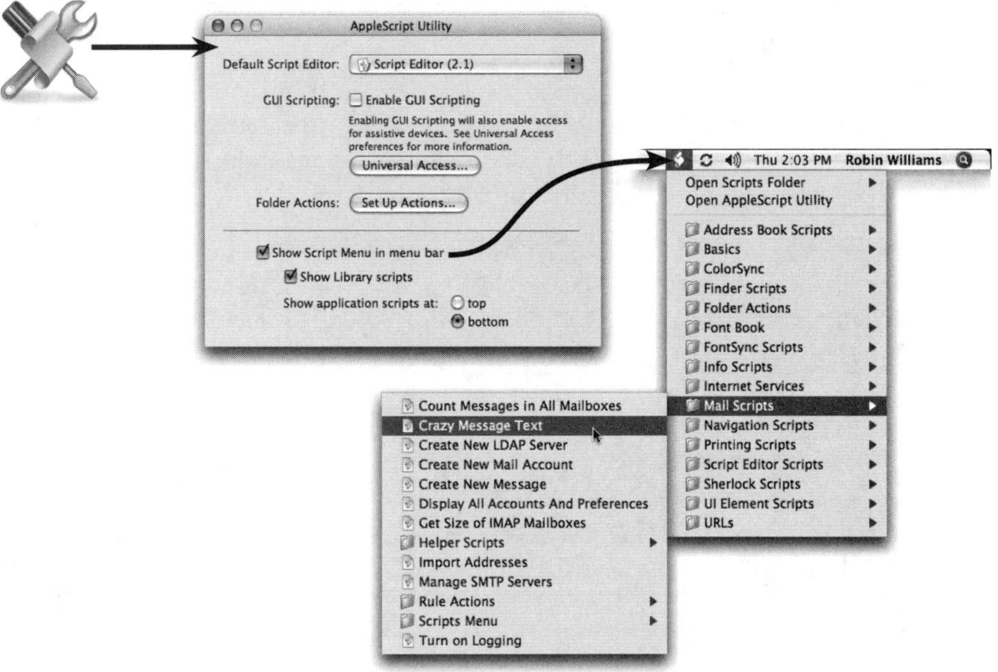

Feel free to experiment with these scripts—just choose one and let it run. Check out the "Crazy Message Text" script.

For full details about AppleScript, go to the website at **www.apple.com/applescript**.

Address Book 16

The **Address Book** is a separate application that works with Mail. Save your favorite email addresses and contact information, enter an email address with the click of the mouse, make a mailing list (a Group) to send a message to a number of people at once, create Smart Groups that add contacts to themselves automatically, and much more.

Are you a .Mac member? If so, once you've got a great Address Book underway, you can share it with other .Mac members.

You can even copy your entire Address Book list of contacts onto your iPod—please see pages 126–127 for that because you'll use iTunes to do it.

The **Address Book** works both independently and with Mail to create Address Cards (also known as **vCards**) that store contact information for individuals or groups. When Mail is open, you can automatically create an Address Book entry for anyone who has sent mail to you.

The Address Book icon, shown above-left, should be in your Dock. It's also in your Applications folder.

The Address Book icon you see in the Mail "New Message" toolbar opens up a limited version of the main Address Book, usually called the Address Pane, as explained on page 411.

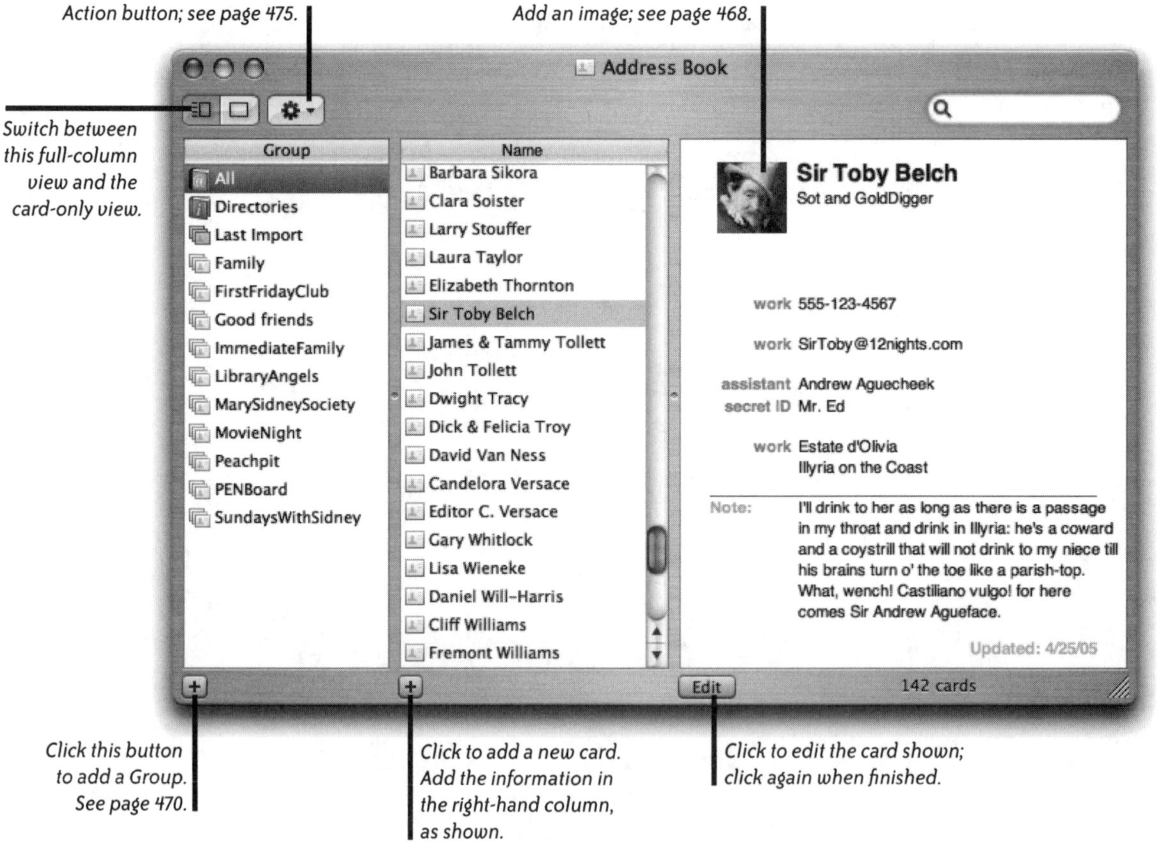

Action button; see page 475.

Add an image; see page 468.

Switch between this full-column view and the card-only view.

Click this button to add a Group. See page 470.

Click to add a new card. Add the information in the right-hand column, as shown.

Click to edit the card shown; click again when finished.

Add New Names and Addresses

There are several ways to **add a new card of information** or just a name and email address to the Address Book, depending on whether you are using Address Book or Mail at the moment.

To add a new address card while using Address Book:

1. Single-click the **+** sign at the bottom of the "Name" column (or at the bottom of the visible card if you are viewing by card only).
2. This makes a new card automatically appear on the right and the name of the person is already selected for you, waiting for you to type.

   Type the person's first name, then hit the Tab key to select the field for the last name.

   Type the last name, then hit Tab.

   Continue to fill in all the information you know.
3. If a label is changeable, you'll see two tiny arrows to its left. For instance, maybe you want to change the label "mobile" to "cell." Single-click the tiny arrows and you'll get a little pop-up menu, as shown below. Either choose one of the pre-named labels, or choose "Custom..." and type in the name of the label you want.
4. Click the green **+** sign to add another label and field; click the red **–** sign to delete the label and field to its right.

   Please see the illustration on the following page!

__To add more fields__ to one card or to all cards, see page 467.

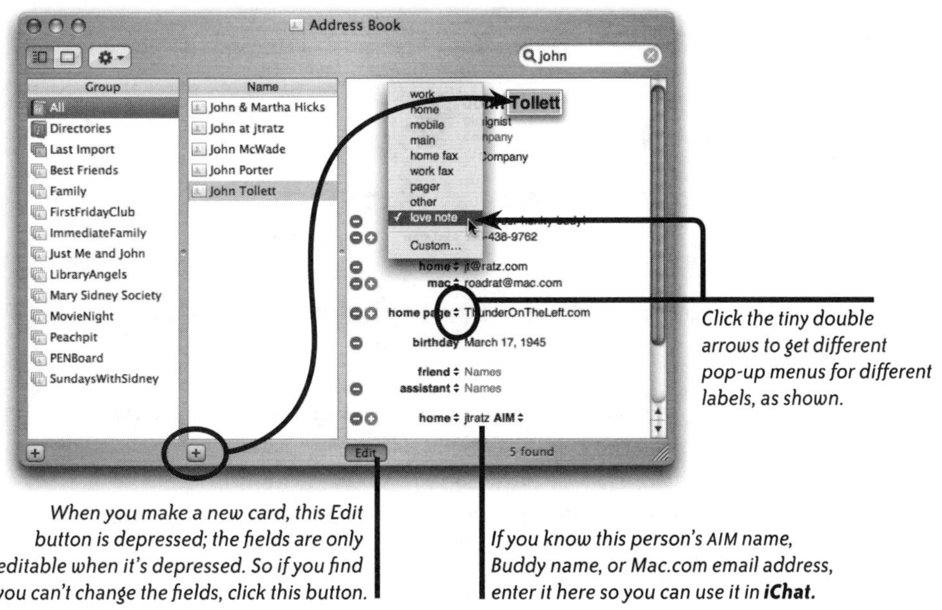

Click the tiny double arrows to get different pop-up menus for different labels, as shown.

When you make a new card, this Edit button is depressed; the fields are only editable when it's depressed. So if you find you can't change the fields, click this button.

If you know this person's AIM name, Buddy name, or Mac.com email address, enter it here so you can use it in __iChat__.

—continued

To add a sender's email address to your Address Book instantly:

1. In the **Mail** program, either single-click on a message in your list, or open an email message.
2. From the Message menu in the menu bar across the top of your screen, choose "Add Sender To Address Book," or press Command Y. The Address Book does not open, but the sender's address is added.

To add someone's address from your "Previous Recipients" list:

1. In the **Mail** program, go to the Window menu and choose "Previous Recipients." This brings up a window, shown below, that has kept track of everyone you have sent email to (not everyone who has sent you email because then you'd have thousands of junk mail addresses).

   If an address has a card icon to its left, that name and address is already in your Address Book.
2. Single-click the name of someone whose address you want to add to your Address Book, then click the button "Add to Address Book."

   Ta da. You won't see anything happen on your screen, but that address has been added.

Have you noticed that when you start typing some addresses, Mail fills in the rest for you? Mail gets that information either from your Address Book or from this list.

Remove any names you don't think you'll be needing anymore.

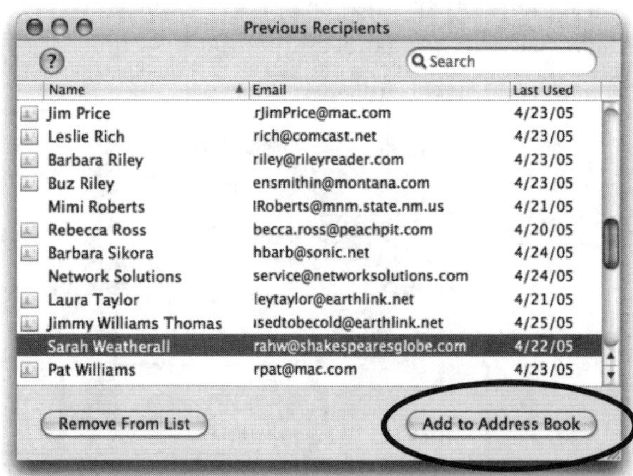

Note: If you scroll down to the bottom of the Previous Recipients list, you'll find all the people you have emailed but whose actual names are not shown. If you add one of *those* addresses to your Address Book, it will show up in the Name column in your Address Book alphabetized by the first letter in the email address.

The Importance of the "Me" Card

When you first set up your Mac, it made a card for you in Address Book and automatically labeled it "Your Card." It's also known as the "Me Card." This is very important! The information in this card is what Safari will use to AutoFill web page forms for you (see page 401). iChat uses the photo you put on this card and the AIM address. If you send automatic updates of your contact information, this is the card that will be sent.

You can have more than one card for yourself, but be sure to designate the appropriate one as your card: Select it, then go to the Card menu and choose "Make This My Card." It will have a little figure next to your name, and a small label, "me," on your photo, as shown below.

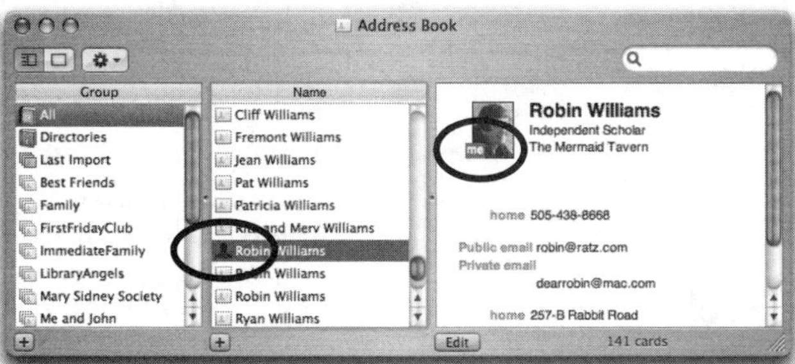

You can make certain information on your card private; see page 482.

Send Email to Someone in your Address Book

Open your Address Book and find the person you want to **send email** to. On that persons's card, single-click on the gray *label* that's to the left of the email address. A menu pops up, as shown below. Choose "Send Email," and a new message window appears with that person's address in the "To" field.

Also see page 411 about using the Address Pane while in the Mail program.

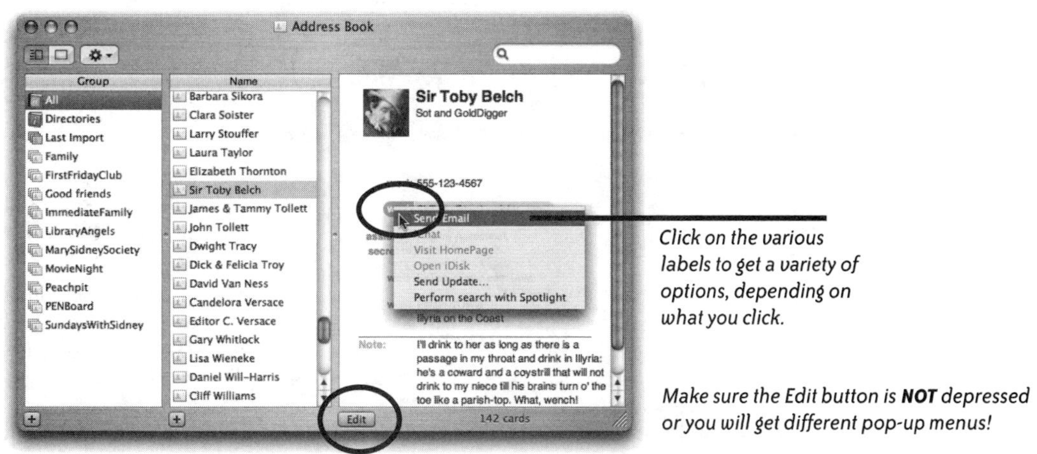

Click on the various labels to get a variety of options, depending on what you click.

*Make sure the Edit button is **NOT** depressed or you will get different pop-up menus!*

Explore the Other Label Options!

Make sure the card is *not* in Edit mode. Single-click on any gray label and check out the options you have for different items.

Omigosh, you can instantly go to a map to this person's house. I can't wait until Address Book uses Google maps (www.maps.Google.com).

See a fax number from across the room

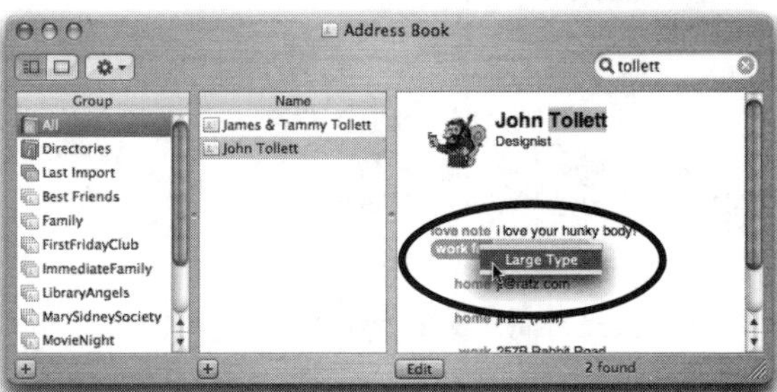

You can choose to see phone and fax numbers in type large enough to fill your screen so you can see them across the room when you fax someone. Try it.

(Or type a love note instead of a phone number and flash it to your sweetheart on the other side of the room.)

Visit a .Mac HomePage (and other options)

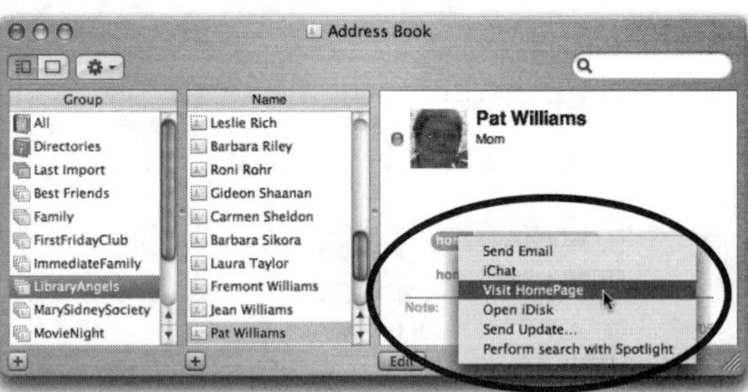

You will see more or fewer options for some labels depending on whether the person is a .Mac member or not.

Go to a web page or open a chat

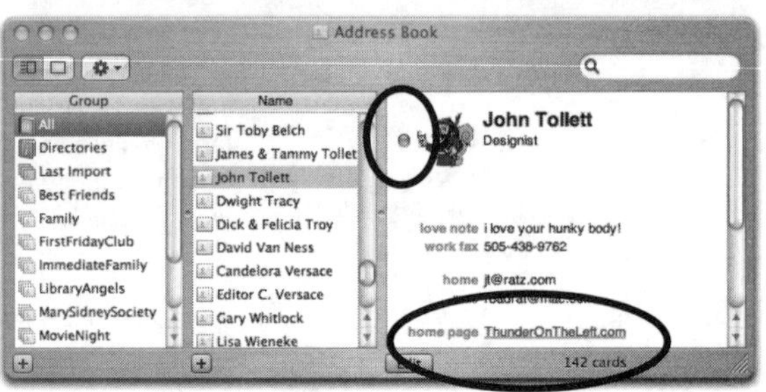

If you see a green orb next to his picture, that means he is online. Click the green orb to open an iChat (see Chapter 17).

If you included a web address in the card, you can go directly to a person's web page—just click the link.

Add New Fields or Edit the Template

You can add more fields to individual cards or to all the cards at once, and delete ones you don't use. This is different from clicking the **+** or **–** buttons on a card; this technique adds *new* fields, not new versions of an existing field.

Once you have a Birthday field in Address Book, go to the iCal preferences and choose to "Show Birthdays calendar." All birthdays that have been noted in your Address Book will be automatically added as events in iCal.

To add new fields to an *individual* card:

1. Select the card and click its Edit button.
2. From the Card menu, slide down to "Add Field," then choose the field you want to add.

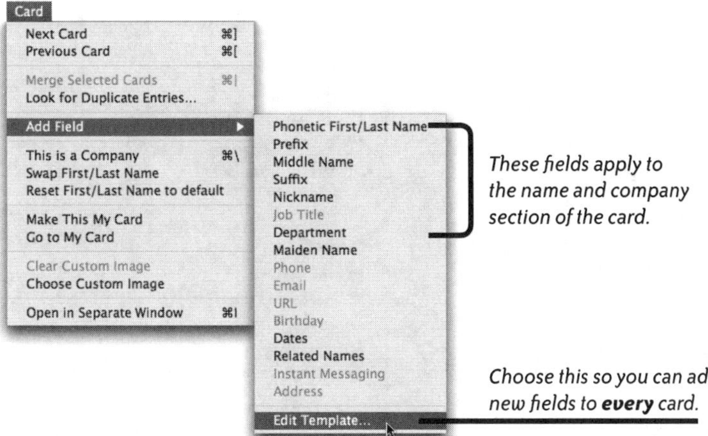

These fields apply to the name and company section of the card.

*Choose this so you can add new fields to **every** card.*

To add new fields to *every* card:

1. You don't have to select any card. Go to the Card menu and choose "Add Field," then "Edit Template...," as shown above.
2. Click the "Add Field" menu, circled below, and choose fields.

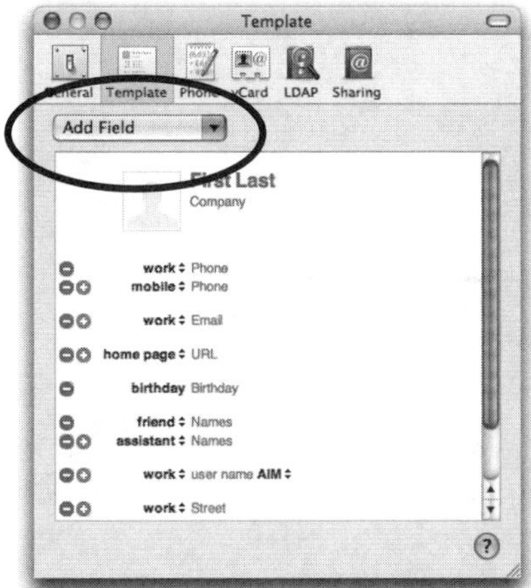

***To delete a field** from all cards, click its red minus button.*

Notice this is actually a pane in the Address Book preferences.

Add an Image to a Card (or delete an image)

You can add any sort of image to a person's Address Book card. Not only can you use photos, but you can also use clip art, drawings, oil painting portraits, or just about any image you have in a digital format.

Once you add an image to a contact's card, it will appear on that person's email messages when they send mail to you. It will also appear in your Buddy List and in iChat sessions with this person; see Chapter 17.

To add an image to a card:

1. Select a card in the Address Book, and then click its Edit button.
2. Double-click the small picture box.

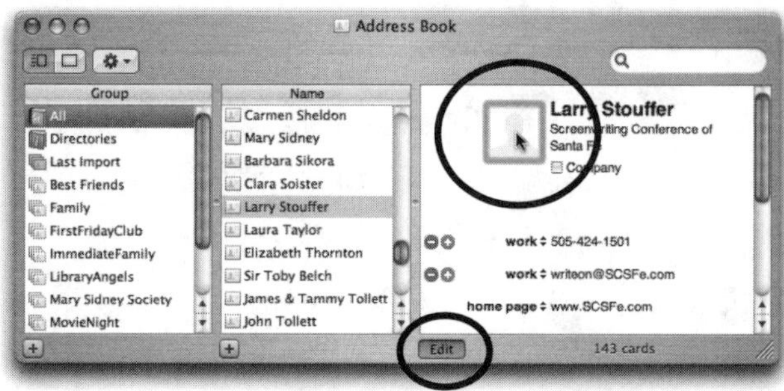

3. Drag an image from your Desktop or from any Finder window and drop it in the empty space shown below. You can use almost any type of graphic image file. If you do this, skip to Step 5.

   Or if you have an iSight or video camera attached and turned on, you'll see a button to "Take a video snapshot." Click it, then skip to Step 5.

   Or click the "Choose…" button and find your graphic, as shown on the next page.

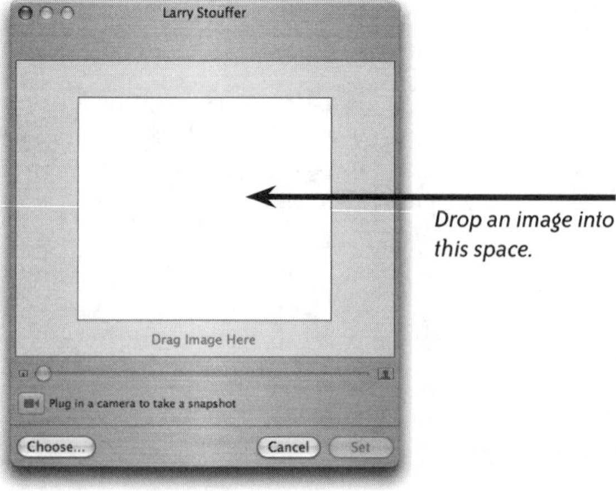

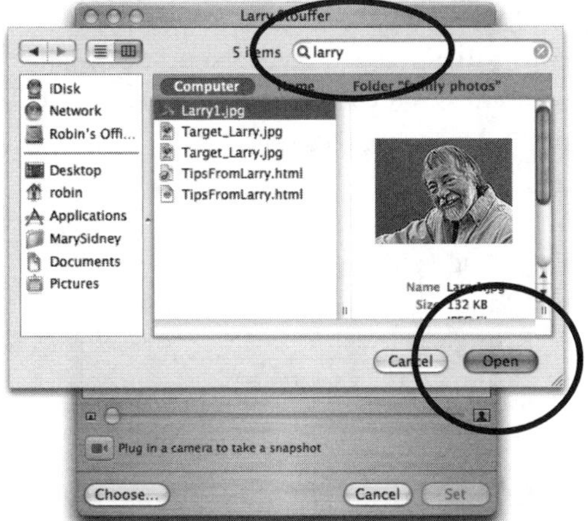

4. In this dialog box, do a search if you need to: Click in the search field and type something you think is in the title of the image.

   When you find the image, select it and click "Open."

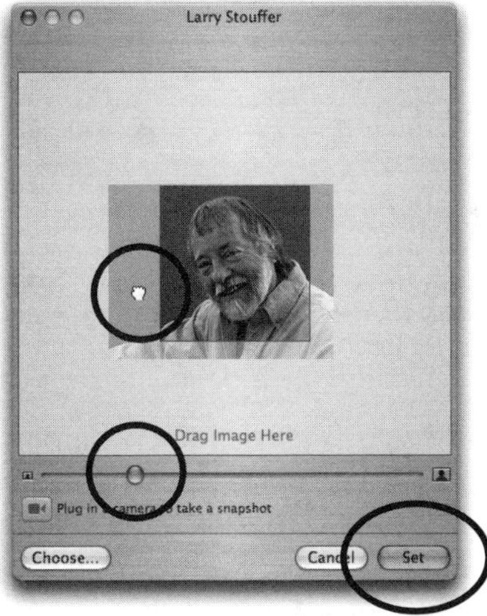

5. In the image box, use the round, blue slider to fit the frame around the image.

   Press on the image to get the grabber hand and drag the image into position within the frame.

6. When you like the size and framing, click the "Set" button.

To delete an image from a card:

1. Select a card and click its Edit button.
2. Click once on the picture.
3. Hit the Delete key.

Create and Use a Group Mailing List

You can make a **Group** in the Address Book, which not only helps organize your address list, but also acts as a **mailing list;** that is, you can send an email message to the Group name and the one message will go to everyone in that list. You can put the same contact name in more than one list.

To make a Group mailing list:

1. In the Address Book, make sure you see all three columns, as shown below, right. (If you only see one panel, the "Card" panel, click the "View Card and Column" button, shown below-left.)

If you only see one card, click this button.

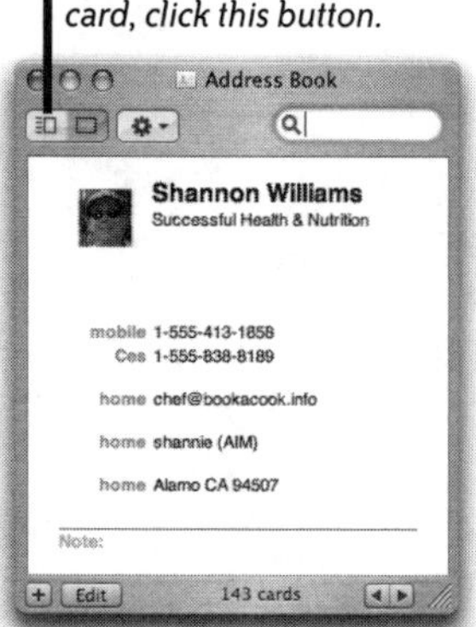

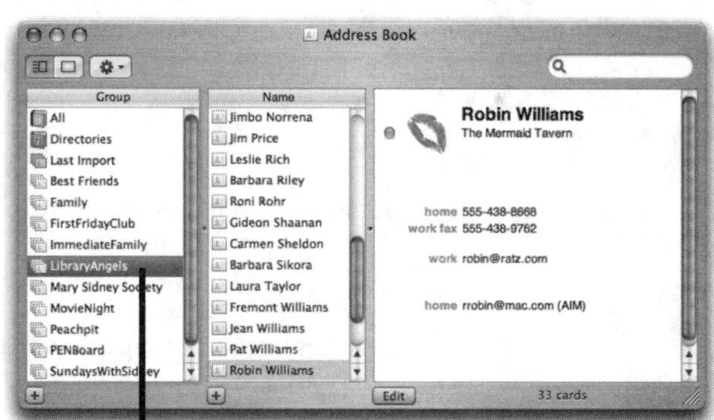

In the left column you see the Groups I have made, and the "LibraryAngels" Group is currently selected. In the center column are all the people in that selected Group.

2. Under the Group column, click the **+** sign. A "Group Name" appears in the Group column, selected and ready for you to type a new name, as shown below. Just type to replace the selected name. When done, hit the Enter key. (If the "Group Name" deselects itself because you waited too long, just double-click it and you can rename it.)

I'm going to name this new group "SFFAI."

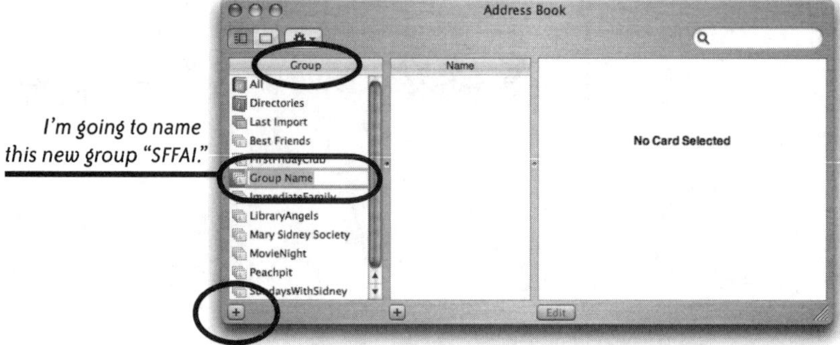

3. Now you can do one of two things: **Either** in the "Name" column, click the **+** sign and add a new address; this new address will be added to your "All" Group *and* to the new Group that you just made (which is still selected, right?).

   Or click the "All" Group so you see all of the addresses in your book. Then drag an existing address and drop it on the Group name, as shown below.

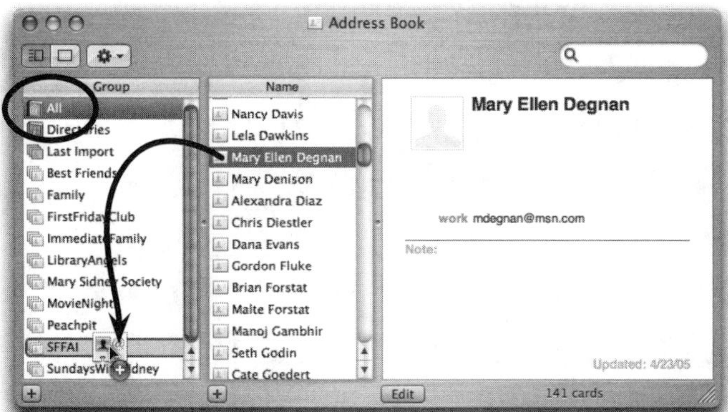

"All" contains the name of every person in every Group, as well as those who are in no Group at all. Each Group actually contains "aliases" to the one address card.

Mary Ellen is now in the "All" list, as well as in the "SFFAI" Group. You can put the same person in any number of Groups.

Shortcut to make a Group

Here's an **even faster way** to make a Group:

1. Hold down the Command key and click on all the names in the list that you want to put into a new Group.
2. Let go of the Command key.
3. Go to the File menu, and choose "New Group From Selection."
4. Change the name of the Group, as shown on the opposite page.

Delete a contact name from a Group

First select the Group name, then select the contact name and hit the Delete key. When you delete a Name from a Group, it is *not* deleted from the "All" list. You will be asked to confirm your action.

Send email to an entire Group

Once you've made a Group mailing list, you can send a message to everyone in that list simply by sending the email to the Group name.

To send an email message simultaneously to every person in a Group:

1. You don't have to have the Address Book open. In **Mail,** start a new email message.
2. In the "To" box, type the name of the Group.

That's all—write your letter, send it, and it will go to everyone in the Group.

Enter the name of the Group here.

If you see a list of all the individual names of the Group instead of the Group name, see below.

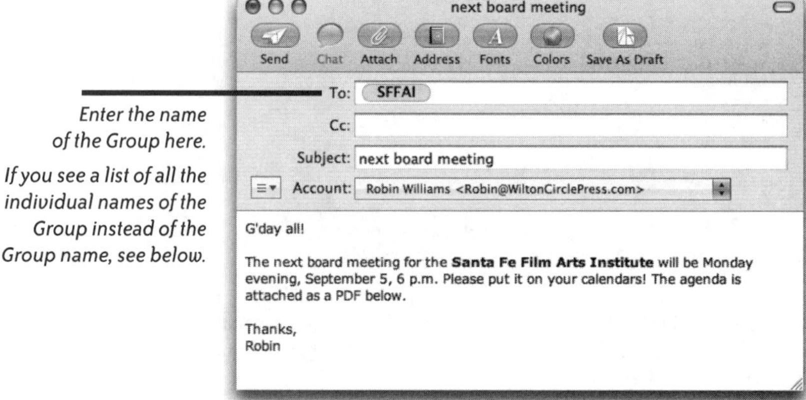

Suppress the address list when sending mail to a Group

It's polite to **suppress the address list** when sending to a Group. For one thing, it's *really* annoying to have to scroll through a long list of addresses to get to the message. For another, *some* people don't want their private email address broadcast to everyone else on the list.

To suppress the Group list of addresses:

1. In the **Mail** program (*not* the Address Book), open the Mail preferences (go to the Mail menu and choose "Preferences…").
2. Click the "Composing" icon in the Toolbar.
3. **UN**check the box (if it's checked), "When sending to a group, show all member addresses."
4. Put the Preferences away (click its red Close button).

Create Smart Groups

Now, a Smart Group is a Group that automatically adds contacts to itself according to the parameters you set. Contacts come and go from this Group according to those parameters. For instance, in the example below, you can create a Birthday Group that adds those contacts whose birthdays are within a certain number of days or weeks. Of course, this means you must have the Birthday field on your cards (if not, see page 468).

To create a Smart Group:

1. Single-click on the Action button, circled below, and choose "New Smart Group…." **Or** hold down the Option key—the **+** sign at the bottom of the Groups pane becomes a gear wheel; click the wheel.

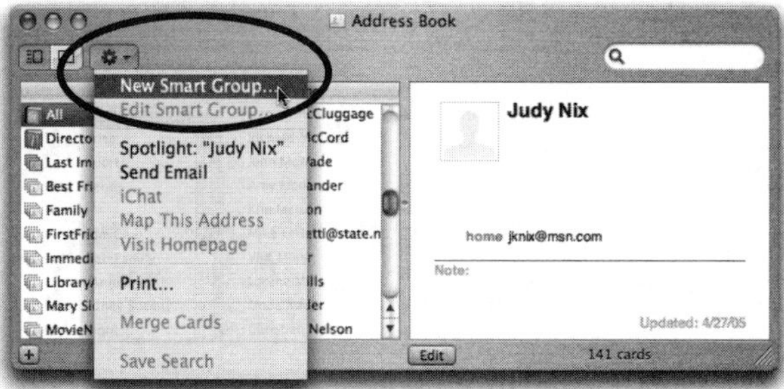

2. Name your new Smart Group. Use the menus to choose parameters. It will only take a few seconds of experimenting to understand the possibilities. You can see what I chose in the example below.
3. Click the **+** button, circled below, to add more parameters. Click the **–** button to delete an existing parameter.
4. If you want to be visually reminded when a new contact has been added to the Smart Group, check the box to "Highlight group when updated." The Smart Group name will appear in bold and in color.

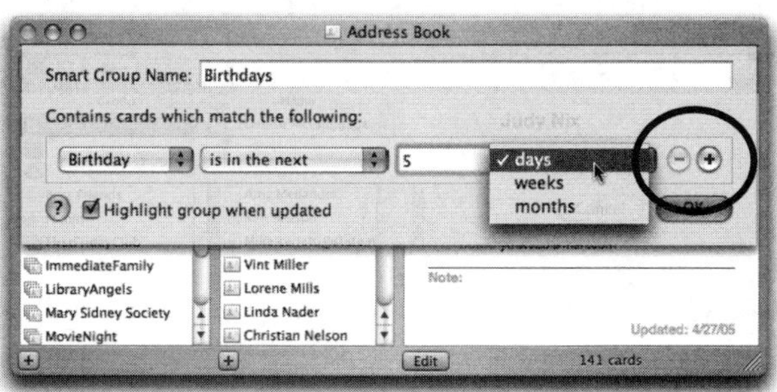

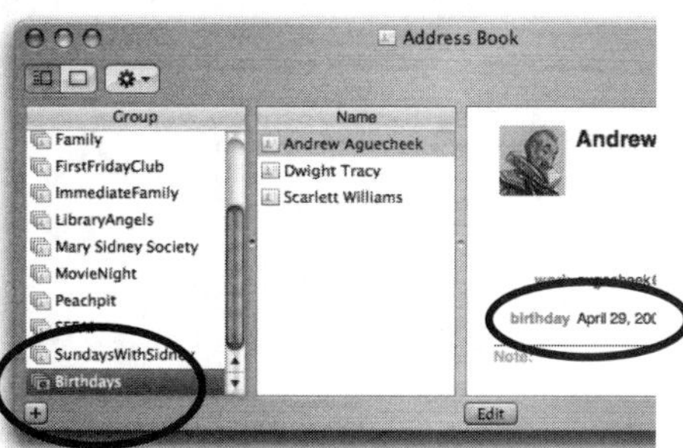

Add a Group to iCal

You can create an event in iCal that automatically includes everyone in a Group. Then with the click of a button, you can send them all a message that details the event. Amazing.

Simply open your Address Book and open iCal. Drag a Group from the Address Book and drop it on the appropriate day in iCal. That's all! Well, you'll probably want to change the title of the event and the time.

As you can see below, iCal added everyone in the Group to the attendee list. **To send them all a message** about the event, click the "Send" button, circled below. You won't get a Mail message form—iCal sends the message itself.

Attendees can then respond to the email. The Notifications box will keep track of who has responded and their responses will be duly noted in the Info drawer. Please see Chapter 13 on iCal for all those details.

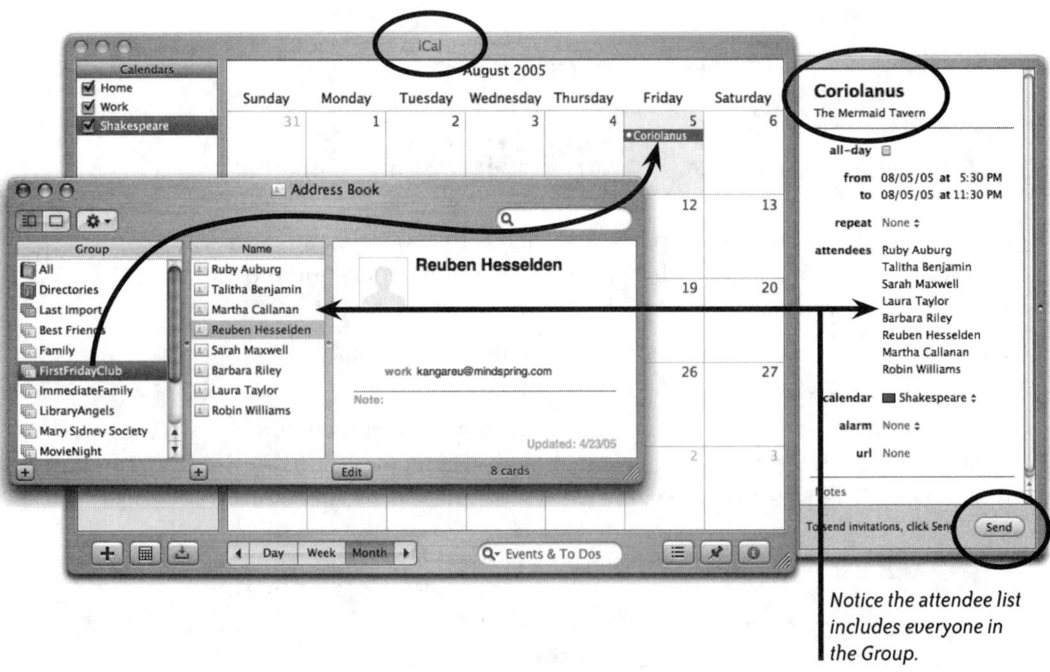

Notice the attendee list includes everyone in the Group.

Export an Address or a Group of Addresses

You can **export** a single address, a collection of selected addresses, or a Group. Once exported, other Address Book users can import the addresses into their applications. There are several simple ways to export:

- Drag a Group, a name, or a collection of names from the Address Book and drop them on the Desktop or inside any Finder window. It will make vCard icons like the ones shown below.

Andrew Aguecheek and 3 others

Drag a selection of cards to the Desktop and the Mac creates a vCard.

LibraryAngels

Drag a Group to the Desktop and the Mac creates a vCard. You'll have to rename it.

- Option-drag a Group name and you'll get a separate vCard for each person in the Group. They all land one on top of the other so it looks like just one card—you have to drag the cards off of each other.
- Select the Group, a name, or a collection of names in the Address Book. From the File menu, choose "Export card..." or "Export Group card...." You will be asked to name the exported vCard and where you want to save it. An icon like the ones shown above appears in the location where you chose to save it.

You can send the vCard to anyone with a fairly recent version of Address Book. The recipient double-clicks the file and those addresses appear in his Address Book. You can also send the vCard to people with any other contact database, even if it's not Address Book. You can even send it to people using PCs.

If any one of the names in the vCard is already in that person's Address Book, a notice appears telling him there are duplicates and asking if he wants to update the existing cards.

Action Button

The Action button in Address Book acts just like any other Action button. The items available and active depend on what you select *before* you open the menu. In this example, two cards were selected, so the "Merge Cards" option is available. I had also clicked on someone's address, so "Map This Address" is available. Generally, the options you see in this menu are the same as you would find in a contextual menu for the same item.

Share your Address Book

If you use a slow dial-up connection, you probably don't want to share Address Books because it will clog up your connection every time it tries to automatically update!

If you are a .Mac member, you can share your Address Book with other .Mac members. Your entire Address Book will have its own space in the other person's Address Book (the contacts are not merged), as you can see in the illustration on the opposite page. When you add or update contacts on your Mac, those updates appear in the other person's shared version.

If you check the box to "Allow Editing," as shown below, the other person can make changes to your Address Book on *his* computer, and those changes are automatically sent to *your* Address Book on *your* computer. At any time, you can go back and uncheck the "Allow Editing" box to stop that; the other person will still be able to edit the cards on his own Mac, but his changes will not be sent to your Mac.

To share your Address Book:

1. The person with whom you want to share must be in your Address Book. Her .Mac email address must be on the card in the email field.
2. From the Address Book menu, choose "Preferences...."
3. Click the "Sharing" icon.
4. Put a check in the box to "Share your Address Book." Wheels will spin for a minute while your Mac prepares for the process.

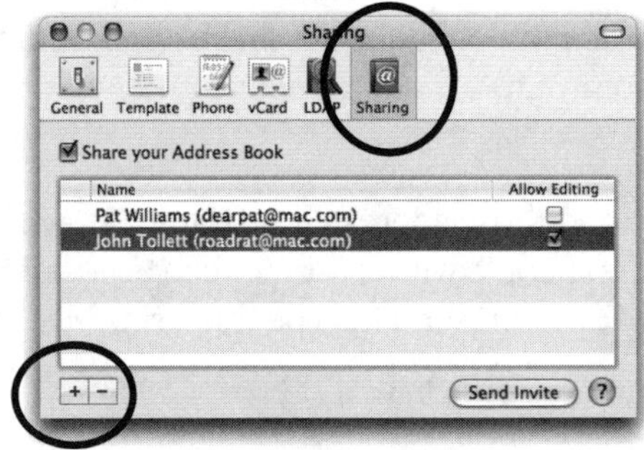

5. Click the **+** sign at the bottom-left of the window. This opens a sheet that contains your Address Book. As mentioned in Step 1, only those people whose .Mac email accounts are listed in the email field will be allowed to share. Just double-click that person's name and she will be added to the list you see above.
6. If you want to allow that person to **edit** your Address Book (*her* edits will appear on *your* Mac), check the box to "Allow Editing."
7. Select names in your list and click the button to "Send Invite."

8. The recipient gets an email message like the one shown below. She clicks the link and her Address Book opens and asks if she wants to subscribe. She clicks OK.

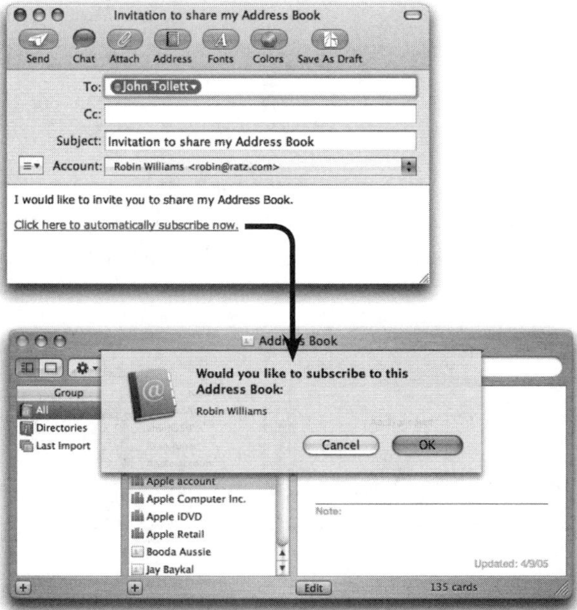

9. The shared Address Book appears in a separated section of the recipient's Group pane, with a different icon. Wow.

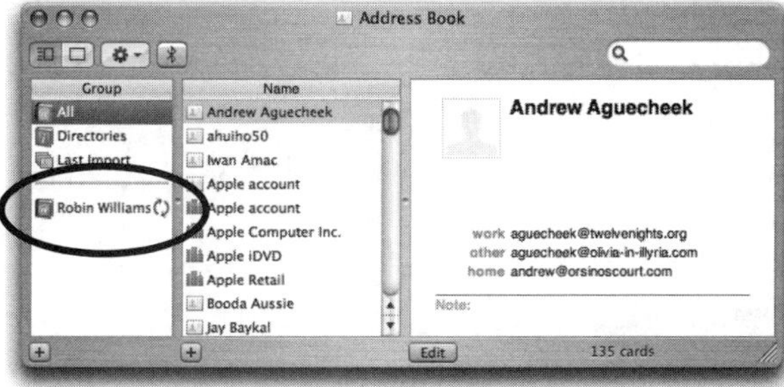

Subscribe to someone's Address Book

You can only subscribe to someone's Address Book if they have already set you up as a person with whom to share, as explained on these two pages. If you know a person has done that, go to the File menu and choose "Subscribe to Address Book...." A small sheet drops down from the Address Book title bar asking you to enter the email address of a .Mac member.

Backup your Address Book

If you depend on your Address Book, be sure to back it up. Apple makes it easy to do this: Just go to the File menu and choose "Back up Address Book...." This puts a file in your Documents folder called "Address Book" and the date, as shown to the left. Copy this file onto a disk or save it to your iDisk for later retrieval.

Restore your Address Book

To restore your Address Book as it was the last time you backed it up, go to the File menu and choose "Revert to Address Book Backup...." In the dialog box that opens, you can search for and choose the file you backed up earlier, as explained above.

Send Updates

Whenever the information in your address card changes (your "Me Card," as explained on page 465), your Mac can send that new information out to your world. You can do this manually or have it done automatically whenever you change the information on your card. You must first have created at least one Group (see pages 470–472).

If you have some information on your card that you don't really want publicized, see page 482 to learn how to make some of the data private.

Anything you have in your "Notes" field will *not* be sent out as updates unless you choose it to be; see page 482.

To send updates of your card manually:

1. From the File menu, choose "Send Updates...."
2. In the dialog box that appears (shown below), choose which Groups to send the information to.

Put a checkmark in the box next to each Group you want to send updates to.

3. The recipients will get email messages that include your vCard, as shown below. They single-click on the card icon.

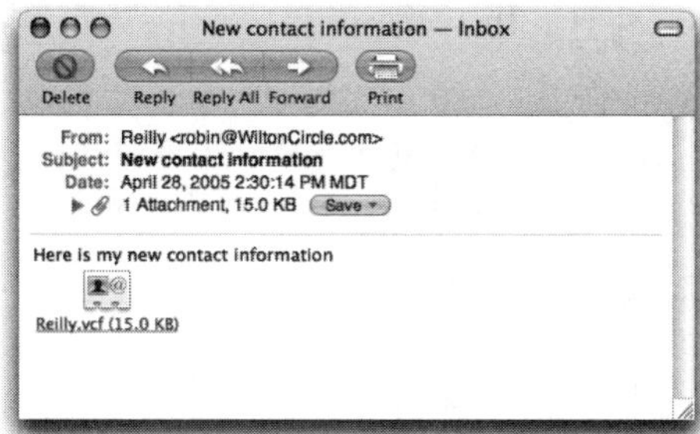

4. If the recipient is on a Mac running some version of OS X, the Mac adds your information to her Address Book. If that person already has you in her Address Book, a window appears asking what she wants to do with the information, as shown below. She makes a choice, and there you are!

A vCard is cross-platform, so even recipients on PCs will receive your updated vCard and be able to add it to their contact programs.

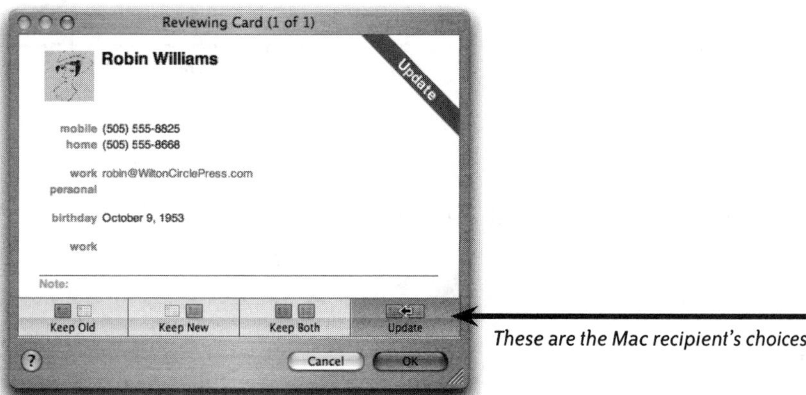

These are the Mac recipient's choices.

To send updates of your card automatically:

You must have at least one Group created before you choose this option.

1. From the Address Book menu, choose "Preferences...."
2. Click the General tab.
3. Put a check in the box to "Notify people when my card changes," as shown on the following page. Close the preferences.

Now whenever you make a change to your "Me Card," the Mac will ask if you want to notify people of the changes. If you click "Notify" in the little window, you will see the window shown in Step 2 on the opposite page. Everything else happens as explained on these two pages.

Other Preferences for Address Book

Two of the preference panes, "Template" (page 467) and "Sharing" (pages 476–477), have already been explained in this chapter. Here are some details about the other preferences.

General: These are pretty self-explanatory. Some items that may be confusing are explained below.

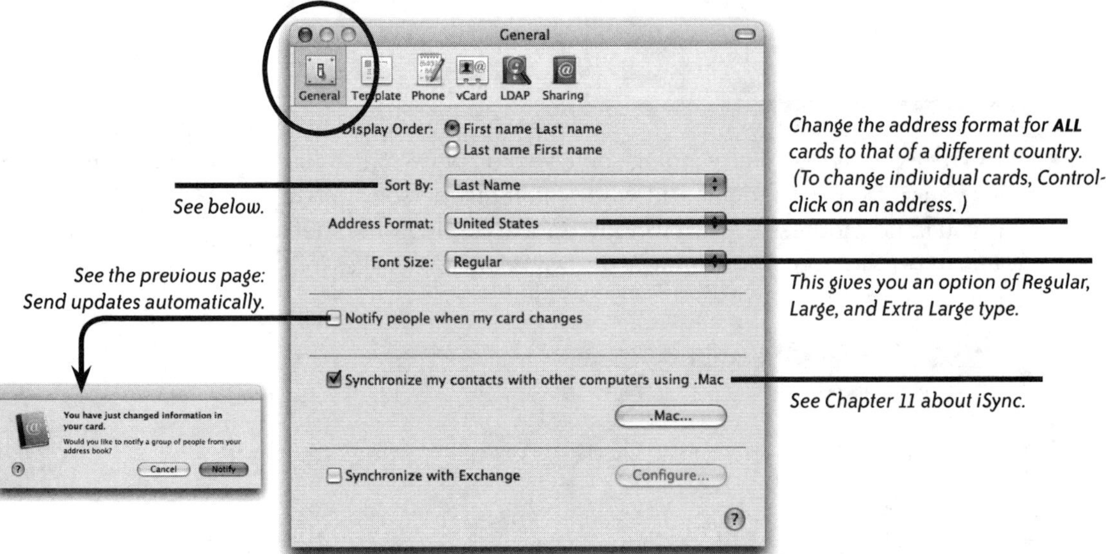

See below.

See the previous page: Send updates automatically.

*Change the address format for **ALL** cards to that of a different country. (To change individual cards, Control-click on an address.)*

This gives you an option of Regular, Large, and Extra Large type.

See Chapter 11 about iSync.

Keep in mind that when Address Book **sorts** (organizes, alphabetizes) by "Last Name," that means it organizes your contacts according to what you typed in the *second* name box. In the illustrations below, the first example will be alphabetized under "a" for "and"; the second example will be alphabetized under "T" for "Tollett."

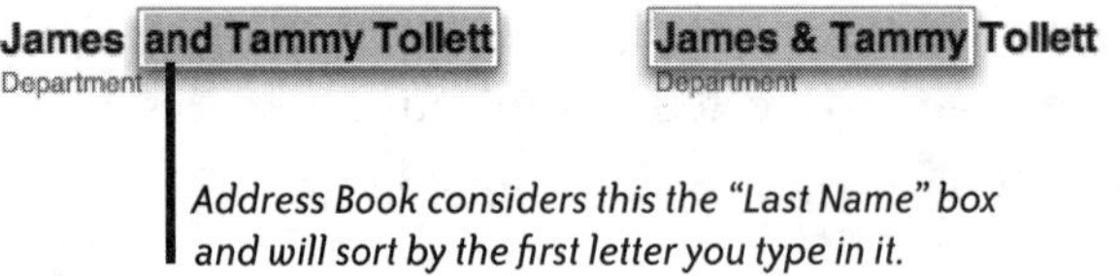

Address Book considers this the "Last Name" box and will sort by the first letter you type in it.

If your company uses **Exchange** 2000, you can **synchronize** your database of contacts through Outlook Web Access. Check with your network adminstrator or the IT personnel to help you set it up.

Phone: When typing phone numbers into your Address Book, you don't have to enter all the parentheses and hyphens yourself—just type the numbers. Address Book displays them for you according to the formats in this preference pane. Try it—just type the numbers in a phone field on the card, then hit Enter or Return or Tab.

In the "Formats" menu, you'll find even **more options.** Or choose "Custom..." and enter a different format altogether.

To edit existing numbers, select one and click the "Edit" button.

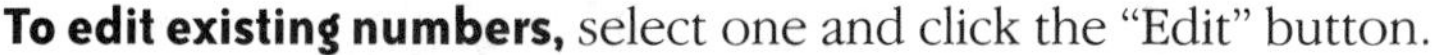

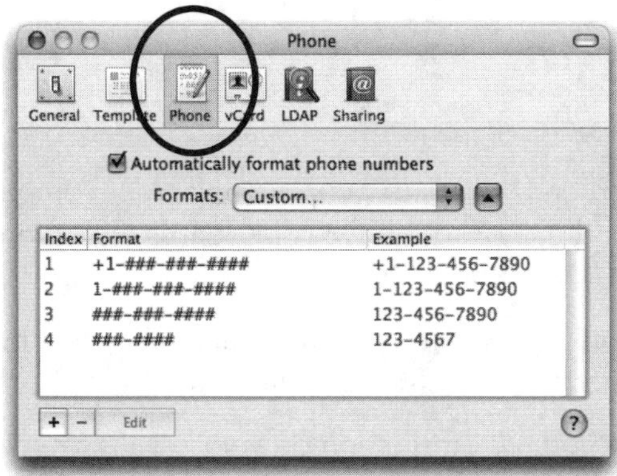

LDAP (Lightweight Directory Access Protocol) is an Internet *protocol,* or set of rules, to look up contact information in directories stored on servers on your network or the Internet. You can tell your Address Book to search specific directories that use LDAP.

For details on how to do it, ask your server administrator. Or open Address Book, then go to the Help menu and choose "Address Book Help." Search for LDAP. (I've had better luck searching for LDAP in all caps rather than lowercase. Weird.)

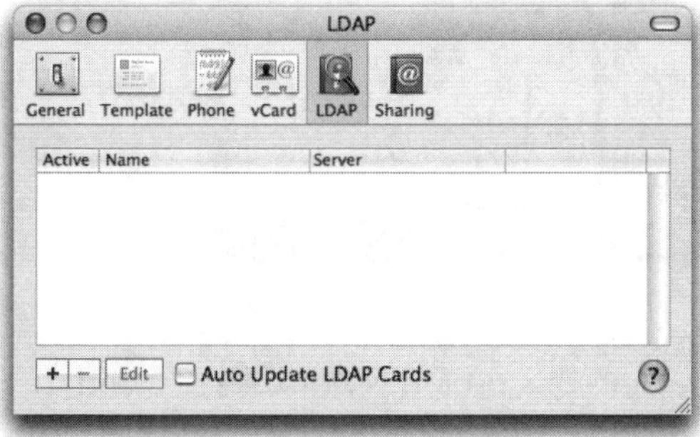

vCard preferences

This pane provides several options for your vCards, or the individual contact cards of information that you might save or send to others.

vCard Format: If you want to send vCards to people using older computers or using older software, you can choose to save your vCards in version 2.1 instead of in the current version of 3.0.

Encoding: Leave this as it is, unless you *know* you need different encoding so you can create vCards in something like Chinese or Korean.

Privacy: You can ensure that certain information on your card is **private** so when you send your vCard to someone or send updates of your contact info, you share just the information you're comfortable with.

1. Check the box to "Enable private 'Me' Card."
2. In the Address Book, select your card. Click its "Edit" button. You'll see checkboxes next to the fields.
3. Check only the boxes next to the information you *want* to share.

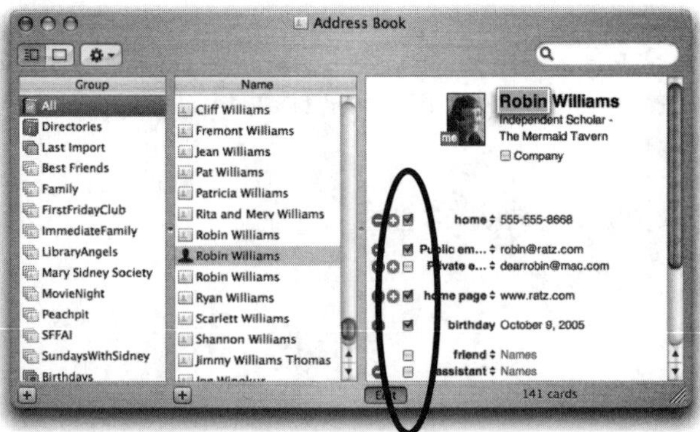

Export notes in vCards: By default, this option is *not* selected, and the contents of the "Note" field are *not* sent when you choose to notify others that your card is updated. If you *do* want your notes sent, check this box.

Email Etiquette

Many people use email everyday without being aware of **email etiquette** and without realizing that they're **1)** annoying co-workers, friends, and relatives; **2)** making themselves look naive and amateurish in the email world; and **3)** turning themselves into junk mailers, albeit well-intentioned.

If no one has complained about your email etiquette, you're probably in good shape. Or it could be that family members and friends do not want to risk embarrassing you. To be safe, consider the following suggestions and see if your email manners are up to date.

1. **Get permission before you add someone to a mailing list.**
   You may be well-intentioned, but most people get so much junk mail that they'd rather not receive the inspirational messages that someone sent you—especially since they probably received five other copies already. Not everyone is a curmudgeon about getting email like this, but it's considerate to ask for permission before putting someone on your mailing list (called a Group in Address Book). And please, don't take it personally if they decline. Privacy on the Internet is hard to come by, and many people try to keep their email address off as many mailing lists as possible. When you add someone's address to your mailing list without their permission, you're publishing private information without permission.

2. **Clean up the email headers.**
   Even if someone *wants* to be on your mailing list, it's extremely annoying to get email that has dozens (or hundreds) of lines of header information before the message. This happens when you receive an email message that was sent to a list (a Group), then someone sent it to their list, then someone else sent it to their list. This kind of email makes the sender look like the clueless amateur he is. Before you forward a message like this, press-and-drag to select the good part of the message. Then when you click the Forward button in Mail, only the selected part will be in the message body for sending.

3. **Hide the mailing list addresses.**
   When you send a message to a Group with all the addresses exposed, you are essentially providing every reader of the message with the email addresses of all your friends and relations. Then if those people forward your message, all of *their* recipients have the email addresses of all *your* friends and relations. Not many people appreciate that. Not only is it

—*continued*

neater to hide these addresses, it is more polite to everyone involved. **To hide the addresses of a Group in Mail,** go to the Mail Preferences, click "Composing," and make sure there is NO checkmark in the option "When sending to a group, show all member addresses."

4. **Take the time to personalize your email.**
   If you send well-intentioned junk email to an acquaintance, friend, or relative, it will be appreciated if you take the time to add a personal note to the forwarded message, such as "Hi Jay, I thought you might enjoy this." To receive an unsolicited, unsigned, almost-anonymous forwarded email makes me wonder when I can expect to start receiving the rest of the sender's postal service junk mail and Sunday supplements.

5. **Identify your email attachments.**
   When you attach a file to an email message, don't make the recipient guess what kind of file it is or what program might open it. Include a description of the attachment and the file type, or what program is needed to open it. Say something like, "Barbara, the attached file is a photograph that I saved as a .tif in Photoshop CS2 on a Mac." Dealing with attachments can be confusing and any helpful information is usually appreciated.

Tip: See page 415 in the Mail chapter for tips on what kinds of attachments to send.

6. **Don't fall for the urban legends and hoaxes.**
   When you get a panic-stricken email from a friend warning you of an apocalyptic virus and to "Please forward this email to everyone you know," *do not* forward it to anyone you know. This email message usually contains the words "THIS IS NOT A HOAX!" That means that this is a hoax. These messages float around the Internet constantly and some of them are many years old. If there's a deadly virus about to destroy the world as we know it, you're more likely to hear about it from the national news services and online news sites than from your cousin who's been using email for three months.

   And anyway, your Mac doesn't get these viruses.

   Also, do not forward the email messages that tell you Microsoft will pay you one dollar every time you use Hotmail. And don't forward the warning that the postal service is going to start charging us for every email, or that the phone company is going to tax every message, and that little boy in the hospital who is waiting for your postcard went home years ago.

   And make darn sure your email recipient has *begged* you to send all those messages that say "Send this to at least ten other people. Do not break this chain!"

iChat AV and Bonjour 17

iChat makes it incredibly easy (and free) to have text chats, audio chats, and video conferences with buddies almost anywhere in the world. You can even do multi-person audio and video chats—up to ten people in an audio chat, and up to four people in a video chat (if your computer and Internet connection are fast enough).

iChat provides Buddy Groups for organizing your iChat buddies, iTunes integration that lets you show the currently playing tune in your iChat Status (your buddies can preview the track with a single click), Jabber support for your friends who chat in the Jabber IM network, and improved video quality.

Bonjour *automatically* detects and connects users and devices (such as printers) on a local area network. Amazing. Bonjour makes it a snap to text chat, audio chat, or video chat with others on your local network. Bonjour integrates with iTunes and iPhoto so you can share music and photos over local networks. Or even Address Book contacts.

iChat AV requires a .Mac buddy name or an AIM (AOL Instant Messaging) buddy name. AIM buddy names are free—go to **www.aim.com** to sign up for one. When you sign up for a .Mac membership, your .Mac member name becomes your buddy name. If you don't want a .Mac membership, sign up for the free 60-day trial membership. When the free trial is over, you can keep your .Mac buddy name.

Text messaging needs only a low bandwidth connection, such as a dial-up modem. Audio and video conferencing requires a broadband connection, such as cable or DSL. To perform multi-person audio or video chats, you must have a faster computer and a faster Internet connection. Minimum requirements for initiating or participating in different kinds of chats are listed on pages 510 (audio chats) and 513 (video chats).

If you're not sure what your Internet connection speed is, do a Google search for "speed test." You'll find many web sites that provide free tests and all you have to do is click a button.

Look for a test page that provides results for both download and upload speeds, such as ***http://nyc.speakeasy.net***

Set Up iChat

Note: You must be connected to the Internet to use iChat!

Bonjour does not require an Internet connection, just a local network.

The first time you click the **iChat** icon in the Dock, a Welcome window opens. Click the "Continue" button to proceed to the next window where you enter information to set up a new iChat account (shown below). The "Account Type" pop-up menu lets you choose between using your .Mac account (if you have one) *or* an existing AOL Instant Messenger account (called AIM; go to **www.aim.com** to get a *free* account; you don't have to subscribe to AOL to get a free AIM account).

If you don't have a .Mac account and you want one, you can click the "Get an iChat Account" button to sign up for it right now. Otherwise, enter your information, and click OK.

Your iChat buddy name (Account Name) is the same as your .Mac membership name (or your AIM buddy name). Your online buddies will use that name to find you and send Instant Messages or files. You can even have both an AOL Instant Messenger buddy name and your Mac.com buddy name and switch between them (only one can be *active* at a time).

Use the pop-up menu to choose a .Mac account or an AIM (AOL) account.

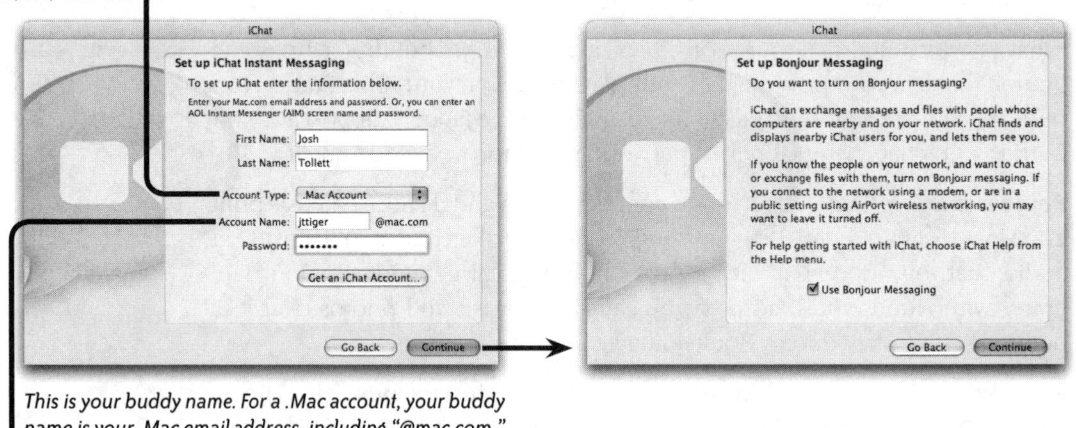

This is your buddy name. For a .Mac account, your buddy name is your .Mac email address, including "@mac.com," which is added automatically. For an AOL or AIM account, enter your AOL buddy name without the "@aol.com" part.

After you enter the information to set up a new iChat account (above-left), click "Continue." The next window lets you set up Jabber Instant Messaging if you have a Jabber account registered to a Jabber server. Enter your account name and password, then click "Continue." The next window opens to ask if you want to use Bonjour messaging (above-right). If you have two or more computers connected to each other on a local network, choose "Use Bonjour Messaging" to make sharing files (or network chatting) easy and convenient. Click "Continue" and one last screen opens. Just click "Done" and start using iChat and Bonjour.

If you're in a public space, such as an Internet cafe, you should quit iChat and turn off Bonjour when you're not using it to ensure privacy and security. Bonjour can be turned off (or on) in the Accounts pane of iChat Preferences.

Create a Buddy List

No matter what kind of chat you plan to do (text, audio, or video), the first thing you need to do is create a Buddy List. If you plan to chat often with certain people, **add them to your Buddy List** so you can easily see when they're online, and with the click of a button you can start a chat or send a file.

This is a typical Buddy List. The people in the list that have a ***green orb*** *next to their names are online and you can start a chat with them.*

An ***amber orb*** *means the buddy is online, but his computer is idle and the AIM service hasn't diconnected him yet.*

A ***red orb means*** *the buddy is away or doesn't want to be disturbed, but is online.*

The ***dimmed*** *buddies at the bottom of the list are offline and unavailable.*

To hide offline buddies, as shown above, in the View menu uncheck "Show Offline Buddies."

Add people to your Buddy List:

1. Click the iChat icon in the Dock, if iChat is not already open. If you don't see your Buddy List, press Command 1 (the number "one"), **or** go to the Window menu and choose "Buddy List."
2. In the Buddy List window that opens, click the **+** button (circled above-left). A sheet containing your Address Book contacts drops down from the top of the window, shown here.
3. If the person you want to add is in your Address Book, select that contact, then click the "Select Buddy" button. The new buddy appears in the Buddy List.

   If you have not yet put that person's buddy name in your Address Book, another sheet opens like the one shown on the next page so you can add the buddy name to the person's contact information.

This sheet contains your Address Book contacts .

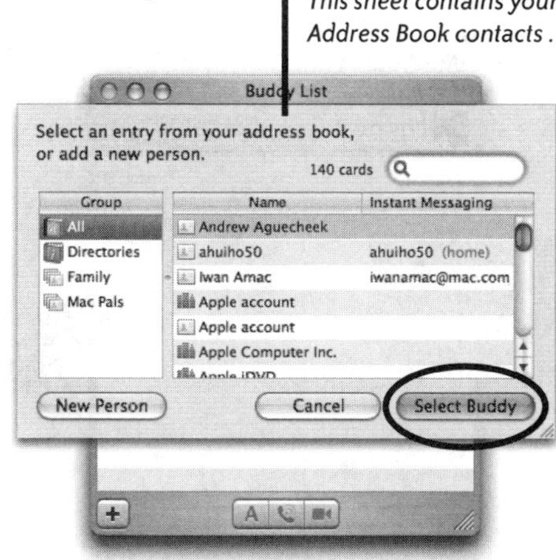

—continued

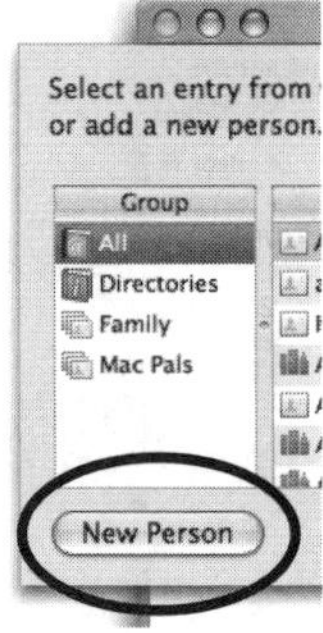

If the Buddy you want to add isn't in your Address Book, click the "New Person" button (shown on the left) to open the sheet shown below.

4. From the "Account Type" pop-up menu, select ".Mac" *if* the new person uses their Mac.com account for instant messaging.

   Or choose "AIM" if the new buddy uses an AOL or AIM screen name.

5. Enter first name, last name, and email information if you want to add this to your Address Book as well.

   The Buddy List uses the entry from the First Name and Last Name field to name the buddy in the list. If you don't enter a first or last name, the Buddy List uses the Account Name entered here. Whatever you enter in this sheet is actually being added to a new card in your Address Book. Later, if you want to change a buddy's information, you can open Address Book and change it there. Or, you can select a buddy in the Buddy List, then from the Buddies menu choose "Get Info" to open an Address Book window for that buddy.

6. To make a photo or custom icon appear next to a buddy's name in the list, drag an image on top of the Buddy Icon window shown below-left. The photo can be a JPEG, GIF, TIFF or Photoshop file.

7. Click the "Add" button to add the new buddy to your Buddy List (and to your Address Book).

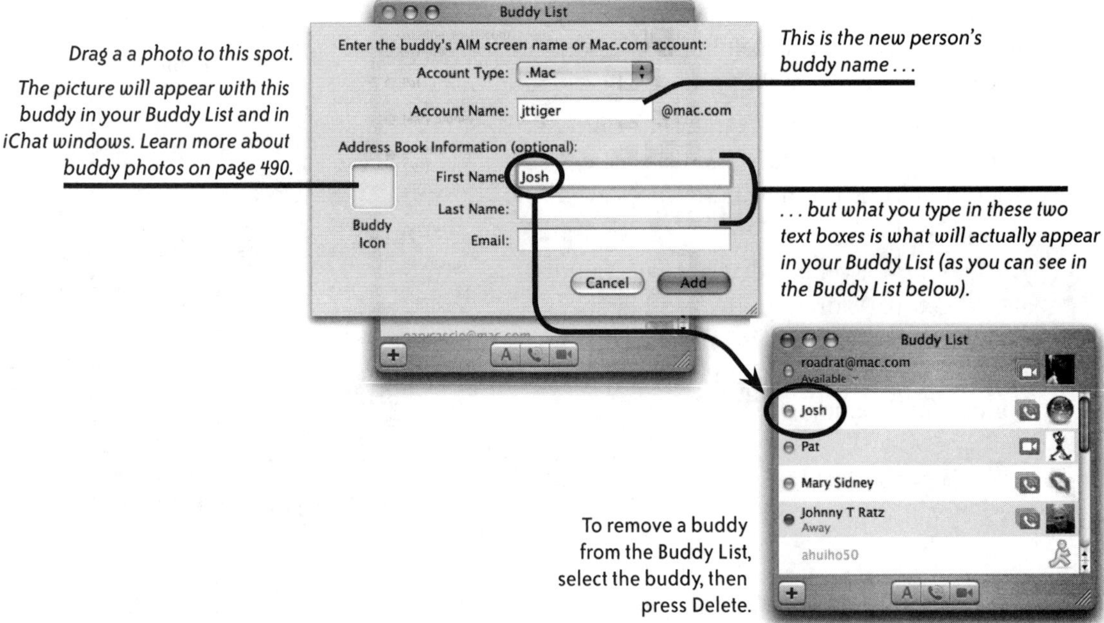

Drag a a photo to this spot.

The picture will appear with this buddy in your Buddy List and in iChat windows. Learn more about buddy photos on page 490.

This is the new person's buddy name . . .

. . . but what you type in these two text boxes is what will actually appear in your Buddy List (as you can see in the Buddy List below).

To remove a buddy from the Buddy List, select the buddy, then press Delete.

Status and messages in your Buddy List

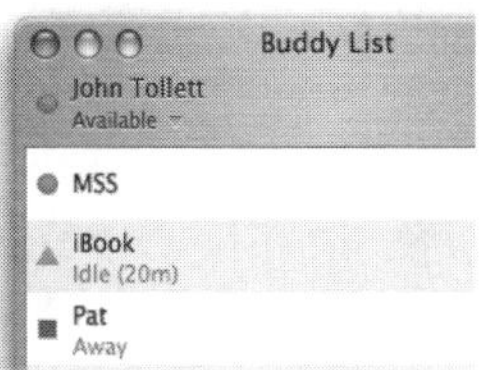

Your name, as it appears in your Address Book, shows in the top-left corner of the Buddy List. If you click on the name, it shows your *buddy name*. The **colored status buttons** in the iChat list indicate the online status of your buddies: Green means "Available," red means "Unavailable," and yellow means "Idle," which usually means that person's computer has gone to sleep due to inactivity.

Tip: If you're colorblind to red and green, you can set the status buttons to display as squares, circles, and triangles.

In the General pane of iChat Preferences, choose "Use shapes to indicate status."

A circle means "Available."

A square means "Away."

A triangle means "Idle."

A **status message** beneath your name indicates your online availablility. Other iChat users on the Internet that have your buddy name can see your status message under you buddy name in the iChat window. Choose "Available," "Away," "Offline," or create a *custom* message. When you choose a status with a *red* dot next to it, buddies can still send you a message.

> **To change the status message,** click the existing message beneath your name to open a pop-up menu (below-left). Choose a status message from the menu list.
>
> **To create a *custom* status message,** click the existing message, then from the pop-up menu choose "Custom…" and type your message in the text field that appears. Hit "Return" or "Enter" to set the new message.

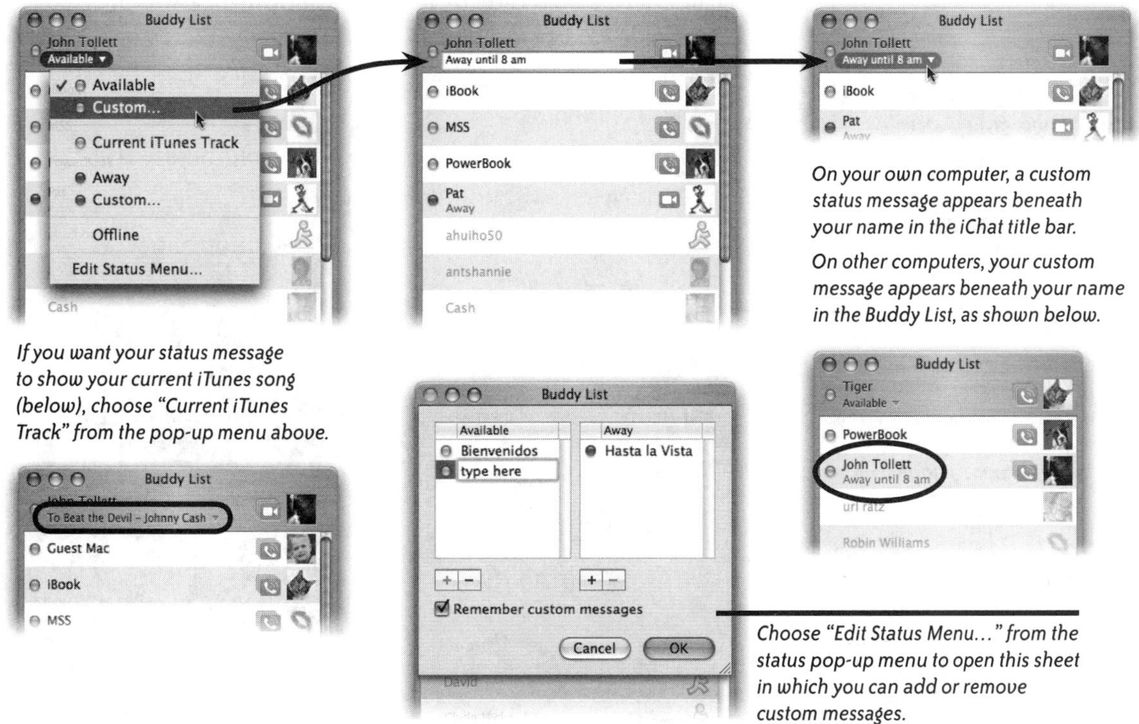

On your own computer, a custom status message appears beneath your name in the iChat title bar.

On other computers, your custom message appears beneath your name in the Buddy List, as shown below.

If you want your status message to show your current iTunes song (below), choose "Current iTunes Track" from the pop-up menu above.

Choose "Edit Status Menu…" from the status pop-up menu to open this sheet in which you can add or remove custom messages.

Photos in your Buddy List

If you've put a **photo or image** of someone (or yourself) in your Address Book, it will appear in your Buddy List and iChat windows. If your AOL Buddy has added a photo or image in AOL, or in their own iChat application, their photo or image will appear instead of the one you placed.

But perhaps you don't like the image your friend uses. **To override his image,** select his Buddy name in your Buddy List, then "Get Info" for that Buddy:

1. From the Buddies menu, choose "Get Info."
   Or press Command Shift I.
2. An Info window opens, shown below-left. From the "Show" pop-up menu choose "Address Card." Drag a photo to the "Picture" well. If the photo you place is larger than 62 x 62 pixels, the "Buddy Picture" window (below-right) opens so you can resize it. **Or,** instead of dragging a photo to the well, you can double-click the well to open the "Buddy Picture" window (below-right).
3. If you dragged a photo into the well in Step 2, it appears here. If the image area is empty, click the "Choose" button to make a Finder sheet slide down in which you can locate the photo you want to use, then click an "Open" button to place it here. **Or** you can drag a photo directly into this window (below-right).
4. Use the size slider (the blue slider button, circled below-right) to adjust the photo size. Press on the image and drag it around to adjust the cropping.
5. Click "Set" to attach the photo to the buddy in your Buddy List.
6. Back in the Info window (below-left), click OK.

You can drag a photo to the "Picture" well.

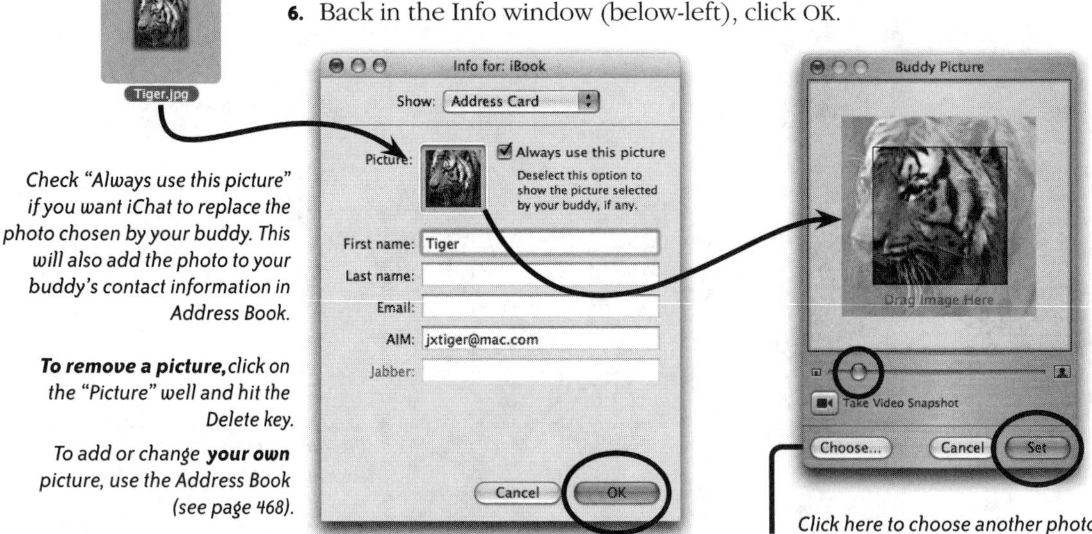

Check "Always use this picture" if you want iChat to replace the photo chosen by your buddy. This will also add the photo to your buddy's contact information in Address Book.

***To remove a picture,** click on the "Picture" well and hit the Delete key.*

*To add or change **your own** picture, use the Address Book (see page 468).*

Click here to choose another photo.

Change your own photo, even while chatting.

To change your own photo that appears to other iChat users, simply drag an image into the Picture well in the top-right corner. You can drag multiple images into the well, and they all are kept in a pop-up menu for you. Click on the Picture well to open the pop-up menu (shown on the right). Click any image in the menu to instantly apply it, even if you're in the middle of a chat. Choose "Edit Picture…" in the menu to open the "Buddy Picture" window (shown on the previous page) and edit its size and cropping. To clear this menu of existing photos, choose "Clear Recent Pictures."

Create actions for a selected Buddy

Every buddy has "actions" associated with it. You can have iChat alert you when a buddy has logged in or out, become available, etc. The "Event" pop-up menu contains all of the events for which you can set an alert. The "Play sound" pop-up menu contains alert sounds you can choose. Choose "Bounce icon in the Dock" for a visual alert. Choose "Speak text" for your computer to actually speak an alert of your choice.

To create actions for a selected Buddy, select his name in your Buddy List. From the Buddies menu choose "Get Info." The Info box *for that Buddy* opens. From the "Show" pop-up menu, choose "Actions," then set your preferences. In this example, when the buddy logs in iChat plays a sound, the iChat icon bounces in the Dock, and the computer speaks the words "who's your buddy?"

Store information about a selected Buddy

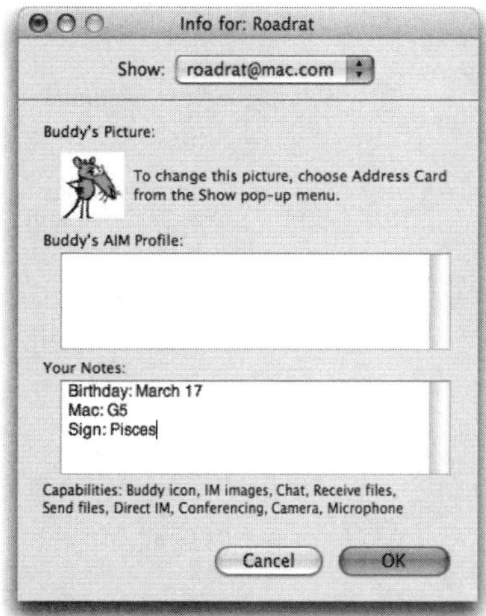

You can store information about a buddy in the same Information window described above.

1. Select a buddy in the Buddy List.
2. From the Buddies menu choose "Get Info"
3. In the Info window, choose the name of your Buddy's account in the "Show" pop-up menu. If the buddy has written a profile in America Online or AIM, it will appear here. You can also type additional notes about this person in the lower area, as shown on the right.
4. Click OK.

Text, Audio, and Video Chats

After you create a Buddy List, you can select a buddy name in the list that's online, then start chatting. You can chat using text-based messaging, audio, or video, depending on the connection speed and the hardware available to both of you.

Text messaging may sound low-tech, but it has some advantages that make it a popular option. It's more private than talking aloud during an audio or video chat. Text messaging also lets you send files to others as you chat. You can include HTML web address links within a message. And you can chat with larger groups of people than you can with audio or video chats.

The icon next to a buddy photo indicates what kind of chat is possible. A *camera icon* means the buddy has a video camera attached and can use text, audio or video to chat. A *multiple-camera icon* shows that a multiple-person video chat is possible. A *phone icon* means the buddy has a mic attached or built in and can use text or audio to chat. *No icon* means the buddy can only use text messages to chat.

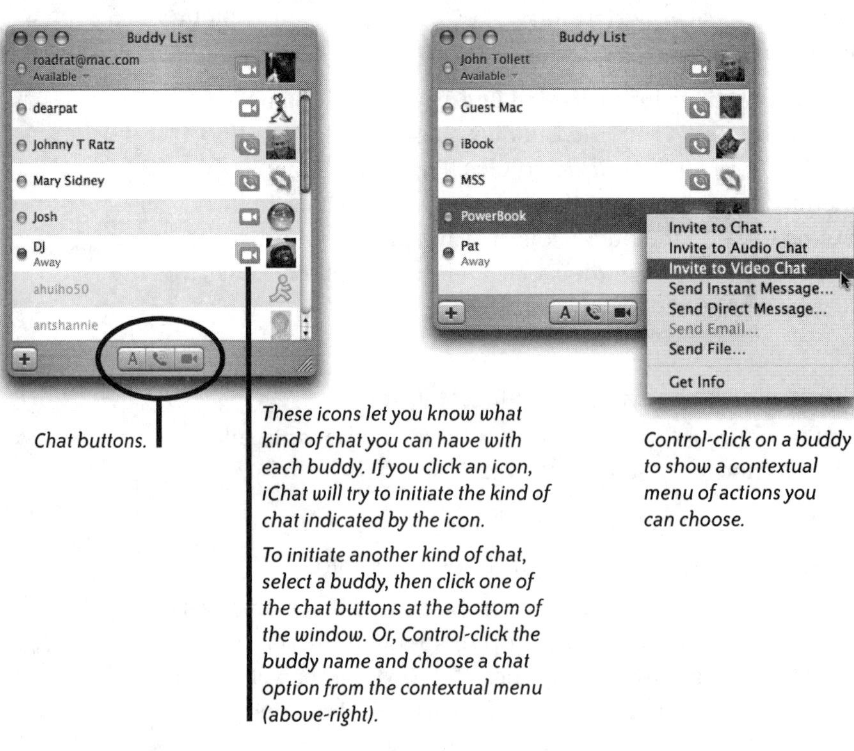

Chat buttons.

These icons let you know what kind of chat you can have with each buddy. If you click an icon, iChat will try to initiate the kind of chat indicated by the icon.

To initiate another kind of chat, select a buddy, then click one of the chat buttons at the bottom of the window. Or, Control-click the buddy name and choose a chat option from the contextual menu (above-right).

Control-click on a buddy to show a contextual menu of actions you can choose.

iChat Text Messaging

To start a text chat:

1. Select a buddy in the Buddy List.
2. Click the Text Chat button (the letter "A") at the bottom of the iChat window to open a message window.
3. Type a message in the message window text box, then press Return. When your buddy answers you, his messages and yours are staggered in the window and tagged with the photos that were set in your chat software (iChat or AIM).

When you receive an iChat invitation, the iChat icon in the Dock alerts you with a red tag and a number to show how many chat invitations are waiting for your response.

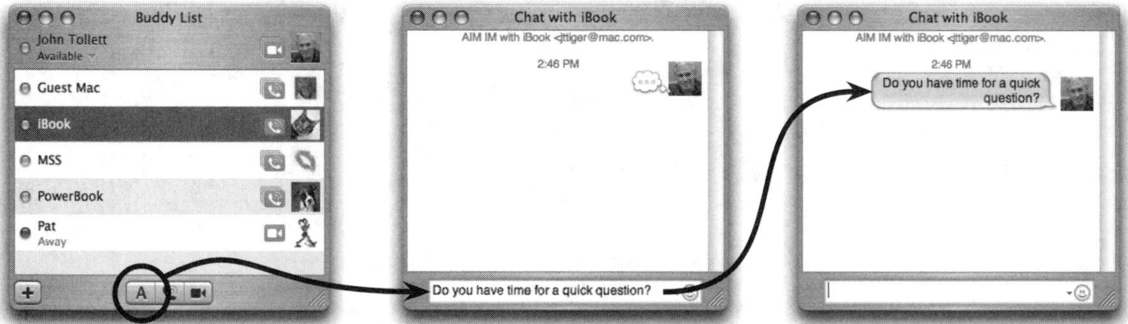

Click the Text Chat button to start a text chat with a selected buddy.

Type your message in the text box, then press Return or Enter. When you start typing, a thought cloud appears so buddies can see that you're responding.

Your sent message appears in your iChat window.

4. When you *receive* a text message, a message window (below-left) opens on your Desktop. The top of the window identifies the buddy sending you a message. Click on the window to expand it (center). Type a response, then click the "Accept" button. When you *accept,* the window expands again (below-right) so you continue the chat. If you choose to *block* the message, an alert asks if you're sure you want to block all future messages from this buddy. If your answer is "yes," click the "Block" button in the alert window. You can remove this block in the Security pane of iChat Preferences.

To remove a block, open iChat Preferences, then click the "Security" tab in the "Accounts" pane. Click the "Edit List…" button next to "Block specific people." A sheet slides down from the Prerences title bar in which you can add or remove buddies to a Block list.

Click anywhere on a received message to open it (right).

Click the "Accept" button to expand the window and continue the chat.

Instant Message, Direct Message, Group Text Chat, and Bonjour

With iChat *text messaging,* you can communicate with others in **four different ways:** Instant Messages, Direct Messages, Group Chats, and Bonjour. Each method is different from the others and each has its own advantages.

An **Instant Message** opens a small window in which you can "talk" back and forth with *one other person,* and your talk is private (unless someone is looking over your shoulder). You must be connected to the Internet.

The easiest way to start a text Instant Message is to double-click a buddy in the Buddy List.

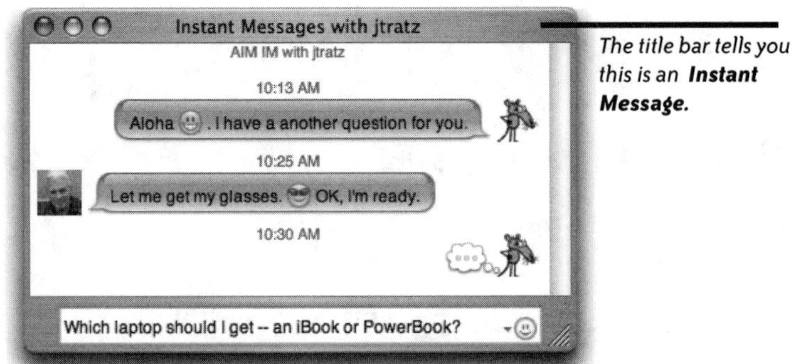

The title bar tells you this is an ***Instant Message.***

To see information about a buddy as you chat: From the View menu choose "Show Chat Participants." A drawer slides open (shown on the next page). Click the buddy name, then from the Buddies menu choose "Get Info." See page 491.

A **Direct Message** looks just like an Instant Message and is even more private. Instant Messages go through a central messaging server on the Internet, while a Direct Message goes directly to *one other person's computer,* bypassing the central server. A Direct Message is between two people —you cannot invite anyone else to join you. Some network or firewall security settings will not allow Direct Messages to be sent or delivered. You must be connected to the Internet.

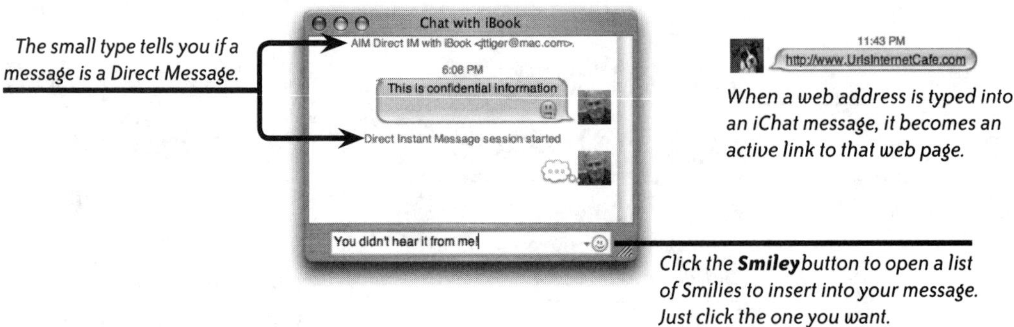

The small type tells you if a message is a Direct Message.

When a web address is typed into an iChat message, it becomes an active link to that web page.

Click the ***Smiley*** *button to open a list of Smilies to insert into your message. Just click the one you want.*

A **Group Chat** is a public "room" where you can invite *any number of people.* These people might be spread all over the world, but you can all gab together. People can come and go as they please and the room stays open until the last person leaves. You can name the Group Chat, allowing anyone who knows the chat name to join in. You must be connected to the Internet. Learn more about groups on pages 498–501.

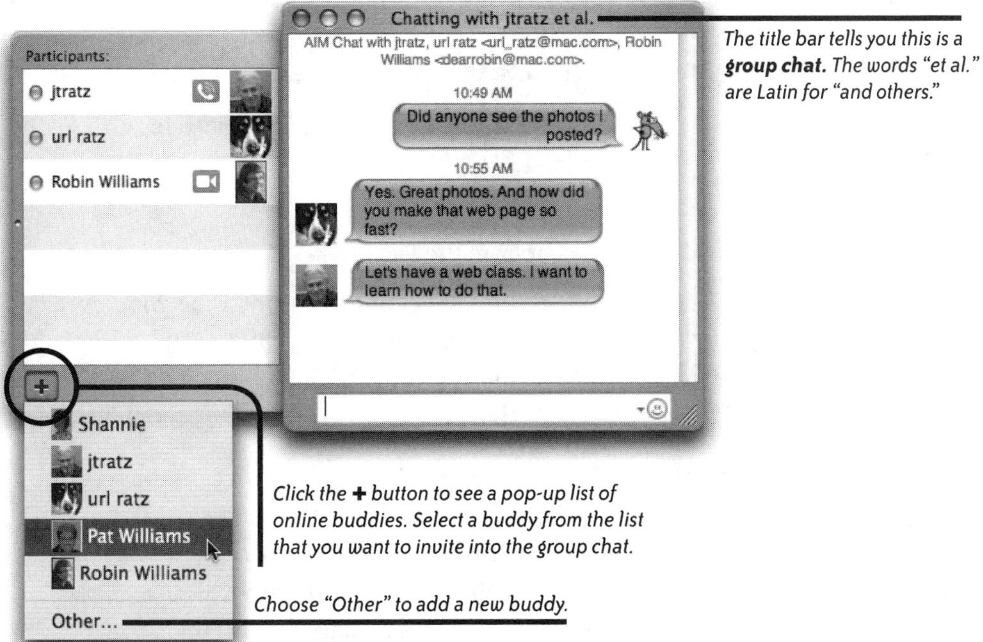

*The title bar tells you this is a **group chat.** The words "et al." are Latin for "and others."*

Click the **+** *button to see a pop-up list of online buddies. Select a buddy from the list that you want to invite into the group chat.*

Choose "Other" to add a new buddy.

A **Bonjour message** does not go through the Internet—it goes through your local network directly to another computer on the same network. Bonjour automatically detects and connects other computers on your local network. You do not have to be connected to the Internet to send Bonjour messages or to transfer files to another computer. See pages 518–520 for details about Bonjour.

To see who's available on your local network, press Command 2 to open this Bonjour window. Select a name and click the Text Chat button (circled above) to send a text message.

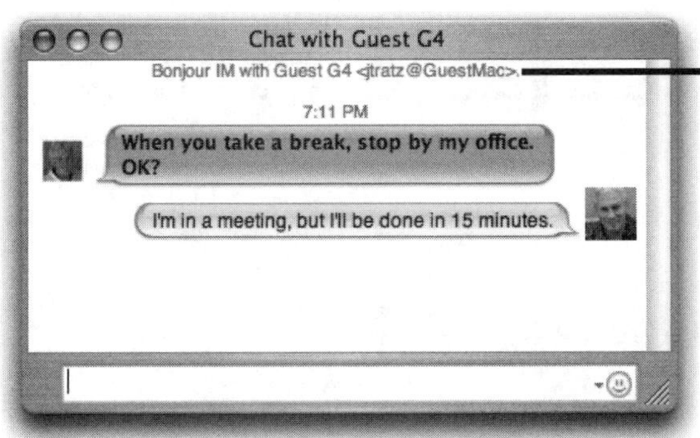

*This **Bonjour** Instant Message looks just like any other instant message except for this small line that identifies it as a Bonjour IM (Instant Message).*

The iChat File Menu

To see a previous chat, choose "Open Recent" from the File menu. If there are any saved chats, they're listed in the submenu, as shown below. See page 503 to learn how to automatically save chat transcripts.

Choose "Open Recent" to open a submenu of previously recorded iChat transcripts. You can set iChat to automatically save transcripts (see page 495).

You can also *start* a chat from the File menu.

From the File menu, choose **New Chat** to open a Chat window such as the one shown below. The chat becomes an Instant Message, a Direct Message, or a Group Chat, depending on which "Chat Option" is set for that particular window, as explained below.

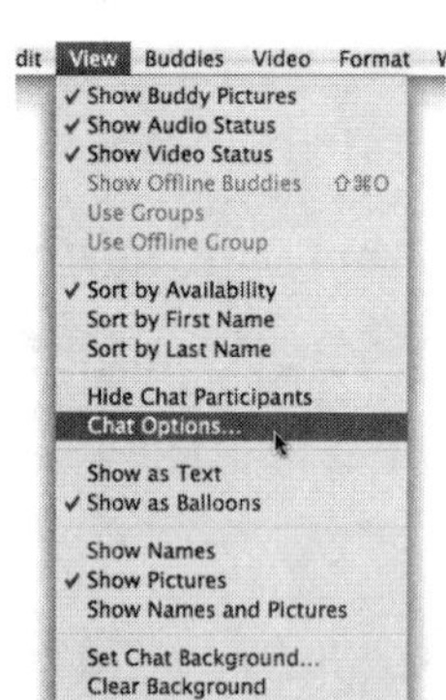

To set Chat Options for a New Chat:

1. From the File menu, choose "New Chat."
2. Before you start a message to anyone, go to the View menu and choose "Chat Options… " (shown on the left).
3. From the "Mode" pop-up menu, choose "Instant Message" for a one-on-one message session. Choose "Direct IM" to start a Direct Message session. Choose "Chat" to start a Group Chat.
4. Click OK. See more details on page 500.

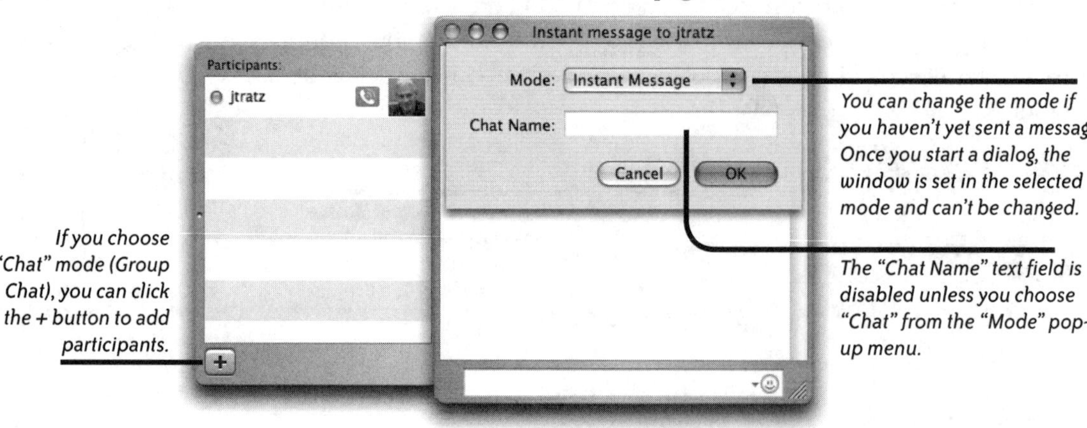

If you choose "Chat" mode (Group Chat), you can click the + button to add participants.

You can change the mode if you haven't yet sent a message. Once you start a dialog, the window is set in the selected mode and can't be changed.

The "Chat Name" text field is disabled unless you choose "Chat" from the "Mode" pop-up menu.

Or, from the File menu, choose **"New Chat with Person..."** to open a **new Instant Message** window with a drop-down sheet, as shown below. Type the Buddy name of the person with whom you want to chat, then click OK.

Or, from the File menu, choose **"Go To Chat..."** to open a **Group Chat** window in which you can invite more than one buddy. Learn more about Groups on pages 498–501.

1. Type a chat name in the "Chat Name" field of the "Go To Chat..." window (right-top), then click "Go."
2. In the chat drawer that opens, click the Plus button to add participants. When you add a participant, an invitation message sheet slides down (right-middle).
3. Type an invitation message in the text field, then click "Invite." As you add participants, the same sheet opens. Click the "Invite" button for each buddy, or you can customize the invitation for some buddies if necessary.
4. To leave a Group Chat, click the red Close button in the top-left corner of the window.

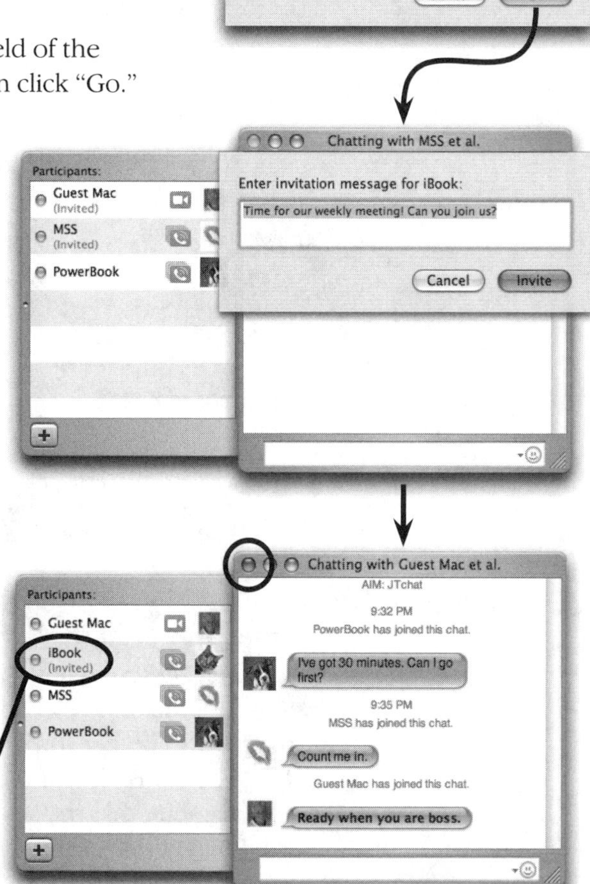

This invited participant has not repsonded to the invitation yet.

More about Group Chats

A **Group Chat** is different from an Instant or Direct Message in that you can have a number of people around the world in the same "chat room" (which looks amazingly like an Instant Message window) all chatting at once.

You can **create a new Group Chat** with a unique name and invite a large number of people to join you, as explained on page 497. .Mac members, AOL members, AIM users, and Jabber users can all be invited into the chat.

You can **join an existing Group Chat** that another buddy has created if you know the exact name of the Group Chat, as explained below.

1. From the File menu, choose "Go to Chat...."
2. In the "Go To Chat" window, type in the name of the Group Chat you want to join (shown bottom-left).
3. Click the "Go" button. If other buddies are already there, you will join them. If you're the first one there, type a greeting and wait for a response from others as they join in.

   Note: If you enter the name of a Group Chat that some other iChat users in the world have already set up, you will land in their room! So you want to be sure to type the correct name of the room you want to join. Caps and lowercase don't matter when typing the name of a Group Chat.

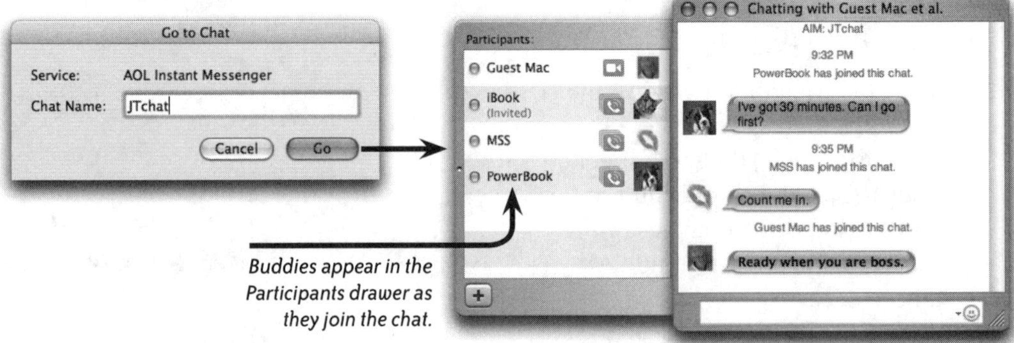

Buddies appear in the Participants drawer as they join the chat.

An easier way to start a group chat

You can quickly **start a new group chat** without having to type an invitation. First, make a multiple selection of buddies by *Command*-clicking on people in your Buddy List that you want to invite to a group chat. Then *Control*-click on any selected Buddy in the list, and choose "Invite to Chat..." from the contextual menu that pops up. A new message window will open and every selected Buddy will receive an invitation in the form of an iChat window popping open on their Desktop.

Create Chat Groups

If you have lots of buddies, you can organize them into *groups*. When you tell iChat to "Use Groups," a default group named "Buddies" appears in the Buddy List that contains all of the buddies you've added to your list.

To use groups:

1. From the View menu, choose "Use Groups" (shown on the right).
2. The default group, "Buddies," appears in the list as a gray row with a black disclosure triangle on the left side. Click the triangle to hide or show buddies in the group.

To create a new group:

1. Click the Add button (in the bottom-left corner of the iChat window) and choose "Add Group…."
2. In the sheet that slides down, type a name for the group, then click the "Add" button.
3. The new group appears in the list as a gray row.

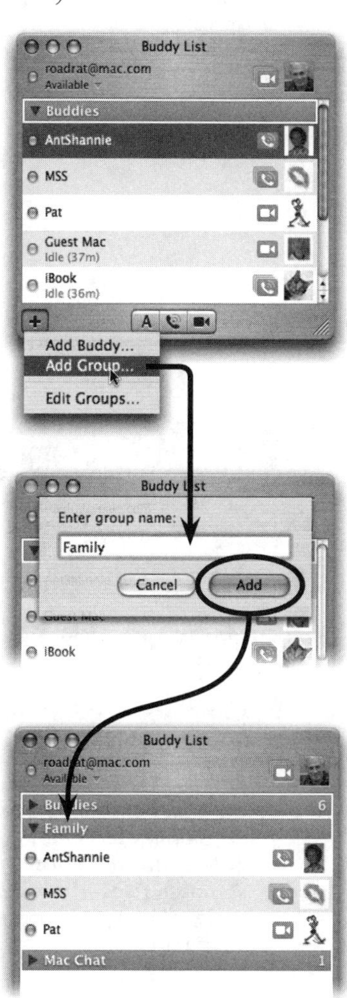

To add a new buddy to a group: Click the Add button (shown right), then choose "Add Buddy…" to open an Address Book window in which you can select a buddy, or click a "New Person" button as explained on page 487.

To move a buddy to another group: Drag a buddy from the current group to another group. The buddy is *removed* from the original group. To keep the buddy in the original group, *Option-drag* to *copy* the buddy to the new group.

To move offline buddies to a different group: From the View menu, choose "Show Offline Buddies," then drag the dimmed-out buddy to another group. Or *Option-drag* to *copy* the buddy to a group without removing from the original group.

To delete a buddy in a group: Select the buddy, then hit Delete. A buddy that you delete from one group remains in other groups.

To delete an entire group: Select a group, then press Delete. An alert asks you to confirm your decision. This will delete all buddies in that group. If those buddies are not duplicated in another group, you'll have to manually add them again later if you want them in your Buddy List. Before you delete the group, drag the buddies you want to keep to another group.

To hide groups: Go back to the View menu and *uncheck* "Use Groups."

Another way to create a Group Chat and invite others to join you:

1. From the File menu, choose "New Chat."
2. A new message window appears. *Before you type anything or choose anyone to invite,* go to the View menu and choose "Chat Options...."
3. From the pop-up "Mode" menu, choose "Chat," as shown below.
4. Type a name in the "Chat Name" text box. Be sure to enter a name that no one else in the world would be using at this moment or you might end up in someone else's chat room. Click OK.

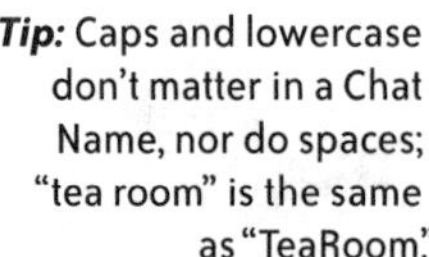

Tip: Caps and lowercase don't matter in a Chat Name, nor do spaces; "tea room" is the same as "TeaRoom."

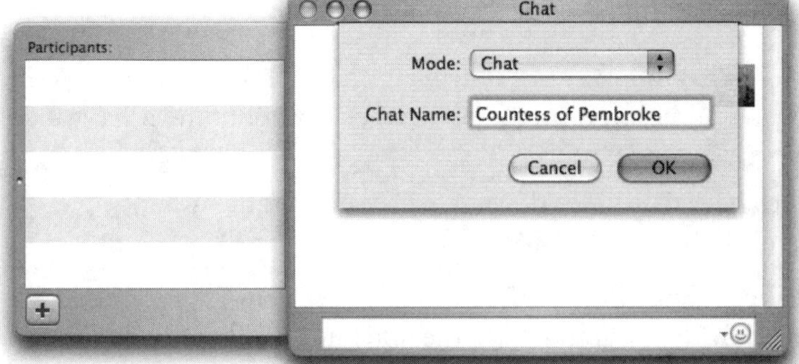

5. **To invite one or more of your buddies** to the new chat, drag them from your Buddy List to the chat's Participants drawer (shown below). **Or** click the **+** button at the bottom of the Participants drawer, then choose people from your list who are online at the moment.

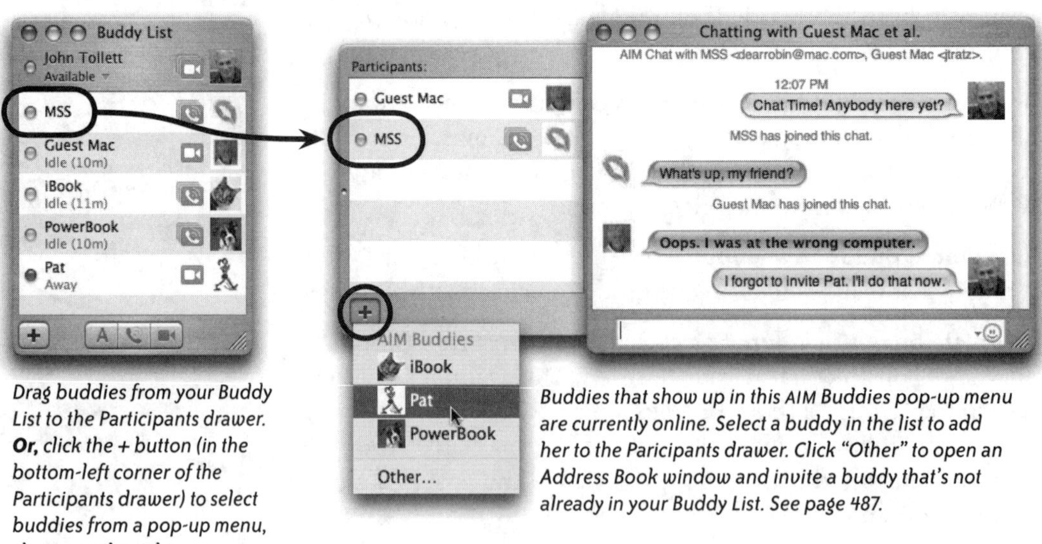

Drag buddies from your Buddy List to the Participants drawer. ***Or,*** *click the + button (in the bottom-left corner of the Participants drawer) to select buddies from a pop-up menu, shown on the right.*

Buddies that show up in this AIM Buddies pop-up menu are currently online. Select a buddy in the list to add her to the Paricipants drawer. Click "Other" to open an Address Book window and invite a buddy that's not already in your Buddy List. *See page 487.*

6. **To invite someone who is not in your Buddy List,** click the **+** button at the bottom of the drawer, then choose "Other…." Type a buddy name in the sheet that slides down from the top of the message window (shown below), then click OK.

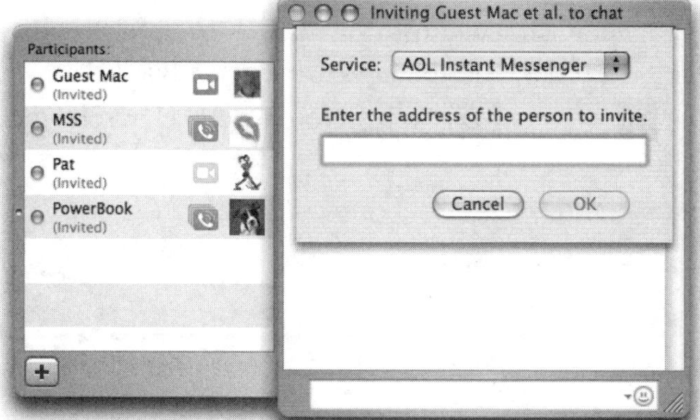

7. Once you've added participants to the list, type a message into the text field at the bottom of the window, hit Return, and that message goes out to everyone in the list.

   You can add more participants at any time, and anyone in the world can enter your Chat Room name and drop in to your window. For instance, if someone is not yet online when you send out an invitation, you can send them an email asking them to join you in that particular room as soon as they are online.

8. All invited participants will see a message on their screens inviting them to the chat. As soon as they respond, they appear in your window.

Join an existing Chat Room

You can **join an existing Group Chat** that another Mac.com member started if you know its name. You cannot join a chat that an AOL user started in AOL.

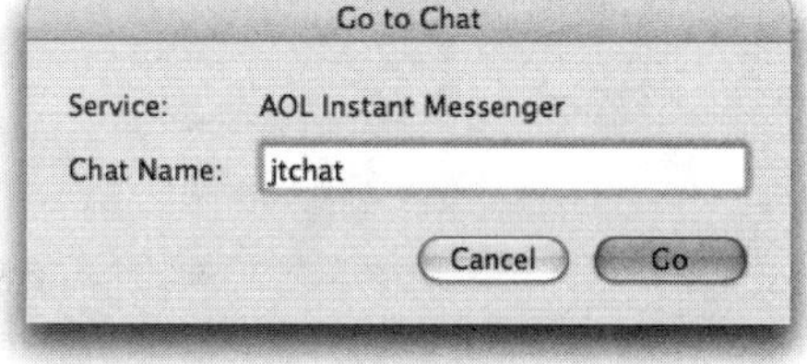

1. From the File menu, choose "Go to Chat…."
2. In the "Go to Chat…" window, type in the exact name of the Group Chat you wish to join, then click "Go."

   If a Chat Room by this name exists somewhere in the world, you will appear in it and it will appear on your screen.

   If there is no such existing room, an "Empty chat room" will open on your screen. People can join you there if they know the chat name.

Send or Receive Files through iChat

You may want to **send a picture or some other file** to a buddy in your list. This technique only works if your buddy is also an iChat user. If he is an AOL user, you'll have to send the file as an email attachment.

To send a file to another iChat buddy in your list:

1. Drag a file's icon on top of a buddy's name in the Buddy List.
2. An alert appears on your Desktop so you can cancel or send the file. Click "Send."

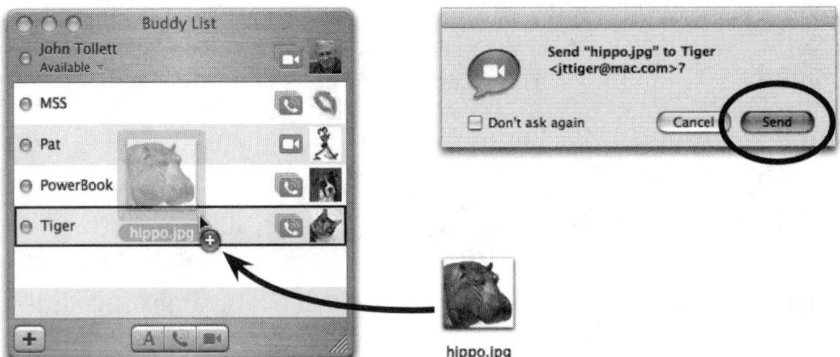

On the recipient's computer (assuming it's an iChat user, not an AOL user), an alert appears warning of an incoming file, as shown below-left.

1. Click anywhere in the white alert panel to transform it into the "Incoming File Transfer" window (below-right) which identifies the sender, the file name, the file type, and the file size.
2. Based on the information in the "Incoming File Transfer" window, you can choose to "Decline" the transfer, or click the "Save File" button and download it. If you save the file, it will appear on your Desktop. You can specify another location to save received files in the General pane of iChat Preferences.

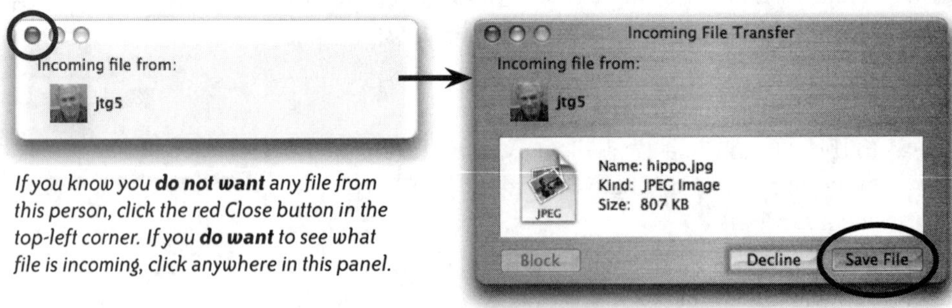

*If you know you **do not want** any file from this person, click the red Close button in the top-left corner. If you **do want** to see what file is incoming, click anywhere in this panel.*

Save Transcripts of Chats

You can save a transcript of any text chat—Instant Messages, Direct Messages, and Group Chats—to document a conversation, to read later, or to store in your digital box of love letters.

To save an individual chat:

1. Make sure the chat you want to save is the active window on the screen.
2. From the File menu, choose "Save a Copy As...."
3. In the sheet that opens (on the right), name the document, choose where to store it, and click "Save."

To automatically save all chat transcripts:

1. From the iChat menu, choose "Preferences...."
2. Click the "Messages" button in the Preferences toolbar.
3. Check the box to "Automatically save chat transcripts." This creates a new folder inside your Documents folder called "iChats." Every conversation you have in iChat will automatically be recorded and stored in this folder—you don't have to choose "Save a Copy As...."

AntShannie on 2005-03-15 at 17.48

The file icon of a saved chat transcript looks like this. The file name includes time and date information.

To open the most recently saved chat transcripts:

From the File menu choose "Open Recent," then choose a file from the submenu.

To read any saved chat:

Double-click the chat file icon. The file will open in a chat window. When you open a saved chat transcript you can scroll through it just like you can an active chat window.

To print a chat:

1. Start a text chat, or open a saved chat transcript.
2. From the iChat File menu, choose "Print...."
3. In the Print dialog box, click the "Print" button. Or, you can click the "Preview" button to see what your document will look like when printed, then click the "Print" button in the Preview window. The chat prints as a text transcript, as shown to the right.

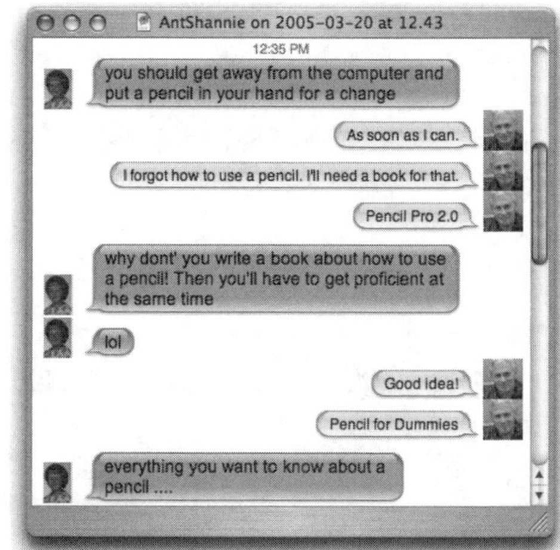

An iChat transcript opens as above, but prints like the sample below.

John Tollett: The fabulous, gorgeous Andrew Wyeth boo been my favorite for a long long time.
antshannie: You're welcome! Sorry it didn't get the
John Tollett: No problem. It's nice stretching out the surp
antshannie: we've seen 2 of his exhibits. I don't mu by my tastes
John Tollett: He is amazing.

Customize the Chat Background

You can **customize the background** of any chat window by adding a picture or graphic. This could be useful if you've got several chats going on and don't want to get confused about who is in which window. Mostly, it's just fun.

This image will appear only on *your* computer—the person you are chatting with will not see it. As soon as you close this chat window, that background disappears and does not automatically re-appear anywhere.

To customize a chat window:

1. Click anywhere in a chat window to select that window.
2. From the View menu, choose "Set Chat Background…."
3. In the dialog box that appears, select an image file that's on your computer, then click "Open."

   Or simply drag any image file from your Desktop and drop it directly into an empty space in the chat window.

Small images will "tile" (repeat over and over) to fill the window space. Large images will display full-sized, cropping off the image where necessary.

Simple or subdued background images are best for readability.

To remove a background, click once in the chat window, then go to the View menu and choose "Clear Background."

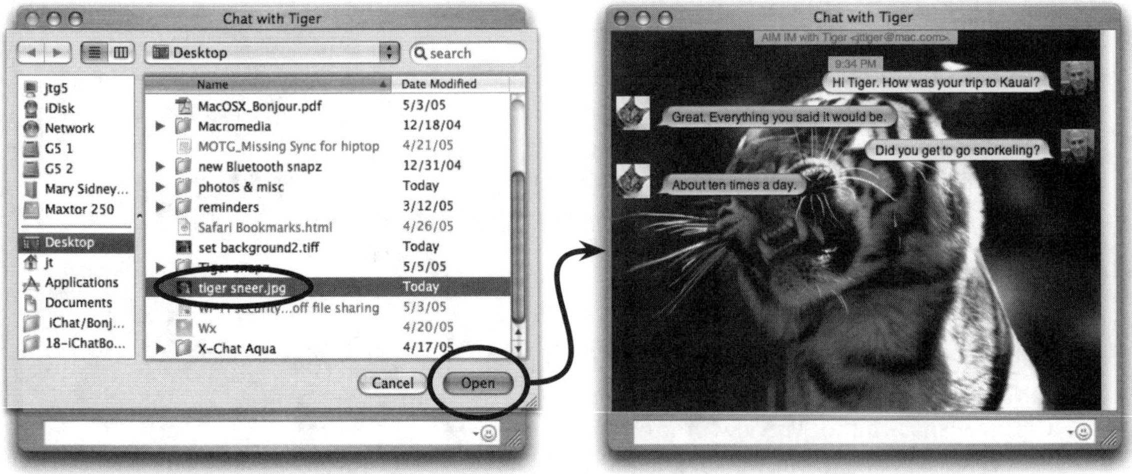

Create Additional Chat Accounts

In addition to your .Mac account, you can also set up an existing AOL Instant Messenger Account (AIM), additional .Mac accounts, or use your AOL screen name as a different account. No matter how many different accounts you have, though, only *one* can be *active* at any time. Each account you create has its own Buddy List. You can switch between accounts whenever you want.

Set up iChat to use another chat account:

1. From the iChat menu, choose "Preferences…."
2. Click the "Accounts" icon in the toolbar.
3. Click the + button beneath the "Accounts" pane.
4. In the sheet that opens (below-left):
   - From the "Account Type" pop-up menu, choose an account type—.Mac Account, AIM Account, or Jabber Account.
   - Enter your account name in the ".Mac Name" text field.
   - Enter the password for that account.
   - In the "Description" field, type another name (such as "SchoolBuddies") if you want the account to be identified as something other than the official account name that you typed into the first text field. The account will be listed as this name in the Accounts pane.
5. Click the "Add" button.
6. Checkmark "Use this account" to make it the active one.
7. The new account is added to the list of accounts (below-right).

After you've set up additional accounts, you can choose one from the iChat menu. From the iChat menu, choose "Switch To," then from the submenu choose one of the accounts you've set up as described above.

To delete a chat account from the Accounts pane, select the account in the list, then click the minus button in the bottom-left corner.

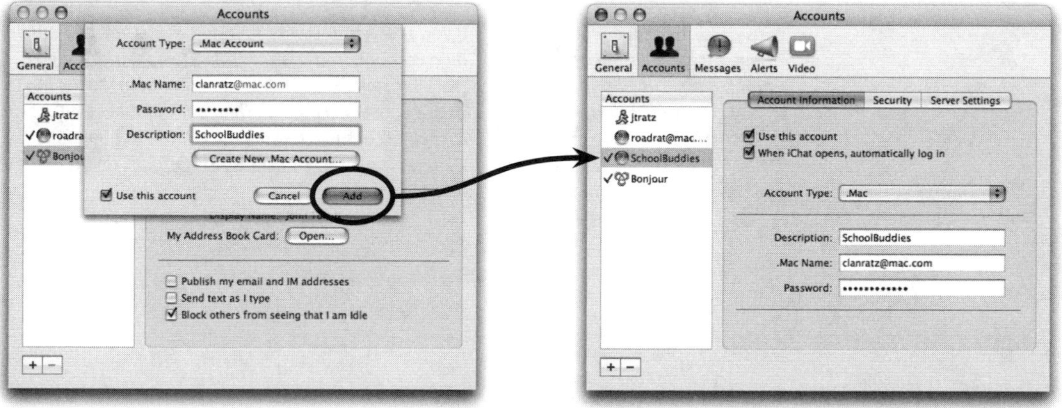

iChat Preferences

To open iChat Preferences, from the iChat menu choose "Preferences…." Click one of the buttons at the top of the Preferences window to show the options for that particular iChat category.

Many of the preferences don't need explanations. The next several pages provide comments and explanations for those that may not be obvious.

General preferences

Use the General preferences to customize some of iChat's behaviors.

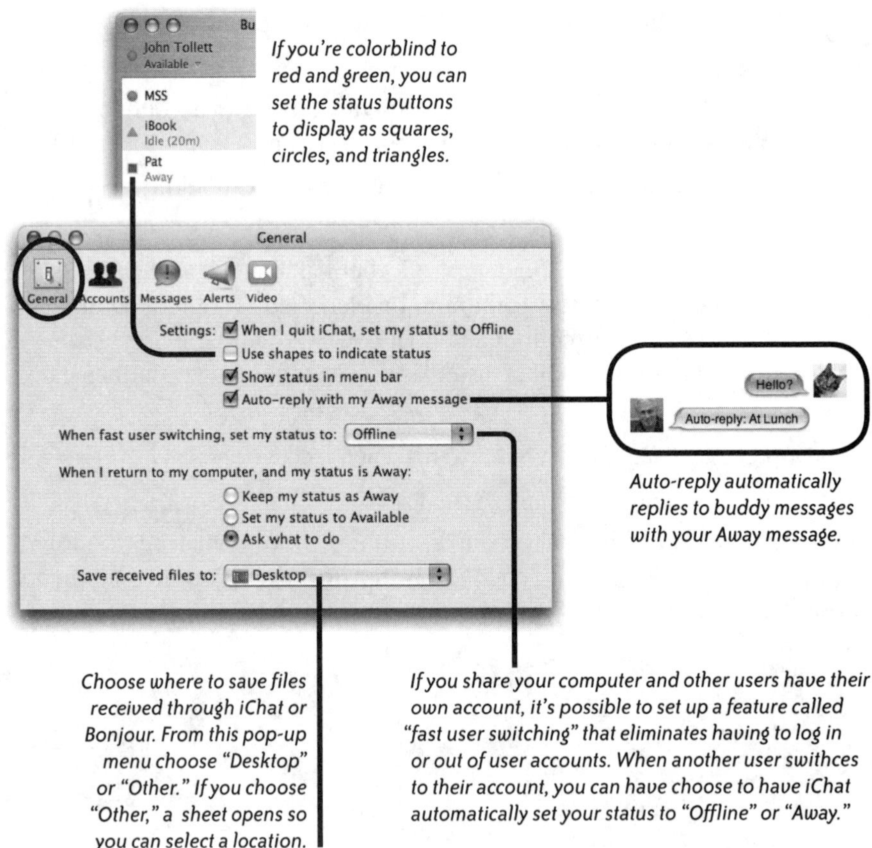

If you're colorblind to red and green, you can set the status buttons to display as squares, circles, and triangles.

Auto-reply automatically replies to buddy messages with your Away message.

Choose where to save files received through iChat or Bonjour. From this pop-up menu choose "Desktop" or "Other." If you choose "Other," a sheet opens so you can select a location.

If you share your computer and other users have their own account, it's possible to set up a feature called "fast user switching" that eliminates having to log in or out of user accounts. When another user swithces to their account, you can have choose to have iChat automatically set your status to "Offline" or "Away."

The Accounts preferences

The Accounts pane is where you add, delete, and manage accounts. The Accounts preferences are separated into three tabs on the right side of the window: Account Information, Security, and Server Settings.

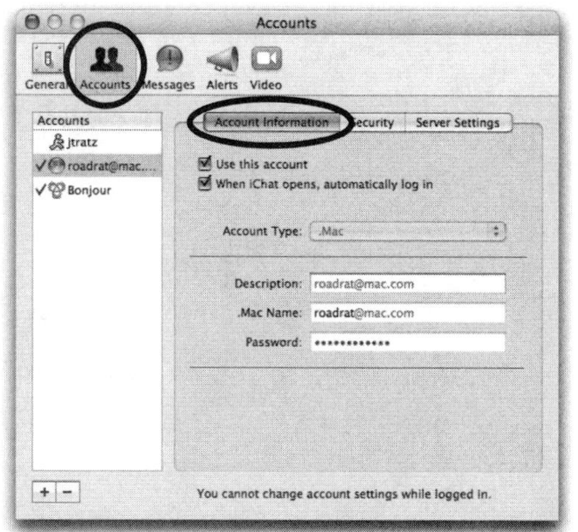

Account Information settings (shown top-right): Your chat accounts are listed in the "Accounts" pane on the left side of the window. Bonjour is automatically listed here (see page 518 for more information about Bonjour).

To add a chat account, click the plus button in the bottom-left corner (see page 505 for details).
To delete an account in the list, select it, then click the minus button.

Check "Use this account" (top-right) to activate the selected account in the Accounts pane.

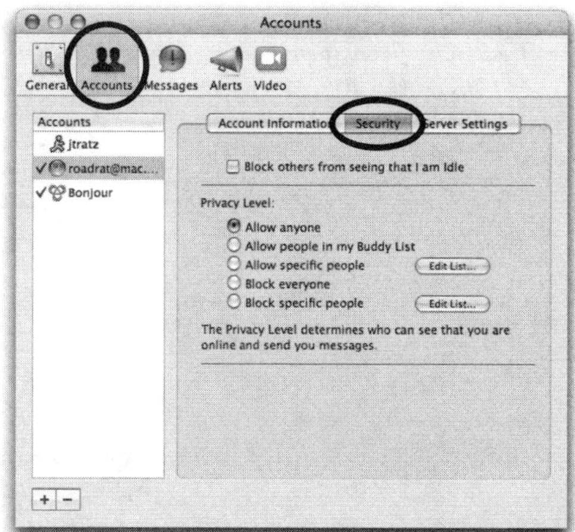

Security settings (shown middle-right): Checkmark "Block others from seeing that I am Idle" if you don't want your online status to show as "Idle" when you've been away from your computer for a while. An Idle status message also shows how long the computer has been idle, and you may not want others to know this information.

AntShannie
Idle (27m)

In the Privacy Level section, choose who you want to allow to see you online and who you want to block. If you choose "Allow specific people" or "Block specific people," click the "Edit List..." button to open a sheet (shown bottom-right) in which you can enter the chat names of specific buddies you want to allow or block.

If you get an unwanted message, you can quickly add that person to your Block list—just click this "Block" button.

To add a name *to the Block list, click the plus (+) button, type a buddy chat name, then click "Done."*
To remove a name *from the list, select it, click the minus (–) button, then click "Done."*

Server settings:
This pane contains server settings for the selected chat service. If you don't know what these settings are all about, you shouldn't try to change them.

Messages preferences

Use the Messages pane to customize the appearance of your Chat windows, such as the color of speech balloons, the font used for your messages and color of your font. You can choose to reformat incoming messages if you don't like the font and balloon color chosen by a buddy. As you change settings, your choices are previewed in the pane shown below.

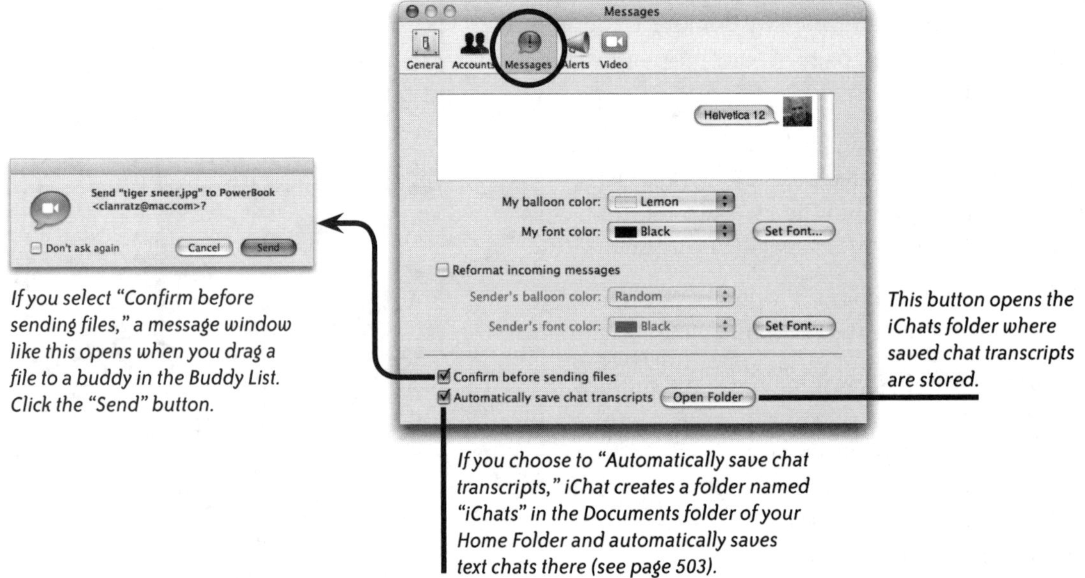

If you select "Confirm before sending files," a message window like this opens when you drag a file to a buddy in the Buddy List. Click the "Send" button.

This button opens the iChats folder where saved chat transcripts are stored.

If you choose to "Automatically save chat transcripts," iChat creates a folder named "iChats" in the Documents folder of your Home Folder and automatically saves text chats there (see page 503).

Alerts preferences

If you're busy working, it's easy to miss a chat opportunity because you didn't see the incoming message alert appear on your screen. iChat can use additional alerts by playing a sound, bouncing the iChat icon in the Dock, or even make the computer speak a message in one of its computer voices.

From the "Event" pop-up menu, choose an event, then set the alerts you want for that event.

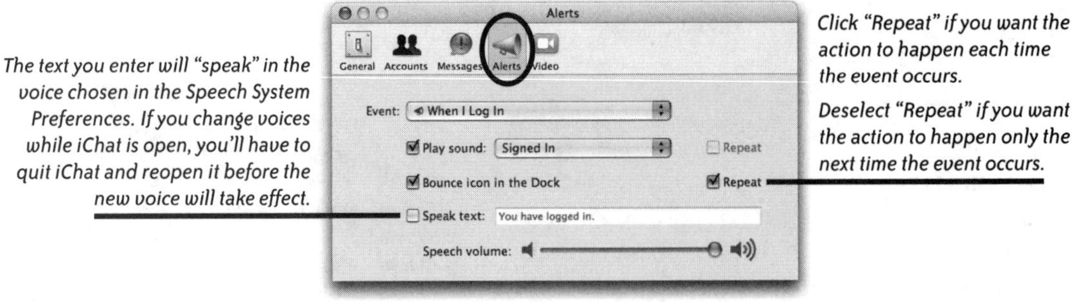

The text you enter will "speak" in the voice chosen in the Speech System Preferences. If you change voices while iChat is open, you'll have to quit iChat and reopen it before the new voice will take effect.

Click "Repeat" if you want the action to happen each time the event occurs.

Deselect "Repeat" if you want the action to happen only the next time the event occurs.

Video preferences

This pane lets you preview your video camera picture, customize various settings for sound input and output, and adjust the bandwidth limit for your broadband connection.

Use the **Microphone** pop-up menu to choose a source for audio. The options that appear in the "Microphone" pop-up menu vary depending on the computer you use and other hardware you may have connected.

- **Choose "iSight Built-in"** if you have an Apple iSight camera connected. If you have some other FireWire video camera connected, the camera name or model number appears in this pop-up menu.
- **Choose "Internal microphone"** if you want to use the built-in internal microphone that may have come with your computer.
- **Choose "Line In"** if you have an external microphone connected to your computer through the Line In port.

Use the **Bandwidth Limit** pop-up menu to set limits for how much bandwidth to use when having a video chat. Lower bandwidth limits are best for slower connections.

- **Choose 100 Kbps** or **200 Kbps** (kilobits per second) if you have a relatively slow broadband connection.
- **Choose 500 Kbps** for a good, average broadband connection.
- **Choose None** or **1 Mbps** or **2 Mbps** (megabits per second) if you have a really fast broadband connection.

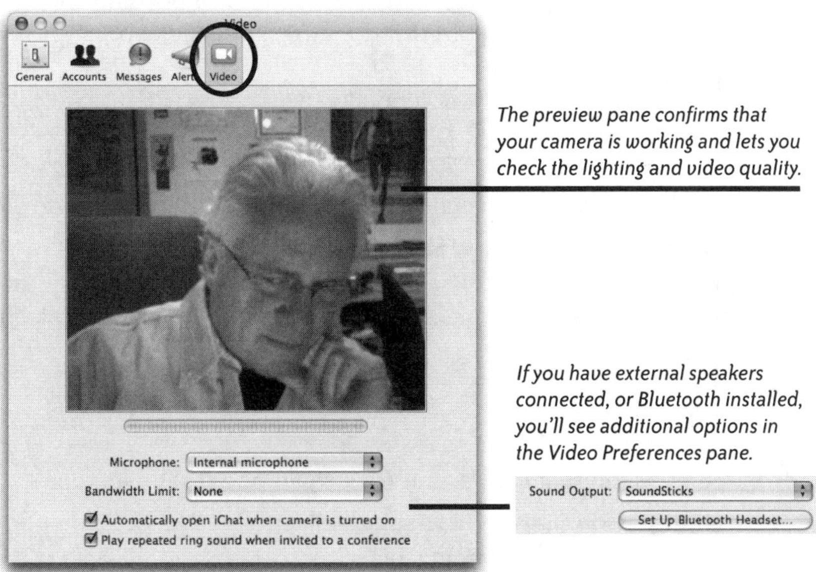

The preview pane confirms that your camera is working and lets you check the lighting and video quality.

If you have external speakers connected, or Bluetooth installed, you'll see additional options in the Video Preferences pane.

Audio Chats

Tip: You need a broadband connection (not a dial-up modem connection) to audio or video chat. Travelers will be pleased to know that many hotels and lodges around the world provide broadband connections. The broadband wireless connections (Wi-Fi) that many coffee shops provide work very well.

Extra tip for frequent travelers: Sign up for a T-mobile Hot Spot wireless account. Starbucks all over the world provide Hot Spot connections. And the connection stays on 24/7, even when Starbucks is closed (as the photo below shows).

You can audio chat with other iChat users that have a microphone connected or built in to their computer. You can audio chat with buddies anywhere in the world for free. If your computer meets the minimum requirements (listed below), you can audio chat with up to ten people at a time. Wow.

Set up for audio chats

Audio chats require almost no setup. In fact, the settings below are automatic and you don't need to change them unless you have a problem connecting.

1. Make sure you have a microphone connected or built in to your Mac.
2. Open iChat. From the iChat menu choose "Preferences...," then click the "Video" icon in the toolbar to open the Video Preferences pane.
3. From the "Microphone" pop-up menu, choose a source for audio. **Choose "iSight Built-in"** if you have an Apple iSight camera connected. If you have some other FireWire video camera connected, the camera name or model number appears in this pop-up menu.
   Choose "Internal microphone" if you want to use the built-in internal microphone that came with your computer.
   Choose "Line In" if you have an external microphone connected to your computer through the Line In port.

Minimum requirements for audio chats

It takes a more powerful computer and a faster Internet connection to initiate a multi-person audio chat than it does to participate in one.

Robin sends messages home from the steps of a closed Starbucks (across the street from Shakespeare's Globe Theatre).

To *initiate* an audio chat, this is what you need:

- **1-to-1 chat:**
  Any G3, G4, or G5
  56 Kbps Internet connection (this could be a dial-up modem)
- **Multi-person chat (up to ten people):**
  1 GHz G4, a dual 800 MHz G4, or any G5, running Tiger
  128 Kbps Internet connection, both ways (upload and download)

To *participate in* an audio chat, this is what you need:

- **1-to-1 chat:**
  Any G3, G4, or G5
  56 Kbps Internet connection (this could be a dial-up modem)
- **Multi-person chat (up to ten people):**
  Any G3, G4, or G5, running Tiger
  56 Kbps Internet connection (this could be a dial-up modem)

Start a 1-to-1 audio chat

The icon to the right of a buddy name indicates what kind of chat is possible. A multi-person phone icon (above) means you can have a multi-person audio chat with that buddy.

1. Open iChat.
2. Select a buddy in the iChat window that shows an "Audio Chat" icon (a telephone) to the right of the buddy name. You can also audio chat with a buddy that shows a "Video Chat" icon (a video camera), in case you're still in your pajamas. Or not.
3. To start an audio chat, click the "Audio Chat" icon next to the buddy name. **Or** click the "Audio Chat" button at the bottom of the window (shown on the right). **Or,** from the Buddies menu, choose "Invite to Audio Chat." **Or** Control-click on a buddy, then choose "Invite to Audio Chat" in the contextual menu.
4. An audio panel opens on your Desktop, waiting for your buddy to accept the invitation, as shown below.

5. On the buddy's Desktop, the audio chat invitation appears. When the buddy clicks on the invitation, it opens into the audio chat panel shown below-right. The buddy chooses to "Decline" or "Accept" the invitation. The buddy can also choose a "Text Reply" if audio is inappropriate at the moment.

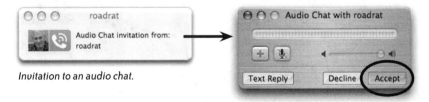

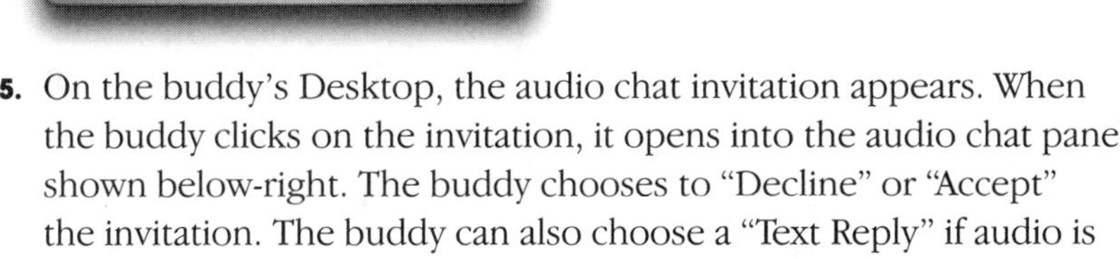

Invitation to an audio chat.

6. Once the audio chat invitation has been accepted, you can talk back and forth just as if you were using a telephone. The audio chat panel shows an animated sound level meter and provides a volume slider so you can adjust the chat volume.

Click this button to mute the sound.

End a 1-to-1 audio chat

To end an audio chat, just click the red Close button in the top-left corner of the "Audio Chat" panel. Either party can end an audio chat at any time.

Start a multi-person audio chat

Once you've started an audio chat with one person, you're just a click away from audio conferencing with up to ten buddies at a time.

1. Start a 1-to-1 audio chat, as described on the previous page.
2. To add another buddy to the chat, Control-click on another buddy in the Buddy List. From the pop-up contextual menu choose "Invite to Audio Chat," as shown below-right.

3. The audio chat window expands (below-left) to show that you're waiting for a response. When the invited buddy accepts your invitation, he appears in your chat window as another sound level meter (below-center).
   To invite another buddy to the chat, click the plus button (**+**) and choose a buddy from the pop-up menu (below-right). **Or** use the procedure described in Step 2.

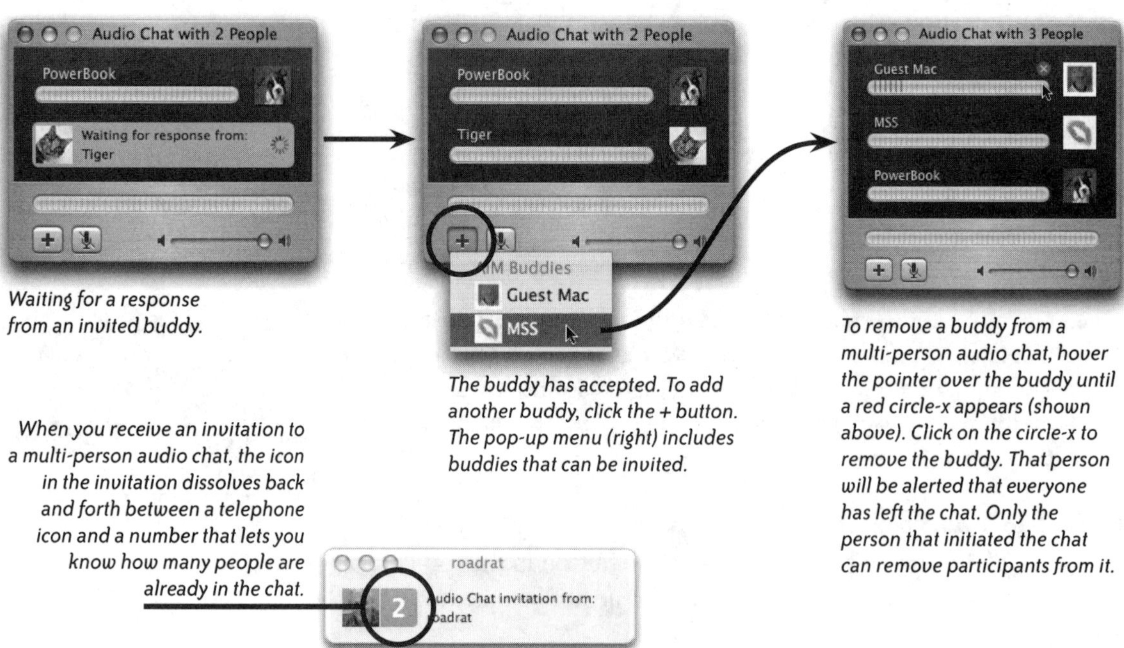

Waiting for a response from an invited buddy.

The buddy has accepted. To add another buddy, click the + button. The pop-up menu (right) includes buddies that can be invited.

To remove a buddy from a multi-person audio chat, hover the pointer over the buddy until a red circle-x appears (shown above). Click on the circle-x to remove the buddy. That person will be alerted that everyone has left the chat. Only the person that initiated the chat can remove participants from it.

When you receive an invitation to a multi-person audio chat, the icon in the invitation dissolves back and forth between a telephone icon and a number that lets you know how many people are already in the chat.

Video Chats

iChat makes video chats so easy that it's just incredible. If your computer and your Internet connection meet certain minimum requirements, you can video chat with one buddy, or with up to three other buddies at the same time.

Minimum requirements for video chats

It takes a more powerful computer and a faster Internet connection to *initiate* a video chat than it does to *participate* in one.

To *initiate* or *participate* in a 1-to-1 video chat:

- You need at least a 600 MHz G3, any G4, or any G5 running OS X version 10.2.5

To *initiate* a 3-way or 4-way video chat:

- **Minimum:**
  Dual 1 GHz G4 or any G5 running Tiger
  600 Kbps Internet connection, both ways (upload and download)
- **Better:**
  Dual 1 GHz G4, 1.8 GHz G5, running Tiger
  128 Kbps Internet connection, both ways (upload and download)
- **Best:**
  Dual 2 GHz G5, running Tiger
  1500 Kbps Internet connection, both ways (upload and download)

To *participate in* a 3-way or 4-way video chat:

- **Minimum:**
  1 GHz G4, or a dual 800 MHz G4, or any G5 running Tiger
  100 Kbps Internet connection, both ways (upload and download)
- **Better:**
  1 GHz G4, or a dual 800 MHz G4, or any G5 running Tiger
  200 Kbps Internet connection, both ways (upload and download)
- **Best:**
  Any G5 running Tiger
  500 Kbps Internet connection, both ways (upload and download)

Set up a video chat

- Connect a FireWire-enabled video camera to your Mac and turn it on. Apple sells a great little camera, called iSight, for $149. If you already own a more expensive digital video camera with FireWire, you can use that too. Make sure the FireWire videocamera is in *Camera* or *Record* mode. Apple iSight cameras are automatically set to record.

1-to-1 video chats

This video icon next to a buddy name means you can have a 1-to-1 video chat with that buddy.

A multi-person video icon next to a buddy name means you can have a multi-person video chat with that buddy.

1. Open iChat. From the iChat menu choose "Preferences...," then click the "Video" button in the Preferences toolbar to open the Video preferences pane. Check your video settings as described on page 509.
2. Select a buddy in your iChat Buddy List whose name has a Video Chat icon (a video camera) next to it. If the icon is a *multi-person* Video Chat icon (a stack of video cameras), that's OK—you can still have a 1-to-1 video chat.
3. Click the Video Chat icon next to the buddy name.

   Or click the Video Chat button at the bottom of the Buddy List window.

   Or, Control-click on the buddy name, then from the contextual menu choose "Invite to Video Chat."

   Or, from the Buddies menu, choose "Invite to Video Chat."
4. An iChat Preview window opens on your Desktop, shown below-left. The Preview pane shows what your buddy will see. While you wait for a response from your buddy you can adjust the camera angle, comb your hair, etc.

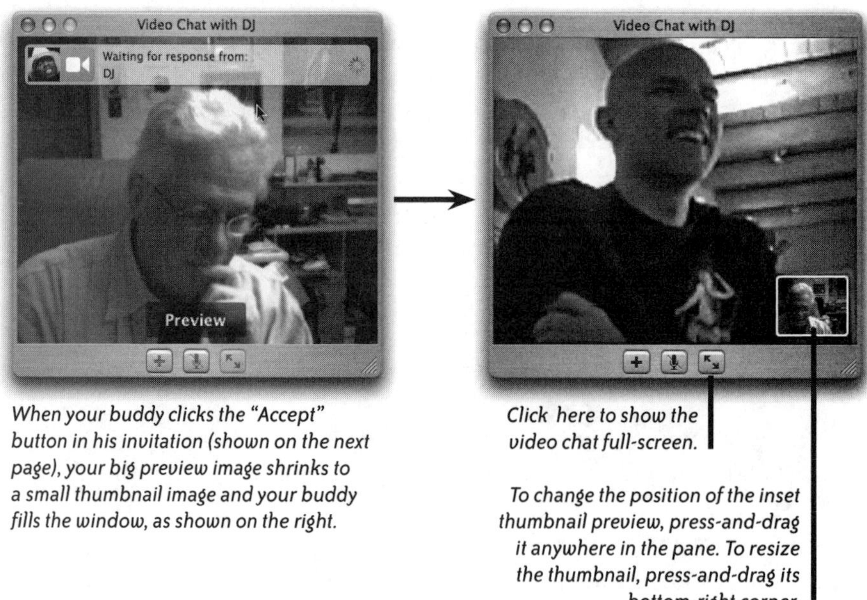

When your buddy clicks the "Accept" button in his invitation (shown on the next page), your big preview image shrinks to a small thumbnail image and your buddy fills the window, as shown on the right.

Click here to show the video chat full-screen.

To change the position of the inset thumbnail preview, press-and-drag it anywhere in the pane. To resize the thumbnail, press-and-drag its bottom-right corner.

5. When your buddy responds by clicking anywhere in the invitation panel (below-left), a video chat window opens on his Desktop with the option to "Decline" or "Accept" (below-right). Or he can choose to respond with a "Text Reply" if a video chat is inappropriate at that time or place.

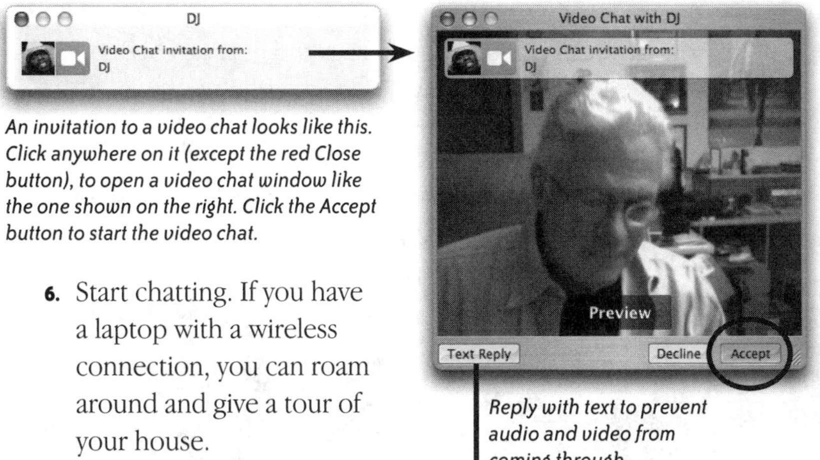

An invitation to a video chat looks like this. Click anywhere on it (except the red Close button), to open a video chat window like the one shown on the right. Click the Accept button to start the video chat.

6. Start chatting. If you have a laptop with a wireless connection, you can roam around and give a tour of your house.

Reply with text to prevent audio and video from coming through.

Tip: You can take a snapshot of a buddy as you video chat. From the Video menu, choose "Take Snapshot." The snapshot is placed on your Desktop.

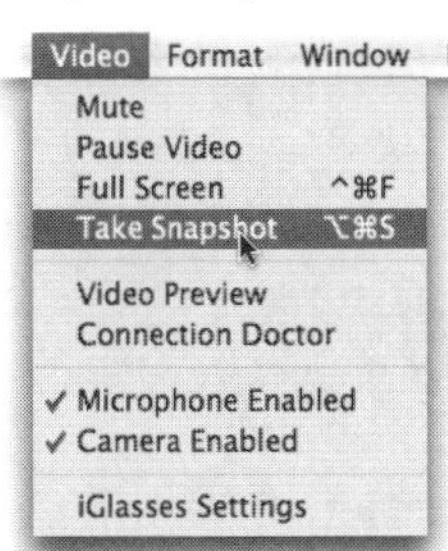

One-way video chats

If you have a video camera and your buddy doesn't, you can have a one-way video chat. Your buddy will see you in a video chat window.

1. Open iChat and select a buddy in the Buddy List (someone that doesn't have a video camera icon next to their buddy name).
2. From the Buddies menu, choose "Invite to One-Way Video Chat."
3. Your buddy receives an invitation like the one shown below-left. When your buddy clicks the "Accept" button, you appear in a video chat window on the buddy's Desktop.

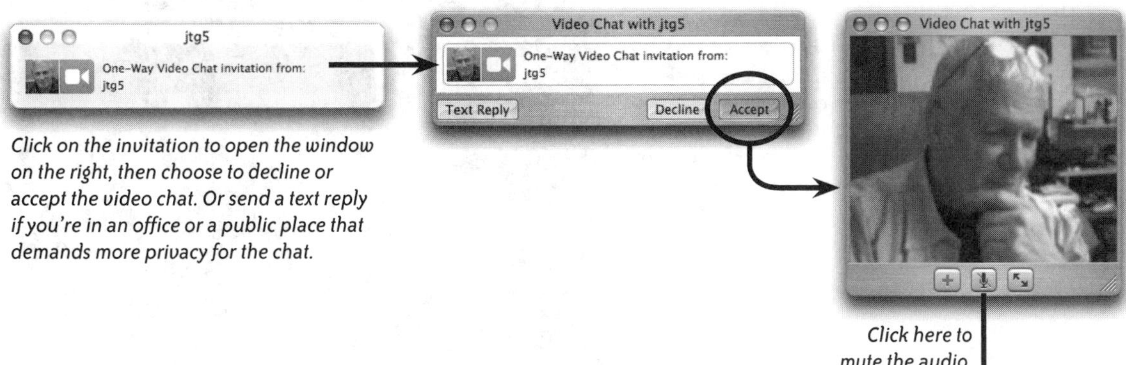

Click on the invitation to open the window on the right, then choose to decline or accept the video chat. Or send a text reply if you're in an office or a public place that demands more privacy for the chat.

Click here to mute the audio.

Multi-person video chats

Now the real fun begins. If you like video chats, you'll love multi-person video chats. Keep in mind the computer and bandwidth requirements listed on page 513 that are necessary for intitiating or participating in a multi-person video chat.

1. Start a 1-to-1 video chat, as explained on pages 514–515.
2. After you've connected with a buddy, click the plus (+) button at the bottom of the screen to show a pop-up menu of other buddies that can be invited to the chat. Choose one of the buddies listed in the pop-up menu.

   If that buddy doesn't have a camera, he joins the chat as an audio participant—an audio sound level meter displays instead of live video (shown at the bottom of the next page).

Click the + button to invite another buddy to the chat.

When you add a third buddy to a video chat, the appearance of the chat window changes as shown here. Your thumbnail image moves to bottom-center and the two other participants are angled above you.

3. To add a fourth participant to your chat, click the plus button again and select a buddy from the pop-up menu. The other participants move over to make room for the new buddy (shown below).

The person that *inititiated* the chat is the only one that can invite additional participants or remove a buddy from the chat.

To remove a participant from a multi-person video chat, hover your pointer over one of the buddies until a red circle-x appears in the corner of the buddy picture. Click the circle-x to remove the buddy.

Invited participants that don't have a video camera connected appear as an audio sound level meter. All participants can hear the audio buddy.

Bonjour

Bonjour is an integrated part of **iChat** in Mac OS X. If you have two or more Macs connected through a local area network (an ethernet network, wireless network, or a combination of both), Bonjour automatically detects and connects all of the computers (or other Bonjour-smart devices, such as a printer) on the network. You can send Instant Messages or files to Bonjour buddies on your local network. You can also have audio or video chats with others on the local network if a microphone or digital video camera is connected to your computer.

To use Bonjour, you don't need a .Mac account, or an AIM account, as required to use iChat. Any computer that you want to connect through Bonjour must have iChat installed (which automatically includes Bonjour) and the computers must be connected through some sort of network (ethernet, wireless, or a combination of the two).

To set up Bonjour:

1. Open iChat: Either single-click on its icon in the Dock, or double-click its icon in the Applications window.
2. The first time you open iChat, a series of dialogs opens to set up iChat and Bonjour (see page 486).
3. One of the set up windows (shown below) is titled "Set up Bonjour Messaging." All you have to do is choose "Use Bonjour Messaging," then click the "Continue" button to finish the setup.

Bonjour automatically goes about its job of detecting others on your local network, so when you're ready to chat or send files, the other user only has to be notified. This is referred to as "zero-configuration" networking.

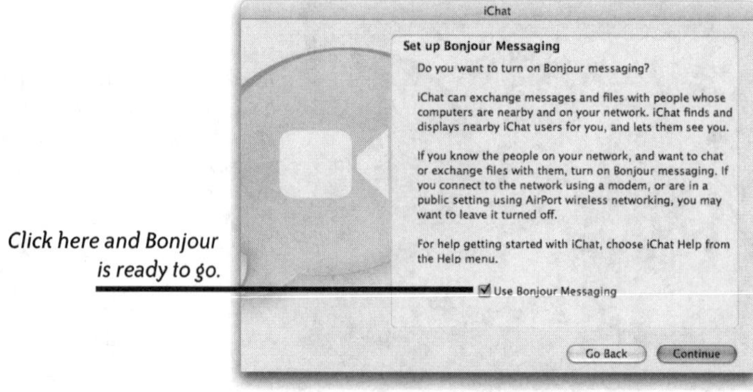

Click here and Bonjour is ready to go.

It's not too late to set up Bonjour

If you previously opened iChat and set it up but did not turn on Bonjour, **or** if you want to change any of the settings (or turn Bonjour off), you can do so at any time:

1. Open iChat, then go to the iChat menu and choose "Preferences…."
2. Click the "Accounts" button in the top bar of the Preferences window.
3. Click the Bonjour item in the Accounts pane on the left to show the Bonjour "Account Information" on the right side of the window.
4. Select "Use Bonjour Instant Messaging" to activate Bonjour. Uncheck the checkbox to turn off Bonjour.

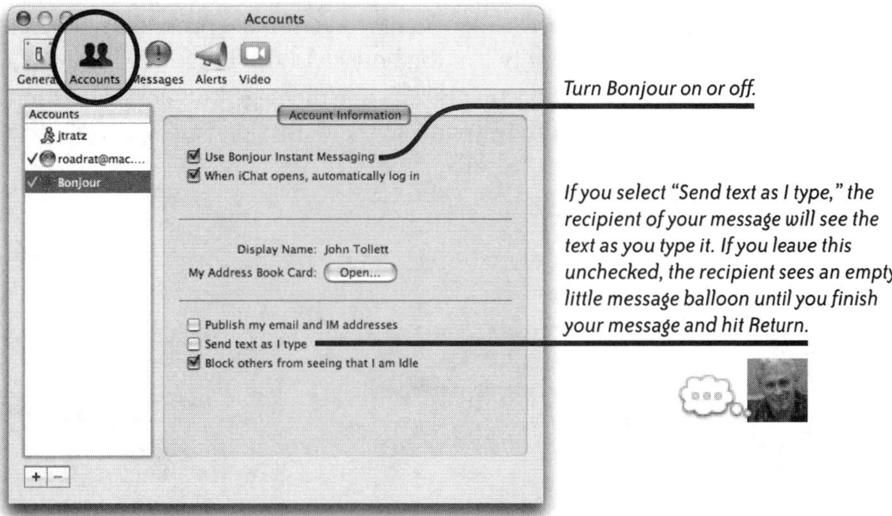

Turn Bonjour on or off.

If you select "Send text as I type," the recipient of your message will see the text as you type it. If you leave this unchecked, the recipient sees an empty little message balloon until you finish your message and hit Return.

Just about everything that applies to **iChat** also applies to **Bonjour.** Read the other pages in this chapter about iChat to learn how to chat or share files using Bonjour. Remember, iChat connects to buddies through the Internet, and Bonjour connects to buddies who are on your local network—otherwise, text chats, audio chats, video chats, and file sharing look and work the same as in iChat. In fact, sometimes it's easy to lose track of which application you're using, iChat or Bonjour. Look at the top of a message window for a line of gray type that tells you if you're using Bonjour or iChat.

Send a file through a Bonjour Instant Message

1. Open iChat, which will activate Bonjour.
2. If the Bonjour window (shown on the left) doesn't appear, press Command 2, **or** go to the Window menu and choose "Bonjour." Other users on your network who also have iChat installed will appear in the Bonjour window.
3. In the Bonjour window, select the user to whom you want to send a file, then click the Text Chat button (the "A" icon), shown on the left. An Instant Message (IM) window opens (below-left).
4. Type a message in the text box, then press Return to send it. The recipient receives an Instant Message notice (shown below-center).
5. When you're ready to send a file, drag the file (or a folder of files) to the text box at the bottom of the Bonjour window.
6. The file name and icon appears in a message bubble. When the recipient clicks the file name in the message, it automatically downloads to her Desktop.

   This also works with iChat.

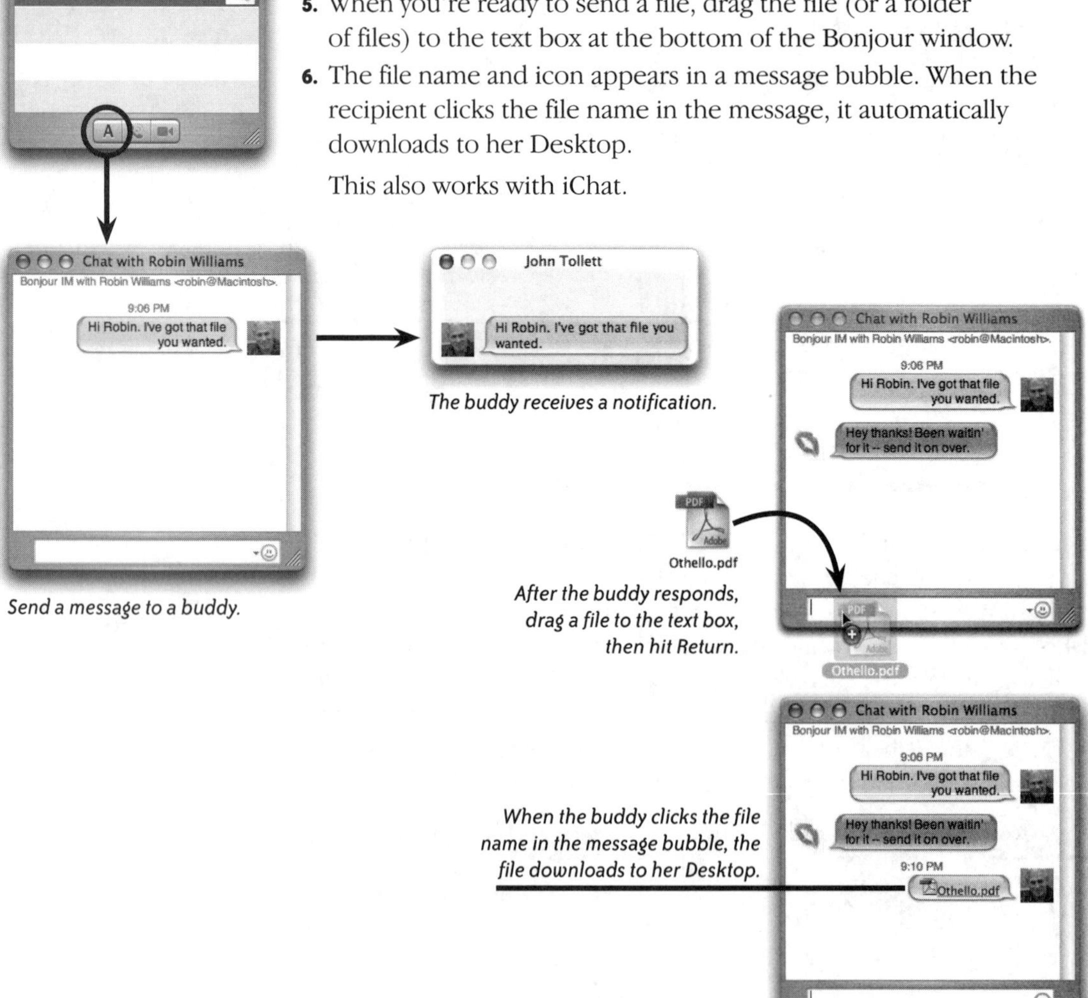

Send a message to a buddy.

The buddy receives a notification.

After the buddy responds, drag a file to the text box, then hit Return.

When the buddy clicks the file name in the message bubble, the file downloads to her Desktop.

the Index

A

H

I

Z